EUROPEAN POLITICS TODAY

FRANK L. WILSON
Purdue University

EUROPEAN POLITICS TODAY
The Democratic Experience

PRENTICE HALL, Englewood Cliffs, New Jersey 07632

Library of Congress Cataloging-in-Publication Data

WILSON, FRANK LEE, [date]
European politics today: the democratic experience / Frank L.
Wilson.
    p. cm.
Bibliography: p.
Includes index.
ISBN 0-13-292012-3 (alk. paper)
1. Europe—Politics and government—1945- 2. Europe, Eastern—
Politics and government—1945- 3. Comparative government.
I. Title.
JN94.A2W54   1990
320.3′094—dc20   89-34425
                CIP

ʃ

Editorial/production supervision: *Edith Riker*
Cover design: *Wanda Lubelska*
Manufacturing buyer: *Peter Havens*

©1990 by Prentice-Hall, Inc.
A Division of Simon & Schuster
Englewood Cliffs, New Jersey 07632

Printed in the United States of America

10 9 8 7 6 5 4 3 2 1

ISBN 0-13-292012-3

Prentice-Hall International (UK) Limited, *London*
Prentice-Hall of Australia Pty. Limited, *Sydney*
Prentice-Hall Canada Inc., *Toronto*
Prentice-Hall Hispanoamericana, S.A., *Mexico*
Prentice-Hall of India Private Limited, *New Delhi*
Prentice-Hall of Japan, Inc., *Tokyo*
Simon & Schuster Asia Pte. Ltd., *Singapore*
Editora Prentice-Hall do Brasil, Ltda., *Rio de Janeiro*

CONTENTS

PREFACE   *xi*

PART ONE
INTRODUCTION: A CRISIS OF EUROPEAN DEMOCRACY?   *1*

The Viability of Democracy   *3*
A Crisis of Democracy?   *4*
Challenge and Response   *16*

PART TWO
BRITAIN   *19*

1   **SOCIAL CHANGE AND TRADITION IN BRITAIN**   *21*

The Legacies of a Glorious Past   *22*
British Society in the 1980s   *26*
Conclusion   *38*

2   BRITISH CITIZENS AND POLITICS   41

The Individual in Politics   *43*
Voting   *46*
Women in Politics   *48*
Conclusion   *49*

3   BRITISH POLITICAL PARTIES AND INTEREST GROUPS   52

Political Parties in Britain   *52*
Interest Groups and British Politics   *62*
Conclusion   *67*

4   BRITISH POLICY MAKING   69

A Constitutional Monarchy   *70*
Prime Ministerial Power   *73*
Parliament   *75*
The British Civil Service   *81*
A Centralized Democracy   *84*
The Public and Policy Making   *87*
Conclusion   *88*

5   DEMOCRACY IN BRITAIN   92

A Troubled Economy: The British Disease?   *92*
Limits on National Sovereignty   *98*
The Overloaded Social-Welfare State   *100*
Human Rights in Britain   *102*
Responses to the Challenges of the 1980s: Why Britain
   Did Not Die   *105*
Britain: A Model Democracy?   *109*

PART THREE
FRANCE   *113*

6   FRANCE: THE HISTORICAL AND SOCIAL BACKGROUND
      TO POLITICS   115

The Incomplete Revolution   *115*
Origins of the Fifth Republic   *121*
France in the 1980s   *124*
A Directed Economy   *131*
Conclusion   *133*

7 FRENCH CITIZENS AND POLITICS *135*

A "Delinquent Community"? *135*
The Individual Citizen in Politics *137*
Voting *143*
Participation and Stability *146*

8 FRENCH POLITICAL PARTIES AND INTEREST GROUPS *147*

Political Parties *148*
Interest Group Politics in France *163*
Conclusions *168*

9 FRENCH POLICY MAKING *170*

The French Constitution of the Fifth Republic (1958) *171*
A Mixed Presidential-Parliamentary Structure
   of Government *172*
The French Civil Service *183*
The One and Indivisible Republic *185*
The Public and the Policy-Making Process *189*

10 DEMOCRACY IN FRANCE *192*

A Retreat from the Planned Economy *193*
The Social-Welfare State *196*
Human Rights *198*
French Responses to the Challenges of the 1980s *201*

**PART FOUR
FEDERAL REPUBLIC OF GERMANY** *207*

**11 DEMOCRACY IN A HOSTILE SETTING? GERMAN HISTORY
AND SOCIETY** *209*

The Emergence of Modern Germany *210*
Legacies of the Past *216*
Germany in the 1980s *220*
Economics and Politics: Good Economics Are Good
Politics *226*
Conclusion *228*

12 CITIZENS AND POLITICS IN WEST GERMANY   *231*

A New German Political Culture? *232*
The Germans in Politics *234*
Women and Politics in Germany *241*
People and Politics in West Germany *243*

13 GERMAN POLITICAL PARTIES AND INTEREST GROUPS   *245*

The German Party System *246*
Interest Group Politics in West Germany *257*
Conclusion *263*

14 GERMAN POLICY MAKING   *267*

The Bonn Republic *268*
The Civil Service *278*
German Federalism *279*
The Public and Policy Making *284*
Conclusions *286*

15 FROM "THE GERMAN PROBLEM" TO "MODEL GERMANY?"   *289*

The German Economy and Politics *289*
Social Policies in West Germany *293*
Civil Liberties in the Federal Republic *296*
German Responses to the Challenges of Governance *301*
Problem Areas in German Politics *304*
Conclusions *307*

PART FIVE
ITALY *309*

16 THE BACKGROUND TO ITALIAN POLITICS   *311*

The Emergence of Modern Italy *312*
Legacies of the Past *317*
Italy in the 1980s *320*
Economics and Politics *327*

17 CITIZENS AND POLITICS IN ITALY *332*

The Italians in Politics *336*

18 ITALIAN POLITICAL PARTIES AND INTEREST GROUPS *347*

The Political Party System *348*
Interest Groups and Italian Politics *361*
Stable Patterns of Political Participation and
    Instability *363*

19 ITALIAN POLICY MAKING *366*

Italian Republican Government *366*
The Constitutional Court *377*
The Bureaucracy *378*
Decentralization *380*
Citizen Control in Italian Politics *382*

**20 THE PERFORMANCE OF THE "UNSTABLE" ITALIAN
REPUBLIC** *386*

Politics and the Economy *387*
Stability and Instability in Contemporary Italy *393*
Human Rights *397*
A Peculiar Stability *400*

**PART SIX
THE OTHER EUROPE** *401*

21 A DIFFERENT POLITICAL SETTING *405*

The Uses of History *406*
Reshaping the Political Culture: Creating a New
    Socialist Citizen *407*
Eastern Europe in the 1980s *408*
Conclusions *414*

22 THE CITIZEN AND POLITICS IN COMMUNIST SYSTEMS *417*

The Individual and Politics *418*
Communist Parties in Power *425*

**23 POLICY MAKING IN EASTERN EUROPE AND THE
    SOVIET UNION**   *431*

Party Policy-Making Bodies *432*
Formal Government Institutions *437*
Parties with States of Their Own *441*

24 REFORM IN REVOLUTIONARY REGIMES   *444*

The Socialist Economy *445*
Total Welfare States *451*
Human Rights *452*
Relations Between the Soviet Union and Other East
    European Communist States *453*
Political Stability *455*

**PART SEVEN
CONCLUSION** *459*

Challenge and Response: European Democracy and the
    Crises of the 1970s to the 1980s *460*
Democracy Without a Vision *467*

INDEX   *469*

PREFACE

Western democracy as we know it today emerged at the end of the nineteenth century in a setting of newly industrializing societies. It responded to the social and political realities of West European and North American countries in that epoch. A century later, the social, economic, and political setting is entirely different in these countries. Some wonder if the political institutions that were fitted for industrial societies a century ago are still the ones that will meet the needs of postindustrial states. During the 1970s and early 1980s it appeared that western democracy was in a state of crisis and many wondered if it would survive until the end of the century in several of the countries where it had worked well for decades.

This book explores the purported crisis of democracy and its effects on West European countries. I contend that it was much less a crisis of democracy than a series of new challenges. In general, the West European countries I study—Britain, France, West Germany, and Italy—have responded well to these crises. They have proved able to reform when such changes were needed and to withstand pressures for changes that would have undermined the essence of western democracy: competitive elections, limited government, and respect for human rights. Of course, there will be new challenges and perhaps real crises to confront in these countries. But their successes in responding to the challenges of the 1970s and 1980s will further strengthen these countries. In facing and overcoming challenges, political systems acquire added public support and institutional flexibility. Their resilience in meeting these recent problems will encourage their citizens to allow them time to overcome future challenges.

This book also includes a brief overview of politics in the "other Europe" where communist political and economic systems are in place. Once viewed as an attractive alternative to western demoncracy, the communist systems have faced their own challenges, some similar to those in the West, others unique to their types of social systems. Indeed, the problems in Eastern Europe and the Soviet Union have reached crisis proportions and major social, political, and economic changes are under way in several of these countries.

Comparisons among these countries, both in Eastern and Western Europe, give insights into the organization and operation of democratic political systems. I believe that comparison is the social scientist's substitute for the laboratory of the physical or biological scientist. By looking at similar institutions in different countries, by comparing how different political systems respond to similar needs or problems, we can gain insight into the political processes. In a text addressed to introductory and intermediate-level students and general readers, I have tried to build these comparisons progressively. The section on Britain makes many references to U.S. political experience; succeeding sections refer back to the countries studied earlier when explaining the differences and similarities in the particular country under examination. While many instructors will prefer to follow the country-by-country organization of the text, those who wish to teach the course in a topical manner will find the chapters in each section are very close to each other in content and structure.

I have benefitted greatly from the readers who have criticized all or part of this text: Alberta Sbragia, University of Pittsburgh; Larry Elowitz, Georgia College; and Arthur M. Hanhardt, Jr., University of Oregon. I am especially grateful to my friend and colleague Rolf H. W. Theen who provided invaluable advice on the section on East Europe and the Soviet Union. Over the years, he has read many of my manuscripts and I have always found his comments to be particularly insightful and helpful. I appreciate my wife and four children who encouraged me and more importantly who helped me to forget this project from time to time.

PART ONE
INTRODUCTION
A Crisis of European Democracy?

The underlying theme of this book is an assessment of the strengths and weaknesses of western democracy in the last decade of the twentieth century. Democracy means, in the words of Lincoln, government of the people, by the people, and for the people. On account of large populations and the disinterest of many citizens in directly governing their countries, modern efforts to achieve this democratic ideal have always assumed a representative form in that the people rule through representatives who are freely elected by the citizens and accountable to the voters for their actions in office.

There are certain conditions that must prevail for democracy through elected representatives to function well. First, elections must be held at regular intervals. Second, the elections must be the means of choosing the principal governmental figures, those actually responsible for making the major decisions. Third, the elections must offer a choice between two or more individuals or teams of individuals with a realistic chance of winning the contest. All sides should have the opportunity to make their viewpoints known to the electorate. Fourth, voters must be able to perceive meaningful differences among the candidates, and these differences should correspond to some of the major divisions among the populace. Finally, the voting results must be honestly tabulated and respected.

These conditions are ideals. Nearly every country, even those where most of the people will grant the presence of representative democracy, falls short on occasion from one or more of these ideal standards. For example, in the United States, it is not clear that all sides have fair opportunities to present their cases during elections because of the high costs of American campaigns, and the often unbalanced finances of alternative candidates. American elections are periodically plagued by problems of electoral fraud. Many observers of electoral behavior, in the United States and elsewhere, have worried about the ability or willingness of voters to select candidates in accordance with the politicians' positions on issues and the voters' own preferences. The fact that these ideals are often not attained in the real world does not mean that representative democracy is fraudulent. Instead of absolute conditions, these ideals represent goals for perfecting the representative form of democracy. Those meriting the democratic label are the countries which come closest to meeting these standards.

About one-fourth of the world's population lives in countries where actual practices correspond closely enough to these ideal conditions to be regarded as democracies. Many of these democratic countries are located in western Europe, and most of the other democracies have patterned their constitutions on European examples. Western Europe is thus an excellent field for the study of the condition of representative democracy as we move toward the twenty-first century. The twenty or so democracies in this relatively small area govern a population well in excess of that of the United States. Most are apparently successful political systems with lengthy histories of stable democracy. They represent a variety of patterns and forms of democracy: centralized states and federations, parliamentary systems, and mixed presidential systems. Western Europe thus offers an excellent laboratory for the study of the strengths and weaknesses of modern democracy. Later in the book, we will compare the experience of these democracies in facing the challenges of a new century with that of Eastern European countries.

The countries included in this book—Britain, France, West Germany, and Italy—are among the most important European democracies. They have the largest populations and two, Britain and France, have legated democratic institutions to several of their former colonies. They constitute laboratories for other democracies in identifying and treating the ills of democracy, and offering examples for other democracies in responding to similar problems.

THE VIABILITY OF DEMOCRACY

Political philosophers such as John Locke, John Stuart Mill, and Immanuel Kant saw democracy as the ideal form of government. Viewing democracy as a natural political end of the civilizing process, they hoped for and predicted an almost inevitable movement toward democratic forms of government. They believed when properly organized, democracy would be durable. Once established, the virtues of democratic government would be so evident that it would become the universal and permanent form of government. Kant went on to predict that the spread of democracy would bring perpetual peace. Such optimism inspired nineteenth and early twentieth-century political reformers, who worked to install democratic governments in many European countries, with the belief that they were ushering in a new and lasting era of liberty and peace.

These optimistic visions were soon dispelled as the new democratic governments that emerged in Europe after World War I proved fragile and transient. Within a decade, most of the democratic regimes installed in central, southern, and eastern Europe had given way to autocracy. Generals and demagogues easily toppled or ignored the carefully constructed democratic constitutions to introduce new authoritarian regimes. Even in those countries where democracy had developed earlier and had functioned reasonably well, there were growing doubts about their ability to confront the rising social, economic, and international crises of the 1930s. Worse still, it appeared to some observers that certain democratic features actually fostered the rise of a new and more menacing autocracy as in the totalitarian rule in Stalin's Russia, Hitler's Germany, and Mussolini's Italy.[1] The historical optimism about the prospects and promise of democracy gave way to the recognition that democracy was neither easily established nor readily sustained.

The new democratic pessimism prevailed in the reconstruction of Europe after World War II. Any lingering hopes for the ultimate triumph of democracy were dispelled by the imposition of authoritarian regimes in the eastern half of Europe and the allure of a new "inevitable" form of government, the proletarian dictatorships of the communist people's republics. Even where democracies were instituted in western Europe, most observers were cautious of projecting long-term success. Few were optimistic about the chances of successful democracies in countries like Germany or Italy which had earlier abandoned democracy and so readily welcomed dictators. The shaky performance of some of them—France's Fourth Republic, Italy, and Greece—only added to fears about the future of democracy in Europe. Democracy was still seen as desirable but as perpetually insecure. The Nobelist Soviet author, Alexander Solzhenitsyn, captured well this pessimism that continues to color people's expectations about democracy:

> You have the impression that democracy can last, but democracies are islands lost in an immense river of history. The water is always rising.

In Western Europe—and the United States—conservatives fretted about the danger of subversion of democracy by foreign or domestic communist agents. On the other end of the political spectrum, Marxists postulated the inevitable destruction of what they labelled "bourgeois democracies" as a result of the internal contradictions of capitalist societies. People of all political persuasions held doubts stemming from their convictions of the internal and international dangers to democracy that democratic governments could survive over the long-term even in the most stable settings.

A CRISIS OF DEMOCRACY?

It is therefore not surprising that, when the politically placid and economically prosperous years of the 1950s and early 1960s gave way to tumultuous politics and economic uncertainty in the 1970s and early 1980s, these long-held concerns about democracy led many to talk about a crisis of democracy and even a possible end of democracy.[2] Without the cushioning effect of expanding economies, western democracies seemed especially vulnerable to a new set of political challenges. Indeed, many came to believe that democracy as it had existed in the western world was the product of a special set of social and economic conditions that had been present during the industrial era and that were no longer present as Western European and North American democracies moved into the new postindustrial era.[3]

The critics on the Left saw the current democratic systems as fatally flawed, and their imminent downfall as part of an inevitable crisis of capitalism long foretold by their doctrine. Conservatives were no less pessimistic but they cited the dangers of big government in endangering human rights and producing unmanageable bureaucracies. I shall argue throughout this book that the crisis of democracy was much overstated by such critics. But it is important to understand the purported symptoms of this new democratic malaise and the reasons for the great concern that it elicited about the ability of democracy to endure in the new social and economic setting.

Government Overload

Nineteenth-century democratic theory was founded on the notion of democratic government being limited government. Government power would be limited in that the rulers would be subject to meaningful restraints on what actions they could take to make and implement decisions. Equally important, democratic governments were limited in the scope of their activities. They shared responsibility for important community activities and decisions with non-governmental bodies such as private enterprises, churches, social associations, and other autonomous organizations of citizens. Many important social and economic decisions lay beyond the scope of governmental powers: prices and wages, investment and production, social and moral norms, care for the poor and elderly, and distribution of wealth. Government's responsibility was defined narrowly as the referee and rule keeper.

During the last half of the twentieth century, this notion of the limited scope of government has been severely challenged. The range of government activity has expanded into virtually all areas of peoples' lives. Table I.1 illustrates this by showing the growth of the government's portion of gross national product in several democracies. In part, this growth in government activity is the product of the need to mobilize society during wartime in order to defend democracies against the threat of totalitarian rule. But the more important explanation for the government's new role is that citizens have demanded that government act in many new areas to control the normal economic cycles and thus assure economic growth, prosperity, and solid currencies; to provide for the impoverished, the sick, the unemployed, and the elderly; to protect the environment; to assure consumer product safety; to promote the cultural arts; to preserve ethnic distinctions and folklore; to provide social and racial justice; and so forth. It is important to stress that this growth of government is not the result of power-hungry public officials seeking to extend their control over society. To the contrary, it is the product of relentless citizen pressure for community action to make collective decisions that in the past were not made at all or were made by private and thus non–representative forces.

There have also been periodic backlashes against this growth in the scope of government. Ronald Reagan in the United States and Margaret Thatcher in Britain based their appeals largely on the resentment citizens had come to feel toward "big government". However, virtually everyone, even vocal opponents of government's growth, wants more government action in some preferred area. Prosperous investors rankle at government's expenditures on the poor but call for regulation of the security markets and control of inflation. Truckers complain about government rules on driving safety but insist on the construction and maintenance of new super-highways. Farmers are displeased with urban renewal but want continued subsidies to protect farm prices. Doctors resist regulation of their fees but demand that government provide them with airports for their private planes. Artists and performers protest huge defense budgets but plead for government support for the arts. With everyone wanting greater or new

TABLE I.1 The Growth of Government

COUNTRY	Cost of Public Programs as % of GDP		Public Employment as % of total employment		Taxes as % of GDP
	1960	1982	1951	1982	1985
Britain	29.3%	44.6%	26.6%	31.4%	38.1%
France	30.2	47.5	n.a.	31.4	45.6
West Germany	28.2	44.8	14.4	25.8	37.8
Italy	26.6	48.5	11.4	24.4	34.7
Sweden	28.7	62.2	15.2	38.2	38.1
USA	25.0	36.3	17.0	18.3	29.2

Sources: Richard Rose, "The State's Contribution of the Welfare Mix," in Richard Rose and Rei Shiratori, eds., *The Welfare State: East and West,* (London: Oxford University Press, 1986), p. 29; Richard Rose, *Public Employment in Western Nations* (Cambridge, England: Cambridge University Press, 1985), p. 6; and US Department of Commerce, *Statistical Abstract of the United States 1988* (Washington, DC: US Government Printing Office, 1987).

state action, it is rare for governments to find sustained demands for the elimination of services or activities. When the economy sours, or social and other problems accumulate, people expect their governments to respond. Indeed, governments now find themselves accountable even for "acts of God". In the early 1980s, an Italian government nearly fell after a major earthquake in southern Italy because of complaints that government disaster preparations were inadequate.

As a result, citizens in western democracies find very few aspects of their lives where government does not intrude in one way or another. It seems likely that the growing expectations on government will continue and perhaps accelerate as the twentieth century comes to an end. The growing size of the world's population and limited natural resources will probably result in shortages of essential goods. No doubt when this occurs, governments will be called upon to control the allocation of scarce resources and perhaps even to regulate family size.

There are four consequences for democracy from this on-going expansion in government activity. First, the erosion of the limited scope of democratic government in itself raises an important question about the effects on democracy: can government powers remain limited while the scope of government continues to grow? As governments are called upon to do more, they necessarily need more power to accomplish the new tasks. The removal of limitations on the scope of government may mean reduction in the restraints on governments' methods of fulfilling these responsibilities.

Second, the vast expansion in government responsibilities means that public officials must make explicit decisions on an enormous range of issues, many of which were previously handled by non-governmental bodies or not made at all. The growing array of public decisions threatens to overload existing decision-making institutions.[4] Faced with growing numbers of public matters, executives and legislators may be unable to make rational decisions on many of them. They lack the time and technical knowledge to make intelligent choices on the often difficult and complicated issues.

Even if they delegate less important matters to civil servants, there are too many decisions for careful action, especially when added to the partisan and personal activities of elected public officials.

Third, the expanding role of government also means the increasing size and complexity of the bureaucracy. Even in countries where the bureaucracy is highly centralized, its growth causes more problems in coordinating the actions of the various departments and agencies. Efforts to coordinate and control only slow the already ponderous bureaucracy and enmesh it further in red tape. A British employer captured well the complexity of modern government regulations:

> It is not for nothing that the Lord's Prayer contains only 56 words, the American Declaration of Independence a crisp 300 words, while the EEC regulations on the export of duck eggs contains nearly 27,000.[5]

Citizens everywhere complain about the difficulty of dealing with large and impersonal bureaucracies. In many European countries, this is aggravated by the persistence of pre-democratic traditions of bureaucratic aloofness and disdain for the citizens they purportedly serve. Incident to the growth of government, the increasing contacts that people must have with bureaucrats results in more friction and more citizen disgust for the bureaucracy.

Finally, as government becomes bigger, it has a greater impact on people's daily lives. Popular expectations that government limit inflation has as a consequence government regulations of the availability and cost of loans for new cars, homes, and other consumer items. As people expect government to promote highway safety, it means that government must enact and enforce speed limits and seat belt laws that have constraining effects on the individual. The impact of government is thus very much in evidence for individual citizens, but they often feel powerless to affect these decisions that have such direct effects on them. In democracies based on public consent, the government must count on citizens to voluntarily comply with most of its regulations. As government's regulation of society increases, it becomes more dependent upon the willingness of the people to abide by the new rules. For example, in several American cities, planners designated certain lanes for car-pool vehicles only in an effort to conserve fuel and reduce traffic. The lanes were well marked and extensively publicized but citizens rejected this imposition of a new rule. There were too many violators for the police to ticket all of them and the program was abandoned. Hence, the growth of government means more impact of the state on people's lives, but it also means that government is more reliant on the voluntary observance of its social regulations.

A Crisis of Confidence

Another major dilemma for contemporary democracies is introduced: just as the need for people to trust their governments and acquiesce in mounting state influence in their lives is expanding, the public's level of trust and confidence in their governments is apparently declining. Polls in the 1970s and 1980s asking people about how much confidence they have in their government and its institutions show a sharp decline compared to responses given to the same questions in the 1950s and early 1960s. But lack of confidence goes beyond simply general attitudes to affect people's political behavior. Several democratic countries have experienced declining levels of participation in established political activities, notably, lower voter turnout for elections and fewer active participants in political parties.

There appear to be two explanations for this phenomenon. Some see a general shift in overall political culture, that is the attitudes, evaluations, orientations, and perceptions people have about politics. Citizens in democratic societies are better educated than in the past and are no longer as willing as they seemed to be in earlier periods to defer to political leaders. Instead, they are prone to question and challenge authority figures of all kinds. Trust in political leaders is being replaced by distrust in a new romantic or populist revolt.[6] The decline in political trust is part of a general questioning of authority and institutions that characterize this populist revolt. Emerging from the student movements that swept across most democracies in the late 1960s, the new populism questions authority of all kinds: rock music challenges established musical standards in form and political authority in its lyrics; "pop art" disregards the rules and practices of art; mod or punk dress ignores the strictures of haute couture; and growing numbers of citizens look to the street for political power they once left safely in the hands of elected officials.

The other explanation of declining public confidence in government is linked with the communication revolution of the postwar era. People are better educated and as a result better informed about their political leaders than ever before. The spread of television to virtually every household in the western world brings political leaders nightly into the homes of their people. Citizens who before had only brief glimpses of their leaders through still pictures in newspapers, are now treated to vivid images of the foibles and frailties of their public officials. The attention focused on leaders by television, including extensive coverage of their private lives and foibles, removes some of the glamour and mystique of the once distant politicians. For example, a generation of Americans will remember the problems that former President Gerald Ford had in controlling his golf shot since he periodically beaned on-lookers crowded along the greens. The always present television cameras took the story to the homes of all Americans. This errant slice in his golf stroke and his tendency to bump his head exiting planes, gave an image of ineptness that diminished his authority and may have contributed to his 1976 election defeat. Television's focus on the warts and follies of public personalities does not always contribute to good democracy. People often expect their leaders to be near the gods and television shows them to be the humans that they are. It may very well be the case that past democratic stability was enhanced to some degree by the ignorance of the people about their leaders.

The media's probing of the lives of political leaders goes far beyond these amusing human interest stories. There is a natural and essential adversary relationship between news reporters and political leaders in western democracies. The leaders want the press to convey their viewpoints and accomplishments, and present them in the most positive way. The reporters have the obligation of assuring that what the government and other politicians claim to be the relevant facts are accurate. In the age of instant news coverage for breaking stories, there are no scoops in the old sense of reporting a major event before your rivals. Nowadays, the competition involves investigative reporting that digs up hidden and usually embarrassing facts that politicians would prefer not to see brought to the public's attention. Much of this investigative reporting is desirable to inform the electorate, but its excesses contribute to public distrust of its leaders.

The tensions between the media and politicians result in a better informed public. The populist revolt brought to the fore new attitudes and patterns of political behavior that may enrich democracy over the long run. But both of these forces are seen as undermining public confidence in democratic government during a trying era. They contribute to a general crisis of confidence at the very moment when the increased activity and impact of the state make public confidence more essential to governments' stability and effectiveness.

The Decline of Parties and Interest Groups

As citizens have lost confidence in their leaders, they have turned away from the political parties where these leaders are recruited.[7] In the United States and many European countries there are signs of party dealignment or the turning away from the established parties by voters who in past years were linked with them.[8] No longer do citizens identify as readily with political parties as they once did. Alignment with a party used to mean that individuals would vote for the candidates of the party with which they identified. Now, voters are less inclined to identify with a single party. Those that do so are more willing to vote for candidates of other parties when they see these other candidates as closer to their own positions or as more attractive than those candidates nominated by "their" party. The decline of established parties is manifest also in the corps of active supporters needed for campaign and other partisan work. Party membership is dropping, and those members who remain are less loyal and less willing to engage in party activities. The old incentives for party engagement—patronage benefits, insider knowledge, pursuit of ideological goals—are no longer either appealing or realistic to prospective party activists. Among those still engaged in party work, both rank-and-file members and elected public officials, are less responsive to calls for party discipline and unity. Without grassroots workers, party organizations decay; without central discipline, they lack cohesion and strength.

A similar process of decay has hit mass membership interest groups—especially trade unions, but also the established women's organizations, student groups, and even some business associations. Members have left these organizations or have decreased the intensity of their commitment when they have stayed on. The political influence of these interest groups is thus affected. It also makes them less reliable partners for government, since they lose their ability to assure their members' compliance with the agreements the group leaders reach with each other and government.

Western representative democracies have relied upon the parties and the groups to structure political participation. The size of modern states makes it difficult for governments to respond to the demands and interests of each individual. The parties and groups have aggregated the disparate interests of individuals and packaged them into meaningful and coherent programs that government can then act upon. The weakening of these political bodies raises questions about their ability to speak for the citizens they claim to represent. The decline of parties is particularly disconcerting since parties are the chief means of linking the people with the state.[9] They organize, structure, and conduct elections—and thus they assure democratic choice and accountability. Their decay threatens the essence of western democracy.

A Crisis of Participation

Even though people are questioning their party loyalties, the rising education level of citizens in western democracies has brought an important increase in the willingness and ability of people to participate in politics on an individual basis. Political scientists have long noted a positive correlation between the degree of education and political involvement: the higher the education the greater the political participation. Before World War II, it was unusual for people in European countries to complete the equivalent of high school; very few attended the then elitist universities. Now, high school education is the rule and a much larger percentage of young people go on for further education in the much more accessible universities and institutions of higher education. Consequently, a larger proportion of the population is aware of politics and more willing to become involved. The effects of higher education in mobilizing citizens for political action are magnified by the heightened sense of government's impact on people's lives. Together, they create a much broader pool of politically interested and aware citizens.

In addition, whole new categories of citizens who in earlier periods were excluded from politics are now able and eager to participate in the political process. Women, for example, once limited in their political roles by socialization patterns and outright discrimination, are now politically active. When the level of education is held constant, they are as likely as men to become involved in politics. Ethnic minorities previously had only limited participation because of language barriers or alienation from the central political system; now they are more willing to become active participants. Students who used to confine themselves to their books now more frequently take up political causes.

This expansion of political participation seems to be on the surface, a positive development for systems striving to provide government by the people. But for some observers of democracy, it is a participation explosion that causes concern. They believe that successful representative democracy requires a delicate balance of two levels of political involvement; some informed citizens who are actively involved in politics to assure democratic control over government, and many less-informed citizens whose political involvement is less-intense but nonetheless positively supportive of the existing system.[10] This balance permits orderly government since too many participants would overcharge the representative bodies and create chaos. Many of the arguments supporting this viewpoint are not relevant to the present participation explosion.[11] The fear that excessive participation would mobilize the poorly educated, who are uninformed and less attached to democratic norms, is no longer a problem since the current mobilization is based on expanded categories of well-educated citizens. Reference to past eras of overpoliticization, when the high levels of participation were motivated by serious crisis and tended to aggravate the problems of maintaining order in unstable situations, do not seem appropriate to either the causes or effects of the contemporary expansion in participation.

Whatever the relevance is of these concerns in the current situation, others criticize these restrictive views on participation as excessively elitist. Being more concerned with the ideal of citizen involvement, they have fewer concerns about overloading democracy with too much citizen participation.[12] For these observers, the higher levels of participation bring new people, often those whose views were neglected by government into the system. Their inclusion reduces possibilities of alienation and portends a more responsive and reform-minded government.

Apart from this philosophical debate over the desirability of mass participation, another concern is that the increase in participation comes at a time when the traditional organs of representation—political parties and interest groups—are in decay. Their stodginess makes them unattractive to new participants, and their organizational weaknesses reduce their ability to absorb and channel the new people seeking a political voice.

Newly mobilized citizens more often wend their way into new social and political movements that rival the older representative bodies: ethnic parties, peace movements, women's groups, anti-tax parties, ecological movements, neighborhood organizations, citizen action groups, and an array of other groups. Because these movements are often organized around a single paramount issue, they are not readily absorbed into broader political coalitions. Their zealous dedication to a single cause makes it difficult for government to meet their demands. Democratic government usually means compromise—or what is called a "satisficing" strategy where most involved groups get some but not all of their demands met by government action. When a group has total commitment to a single purpose, such partial solutions are not enough. Even part success is failure and leads to the political alienation of those who have often devoted large amounts of time and energy to the cause only to see it fail to decisively change public policy. These movements lack formal membership and internal decision-making procedures. There is little organizational patriotism and few material or status incentives from working in the movement. As a result, the new movements often serve as vehicles for episodic, if intense, involvement. They are unable to provide the long-term, sustained participation through periods of partial achievement and failure, that is needed for success in democratic politics.

It is not only the extent of political participation that causes concern. Observers worry also about the new forms of participation. The repertoire of political action has expanded considerably, offering a broader range of alternative political tactics to those seeking involvement.[13] In addition to the conventional avenues of political participation such as election campaigns, letters to elected representatives, and membership in established interest groups and political parties, concerned citizens are using new and unconventional forms of participation. The new forms range from policy noncompliance and sabotage, boycotts, demonstrations, political violence, and revolt. Such approaches bypass traditional representative institutions in favor of direct action; in fact, some are explicitly designed to disrupt those institutions. Unconventional forms of political action are not new in western democracies. What is novel, is the greater frequency and more rapid recourse to these techniques. New participants who find existing representative bodies unresponsive to their concerns or too slow in acting on them, turn to direct action.

These unconventional forms of political participation are seen as disruptive and destabilizing to democratic processes. They bypass the usual representative structures. They are often more adapted to publicizing an issue than to resolving it. As an example, a few years ago, an international commission met in London over several weeks to discuss the whaling industry and the need to protect whales. One morning, delegates were surprised to find the hall filled with reporters and television cameras as they convened the session. Then a group of demonstrators—the first to appear during the conference—burst into the room, threw blood on the Japanese delegation because of its support for continued whaling, and then left. The media recorded the dramatic episode and departed too. That evening, the event made headlines and was featured on the television news—the only coverage that the conference received in the general press. The anti-whaling group had staged a media event and caught the fleeting attention of the public, but it had no impact on the policy set by that conference. And such is often the case with the new forms of action. Unless sustained by traditional forms of participation, they rarely succeed in shaping public policy. They thus appear to many as disruptive, ineffective, unnecessary, and destabilizing in western democracies.

The more extreme forms of unconventional participation involve violence and these too have become more common in western European democracies. Political terrorism has become a particularly grave menace to these democracies. The destruction and casualties caused by terrorist acts promote insecurity among the citizenry and lead to doubts about the ability of government to provide for the safety of its people. It is nearly impossible to eliminate the tiny terrorist groups while still observing democratic guarantees needed for the protection of the rights of more responsible political actors. When an authoritarian regime captures suspected terrorists, it can torture them, find their accomplices, and thereby more readily eliminate terrorism. In contrast, democracies are bound by the due process of law and real restraints on their abilities to interrogate and investigate suspected terrorists. The elimination of the small secret societies that are still capable of wreaking major damage is thus much more difficult in the democratic setting. Indeed, terrorists hope that their actions will unleash a reaction in the form of restrictions that will affect all people and build sympathy for their cause. The reactionary policies will presumably reveal to all the fraud they contend "bourgeois" democracy to be. This conservative reaction in turn will extend dissatisfaction with the regime and make it easier to recruit a broader range of supporters for the cause of the terrorists. The facility with which a small handful of extremists can attract attention and feel that they are pursuing their goals, and the difficulty of democratic governments in countering terrorist violence makes terrorism attractive to the very discontent. Terrorism has thus become a major challenge to contemporary democracy.

Institutional Sclerosis

Many of the most important formal institutions of democratic government appear to some to be in an advanced stage of decay. The basic element of parliamentary democracy, the popularly elected legislature, has suffered a sharp decline in its power and prerogatives.[14] With the exception of the United States Congress and a few other democratic parliaments, the legislative branch has lost power to the executive. In theory, parliament still controls the prime minister and cabinet, known collectively as the "government". But in practice, the government often dominates parliament through its disciplined parliamentary majority. The government also controls the parliamentary agenda in most European democracies. While it is rare for the government to fail to win legislative endorsement of its proposals, very few bills that are initiated by members of parliament are adopted. At times, it appears that the legislative body has become little more than the ratifier of the executive's proposals.

Political executives, prime ministers or premiers, and their cabinets, are not immune from the danger of institutional decay. I have already noted the effects of the media's close scrutiny on public confidence in leaders. Frequently, national leaders win impressive electoral victories and then, after a brief honeymoon, find their public approval ratings dropping rapidly and precipitously. Even successful leaders face such serious difficulties in imposing their imprint on public policy. They usually must settle for only incremental adjustments to existing policy so that even they look ineffective and weak. Often it appears that the skills that brought political victory are not those needed to direct the modern state. The problems of coordinating the vast enterprises of modern government and the inevitable discovery of inefficiency or corruption in some part of it soon erode the public standing of once popular leaders. In addition, executives are held accountable for the state's inability to do all that is expected of it. For example, while governments are held accountable by their electorates for the health of the economy, it often appears that the problems of inflation and unemployment do not respond to a government's best efforts to cure them. The failure to manage these intractable problems, nevertheless, leads to a deterioration of public confidence in the leaders and to the diminution of their authority.

Decision-making power appears often to be slipping out of the hands of elected officials and into the hands of technocrats. Highly technical matters, which are increasingly prominent on the political agendas of modern democracies, require technical expertise that even well-educated politicians do not have. For example, decisions on the need for a new power plant or on the safety of nuclear power plants are highly technical issues requiring expertise that politicians rarely possess. As a result, parliament has accorded the bureaucracy more direct power to decide important issues which the elected body lacks the expertise to make on its own. It is not only the legislative branch that finds its powers shorn by the complicated policies of modern democratic states. The elected and politically responsible officers in the executive branch, too, are increasingly obliged to defer to the experts on important public issues that require specialized knowledge that they do not have.

The expanding decision-making powers of these technical experts have led some to see the emergence of a "technocracy" where highly trained specialists in the bureaucracy rule behind the facade of a democratically elected government.[15] While the technocrats have the needed expertise, they often neglect or ignore political and human dimensions. For example, experts may correctly predict energy needs and determine the appropriate site for a nuclear energy plant from the economical and technical standpoint. But they are less sensitive to the political costs of dislocating people, to the social effects of disrupting neighborhoods, to public concerns about nuclear accidents, and other human and social factors than would be elected public officials. With the power of technocrats on the rise, politicians face growing difficulties in controlling those who claim to support their positions on the basis of their superior knowledge of "scientific facts."

Among the many instances when technocrats have manipulated their technical knowledge to control decisions was a British cabinet decision a few years ago on whether to authorize the expansion of a nuclear energy plant. Senior civil servants in the energy department, committed to the expansion of the country's nuclear energy capacity, concealed information about a nuclear accident in the plant until after the cabinet had acted. They feared that the news of the accident would tip the decision against the new plant. And yet that information should have been available to the politicians making the decision. These examples are all drawn from nuclear energy but this is by no means the only policy area where technocrats have demonstrated their power. The increased role of government in society and the economy necessitates public decisions on highly technical matters. This gives unelected and politically unaccountable experts the ability to control or subvert the decisions of elected public officials over a wide range of issues that affect people's lives in a direct and constant manner.

Beyond the manipulation of technical knowledge, the control of the immense bureaucracies in modern democracies presents a real challenge for elected political leaders.[16] The various government agencies and departments develop departmental policies and loyalties that endure through the changes in political leadership produced by elections. The bureaucrats often resist policy changes that go against the department's viewpoint through controlling the information given to the political leadership or through deliberate slowness in doing what is asked of them when they believe the politicians' decision to be a wrong one. They are even better at blocking government efforts to enact reforms that strike at their vested interests: their jobs, salaries, privileges, their established recruitment patterns, and their procedures and chains of command. Reform of the bureaucracy is thus one of the most difficult and least successful reforms undertaken by democratic (and nondemocratic) politicians.

Most European democracies are highly centralized in that nearly all political power is concentrated in the national government with few prerogatives reserved for regional or local governments. Centralization has caused popular resentment as government regulations impinge more directly on people's daily lives and activities. People feel that those who make the policies that affect their lives are unresponsive. They see public officials as beyond their control and unaware of local needs and regional variations. But efforts to decentralize government have been few and limited. National politicians are loathe to give up their power; bureaucrats oppose measures that might reduce their established procedures and prerogatives; and even local politicians, the presumed beneficiaries of decentralization, prefer the system they know and have learned to work with to uncertain experiments in decentralization.

Many observers see democracies as increasingly handicapped by the stagnation and decline of the traditional political institutions. The representative and elected bodies are seen as unable to carry out their governing duties and thus as failing to maintain the link between people and their government. In a time of general crisis in democracy, the institutions that should lead in the adaptations to a new social and political setting are themselves in decay.

The Erosion of Civil Liberties

A variety of changes threaten to undermine basic human rights that are essential parts of democracy. Modern electronic technologies permit greater intrusion into the lives of individuals. The accumulation of vast banks of information about individuals, and the availability of sophisticated computers to keep track of the data, permit the monitoring of people's activities. The availability of these data can be used to attack organized crime, but they can also be abused to the detriment of the individual's right to privacy.

The danger of internal subversion and spying by enemies of democracy seems to require the use of methods such as wiretaps and surveillance that would be unacceptable violations of the individual's political rights. Western

Europe, sharing a long frontier with eastern bloc countries, is particularly sensitive to the need to defend against such dangers. The rise of terrorism justifies abridging important rights in order to counter this threat to public order. The search for subversives, however, often leads to the use of these security provisions against political rivals. For example, in 1986 in West Germany, there was a major controversy over alleged government efforts to use intelligence agencies against the Greens, a responsible party with elected representatives in the Bundestag.

In all these areas of concern, there is a delicate balance to be struck between the state's need to maintain its internal security and the individual's rights. It is a balance that might easily tip one way or the other with potentially disastrous consequences for democracy either way.

Many European countries are facing for the first time the danger of racism. Large scale immigration of manual workers from Third World countries and of refugees from former colonies have introduced important racial minorities into racially homogeneous societies. Once welcomed as a source of inexpensive manual laborers, the immigrants were seen as guest workers. As the number of immigrants mounted to the point that they constituted significant percentages of the total population, tolerance for the newcomers wore thin. When the prosperous years of the 1950s and 1960s gave way to leaner times, resentment grew stronger. Foreigners were seen as taking jobs that otherwise might have gone to natives. Often vying with lower-income natives for jobs and social benefits, the immigrants were blamed with overburdening schools, public housing, and social welfare. They were also held accountable by some for rising urban crime rates.

Some politicians responded to the growing intolerance for immigrants by advocating discriminatory laws and even mandatory repatriation. Politicians from all points on the political spectrum insisted on tightening immigration laws even to exclude family members of immigrants already resident in European countries. Several countries enacted programs to pay large bonuses to immigrant workers who agreed to return to their homes. Heightened tensions caused by the new intolerance and the immigrants' reactions resulted in racial violence. In several countries, notably in Britain, high unemployment in the 1980s severely affected the immigrant workers and contributed to rioting in their depressed neighborhoods. The question seems to be whether countries which have never had to deal with racially distinct populations can develop the tolerance necessary to grant these peoples the equality and liberty the natives have insisted on so strongly.

A changing society, the growth of government, economic constraints, new technologies, and the arrival of large numbers of racially distinct peoples all pose challenges to the maintenance of civil liberties in twenty-first century democracies. They will challenge the historical commitment of most Western Europeans to respecting a broad range of human rights.

CHALLENGE AND RESPONSE

I have spelled out in some detail the elements of the crisis many see facing democracy in the last years of the century. Some parts of this purported crisis may well be more imaginary than real; others may be exaggerated;

other elements are indisputably serious problems for western democracies. In fact, my own view is that there is no crisis of democracy. Instead, democracy faces a series of important challenges that pose difficulties but do not threaten its very existence. As democratic governments face these challenges, as they must, and surmount them, as I believe they are doing, democracy will emerge strengthened and better able to meet a new set of challenges in the next century.

It is the conviction that citizens can learn from the experience of other countries and that they have the ability to strengthen and refine their democracies, that leads me to believe that it is useful to see how Western European democracies are coping with these challenges. The experience of four countries—Britain, France, West Germany, and Italy—will be our real-world laboratory for examining the impact of these problems and the ways some democracies have tried successfully and unsuccessfully to respond. It is also useful to assess whether these problems afflict the non-democratic countries of Eastern Europe and if so how these Communist countries have responded. In the conclusion, I will return to these symptoms of crisis to evaluate the extent of the danger and explain the viability of western democracy.

NOTES

1. J. L. Talmon, *The Origins of Totalitarian Democracy*, (New York: Praeger, 1970).
2. For a summary of these arguments, see Michel Crozier et al., *The Crisis of Democracy: Report on the Governance of Democracies to the Trilateral Committee*, (New York: New York University Press, 1975).
3. On the political consequences of the postindustrial era, see Samuel P. Huntington, "Post-Industrial Politics: How Benign Will It Be?" *Comparative Politics*, 6 (January 1974): 163–91.
4. Anthony S. King, "Overload: Problems of Governing in the 1970s," *Political Studies* 23 (Nos.2–3 1975): 284–296; Samuel Brittan, "The Economic Contradictions of Democracy," *British Journal of Political Science* 5 (No.2 1975):129–159; and A.H. Birch, "Overload, Ungovernability and Delegitimation," *British Journal of Political Science* 14 (No. 2 1984):135–160.
5. L. Neal, "Industrial Democracy in the United Kingdom, An Employer's View," in *Proceedings of the International Conference on Industrial Democracy*, (Sydney, Australia, 1978), p. 115.
6. See Samuel H. Beer, *Britain Against Itself: The Political Contradictions of Collectivism*, (New York: Norton, 1982), pp.107–208; and Vivien Hart, *Distrust and Democracy: Political Distrust in Britain and America* (Cambridge: Cambridge University Press, 1978).
7. See Kay Lawson and Peter H. Merkl, *When Parties Fail*, (Princeton, NJ: Princeton University Press, 1988).
8. See Russell J. Dalton et al., eds., *Electoral Change in Advanced Industrial Democracies: Realignment or Dealignment?* (Princeton, NJ: Princeton University Press, 1984).
9. See Kay Lawson, ed., *Political Parties and Linkage: A Comparative Perspective* (New Haven, CN: Yale University Press, 1980).
10. See, for example, Gabriel A. Almond and Sidney Verba, *The Civic Culture: Political Attitudes and Democracy in Five Nations* (Boston: Little, Brown, 1965).

Britain has long been regarded as one of Europe's, and indeed, the world's, most durable and successful democracies. With political traditions dating back to medieval times, it has preserved a sense of continuity while changing into a modern democracy.

This long, successful, tradition of democracy faced such challenges in the 1970s that a spate of alarmist books raised questions about Britain's ability to survive: *Britain in Decline, Britain: The Future That Doesn't Work, Britain Against Itself,* and *Is Britain Dying?* Yet Britain has survived and done quite well. Its record should be useful in understanding the strength of western democracy in a time of trials.

CHAPTER ONE
SOCIAL CHANGE
AND TRADITION
IN BRITAIN

I was brought up in a faith untroubled by doubts . . . We were all wonderfully optimistic then; believed in progress . . . in Mr. Gladstone [prime minister 1868–74, 1880–85, 1892–94] and in our moral and intellectual superiority. . . . And no wonder. For we were growing richer and richer every day. The lower classes, whom it was still permissible to call by that delightful name, were still respectful, and the prospect of revolution was still exceedingly remote.

Aldous Huxley,
Those Barren Leaves

One of the most notable features of British history is the sense of political continuity. In the other European countries to be examined in this book, there have been a series of regime changes during the twentieth century. France has gone through three republics, a fascist dictatorship, and a provisional government; Germany has experienced an empire, two democratic republics, Hitler's totalitarian state, and an occupational government; Italy has had a constitutional monarchy, a fascist dictatorship, a provisional government, and a democratic republic. In Britain, however, one has to go back to the seventeenth century to find a regime change— Cromwell's military and parliamentary dictatorship. And then it was only a twelve year aberration in over a millenium of political continuity under the monarchy.

However, the various social, political, and economic changes that swept over Europe in the eighteenth and nineteenth centuries did not miss Britain. Indeed, some of them, such as the Industrial Revolution, appear to have originated in England. But Britain's uniqueness was the ability of its existing political and social order to accommodate these changes without violent breaks with the past. One historian notes:

> The true "miracle of modern England" is not that she has been spared revolution, but that she has assimilated so many revolutions—industrial, economic, political, cultural—without recourse to revolution.[1]

Thus, at the end of the twentieth century, the British face the task of adjusting to new social changes and a difficult economic situation within the context of a political order shaped over a thousand years.

THE LEGACIES OF A GLORIOUS PAST

A Respect for Tradition

Contemporary British democracy emerged out of seven hundred years of gradual change from the Magna Carta in 1215, when the first limits were placed by the nobility on the powers of the monarch, to the Parliament Act of 1911, that transferred final decision-making power from the aristocratic House of Lords to the popularly elected House of Commons. Unlike other countries where the institutions and practices of the past have been abandoned as they have been replaced by more modern forms, the British have carefully preserved their traditions and historical bodies even as they have changed or sometimes completely lost their functions. This careful preservation of colorful tradition does more than simply attract tourists: It evokes historical memories that add legitimacy to the overall political system. It impresses public office-holders with the dignity and responsibility of their positions. It stimulates patriotism, national pride, and unity among the British people.

While old institutions and practices persist, they often do so with entirely new purposes and derive their public acceptance for completely different reasons. This can be illustrated easily in the case of the monarchy. The monarch's role changed from that of a feudal overlordship (legitimized by military strength and dynastic claims during medieval times), to a royal absolutism (based on a claim of "divine right" during the Tudor period [1485–1603]), to a monarchy (ruling with the consent of Parliament in the seventeenth century), to a limited constitutional monarchy (legitimized by the monarch's acceptance of limits on his or her political role during the eighteenth and nineteenth centuries), to finally, a ceremonial figurehead in a parliamentary democracy (legitimized by tradition and by the monarch's total abstention from politics in the twentieth century).[2] In a like manner, other medieval institutions persist today, often still bearing the paraphernalia of bygone days. But their tasks in today's democratic regime are much different from their past functions. While institutions continue and their outward forms remain imbued with the past, their actual performance has changed completely to accommodate the needs of a modern industrial democracy.

Democracy Through Gradual Reform

Over the past three hundred years, while revolution and political turmoil shook and divided other European countries, Britain's political institutions evolved gradually and rather peacefully into their contemporary democratic forms. Insulated by its island status from invasion and conquest, Britain could develop politically at its own evolutionary pace. The evolution toward democracy was aided by the absence of political absolutism. By the seventeenth century, the powers of the monarch were limited by Parliament. However, the residual royal powers served to prevent a new absolutism by Parliament, prime ministers, or military figures.

Despite many sources of social unrest, discontent was often manifest in religious dissidence rather than political dissent. Methodism, Puritanism, Congregationalism, and other "nonconformist" religions diverted social and economic unrest thereby reducing possible sources of support for violent revolution. As Walter Bagehot noted, even the most miserable and discontented did "not impute their misery to politics."[3] In addition, British colonies in North America, New Zealand, and Australia served as safety valves for social unrest. Groups and individuals with religious or political grievances could emigrate; occasionally such dissidents were driven out by oppressive governments.

Also important in the evolutionary nature of British politics was the ability of those holding power to recognize growing pressures for change and their willingness to respond to this pressure by both, deflecting demands for more radical change and preserving their own political power. The Conservative party, long the most important and successful political party, was particularly adept at this. Driven by a powerful will to rule, the Conservatives were quick to accept and enact reforms proposed by others. In many cases the Conservatives, though they represented the most privileged sectors of the population, took the initiative in carrying out far-reaching social and political reforms. This Tory reformism was not simply a means of perpetuating their hold on political power but was also a result of the British aristocracy's genuine commitment to a notion of *noblesse oblige,* that is, the responsibility of the privileged to care for the general well-being of all people. Though paternalistic and often neglectful, the aristocratic sense of obligation led Conservative governments to press for political and social reform.

The Conservative tendency to accept change was complemented by the willingness of those wanting change to seek it through reform and compromise. The "practical good sense of the British workingman" led the working class to use its political strength to encourage reform rather than to promote revolt.[4] Rather than insisting upon radical and rapid change, the socialist and liberal forces adopted a gradualist approach to their social and political goals, often accepting the partial reforms handed down by Conservative governments.

For many observers, the moderation of British workers and other advocates of change was the central element in the peaceful evolution of modern Britain. Writing over a century ago, Bagehot labeled England as "a deferential country." He saw in this deference a reciprocal willingness of the upper classes to reform and the lower classes to consent to government by their social betters. For him and others, this deferential political culture was the secret to the British success.[5] Some now assert that this deferential society disappeared by the 1970s[6] but it appears to have had a major impact on the development of modern British democracy.

A Strong and Stable Ship of State

One important legacy of Britain's deep traditions is the sense of permanence and durability that they confer upon modern institutions. Centuries of uninterrupted history give the impression that a future with similar political characteristics lies ahead. The polity has met and adapted well to challenges that have toppled other regimes: the social disruptions of the industrial revolution, the emergence of genuine democracy in an aristocratic setting, the egalitarianism of a powerful and well organized working class, the military threats of two Napoleons and Hitler's blitz, and the building and eventual loss of history's largest empire. Survival of so many trials and challenges in the past gives modern Britons the feeling that whatever the difficulties of the present, "there will always be an England."

The evolutionary nature of the adjustment to these various challenges has made the state appear strong and stable. And indeed it has been so. As a legacy of the American struggle for independence against this strong but distant British state, Americans have come to mistrust concentrated political power and to regard it as dangerous in itself. The British do not have such fears of a strong state. They see the state as having permitted the transfer of ultimate control from a narrow elite to the general citizenry. With the Crown still holding formal ownership of most public property and enjoying theoretical sovereignty, but with the monarch politically impotent, the British are reminded that even concentrated power is subjected to the rule of law. They admire strong political leaders capable of using fully the powers of office. For example, Prime Minister Margaret Thatcher won plaudits (and the next election) for her strong and successful reaction to the Argentine invasion of the Falkland Islands in 1982. Britons recognize the unusual virtue of their government which respects civil liberties and practices representative democracy in trying times of war and peace. They are willing to accord the state considerable power to meet collective needs in an efficacious and efficient manner.

The British have considerable pride in the success of their political institutions. There are many reasons for such pride; the country's cultural heritage, its physical beauty, its economic success, as well as its political features. In Britain, public approval of the political institutions is one of the principal sources of national pride. The ornamental monarchy instills great pride in British people,[7] but so do the less glamourous but more practical institutions such as Parliament and the government. Britons are rightfully proud that their Parliament has served as the model for successful copies in countries as disparate as Canada, Kenya, and India. Such pride in political institutions buffer the state from the ineptitude of particular leaders and give citizens confidence in the ability of the system to ultimately prevail over contemporary problems.

A Royal Past or Delusions of Grandeur?

In any country with such a positive record in the past, there is the danger of complacency. The feeling that "there will always be an England" may lead citizens and leaders to procrastinate in responding to real needs for adaptation. Past successes may become contemporary liabilities when political leaders fail to note soon enough the changed setting. For example, Britain's far-flung empire was gradually dismantled in the twenty years after the Second World War but Britain's pretentions to a continued world power status were expensive and contributed to its economic decline in the 1960s and 1970s. The absence of social revolution has left Britain with an archaic aristocracy. The traditional problem-solving strategy of compromise and accommodation—the seeming explanation for past success of British politics—appears as unprincipled "muddling through" and as ineffective in responding to the multiple challenges of the last decades of the twentieth century. Finally, and most tragically, three hundred years of near-continuous conflict in Ireland left a legacy of heroes, slogans, and battle tactics for modern combatants in Northern Ireland. A common, schoolyard, rope-jumping rhyme captures well the tendency even among the youth to look backwards in this sad conflict:

> To hell with the future
> And long live the past,
> May God in his mercy
> Look down on Belfast.

TABLE 1.1   Extent of National Pride, 1981

Percent expressing pride in their country:

Country	Proud	Not Proud	Don't Know
United States	96%	2%	2%
Britain	86	11	3
Italy	80	17	2
France	76	17	7
West Germany	59	29	12

Source: Adapted from Richard Rose, "National Pride in Cross-National Perspective," *International Social Science Journal,* 37 (No. 1, 1985), p. 86.

Britain's history, like that of most other countries, passes on to its present leaders both challenges, in the form of unsolved problems and resources, in the form of past successes and emotion-laden historical symbols that can unite and mobilize the population. How these historical assets and liabilities are used depends largely, on the leadership's perceptions of the problems and resources of this legacy, and on its skill in using its strengths from the past to solve contemporary challenges. Current problems may have taken some of the luster off Britain's glorious past, but few advocate a break with this past through radical change or revolution.

BRITISH SOCIETY IN THE 1980s

Social Changes

Social Class Decomposition.   The evolution of democracy was not accompanied by a leveling of British society. The industrial revolution produced sharp economic and social differences between the privileged classes and the impoverished, new, industrial working class. The oppression inspired not only Dickens' novels, but also Karl Marx's critique of capitalism and his prediction of an inevitable proletarian revolution. Even the gradual spread of egalitarian ideas in the twentieth century did not affect the well-structured social classes. The result was the anomaly of a flourishing class system replete with dukes, duchesses, barons, lords, and ladies alongside a nonetheless democratic government. The education system perpetuated these class lines dividing children at an early age between the privileged, who attended elite private boarding schools (paradoxically known as public schools), and the others in state-owned schools. Within the state schools there was further distinction as the students were tested at 11 years of age. Those with more potential (usually from the more affluent homes) were directed to the grammar schools to be groomed for higher education, while those who did poorly on these exams went to "modern" schools for technical training. Education patterns and tradition combined to draw sharp distinctions between the working class and the middle and upper classes as reflected in their entire lifestyles—from diet to preferred sports, religion to recreation, and access or the lack of to consumer goods.

Despite these clear class differences, social tensions have generally been minimal in twentieth-century Britain. Class, however, has had important political consequences. For most of this century, social class has been the most reliable predictor of voting behavior. The Conservative (Tory) party drew its strength principally from the middle and upper classes, and the Labour party relied heavily on working-class voters. There were some deviations from this pattern, notably the presence of "working-class Tories," industrial workers who were expected to vote Labour. The deviation was understandable in the light of other intervening factors; religion, parental influence, and social deference. But the strength of class in the citizens' voting decision was stronger in Britain than in any other western democracy.[8]

In the past two decades, however, social class has lost much of its political saliency. Whereas in the 1964 elections, the voting decision was primarily a reflection of the voters' social class, by the 1983 elections voting reflected a rational choice based on the voters' perception of the parties' positions on the issues and their own stands on those issues.[9] Table 1.2 illustrates the declining hold of the Conservatives on middle class voters and the Labour party on workers. Britain's once class-ridden society has given way to one where class distinctions are poorly perceived and of little political consequence. Thus the percent of voters who voted for their "natural" class party has declined steadily in nearly every election, dropping from 67 percent in 1951 to 47 percent in 1983.[10]

There has been a striking decline in the willingness of Britons to identify with a social class. In 1964, 50 percent of those polled felt they belonged to a particular class; the same question in 1981 found only 29 percent feeling part of a class.[11] Even among those still sensing a class loyalty, the identification is merely formal with few consequences for the individual's political or social behavior.[12] While the shift to issue voting from class determined voting reflects a more sophisticated public, the rapid decomposition of social classes portends political disruptions.[13] Class identification was linked with partisan identification and thus provided a secure political base for the major parties which in turn provided support for party government. The decay of class solidarity weakened the ability of leaders to speak for their followers and fostered more independent action on the part of workers.

Among the most important reasons for the decline of class is the diminution of objective differences in class. There has been a leveling in British society since the Second World War produced by progressive tax structures, which have taxed the wealthy more heavily than the poor, and by the use of these tax revenues, to provide an extensive set of social welfare programs to insulate the less advantaged from economic uncertainties. Until recently, Britain had one of the most equitable distributions of income in western countries and one of the best developed systems of social benefits. Educational reforms, including the introduction of com-

TABLE 1.2 Social Class and Voting

	1964		1983			1987		
	Conservative	Labour	Conservative	Labour	Alliance	Conservative	Labour	Alliance
Higher managerial	86%	14%						
Lower managerial	81	19	60%	10%	28%	57%	14%	26%
Supervisory	61	39						
Office and clerical	61	39	51	20	27	51	21	26
Skilled manual	29	71	40	32	26	40	36	22
Semi- and Unskilled	25	75	33	41	24	30	48	20

Source: 1964: Samuel H. Beer, *Britain Against Itself,* (New York: Norton, 1982), p. 81; 1983 and 1987: *The Sunday Times,* 14 June 1987.

prehensive secondary schools to eliminate the old division between grammar and modern schools and expanded opportunities for higher education, have facilitated upward social mobility for working-class children.[14] Working-class solidarity, the keystone of social awareness, has been undermined by the growing complexities of the contemporary economy. Heavy industry, the traditional bastions of worker solidarity, is in decline in Britain thus providing fewer people the setting in which working-class awareness flourishes. The old rift between skilled, semi-, and un-skilled workers remains. It is supplemented by new divisions between: employed and unemployed workers, workers whose jobs are secure and those whose are not, workers in public employment and those in the private sector, workers consuming private services and those living in public housing or benefitting from public services, workers in innovative new technologies and those in declining industries, and so on. Most importantly, the workers who were once seen as excluded from the political system, now appear well integrated into the modern British state. In its traditional sense, social class seems to have lost much of its political saliency in Britain.

Among those who see the working class as an important force for desirable social change, there has been efforts to seek a new basis for class politics. They challenge the integrative effects of class mobility and see the decline in class tensions as temporary.[15] Some expected important sections of the burgeoning middle class of technical and supervisory employees would feel similar oppression to that of manual workers and align themselves with the working class, but this alignment has not occurred.[16] Some have sought to redefine class by basing it not on self-identification nor on occupation but rather on "consumption sectors."[17] Under this conception, new class lines are inherent in the public or private nature of three crucial arenas whether individuals are employed in the private or public sector, they rely for housing, transportation, and other vital services on public or private sources, and their income comes in the form of public benefits (pensions, unemployment aid, etc.) or of private payments. The consumption pattern is then linked with voting and other political behavior. There is political potential in this new bloc of citizens dependent on the public since over half the adult population derives its primary income (as pensioners or government employees) from the state. It is doubtful though that such new social categories will have the unifying force or political impact that traditional class structures once had.[18] In Sweden, a switch in the 1960s from a pure working class party to one based on this state clientele proved successful for Swedish Social Democrats. But the British Labour party has yet to try such a strategy and remains tied closely to its shrinking trade union base.

The Resurgence of Ethnic Nationalisms. The proper name for modern-day Britain is the United Kingdom of Great Britain and Northern Ireland. It is the union of the three nations inhabiting the island of Great Britain—England, Scotland, and Wales—and the people of northeastern Ireland.[19] This amalgam of nations is symbolized by the national flag, the Union Jack, which is the overlapping of the crosses of St. George, St.

Andrew, and St. Patrick, the patron saints of England and Wales, Scotland, and Ireland. These peoples once had separate political units. Their unification under the English crown was achieved through conquest, Wales in 1535, Ireland in 1542, and Scotland in 1603.

The numerical superiority of the English often leads to the overlooking of the ethnic diversity of the United Kingdom (see Table 1.3). Since the English make up nearly 80 percent of the total population, there is a tendency to equate Britain with England. But the various nationalities still identify themselves first as English, Scot, Welsh, or Irish rather than as British.[20] While most have political loyalty to Britain, they still feel themselves distinct from other nationalities in the United Kingdom. Someone from Scotland or Wales would probably be offended if a foreigner labeled them as English.

By the end of the Second World War, all three of the minority nationalities seemed well integrated and satisfied with terms of their union with England. However, in the 1970s, ethnic nationalism reemerged with a vengeance and threatened the unity of Britain. In Scotland and Wales, nationalist parties suddenly gained unexpected electoral strength and began calling for autonomy or even independence for their nations. In Northern Ireland, the rebirth of Irish nationalism brought near civil war as the non-Irish Protestants of Ulster resisted any hint of concessions to the Irish minority.

It is difficult to explain the resurgence of these nationalist causes. In part, renewed ethnic awareness was stimulated by an international contagion. Decolonization in the Third World, the American civil rights movement, and French-Canadian separatism provided examples of oppressed people rising up to insist on their right to self-rule. The Irish, Scots, and Welsh drew inspiration from these struggles and successes. In addition, dissatisfaction with both the major parties left many voters looking for alternative parties, and they found them in the nationalist parties. In Scotland, the discovery of important oil deposits offshore led to nationalist desires to keep Scottish oil for Scotland.

Nationalism was revived in times of growing economic hardship in regions that were on the periphery and had not shared fully in the prosperity of the 1950s and 1960s. That the nationalist revival coincided with the decline of social class may be no coincidence. With class conflict no longer a fashionable explanation for social and economic discontent, people looked for other causes for their continued dissatisfaction. Many in Northern Ireland, Scotland, and Wales found them in ethnic discrimination by the English and believed greater autonomy could be the answer.

While there can be no doubt of the sincerity of beliefs in discrimination, it is difficult to make an objective case for it in either Scotland or Wales.[21] Minority groups have been overrepresented in Parliament and for the country's political leadership. With 17 percent of the total population, Scotland, Wales, and Northern Ireland account for 22 percent of the members in Commons and have provided six of the eighteen twentieth-century prime ministers.[22] Government expenditures on local services are higher on a per capita basis in Scotland, Wales, and Northern Ireland

FIGURE 1.1   Map of the United Kingdom. *Source:* Rolf H. W. Theen and Frank L. Wilson, *Comparative Politics: An Introduction to Six Countries* (Englewood Cliffs, NJ: Prentice Hall, 1986). Reprinted with permission.

TABLE 1.3 Population by Region in the United Kingdom

	1981 POPULATION	PERCENT OF TOTAL POPULATION	PERCENT OF TOTAL LAND AREA
England	46,363,000	83.1%	53.8%
Scotland	5,130,000	9.2	32.0
Wales	2,792,000	5.0	8.6
Northern Ireland	1,491,000	2.3	5.6

Source: Whitaker's Almanack 1985 (London: Whitaker, 1984), pp. 618, 629, 676.

than in England. The fact that these regions are less economically developed than England is due to their lack of resources and their distance from the European markets. Their economic problems stem from changes in the world economy rather than from English exploitation.[23] For many in Scotland and Wales, the issue was less economic than cultural. The spread of a national culture was threatening distinctive Scottish and Welsh cultures. This was dramatized in Wales by the decline of those speaking Welsh from 37 percent of the population in 1921, to 29 percent in 1951, and to 19 percent in 1981.

In Scotland and Wales, the nationalist surges have already receded. At their peak in the mid-1970s, the Scottish Nationalist party took 30 percent of the Scottish vote and the Welsh nationalists won nearly 11 percent of voters in Wales. Parliament passed devolution measures creating regional assemblies in Scotland and Wales with some powers over local matters. The decentralization was conditioned on the acceptance of the reforms in separate referendums in May, 1979 for Scotland and Wales. Neither was approved by the voters: In Scotland a bare majority of voters supported the devolution measure but this was only 32.9 percent of the registered vote, well below the 40 percent stipulated by Parliament for ratification. In Wales, the vote actually went four to one against devolution. In the aftermath of these electoral rebuffs, Scottish and Welsh nationalist movements went into rapid decline.

The referendum defeats are striking evidence of the public's uncertainty about the wisdom of decentralization. In abstract, the notion of bringing government closer to the people is appealing. But when concrete proposals are made, voters and politicians are hesitant to endorse them. Decentralization or devolution involve departures from existing patterns of behavior and power relationships. Uncertainties about how the new system will affect these patterns, worries about who will pay for the new layers of government, and concerns about the effects on national unity make decentralization appear too risky to many. In effect, the nationalists appear to have been satisfied with a few token reforms embellished with greater respect for the separate cultural traditions and, in the case of Wales, for the local language.[24]

The situation in Northern Ireland has not been as easy to resolve. The clash between Protestants of Scottish and English ancestry and Irish Catholics is often cited as an example of the violent potential of the modern

TABLE 1.4 Electoral Support for the Scottish and Welsh Nationalist Parties

Election Year	Welsh Plaid Cymru			Scottish Nationalist Party		
	Votes	% Welsh vote	Seats won	Votes	% Scottish vote	Seats won
1959	77,571		0	21,738		0
1964	69,507	4.8%	0	64,044	2.4%	0
1966	61,071		0	128,474		0
1970	175,016		0	306,802		1
1974	171,264		2	632,032		7
1974	166,321	10.8	3	839,617	30.4	11
1979	132,544	8.1	2	504,259	17.3	2
1983	125,309	7.8	2	334,676	11.8	2
1987		7.3	3		14.0	3

Sources: L. J. Sharpe, "Devolution and Celtic Nationalism in the United Kingdom," *West European Politics* 8 (July 1985): 85; Ian Richardson and Richard Rose, *The Nationwide Competition for Votes* (London: Frances Pinter 1984), p. 19; and *The Sunday Times,* 14 June 1987.

crisis of democracy. They are in fact, simply the modern continuation of a centuries old conflict. The causes of strife go deep into the history of the British conquest of Ireland. Whereas most of Ireland was divided up among absentee landlords, in the north, colonists from Scotland and England settled in permanently. When the Irish, at last, won their independence after the First World War, the descendants of these settlers insisted on continued union with Britain. The island was partitioned with six counties in the northeast, basically the province of Ulster, remaining part of the United Kingdom. Whereas the rest of Ireland had an overwhelming Catholic, Irish majority, Northern Ireland was predominantly Protestant and non-Irish. The Irish, both in and out of Northern Ireland, rejected this partition as unnatural and an unacceptable relic of English domination. Northern Ireland's Protestants, however, outnumbered Catholics in the region by two to one. They used their majority to establish Protestant hegemony and their threat of violence to extract a concession from the British government never to change their status, that is, permit Northern Ireland to be incorporated into Ireland without the consent of a majority of the inhabitants of that region.

Despite blatant political and economic discrimination against the Irish Catholic minority in Northern Ireland, the issue remained quiescent until the mid-1960s. Then a better-educated, young generation of Catholics organized a civil rights movement patterned on the American one to insist on the end to discrimination. The Protestant majority rejected even minor concessions. By 1968 Catholic civil right demonstrations and Protestant, counter demonstrations brought rioting. With the local police biased toward the Protestants, the British sent in the military, principally to defend Catholics against Protestant violence. However, the presence of British troops revived Irish nationalism and the Irish Republican Army. A variety of other Irish extremists reorganized to fight British oppression. Fueled by the memories of 300 years of conflict, contemporary religious bigotry, and extremism on both sides, the "troubles" have lasted two decades, taking a terrible toll of lives lost and scarred in the violence. (See Table 1.5)

It is difficult to fault the British government for the continued problems. It intervened to protect the Catholics from Protestant violence; it suspended the Protestant Northern Irish parliament in 1972 when it was clear that the body would not accept Catholic political equality. While Irish Catholic nationalists in Northern Ireland have loudly called for British withdrawal, the Irish government in the south has quietly urged Britain to stay on and prevent further deterioration of the situation. The intransigence of both sides in Northern Ireland has left Britain trapped. Extremists have quieted more moderate elements and prevented compromise solutions.

Both Protestant loyalists and Catholic nationalists have engaged in random acts of violence, assassinations, and bombings and then escaped into the sympathetic crowds of their supporters. IRA provos on occasion, have carried the terror to Britain. This urban terrorism has proved difficult

TABLE 1.5 Deaths from the Conflict in Northern Ireland, 1969–1985

Police and military	757
Irish nationalist fighters	240
Protestant loyalist fighters	62
Civilians	1,383
Prison officers	24
Total	2,466

Source: The New York Times, November 24, 1985, p. E-3.

TABLE 1.6 Principal Actors in the Northern Conflict

Loyalists		Nationalists	
POLITICAL PARTIES	BATTLE GROUPS	POLITICAL PARTIES	BATTLE GROUPS
Democratic Unionist Party (Ian Paisley's hard-line loyalists opposed to any compromise) *Official Unionist Party* (slightly more moderate but still hard-line Loyalists)	*Ulster Volunteer Force* (terrorists) *Ulster Defense Force* (vigilante type body) Orange Lodges (fraternal organizations with para-military organizations) A variety of neighborhood defense organizations	*Sinn Fein* (Political wing of IRA, demands British withdrawal and integration with Ireland) *Social Democratic Labour Party* (Moderates opposed to violence but favorable to eventual integration with Ireland)	*Irish Republican Army Officials* (Marxist-oriented group. *IRA Provisionals* "Provos" (Terrorist body) Variety of schismatic groups of terrorists

to control. When the government tried preventive detention of suspected terrorists, the prisons became a boon for terrorist recruiters. If young people were going to be jailed on suspicion of terrorism, many decided they might as well deserve the punishment by perpetrating terrorist acts. When preventive detention was suspended in 1974, IRA terrorism declined and extremist groups had a more difficult time recruiting activists. But the terrorist threat remains important in Northern Ireland and is likely to continue to be so.

In 1985, Britain adopted new measures for Northern Ireland in the hopes of moving the opposing sides closer to compromise. To placate Irish Catholics, the British agreed to grant Ireland a consultative voice in Northern Irish affairs through a new Anglo-Irish Conference. The Irish agreed to assist in tracking down suspected terrorists who take refuge in the Republic. The Irish government recognized formally that no change in the status of Northern Ireland can take place without the acquiescence of the majority of the people there, and, at the present, the majority was hostile to such a change. Protestants reacted vigorously against this Anglo-Irish agreement interpreting it as allowing the Irish government to meddle in the affairs of Northern Ireland. In an attempt to mobilize opinion, all Unionist members of Parliament resigned their seats. In the ensuing elections, Protestant hard-liners hoped to demonstrate massive rejection of the accord. The level of Unionist support fell below expectations, and the moderate Social Democratic Labor Party fared better than the extremist Sinn Fein among Catholics. This support was a promising start for what will be a long process of easing tensions and paving the way toward ending the blood feud between the two peoples of Northern Ireland.

Immigration and Racism.   One legacy of the imperial era was the immigration of large numbers of people from Britain's former colonies. Originally, citizenship in any British Commonwealth, country or colony, included citizenship in the mother country as well. Tens of thousands of people from the colonies moved to Britain in the 1950s and 1960s. Violence on the Indian subcontinent prompted the emigration of large numbers of Indians, Pakistanis, and Bangladeshis. African independence often meant the large Indian class of merchants in East Africa had to leave their African homes, and most came to England. Many also emigrated from the West Indies as these Caribbean Islands achieved self-rule. As the flow of immigrants grew, citizenship was redefined and immigration strictly limited in the late 1950s and early 1960s.

By that time, however, the nature of Britain's population had been forever altered. In 1951, the non-white or "coloured" population totalled 74,000 or 0.2 percent of the total population; by 1971, it had increased to 1.5 million or 2.3 percent; in 1981, the coloured accounted for 3.5 percent of the population. Through normal growth patterns, the non-white population will reach 3.3 million or 6.7 percent by 2001. Already, by the mid–1980s, many coloureds were born in Britain (48 percent of the West Indians and 43 percent of the Pakistanis and Bangladeshis residing in Britain). Clearly they can not be dismissed as foreign immigrants who will return to their homes someday. They are durable features of British society.

The very rapid growth of the non-white population, its concentration in industrial centers, and its resistance to assimilation created animosity among the indigenous people with whom they competed for jobs and social services. When the economy worsened in the late 1970s, and many native Britons found themselves out of work, there was a tendency to blame the immigrants for unemployment. Racial hatreds mounted, despite government efforts to promote tolerance, and sometimes were manifested in beatings of blacks by discontented whites.

The immigrants suffered too from the economy's problems. Living in deteriorating council (public) housing, their children went to overcrowded schools, and they faced overburdened social service providers. With unemployment very much higher among the immigrants than in the general population, social unrest rose in black neighborhoods. By the early 1980s, tensions exploded into riots in Brixton, Totenham, Birmingham, and elsewhere. These were not racial riots since the participants and victims were nearly all black. But they did reflect the economic unrest and frustration with discrimination felt by the non-white immigrants.

The political consequences of racism have been limited. So far, the coloured vote has not been an election factor except in a very few districts. This will change as the size of this population grows, and as the racial minority comes to see political answers to their problems. There has not been much of an electoral backlash among native voters. Unlike in France where an anti-immigrant National Front posed a serious challenge, the British National Front proved to be an electoral failure. It organized several large demonstrations against immigrants in the late 1970s but then virtually disappeared after an election disaster in 1979. The major parties have avoided demagoguery despite efforts by Enoch Powell to bring the issue into the Conservative party in the early 1970s.

After centuries of isolation from regular contact with other racial groups, the British now face the challenge of learning to live harmoniously with an increasing number of nonwhite citizens. For the government, the task of balancing conflicting claims from natives, immigrants, and people abroad wanting to immigrate will continue to be difficult. At the same time, the government must avoid pushing native whites toward extremist backlash groups, promote the integration and acceptance of those immigrants in Britain, and accommodate requests for immigration from dependents of those already here. Above all there is the need to promote racial understanding. While democratic governments can enact laws insisting on racial equality and nondiscrimination, they have much more difficulty in changing people's attitudes and legislating tolerance.

Religion and Politics

The clash in Northern Ireland is in part a continuation of religious wars of the past. The historic rhetoric continues to give this conflict a religious dimension. Northern Protestant leaders are often clerics who denounce growing Irish influence as leading to an inevitable rule of Northern Ireland by the pope. But it is now more an ethnic conflict than a religious one: The issues at stake are economic and political power rather than doctrinal viewpoints.

Elsewhere in the United Kingdom, religion has only minimal effects on politics. The link between party preference and religion in Britain is of much less consequence than in France, Germany, and Italy where religious faith has an important effect on electoral choice. There is some historical association between religious preference and party identification: Members of the Church of England tend to vote Conservative while members of the "nonconformist" religions—Methodists, Congregationalists, Baptists—are more likely to vote Labour. But the religious factor has little explanatory value in understanding contemporary voting behavior.[25]

The Church and State remain formally linked in Britain. The Queen is at once head of both the Church of England and the Church of Scotland (Presbyterian). Clerical appointments in these established churches have to be cleared by the government. Ordinarily, that is a routine matter but politics can intrude. In 1987, the nomination of a Church of England bishop was blocked by Prime Minister Thatcher when the local Conservative member of Parliament complained that the people in his district "had had enough left-wingers and did not need another tub-thumping bishop."[26] Tax revenues are distributed to all churches to match contributions by individual members. Despite such links, the British state is essentially secular and religious influences in politics and vice versa are minimal.

Politics and the Economy

Unlike the strong sentiment in the United States opposed to government management of the free enterprise economy, Britons have expected a much larger role for the state in the economy. From the nineteenth-century mercantilism of the Conservatives to the twentieth-century socialism of the Labour party, the tradition of state economic intervention was well accepted. The result was a mixed economy with an important public sector of nationalized industries interacting with a large sector of privately held enterprises. For most of the postwar era, the public sector has grown in size under both Conservative and Labour governments. In addition, both parties supported an extensive system of social welfare benefits.

Britain's economy has not performed as well as elsewhere in Europe. Concern about this decline in the mid-1970s destroyed the consensus on a managed economy and social-welfare society. Thatcher launched an assault on the public sector, trimming social welfare benefits and selling off public corporations. The Labour party took another approach promising to extend the public sector when they returned to power. Despite both parties' ideological goals, the economy remains a mixed one with extensive social-welfare programs with broad public support of the active sociopolitical role of government.

Beyond the balance between the economy's private and public sectors, the employment structure is changing also. The agricultural population is amongst the smallest in Europe and has been through most of the century. British peasants had moved to the cities in the nineteenth century and found employment in the thriving blue collar factories. But since World War II, a new shift has taken place. Whereas two or three decades ago, most Britons earned their livelihoods in industry, the majority are employed now in the service sector, for example, education, sales, health care, finance and banking, communication, transport, and government. (See Figure 1.2) Between 1973 and 1985, industrial employment declined by 26 percent in Britain. Part of the continuing problem of unemployment has been the failure of the service sector to offer jobs for all those displaced by this shift. The shift has also weakened class alignments since the industrial setting has been a key element in the development of class awareness and solidarity.

The growing international economic interdependency was another complicating factor. Britain joined the European Economic Community (the Common Market) in 1973, 15 years after the body was created. Britain had missed the growth era of the Common Market and joined late with a stiff buy-in price just as the boom ended. Britain's adjustment to the taxing and price policies of the Common Market fed inflation and economic disarray. It placed restraints on the kinds of policies that Britain could use to manage its economy.

Other restraints came from the international banking community whose confidence was essential for loans and investments from abroad. In effect, both the Common Market and the international banking community placed new limits on the ability of Britain (and other governments as well) to select their own economic and social policies. This was graphically demonstrated in 1976 when Britain turned to the International Monetary Fund for assistance in fighting a run on the pound. The needed loan was granted but only after the IMF attached conditions placing strict limitations on British government expenditures forcing the government to drop several

FIGURE 1.2   Employment by Economic Sector in Britain. *Source: The World Almanac and Book of Facts* (New York: World Almanac, 1988).

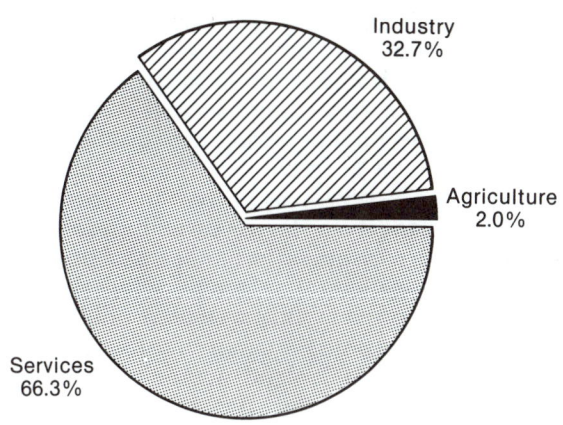

Industry
32.7%

Agriculture
2.0%

Services
66.3%

economic and welfare programs that it was committed to carrying forward. This intervention by unaccountable financeers into the ability of sovereign states to determine their own domestic policies demonstrated the curtailing of national sovereignty by growing interdependency.

Economic changes such as these and the increasingly complex economic relations made the government's task of managing the economy very difficult. Indeed, the situation became so complex and dissatisfying that the economic roles were seen by observers from all political perspectives as the principal cause of government overload in the 1970s.[27] The mid-1970s were a real trial of the government's economic skills. There was the oil shortage, the resulting worldwide recession combined with rampant inflation, the adjustment to membership in the Common Market, and unhappy and unruly union workers. The tried solutions of the past did not work in this novel situation. Without clear guidelines of its own and receiving conflicting and changing advice from both labor and management, the British government stumbled through the mid-1970s, sometimes trying to prod the economy and then, only a few months later, trying to cool it down. It is not surprising that these stop and go policy shifts did not solve Britain's economic decline; instead, they added to citizens' concerns about the ability of their government to manage the new and unpredictable economic forces. It was in this troubled setting that parties reexamined the postwar socioeconomic consensus and sought new answers to the challenge of mastering the new economic forces. The results of the search and the question of whether governments can still manage the economy will be examined in Chapter 5 of this section.

CONCLUSION

British political history and contemporary social and economic patterns pose important challenges to the state; adjusting the legacies of the past to the realities of the present, the loss of class as an organizing force in society and politics, the tragic conflict in Northern Ireland, racial conflict, and a stagnant economy with staggering unemployment. The open expression of the tensions from these and other problems permits the government to perceive potential difficulties, to respond to the needs of special sections of society, and to prevent the deepening of social cleavages. The consensus on the political and socioeconomic structures produced by centuries of conflict and compromise helps keep conflict at manageable levels. It is only when this consensus breaks down, as it has in Northern Ireland, that democratic stability is endangered. There three hundred years of violence and hatred fuel modern terrorism and prejudice and pose serious problems for contemporary political leaders. The geographic isolation of the conflict on a separate island helps prevent this serious problem from becoming a national crisis; most Britons dismiss it as an "Irish" problem, not a British one. The troubles in Northern Ireland are an ancient rift, not a crisis produced by modern social tensions. Britain offers little evidence of a breakdown in the social and economic systems underpinning modern representative democracy.

NOTES

1. Gertrude Himmelfarb, *Victorian Minds*, (New York: Knopf, 1968), p. 292.
2. Keith Thomas, "The United Kingdom," in *Crises of Political Development in Europe and the United States*, ed. Raymond Grew, (Princeton, NJ: Princeton University Press, 1978), pp. 56–59.
3. Walter Bagehot, *The English Constitution*, (Ithaca, NY: Cornell University Press, 1963), p. 249.
4. Samuel H. Beer, "The British Political System," in *Patterns of Government: The Major Political Systems of Europe*, 3rd ed., Samuel H. Beer et al., (New York: Random House, 1973).
5. Bagehot, *The English Constitution.*
6. See Dennis Kavanagh, "Political Culture in Great Britain: The Decline of the Civic Culture," in *The Civic Culture Revisited*, ed. Gabriel A. Almond and Sidney Verba, (Boston: Little, Brown, 1980), pp. 124–176; and Samuel H. Beer, *Britain Against Itself: The Political Contradictions of Collectivism*, (New York: Norton, 1982), pp. 107–208.
7. See Richard Rose and Dennis Kavanagh, "The Monarchy in Contemporary Political Culture," *Comparative Politics*, 8 (April 1976), 548–576.
8. Robert R. Alford, *Party and Society*, (Chicago: University of Chicago Press, 1963); and Paul R. Abramson, "Social Class and Political Change in Western Europe: A Cross-National and Longitudinal Analysis," *Comparative Political Studies*, 4 (July 1971): 131–155.
9. Mark N. Franklin, *The Decline of Class Voting in Britain: Changes in the Basis of Electoral Choice, 1964–1983*, (Oxford and New York: Oxford University Press, 1985).
10. Anthony Heath, Roger Jowell, and John Curtice, *How Britain Votes*, (London: Pergamon, 1985).
11. Martin Harrop, "The Changing British Electorate," *Political Quarterly* 53 (October–December 1982): 393.
12. Gordon Marshall et al., "Class, Citizenship, and Distributional Conflict in Modern Britain," *British Journal of Sociology* 36 (June 1985): 259–284. See also David Robertson, *Class and the British Electorate*, (London: Basil Blackwell, 1984).
13. Beer, *Britain Against Itself:* 79–103.
14. John H. Goldthorpe, *Social Mobility and Class Structure in Modern Britain*, (Oxford: Clarendon Press, 1980).
15. Ibid.
16. See, for example the difficulty of situating technical employees: Peter Whalley and Stephen Crawford, "Locating Technical Workers in the Class Structure," *Politics & Society* 13 (No. 3, 1984): 239–252.
17. Patrick Dunleavy and Christopher Husbands, *British Democracy at the Crossroads*, (London: Allen & Unwin, 1985).
18. Franklin, *The Decline of Class Voting in Britain*, pp. 156–57.
19. On the multinational character of the modern United Kingdom, see Richard Rose, *The Territorial Dimension in Government: Understanding the United Kingdom*, (Chatham, NJ: Chatham, 1982).

20. See Richard Rose, *Governing Without Consensus: An Irish Perspective,* (Boston: Beacon Press, 1971), pp. 42–73.
21. For an attempt to make such a case, see Michael Hechter, *Internal Colonialism: The Celtic Fringe in British National Development, 1536–1966,* (London: Routledge and Kegan Paul, 1975).
22. Anthony H. Birch, "Minority Nationalist Movements and Theories of Integration," *World Politics* 30 (April 1978): 325–344.
23. Philip M. Rawkins, "Outsiders as Insiders: The Implications of Minority Nationalism in Scotland and Wales," *Comparative Politics* 10 (July 1978): 519–534.
24. For example, the Welsh, Scots, and Northern Irish are the only subnational units permitted to participate in European Cup soccer competition alongside other fully independent countries.
25. Franklin, *The Decline of Class Voting,* pp. 17, 85.
26. *The Times* (London), 9 April 1987.
27. See Anthony S. King, "Overload: Problems of Governing in the 1970s," *Political Studies* 23 (Nos. 2–3 1975): 284–296; and Samuel Brittan, "The Economic Contradictions of Democracy," *British Journal of Political Science* 5 (No. 2 1975): 129–159.

CHAPTER TWO
BRITISH CITIZENS
AND
POLITICS

Political scientists usually find that the political culture, or the underlying sets of political values, orientations, and attitudes, are important in understanding a country's politics. As we have seen, a deferential political culture stressing acquiescence to social betters as governors, and a corresponding sense of responsibility to the broader community amongst those who rule seem to have played an important part in the evolution of modern democracy in Britain. Ordinarily, such deep-seated values and feelings are durable, and they have seemed particularly long-lived in Britain. But this traditional political culture faces challenges in contemporary social change.

Elsewhere in Western Europe, people are acquiring new political values as a result of the relative prosperity and security of the past forty years.[1] With the fear of war and the need to provide for the material necessities of life no longer the pressing concerns they were in the past, citizens are shifting their focus from "materialist" concerns with protection and basic needs to newer "postmaterialist" values promoting self-expression and equality, protecting and enhancing the environment in which they live, and achieving a sense of aesthetic potential. Younger people are especially prone to express these new postmaterial political values. Many observers believe that the new values will bring different priorities to government in much of Western Europe in coming years as these postmaterial younger generations reach the age where they dominate politics. But in Britain, the trend toward postmaterial values is less clear. Britain has lagged behind in this revolution of values because its slower economic growth has kept people, young and old, concerned with jobs, inflation, and the future.[2]

Nevertheless, political values in Britain are changing in other ways. The deferential political culture sustained twin attacks from first a technocratic revolution and then a populist revolution that challenged both the old deferential patterns and the new technocracy.[3] As government became more complex, there was less place for the gentleman politician who governed through the deference of the general population and more demand for technical experts whose governing role came not from social station but from specialized education. The revolt of the 1960s and 1970s questioned authority of all types and undermined the elitism of both traditional deference and technocracy. A populist mood of egalitarianism and participation rejected the notion that power should be left in the hands of the privileged or the specialists.

Under these attacks, the deferential political culture evolved. But, in typical British tradition, the changes refined the previous cultural pattern rather than rejecting all of it. Deference is not dead; some its features have changed while others remain the same.[4] No longer does British political deference mean popular acquiescence to government by some aristocratic Tory ruling class. Two contemporary Tory prime ministers (Edward Heath and Margaret Thatcher) were even far from this traditional mold of Conservative leaders. But support for strong leaders, another key element in the deferential political culture, remains and helps explain the popularity of a Margaret Thatcher.

The nobility no longer rules but the underlying principle of *noblesse oblige*, that the governors exercise their authority in the general interest rather than their own narrow interests, persists and limits both Labour and Conservative governments. Few believe that the Queen has political power but, and perhaps for this reason, nearly all British citizens strongly support the continuation of her ceremonial political roles. Blue-collar workers no longer vote Conservative out of admiration of the aristocracy's social standing, but a sizable number of them regularly vote Tory out of conviction that the Conservative party defends their interests better than does the Labour party. People are better educated and able to form their own political views, but more than half the people (see Table 2.1) betray a deferential attitude when they declare that they have little or no interest in politics and still remain supportive of the existing system. In contrast with Americans, the British still appear more trustful of government, more elitist, and less participatory.[5] What is surprising is how much of the deferential culture still persists with all the social changes, after the onslaught of the 1970s.[6]

The British remain remarkably loyal to their political system. An overwhelming 94 percent evaluate their representative government as very good or fairly good.[7] Antisystem parties, such as the Communists on the far Left and the neo-fascist National Front on the far Right, together poll less than 0.2 percent of the vote in general elections. The public shows strong support for the traditional British approach to gradual improvement of society through reform (71 percent) with only 5 percent claiming to

TABLE 2.1   Level of Political Interest

	BRITAIN	FRANCE	GERMANY	ITALY
Level of interest				
a great deal	12%	11%	14%	4%
to some extent	38	33	37	17
not much	35	29	37	37
not at all	15	27	11	42

Source: Eurobarometer, (No. 19, June 1983), p. 44.

see a need for revolutionary change.[8] Nor is there evidence of increasing levels or alarming current levels of mistrust of political institutions among the British.[9] A solid majority report satisfaction with the way democracy works. Most of those who express reservations do so out of dissatisfaction with the current government rather than with the system itself. Above all, the British in their respect for their institutions, their voluntary compliance with the law, and their support for peace and order exhibit a "civic decency" conducive to stable democracy.[10]

THE INDIVIDUAL IN POLITICS

The debate over whether or not too much participation destabilizes democracy is a moot one in Britain. Indeed, one observer believes that the proportion of the adult population actively involved in politics now is little different from what it was 100 years ago before the completion of democratization.[11] Few Britons do more than vote and read about politics in newspapers (see Table 2.2). More demanding political actions; membership in a party, election campaign work, involvement in local communities, and candidacy for public office, attract only a very small group of political activists.

TABLE 2.2   Frequency of Political Actions, Britain

Percentage of respondents claiming to engage in activity:

	OFTEN	SOMETIMES	RARELY	NEVER
Read about politics in paper	36	30	19	15
Discuss politics with friends	16	30	23	30
Work to solve community problem	4	13	13	69
Convince friends to vote as self	3	6	8	82
Contact officials or politicians	2	9	13	74
Attend political meetings	2	7	12	78
Campaign for candidate	1	3	3	91

Source: Adapted from Samuel H. Barnes, Max Kaase et al., *Political Action: Mass Participation in Five Democracies,* (Beverly Hills, CA and London: Sage, 1979), p. 541.

The low level of participation is not necessarily a positive feature. Public apathy is linked in some countries with alienation but this does not appear to be the case in Britain. It does weaken efforts by parties and politicians to link people with their political processes. It can lead to actions that do not represent the views of the general public. For example, the low level of individual involvement in the Labour party facilitated the capture of that party in the 1980s by factions unrepresentative of the overall Labour electorate. Group leaders, unaware of or unresponsive to their members' views, make demands on government that are not those of the membership they claim to represent. A democratic government that arouses so little public enthusiasm prompts questions about its legitimacy. This is not a new phenomenon in Britain but one that has characterized British democracy since its inception. Indeed, some see it as a sign of the deference which has been a source of strength and stability.[12]

The British public appears moderate in its political orientations. Figure 2.1 shows how British respondents place themselves on a Left/Right political spectrum. An overwhelming majority of Britons eschew political extremes and see themselves as near the political center. This public disinterest in political extremism serves to limit the appeal of antisystem parties and to encourage leaders of the major parties to opt for moderate policies.

This moderation reflects the depth of the public consensus on politics. There is a general feeling that the institutions and procedures of politics are working well and ought to be observed. The public expects political leaders to observe basic rules of fair play in their competition with each other over control of government. There is also strong public support for

FIGURE 2.1   The Self-Placement of British Voters on a Left/Right Spectrum. *Source: Jacques-René Rabier, Hélène Riffault, Ronald Inglehart, Eurobarometer 23: The European Currency Unit and Working Conditions, April 1985* (Ann Arbor, MI: Inter-University Consortium for Political and Social Research) 1986, pp. 81–82.

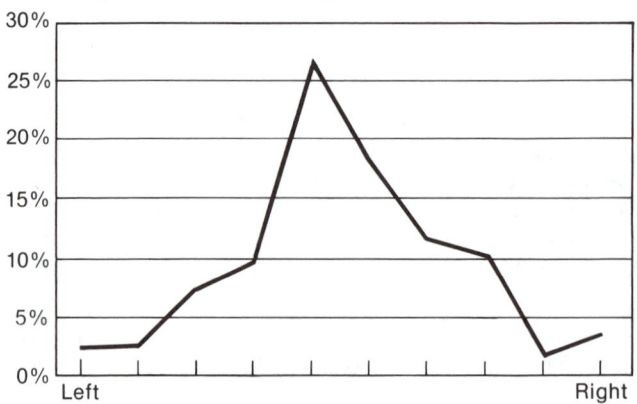

Percent of voters locating their political position at each of ten points

compromise and accommodation in the style of public policy decision-making. In recent years, this consensual approach to politics has been challenged by Margaret Thatcher. Unlike other postwar political leaders, she has declared herself to be opposed to consensus politics and in favor of a government of principle and conviction. Her preference for this leadership style has made her a powerful and often abrasive leader. It is not clear whether her departure from the usual consensual style will mark a break with the past or simply a temporary aberration. After a decade of Thatcherism, however, there is little evidence to indicate that her dogmatic approach has been adopted by many of her fellow political leaders or by the general public. The public has supported Thatcher not for her doctrinaire views, but out of admiration for her leadership qualities and out of disappointment with the political options offered by her rivals.

Concerns about new, less orderly forms of political participation are also out of place in Britain. While Britain had a few bouts of street politics in the 1960s and 1970s, they were far fewer and less disruptive than elsewhere in Western Europe. That they had occurred at all was viewed with alarm by some observers who were unduly impressed with the tranquility of British politics in the late 1940s and 1950s. The usual emphasis on the evolutionary nature of British political development sometimes obscures the turbulence and violence that has often accompanied change. The demonstrations and rare episodes of political violence of the late 1960s and 1970s were actually better controlled and less threatening to democracy than were the turbulent events in the 1920s and 1930s.

In both absolute and comparative terms, the recourse to unconventional methods of political participation is rare in Britain. In a recent poll, only 9 percent of British respondents claimed to have participated even in a lawful demonstration; 6 percent said they had taken part in political boycotts; even fewer admitted to other unconventional political actions such as painting slogans, or occupying buildings.[13] These levels were lower than any of the other eight European countries studied (Denmark, France, Italy, Germany, the Netherlands, Spain, Ireland, and Belgium) as were the numbers of Britons expressing willingness to use such tactics in the future. The use of extraordinary political tactics is restrained by the expectation that groups will be heard and considered provided that they present their views in a moderate and reasonable way.[14] Most Britons still define narrowly the repertoire of acceptable political actions to those of traditional representative democracy.

Britain has not experienced the surge of terrorism that seemed to threaten democracy in Germany and Italy. There have been terrorist incidents but their frequency has been less than elsewhere. Furthermore, the political impact of these terrorist acts has been minimal. They have not provoked the soul-searching selfexamination that occurred in Germany, nor the criticism of the government's effectiveness in responding to the threat that discredited the Italian government in the early stages of its battle against terrorism.

There has been little domestic terrorism by extremists from the left or right. Most of the terrorism has been easy for the government to use to rally support rather than to weaken its position. Much of the terrorism in Britain has been the work of international terrorists, usually from the Middle East. Such terrorist acts have been less directed at the British government than at attracting world attention to the plight of the peoples in troubled Middle Eastern countries. Such events have disrupted domestic order but they are not really challenges to the established political system in Britain.

A more important cause of terrorism has been the violence in Northern Ireland. At times, the extent of violence in that troubled land has approached the level of civil war. But the conflict rarely crossed the Irish sea and Britons have come to sustain the news of violence there with regret but not fear for its consequences to their lives or to their political system. Despite frequent IRA threats to bring the violence to the British people, there have been relatively few Irish nationalist terrorist acts on the island of Britain. That fact in itself conveys to the citizenry a sense of government efficacy in warding off the oft-repeated IRA threats.

VOTING

Voting is the most common political action and for many Britons the only outward political act. As in most parliamentary systems, the only national election is the general election of members of the House of Commons. Voter turnout for these elections is generally high, with 73–78 percent of the eligible voters typically voting. This is much higher turnout than the poor turnout in recent American presidential elections, but it is a lower voter participation rate than in elections in France, Germany, Italy, and other Western European countries.

The electoral system used for all British elections (except regional elections in Northern Ireland) is the "first past the post" plurality system. It is similar to the system used in most United States elections. Each of the 650 districts elects a single member to the House of Commons with the candidate gaining the most votes, whether or not that is a majority, winning the seat. The advantage of this electoral system is that it usually assures that a single party wins a parliamentary majority. It has the additional asset of being straightforward and easy to understand.

But the simple majority single member district electoral system distorts the representation of the public's political preferences in the legislative body. This system overrepresents the strength of the larger parties and underrepresents smaller parties. For example, in 1987, the Conservatives won an overwhelming majority in Commons with only 42.3 percent of the vote. In the same election, the Liberal Social-Democratic Alliance took 22.8 percent of the vote but won only 22 seats or 3.4 percent of the seats. For every one percent of the vote, Conservatives elected 9 Members of Parliament (MPs) and Labour elected 7.5 MPs, but the Alliance elected only 1 MP for each percent of the total vote. In effect, nearly one out of four voters were left very underrepresented in the new House of Commons. Periodically, these distortions produce calls for electoral reform but the chances of a change to a more equitable system of proportional representation are virtually nil. Such a reform would have to be voted by the very parties that profit from the existing system.

British general election campaigns differ significantly from American elections. The most notable differences are that the British campaigns are shorter and much less expensive than are United States campaigns. British parties nominate their own candidates without the lengthy and costly American system of primary elections. Television time is made available to the major parties free of charge usually in large enough blocks of time to permit the party to present a coherent argument instead of the two minute ads characteristic of American campaigns. In Britain, television political advertisements are barred thus eliminating the major cost item in American campaigns. The campaigns tend to stress party positions rather than the personalities of individual candidates for the House of Commons. However, the image and personality of the parties' prime ministerial candidates are becoming more important in British campaigns.

There are also municipal elections held every three years to elect local authorities. Voter interest in these elections is generally less than in general elections but higher than what is common in the United States. Direct consultation of the public on specific issues through referendums is alien to the British tradition. British constitutional theory stresses the supremacy and sovereignty of Parliament; referendums are seen as detracting from Parliament's supremacy and as shifting sovereignty from the Crown and Parliament to the people.

During the 1970s, several referendums were held, always with the stipulation that the outcomes were advisory to Parliament in order to preserve the constitutional principle of parliamentary supremacy.[15] Three of the referendums were regional in that they took place in only part of the country; one in 1972 in Northern Ireland on constitutional reform of regional government; and two in 1979 in Wales and Scotland on proposals for regional autonomy. The only national referendum was in 1975 when voters approved membership in the European Common Market. There have been suggestions that other issues also should be submitted as referendums, and it is likely that the referendums of the 1970s will be used as precedents for additional experiments in the future. This would be a logical extension of the gradual shift of sovereign power from the monarch to Parliament, and now to the people—in fact, if not yet, in constitutional precept.

Considerable research has been devoted to determining how voters make their election decisions. The low levels of political interest and knowledge raise questions about how rational such decisions can be. The decision is simpler than in the United States because of the homogeneity and unity of British parties. In the United States, a voter would not be able to tell much by the party label. In Britain the party label means more. Voters who elect a Conservative can be assured that their MP will always support the position of the Conservative party. But early studies of the voting decision suggested that the willingness of voters to make such choices was diminished by long-standing partisan commitments and class loyalties.[16]

There appears to be a growing volatility in partisan choice among British voters.[17] Voters shift from one party to another, decreasing the reliability of voters' past habits in predicting current voting choices. The reduced salience of class opens up opportunities for voters to express individual preferences on the candidates' issue positions. In doing so, voters exercise rational choices grounded in their own issue positions.[18] The swing away from the Labour party in the last three elections is thus explained by the fact that voters do not share that party's views on labor relations, education reforms, and economic policies.[19] The clear distinction between a party controlling government and a party in opposition makes it easy for British voters who are unhappy with the performance of the current government to express their dissatisfaction by voting for the opposition. Their votes, for or against, the incumbent government can represent a reasoned decision to affirm or reject the current government even if their interest and knowledge prevent voters from choosing rationally between candidates on the basis of issue positions.

WOMEN IN POLITICS

British women lacked a mobilizing issue—such as the Equal Rights Amendment in the United States or the legalization of abortion in Catholic European countries—to invigorate the feminist movement during the 1970s and 1980s. The women's movement was active in Britain but not as politically visible as in countries where feminist issues had a place on the political agenda. Equal pay and antidiscrimination laws were adopted in the early 1970s without much pressure from women's movements. The important struggle to enforce these provisions involved prolonged court action and bureaucratic debates over job definitions and equivalencies. Such feminist causes were too abstract and arcane to rally women into political action.

One of the most interesting features of the women's role in British politics is the declining significance of gender in politics. Women's attitudes on political issues, even specifically feminist issues, differ little from those of men.[20] By the 1983 elections, the once Conservative bias of women voters had disappeared and for the first time since women's enfranchisement men were more likely to vote Conservative than women.[21] Nor does there appear to be significant differences in the ability of women candidates to attract voters.[22]

Where gender counts still is in the number of women serving in public offices. At the local level, women make up only 19 percent of the members of local councils.[23] There has been a greater emphasis in all parties to nominate women for House of Commons seats; in the 1987 elections a record number of women ran for office. But the women generally found themselves showing their party colors in unwinnable districts (see Table 2.3). After the 1987 election, the number of women in parliament hit an all time high but still remained low in absolute terms, 41 women out of 650 members (6.3 percent). And Britain remains the European country with the second lowest percentage of women members of parliament. Part of the explanation is that local party units still discriminate against potential women candidates.[24] But a more important part is attributable to socialization patterns. A woman MP captured well the dilemma of the younger women now tempted by political careers:

> Look back on the women MPs of a generation ago; a very high proportion were single or widowed, some succeeding their deceased husbands for the same constituency. Of today's women MPs and candidates, many are trying to keep a family and a job going at the same time. Parliament's timetable ensures that any reasonably responsible parent will live in a perpetual state of mild guilt . . .[25]

There was one spectacular exception to this pattern of few women in high places and that was Margaret Thatcher. Selected as Conservative party leader in 1975, she became the first woman prime minister of a major western European democracy when her party won the 1979 election. But it is difficult to view this as a victory for women's rights. The prime minister was the sole woman in the cabinet until 1987. Out of the 89 members of the government in 1987, only 5 were women. In addition, Thatcher's government showed little interest in women's issues and actually undercut some earlier gains of the women's movement.

The British feminist movement is weaker than those in the United States and some other European countries. An attempt in 1970 to organize a unified women's liberation movement ended in immediate division. However, informal networks of people interested in promoting political and social equality for women have managed to keep some issues on the public agenda. This interest has done little, however to redress the imbalance in the number of women in politics. Because this imbalance is the product of people's attitudes and women's selfrestraint, change will probably be gradual and slow. It is one thing to eliminate legal barriers to participation; it is quite another to change the attitudes of men and women toward their social and political roles.

CONCLUSION

There are few signs that the level and nature of political participation have reached the point where they might endanger British political stability or democracy. Levels of political interest and involvement still remain

TABLE 2.3 Women Candidates in the 1987 British Election

Party	Number of women candidates	Percentage of total candidates	Women elected
Conservatives	46	7.3%	17
Labour	92	14.5	21
Alliance	109	17.2	2
Other	not available	not available	1

modest. Those willing to engage in the more dramatic and unconventional forms of participation are a small minority and seem to actually use these forms only on rare occasions.

Much of the political deference that characterized British political attitudes in the past appears to have disappeared. But the passing of deference has not been accompanied by challenges to the political order created earlier. Support for the regime, and for the "fair play" considered an essential part of the British way, still remains very high.

NOTES

1. Ronald Inglehart, *The Silent Revolution*, (Princeton, NJ: Princeton University Press, 1977).
2. Alan Marsh, "The 'Silent Revolution:' Value Priorities and the Quality of Life in Britain," *American Political Science Review* 69 (March 1975): 21–30; see also Alan Marsh, *Protest and Political Consciousness* (Beverly Hills, CA: Sage, 1977).
3. See Samuel H. Beer, *Britain Against Itself: The Political Contradictions of Collectivism* (New York: Norton, 1982), pp. 107–208; and Dennis Kavanagh, "Political Culture in Great Britain: The Decline of the Civic Culture," in Gabriel A. Almond and Sidney Verba, eds., *The Civic Culture Revisited*, (Boston: Little, Brown, 1980), pp. 124–176.
4. See Philip Norton, *The British Polity*, (New York: Longman, 1984), pp. 25–36.
5. Vivien Hart, *Distrust and Democracy: Political Distrust in Britain and America*, (Cambridge: Cambridge University Press, 1978), pp. 42ff.
6. Norton, *The British Polity*, p. 34.
7. Richard Rose, *Politics in England*, 4th ed. (Boston: Little, Brown, 1986): p. 125.
8. *Eurobarometer*, No. 25 (June 1986), p. 6.
9. Norton, *The British Polity*, pp. 350–363.
10. Geoffrey Smith and Nelson W. Polsby, *British Government and Its Discontents*, (New York: Basic Books, 1981), pp. 173–174.
11. Richard Rose, *Politics in England*, 3rd ed., (Boston: Little, Brown, 1980), pp. 176–177.
12. See Gabriel A. Almond and Sidney Verba, *The Civic Culture: Public Attitudes and Democracy in Five Nations*, (Princeton, NJ: Princeton University Press, 1963).
13. Elizabeth Hann Hastings and Philip K. Hastings, eds., *Index to International Public Opinion, 1982–1983*, (Westport, CT: Greenwood, 1984), p. 546.
14. F. F. Ridley, "The Citizen Against Authority: British Approaches to the Redress of Grievances," *Parliamentary Affairs* 37 (1984): 1–32.
15. See David Butler, "The United Kingdom," in *Referendums: A Comparative Study of Practice and Theory*, eds., David Butler and Austin Ranney (Washington, DC: American Enterprise Institute, 1978).
16. One study found that 4 out of 5 voters claimed to always support the same party. David Butler and Donald Stokes, *Political Change in Britain*, (New York: St. Martin's, 1971), p. 27; on class voting, see Robert Alford, *Party and Society*, (Chicago: University of Chicago Press, 1963).
17. Hilde Himmelweit et al., *How Voters Decide: A Longitudinal Study of Political Attitudes and Voting Extending Over Fifteen Years*, (London: Academic Press, 1981), pp. 193–194.

18. See Mark N. Franklin, *The Decline of Class Voting in Britain: Changes in the Basis of Electoral Choice 1964–1983*, (Oxford: Clarendon Press, 1985); For a critique of this rational choice model of electoral behavior, see Patrick Dunleavy and Christopher T. Husbands, *British Democracy at the Crossroads: Voting and Party Competition in the 1980s*, (London: George Allen & Unwin, 1985).

19. Bo Sarlvik and Ivor Crewe, *Decade of Realignment: The Conservative Victory of 1979 and the Electoral Trends in the 1970s*, (Cambridge: Cambridge University Press, 1983).

20. See Richard Rose, *Politics in England*, 4th ed., (Boston: Little, Brown, 1986), p. 155–60.

21. See Ivor Crewe, "How to Win a Landslide Without Really Trying: Why the Conservatives Won in 1983," in Austin Ranney, ed., *Britain at the Polls, 1983*, (Durham, NC: Duke University Press, 1985), pp. 167–168.

22. Jorgen Rasmussen, "Women Candidates in British By-Elections: A Rational Choice Interpretation of Electoral Behaviour," *Political Studies* (No. 2, 1981): 265–271.

23. Equal Opportunities Commission, *Women and Men in Britain: A Statistical Profile*, (London: Her Majesty's Stationery Office, 1986).

24. Jorgen S. Rasmussen, "Women's Roles in Contemporary British Politics: Impediments to Parliamentary Candidature," *Parliamentary Affairs* 36 (Summer 1983): 300–315.

25. Anthony Sampson, *The Changing Anatomy of Britain*, (New York: Vintage, 1982), p. 20.

CHAPTER THREE
BRITISH POLITICAL PARTIES AND INTEREST GROUPS

With levels of individual political participation generally low, political parties and interest groups become key political actors. They are the intermediaries linking citizens and their government. Political parties have the essential task of organizing and giving meaning to the periodic elections; interest groups assemble like-minded individuals to express collectively concerns and demands for government action. Given their key political roles, political parties and interest groups merit close examination for their contribution to contemporary British democracy.

POLITICAL PARTIES IN BRITAIN

More so than in most other countries, Britain represented in practice the notion of party government—a government linked closely with a single party and forced to accept responsibility for its policies and performance before an electorate, which if dissatisfied may select an alternate as the new government party. This British pattern became an esteemed ideal for other countries because it seemed at once to provide effective government and accountability to the voters. In recent years, this "model" form of party government seemed to falter with serious questions being raised about the health of the parties that are needed for party government, and about the reality and even the desirability of that form of party/ government relationship.

In contrast to the poorly organized and undisciplined American political parties, British parties are highly structured, centralized, and cohesive. They present developed party programs to the voters and have a record of fulfilling these pledges once in office. Their members in parliament vote as a bloc with only rare instances of cross-party voting. Party uniformity and discipline are enhanced by the absence of primary elections. Nominations of candidates are made by the local parties without consulting the electorate and then, are subject to approval by the central party organization. While the central headquarters normally defer to the local party in candidate nominations, they do occasionally bar the use of the party label to candidates that seem to be out of harmony with the party philosophy. The result is that the British parties offer clearly defined and coherent options to the voters. Unlike the variations among Republicans and among Democrats in the United States, Conservative politicians throughout Britain stand for approximately the same values, and likewise, Labour politicians.

For most of the twentieth century, British politics has been dominated by two political parties: the Conservative (or Tory) party and the Labour party. This is a much simpler party system than those of many other European countries, which have large numbers of parties competing for political control. But the British system is not a two-party system such as in the United States; the two major British parties have nearly always faced important rivals at the polls. They are assured of a near monopoly in the House of Commons by a simple majority electoral system that works to their advantage and to the great disadvantage of smaller contenders. In fact, in the last 15 years, the dominance of the Conservative and Labour parties at the polls has dropped sharply. Whereas the two parties captured over 90 percent of the vote in elections between 1945 and 1970, their share of the vote has dropped to near 70 percent in elections during the 1970s and 1980s. (See Table 3.1 and Figure 3.1.)

TABLE 3.1 Political Parties in British General Elections

	Percentage of Votes			Seats Won in House of Commons		
	1979	1983	1987	1979	1983	1987
Conservative	43.9	42.4	42.3	339	397	375
Labour	36.9	27.6	30.8	268	209	229
Alliance	13.8*	25.4	22.8	11*	23	22
Plaid Cymru (Welsh nationalist)	0.4	0.4	0.4	2	2	3
Scottish Nationalist	1.6	1.1	1.	2	2	3
Others	3.4	3.1	3.	13	17	16

* Results for the Liberal party.

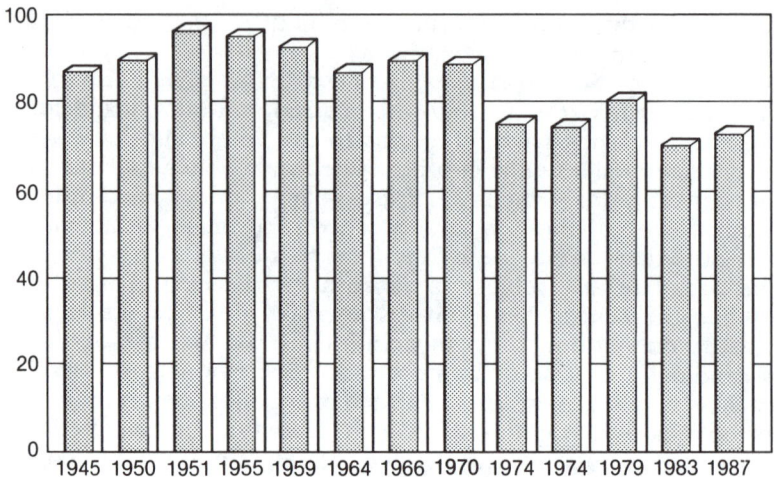

FIGURE 3.1   Percent of Vote Cast for the Conservative and Labour Parties in National Election.

While they were arch rivals and distinctive in their political philosophies, the two parties represented alternative sets of leaders not alternative societies. Indeed, for 25 years, from 1950 to 1975, the two parties converged on a political and social consensus built around mutual acceptance of a social-welfare state and mixed economy. The British public has rejected political extremism of both sides, with most voters situating themselves at or near the political center. (See Figure 2.1 in Chapter Two.) The clustering of voters at the center was an incentive for both parties to moderate their policies. There did remain significant differences in style and emphasis between the parties, although they disappeared sometimes when the party in power faced the political, economic, and international constraints of governing.[1]

In the mid–1970s, both major parties began to move from the political center toward their respective ideological poles. Disillusioned with their inabilities to solve Britain's long-term economic decline and the current social malaise, the parties sought new answers in ideologies. Under Margaret Thatcher's leadership, the Conservative party abandoned the consensus on a planned economy with a social welfare state, and called for a return to free enterprise. Once in power after 1979, the Conservatives pioneered in implementing "supply side economics": cutting back on welfare programs, lowering progressive income taxes, reducing government industrial investment funds, eliminating government economic controls, and selling off, "privatizing", nationalized industries.

The Labour party had moved sharply to the left in 1973 with a new party program, by far the most radical document in its history, calling for "a fundamental and irreversible shift of power and wealth in favour of working people and their families." The Labour party's parliamentary leadership succeeded in keeping this radical posture from affecting its leadership succeeded in keeping this radical posture from affecting its government and campaign platform until it lost office in the 1979 elections. Then under a new leftwing leader, Michael Foot, the party program was given an increasingly militant interpretation with calls for many new nationalizations of privately held firms, vast expansions of welfare, public housing, and other social services, extended government powers over the economy, the abolition of the House of Lords, immediate withdrawal from the Common Market, unilateral nuclear disarmament, and the elimination of all United States nuclear weapons on British soil.[2]

Already in the 1970s, voter dissatisfaction with the seeming ineffectiveness of the solutions of both major parties led large numbers of voters to turn to minor parties: the nationalist parties and even the old Liberal party. By the end of the decade, with the two major parties adopting unusual and extreme positions, there was room at the center for more moderate parties. This space was filled by the Liberal and the Social Democratic parties which joined in "the Alliance" for the 1983 and 1987 elections. But the operation of the electoral system worked to the disadvantage of this centrist alliance so that by the end of the 1980s, the traditional parties, the Conservative and Labour parties, seemed to be regaining their old dominance of the voting public.

The Conservative Party

The Thatcher era marked a departure from tradition for the Conservative party.[3] While always the defender of privilege and the interests of the middle and upper classes, the Conservative party was above all, characterized by its willingness to accommodate change in order to retain its hold on power. This pragmatic approach was evidence of the Conservatives' "will to rule," and their readiness to adapt to changing times in order to remain appealing to the electorate. Conservatives thought of themselves as the natural government party accepting the duty to govern moderately and in the general interest that such a calling obliges, and that is required to make that calling possible in a democratic system.

Thatcher's doctrinaire style and the radical content of her policy thus depart from traditional Tory pragmatism. Her dogmatic commitment to free enterprise contrasts with traditional Tory mercantilism, based on the recognition of the state's important economic role, and with the Conservatives' postwar embracing of nationalizations and the social welfare state. Because her agenda deviates from traditional principles, Thatcher has encountered opposition from moderates, dubbed "wets," throughout her leadership. Her firmness and political skills, coupled with traditional Tory deference to their winning leaders, keeps her secure as party leader and prime minister.[4]

The Conservatives make few pretensions about internal democracy within the party. The party has 1.5 million members. With about 300 full-time paid constituency agents and a secure financial base, the Conservatives have the best organized and largest party in Britain. The party organization serves the Conservative members of parliament. It is carefully controlled by the party leader, who is also the parliamentary leader (prime minister when the Conservatives have a majority or leader of the opposition when out of office). The absence of internal party discussion saves the party from the embarrassments and weaknesses of lengthy public squabbles over doctrine and leadership. But driven by its "will to rule," the Conservative party adjusts quickly to needed change both in doctrine and leadership. Even the Thatcher deviation is understandable in these terms. Frustrated by problems that did not respond to traditional answers and by two election losses in 1974, the party elected a new leader, Margaret Thatcher, and accepted, albeit with reservations, her new economic and social views.

Thatcher is the first postwar prime minister to be selected in three consecutive parliaments. But there are important limits on her success. Her party controls a majority in Commons but its mandate is unclear. The percent of voters supporting her victorious party between 1979 and 1987—between 39 and 44 percent of the voting electorate—is far from a majority of the voters. In addition, voting analysis suggests that many who vote Conservative do so more out of appreciation of Thatcher's leadership style than out of support of her radical policies. Her party's success is due less to public enthusiasm for the Conservatives' new agenda than to public disenchantment with the Labour party and the division of opposition vote between Labour and the Alliance.

Perhaps more important, for a party that has always aspired to unite Britons of all social backgrounds, the Conservative party has become a regional party with nearly all of its elected officials located in England, and especially in its more affluent south. Conservative support in Scotland, Wales, and in the industrial cities of northern England has dwindled to record low levels. Over the long run, this new regional political division may heighten nationalist feelings in the Celtic countries of Scotland and Wales and feelings of despair and alienation among the seemingly neglected poor in northern England.

After a third general election victory in 1987, Margaret Thatcher's position at the head of the Conservative party is secure. But many in the party are concerned by the Thatcher government's apparent callousness to the problems of those disadvantaged by her economic programs. The party has long been close to the Church of England—so close that the Church has been described as "the Tory party at prayer." But the relationship has been strained by the party's recent social and economic policies. Thus in 1985, the Church of England issued a strident attack on the failure of Thatcher's government to alleviate the misery of the urban poor. Many in the party share that judgment but are stilled by Thatcher's continuing political success. Many also worry about the long-term consequences of ignoring the party's decline outside of the affluent portions of England. As her third term proceeds, Thatcher's ability to restrain such internal party tension may well decline. Long noted for its openness to the kinds of change needed to win elections and to unite the country, the Conservative party has been known to put aside its leaders—even successful ones—who do not seem able to make those adjustments.

The Labour Party

The modern Labour party developed out of a schism during World War I by the trade union branch of the old Liberal party. By 1922, Labour had succeeded the Liberals to be one of the two principal British parties. Rejecting the revolutionary and radical paths often advocated by continental socialist parties, the British Labour party chose instead a gradual reform agenda based on the achievement of a democratically planned economy and social-welfare state. Most of this program was implemented in the postwar government of Clement Attlee with the expansion of the public sector in the economy through nationalizations and the development of a large and popular system of social services.

The party's move to the left during the 1970s was due in part to its close links with the trade union movement. The Trades Union Congress (TUC) is still affiliated with the party and provides the bulk of its members. Membership in a union brings automatic membership in the party except in the rare cases where the union member explicitly opts out of the party. As a result, the TUC has a preponderant weight in party matters. (At present, for example, the TUC has a firm majority on the party's National Executive Committee [NEC], controls 40 percent of the votes in elections for party leader, and provides 70–80 percent of the party's funding.) Faced with a decade of industrial decline and growing labor/management problems, several of the key union federations elected radical leaders who moved the TUC and then the party to the left at the end of the 1970s.

Reinforcing the leftward pressure of the unions was the radicalization of the constituency party organizations at the grass roots. The number of individual Labour party members fell steadily during the 1960s and 1970s, and in many districts, the remaining members tended to be the most militant.[5] In addition, the loss of a mass membership made it easy for extreme elements to come into the party and quickly dominate it. They were more assertive, more active, and more middle-class intellectual than traditional party members. As a result, many constituency units fell under the influence of Trotskyites, Leninists, and revolutionary Marxists from the "Militant Tendency" and other far left factions.[6] Never very numerous—in 1985 there were approximately 5,000 militants out of a total individual party membership of 250,000—the militants counted on their ability to dominate poorly attended local party meetings. These militant activists brought to the party ideas and positions that broke sharply with earlier traditions of British socialism and the current aspirations of the typical industrial worker. With the gap between the views of Labour activists and their party's voters "wider than that between Hawaii and mainland America,"[7] the Labour party was pushed into positions that reduced its chances for electoral success.

Fearing dilution of the party's new leftist agenda by more electorally aware Labour MPs, the radicals sought to enhance internal party democracy which they rightly believed would assure their control. The party leader, who in the past was elected by Labour MPs alone, is now elected by an elaborate procedure giving 40 percent of the say to the TUC, 30 percent to the constituency units, and 30 percent to the Labour MPs.[8] The party's election manifesto was now written by the NEC so that the leadership of the parliamentary party could no longer shape the campaign platform. This change was in reaction to the party leaders of 1974 and 1979, who had lowered the increasingly radical tone of the party's program to appeal to the still moderate electorate. Finally, sitting moderate Labour MPs were threatened with disavowal by their constituency parties as mandatory "re-selection" or renomination processes were instituted. By the 1987 election the party's shift to the left was even apparent in the usually more moderate parliamentary Labour party: The number of militant leftists in parliament was at a record high (57 MPs) with radical and traditional leftists outnumbering the moderates 141 to 88 in the Labour party in Commons.

The paradoxical result of this democratization process was to make the party more democratic internally but less representative of its general supporters. This occurrence is neither unusual nor unexpected. In the United States, the most participatory national party conventions have produced some of the least representative (and most electorally disastrous) presidential candidates; Barry Goldwater for the Republicans in 1964 and George McGovern for the Democrats in 1972. The explanation is that internal democracy within the party heightens the influence of activists who are more radical and less representative of the party's electorate. In addition, the democratic exchange within the party creates a public image of party division and weakness that lessens its electoral appeal. Thus excessive internal party democracy may undermine the more important democratic choice in national elections. These perils lead many to believe that one ought to look for democracy not within parties but between them.[9]

All of these problems of internal party democracy have plagued the Labour party in the last decade. Its attractiveness to the voters has been reduced by its internal divisions and its radical posture. In addition, it has lost electoral support as social changes—the decline in class awareness and the reduction in blue collar jobs due to economic changes—have eroded its natural political base in the industrial working class.[10] Many of the remaining workers fail to recognize the new priorities of the intellectual leftists now dominant in the party as their own. In 1983, for example, only 35 percent of the blue collar vote and 40 percent of the trade union vote went to the Labour party; the 1987 elections showed little improvement in these figures.

With a total share of the vote at 27.6 percent in 1983, Labour had its worst result at the polls since 1918. After this defeat Labour quickly replaced its inept party leader, Michael Foot, with Neil Kinnock, another leftist leader.[11] Kinnock tried to gently nudge the party toward the center. But he was embarrassed by militants in the trade unions—notably the disastrous miners strike of 1984—and in local governments—especially in London and Liverpool. The new democratic party procedures and a more leftist parliamentary party than ever before, (usually the parliamentary party is the center of moderation in the party) limited his ability to change the party's strategic position. The moderation was welcomed by the public but electoral recovery in 1987 was modest. The party increased its support to 30.8 percent of the vote but this was still the second lowest vote for the party since the Second World War. The results were especially disappointing. Kinnock had achieved some popularity and the party's image was better than in 1983. Kinnock had run an effective modern campaign. Continued economic problems and high unemployment should have helped Labour. But nothing succeeded in winning back many former Labour voters.

The Labour party faces a difficult task in building for the future. Its traditional economic policies have lost their attractiveness and the party's recent emphasis on unilateral nuclear disarmament has been unappealing to most voters. The party's base in the working class vote has been eroded by the decreasing numbers of blue collar workers and the defection of many of the remaining industrial workers from the Labour party. Changes over the last decade have left many of its traditional supporters confused. A former Labour MP caught this disorientation, "The Labour party just isn't the same cuddly party of the center which I joined 30 years ago." To attract more voters, Labour will have to further moderate its policies, but in doing that it will antagonize the more militant activists. Indeed, the increased militancy of new MPs has hampered the party's ability to convey a moderate image. Despite the slight recovery in the 1987 election, some observers regard the Labour party as unelectable unless it undergoes substantial internal reform and reorganization. But the strength of the militant left in the party makes such adaptation unlikely.

The Alliance

The Alliance was a political coalition of two centrist parties during the 1980s: the Liberals and the Social Democrats. The Liberal party is a relic from the past, one of the two major parties until the First World War. With a small political base in local politics, the Liberals had succeeded in staying barely alive until reviving in the 1970s. The Social Democratic party developed out of a schism of the moderate and right wings of the Labour party in 1981 as that party moved sharply to the left.

The Liberals and Social Democrats soon joined in the Alliance to compete effectively against the larger parties. Together they constituted the most serious "third party" threat since the 1920s. They won a string of by-elections (to fill vacancies caused by deaths in the House of Commons) and gained a large following according to public opinion polls. In the 1983 elections, the Alliance did well but not well enough to overcome the obstacle posed by the plurality electoral system. The Alliance had the support of nearly 8 million voters (25.4 percent) but won only 23 of the 650 House of Commons seats. In 1987, they had the support of more than one of five voters—22.8 percent of the votes—but still could not win a foothold in Parliament.

The Social Democratic-Liberal Alliance has faced three serious handicaps in trying to break into the system. One has been the Alliance's difficulty in conveying a distinctive position on major issues to the public.

Reacting against the excesses of program writing in the Labour party, the Social Democrats were hesitant about producing yet another party manifesto. One of its leaders responded to a woman's question on the party's position, "True love, if you want a manifesto, go and join one of the other parties."[12] This image of a party without a distinctive program prevailed in the press even after the Alliance presented a series of well-stated position papers. The difficulty was that, with a few notable exceptions, they represented familiar positions not far removed from those defended by the Conservative and Labour parties during the era of consensus. They seemed old hat and dated even for those who found the alternatives in the main parties too extreme or doctrinaire. In addition, disagreements between Liberals and Social Democrats on several issues, notably on disarmament which many Liberals supported and the SDP opposed, created further uncertainties over key Alliance positions.

Second, the Alliance lacked an attractive leader as its prime minister candidate. There were too many leaders with a Liberal party leader, David Steel, and five Social Democratic leaders all running. When the Social Democrats finally selected a single leader, Roy Jenkins, the Alliance's prime minister candidate for the 1983 election, he was ineffective both within the Alliance and in the electorate. After the 1983 election, Jenkins was replaced by David Owen as Social Democratic leader. Owen ran jointly with Liberal leader, David Steel, at the head of the Alliance in the 1987 election campaign. While both were seen as able men, the dual leadership left unresolved questions about who really led the Alliance.

Finally and most seriously, the Alliance suffered as a third party in an electoral system that discriminates in favor of the two major parties. Alliance candidates took one out of four votes in the 1983 election, only two percent fewer than Labour, but were nearly excluded from Commons by the workings of the plurality electoral system. To break into the system requires close to one-third of the total vote, a figure that seems to elude the Alliance except during the by-elections when voters are more willing to convey messages of disappointment to major parties by voting for minor parties. But when the real contest comes in general elections, voters fear "losing" their vote by casting it for a third party and instead vote either Conservative or Labour.

The 1987 election dealt a death blow to the Alliance. The poor results confirmed the impression already created by the 1983 election that the Alliance was unable to transform its electoral potential into seats in Parliament. In future elections voters will be less inclined to "waste" their vote on a party that cannot elect MPs.

The 1987 defeat opened serious personality and doctrinal differences within the Alliance. The two leaders who had fought the election as partners—Owen and Steel—began feuding over the appropriate future course for the coalition. Steel proposed a fusion of the two parties, and a narrow majority of Social Democrats approved the merger. Owen, however, rejected the merger. He resigned as SDP leader and led a minority of his party in a rump party still claiming the SDP label. The rest of the Social Democrats and the Liberals formed a new party, calling themselves the Social and Liberal Democrats. They selected a new leader, Paddy Ashdown, and seemed to win the majority of those voters still identifying with this political current. The tensions between these two groups eroded popular support. By the end of the 1980s, polls suggested that only one voter in ten would be willing to support the social democratic and liberal parties in national elections.

While Britain is unlikely to ever have a "pure" two-party system, third party challengers will always find themselves in a difficult position. The fate of the Alliance illustrates these problems. It gained political support as the two major parties moved to their respective extremes on the political spectrum and left open the center for the new political force. But the electoral system worked to limit the ability of the Alliance to translate its voting potential into political power. As the parties moderated their stance, as is usually the case in British politics, the centrist political space occupied by the Alliance shrunk, further diminishing its political appeal.

Party Decline?

Britain is often cited as a prime example of the decline of parties. In fact, the crisis really affects only one party, the Labour party, and even this party continues to show remarkable ability to recover from disaster. Most Britons (71 percent) still align themselves with the one of the major parties (see Table 3.2). If there is a decline of parties, it is not part of a disaffection with parties in general but with a particular party, its leadership, and/or policies of the moment. Rather than a crisis, this appears much like the action of a democratic "market" situation where voters shift from ineffective, unresponsive, and unpopular parties to others.

The success of the Conservative and Labour parties throughout this century has been due to their alertness to warnings of electoral decline and their skill in responding with changes that enable them to recapture the loyalty of their voters or to extend their appeal to new voters. Buffered from immediate threats by an amiable electoral system, and profiting from important pockets of loyal voters and their organizational strengths, they weathered the challenge of the nationalist parties in the 1970s and now appear to have surmounted the challenge of the Alliance during the 1980s. Even if one of them gives way to the new party, such a change is to be expected in an open democracy that permits voters to eliminate parties

TABLE 3.2 Identification With Parties, Britain, 1984

	Total	Conservative	Labour	Alliance
Supporter of a party	46	24	17	5
Closer to one party	25	9	11	5
Independent	29			

Source: Roger Jowell and Colin Airey, eds., *British Social Attitudes: The 1984 Report* (Aldershot, England: Gower, 1984), p. 166.

that do not change with the times. The party system seems likely to continue as a source of stability in British politics.

INTEREST GROUPS AND BRITISH POLITICS

For many Britons, it is natural to turn to an organized group in order to press for government action on a matter of concern. Consequently, groups emerge freely to champion small and large causes as the need arises. For example, early in the 1980s some citizens became concerned when they discovered that hundreds of hedgehogs were falling into the pits under cattle guards and perishing. They organized themselves into the British Hedgehog Preservation Society and successfully urged local governments to install concrete escape ramps to permit the trapped hedgehogs to climb out from under the grids.

There are countless groups desiring to affect public policy ranging from such narrow interests as the hedgehog advocates to large occupational groups such as trade unions and employers' groups. In some ways, the British political system appears less vulnerable to group pressure than does the United States system. Tight party discipline restricts the ability of groups to enlist the support of individual MPs. Shorter and far less expensive election campaigns reduce politicians' need for the financial resources offered by some interest groups. But British groups succeed in wielding their influence and shaping public policy in less visible manners, working unobtrusively in the offices of ministers and civil servants.

There is a place for the views of affected interests in a democracy. The challenge is to provide opportunities for concerned groups to voice their opinions while preventing the distortion of public policy by unrepresentative special interests. The presence of disciplined and coherent government majorities supporting governments which, usually have a clearer policy agenda than do their American counterparts, prevents such distortions of the policy process. However, the growing complexity of public policy has made government more dependent upon the cooperation of groups that it must regulate. For example, in operating the National Health Service, Britain's highly regarded national health system, the government must have information on medical needs and resources which often can be supplied only by the medical practitioners themselves. This lends medical professionals some control, since they usually interpret the needed data in a way that supports their own interests. They can threaten to sabotage unwanted policies through noncompliance in order to shape policy in ways that better respond to their needs. And the doctors are not alone in having such power; many other socioeconomic groups regulated by government have similar or greater impacts on the policy process for the same reasons.

The government's need for group cooperation has led it to sometimes invite the groups to participate directly in the policy process. Parliament sets the broad guidelines and then "hives" off the decisions on important technical details to official committees, councils, or work groups made up of civil servants and representatives from concerned interest groups. During the 1960s and 1970s, the number of these semi-state bodies—dubbed quangos, for quasi-autonomous national government organizations—grew rapidly.[13] These quangos allowed direct interest group involvement in the making and implementing of public policy. For example, the Manpower Services Commission set up and administered occupational retraining and job creation programs; the Health and Safety Commission defined and enforced occupational safety regulations.

This trend was so strong that many saw a neocorporatist form of interest group/government relationship developing.[14] Under neocorporatism, powerful interest-group monopolies collaborate with each other and government in deciding policies affecting their members. The extent of such a neocorporatist trend in Britain seems to have been exaggerated.[15] Even at the height of the quango era in the 1970s, the government still held the upper hand in the process. The groups could not exercise their full potential influence because of divisions among them and because of their inability to insure that their followers would in fact accept the policy arrangements they had agreed upon.

One of the dangers of neocorporatism is that the interest groups become accustomed to dealing with each other and forget the interests of their rank-and-file members. Trade unions are particularly vulnerable to such co-optation into a system that may disadvantage the workers. There is some indication that this has happened in Britain as union leaders have lost touch with the grass roots and become defenders of the status quo.[16]

The quangos also seemed a threat to Parliament's supremacy and Margaret Thatcher's government launched a major attack on them. In due course, many were dissolved—approximately one fourth of the 2,000 in existence in 1980—and others had their policy powers curtailed. The majority of the others continue to operate because the government found them to be useful and no threat to its authority. The dominance of democratic policy processes by nonrepresentative and self-serving groups that some had feared did not occur. Nor did the manipulation of groups by government that others had claimed to see in the corporatist trends. Both government and groups remained vigilant of their own autonomy and when a government was elected that interpreted the group-government relationships as endangering its prerogatives—probably an exaggerated fear—it was able to end them without difficulty.

Occupational Interest Groups

Because of their organizational strength, their large memberships, and their consistent interest in broad areas of public policy, occupationally-based groups are among the most important interests in the policy-making process. Perhaps the most successful of these was the National Farmers' Union (NFU). It based its strength on its bipartisan support from both major parties during much of the postwar era. It was able to get what it felt farmers needed despite the very small agriculture population because it succeeded in convincing Labour and Conservative policy makers that the interests of the farmers were the interests of the nation as a whole. While the relationship remains much the same today, NFU influence has waned. This is because the most important farm policy decisions are no longer made in London but rather in Brussels through the Common Market institutions. While still able to get support from their own government, British farmers now face powerful counter forces from farmers in other countries and their governments as the European Community shapes a common agricultural program.

The Trades Union Congress (TUC) is an umbrella organization, like the American AFL-CIO, that links most of Britain's labor unions. As in other western trade unions, British unions are experiencing a sharp loss of members, declining from a peak of over 12 million union members in 1979 to 9 million in 1987. Whereas 51 percent of eligible workers belonged to unions in 1979, only 37 percent did so in 1987.

The TUC is intimately linked with the Labour party. Unless they deliberately opt out of party membership, those who join the union also adhere indirectly to the Labour party. The TUC provides much of the financial backing for the party. This gives the TUC a powerful position. Trade union leaders cast enormous blocks of votes on behalf of their members in Labour party congresses. Of the 229 Labour MPs elected in 1987, 129 were union sponsored and financed. The TUC holds twelve of the twenty-nine seats on the party's National Executive Committee. Despite this powerful position in the party, the TUC no longer is able to deliver the most essential resource—votes. In the 1987 election, only 42 percent of union members voted for the Labour party.

The unions have also seen their political influence decline dramatically. Part of this fall is due to their intimate association with the Labour party which has been out of power for the last decade. More importantly, the TUC has lost influence because of a widespread public perception that the unions abused their powers during the 1970s when they moved to more radical, leftwing postures. This shift to the left was not due to a radicalization of the workers but rather to the work of militants in the TUC who successfully wrested union power from more moderate trade unionists.[17] The radical leaders had difficulty maintaining the confidence of union members and of the general public.

Thatcher's government took advantage of this sentiment to pass restrictive legislation during the 1980s: barring secondary strikes, requiring unions to hold secret ballots on strikes, leaders, and allocating union funds to political parties, and permitting stiff fines for illegal strikes. While this legislation reflected her own anti-union sentiments, it also built on earlier Labour party legislation introduced in the 1960s and 1970s to counter growing trade union excesses.[18] The TUC grudgingly accepted these provisions but hoped to convince a future Labour government to repeal them.

The political influence of the unions is diminished, no matter who is in power, by the internal divisions of the trade union movement. With over 100 unions in the TUC, many have conflicting interests and different philosophies; its unity is fragile. Often, it is held together by ambiguous compromises that leave leaders of separate unions free to interpret them in conflicting ways. The leaders of the TUC and many of its affiliates face growing problems in convincing rank-and-file members to support their decisions not only on political issues but on work place disputes: The miners' union split after a long and failed strike in 1984; The railway workers voted down a strike call from their leaders; The electrical workers union was expelled from the TUC for violating the central's policy on accepting government funds for mail ballots. These and the many other incidents of internal division illustrate the disarray of the unions that lessens their political impact.

The weakness of the British trade union movement is similar to problems in other European unions. British trade unions have also suffered from the general decline in the heavy industries that provided much of their support. The long-term problem of very high unemployment has further weakened the unions. Workers have been hesitant to engage in strikes and political actions that might endanger their jobs when more than 10 percent of the population is unemployed.

The weakening of the trade unions may well have proceeded too far. Unions remain an important means of representing less advantaged sections of the population and of integrating workers into a capitalist economy. Too sharp a reduction in their power may well result in growing disaffection of important parts of the population. Paradoxically, the Thatcher reforms may (unwittingly) serve the long-term interests of the trade union movement. By increasing democratic controls in unions, their leaders may well become more representative, more effective in gaining membership support, and thus more influential in politics. The more orderly state of labor/management relations emerging out of the Thatcher era may also help rebuild public sympathy for the unions and heal rifts within the TUC.

The business community is well represented in politics by a plethora of associations advocating the interests of each of the many industrial and commercial trades. In addition, there is a strong central association, the Confederation of British Industry (CBI) to represent business interests in general.[19] Its diversity diminishes its political impact since the various CBI affiliates often have differing, even clashing, interests. Thus, much of the real representation of business interests comes from the specific trade associations.

There are no formal ties between the business groups and the Conservative party but their political affinity is apparent. The party and business people share common economic and social perspectives. Business interests provide about half of the financial backing for the Conservative party. They see the Conservative party as a privileged ally that should be supported at all costs. Thus, criticism of the Conservative government by the CBI leader in 1981 provoked a major conflict in that organization and the temporary withdrawal of several industrial firms to protest the CBI leader's indiscretion.[20]

New Social Movements

The wave of mass social movements that has swept across the rest of western Europe has had surprisingly little impact on British politics. There are British parallels to the German ecologists, the Danish anti-tax movements, the Dutch peace movement, the French feminists, and so on. But the British groups are nearly always a pale reflection of their sister organizations. It is not that the British are reluctant to organize such groups. Instead, it appears that the British are reluctant to engage in the street politics that such movements have utilized elsewhere. Citizens appear basically satisfied with legislation emerging from their existing institutions. A 1984 poll, for example, asked what people have done when they have felt a law to be unjust or harmful: Fully 69 percent claimed that they had never considered any law as meriting such a description![21] Only 2 percent claimed they had reacted to an unjust law by joining a protest or demonstration. With confrontation politics viewed widely as "un-British," social movements must tread a narrow path between such moderation that they are ignored and such radicalism that they are spurned, even by sympathizers, for inappropriate tactics.

A second explanation has been the general unresponsiveness of the British political system to pressure from such movements. Governments are usually secure in their parliamentary majority and are able to persevere in their policy paths even when large groups attempt disruption. Thatcher demonstrated this strength against both the miners' turbulent strike and the mass protests for nuclear disarmament. Even governments with uncertain majorities, such as those in the 1970s, have proved resistant to extra-parliamentary pressure as, for example, in their handling of the nationalist revival in Scotland, Wales, and Northern Ireland.

The only social movement with an important following is the peace movement. In the early 1980s, while decisions on deploying new missile systems in Britain were under consideration, the Campaign for Nuclear Disarmament (CND) mobilized tens of thousands of protestors. For over two years, a women's peace group camped in tents on the fringe of the Greenham Common air base which was scheduled to receive new American missiles. Unable to stop the arrival of the missiles, the camp became a sanctuary for peace advocates and activists pressing for disparate radical feminist causes. Elsewhere, demonstrations and rallies gathered thousands to protest nuclear weapons.

While similar on the surface to peace movements in other European countries, the CND is a continuation of a campaign for unilateral disarmament that has played a vocal but ineffective role in British politics since the 1950s.[22] The CND has received support from the Labour party, which has incorporated antinuclear pledges in its program on several occasions. While popular among activists, Labour politicians have recognized their limited appeal to the general public and have muted that theme in most election campaigns. Once in office, previous Labour governments have ignored those party commitments to disarmament. Reacting against past vacillation, the party made unilateral dismantlement of British nuclear forces and opposition to the deployment of new NATO missiles central planks in Labour's 1983 and 1987 election platforms. However, after both elections, Neil Kinnock, Labour's new leader, eased back on this unpopular position.

By the mid-1980s, the CND was in decline again. Its supporters lost badly in the 1983 election, the new missiles were installed on schedule, and popular opinion expressed overwhelming support (77 percent) for retaining Britain's nuclear arms and for Britain's loyalty to NATO (79 percent).[23] With little chance of success and the mobilizing issue of new missile deployment now in the past, the CND lost membership and those peace advocates who remained slackened their activity.

CONCLUSION

There is little evidence in Britain of a participation crisis provoked by modern social and economic tensions. The abrupt and simultaneous emergence of several issues in the late 1960s and 1970s appeared unsettling because of the unusually tranquil 1950s. But the causes, tactics, and passions were not new when compared with prewar politics and older political traditions. When looking at British citizens' politics in the 1980s, what is still impressive is the high level of commitment to old institutions and traditions. It is surprising to still find so much political self-restraint in a country where people feel able to influence the government and in a time when participation is so widely praised as a civic virtue. Despite the challenges of economic decline, unemployment, nationalist revivals, and parties that lost their orientations, the British remain characterized above all by a civic decency. The crisis of the 1970s and 1980s was more one in perceptions of the Jeremiahs and Cassandras than in real actions and feelings of typical Britons. In the last analysis, the British have remained, as always, imperturbable.

NOTES

1. Richard Rose, *Do Parties Make a Difference?*, 2nd ed. (Chatham, NJ: Chatham, 1984).
2. See *Labour's Plan: A New Hope For Britain* (London: Labour Party, 1983).
3. On the Conservative party's background and philosophy, see Philip Norton and Arthur Aughey, *Conservatives and Conservatism* (London: Temple Hill, 1981).
4. On the period of change, see Robert Behrens, *The Conservative Party from Heath to Thatcher* (London: Saxon House, 1979).
5. Paul Whitely, "The Decline of Labour's Local Party Membership and Electoral Base, 1945–1979," in Dennis Kavanagh, ed., *The Politics of the Labour Party* (London: George Allen & Unwin, 1982).
6. Philip Williams, "The Labour Party: The Rise of the Left," *West European Politics* 6 (October 1983). See also David Kogan and Maurice Kogan, *The Battle for the Labour Party*, 2nd ed. (London: Kogan Page, 1983).
7. *The Economist*, 5 November 1984. See also Paul Whitely, *The Labour Party in Crisis* (London: Meuthen, 1984).
8. This poses a constitutional problem since the selection of the potential Labour prime minister is now by a process in which the popularly elected MPs are in a minority.

9. See Robert McKenzie, "Power in the Labour Party: The Issue of 'Intra-Party Democracy,'" Kavanagh, ed., *The Politics of the Labour Party.*

10. Ivor Crewe, "The Labour Party and the Electorate," in Kavanagh, ed., *The Politics of the Labour Party.*

11. Robert Harris, *The Making of Neil Kinnock* (London: Faber & Faber, 1984).

12. *The Times* (London), 27 March 1981.

13. See Anthony Barker, ed., *Quangos in Britain: Government and the Networks of Public Policy-Making* (London: Macmillan, 1982).

14. See J.T. Winkler, "Corporatism," *European Journal of Sociology* 17 (1976): 100–136.

15. Andrew Cox and Jack Hayward, "The Inapplicability of the Corporatist Model in Britain and France," *International Political Science Review* 4 (No. 2, 1983): 217–240.

16. Joel D. Wolfe, "Class Formation and Democracy: The Decline of Working-Class Power in Britain," *West European Politics* 9 (July 1986): 354–357.

17. Ibid., p. 355.

18. Stanley McBride, "Mrs. Thatcher and the Post-War Consensus: The Case of Trade Union Policy," *Parliamentary Affairs* 39 (July 1986): 330–340.

19. Wyn Grant and David Marsh, *The Confederation of British Industry* (London: Hodder & Stoughton, 1977).

20. Philip Norton, *The British Polity* (New York and London: Longman, 1984), p. 157.

21. Roger Jowell and Colin Airey, eds., *British Social Attitudes: The 1984 Report* (Aldershot, England: Gower, 1984), p. 21.

22. See Richard Taylor and Colin Pritchard, *The Protest Makers* (London: Pergamon, 1980).

23. Jowell and Airey, eds., *British Social Attitudes, 1984*, pp. 170–171.

CHAPTER FOUR
BRITISH POLICY
MAKING

We have made, or rather stumbled on a constitution which . . . has two capital merits: it contains a simple efficient part which, on occasion, and when wanted *can* work more simply and easily, and better, than any instrument of government that has yet been tried; and it contains likewise historical, complex, august, theatrical parts, which it has inherited from a long past.

Walter Bagehot,
The English Constitution

Unlike the other countries included in this book which have written and rewritten their constitutions to form more perfect democracies, the British political institutions are the product of centuries of political and social evolution. Changing society and ideas have molded an absolute monarchy into a modern constitutional democracy. As a consequence of this evolutionary development, Britain, alone among major democracies, has no written constitution. While Britons refer to their Constitution, there is no single document codifying political institutions and rules. Instead, the constitution is composed of customs, traditions, individual acts of Parliament, treaties, and other historical documents of which only some have actually been put down in writing. The fact that the constitution has never been written out or formally adopted detracts in no way from the respect that the British people have for their constitution. Nor does its unwritten status reduce its effectiveness in organizing government action and in restraining the exercise of power.

Written constitutions usually have elaborate procedures for amending them in order to limit frivolous change. But these procedures can hamper rapid adaptation to changing needs. The British unwritten constitution is remarkably easy to change when necessary. For example, during World War II the normal five-year limit on the life of a parliament was extended by a simple act of Parliament. This avoided the inconvenience of a national election during the war. Once the war was over, and the exceptional circumstances gone, the rule of general elections at least every five years was reinstated. The constitution can also be changed simply by new practices and informal understandings. Just in the last two decades, it has become accepted as constitutional for an individual to renounce his hereditary peerage in the House of Lords in order to become eligible to become prime minister. The apparent ease of amending the constitution does not mean that change comes easily. Modification of the constitution is a weighty matter even if it can be done by a simple act of Parliament or even by a change in expectations.

Occasionally, the constitution has been changed by the unchallenged violation of what was once believed to be constitutional principle. For years, British constitutional experts believed that prime ministers were required to resign if they were defeated on important votes in Commons. Then in the 1970s, both Conservative and Labour governments refused to resign after they were defeated on votes they had identified as vital. The old principle became a "constitutional myth" and a new principle that the government need resign only if it lost a vote of confidence or censure replaced the old.[1]

Despite the potential for confusion with no final written authority, there is in practice, little division over the content of the constitution.[2] For Americans used to venerating their constitution, the fluidity of the British constitution seems to offer the potential for abuse. But a broad consensus exists in Britain among political leaders and the informed public about what is and what is not permitted by the constitution. Those in power are in fact restrained from violating constitutional principles by the threat of public outcry and the fear of voter retaliation at the next election, sanctions that are in some ways more effective than documents and courts. The British have constitutionalism without a written constitution.

A CONSTITUTIONAL MONARCHY

Over a century ago, Walter Bagehot in his classic treatise on the constitution, distinguished between two aspects of the British government: the dignified parts (those institutions and practices that excite and preserve the reverence of the population) and the efficient parts (those actually responsible for the conduct of government).[3] Chief among the dignified elements is the monarch. More than any other modern state, Britain has preserved the traditions and institutions of its monarchical past, while placing them in a democratic context.

In theory and in law, all acts of government are performed in the name and by the authority of "Her Most Excellent Majesty Elizabeth the Second": She promulgates laws, negotiates treaties, selects the prime minister, names other political and religious leaders, and grants pardons. In actual practice, the Queen exercises virtually no political power whatsoever. All the acts performed in her name are undertaken by the prime minister and the cabinet who are accountable to the popularly elected House of Commons. In fact, the political prerogatives of the Queen are less extensive than those of the ordinary citizen. She does not have the right to take a partisan position; she cannot vote. Any temptation to political involvement is countered by the certainty of a public reaction that would endanger the very existence of the monarchy. A monarchy can be democratic only so long as the unelected monarch completely abstains from interfering with the actions of elected leaders.

The monarch does have the right to be informed on the actions of the government and to privately advise the prime minister. For over 35 years, Queen Elizabeth has met weekly with her prime ministers, read cabinet briefs, and interacted with foreign heads of state. Her long experience permits her to provide continuity and give invaluable and totally confidential advice to the prime minister. One former prime minister likened his weekly visits with the Queen to going to a psychiatrist, admitting he could tell her things he could not say even to his closest political colleagues.[4] Another area of possible discretion is in the selection of the prime minister. Ordinarily, the monarch calls upon the leader of the party that wins a majority in Commons. When no single party has a majority, the monarch may have some option in whom is selected. In 1974, the last time this situation existed, the queen minimized her discretion by turning first to the outgoing prime minister and, when he failed to form a gov-

FIGURE 4.1 **British Political Institutions.** *Source:* Rolf H. W. Theen and Frank L. Wilson, *Comparative Politics: An Introduction to Six Countries* (Englewood Cliffs, NJ: Prentice Hall, 1986, p. 57. Reprinted with permission.

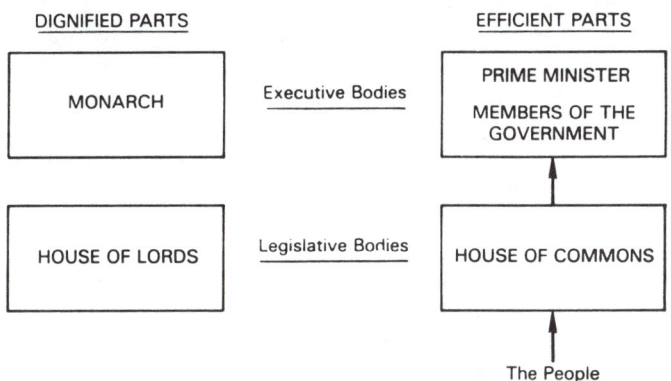

DIGNIFIED PARTS   EFFICIENT PARTS

MONARCH	Executive Bodies	PRIME MINISTER / MEMBERS OF THE GOVERNMENT
HOUSE OF LORDS	Legislative Bodies	HOUSE OF COMMONS

The People

ernment, she turned to the leader of the opposition who succeeded in forming a minority government. If a third party were to emerge and prevent either of the major parties from winning a majority, the monarch may once again face a Commons without an obvious prime minister. If this happens, it is likely that she will again try to resolve the issue with a minimal public role for herself by relying on the elected leaders.

The monarch is at once titular ruler of the United Kingdom and head of the Commonwealth of Nations—the loose assembly of now independent states that formerly made up the British empire. Queen Elizabeth found that these dual roles conflicted on occasion as the interests of Commonwealth countries increasingly differed from those of the United Kingdom. In 1986, the Queen's sense of conflict between these two roles led to the one semipublic political clash between Elizabeth and her government. Concerned about the possible consequences for the Commonwealth of Britain's refusal to impose sanctions on South Africa, the Queen attempted to persuade Thatcher to take a firmer stand against apartheid. When this royal pressure became public knowledge, all sides denied that it had occurred. The Queen's intervention was criticized even by Labour party figures who shared her endorsement of sanctions but who rejected the notion of any interference by the monarch.

Occasionally, radicals propose the abolition of the monarchy but such appeals have found little support in the general public. A 1984 poll found only 3 percent advocating the abolition of the monarchy with two thirds feeling that the continuation of the monarchy is very important.[5] At a time when other public institutions were losing public esteem, the monarchy retained its popularity and cast some of its luster by reflection on the whole political system. In the words of one former minister:

> The monarchy has become our only truly popular institution at a time when the House of Commons has declined in public esteem and the Lords is a matter of controversy. The monarchy is, in a real sense, underpinning the other two estates of the realm.[6]

The monarch serves a useful role by relieving the prime minister of many of the ceremonial duties required of a chief of state: receiving ambassadors, public appearances, state visits abroad, and recognizing artistic, scientific, and industrial accomplishments. More importantly, the monarch personalizes the state, embodies national unity, and links the present with a glorious past. The monarch is an important political symbol producing strong emotional ties in the general public.[7] These affective sentiments contribute to patriotism and to a willingness to accept political rule by less glamorous, real politicians. As one analyst noted during the surge of patriotism that developed during the celebration of Queen Elizabeth's 25 years as monarch, the Queen was "a historical figure whose presence not only gave pleasure to her people but identity and confidence too."[8]

PRIME MINISTERIAL POWER

In the 1960s, there was concern that the prime minister had accumulated too much power. Originally, the presiding officer of a collegial body created and beholden to Parliament, prime ministers had gradually become the dominant political figures, able to control the parliamentary procedures and dominate their colleagues in the government. Some critics felt that the prime minister's powers had grown so much that collegial "cabinet government" had been replaced by government by a dominant prime minister.[9] However, in the fifteen years from 1956 to 1971, a series of five relatively weak prime ministers provoked concerns of an opposite trend: The executive lacked the power to meet the demands of a modern industrial society. These conflicting concerns about prime ministerial powers reflect the delicate balance needed in democracies: Executives need to be strong enough to govern efficiently and effectively; they must also be subject to enough restraints that they will not be tempted or, if tempted, they will not be able to abuse their powers.

One key power of prime ministers is their role in creating the government. Once designated by the Queen, they have considerable leeway in choosing other ministers and ultimately in dismissing them. In practice, however, there are important limits on the prime minister's ability to exercise this discretion.[10] Except during rare coalition governments, prime ministers are limited to their fellow party members in Parliament and to those with the skill to administer a government department. They must balance various factions and which often include powerful rivals, simply because of the political importance of these key party leaders.

From the members of the government, the prime minister selects twenty or so of the most important ministers to form the cabinet.[11] The cabinet meets weekly to discuss major issues and to collegially set government policy. Unlike United States cabinets whose members are usually not the most important leaders, British cabinet ministers are powerful and independent political figures, not lackeys of the prime minister. They have important places in a collegial decision-making process and are not simply administrators of their departments. The prime minister controls the agenda and presides over meetings of the cabinet. After full discussion, the prime minister determines (usually without a formal vote) the collective decision of the cabinet. The government is in turn confident of the cooperation of a loyal majority in Commons that will support its actions and legislative program with a minimum of delay and change. In this regard, British prime ministers are more powerful than American presidents who must struggle to get their programs approved by an independent and powerful Congress.

Once a decision is reached, the guiding principle is the *collective responsibility* of the cabinet to Parliament and the people. Cabinet decisions are collective in that all ministers are presumed to have assented to the decision. Ministers who are not able to support the government's position are expected to resign. This permits clear lines of accountability. Unlike the United States—where a president might blame failures on Congress, the cabinet, or the bureaucracy—in Britain the cabinet stands permanently responsible for all government action or inaction.

In the past, a convention of secrecy insulated cabinet debates from the public and even Parliament thus enhancing the strength of the prime minister. This privacy has broken down with former ministers now disclosing internal debates and the prime minister's maneuvers to get his or her way. Disgruntled ministers have resigned and gone to the press with their stories of autocratic abuses by the prime minister. The press is more eager to report indications of dissent within the government and their likely political ramifications than it is to cover the substance of the disagreement. Lifting the veil of secrecy has diminished prime ministerial power. For example, the 1986 resignation of Thatcher's defense minister, in a disagreement over the sale of Britain's last helicopter firm to an American company, disclosed tensions within her government and reduced her ability to coerce her colleagues down paths they were reluctantly treading on a variety of completely unrelated issues. Press coverage of the division weakened Thatcher's control over her colleagues and encouraged speculation on her ultimate successor.

The modern, political executive faces important hindrances to effective control of the state he or she presumably masters. The sheer size of the bureaucracy, the multiple political tasks placed on leaders, the constraints of political and social reality, and eager rivals for power all diminish the potential authority of the prime minister. One analyst captured well the challenges of executive political control:

> Viewed from the top, British government looks more like a mountain range than a single pyramid of power. The Prime Minister is preeminent among these peaks, but the political significance of this preeminence is ambiguous. . . . Perhaps the person on top is better described as the "least weak" member of government instead of the most powerful.[12]

Three idiosyncratic elements play important parts in determining the prime minister's powers. First, the events the prime minister is called upon to manage often enhance or limit the exercise of executive power. Obviously, war or foreign crises facilitate prime ministerial power because such critical moments demand solidarity, rapid action, and secrecy. Margaret Thatcher profited from the brief Falklands War. She extended her powers and established decision making by a small group of her intimate advisors that continued long after the end of the war.[13] More mundane events limit the opportunities for expanding the prime minister's control. Second, the prime minister's personality affects accumulation of power. A prime minister dedicated to collegial consensus is less likely to become a dominant leader than someone with strongly held goals to implement. Thatcher's reputation for firmness, her ideological commitments, and her obvious relish for confrontation made her one of the most powerful prime ministers since the war. Finally, the public's view of the prime minister is important. Even ambitious prime ministers find their power declines when their public approval drops. They are less able to impose their will on colleagues worrying about reelection or on civil servants anticipating a change in leadership. Thus, Thatcher faced growing rebellion against her strong leadership style as her public standing fell after 1985.

It is paradoxical that, in any given year, one can find knowledgeable observers worried about insufficient executive leadership and equally qualified on-lookers complaining about excessive executive power. In this paradox, we can perhaps see a healthy struggle to maintain that delicate balance between granting the leader too much power and denying him or her the power needed for effective government. The British record has been admirable. Periods of inadequate leadership, such as during the 1960s and 1970s, were not due to institutional weaknesses but to the lackluster individuals who led the government. Even these leaders had adequate power (and were sometimes accused of excessive use of it) but used it ineffectively. When powerful leaders have emerged they have been committed democrats unwilling to abuse their powers, and they have faced a skeptical public and vigilant colleagues.

PARLIAMENT

Rich in more than 700 years of tradition, Parliament offers a spectacular pageant. But behind this pageantry is the heart of British politics. In the House of Commons rests the Mace, the symbol of royal authority, conveying the essential principle of British politics: the supreme sovereignty of Parliament. Officially, Parliament refers to three distinct elements: the monarch, the House of Lords, and the House of Commons. Together they exercise sovereign legislative power with the Queen affixing the Royal Assent to legislation passed by the two chambers. Two of these elements, the monarch and the House of Lords are "dignified" institutions with more ceremonial than practical importance. The monarch has not refused the Royal Assent since 1707 and the House of Lords can do no more than delay legislation that it dislikes. In terms of real political power, it is held by the 650 elected members of the House of Commons.

The House of Commons

During the 1960s, many viewed the House of Commons as a body in decline and in desperate need of reform to escape further eclipsing by the increasingly powerful executive.[14] The rise of the executive government supported by a disciplined party majority had reduced the role and importance of Commons. Then, during the 1970s, a series of new issues—immigration, the Common Market, and devolution—divided parties and undermined their unity.[15] With slim majorities and two minority governments, Commons changed and periodically challenged the powers of the government. Between 1945 and 1970, the government suffered major parliamentary defeats only eleven times; between 1970 and 1979, the government went down to defeat on major votes 65 times.[16] Commons came to be viewed as unruly and as having contributed to the political instability of that decade but without having regained its power.[17] The evidence of this disruptive role is slim. Dissent remains unusual and actual defeat for government in Commons is still very rare.[18] What seems to be occurring is the evolutionary process of typical, British, political change. Commons has not regained the law-making and government-creating functions but it has changed, keeping some responsibilities and acquiring others to maintain its vital role in British democracy.[19]

One of these tasks is its role in training and recruiting top political leaders. Unlike the United States where politicians may prepare for office in local politics, businesses, or even professional sports and acting, all Britain's political leaders emerge from Parliament, mostly from the House of Commons with only a few drawn from the House of Lords.[20] Leaders serve long apprentices in the "backbenches" and then, in junior ministerial posts learning the legislative process and proving themselves as able party supporters. On average, prime ministers have served 27 years in Commons prior to their elevation to the top political position. Margaret Thatcher had served fifteen years in Commons before becoming her party's leader; Neil Kinnock had served thirteen years before his selection as Labour party leader. This pattern of recruitment emphasizes party loyalty, the development of cohesive leadership teams, and the gentility that make British "Watergates" unlikely. But it also runs the risk of inhibiting innovation and initiative. Too much inbreeding of leaders may accentuate the already elitist nature of leadership and inhibit bold departures from established policies by either party. This closed recruitment prevents the involvement of bright people who are not members of parliament. Some feel that this explains Britain's inability to respond to the economic challenges of the postwar era.

Commons plays a vital role in representing the people in politics. It is not representative in that its membership is far from a good reflection of the general population. Its members are more affluent, higher in social class standing, far more male, and better educated. Nor do they reflect accurately political preferences since the electoral system gives the large parties disproportionate shares of the seats. The House of Commons' claim to representativity comes from the fact that this membership is the one selected by the voters in free, competitive elections.[21] Individually, members of Commons seek to bring the concerns of their constituents into the policy process, either directly to the floor of Parliament or indirectly through the offices of ministers and department heads. They meet nearly daily with individuals and groups and hold regular "surgeries," office hours, in their constituencies to listen to the views of voters. On occasion, such constituency considerations lead MPs to defy party discipline to protect their voters' interests.[22] More frequently, MPs convey quietly, but not ineffectively these concerns to government or party, policy makers. Clearly, the mood of the public affects successful politicians who shape the mood of Parliament which in turn places limits or demands on even the strongest government.

Another task is that of informing the public on different ways to deal with key issues. The debate on the floor of the House of Commons presents the public with alternative approaches to the nation's problems. The clear division between the government and the opposition clarifies differences and choices. The opposition has the opportunity to criticize the government's policies and to present its own approaches in a public forum. It controls the agenda in Commons on "Opposition days" and can challenge the government's performance through public debate on a topic of the opposition's choice. There are nineteen Opposition days distributed through the year. In addition, the opposition can force debate on a given issue by filing a motion of censure. A censure motion has priority over other legislative matters and must be debated. Even if the motion is doomed to failure by the presence of a disciplined majority, as it usually is, the debate on the censure motion permits the opposition to criticize the government and force it to defend its conduct before the public. Despite the opportunity for informative dialogue, the "mewing and bawling" that actually occurs is often disappointing. Public awareness of these debates is low despite radio broadcasts of key debates and better press coverage of Parliament than what is available in the United States. Nevertheless, Commons provides a forum for clearly contrasting approaches to government by Britain's major parties.

While it is indisputable that priority in the legislative process has shifted from Commons to the government, Commons retains an important place in the legislative process. While government bills rarely are defeated, Commons does scrutinize and refine pending legislation. Governments often withdraw proposed bills that have elicited backbench reservations or accept amendments that improve or alter the bill. The ability of Commons to carry out legislative responsibilities has increased in the last decade with the creation of "select committees."[23] The older "standing committees" were large, unwieldy bodies which lacked special areas of competence. The new select committees are smaller and oversee specific ministries. This focus permits more expertise to develop among committee members giving them greater potential influence on legislation within their specialization. More important than their role in reviewing proposed bills—a task still exercised by the old standing committees—the new select committees have investigative and oversight responsibilities. Thus, a select committee led the investigation of the Thatcher government decision to abandon the Westland helicopter in favor of an American competitor. The report was sharply critical of the government's action and censured key advisors to the prime minister. The select committees are still new—most were created in 1979—and they have received little cooperation from a government that recognizes them as potential rivals. They have not yet acquired the status and power of Congressional committees in the United States but they do represent a modest reassertion of parliamentary scrutiny of government: "A small squad of Davids facing an army of departmental Goliaths."[24]

Finally, Commons exercises restraint on the power of the executive. The ultimate weapon is that of censure which compels the resignation of the prime minister and cabinet. This has been used successfully only once in the last 60 years—in 1979 to oust James Callaghan. Then, it represented the loss of the government's majority in Commons rather than a direct repudiation of the government's actions. The prime minister does have the power to order dissolution of the House of Commons if faced with a vote of censure. In such a case, voters go to the polls after a brief campaign to elect a new Commons. This power of dissolution deters MPs from the prime minister's party from supporting censure motions or from voting against their government in confidence votes. The results of such elections, of course, are unpredictable. In some cases, they result in the sustaining of the prime minister and government just defeated in a censure vote by the outgoing parliament. But in other cases, as in Callaghan's case in 1979, the election brings a new majority and a new prime minister.

The prime minister's power to dissolve Commons can also be exercised in order to permit the government to select the most advantageous moment for new elections. While Commons is elected for a five year term, most parliaments are dissolved by the prime minister in their fourth year. They do so in order to prevent giving the electorate the impression that the government fears to go before the people. They also avoid waiting until the term expires in order to pick a moment when they and their advisors believe their party will have the best chance. When the majority is uncertain or narrow, dissolution can be ordered by the prime minister to ascertain the voters' mandate or to improve the majority party's parliamentary margin when polls indicate a favorable evaluation of the government.

Unlike American presidents who cannot be questioned by Congress, prime ministers know that their actions must be defended daily and in person against a group of peers not noted for their respect of position. Twice each week during Question Time, MPs from all parties can pose questions to the prime minister and other ministers regarding government policies or performance. With many of these questions designed to embarrass or criticize a minister, Question Time is an important parliamentary check on executive power. Skillful questioning can embarrass the government or force it to direct attention to specific matters or issues. That this questioning is an effective restraint is attested to by a former prime minister:

> . . . no prime minister looks forward to "PQs" [parliamentary questions] with anything but apprehension; every prime minister works long into the night on his answers; and on all the notes available to help him anticipate the insistent and unpredictable supplementary questions that follow his main prepared answer. . . . If Britain ever had a prime minister who did not fear Questions, our parliamentary democracy would be in danger.[25]

More recently, Margaret Thatcher admitted her nervousness kept her from eating much on the days when she faces Question Time. "I find that if you have got to have all your concentration on answering questions, you do not want too much in your tummy."[26]

In comparison with the powerful and independent United States Congress, the British House of Commons appears weak and subordinate to the executive. It lacks the resources for developing real power. Its committee system is weak; its members poorly paid (only about £24,107—

US$42,000 in 1989 terms; they lack adequate secretarial and legislative staffs; office space is very limited. These perquisites of office, less than what is available to middle-level management in industry or commerce, are not likely to attract the best and the brightest into government service. Perhaps the comparison with the American Congress is unfair since the power of Commons compares well with parliaments in France, Germany, Italy, and in other democratic countries with powerful parties and parliamentary traditions. Above all, it is important to remember that Commons still has the power to reassert itself should a majority of its members wish to do so. The government defeats in the 1970s demonstrate the ability of Commons to act independently when members feel that the leaders are not acting in accord with party philosophies or the needs of the country. The fact that the rise of executive power came from the voluntary acquiescence of Commons means that prime ministers and ministers cannot afford to and, in fact, do not ignore Commons.

The House of Lords

Most democratic countries have sensed a need for two legislative chambers to assure carefully drafted laws and to serve as checks on each other against hasty action or abuse of power. But the problem is to find a basis for the second chamber's existence. In the United States, this is provided by the notion of senators representing entire states instead of smaller districts. But in countries lacking federal structure, there is often uncertainty on how to differentiate the second chamber from the one directly elected to represent the people.

Britain's answer is a unique one: Its second chamber, the House of Lords, is based on representation of the nobility. Its membership is composed of titled nobility who have inherited their positions, lifetime peers (named by the government as an honor), law lords who serve as the ultimate court of appeal, and "lords spiritual" from the Church of England. (See Table 4.1) Theoretically the upper chamber, the House of Lords, plays a much less important political role than does Commons. The process of democratization has stripped nearly all power from the Lords. It no longer has the ability to block legislation passed by Commons, though it can delay most legislation for a year (financial matters can be delayed for only a month).

Nevertheless, the presence of a legislative body based largely on hereditary members is an object of debate in Britain. Public opinion generally supports the House of Lords as it is—57 percent in 1984.[27] But the Labour party has advocated its abolition. Alliance politicians and others have demanded its reform to eliminate the hereditary members and to provide a stronger second chamber; still others have insisted upon its continued utility. Those advocating abolition or change claim that the House of Lords is undemocratic and frivolous. They protest a hereditary body still operating in a supposedly democratic decision-making process. They see it as remote from the real needs of the nation as, when in the midst of crippling strikes in 1979, it serenely debated the reality of un-

TABLE 4.1   Composition of the House of Lords

Nature of peerage (1983)

Hereditary peers	790
Life peers	334
Lords spiritual and law lords	47
Total	1170

Party affiliation (1986)

Conservative	419
Labour	119
Alliance	86
Cross-bench	244
Others	53
Lords Spiritual	26

Source: Paul Silk, *How Parliament Works* (London Longman, 1987), pp 17-18.

identified flying objects and the impact on religion of belief in such phenomena. For those wanting a second body, they contend that the hereditary House of Lords lacks the power to serve as a needed check on Commons.

The defenders of the present House of Lords point to the difficulty other countries—such as France and Germany—have had in finding a basis for a second chamber. The Lords serves well in providing a second examination of pending laws and a constitutional safeguard against abuse of power by the Commons without challenging the supremacy of Commons as a second popularly elected chamber would do. The nonelected nature of the House of Lords gives it independence and makes it a less partisan forum for debating public issues. The House of Lords has conducted useful and intelligent debates of important but politically sensitive issues such as legislation on homosexuality and the death penalty. Because their agenda is less charged, the Lords can devote greater time to the tedious but important review of technical passages in proposed laws.

Some sort of change in the House of Lords appears likely since the Labour party has made its abolition a central plank in its program and the Alliance wants its reform. Informal changes are already evident. The hereditary nature of the body is diminished by the growing numbers of life peers, and the disinclination of about one third of the hereditary peers to exercise their right to sit in the House of Lords. Life peers were first created in 1958. Since then only two new hereditary peerages have been created. The life peers, (mainly former Commons' politicians elevated to the House of Lords) already make up nearly a third of the potential membership and a solid majority of those actually engaged in the chamber's activities. Despite the controversy surrounding it, the House of Lords has actually become more active in the last decade with many more Lords participating and doing so in more frequent and lengthier sessions.[28] The Lords generally avoid conflict with Commons by deferring to the elected body when it is clear that the Commons is resolute. They focus on technical details and provide amendments that often improve the legislation and are welcomed by the government.

THE BRITISH CIVIL SERVICE

The bureaucracy must be subject to the political leaders in a democracy if the people are truly to retain control of their government. Elected officials subject to the voters' sanctions must control the unelected and thus, democratically irresponsible bureaucrats. But it is unrealistic to expect bureaucracies to have no say in policy making. It is also undesirable, since bureaucrats represent not only their own interests but also the interests of the clientele they serve. For example, government social workers often defend the interests and needs of their clients, the poor and disabled. However, if the lines of democratic responsibility are to be maintained, it must be an elected official who ultimately regulates the bureaucracy's actions.

In Britain the burden of controlling the civil service falls on comparatively few politically responsible leaders. This system contrasts with the United States where each federal department has many—sometimes as many as several hundred—top-level political appointees who oversee the permanent bureaucrats. In the typical British government department, there are only three or four political leaders: the minister and a couple of parliamentary secretaries, all MPs. (See Figure 4.2) The rest of the managerial positions, including the permanent secretary, the deputy secretaries, and the minister's private secretary are all career civil servants removable only on grounds of malfeasance in office. The American principle of control has been to staff all policy-making positions in the administration with politically reliable appointees to assure that the civil service implements the president's policies. The British have based their approach to political control of the administration on the principle that civil servants will be neutral and will faithfully execute the policies of whatever government is in place.

Over the last decade, a growing chorus of complaints has been directed at Whitehall (a term used to refer collectively to the British civil service) by former ministers and politicians who feel that the bureaucrats have failed to live up to their obligation of total fealty to the minister in place. These criticisms have come from politicians on the Left and the Right.[29] The complaint is not so much of a political bias for or against any party but rather Whitehall's proclivity to defend the existing department policy and procedures. Civil servants, who will be in a department for their whole career sometimes work subtly to shape the minister's view and policy to conform with department policy. They do so by selecting issues and information to bring before the minister, by invoking prior practices, and by retarding implementation of undesired changes in the

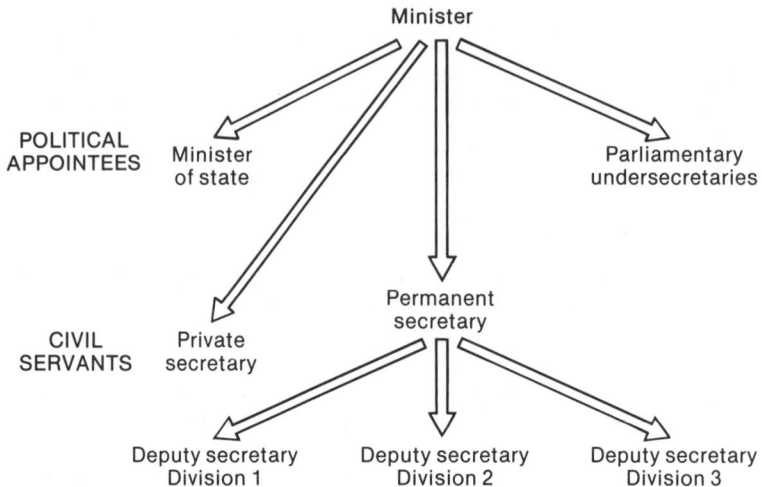

FIGURE 4.2   A Typical British Department

hope that the minister's mind will change or, a new minister will be more amenable to Whitehall's view.[30] This kind of subtle distortion practiced by civil servants is easily remedied by alert and capable administrators, but such individuals are not always found in ministerial posts. Ministers are all experienced politicians and many have developed substantive expertise in their departments. But they often lack the administrative and managerial experience needed to control complex organizations. With multiple responsibilities in their home districts, on the floor of Commons, and as party leaders they have inadequate time to devote to their departments. One author cites a soon-to-be appointed minister as saying that "only about one minister in three runs his department." When queried about this estimate after he had served as a cabinet minister, he replied that "on reflection, I think it was probably an overestimate."[31]

In an attempt to provide ministers with independent, outside viewpoints, the 1974 Labour government appointed one or two special advisers to each department.[32] Based in part on French *cabinets*, these special advisers were politically loyal to the minister and provided expert advice on department affairs. Free from any regular administrative duties, they gave political, as opposed to technical, advice on policy decisions as well as assisting the minister in developing new approaches. The Conservatives criticized the use of special advisers as politicalization of the civil service. Once back in office, the Thatcher government cut back on the use of special advisers, limiting them to only some departments.

We have seen that while civil servants are apolitical, they do develop and defend "department policies." They are also very ready to defend the prerogatives and interests of the bureaucrats against challenges from both Conservative and Labour governments. A good illustration is the civil service reforms proposed by the Fulton Committee. These reforms were designed to eliminate some of the worst bureaucratic ailments, but civil servants resisted or distorted those parts they deemed detrimental to their interests. One of the authors of the Fulton Report claimed that the civil servants "tore the heart out" of the reform recommendations while maintaining that the changes were being implemented in full.[33] Similarly, the Thatcher government sought to cut the size of the civil service but encountered opposition as civil servants resisted their ministers with delays, half gestures, and outright noncompliance. It took five years before the government had succeeded in reaching its goal of reducing the civil service by 15 percent.

This section has focused on abuses for such abuses endanger democratic control. But the overall picture is still one of remarkable loyalty on the part of senior civil servants to changing political leaders. Most of them do try to accomplish the goals outlined by their ministers. The problems of abuses of technical knowledge have been few in Britain, in comparison with France and Germany, for example. A principal reason is the British preference for generalist, liberal arts training for senior civil servants. Prime ministers and former ministers from all parties have given testimony of the ability and obedience of their civil servants. One recent Labour prime minister reported that when he took office after thirteen years in opposition, his ministers arrived at the Westminister offices on the day of their appointment and found that the civil servants had already drawn up proposals to implement the policies the ministers had pledged during the campaign. The proposals were ready for submission and the cabinet was able to act on some of them the next day.[34] Such loyalty and efficiency contrast markedly with the chaos produced by a change in the American presidency when literally thousands of political appointees are reshuffled. There are times when the British civil service escapes the controls of their political masters but these situations are checkable by skillful and attentive ministers.

The problem of maintaining political control over the burgeoning bureaucracy is one shared by all modern states. Governments have tried a variety of means to exercise this control ranging from the American practice of flooding the top levels of the administration with political appointees to the Soviet technique of elaborate parallel bureaucracies that check on each other. Britain's approach has been to rely on civil servants to accept the norm of subservience to political leaders. The norm holds well in deterring civil servants from favoring one party's politics over the other's. But it does not deter the civil servants from defending their own corporate interests: their jobs, their established procedures, their expertise. In an era when the bureaucracy's size and cumbersomeness have become key political issues, the bureaucrats' resistance to internal reforms becomes a clear challenge to the political authority and preeminence of the elected leaders.

A CENTRALIZED DEMOCRACY

Americans often see their federal structure as assuring democracy by dividing power between the federal government and the states. Britons have fewer concerns about the effects of concentrated power on democracy. The British government is highly centralized in that the national government has all the power and has the discretion to grant or withdraw prerogatives and power to local authorities. Despite this centralization of political power, the all-powerful national government does not seem inclined to abuse it. The restraint of British government suggests that the American fear of misuse of power by centralized government is unwarranted. Americans have followed Madison's notion of offsetting power with power and have used structural impediments to prevent their leaders from abusing political power. The British have spurned separation of power and instead have developed informal and internal norms in their political leaders that keep them from exceeding democratic limits even while their institutions give them extensive power.

The Local Authorities

The various "national" groups in Britain—the Welsh, the Scots, and the Northern Irish (since 1972)—lack their own regional governments. There are only two levels of government: the central government and the local authorities. The pattern of local government is very complicated. The structures vary from one part of Britain to another with England and Wales having one set, Scotland a different one, Northern Ireland yet another, and metropolitan London its own. Even in the same part of the country, the levels of power vary from one community to the next because Parliament has given some communities authority that it has not conferred upon others.

A major reform in 1972 established a two-tier system.[35] The broader layer is made up of county councils (or regional councils in Scotland) providing major governmental services such as education, social services, police and fire protection, and highways. The lower level is made up of a greater number of smaller district councils responsible for local services such as recreation, housing, garbage collection, and street cleaning. At both levels of government, the members of the councils are elected by the general public to four-year terms. In London, borough and district councils provide elected local government.

In general, local authorities administer policies established by the national government. They are expected to follow the government's guidelines in administering these policies. Central control is assured by the supervision of the government's ministers and their inspectors, and through the allocation of government funds. In addition, the *ultra vires* rule (beyond authority) bars local authorities from doing anything that has not been specifically authorized by Parliament. These limits are not entirely unsatisfactory from the standpoint of elected local officials. New services or programs locally developed would have to be financed by raising local rates (taxes). The rates are not popular and efforts to raise them are always politically risky.

Local authorities often can delay or even alter the application of unwanted policies. For example, local authorities slowed the consolidation of secondary schools passed by Parliament in 1965 for nearly a decade. Programs to contract or sell council (public) housing were effectively blocked in many communities by reluctant local authorities. The London government subsidized public transportation and raised rates to pay for it in contradiction to national policy. The central government ultimately has the upper hand. The Thatcher government dealt with resistance from metropolitan councils in London and other large cities, that were dominated by far leftists bent on attacking the government, by simply abolishing the councils in 1986 and devolving their responsibilities on the borough councils.

Despite such central supervision, British local authorities do have important powers that they can exercise. There is a long tradition of local control over schools and police, vital governmental functions reserved for the central governments in France, Italy, and other unitary states. Despite this apparent autonomy, British local authorities lack the political weight of their counterparts in France. There is no equivalent in Britain to the great prestige and power of French mayors. Nor do British local officials play the brokerage role between the central government and the citizens as their French and Italian colleagues do. Finally, the local authorities' lack of real power in Britain is well demonstrated by the 1972 reform imposed by the central government that reduced the number of municipal councillors by one third. It would be unthinkable and political suicide for a French government to propose such a reform even though the number of French local officials is twenty times larger than in Britain and far in excess of the needs of the country.

Decentralization and Devolution

The growing impact of government on the lives of British citizens has stimulated interest in decentralizing government decision making. It is widely accepted that decentralization to local government would permit greater responsiveness to the public and increase citizen involvement in making the decisions that affect their lives. But these assumptions about the greater responsiveness of local or regional governments have never been proved. Indeed, there is reason to question them. It is not at all clear, for example, that decentralization would lead to greater citizen participation. The public's interest in local government is lower than its interest in national politics—as suggested by the fact that voter turn-out for local elections is much lower than for national elections. Very few people attend county or district council meetings or can name their locally elected councillors. Press coverage of local politics is minimal. This widespread disinterest in local politics makes local authorities less representative of the public. It insulates them from their constituents and makes them less responsive to the public when compared to national political figures who are more visible to their electorate. There is the tendency for voters to use local elections as opportunities to make a midterm evaluation of the national government. Consequently, local councillors know that their fate hangs less on their performance or local issues than it does on the public's feelings toward the national government.

Local governments may be more vulnerable to the influence of special interests than is the national government for two reasons. First, disinterest on the part of the general public makes local governments more susceptible to pressure by special-interest groups threatening to mobilize their followers against uncooperative officeholders. Second, at the national level the presence of many groups provide countervailing forces to prevent a single group from insisting on its way; at the local level, however, officials may find it more difficult to refuse the demands of a firm that dominates its economy. For example, the fear of losing large industries kept many British communities from enforcing air pollution regulations despite the fact that the polluted air adversely affected the lives of their residents and those of surrounding communities.

There is another danger—the tyranny of local majorities over minorities, that is well illustrated by Britain's only genuine experiment in devolution before the 1970s. The assembly in Northern Ireland was dominated by Protestants who used their majority status to discriminate against the Catholic minority. The greater pluralism and diversity in the national unit made such discrimination unlikely. To end it in Northern Ireland, the central government had to prorogue the assembly and transfer power to London in 1972. Since then, Northern Irish Protestants have made their intention clear to use any new devolution to reestablish their political dominion over minority Catholics.

Interest in decentralization is uncertain. After centuries of strong central rule, there is no natural basis for British decentralization like the German länder or Italian regions. Political parties seem to be politically motivated in their support for decentralization with the party controlling Commons favoring central control and those out of power seeing local control as a counterbalance to their lack of influence over national politics. Thus, the Labour party opposed decentralization when hoping for power because they feared that local authorities might retard the implementation of the reforms they planned to make. Then, when out of office nationally but in control of several major cities, they championed local rights in order to begin their reforms at the grass roots. Similarly, Conservatives have long advocated some local autonomy to check on the central government but under Thatcher they slashed local powers in order to impose fiscal responsibility and control inflation. The Liberals have been consistent advocates of local government power, but again, it is in their political interest to do so since they have been more successful in local elections than in national politics.

The general public's reaction to proposals for devolution of new powers to local authorities is lukewarm at best. A 1984 poll found only 34 percent advocating more autonomy for local government with 13 percent wanting more central control and 45 percent favoring the existing relationship.[36] Even more revealing was the lack of enthusiasm for devolution shown by voters in the two areas—Scotland and Wales—where sentiments for local autonomy seemed strongest. In 1979 referenda on devolution, measures that would have given each its own regional assembly and limited local autonomy, failed to be endorsed. In Wales, voters overwhelmingly rejected the proposal; in Scotland there was a narrow majority favoring devolution among those voting, but this number fell well short of the 40 percent of registered voters needed for ratification. In contrast to American fears about the growth of big central government, it appears that the British are more fearful of the centrifugal and divisive effects of decentralization. Indeed, the one experience with devolution, Northern Ireland, had an overall effect that was "decidedly negative" even apart from the fanning of ethnic tensions.[37] In practice, devolution did not achieve the responsiveness, flexibility, and reduced workload on central governments that decentralization is touted to provide.

THE PUBLIC AND POLICY MAKING

The very nature of representative government produces a gap between the public and the leaders. Some of this distance is desirable since it buffers the state from the changing whims of public opinion and permits governments to take necessary steps which may not be popular in the short run but which are necessary in the long run. Some of the gap is unavoidable since at best citizens lack well-formulated opinions on more than a few public issues. Thus, the link between public opinion and public policy in Britain is lengthy but nevertheless brings public policy into conformity with the general public will. Public opinion, rather than compelling government to act in certain ways, establishes outer limits of acceptable policy leaving the elected officials considerable leeway in setting the actual policy.[38] These "opinion dikes" may expand permitting more leader discretion on uninteresting or complex issues. Or they may contract as the public becomes interested in an issue or sees a particular approach as imperative. Then even reluctant politicians find they cannot resist an idea whose time has come.

With politicians schooled in a historical tradition emphasizing the importance of avoiding the unacceptable, Britain's political system seems well adapted to the democratic need to be attentive to these opinion dikes. With party competition between Conservatives and Labour as intense as it is, both have found that they must respond and respond quickly to changing opinion or risk electoral disaster. The threat of third parties in the 1970s and 1980s has added to the parties' recognition that they cannot survive if they stray too far from their publics.

Britain has also developed a system of "party government" that facilitates the maintenance of democratic accountability.[39] Party programs set out a fairly clear agenda for a future government. The electoral system usually provides one party with a parliamentary majority and party discipline assures the votes so that the government's program will be enacted. The government is reasonably certain that its laws will be implemented by the civil service. The result is that the voters' mandate through their choice of alternative parties and programs can be enacted. In addition, voters know who is responsible for public policy and they can then reward or sanction that party at the next election. This is a very tidy system of accountability that helps link people with their government. Government is responsible in the eyes of the electorate and permits even modestly informed citizens to exercise rational choices at the polls. Thus, voters who were unhappy with the government's efforts to remedy high unemployment in the mid-1980s knew that it was Thatcher's Conservatives who were responsible and they could vote against them the next time.

Contrast this clear accountability with the situation in the United States where the conflict between the president and Congress and the near absence of party cohesion in congressional votes make it nearly impossible for even a very informed citizen to know who is responsible. When President Reagan and congressional Democrats blamed each other for the mounting federal deficit, there was no way for the concerned citizen to determine who was right. The president's proposals are always modified in Congress by votes that include members from both parties. The lines of accountability in the United States are thus muddied and impossible to trace whereas in Britain, party government brings accountable or responsible government.

CONCLUSION

The one thing that saved England from the fate of other countries was not her insular position, nor the independent spirit nor the magnanimity of her people . . . but only the consistent, uninventive, stupid fidelity to that political system which originally belonged to all the nations that traversed the ordeal of feudalism.

Lord Acton

The persistence of quaint political institutions dating back nearly a thousand years makes Britain particularly attractive for tourists. These traditional political institutions and practices have important value beyond their picturesqueness. The durability of these institutions through the centuries adds to the public's respect for their current decisions and actions. They confer *legitimacy* on the political system—in the sense that the political system in place not only has political power, but *ought* to have this power. They contribute to the public's willingness to accept government decisions as authoritative and as deserving obedience.

It is remarkable that these feudal institutions provide the framework for a highly successful democratic government. This government is possible because the procedures and power relationships change in pace with the time, permitting their democratization and their continued relevance for modern political challenges. They continue to change in the 1980s. This conservation of traditional institutions through gradual change and compromise helps create and perpetuate a political style based on accommodation and adjustment rather than on conflict and radical revolution.

Political scientists often debate the effects of particular political frameworks on the overall nature of politics in a given country. Some argue that the social setting, the prevailing political culture (the pattern of political attitudes and values), and the behavior of political actors have much greater effects on the shaping of the political system than do the particular political institutions present in the country. Others insist that the nature of the institutions can affect and in certain cases even determine the political culture and behavior. In Britain, it appears that the relationship between institutions on the one hand and political culture and behavior on the other is one of interdependency. The practices and power relationships of British political institutions have evolved gradually and harmoniously with the democratization of political attitudes and behavior. This agreeable congruency of institutions and complementary political culture and behavior patterns does not always occur. As we shall see, democratic political institutions were artificially established in Germany during the Weimar era (1919–1933) with disastrous effects; the failure of these institutions in the unfavorable attitudinal and behavioral setting contributed to Hitler's rise to power. This experience stands in sharp contrast to Britain, where the durability of honored political institutions and the presence of congruent patterns of political culture and behavior have given Britain a remarkably stable political order.

NOTES

1. Philip Norton, *The Constitution in Flux*, (Oxford: Martin Robertson, 1982), pp. 67–69.
2. For recent constitutional developments, see James B. Kellas, "The Politics of Constitution-making: The Experience of the United Kingdom," in Keith G. Banting and Richard Simeon, eds., *Redesigning the State: The Politics of Constitutional Change*, (Toronto: University of Toronto Press, 1985); and Nevil Johnson, *In Search of the Constitution*, (London: Meuthen, 1980).
3. Walter Bagehot, *The English Constitution*, (Ithaca, NY: Cornell University Press, 1963).
4. F. N. Forman, *Mastering British Politics*, (London: Macmillan, 1985), p. 133.
5. Roger Jowell and Colin Airey, *British Social Attitudes: The 1984 Report*, (Aldershot, England: Gower, 1984), p. 30.
6. Norman St. John-Stevas, quoted in Anthony Sampson, *The Changing Anatomy of Britain*, (New York: Vintage, 1982), p. 10.
7. See Richard Rose and Dennis Kavanagh, "The Monarchy in Contemporary Political Culture," *Comparative Politics* 8 (July 1976): 548–576; See also Tom Nairn, *The Enchanted Glass: Britain and its Monarchy*, (London: Radius, 1988).
8. Brian Redhead, "James Callaghan," in John P. Mackintosh, ed., *British Prime Ministers in the Twentieth Century*, vol. 2 (New York: St. Martin's, 1978).
9. R.H.S. Crossman, *The Myth of Cabinet Government* (Cambridge, MA: Harvard University Press, 1972).
10. R.K. Alderman and J.A. Cross, "The Reluctant Knife: Reflections on the Prime Minister's Power of Dismissal," *Parliamentary Affairs* 38 (Winter 1985), 387–408.

11. Peter Hennessy, *Cabinet* (London: Basil Blackwell, 1986).
12. Richard Rose, "British Government: The Job at the Top," in Richard Rose and Ezra N. Suleiman, eds., *Presidents and Prime Ministers*, (Washington: American Enterprise Institute, 1980), p. 1.
13. Martin Burch, "Mrs. Thatcher's Approach to Leadership in Government," *Parliamentary Affairs* 36 (Autumn 1983): 399–415.
14. See Bernard E. Crick, *The Reform of Parliament*, 2nd ed., (London: Weidenfeld & Nicolson, 1970).
15. John E. Schwarz, "Attempting to Assert Commons' Power: Labour Members in the House of Commons, 1974–1979," *Comparative Politics* 14 (October 1981): 17–29; and John E. Schwarz, "Exploring a New Role in Policy-Making: The British House of Commons in the 1970s," *American Political Science Review* 74 (March 1980): 23–37.
16. Philip Norton, *The Constitution in Flux*, (Oxford: Martin Robertson, 1982), pp. 68–69.
17. See S.A. Walkland and Michael Ryle, eds., *The Commons in the Seventies*, (London: Martin Robertson, 1978).
18. Richard Rose, "Still the Era of Party Government," *Parliamentary Affairs* 36 (Summer 1983): 282–299.
19. Philip Norton, *The Commons in Perspective*, (London: Martin Robertson, 1981), pp. 47–79.
20. The only exception since the war was Harold Wilson's naming of two non-members of Parliament in 1964, an unsuccessful move that confirmed the rule.
21. A poll found that voters prefer strongly for their MPs to be well educated. Jowell and Airey, eds., *British Social Attitudes*, 1984, pp. 19–20.
22. Philip Norton, *Dissension in the House of Commons, 1974–1979* (London: Oxford University Press, 1980); and Philip Norton, *Conservative Dissidents* (London: Temple Smith, 1978).
23. Gavin Drewry, ed., *The New Select Committees: A Study of the 1979 Reforms* (Oxford: Clarendon Press, 1985).
24. Gavin Drewry, "Scenes from Committee Life—The New Committees in Action," in Drewry, ed., *The New Select Committees*, p. 353.
25. Harold Wilson, *The Governance of Britain* (London: Weidenfeld and Nicholson, 1976), p. 132.
26. Jane Einer, "The Most Powerful Woman in the World," *The Philadelphia Inquirer Magazine*, 7 June 1987, p. 41.
27. Only 8 percent wanted its abolition. Jowell and Airey, eds., *British Social Attitudes, 1984*, p. 31.
28. Average daily attendance in 1982–84 was 321, up from 136 in 1959–60. Donald R. Shell, "The House of Lords and the Thatcher Government," *Parliamentary Affairs* 38 (Winter 1985), 16–32.
29. Some of these accounts provide more evidence of inept ministers than they do bureaucratic obstruction. But there is still evidence of bureaucratic abuses. See for example, Peter Kellner and Lord Crowther-Hunt, *The Civil Servants: An Inquiry into Britain's Ruling Class* (London: McDonald Futura, 1980).
30. See Maurice Wright, "Ministers and Civil Servants: Relations and Responsibilities," *Parliamentary Affairs* 30 (Summer 1977): 293–313.
31. Philip Norton, *The British Polity* (New York: Longman, 1984), p. 193.
32. Rudolf Klein and Janet Lewis, "Advice and Dissent in British Government: The Case of the Special Advisers," *Policy and Politics* 6 (September 1977): 1–25.

33. Kellner and Crowther-Hunt, *The Civil Servants.*
34. Wilson, *The Governance of Britain,* pp. 42–43.
35. Peter G. Richards, *The Local Government System* (London: Allen & Unwin, 1983); and Lord Radcliffe-Maude and Bruce Wood, *English Local Government Reformed* (Oxford: Oxford University Press, 1974).
36. Jowell and Airey, eds., *British Social Attitudes, 1984,* pp. 29–30.
37. Norman Furniss, "Northern Ireland as a Case Study of Decentralization of Unitary States," *World Politics* 27 (April 1975): 387–404.
38. V.O. Key, Jr., *Public Opinion and American Democracy* (New York: Knopf, 1961).
39. Richard Rose, *The Problem of Party Government* (London: Macmillan, 1974).

CHAPTER FIVE
DEMOCRACY
IN BRITAIN

A decade ago, observers were highly skeptical of Britain's future: Democracy itself was in danger of collapsing.[1] The signs were indeed troubling: a perpetually sick economy; an overly expensive, social-welfare system; a tense, social climate featuring lengthy strikes by unruly leftist trade unions; political parties no longer able to maintain their internal cohesion and unable to retain the loyalties of their followers; a series of weak and minority governments; a bloated and uncontrolled bureaucracy; and separatist tendencies in Scotland, Wales, and especially in Northern Ireland where a near civil war had drug on for a decade. To many, Britain, once the bulwark of democracy, had become Europe's "sick man" with serious, perhaps irremediable political, economic, and social problems. In retrospect, these Cassandras and Jeremiahs seem short-sighted and overly pessimistic. Britain's democracy is still alive and well and likely to remain so as the new century approaches. There remain challenges from the past decade's problems and there are likely to be new difficulties to overcome in the coming years. It is useful to assess the present strengths and weaknesses of British democracy.

A TROUBLED ECONOMY:
THE BRITISH DISEASE?

Between 1950 and 1975, a broad political consensus favorable of government management of the economy and of extensive social-welfare benefits prevailed in Britain. The public sector grew under both Conservative and

Labour governments through nationalizations motivated by desires for reform or by the need to rescue faltering but vital industries. Tentative steps were taken for noncompulsory, indicative economic planning where the government set priorities and general investment direction in consultation with trade unions and industrialists. An extensive and popular system of social-welfare programs provided all Britons with health care, pensions, and unemployment benefits and many Britons with housing, education, and a variety of other services.

This consensus broke down in the mid-1970s largely as a result of the failure of successive Conservative and Labour governments to assure more rapid economic growth. In comparison to the booming economies of other European countries, Britain's economy was sluggish at best. From one of the most prosperous countries in the world, Britain fell to one of the weakest economies in Europe (see Table 5.1). By the mid-1970s, the economy was sufficiently shaky that the government had to abandon promises to increase social-welfare benefits and pledges to assure full employment in order to win International Monetary Fund approval of necessary international loans.

Some critics of the British economy contended that the causes of the economic malaise were much deeper than apparent. Leftists attributed the problems to a general and unavoidable crisis of capitalism that could be overcome only by a radical change in the socioeconomic structures to bring socialism into reality.[2] Even more common were critics from the Right who saw a whole social-welfare state syndrome as fatally weakening Britain.[3] These critics argued that the economy was faulted by excessive government intervention into what once was a free enterprise system, by confiscatory taxes that inhibited initiative and innovation, and by the diversion of private funds, that might have gone into investment and economic development, into increasingly expensive welfare programs. The social-welfare

TABLE 5.1   Economic Performance of Selected Industrial Democracies

	National Income Per Capita, 1976 $U.S.	Growth of Gross Domestic Product (Percent)		Inflation (Percent Annually)
		1970–76	1960–70	1970–76
Belgium	$6371	4.0%	5.0%	8.5%
France	5859	4.1	5.8	8.9
West Germany	6451	2.5	4.7	5.9
Italy	2723	2.9	5.5	12.2
Japan	4465	5.5	10.8	11.1
Netherlands	5892	3.6	6.0	8.7
Sweden	8043	2.2	8.5	8.3
Switzerland	8246	0.3	4.7	6.7
United Kingdom	3550	2.0	2.8	13.6
United States	6996	2.9	3.9	6.6

Source: The Economist, *The World in Figures* (New York: Facts on File, 1980). Reprinted from Rolf H. W. Theen and Frank L. Wilson, *Comparative Politics: An Introduction to Six Countries* (Englewood Cliffs, NJ: Prentice Hall, 1986), p. 99.

programs were seen as not only costly but as producing so secure a setting that workers were not willing to work hard and sometimes not even willing to work at all. By offering subsidized housing, medical care, disability and unemployment benefits, welfare programs supposedly fostered laziness, absenteeism, and unemployment. The strength of the trade unions was seen as compounding these problems by excessive wage demands, lengthy strikes, and uncooperative workers imbued with a class warfare ideology. Worker productivity was discouraged but more importantly, the social-welfare state was undermining the social basis for democracy. Finally, there were political consequences as well. Burdened with social and economic roles that it ought not to have undertook, the state was seriously overloaded. Struggling to meet these demands, the state acceded to excessive influence from business and labor groups, undermining the sovereignty of Parliament. The growing gap between what it tried to do and what it actually accomplished promoted public disenchantment with the government and the whole political system. In short, the growth of social welfarism was seen as a threat to the social fiber of the nation and its democratic order. Together, these various problems added up to what became known as "the British disease"—an economic illness likely to affect all industrial social-welfare states but at its most virulent stage in Britain.

The inability of the British governments to reverse this economic decline led elements of both major parties to turn to their respective ideological poles for answers to the economic dilemma. The leftwing of the Labour party advocated: new nationalizations of private industry, greater government direction of the economy, increases in existing social programs, and an array of new social-welfare benefits. The Conservatives under Margaret Thatcher proposed almost the exact opposite: reduced government economic intervention, sale of public enterprises, less planning, sharp reductions in social-welfare programs, and lower taxes. The Labour party has not had a chance to try its proposals out but a similar approach was used by the French Socialists in the early 1980s; we shall evaluate its effectiveness when we turn to France. The British Conservatives have had over a decade in office to try their economic ideas.

The Conservatives began with an analysis of Britain's poor economic performance close to the "British disease" approach. A strong, Conservative, parliamentary majority permitted Thatcher to enact most of her slate of economic reforms with the goal of reducing the social-welfare state. Many previously nationalized industries were "privatized," or sold off to private investors. Government economic intervention was curtailed by both eliminating regulations and reducing public investment funds and incentives. Britain's once very progressive income taxes were slashed to encourage the wealthy to invest and undertake entrepreneurial risks. Social-welfare programs were reduced and users' fees were imposed on the remaining programs. New legislation was passed restricting trade union activities and imposing restraints designed to weaken their ability to call strikes and to support the Labour party.

But the results were disappointing. Private investment did not compensate for reduced public investment; economic growth was negative for several years before showing only slow progress; unemployment rose and then held at nearly 12 percent of the workforce. The more positive results, lower inflation and slightly improved productivity, were similar to those in other European countries which had not adopted the Thatcher approach. What made the lack of success more distressing was that the North Sea petroleum deposits reached their peak of production at this time and should have provided a strong boost to the British economy both from the income providing royalties to the British government and from the ending of Britain's dependency on expensive imported petroleum. Thus, the reduction of Britain's trade deficit was a major economic improvement, but it was not due to Thatcher's policies.

In retrospect, it seems clear that Thatcher's diagnosis of the causes of Britain's economic ills was incorrect. If it was "creeping socialism" that was causing Britain's economic decline, other countries with extensive welfare and government economic intervention would have experienced problems similar to those of Britain. In fact, most other western European countries, the ones whose strong economic growth made Britain look weak, have social-welfare programs that are as sweeping and costly as those in Britain; indeed, Britain ranked among the lowest in terms of the economic burden of social-welfare programs even before Thatcher's cutbacks took full effect (See Table 5.2). All of the industrial countries listed in Table 5.3, with the exception of Japan and the United States, have tax burdens that are as heavy or heavier, welfare programs that are as extensive or more extensive, and government involvement in the economy as great or greater than in Britain. Many industrial democracies have public sectors—those parts of the economy controlled directly by the government such as the civil service and nationalized enterprises—that are as large or larger than Britain's public sector. These countries have economically done much better than Britain and as well as countries with smaller public sectors. British workers receive less in unemployment benefits than do workers in all other industrial countries. But it is British workers, not the more highly insured French, German, or Danish workers, who are accused of avoiding work because of unemployment protection (see Table 5.4). British trade unions are powerful, but labor unrest cannot be blamed for the economic problems. In the 1950s and early 1960s, when Britain's economic growth was slowest, there were far fewer strikes in Britain even though wages grew more slowly, than in most of the economically booming countries. Serious labor problems came only in the 1970s when the economic crisis was already critical and only after real wages, adjusted for inflation, had fallen in Britain while they had risen elsewhere in Europe.

There is no question that Britain has had serious economic problems. What is doubtful is that the Thatcher diagnosis is the correct one. There are simply too many other democratic states where extensive social-welfare systems have coexisted with healthy and expanding economies. More likely explanations of Britain's economic difficulties focus on: the decline of productivity due to a failure to invest in new factories after the war; the costs of maintaining a large military force spread across the globe; the difficulties of adjusting to the economic effects of the loss of the Empire;

TABLE 5.2   Economic Burden of Social Welfare Programs, Selected Countries

	Percent of GNP devoted to social benefits to retired persons, invalids, family allowances unemployed, medical services, etc.
France	24.4%
West Germany	25.6
Italy	22.5
United Kingdom	19.8

Source: Office Statistique des Communautés Européenes, *Le Monde*, 6 March 1979. Reprinted From Rolf H. W. Theen and Frank L. Wilson, *Comparative Politics: An Introduction to Six Countries* (Englewood Cliffs, NJ: Prentice Hall, 1986), p. 100.

TABLE 5.3   Tax Burden in Selected Industrial Democracies

	Total tax revenue as Percent of GNP (1982)
Belgium	46.7
France	43.7
West Germany	37.3
Italy	39.9
Netherlands	45.5
United Kingdom	39.6
United States	30.5

Source: Bureau of the Census: *Statistical Abstract of the United States, 1985* (Washington, DC: U.S. Government Printing Office, 1985), p. 850.

TABLE 5.4   Unemployment Benefits in Selected Countries

	Percentage of prior earnings replaced by unemployment insurance
Belgium	60%
France	70
West Germany	68
Japan	60–80
Netherlands	80
United Kingdom	52–66

Source: *The Economist*, 6 June 1981. Reprinted from Rolf H. W. Theen and Frank L. Wilson, *Comparative Politics: An Introduction to Six Countries* (Englewood Cliffs, NJ: Prentice Hall, 1986), p. 101.

the weaknesses of both the trade unions and the employers' groups in giving direction to the government on an economic course to follow; the succession of different and often contradictory economic policies followed by the government in the 1970s—sometimes inflating and then deflating the economy within a few months; Britain's late entry into the European Common Market when the rapid economic expansion of the European market had already ended.[4]

While Thatcher's analysis of Britain's economic problems may have been faulty, her tenure as prime minister has been marked by relative economic success. The old problem of inflation was mastered, and Britain's rate of economic growth at the end of the 1980s was among the highest in the industrialized world. The government's budget deficit was reduced. Britain's trade balance with its economic partners was improved, and the value of the pound sterling was stabilized.

These impressive accomplishments must be balanced against two considerations. First, the positive economic results came at a time of relative advantage for Britain. Production of North Sea oil peaked during the 1980s with sufficient oil to not only meet British needs but also, to permit the export of oil to other countries. This oil eliminated a costly import and provided an important source of export. But the known North Sea oil deposits will be depleted during the 1990s. Unless new deposits are found, Britain will once again be dependent upon imported oil and will lose this valuable source of foreign income. Another temporary boon to the economy was the proceeds from the sales of state-owned enterprises. These receipts permitted the Thatcher government to keep taxes down during the mid-1980s. But these proceeds are also a temporary economic resource that will soon be exhausted as privatization runs its course.

The second consideration is that the economic recovery has not helped everyone. Unemployment has remained very high, staying at or above the unemployment levels during the Great Depression of the 1930s. The Thatcher economy has really been a dual one: a new, service industry-based economy that has thrived under Thatcher and an industrial economy that has continued to falter. Many of those who have been without work face long-term unemployment. Parts of the country have been booming but in the blighted industrial cities of the north there has been unrelenting economic decline. The high social cost for this economic dualism has characterized the Thatcher economic recovery. It has left an important part of Britain with little hope of economic improvement while the rest of the country has prospered.

Some express concern that the resulting "underclass" of people facing long-term unemployment and economic deprivation may become an important source of political and social instability in the future. It is impossible to tell yet how much credence to place in these fears. Earlier, in the 1970s, there were fears that the general economic decline would undermine essential, popular support needed for a stable democracy.[5] But these fears proved premature. Then, Britain's economic decline was relative compared to the other more rapidly growing economies. The current problems of the unemployed are also relative. Average Britons live better today than they did twenty years ago and far better than their grandparents did fifty years ago. The social-welfare benefits provide a safety net that protects citizens from genuine economic disaster. Economic fears have not undermined popular support for democracy. The expected alienation of the unemployed against the government that had permitted their loss of employment has not yet occurred. In 1983 and again in 1987, less than half of the unemployed voted for the Labour party whose program came closest to suggesting a radical break with the existing socioeconomic system; Nearly one in three unemployed voted Conservative!

The slower economic growth in Britain reflects to some extent a deliberate choice of life style which places other values higher than economic expansion.[6] Thus, the British protect the beautiful rolling fields, criss-crossed by hedgerows and trees, because of their aesthetic value rather than flatten and extend the fields for more economical farming. Workers prefer remaining in their neighborhoods, where they have established friendships and families, to moving away where jobs pay more. It would take far more serious economic problems than those that exist today, before democratic stability in Britain would be endangered. In the 1970s, voters seemed to sanction poor economic performance of governments headed by both the Conservative and Labour parties by voting for the opposition or for a third party. In the 1980s, it is possible that the voters no longer expect economic miracles from either party. Perhaps this lower expectation explains Thatcher's reelection in 1983 and 1987 in times of record high unemployment and continued poor economic development. It may be that voters are coming to realize that there are many factors at play in determining the performance of a modern industrial economy that are beyond the control of elected officials. This realization seems to have reduced economic performance as a political issue.

LIMITS ON NATIONAL SOVEREIGNTY

Britain's economy shows the impact of the growing interdependency of European democracies. National sovereignty refers to the ability of a country to make autonomously all decisions affecting its people. Once thought to be an essential characteristic of an independent country, national sovereignty is being eroded everywhere by growing political, economic, and military interdependence of all polities. The British decision in the 1950s to turn down the invitation to join other European countries in forming the European Common Market was motivated in large part by a desire to avoid entanglement in an international body that might restrict British sovereignty or control over economic matters. But even this independent course demonstrated unescapable interdependency in that Britain, on the outside, was not able to participate in the economic expansion produced in the earlier years by the European economic unification. Britain, like other European nations, relies heavily on imports and exports for its economic activity. The resulting trade, loans, and financial transactions make it impossible for any government to undertake a major economic program without considering its international consequences.

When Britain was finally able to join the European Community in 1972, independent economic action declined further but with the compensation of participating in forming the Community's economic policies. Important policy issues affecting the daily lives of British citizens are now handled in Brussels rather than London: tariffs, all agricultural policies, and many energy, transportation, social, and communication policies. This shift of important economic policy-making powers to Brussels will become even more important as the European Community moves toward the 1992 target for the elimination of all barriers to economic exchanges among its twelve members.

In 1976, a Labour government faced rampant inflation and needed a loan from the International Monetary Fund in order to sustain the value of the pound. The IMF agreed to grant the essential loan only if the government cut back social expenditures and imposed taxes to reduce the budget deficit. There was no choice but to give in to this international body. But in doing so the government broke its campaign pledges to the voters and informal agreements with trade unions to provide new social benefits in exchange for the unions' restraint in wage demands. While it made sense for the IMF to require action in exchange for its loan, the problem of democratic accountability arose. The elected British government found itself forced to abandon its obligations to its voters and to comply with the social dictates of a non-elected, non-British body of unaccountable international bureaucrats.

Defense is another policy area that has largely escaped the mastery of British government. Even with its own nuclear force, Britain is heavily reliant upon the United States and its NATO partners. This dependence was graphically illustrated thirty years ago when Britain joined France and Israel in an attack on Egypt. Soon after the United States criticized the venture, it collapsed with Britain and France hastily withdrawing from the Middle East. Today, British defense strategy, tactics, and even specific weapons are jointly planned and developed with one or more of its NATO partners. Both Labour and Conservative governments have found remarkable little leeway in these issues. This security interdependence explains in part why Labour governments once in office have ignored their party's commitment to unilateral disarmament that was made before the election.

The declining national sovereignty poses challenges. Important parts of national policy can no longer be decided by those elected to make policy. The accountability of democratic systems diminishes since the citizens no longer have a way of disapproving of a social policy imposed by the IMF, or a farm policy decided by the European Community, or a defense decision made by NATO. Such instances of policy change imposed by outside forces are common in Third World countries which are dependent upon foreign countries and international bankers for their economic and political existence, but they are not absent even in mature, developed democracies. And it is likely that these international controls will become more common.

One response has been to "democratize" the international bodies. For example, the European Community made its parliament directly elected by the citizens of the member countries in 1979. But the physical and emotional distance between the citizens and these still very bureaucratic institutions is great and voters have shown little interest in these European elections. (For example, voter turnout in Britain for the 1979 and 1984 European elections was only 33 percent.) Even if public interest could be aroused, the powers of the European Parliament are limited. Among the many other international bodies which affect social and economic policies, no others even make the pretense of accountability to the people. The ultimate sanction for voters dissatisfied with the policies that are imposed from without, is to oust their government even if it cannot control the international forces. The opposition party sometimes fosters this coercive measure by threatening withdrawal from the UN, NATO, or the European Community as a platform. But once in office the new government soon finds itself in the same situation because no modern nation can cut itself off from the outside world.

THE OVERLOADED SOCIAL-WELFARE STATE

While the economic burden of social-welfare programs cannot be blamed for problems of the British economy, there is still the charge that the excessive involvement of the state has overloaded the decision making and the administrative processes of British democracy. Social welfare is not a new concern for the British government. As early as 1908 the government enacted an old age pension program, and in 1911 it passed the National Health Insurance Act providing governmental assistance to meet the medical needs of the poor. After World War II, welfare services were greatly expanded so that in the 1980s government-sponsored programs care for the individual from the cradle to the coffin. They represent an important part of the economy with government expenditures on social programs accounting for 25.4 per cent of gross domestic production in 1981.

Attempts to reduce the gap between the wealthy and the poor had included progressive taxation and the provision of necessary social services to all. A major share of the government's receipts came from a steeply progressive income tax. In addition, estate taxes helped to minimize the inheritance of wealth. The government spent heavily on social services targeted toward lower-income groups: housing, health care, education, and retirement pensions. Thus, income was redistributed by taxing the wealthy to assist the poor. Through such programs, Britain had reduced the inequality of income distribution and by the end of the 1970s was among the most equal of western democratic societies. Such programs also had had the added advantage of integrating into society groups that historically had sensed alienation in capitalist societies, especially the working class. Much of the contentment of British workers with their place in society was due to these social-welfare guarantees that removed some of the uncertainties and risks of a free enterprise system.

Although previous Conservative governments had accepted the social-welfare programs, after 1979, the Thatcher government reduced many of these benefits and imposed user fees (similar in cost to free market values) on others. She cut back on progressive income taxes, shifting more of the tax burden to lower- and middle-income persons. Thatcher's programs have had their effects on social equality. The equalizing trend, which had operated up to the end of the 1970s, has now been reversed with a growing concentration of income and wealth in the hands of the wealthiest. However, there are no signs that these recent trends have yet had an impact on social cohesion in Britain. As we have seen, social class relations remain calm with the salience of class in politics and in society seeming to diminish even as the trend of leveling income has ended.

Whether these programs "overload" government is highly controversial. The whole notion of overload is difficult to implement since it means different things to different people. If it means that the programs are too costly and damage the country's economic development, then the allocation of one fourth of the nation's economy to such welfare programs seems great. But we have already noted that other countries with more expensive programs have healthy and growing economies. If overload means the inability of the state to efficiently administer such massive programs, then there are clearly problems in doing this. But the most costly and extensive of these programs—the National Health Service (NHS), education, and council housing—are functioning well. For example, the NHS which provides virtually free medical care of all kinds to Britons has its administrative problems. But it has proved, in its nearly forty years of history, to not be unduly expensive, successful in providing an outstanding level of health to the British people, and sufficiently satisfying to those who choose medicine as a career that the oft predicted flight of doctors to other countries has not taken place.[7]

If overload means that the government programs arouse hopes that are impossible for it to fulfill, then this may be true in the various programs designed to eliminate poverty but not in the other social programs. They are highly popular in the eyes of the citizens even with their problems. The NHS has had many difficulties but it is enormously popular—nearly as highly supported among citizens as the monarchy. Along with other popular programs, the NHS has been "a successful instrument for delivering support to the political system."[8] In short, whatever view of overload is used, the concept is not applicable to Britain at the end of the 1980s.[9]

There, no doubt, will continue to be pressure for new social and economic programs. New groups arise with new programs and seek to make their voices heard in an effective forum. They often have new demands for government action. Despite the cutbacks in government programs in recent years, it is likely that the British government will continue to provide a wide range of social programs. It very well may be that democratic governments do not have the means or the funds to eliminate poverty and British government has moved back from such ventures in recent years. But it does have the means to respond to some of poverty's problems without the risk of overload. Britain provides subsidized public housing to 29 percent of its households. And such housing is very popular, more for social and cultural reasons than for financial considerations, even among families able to find housing on the private market. The education system needs expansion, especially at the higher level. With only 20 percent of young people between 20- and 25-years-old enrolled in higher education, Britain lags behind France and Germany (which have 25 percent in higher education) and far behind the United States (close to 60 percent). Improved educational opportunities represent an important investment in future economic growth. The British government will find it expedient to make this investment.

There will be additional social tasks that government will be expected to handle in the next decades. There may again be periods of difficulty as the government responds to these needs and as the public alters its expectations about what the government can and should do. For the foreseeable future, the financial, technical, and personnel means at the disposal of the British government appear adequate to respond to these new activities without risk of overload.

HUMAN RIGHTS IN BRITAIN

Britain lacks a constitutional document that is equivalent to the American Bill of Rights. There is a British "Bill of Rights" but it defines the rights of Parliament in relationship to the monarch rather than specifying individual rights. Despite the lack of formal constitutional guarantees, Britain has a long tradition of respect for civil rights. These rights are jealously guarded by an independent judiciary, a free press, and a Parliament whose opposition members are ready to seize a human right's violation to criticize the government. In addition, Britain has signed the European Declaration of Human Rights and has consequently accepted the right of its citizens to appeal to the European Court of Human Rights.

There is public debate in Britain now over the advisability of a constitutional document specifically stating basic human and political rights.[10] The concern of those who advocate a Bill of Rights is not about what has happened so far but about what a Parliament might do in the future. In general, those seeking a constitutional document appear worried about possible encroachments on human rights as government continues to increase its impact on the lives and activities of individual citizens. The Bill of Rights would define those rights that would be inviolable as the government's influence expands. The proposals face opposition from both the Right (which fears the politicization of the judiciary) and from the Left (which resists measures that might limit its future ability to enact radical social and economic reforms). There is also a constitutional issue at stake since the existence of a Bill of Rights would place limits on the absolute sovereignty of Parliament which goes against a basic principle of Britain's unwritten constitution. There is no immediate prospect that such a statement of rights will soon be adopted in Britain.

Parliament may suspend human rights in national emergencies. This power has been used with restraint in the on-going troubles in Northern Ireland. A 1973 law permitted the preventive detention of suspected terrorists in Northern Ireland, but the law was repealed when it was found to be counterproductive. When a new rise in terrorism in 1988 led the government to seek a strong response, the proposal to return to preventive detention was put aside, not only on the grounds of its damage to human rights, but also because it had proved ineffective earlier. However, the new law did permit judges to lift the usual right of a defendant to refuse to give evidence in terrorist-related crimes. While the accused may decline to testify, that fact may be used against him or her by judge and jury.

This illustrates the dilemma faced by democracies in handling political violence. These terrorists often use their civil liberties to shield acts of violence against other citizens and the government. In respecting their rights, the government is handicapped in its efforts to assure public security. In violating these liberties, the government establishes precedents that might be used against nonviolent critics of its policies or individuals accused of nonpolitical crimes. Finding the correct balance between protecting human rights and countering terrorism has been a major test in Britain as well as in West Germany and Italy.

The overall record of the British government has been admirable in observing human rights in the midst of a near civil war in Northern Ireland. Despite the use of indiscriminate violence and the dangers associated with terrorism, the government has handled suspected terrorists with a respect for their rights. Early in the Northern Irish conflict, several Irish nationalists were arrested by the British army on suspicion of terrorism. They claimed that they were tortured during their interrogations and carried the case all the way to the European Human Rights Commission. The panel agreed that the interrogation methods (which threatened possible violence but did not include actual physical torture) had violated the European Human Rights Convention. The British government admitted it had used such practices in the past but stated it had ceased using them in 1972 and had compensated the victims. As deplorable as such a case was, it was the worst incident of government abuse of civil rights during twenty years of near guerrilla warfare in Northern Ireland. It is remarkable that more extreme restrictions on civil liberties have been avoided in this long, sad conflict.

Another potential area of human rights abuse is the Official Secrets Act of 1911. Originally designed to be used against spies and saboteurs, it has occasionally been used by the government to hinder the press investigation of sensitive public issues. A recent case involved government suppression of a book exposing dubious actions by the British secret service: Peter Wright's *Spycatcher*. The book was published abroad but could not be published or sold in Britain, nor could the British press publish accounts of some legal actions abroad to bring the book into the United Kingdom. In a related area, the government has, in rare instances, attempted to block broadcasts of BBC programs thought to be damaging. Again, the issue has been most sensitive in the dealing with the troubles in Northern

Ireland. In 1988 the Thatcher government wanted to deprive terrorists involved in this conflict "the oxygen of publicity." The government decided to bar British radio and television broadcasters from interviewing terrorists involved in the Northern Irish conflict. The new regulations faced a storm of criticism but still were adopted.

Unlike the situation in the United States, where "sunshine laws" require open public decision making, the British have always insisted that effective government action required that many decisions be made in secret. Indeed, secrecy has been equated with effective government power. The obsession with secrecy in government is such that secrecy has become "a substitute for the mystery of religion" among public officials.[11] The Official Secrets Act authorizes the government to issue "D-notices" that prevent publication or broadcast of material deemed to be sensitive by the government.

The law was designed to protect national security against the unauthorized revelation of secret materials to foreign governments. Occasionally, however, "D-notices" have been used to prevent politically embarrassing information from being revealed to the British public. In such cases, it is not national defense that motivates the censorship but the desire to shield British politicians or civil servants from criticism by domestic critics. But such abuses are rare and nearly always elicit a critical response from the media and both friendly and unfriendly politicians. The political costs of interfering with the freedom of information are too high for governments to risk such abridgements of the printed or electronic press. Indeed, the British press and even the BBC are renowned for their political independence and their willingness to subject the government (and other powers that be) to critical and even irreverent inspection.

Perhaps the greatest, human rights problem comes not from the government but from individual citizens. Certain people refuse to accord equal treatment to their fellow citizens because of religious intolerance (especially in Northern Ireland) or racial prejudice (especially toward the growing nonwhite population). The resulting discrimination abridges the political, social, and economic rights of minorities. There are laws to deal with such discrimination and the government makes conscientious efforts to enforce them, but it is not easy for a democratic government to overcome the prejudices of its people as they deal with each other.

In the resulting setting of poverty and despair in which some minorities find themselves, crime thrives and the police become "the anvil on which society beats out the problems of political and social failure."[12] Overworked police agents, sometimes feeling neglected and even betrayed by politicians, occasionally use brutal methods and are ensnared by racism too.[13] Consequently, the deprived periodically resort to violence in desperation, more than in hope that such actions will bring a change in their status. The situation is often tense with some cases of police abuse of their powers, but there is no evidence of a fundamental breach in the usual democratic controls on the police.

In balance, while there are some problem areas, there are few signs of erosion in the condition of civil liberties in Britain. The trend is toward greater, citizen vigilance with an alert press willing to probe possible abuses of human rights. Even if the debate over a written Bill of Rights is not resolved, the debate itself focuses public attention on the state of human rights. A growing tendency toward judicial activism is bringing better protection by the courts for the rights of the individual against abuses by public officials.[14] The recent adjudication by the European Court of Human Rights of several British cases indicates a new channel for Britons to use in seeking redress for abuse of their civil rights. The British government's response to these cases indicates that the Court's rulings will be accepted as binding even on marginal issues.

RESPONSES TO THE CHALLENGES
OF THE 1980s: WHY BRITAIN DID NOT DIE

The doomsayers of the 1970s have been proved wrong by the events of the 1980s. Britain did not die nor did its democratic institutions falter. There remain important social, economic, and political problems—in many ways as severe or more so than those of a decade ago. But there is new optimism that government can cope with these trials. The democratic political system is not in doubt.

Stability and Security in Troubled Times

One of the most important changes in Britain has been the decline of personal security. During the 1950s and 1960s, Britain appeared to be an island of tranquility surrounded by the troubled waters of other democratic and nondemocratic governments. But in the 1970s and 1980s, public order was undermined by the open conflict between Catholics and Protestants in Northern Ireland, periodic incidents of terrorism throughout Britain, and the rapid growth of violent crime in large cities. Despite the very real problems in these areas—and public opinion polls showing greater public concern about personal safety—Britain remains remarkably stable and orderly.

The strife and violence in Northern Ireland have little impact on the British political unit as a whole for three reasons. First, Northern Ireland is geographically isolated from the rest of Britain, remote from the areas of densest population, and far from the center of political power. Attempts by Irish nationalists to enlarge the area of conflict by bombings or other acts of terrorism in London and other cities have failed. Second, since conflict has been restricted to Northern Ireland, only 2.6 percent of the total population is in a position to be directly affected by it.

Third, the rest of Britain considers the conflict a Northern Irish, rather than a British, problem. Most Britons do not understand why Irish Catholics and Ulster Protestants cannot get along. With the exception of some Scots with religious and fraternal links to Ulster Protestants, both Catholics and Protestants elsewhere in Britain are dismayed and puzzled by the conduct of their coreligionists in Northern Ireland; to them, the behavior of both sides in the conflict is "un-British" and therefore baffling. The predominant feeling in Britain is aloofness from the conflict in Northern Ireland, accompanied by a frustrated sense that there is no way for Britain to get out of the conflict. The conflict is acceptable to the bulk of the people as a peculiarly Irish problem. Irish nationalists try to convince world opinion, and especially Irish-Americans that the battle in Northern Ireland is a "colonial war" with Britain hanging on to one of its last colonies. Nothing could be farther from the truth. Neither the government nor the general public is eager to maintain British rule in Northern Ireland. The general public would have Britain pull out immediately. A recent poll showed a majority for the unification of Northern Ireland with the Republic of Ireland (58 percent as opposed to only 28 percent who want to keep it in the United Kingdom) and the withdrawal of British troops (59 percent).[15] The government keeps the British army in Northern Ireland, with the encouragement of the Republic of Ireland, because it feels an obligation to maintain peace between the warring parties and to protect Catholics against likely violence, even civil war, if the Protestants were to feel more threatened. While the British people do not understand the conflict and have little sympathy with either side, they seem resigned to continuing their role as peacekeeper in that tense province.

The rise of terrorism has had its impact on the people's sense of security as well. A 1985 opinion survey found that nearly three quarters of those polled expected acts of terrorism to become common events within the next ten years.[16] Even with the increase of terrorism, such acts are still remote to most Britons. Many of these incidents are linked to the Northern Irish troubles and are grudgingly accepted as part of that burden. Londoners—who endured the systematic bombings of the Nazi Blitz— were not deeply troubled by the scattered terrorist bombings or assassinations of the 1980s and, in fact, seemed to become more determined to resist extremist demands. The government's response to terrorism has been moderate and within the constitutional bounds of normal law enforcement. In general, Britain has weathered the rise in terrorism relatively well. The public has not panicked or insisted on excessive repression. Security forces have been successful in arresting many terrorists and in prosecuting them without suspending basic civil liberties.

Britons often bemoan the growth of violent crime in the streets of their cities. Anyone familiar with Dickens' novels, however, cannot deny that there are certainly precedents for these problems in the poverty and social distress of the last century. But even with the rising crime rate, the incidence of violent crime in Britain is strikingly low. For example, the 1985 figure on homicides of 1.2 per 100,000 people was less than one seventh the rate in the United States (7.9 murders per 100,000 population). Most British police officers still take to their beats unarmed. The majority of Britons (58 percent in 1981) feel that the police "are efficient and do the job well."[17]

A sense of "civic decency" still prevails and helps to preserve public order.[18] Britons respect the authority and obey the laws. They comply with traffic laws giving Britain one of the lowest accident rates in the world. In contrast to the disorderly lines and crowding that are part of daily life in France or Italy, Britons queue up politely to wait their turn. This orderliness is voluntary and spontaneous, not the product of state repression. It contributes to a sense of security that has been challenged by recent trends but not destroyed.

Resilience of Political Institutions

The strength of British political institutions is attested to first by their durability: Parliament had its origins over 700 years ago; the House of Commons emerged as a separate chamber by the middle of the fourteenth century; The cabinet dates back to the fifteenth century and assumed its modern form by the early eighteenth century; The major political parties date back to the beginning of this century. The persistence of these British political institutions contrasts sharply with the much more recent origins of their counterparts in Italy and West Germany, where the government bodies and parties date back only to the end of the Second World War, and in France, where contemporary parties and institutions emerged only after 1958.

The significance of age in these British institutions is not simply that they have survived, but that they and other ancient structures have continued to prove their utility by adapting to changing circumstances. British political institutions were capable of incorporating new participants and responding to the new political demands during earlier eras of rapid social and economic change. This adaptive experience and the legitimacy acquired over the centuries facilitates their adaptation to the new demands of a still changing world. The durability of traditional structures, including such seeming anachronisms as the House of Lords and the monarchy, provides the British regime with powerful political symbols that unite Britons and link the present with a glorious past. They enhance the stability of the regime.

Britain's institutions are by no means rigid, despite the years of tradition they embody. Confronted with a crisis, the regime has proved highly flexible. In 1976 to 1979, the political system quickly adjusted to the absence of any majority party in Commons by providing stability through a governing minority party. When the minority Labour government was finally ousted by a vote of censure, the voters gave a solid parliamentary majority to the Conservatives in 1979. Also, during the 1970s, when facing difficult issues that divided the major parties, the political leaders "invented" the use of consultative referendums to seek the will of the general public on specific issues such as membership in the Common Market and devolution in Scotland and Wales. Both the Conservative and Labour parties have responded to threats to their very existence and have adapted in such a way as to win back the loyalty of many of their voters. This institutional flexibility contributes to the strength of British political institutions, allowing them to evolve in response to new needs while retaining the traditions and grandeur that convey legitimacy.

The process of recruiting political leaders in Britain tends to favor individuals with leadership skills well suited to the management of conflict. The leaders who gain the top party and government posts have served long apprenticeships in the party and in Parliament. They are skilled in compromise and accommodation. They have already proved that they are sensitive to the need for change and capable of making the required adaptation. The result is a set of leaders who are particularly skillful at balancing contending party and interest group viewpoints in pursuit of a consensus.

There are some disadvantages in this pattern of political recruitment. The search for a democratic solution in Northern Ireland despite the refusals of both the Protestant majority and the Catholic militants to compromise may have exacerbated the situation. The reluctance of British leaders to intervene forcefully and decisively to impose a settlement early in the conflict (1968 to 1970) permitted both sides to become intransigent. The emphasis on party and parliamentary service in the training of top leaders brings to the fore individuals whose ideas have not been so innovative that they have troubled the rank-and-file. Such a recruitment pattern has both good and bad effects. While such individuals may be trusted to avoid the dangers of extremist solutions and of blundering because of political inexperience, they may not have the new ideas needed to adapt to a changing world, and they may lack the forceful personality needed to push through such changes. But in democracies there usually is less harm in erring on the side of accommodation than in bringing abrasive and possibly demagogic individuals into leading political positions. The system has permitted the emergence of dynamic, innovative, and powerful leaders when the need has developed as with Disraeli in the 1870s, Churchill in the 1940s, and perhaps even Thatcher in the 1980s.

The "Level-Headedness" of the British People

With all the political doubts and turmoil that have spilled out of academic circles into the public debate during the past two decades, it has been surprising how little effect these doubts have had on public support for existing democratic forms in Britain. Despite the purported disillusionment of the citizenry, political opinion polls continue to show high levels of support for the system and its institutions. More importantly, voters spurn the appeals of antiregime parties and such parties, on both the far left and far right, have virtually no support in Britain. It is indicative of the underlying support for the regime that the most successful third party challenge did not come from the political extremes or from regional or nationalist causes. It came instead from the Social Democratic-Liberal Alliance—a proregime coalition of familiar, moderate politicians who rejected the polarization of Conservative and Labour parties. They did not offer a new regime or even a new program but a return to traditional moderate solutions to the accumulating economic and social problems.

The nationalist movements in Scotland and Wales have demonstrated the readiness of even those feeling discontent to accept proffered reforms that fall short of the ultimate goal of their movements. With a few token reforms and the passage of time, the nationalist movements in both these areas have lost political salience. For their leaders, the dilemma has been either to accept the modest reforms and abandon their ultimate goal of autonomy or to take the path of an antiregime party and lose all but a small handful of true believers.[19] Neither alternative offers much hope of an immediate revival of these nationalist causes as the voters, who once backed them, return to prior political loyalties or discover new ones unrelated to the regional or ethnic struggle. Indeed, never in British political history has there been evidence of mass support for radical change. The gradual approach prevails, now, as it did in the past and, as in the past, often rewards patience with the desired reforms.

A thoughtful Italian intellectual, Luigi Barzini, found a key to understanding the "imperturbable British" in their clinging to certain stoic virtues that made them great and powerful:

> . . . virtues they distilled from their native land, the surrounding seas, the weather, and the vicissitudes of their history. They are the virtues of sailors on sailing ships who face raging seas and hurricanes or wait weeks for the windless calm to end; farmers on inhospitable land, resigned to the unpredictable weather; fishermen on the stormy and fog-bound seas of the North; lonely shepherds on deserted moors; . . .[20]

Barzini claimed that such virtues are obsolete in the modern world. The British loyalty to them explains why Britain failed to grasp the vision of a united Europe early enough to have avoided its own economic decline. But these stoic virtues of selfconfidence, resoluteness, and patience serve Britain well in troubled times. They grant the political system time to resolve its own problems and give it latent support based on its past successes.

There remain important problems and sources of unrest for the British political system to overcome. We have noted the continuing economic problems of high unemployment, rising crime rates, racial tensions and the growing alienation of the coloured population, and the never-ending violent troubles in Northern Ireland. There will be new challenges from evolving social and political developments that will test the mettle of Britain's politicians and the adaptability of its institutions. The successes of the past will give the political leaders time and legitimacy in responding to the continuing and new challenges.

BRITAIN: A MODEL DEMOCRACY?

In the study of comparative politics, England is important as a deviant case, deviant because of its success in coping with the many problems of the modern world. Just as Alexis de Tocqueville travelled to America in 1831 to seek the secrets of democracy, so today one might travel to England in search of the secrets of stable representative government.[21]

This statement was made over 25 years ago by a respected American observer of the English political scene. The intervening years have been difficult ones for British democracy and the statement disappeared in subsequent editions of his book. Many of the presumed strengths of British politics have faced challenges or have been eroded. The supportive deferential political culture has yielded some to new political attitudes much less accepting of tradition and hierarchy. The much-vaunted two-party system has faced the twin threats of internal decay of the main parties and of strong electoral challenges from third parties. Governmental stability, long thought to be a particularly important virtue of British democracy, has been challenged by the indiscipline of MPs and the narrowness of governmental majorities in Commons. Violence and terrorism have shattered the presumably normal calm of British politics. The ability of the government to govern, and to manage the economy has been called into serious doubt. Some radicals believed that the only way out of the crisis was major socioeconomic change to give Britain a more secure basis for a more democratic society.[22]

Predictions about the demise of British democracy, however, were premature. The "crisis" of the 1970s and early 1980s appears, in retrospect, to be less a harbinger of future disaster than a sign of temporary maladjustments and leadership inadequacies. The political problems of that era were exaggerated. Other countries experienced or are still experiencing similar disorders without the degree of concern of catastrophe that was expressed about Britain's problems. The successful weathering of these problems, and of the state of near crisis provoked by alarmist cries, gives evidence of the vitality and strength of British democracy. It survived these dangers without compromising its basic democratic and civil libertarian traditions. Even in the 1990s we might suggest Britain as an example of how democracy ought to work. The applicability of these lessons for other countries might be doubted because Britain's response to crisis draws so heavily on its unique history and development pattern. For this reason, it is useful to look at other European countries to see how they responded to the political, economic, and social crises of the 1970s.

NOTES

1. See Isaac Kramnick, ed., *Is Britain Dying?* (Ithaca, NY: Cornell University Press, 1979); Stephen Haseler, *The Death of British Democracy* (New York: Prometheus Books, 1976); Robert Moss, *The Collapse of Democracy* (London: Sphere Books, 1977); Robert Emmett Tyrrell, Jr., ed., *The Future That Doesn't Work* (Garden City, NY: Doubleday, 1977); and Robert Moss, *The Collapse of Democracy* (London: Temple Smith, 1975).
2. See, for example, Tom Nairn, ed., *The Breakup of Britain* (London: New Left Books, 1977) and Ralph Miliband, *Capitalist Democracy in Britain* (London: Oxford University Press, 1982).

3. See especially, Tyrrell, *The Future That Doesn't Work;* and Haseler, *The Death of British Democracy.* For a fictional account of what was to be, see Anthony Burgess, *1985* (London: Hutchinson, 1978).
4. See Richard E. Caves and Lawrence B. Krause, eds., *Britain's Economic Performance* (Washington: Brookings Institution, 1980).
5. See Kramnick, *Is Britain Dying?;* Haseler, *The Death of British Democracy;* and Tyrrell, *The Future That Doesn't Work.*
6. See Bernard Nossiter, *Britain: A Future That Works* (Boston: Houghton Mifflin, 1978).
7. Rudolf Klein, *The Politics of the National Health Service* (London: Longman, 1983).
8. Ibid.
9. See Anthony H. Birch, "Overload, Ungovernability and Delegitimation: The Theory and the British Case," *British Journal of Political Science* 14 (April 1984): 135–160.
10. Philip Norton, *The Constitution in Flux* (Oxford: Martin Robertson, 1982), pp. 244–260.
11. Cited in Anthony Sampson, *The Changing Anatomy of Britain* (New York: Vintage, 1982), p. 240.
12. Ibid., p. 206.
13. See Robert Reiner, *The Politics of the Police* (New York: St. Martin's, 1985).
14. J.A.G. Griffith, *The Politics of the Judiciary,* 2nd ed. (London: Fontana, 1981), especially chapter 9.
15. Roger Jowell and Colin Airey, eds., *British Social Attitudes: The 1984 Report* (Aldershot, England: Gower, 1984), pp. 33–34.
16. *British Politics Group Newsletter* 40 (Winter 1986): 17.
17. N. Webb and K. Wybow, *The Gallup Report: Your Opinions in 1981* (London: Sphere, 1982), p. 123.
18. Geoffrey Smith and Nelson W. Polsby, *British Government and Its Discontents* (New York: Basic, 1981).
19. Phillip Rawkins, "Living in the House of Power: Welsh Nationalism and the Dilemma of Anti-System Politics," in Edward A. Tiryakian and Ronald Rogowski, eds., *New Nationalisms of the Developed West* (Winchester, MA: Allen & Unwin, 1985).
20. Luigi Barzini, *The Europeans* (Harmondsworth, England: Penguin, 1983), p. 61.
21. Richard Rose, *Politics in England,* 1st ed. (Boston: Little, Brown, 1964), p. 1.
22. For a radical critique of British politics, see Colin Leys, *Politics in Britain: An Introduction* (Toronto: University of Toronto Press, 1983).

PART THREE
FRANCE

In contrast to Britain's steady, evolutionary path to democracy, France has had a much more turbulent past. The bicentennial of the French Revolution was celebrated in 1989. But it has taken the formation and reformation of five separate democratic republics to achieve the generally stable and effective democracy of contemporary France. Even with this success, it is not unusual to read of strikes, demonstrations, and other signs of apparent political unrest. France's long history of dealing with political turbulence makes such events less significant than they might be in other democracies. Its troubled political past, in some ways, helped to insulate France from the crisis of confidence found in other western democracies during the 1970s and early 1980s.

France has long been viewed as the exception to the usual patterns of European democracy because of its past instability and ineffectiveness. The transformation of this troubled political system into a bulwark of democracy offers insight into ways other democracies might respond to the challenges of the last years of the twentieth century. Perhaps France is no longer a problem area of Europe but an example to others of how democracy can adjust to the more turbulent politics of this era.

CHAPTER SIX
FRANCE: THE HISTORICAL AND SOCIAL BACKGROUND TO POLITICS

> Disputes of the past accumulate, so that present issues are still debated in terms of historical precedents, and old allegiances produce permanent animosities.[1]

In 1989, France celebrated the bicentennial of the French Revolution. This great political, social, and economic revolution marked the end of feudal and traditional practices, but it failed to resolve the political future of the country. While the Revolution produced sweeping political and socioeconomic changes, it did not result in a consensus that could serve as the basis for a stable democracy. The violence and terror associated with the Revolution brought divisions that are only now disappearing. Indeed, as recently as the 1970s, when a unanimous American population was feting the bicentennial of their revolution, polls showed a sharp division among the French over the desirability of its Revolution of 1789. Many French citizens still regard the Revolution as a catastrophe while many others regard it as one of France's major contributions to modern world history.

THE INCOMPLETE REVOLUTION

The 800 or so revolutionaries who on July 14, 1789 took the Bastille, a near empty prison that had come to symbolize royal oppression, triggered a decade of violence as revolutionaries first battled reactionary forces and then each other. In the pursuit of "liberty, equality, and brotherhood," an estimated three hundred thousand people were imprisoned during the Reign of Terror; forty thousand people were executed by guillotines in Paris or by drowning in the provinces. Churches, the homes of the wealthy, and other symbols of oppression were destroyed by unruly mobs. In Paris, the zealous effort to destroy all statues of France's kings led to the beheading or smashing of the row of Israelite kings on the facade of Notre Dame Cathedral.

The revolutionary violence was understandable given the oppression that had afflicted many French citizens under the old regime. The peasants had suffered in particular from abuse by often insensitive and authoritarian noble landowners. Heavy seigniorial dues left over from feudal times accentuated the growing shortage of food in the countryside. The king lacked the will and the means to bring about essential reforms.

If the great loss of life during the Revolution was a tragedy, so too was the incomplete nature of the change. The excesses of the Revolution prevented the emergence of a consensus on the democracy it was supposed to create. In the 200 years that followed the Revolution, while Britain's monarchy slowly evolved toward democracy and the American constitution gave shape to a republican democracy, France went through a series of political regimes, revolutions, and near revolutions. In marked contrast to the evolutionary pattern of political development in Britain, the French have had a turbulent political history. In the 200 years from 1789 to the present, the French have tried five republics, three monarchies, two empires, a fascist state, and several provisional governments. On the average, the entire political system would have changed every eighteen years. Unlike in Britain, where the crisis of democracy represents a new problem, France is used to near-permanent regime-threatening crises.

The impact of these regime changes on ordinary people should not be overexaggerated. Often even dramatic regime changes have had little impact on the general public. Republics and authoritarian regimes have come and gone but it was usually the same people who collected taxes or sold stamps in the post office. The same laws have remained in effect. A visitor to France today will still note on bus-stop shelters small warnings that posting bills is forbidden by law. The laws cited on these warnings originated from 1877 and 1942; the regimes that passed them are long dead and discredited—one for its instability, the other because it was a German-imposed fascist dictatorship. But the laws are still on the books and enforced.

The emotional scars from the regime changes are long lasting and divisive. These grudges are well illustrated by the powerful tensions still evoked by the division between the supporters of the Vichy regime during World War II and those who sided with the Resistance. Some forty-five years later this cleavage lingers in the shadows of the French politic. These tensions reemerged to the forefront of French life in the 1980s when a wartime Gestapo commander who was stationed in Lyons was returned to France for trial after hiding for thirty-five years in South America. Klaus Barbie was accused of direct complicity in the deaths of thousands of

Resistance workers, Jews, and other enemies of the Germans. The initial satisfaction in being able to bring this war criminal to justice was soon replaced by fears about reopening old wounds and by apprehension that his testimony might implicate other now respected citizens for wartime improprieties—both as friends of Vichy and as rivals in the Resistance. Four years later, the usually rapid French system of justice had yet to begin Barbie's trial.[2] When Barbie was eventually convicted, the end of the trial was greeted with a collective sigh of relief as the old divisions and rancour were once again put aside.

The Concept of the Exalted State

Through all the regime changes, the French concept of the state has remained relatively unchanged in the 300 years since Louis XIV when the absolute monarch pronounced: *"L'Etat, c'est moi"* (I am the State). The French think of the state as a political entity separate from the divisions and conflicts of everyday politics. Unchanging and symbolic of all national virtues, it is distinguishable from the current government that reflects partisan divisions and human imperfections. Aloof from the petty squabbles of these self-seeking groups and individuals, the state represents the overall public interest—the Rousseauian notion of a general will that can command the unanimous support of the people. The state represents the *general interest* in its pure form as opposed to the attenuated versions from specific governments.

The state is not, however, simply an abstract entity. It is embodied in the administrative services of the bureaucracy. The French bureaucracy was already well developed by the time of the Revolution. Modernized by Napoleon, it has continued without major reform through revolutions and counterrevolutions to the present. The pervasive power of the Napoleonic civil service led critics of French democratic regimes to complain that while the republic was above the surface, the empire still prevailed below, through the bureaucracy. Imbued with the notion of the state's sanctity and convinced that they are better aware of the citizens' interests than the people themselves, civil servants (then and now) attempt to foresee and to take care of everything through state regulation.

To a large extent, the people accept this powerful state presence in their lives as natural and desirable since it represents the general will. With this positive notion of the state, the French rarely exhibit the fear of government intrusions that Americans often express. The state has always had a key role in the social and economic life of the nation. Under the prerevolutionary monarchy, the state already regularly intervened in agriculture, commerce, and the crafts. The Revolution only eliminated the feudal aspects of this interference. Succeeding regimes maintained the interventionist approach to the economy. Of particular importance were the state's efforts, not always successful, to promote industrialization.[3] Government price controls on bread illustrate state economic intervention. First established during the Revolution of 1789, they continued in effect without interruption until 1979.

Political Pluralism

Unlike the British pattern of politics, which for more than a century has been distinguished by competition between two broad political camps, France has always had a large number of small political factions contending for public office. During the Revolution, there was no united revolutionary movement but a large number of loose factions, which eventually turned on each other with the same violence they had earlier directed at the monarchy. Even during authoritarian regimes, political pluralism proved impossible to repress with numerous competing political groups and clubs meeting clandestinely to prepare for the eventual reopening of politics.

The French political spectrum runs today from fascists, monarchists, and Bonapartists (dreaming of the restoration of the Napoleonic empire) on the far Right to anarchists, Trotskyites, and Maoists on the far Left. As in the past, these groups often have all-encompassing ideologies that shape their political actions and interpretations of the world such as communism, socialism, fascism and liberalism. Others profess vaguer principles of political action, such as anticommunism, anticlericalism, or antiGaullism, which prove to be equally firm obstacles to interparty cooperation despite their relative lack of rigor. These political belief systems often persist as guidelines for action years after the problems that inspired their conception have ceased to have political significance. Public division over the Catholic Church's political role continued long after the issue had been resolved by the church's loss of influence. Many older French leftists still refuse to believe that a practicing Catholic can be a leftist or even a supporter of a republican government. This attitude stems from battles fought in 1791 and again in the first decade of this century, when Catholics opposed the republic because it had severed the tie between church and state. Thus, political disputes of the past are perpetuated even though the issues and personalities change.

French political leaders often show great skill in compromising their ideological beliefs when circumstances demand it. But compromise is not considered as heroic or desirable a style of political action as it is in Britain. In France, loyalty to abstract principles and ideologies is the norm. Fidelity to these doctrines hinders political accommodations and may ultimately undermine those compromises that are successfully negotiated. The Socialist government worked out a compromise in the early 1980s with the supporters of parochial schools to impose government controls on private church schools that receive government subsidies. The compromise collapsed—and the whole reform was eventually abandoned—when Socialist deputies in parliament insisted on a more ideologically pure, harder line toward the parochial schools.

These political and ideological divisions are not restricted to the party system. They permeate other social groups. There are conservative, socialist, and communist farmers' organizations; lawyers, doctors, and other professionals may join conservative or leftist groups; the parent-teacher associations reflect divisions between socialism and moderate conservatism. In the trade union movement, three different unions, all claiming some ties to the Left, compete for members with the smaller conservative unions. Thus political pluralism in the party system spreads throughout society.

A Propensity for Revolt

The French state has been a strong one, even during democratic regimes. The notion of the state as the embodiment of the general will brings with it an impulse for elected officials and civil servants to stand aloof from the contention of divisive and self-serving interests that might distract them from the pursuit of the general will. This independence tends to give politics an authoritarian air even when free elections and civil liberties are present.

Coexistent with this usually authoritarian power relationship is a tendency for the citizens to resist the government and to revolt periodically. A prominent French political thinker explained this seeming paradox in a people tolerating both authoritarianism and revolt:

> Resistance and obedience are the two virtues of the citizen. By obedience he guarantees order; by resistance he guarantees liberty.[4]

This is, in essence, a tradition of revolt against tradition and dates back at least 400 years.[5] Once established, this "right" of revolt has justified yet further rebellions. Indeed, there is a long history of popular resistance to changing economic structures and the extension of the powers of the state. There is, by now, a well-established ritual of revolt with traditional targets, rallying points, march routes, songs, slogans, and other tactics that are used by successive generations of rebels.

While the French routinely accept rule by aloof governors in both authoritarian and democratic garb, they retain the right to protest vigorously against specific actions which they view as detrimental to their interests.[6] At times this protest explodes spontaneously into a more general revolt. There is a long string of such popular uprisings, so much so that they are viewed as "a national way of life" or even as "the national sport."[7] The results of protest actions are usually limited as the state has developed the means to counter them. Successful or not, they become historical precedents that future generations will draw upon as patterns for future revolts. Many of these events—especially the Revolutions of 1789 and 1848, the Paris Commune of 1870 to 1871, and the Events of May 1968— are imbued with a mystique of revolutionary camaraderie, spiritual uplift, and glamour that make them attractive models for modern discontented groups. Thus, when discontent rises there is always the temptation to recreate the glamourous past by patterning a new revolt on the episodes of an earlier time.

Such an instance was the student/worker revolt in May 1968. Student unrest was based on seriously overcrowded universities, archaic university procedures and aloof professors, restraints on the freedom of political expression, limited guest hours in dormitories, and uncertain job prospects.

The French students were also influenced by the student unrest and rioting that beset most Western democracies at the end of the 1960s.[8]

When demonstrations led to rioting and police repression, a one day general strike was called to show the workers' sympathy with the student rebels. The overt goal of the strike was to support the students, but the strikers used the occasion to protest a wide range of grievances from salary levels, vacation benefits, reduced social security payments, to the length of the workweek. Many workers were swept up in the protest movement and failed to return to work the next day; others who had not taken part in the initial protest joined in the strike and demonstrations in the following days. Instead of simply going home, the workers and students conducted sit-ins of their plants, offices, and classrooms. It was not an organized movement, labor leaders and politicians from opposition parties were taken by surprise at the course of events. It was a spontaneous outpouring of revolutionary fervor: a chance for the French to recreate in real life the revolutionary dramas they had read about in history books.[9]

The strikes, student riots, and the occupation of factories, universities, and public buildings continued for over three weeks. The rebels claimed that "imagination was in power" and that "power was in the streets." It was a remarkable political-cultural event: Art students covered city walls with bold posters often featuring the profile and prominent nose of President de Gaulle; students occupied their classrooms, sleeping on the floors, turning lecture halls into debating centers or emergency hospitals, and taking time out to learn traditional revolutionary songs; even theater companies and soccer teams put aside their regular routines to debate political issues. Unable to gain control of the mounting rebellion, de Gaulle fled the country only to be persuaded by his prime minister and military leaders to return. The beginning of the end of the "psychodrama" came when de Gaulle dissolved the National Assembly and called for new elections. This shifted the focus of conflict from street politics and strikes to electoral politics. The strikes quickly ended, student rioting abated, and order was restored as politicians and social leaders concentrated on the election. The overwhelming victory of the Gaullists and the decisive defeat of all left-wing forces—including those even remotely associated with the crisis marked the end of this near revolution.

The romantic attraction of this revolt explains the intensification of conflict to the point of endangering the regime. Many participants consciously patterned their goals, their actions, and even their vocabulary on past revolutionary eras: the Revolutions of 1789 and 1848, the Paris Commune of 1870, and the General Strike of 1936. Current events provided the opportunity to experience firsthand the romance and glory of revolution, which could otherwise be experienced only through books. With such a tradition of revolt joined with the glamour that surrounded previous revolts, France will always be vulnerable to periods of rapidly accelerating social conflict and near revolution because serious conflict has been manifested thus in the past. The Events of May 1968 belong to a long history of glorious revolutionary episodes that will doubtlessly incite similar ventures in the future.

A Civilizing Mission

De Gaulle used to say that France could not be France without grandeur. That sense of France's importance to the rest of the world dates back well before de Gaulle. Enlightenment thinkers were convinced that all people everywhere were potentially French and really wished to be French.[10] The pre-revolutionary pride in their cultural achievements was supplemented by revolutionary expansionism after 1789: The Revolution was obligated to bring the liberty and equality achieved in France to other oppressed peoples in Europe. Indeed, the Revolution produced modern mass-based nationalism by replacing the mercenary armed forces of the past with popular armies mobilized by the desire to spread the Revolution and French culture to other peoples.

French nationalism manifested itself, after the messianic fervor of the revolutionary era, in the expansionist imperial eras of the nineteenth century. Motivated by its perceived mission to civilize, France built an empire second only to the British empire. Despite the tragic colonial wars during the decolonization of French Indochina and Algeria, French political, economic, and cultural influence remains more important in its former empire than does British influence in the contemporary Commonwealth:

> Today a subtly structured empire, as rewarding as any in history, maintains France as a world power, perhaps the only cultural superpower, one that is based firmly and squarely on illusions. Freed of its colonies, it is master. Having killed hundreds of thousands in colonial wars, France is a Third World symbol of liberty, equality, and brotherhood.[11]

ORIGINS OF THE FIFTH REPUBLIC

The democratic political system that emerged in France after the Second World War—the Fourth Republic (1946 to 1958)—was very similar to the Third Republic that had collapsed in 1940 when Germany dealt France an early defeat. The efforts to remedy certain problems that had led to governmental paralysis and ineffectiveness before the war failed, and the same problems reemerged in the Fourth Republic. The French parliament was presumably all powerful, but there were so many parties that it was difficult to form the stable coalitions needed to keep the premier and cabinet in office. The weakness of the executive was compounded by the numerous political parties being poorly disciplined, and ideologically based. Because of divisions within and between parties, parliament, very powerful on paper, was in fact only able to exert its power in a negative way by blocking proposed reforms and by overthrowing governments. The result was governmental instability with twenty-seven separate governments in the twelve years of the Fourth Republic. Since the various governments faced the constant threat of a collapse of their parliamentary base, which

FIGURE 6.1   Map of France. *Source:* Rolf H. W. Theen and Frank L. Wilson, *Comparative Politics: An Introduction to Six Countries* (Englewood Cliffs, NJ: Prentice Hall, 1986), p. 114. Reprinted with permission.

would force their resignation, they were often unable to act on the major problems facing the country.[12]

The issue that eventually brought down the Fourth Republic was decolonization. Already weakened by an internally divisive and futile colonial battle in Indochina (Vietnam, Cambodia, and Laos), the Fourth Republic faced an even more bitter struggle in Algeria.[13] This North African territory had been more than a typical colony. Most French regarded it as an integral part of France, and large numbers of French citizens had emigrated to Algeria with government encouragement. Alongside the indigenous population of 9 million Moslem Algerians lived some 1.2 million Europeans, mostly of French extraction. In 1954, Algerian rebels began an armed insurrection to achieve independence. The French military, called in to control the revolt, soon came to believe that the civilian regime in Paris was hindering its ability to conduct the war because of its internal division, instability, and general incompetence.[14] In France, the colonial war became increasingly unpopular. Politicians wavered between negotiations with the rebels and military actions. The public split between those wanting to end the war, even at the cost of an independent Algeria, and those defiantly insisting on keeping Algeria French.

Eventually it was the French population in Algeria—fearful that the government in Paris would capitulate to calls for Algerian independence—that precipitated the insurrection which toppled the Fourth Republic. On May 13, 1958, rebellious French civilians seized public buildings in Algiers and set up a "Committee of Public Safety" to govern in place of the Paris-appointed officials. The military and the police joined with the French rebels instead of defending the Parisian government. Afraid that a new national government intent on appeasing Moslem Algerian nationalists might soon come to power in Paris, the French colonialists in Algiers also called for a revolutionary Committee of Public Safety in Paris. It succeeded in setting up such an insurgent government in Corsica. A few days later, the rebels threatened to drop paratroopers on Paris if their demands were not met. Such an action, politicians feared, would trigger a civil war.

To prevent further chaos, the leaders of the Fourth Republic turned to General Charles de Gaulle, leader of the wartime Resistance movement and an outspoken critic of the Fourth Republic. Associates of de Gaulle had encouraged the rebellion in Algeria, but there was no evidence that de Gaulle himself had taken part in it. Despite the treasonous activities of his friends, de Gaulle appeared to be the only person capable of averting anarchy and civil war. On June 1, 1958, the National Assembly invested de Gaulle as premier and voted full powers to him. The National Assembly also granted de Gaulle the authority to revise the constitution. Instead, he and his supporters drafted an entirely new constitution, ratified by the voters in a special referendum at the end of 1958. Then, on January 1, 1959, the Constitution of the Fifth Republic took effect, putting an end to the Fourth Republic.

Once in power, de Gaulle proceeded to do exactly what some people had feared the old regime would do: Within a year he had announced that Algeria would be allowed its self-determination. Algerian independence was overwhelmingly approved by the French public in two referendums. Die-hard advocates of a French Algeria formed a Secret Army Organization (OAS) and resorted to terrorism. They made several attempts to assassinate de Gaulle, and in one ambush the president's car was riddled with bullets. De Gaulle, however, emerged, unscathed, with his wife, and dismissed the episode with a laconic, "They can't shoot straight." In Algeria, the military and French settlers organized two abortive uprisings; but the decision to terminate colonial rule held; and in 1963, Algeria became an independent state.

The end of the Algerian war marked the consolidation of the Fifth Republic. In successive elections and referendums, the French voters showed strong support for the new constitution. But leftist parties, both the Communists and Socialists, contested its legitimacy and democratic credentials for another fifteen years. Many observers felt that it was a special regime, so tailored to the style of its founder that it would not last. But the Fifth Republic survived de Gaulle's retirement. It continued unchanged even when political power shifted from the hands of de Gaulle's supporters to the once-hostile Left. Indeed, it was the election of a Socialist president in 1981 and his use of broad presidential powers that signified the final acceptance of the Fifth Republic by all major parties. After thirty years, the Fifth Republic is solidly in place providing France both effective and democratic government.

FRANCE IN THE 1980s

It has long been fashionable to claim that France has been afflicted by multiple social cleavages and a backward economy. Furthermore, the political disruptions and ineffective governments have been blamed for producing a stalled or a stalemate society where social and economic problems have been impossible to overcome.[15] But there is increasing evidence to suggest that France is a much more consensual and dynamic society than usually believed.[16] French society has dramatically changed since the 1950s and its economy is among the strongest in Europe. These social and economic changes have had important political consequences.

Social Class and Politics

Among the most important divisions in French society are those dividing the French into socioeconomic classes. The French have a stronger sense of class membership than do Americans, but they do not have as strong a sense as the British. As in Britain, once prominent social class distinctions in attitudes and demeanor have been diminishing. Modern communications and broadened affluence have created a more uniform national culture and life style to supplant the once distinctive class and regional patterns. The expanded access to consumer goods is impressive: In 1958, 71 percent of French households did not have a refrigerator, washing machine, or television: By 1978, 71 percent of the households had *all* three. There has also been some leveling of income between the industrial worker and the white-collar worker. In 1954, the median income of the white-collar worker was 13 percent higher than that of the industrial worker; by 1974 this income differential had dropped to only 4 percent.[17] With these changes has come a growing sense that class distinctions are giving way to a more uniform society. A 1983 poll reported that, of French people who identified themselves as either working class or middle class, 62 percent of the workers and 71 percent of the middle class felt that the two social classes are gradually integrating into a large middle class.[18]

These changes in social structures and in people's ideas about classes have led some to conclude that France (along with other European democracies) is experiencing the leveling or "embourgeoisement" of society. According to this school of thought, the old image of the social hierarchy as a pyramid with a large working class supporting a smaller but politically and economically dominant "bourgeois" class is replaced with a diamond shaped social structure with a very large middle class encompassing much of the population. Embourgeoisement comes with a decline in the social class tensions of the past. Since most people see themselves in this broad middle class, social class is seen as having less impact on political attitudes and behavior. These are abstract models of class relationship that are difficult to verify empirically. And there is little consensus among politicians or citizens on which most accurately portrays the reality of French social class relationships.

Until very recently, many French political leaders, notably those on the Left, rejected this embourgeoisement model of social class change insisting on the validity of traditional class politics. They recognized improvements in the living standards of workers but insisted that a "new working class" was emerging among white collar employees of large firms and the government. These employees experienced relations with aloof employers that differed little in quality from those of the blue collar

FIGURE 6.2 Alternative Views of Class Structure

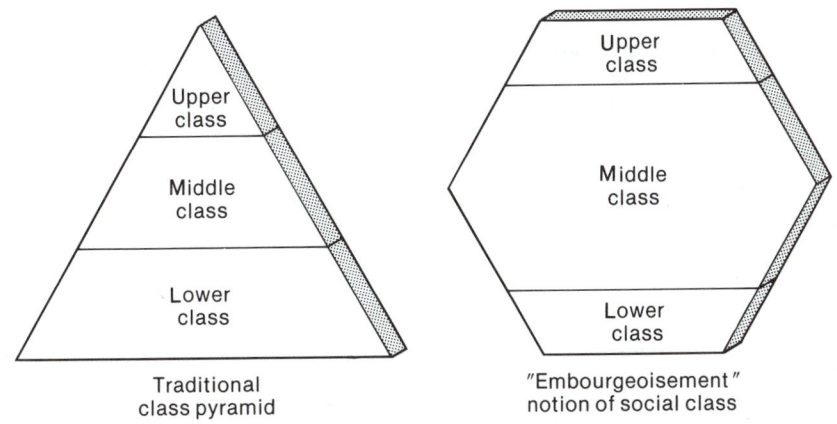

Traditional
class pyramid

"Embourgeoisement"
notion of social class

workers. They saw evidence of this new alliance of blue and white collar workers in the breadth of the support for the 1968 general strike. More recently, the victory of the Left in the 1981 elections offered evidence of the political viability of such a coalition. Together, the traditional working class and this new working class might still achieve the social revolution sought by radical reformers. As a result, throughout the 1970s and into the 1980s, the trade unions and leftwing parties used traditional class warfare symbols and terminology.

The loss of public support for the Socialist government after 1983, however, led to a revival of the embourgeoisement thesis of social change in France. By the end of the 1980s, it was clear that traditional working class appeals had a very limited audience in France. Leftist political parties and trade unions dropped their class warfare rhetoric and shaped their appeals to a more contented and consensual audience. While it is still too early to say whether this will mark a definitive change in French political style, it should be noted that the one party that continued to harp on traditional class themes, the Communist party, experienced sharp declines in its level of electoral support.

Social class divisions are reflected in the voting patterns in France but not as strongly as they are in Britain. The working class is more likely to vote for the leftist parties and the middle and upper classes tend to support the Center-Right parties (Giscardians and Gaullists). Table 6.1 illustrates this class impact on the vote by showing how various occupational categories divide their votes among the principal parties. With the exception of the Communist party, which draws the majority of its vote from the working class, French political parties are catch-all parties in that they draw upon several occupations or classes. Even the working-class vote is divided among all parties. In France, other factors such as the voters' degree of religious commitment or geographic location are more important than the voters' class identities in explaining electoral choices.

TABLE 6.1   Occupation and Voting Preferences, 1986

Party respondent voted for in 1986:

Occupation	Communists	Socialists	Conservatives	Far Right
Farmers	7%	21%	54%	11%
Small business	5	14	61	14
Professionals and managers	4	32	49	9
Mid-level management	9	38	36	10
White collar workers	12	44	33	7
Blue-collar workers	20	34	29	11
Service personnel	15	31	40	6
No occupation	11	29	45	9

Lines do not total 100% because "others" omitted.
Source: Bull-BVA exit polls reported in *La Libération,* 18 March 1986, p. 18.

Despite verbal attachment to "equality and brotherhood," the French support several practices that hinder greater social equality. Income distribution in France is one of the least equitable among industrialized countries.[19] Efforts to redress this inequity are unpopular. There is a progressive income tax but it is weakened by loopholes and widespread evasion. Taxes used in other countries to redistribute wealth from the rich to the poor—such as wealth, inheritance, and capital gain taxes—are minimal or nonexistent in France. Opinion polls show strong opposition from people of all backgrounds to such taxes. As a result, much of government revenue comes from regressive value-added taxes, a hidden tax on most purchases amounting to as much as 30 percent of an item's cost to the consumer.

Social mobility is also lower in France than in many other European countries.[20] Children from modest backgrounds now have greater opportunities to acquire higher education which might be expected to improve upward mobility. But the effects are limited. The large number of university graduates has diluted the value of the degree. At the same time, the number of attractive job opportunities has decreased. In this tight job market, the competitive advantage goes to the young people who inherit prestige, poise, personal contacts, and other social assets thus perpetuating inherited class lines.

A further limit on the benefits of expanded university education is a system of elite schools known as the *grandes écoles*.[21] Theoretically, these schools are open to all qualified young people but in practice applicants from modest social backgrounds are generally ill prepared for the style and content of the highly competitive admission examinations. As a result, it is usually the children of former graduates and privileged families that succeed in winning admission. It is true that such elite schools are not unique to France; in Britain they exist as the "public" schools and Oxford and Cambridge Universities. But in Britain the elite schools are private institutions. The state has worked to reduce their influence through improvements in the state-run schools. In France, the elite schools are state run, and all educational reforms have avoided any challenge to the preeminence of these *grandes écoles*.

Religion and Politics

Despite the fact that most French are Roman Catholic (87 percent), a division among Catholics themselves has been the source of social tension. One of the oldest and deepest cleavages in French society is between those who sought to reduce the political and social role of the Roman Catholic Church (the anticlericals) and those who defended the church's place in French politics (the clericals). From roots dating before the Revolution of 1789, the religious cleavage continued even after the formal separation of church and state in 1905. Anticlerical forces, generally from the Left, attacked remaining areas of church influence, such as the parochial schools; clericals, generally from the Right, often contested the democratic parliamentary system as a whole because of its past violent attacks on the church.

In the eyes of most republicans, loyal Catholics could not be loyal democrats; in the eyes of many Catholics, devotion to the republican state, especially when accompanied by identification with a leftist party, signified the individual's loss of religious faith.

Since World War II, changes in the church and in French society have eased the tensions between clericals and anticlericals. The active role of many practicing Catholics in the wartime Resistance movement served to integrate Catholics into the political system and to demonstrate that they could be devout and democratic at the same time. The church no longer condemned the Left as heretical, and the leftwing parties reduced their dogmatic anticlericalism.

The only significant issue left over from the old conflicts is the question of state financial support to church schools. Among the general public, this issue seems to stir little passion since a compromise reached in 1960 allowed state subsidies to the private schools that conform to state-dictated educational curricula and standards. Political elites on the Left still pledge the elimination of subsidies to church schools and even the nationalization of all private schools. The most recent flare-up of this old issue came in the mid-1980s when the Socialist government sought to reduce the subsidies. Both sides of the controversy mobilized hundreds of thousands of marchers to demonstrate their support. At the height of the movement, the supporters of church schools brought over a million people to the streets of Paris to oppose the Socialist plan. Eventually the government retreated and withdrew its legislative package leaving the 1960 compromise in force. While the symbols and rhetoric recalled the old clerical/anticlerical battle, the issue was much broader. The government's educational subsidy reform was viewed by opponents as an attack on freedom to choose private education. It was this broader issue, plus the rallying of diverse opponents who saw the issue as an opportunity to attack the leftist government, that mobilized the general public.

Aside from such symbolic outbursts, the most important political manifestation of the religious cleavage is voting behavior. For nearly a century or more, the single best indicator of likely partisan preference has been the voter's level of religious conviction. The more faithfully individuals practice Catholicism, the more likely they will vote for rightwing parties (see Table 6.2). This religious impact on voting behavior reflects intense feelings engendered by the long struggle between the anticlerical republican forces and the church-supported conservatives. For a devout Catholic to vote for the Left was for many decades tantamount to apostasy, or at the very least to disobedience. Parish priests no longer tell their parishioners how to vote from the pulpit, but the strong association between religious practice and voting makes the level of religious dedication a better predictor of partisan ties than any other factor including social class identity.

There is evidence that this influence is declining.[22] There is an overall decline of religious commitment among the French. There are simply fewer devout Catholics today than there were 25 years ago.[23] In addition, loyal Catholics seem less closely tied to the parties of the Right and the Center than before. The church no longer plays as central a role in shaping

TABLE 6.2 Religion and Voting Preference in France, 1988

	Voted for	
RELIGIOUS LOYALTY	LEFTIST PARTIES	RIGHTIST PARTIES
Regularly practicing Roman Catholic	23%	77%
Occasionally practicing Roman Catholic	34	66
Nonpracticing Roman Catholic	57	43
Other religions	69	31
No religion	80	20

Source: CSA exit polls reported in *Le Journal des Elections,* No. 3, June 1988, p. 9.

values, including political orientations, as it once did. Leftwing parties have put aside their traditional mistrust and have begun courting the votes of loyal Catholics. They have also welcomed practicing Catholics into their ranks. Despite the slight loosening of the linkage between religious practice and electoral choice, religion still provides the most reliable predictor of likely voting choice.[24]

Ethnic conflict

As in Britain, ethnic minorities in France long thought to be well integrated have reemerged as important social and political forces. Despite surface unity, France has always included a number of distinctive peoples. In a country that is proud of its national language and almost defiant in its efforts to preserve that language, it is surprising to find that over a third of the French also speak a regional language. Many of the linguistic and ethnic groups have renewed their political activities in the last two decades. Those with the greatest political impact are the Bretons, Basques, and Corsicans.

The Bretons have resented the economic isolation of their part of the country. Located on a peninsula on the western extremity, Brittany has not shared the economic growth of other regions. The distinctive Breton culture and language are threatened with extinction as a result of the inroad of the national culture. During the 1970s, a small but noisy and occasionally violent separatist movement claimed autonomy for Brittany. While the movement declined during the 1980s, the continued resentment of the economic underdevelopment and cultural decline of Brittany may bring its revival in the future.

The economic situation in the Basque regions of southwestern France is similar. But their conflict with the government is over policies with Spain where the major Basque nationalist cause is contested. Until the death of Franco in 1977, the French government sheltered Basque nationalists. But since the mid-1980s, the French government has cooperated with the now democratic regime in Spain by extraditing Basque nationalists accused of acts of violence. In reaction, the Basques have carried out terrorist acts in France too.

In the 1980s, the most virulent nationalist cause has been that of the Corsicans. This island lies 100 miles off the French coast in the Mediterranean Sea. It has been a part of France since 1769. While remote from industrial centers, the main grievance of Corsicans has been too much of the wrong kind of economic development. The rapid expansion of resorts and hotels on Corsican beaches by mainland French entrepreneurs in the 1960s and 1970s produced resentment among Corsicans over the destruction of their island's beauty by "alien" developers. Corsican nationalist movements have emerged including several that are intent on achieving independence through terrorism if necessary. Over the past few years, an average of two bombings a day have hit businesses owned by mainland French firms.[25] In addition, less extreme nationalist movements have emerged as powerful forces in regional politics and elections.

Elsewhere nationalist movements have had much less political impact. Unlike the situations in Scotland and Wales, the French national minorities have not succeeded in developing political parties capable of cutting into the electoral support of the major parties. There are several ethnic parties that often run candidates in national and local elections but without any success. Even the Corsican nationalist parties have been unsuccessful in national elections. French voters feel that too much is at stake in the choice between the major parties of the Left and Right to cast votes for minor regional parties in national elections.[26]

There have been some important steps to provide regional governments with greater powers and thus defuse ethnic separatist causes. The Corsican regional government was set up to deflect calls for independence. The results of these experiments have been mixed. In Corsica, the success of the nationalist parties in regional elections was not great enough to replace the main parties, and the result was a highly divided regional assembly that has been prone to stalemate. Everywhere, the gains for nationalist groups have been more symbolic than real: The Corsicans got a university; the Bretons obtained some television programming in their language; the Alsatians were allowed to operate state nursery schools using their dialect; even smaller ethnic groups, such as French Jews, were given museums, libraries, and theaters to promote their distinctive cultural expressions. While the state has been willing to spend more for ethnic minorities to preserve their culture, it has conceded little real political power to regional governments.

As in Britain and West Germany, the French have experienced major problems from the presence of large numbers of immigrants. During the years of economic boom in the 1960s and early 1970s, there were not enough native French workers to fill all the jobs. Immigrant workers were permitted to enter France to fill the gap. Once in France, many brought their families and permanently settled in. By 1979, the immigrant population reached 4.1 million or nearly 8 percent of the total population, with much of it concentrated in the larger cities. In Paris, immigrants made up over 16 percent of the population in 1982. The foreign workers came from lesser-developed European countries, such as Portugal, Spain, Greece, and earlier, Italy and North Africa, especially Algeria.

When the economy slowed in the late 1970s, resentment toward the immigrants began to increase. But the resentment was not only economic in nature. Native French citizens were angered by the unwillingness of many of these immigrants—notably the Moslems from North Africa—to assimilate into the French style of life. They also associated the rise of urban crime and drug use with the immigrant populations. The French have long prided themselves on their racial tolerance, and indeed, their attitudes conveyed to public opinion pollsters suggest that they are more tolerant than the British.[27] But there are deep-seated suspicions and stereotypes about foreign workers, especially those from North Africa, that are often not admitted to pollsters. By the mid-1980s, racial relations had become very tense. While France had been spared the rioting of immigrant populations that had hit British cities, nasty racial incidents involving individuals and small groups had become commonplace in many parts.[28]

Public opinion became openly hostile to the immigrants with racial graffiti common in subways and on billboards. The major parties, however, avoided the immigration issue. Both conservative and leftist governments tried to stem new immigration and tried to encourage the voluntary departure of those already in France through bonuses for workers who agreed to return to their homelands. Both Right and Left political leaders tried to encourage nondiscrimination and racial understanding.

The failure of the major parties to respond to the changing public mood offered opportunities for extreme rightwing groups. One, the National Front, emerged as a powerful political force bent on exploiting the racial issue. With a platform calling for the compulsory repatriation of immigrants, the National Front won over 10 percent of the vote in the 1986 National Assembly elections and 14.5 percent on the first ballot of the 1988 presidential election. The rise of the National Front was made possible by conditions that may prove temporary as will be discussed in Chapter Eight. But the issues of immigration and racial tolerance are not likely to go away even if the National Front declines. As in Britain, the French face the difficult challenge of learning to live with a racially diverse population after centuries of relative racial homogeneity.

A DIRECTED ECONOMY

From Colbert's mercantilism of prerevolutionary France to the Socialist nationalizations in 1981, the French government has always played an important part in regulating and directing the economy according to the wishes or visions of its leaders. As one recent observer notes:

> The French love regulation. They judge their public officials by the quantity of laws they produce. Rare is the minister who advocates deregulation, rarer still the minister who achieves it.[29]

The resulting economy is a mixed one with a substantial public sector coexisting with private enterprises in a market economy. By the mid-1980s, the public sector of nationalized enterprises accounted for 30 percent of French industrial output. Privately held businesses were also heavily influenced by the state through its long-term purchase agreements, subsidies, and research funding. Unwilling to rely on market forces, the French government engages in indicative economic planning. Four year economic plans are drawn up by the government in consultation with business, financial, and labor leaders. The plans serve as voluntary guidelines for investment and development. The government also seeks to direct the economy through a series of "industrial policies" designed to enable France to compete effectively on the world market and to maintain (or achieve) national independence in vital defense-related industries. It uses state-defined industrial policies more so than any other major industrial country, with the exception of Japan. Even though not always successful, these industrial policies have made France highly competitive in several industrial sectors.

The nature of the French economy has changed dramatically since the end of the Second World War. Most notable has been the movement of people from agricultural occupations to industrial and service employment. The farm population dropped from 26.7 percent of the 1954 work force to 9.3 percent twenty years later. Some two million people from families once involved in farming have been assimilated into the industrial and commercial sectors in less than two decades. The decline of heavy industries, such as steel and automobile, has brought new shifts in occupation patterns toward the service sector. By the mid-1980s, the service sector has become the largest source of employment. (See Figure 6.3.)

The French economy has performed well through much of the postwar era. Since the late 1970s, it has experienced difficulties coming from the worldwide recession and the decline of smokestack industries that were

FIGURE 6.3 Employment by Economic Sector in France. *Source: The World Almanac and Book of Facts* (New York: World Almanac, 1988).

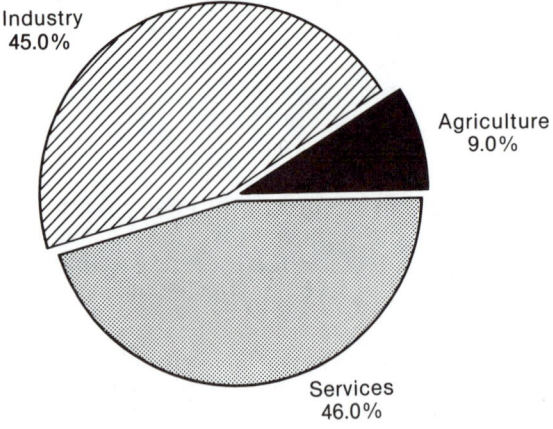

Industry
45.0%

Agriculture
9.0%

Services
46.0%

large employers. Its response has differed from other European countries. It experimented briefly, under the Socialist government, with a more interventionist approach to solving the economic decline while other industrial countries were reducing government economic controls. (An evaluation of this effort will be made in Chapter Ten.) It is important to note that government economic intervention has been a long-term pattern that is likely to continue for the years to come.

CONCLUSION

The persistence in France of traditional patterns of political action and of social cleavage has produced a widely used adage: *le plus ça change, le plus c'est la même chose* (the more it changes, the more it is the same thing). There is some truth in this dictum; France has not escaped its past despite the revolutionary and evolutionary sociopolitical changes of the last 200 years. But it is also wrong to overstate the continuity. France at the beginning of the 1990s is a remarkably different place than it was twenty years ago. Dramatic changes have occurred as new political patterns have emerged and as society has evolved. The legacies from the past have not disappeared but skillful politicians and citizens have found ways to overcome traditional political and socioeconomic patterns to create a modern and dynamic France.

NOTES

1. Theodore Zeldin, *France 1848–1945; Politics and Anger* (New York: Vintage, 1979), p. 1.
2. Erna Paris, *Unhealed Wounds: France and the Klaus Barbie Affair* (New York: Grove, 1986).
3. J. H. Clapman, *Economic Development of France and Germany 1815–1914* (Cambridge, England: Cambridge University Press, 1966); Richard F. Kuisel, *Capitalism and the State in Modern France: Renovation and Economic Management in the Twentieth Century* (Cambridge, England: Cambridge University Press, 1981); and John H. McArthur and Bruce R. Scott, *Industrial Planning in France* (Cambridge, MA: Harvard University Graduate School of Business Administration, 1969).
4. Alain [Emile Chartier], *Elements d'une doctrine radicale* (Paris: Gallimard, 1933), p. 281.
5. Charles Tilly, *The Contentious French* (Cambridge, MA: Harvard University Press, 1986).
6. Stanley Hoffmann, *Decline or Renewal? France Since the 1930s* (New York: Viking, 1974), pp. 111–144.
7. Ibid. Hoffmann uses the term "national way of life" in discussing protest; Roger Peyrefitte labels rioting "the national sport" in France in *The Trouble With France* (New York: Alfred A. Knopf, 1981), p. 263.
8. For an interesting discussion of various explanations of the events of May 1969, see Bernard E. Brown, *Protest in Paris: Anatomy of a Revolt* (Morristown, NJ: General Learning Press, 1974).

9. Raymond Aron, *The Elusive Revolution: Anatomy of a Student Revolt* (New York: Praeger, 1969).
10. Crane Brinton, *The Americans and the French* (Cambridge, MA: Harvard University Press, 1968), p. 45.
11. Mort Rosenblum, *Mission to Civilize: The French Way* (New York: Harcourt Brace Jovanovich, 1986), p. 4.
12. On the Fourth Republic, see Duncan MacRae, Jr., *Parliament, Parties, and Society in France, 1946–1958* (New York: St. Martin's, 1967; and Philip M. Wright, *Crisis and Compromise: Politics in the Fourth Republic* (Garden City, NY: Anchor Books, 1966).
13. See Tony Smith, *The French State in Algeria: 1945–1962* (Ithaca, NY: Cornell University Press, 1978).
14. See John S. Ambler, *Soldiers Against the State: The French Army in Politics* (Garden City, NY: Anchor Books, 1968).
15. See for example, Michel Crozier, *The Stalled Society* (New York: Viking, 1973).
16. See John Ardagh, *France in the 1980s* (Harmondsworth, England: Penguin, 1983).
17. Gilbert Matthieu, "Wage Differentials: A Steady Narrowing Since '68," *The Guardian*, 16 May 1976.
18. *L'Expansion*, 6 May 1983.
19. Malcolm Sawyer, "Income Distribution in OECD Countries," *OECD Economic Outlook: Occasional Studies*, July 1976, pp. 3–36.
20. Jane Marceau, *Class and Status in France: Economic Change and Social Immobility 1945–1977* (London: Oxford University Press, 1977).
21. See Ezra N. Suleiman, *Elites in French Society: The Politics of Survival* (Princeton, NJ: Princeton University Press, 1978).
22. Guy Michelat and Michel Simon, *Classe, religion, et comportement politique* (Paris: Presses de la Fondation Nationale des Sciences Politiques, 1977).
23. A 1985 poll found that only a third of the respondents ever attended mass. SOFRES, *Opinion publique 1986* (Paris: Gallimard, 1986), p. 242.
24. Michael S. Lewis-Beck, "France: The Stalled Electorate," in Russell J. Dalton, Scott C. Flanagan, and Paul Allen Beck, eds., *Electoral Change in Advanced Industrial Democracies: Realignment or Dealignment?* (Princeton, NJ: Princeton University Press, 1984).
25. Rosenblum, *Mission to Civilize*, p. 60.
26. Frank L. Wilson, "When Parties Refuse to Fail: The Case of France," in Kay Lawson and Peter Merkl, eds., *When Parties Fail* (Princeton, NJ: Princeton University Press, 1988).
27. Gary P. Freeman, *Immigrant Labor and Racial Conflict in Industrial Conflict: The French and British Experience 1945–1975* (Princeton, NJ: Princeton University Press, 1979), pp. 259–280.
28. Tensions were particularly high in areas where large numbers of the French settlers, expelled from Algeria after that country's independence had congregated.
29. Raymond Levy, "Industrial Policy and the Steel Industry," in William J. Adams and Christian Stoffaes, eds., *French Industrial Policy* (Washington, DC: Brookings, 1986), p. 63.

CHAPTER SEVEN
FRENCH CITIZENS
AND POLITICS

> Undisciplined by temperament, the Frenchman is always readier to put up with the arbitrary rule, however harsh, of an autocrat than with a free well-ordered government by his fellow citizens, however worthy of respect they be. At one moment, he is up in arms against authority and the next we find him serving the powers-that-be with a zeal such as the most servile races never display. So long as no one thinks of resisting, you can lead him on a thread, but once a revolutionary movement is afoot, nothing can restrain him from taking part in it.[1]

These words, penned by Alexis de Tocqueville over a century ago, have been cited by countless observers of French politics to explain the cycle of submission followed by mass revolt. De Tocqueville helps explain the volatility of French politics which is periodically upset by unexpected mass strikes or demonstrations that seem to threaten the very existence of the regime. The reminder of the ever-present threat of popular uprising, accurately warns of that unpredictable element in French political life. But the passivity that de Tocqueville attributed to French citizens may no longer describe the nature of citizen political involvement.

A "DELINQUENT COMMUNITY"?

Political scientists and historians have stressed the importance of Britain's deferential political culture of the nineteenth century in the development of its stable democracy. The same analysts then blame the political turmoil in France on its much different set of political attitudes and values. Unlike the British who trusted their public authorities, the French held those with power in suspicion. Alain, a popular political theorist, early in this century, urged his fellow citizens to build barriers daily to impede the exercise of authority. For him and other like-minded French citizens, this drastic conduct was the only means to preserve liberty. This inherent mistrust of any authority may explain why the French are usually among the least likely to express satisfaction with the way democracy works in their country. (See Table 7.1.) This resistance to authority produces a "delinquent community" in which citizens fail to fulfill normal civic responsibilities. One indication of this has been the exceptionally high rate of income tax evasion in France; as recently as 1977, less than six out of ten households paid any income tax at all.[2]

There is also great ambivalence about political participation that derives, paradoxically, from ardent attachment to personal political liberty. The French recognize that to participate is to lose one's freedom.

> It means abandoning the normally comfortable sheltered position of the critic; it means running the risks of emotional commitment; it means submitting to the constraints of someone else, to the group or unit in whose decision-making process one participates.[3]

They fear the constrictions placed on their own conduct by face to face democratic bargaining. They prefer decisions to be made at a higher level and to maintain their right to oppose those decisions. They are disinclined to participate in civic affairs because they fear that their own conduct will be controlled by those with whom they participate. On the other hand, a strong commitment to political equality leads them to oppose the participation of their peers since that would give the others more say and threaten their equal status. The result is a preference for decisions to be made by clearly superior and aloof figures whose authority they can periodically challenge through revolt.

A recent illustration of this paradox came in the bitter and long railroad strike of 1987. One of the points hindering settlement was the government's intention of giving control over merit raises to local managers,

TABLE 7.1 Satisfaction With Democracy, 1987

Percent indicating satisfaction with the way democracy works in their country

	Very Satisfied	Fairly Satisfied	Not Very Satisfied	Not At All Satisfied	No Response
Britain	11%	45%	27%	13%	4%
France	3	39	34	15	9
Germany	6	62	25	4	3
Italy	2	24	46	26	2
Average for 12 European countries	7	44	31	13	5

Source: *Eurobarometer*, No. 28 (December 1987): B13–B23.

who would act on the basis of reports from boards that would include union representatives. The workers preferred that raises be accorded from above, even if based solely on seniority, rather than have the decisions made at this lower level despite their union participation.

Notwithstanding their peculiar attitudes toward authority, the French are much like other European people in terms of their distribution on a Left/Right political spectrum. The presence of a prominent Communist party and an equally powerful party of the extreme Right does not affect the basically centrist orientation of the overwhelming majority of French voters.

A common view of the French includes the notion of a people highly attached to sharply opposed ideologies. In fact, historians now question this view of an ideologically divided country as one that is old and belongs in the past.[4] The French now appear to be disinterested in ideologies and are pragmatic in their approach to political and social issues. There is growing evidence that the general public has developed a broad consensus on the major sociopolitical questions that once seemed to divide the French: the constitutional framework, role of government in society, church/state relations, and foreign and defense policies. Political leaders have been slow to acknowledge the depth of this popular consensus. Even as they act pragmatically when in office, they still employ the ideological shibboleths of the past. The result is that most French voters feel that their party leaders use a vocabulary out of touch with the modern world.[5]

THE INDIVIDUAL CITIZEN IN POLITICS

Foreign visitors in France often come away with the impression that the French are very highly politicized. They see political posters everywhere, slogans painted on buildings, and frequent street demonstrations. Despite

FIGURE 7.1   The Self-Placement of French Voters on a Left/Right Specturm. *Source: Jacques-René Rabier, Hélène Riffault, Ronald Inglehart, Eurobarometer 23: The European Currency Unit and Working Conditions, April 1985* (Ann Arbor, MI: Inter-University Consortium for Political and Social Research) 1986, pp. 81–82.

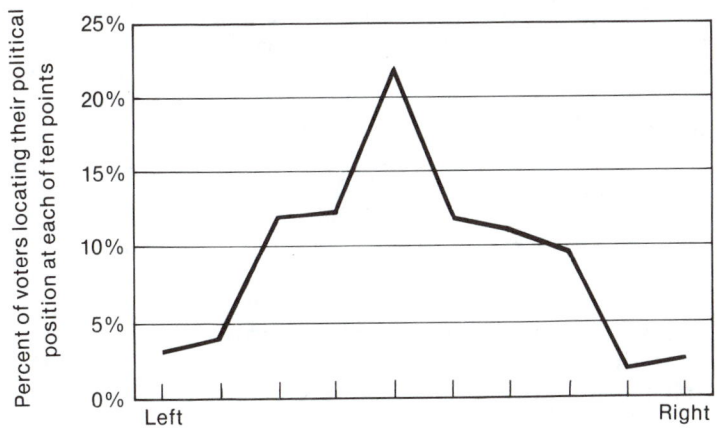

such visible indications of great political activity, the French are no more interested in politics than people in other Western democracies. In 1985 with an important election only six months away, only 16 percent claimed to be very interested in politics, 44 percent a little interested, 23 percent very little interested, and 16 percent not at all interested.[6] Another poll found that 28 percent of the French admit to never reading the political news in their daily papers, a higher percentage than in any other European country.[7] There are other sources of political news than the newspapers, of course, but many French ignore political coverage on television and in magazines as well.

For those who are interested in political involvement, the forms of possible action vary greatly. The range includes joining a political party or interest group, participating in political meetings or rallies, taking part in political demonstrations, standing as a candidate for elective office, and so forth. In France, there is an unusually large number of opportunities to serve in elected offices. There are many small communities, each with its own elected municipal council, providing some four hundred seventy thousand local elected offices. (In contrast, in Britain, there are only about twenty-four thousand municipal councilors.) With so many positions, about fourteen people out of every 1000 voters serve in an elected capacity and at least twice that number run for public offices every six years.

Parties actively recruit citizens in their ranks for sustained political activity. The French notion of party membership is more than the simple self-identification with a party that Americans claim as either Democrats or Republicans. Party membership in France involves paying regular dues, attending meetings, and propagating the party's ideals through distributing tracts, putting up posters, and organizing rallies. For these reasons, the French refer to their rank-and-file party members as *militants,* not because of their radicalism but because of their active commitment to their parties. Party membership is very low. Party membership claims are always inflated but even if we accept these figures, the total number does not exceed three million party members. The number of even partially active party members is less than half the claimed membership.

Many French citizens get sporadically involved in politics as they feel their interests endangered and therefore mobilize to fight for a certain cause. Residents in an area where the government proposes to build a nuclear energy plant may become deeply involved in the political battles over location and safety measures. Parents may mobilize to urge the installation of traffic lights to protect children on their way to school. University students, concerned about the lack of employment prospects, may organize to demand governmental action to create new jobs.

These movements are usually ad hoc in that they produce their own temporary organization rather than develop out of existing political groups or parties. They are protesting government action or inaction they feel seriously damages their immediate interests. There are some problems with this kind of specific, issue-related political participation. These protests may lead to confrontation and violence, as has happened with citizens' efforts to block the construction of nuclear plants. Furthermore, when the government decision goes against the small interest groups that are mobilized, as it must from time to time since these groups represent only a section of the population and not the general interest, the participants are disillusioned, embittered, and unwilling to trust "democratic procedures" in the future. In contrast to members of established groups with many battles to fight, these citizens have fought for a single issue and lost; they do not look to the future for satisfactory results from their participation.

Protest Politics

Earlier noted was a recent trend toward protest politics in Britain. In France, however, protest politics has always been the norm, not the exception.[8] The Events of May 1968, are the most vivid, recent manifestation of a long tradition of spontaneous protest and revolt. In addition to major revolutionary or near-revolutionary actions, there have been numerous less spectacular but nevertheless disruptive protests. Indeed, there has rarely been a period in French history when some spontaneous or organized protest was not underway. At times there appear to be few French citizens who are not protesting in one way or another. It is not that protest is the only form of political action, but it is one that is frequently adopted. As one French observer noted, his fellow citizens have "a begging bowl in one hand and a Molotov cocktail in the other."[9]

In comparison with other Europeans, the French are more likely to engage in political demonstrations. Farmers spread wet manure on freeway curves; workers occupy their plants; truckers clog narrow downtown streets; shop owners shutter their stores to show hostility to visiting government officials. The frequency of such protest politics has robbed them of their shock effect that demonstrations have had in the usually more placid Britain or Germany. While such street politics lead to concerns about the health of democracy in these other countries, in France they are viewed as ordinary and expected developments. And the French have proved more adept in controlling them through a "feather quilt strategy"[10] that absorbs blows from discontented elements even when these protests involve some violence.

TABLE 7.2 Attributes of a Good Citizen

Percent selecting the following as part of their ideal of a good citizen (multiple answers were allowed):

Respects the rules	59%
Minds his business without making an issue	31
Raises his children well	50
Pays taxes without cheating	31
Votes regularly	43
Seeks to be informed about the life of the country	57
Joins a union	7
Joins a party	3
No opinion	2

Source: *L'Expansion*, 6 May 1983.

With an experienced police force and a public that expects such events, the government rarely is forced to concede to the demonstrators anything more than a few symbolic gestures.

Despite this propensity for protest, the French are no more interested in revolutionary change than any other European people. Table 7.4 shows that only a small percentage of French respondents would like to radically change the whole way society is organized through revolutionary action; most prefer some change through gradual reform. The French profile on this issue is very near the average for twelve European countries.

VOTING

Voting is the only political act for the vast majority of French citizens. All citizens eighteen years and older are eligible to vote. Election turnout is generally quite high with 80 percent or more customarily voting in national elections. This is slightly higher than the participation rates in Britain and much higher than voter turnout in the United States. The high turnout in France is facilitated by automatic registration, with annual revisions to keep the lists of voters current, and by holding elections on Sundays when voters have all day to make it to the polls.

French citizens have frequent opportunities to go to the polls (See Table 7.5) but each time they make only a single decision: a vote for a presidential candidate in presidential elections, a vote for a deputy in

TABLE 7.3 Participation in Political Demonstrations

Percent reporting participation in a demonstration in the previous four years:

Britain	9.6%
France	20.2
West Germany	11.9
Italy	18.0

Source: Jacques-René Rabier, Hélène Riffault, Ronald Inglehart, *Eurobarometer 21: Political Cleavages in the European Community, April 1984* (Ann Arbor, MI: Inter-University Consortium for Political and Social Research, 1985): 16–17.

TABLE 7.4 Attitude Toward Social Change, 1986

	Revolutionary Change	Gradual Reforms	Defense Against Subversion
Britain	5%	71%	24%
France	6	65	29
West Germany	3	56	41
Italy	8	65	27
Average for 12 European countries	5	67	28

Source: *Eurobarometer*, No. 25 (June 1985): 18.

National Assembly elections held on a different date, and so on. Before the election, each voter receives a packet in the mail that includes a statement from each candidate and slips of paper. Each slip, with a candidate's name on it, serves as the actual ballot. Voting is secret with booths available.

The presidential and National Assembly elections are the two most important because they determine who controls national politics. The president is elected for a seven-year term in a direct election. If no candidate receives an absolute majority, a run-off election is held two weeks later between the two leading candidates. The 577 deputies in the National Assembly are elected for five-year terms. There has been controversy surrounding the rules for organizing these elections; when in 1985, the Socialist government of the time introduced a system of proportional representation (PR) for National Assembly elections. Under this system, there were multi-member districts varying between two and twenty-one deputies according to the size of their population. Instead of one candidate, each party proposed a list of several candidates. (This system will be explained more fully in the sections on West Germany and Italy where proportional representation remains the means of selecting deputies.)

After the conservative victory in 1986, a two ballot majority system was readopted. Under the present electoral laws, it takes an absolute majority of votes to win on the first ballot. Having a majority occurs in

TABLE 7.5   Elections in France

TYPE	FREQUENCY	ELECTING BODY
National elections:		
Presidential	7-year terms	Entire electorate
National Assembly	5-year terms	Entire electorate
Senate	⅓ elected every 3 years for 9-year terms	Electoral college of 104,000 locally- and nationally-elected officials
Referendum	At initiative of the president (6 since 1958)	Entire electorate
Local elections:		
Regional councils	6-year terms	Entire electorate
General councils	½ elected every 3 years for 6-year terms	Entire electorate
Municipal councils	6-year terms	Entire electorate
Mayors	6-year terms	Municipal councilors in each town

Source: Rolf H. W. Theen and Frank L. Wilson, *Comparative Politics: An Introduction to Six Countries* (Englewood Cliffs, NJ: Prentice Hall, 1986), p. 159. Reprinted with permission.

about a third of the districts. If no candidate has a majority, a runoff is held one week later. All candidates with fewer than 15 percent of the registered vote (or about 18 to 20 percent of the votes cast) on the first ballot are eliminated; other candidates may withdraw. In most cases, the second ballot involves a duel between the strongest candidate on the Right and the strongest candidate on the Left. In those unusual cases where more than two candidates are present on the second ballot, a simple plurality is sufficient for election. An example from a recent election will illustrate.

FIRST BALLOT		SECOND BALLOT
Republican candidate	29%	49%
Socialist candidate	29	51 *Elected*
Communist candidate	17	Withdrew, supported Socialist
Gaullist candidate	15	Eliminated, supported Republican
Eight other candidates	10	All eliminated

This two ballot system has won wide support among the general public. It is relatively straightforward and easy to understand. Its runoff procedures encourage similar parties to coalesce and reduce the political impact of marginal or extremist parties. It also facilitates the winning of solid parliamentary majorities to support government coalitions. But, as with Britain's plurality system, it leads to distortions of the public's support. A comparison of the results from the 1986 election under proportional representation with computer projections on the outcome of the same election using the two ballot majority system illustrates the tendency to exaggerate the strength of the largest coalition and to reduce the representation of extremist parties (see Table 7.6). After the return to the two-ballot majority system for the 1988 National Assembly elections, the representation of these extremist parties was sharply reduced: The Communists went up in percentage of total vote (to 11.3 percent) but elected only twenty-seven deputies; The far right National Front had a comparable percentage of the vote (9.8 percent) but elected only a single deputy.

The Socialists had adopted proportional representation in 1985 as their popularity waned in an unsuccessful effort to stem their party's losses.

TABLE 7.6   Effects of Alternative Electoral Systems in France

Party	1986 % of vote	Actual seats won in 1986	% of seats in National Assembly	Projected seats under 2 ballot system	Projected % of seats in Assembly with 2 ballots
Communists	9.78%	35	6.3%	14	2.5%
Socialists	31.72	211	38.0	129	23.2
Guallists and Giscardians	40.98	277	49.9	404	72.8
National Front	9.65	35	6.3	8	1.4

Source: Projected electoral outcome from SOFRES, reported in *Le Monde*, 9 October 1986, p. 8.

When the conservatives returned to the 2 ballot system in 1986 it was, at least in part, to assist them in fending off threats from the far Right. Indeed, there is a long history of changing the electoral rules in France with the party in power trying, often unsuccessfully, to rig the system to help them stay in power. Thus, between 1871 and 1988, there have been eleven different electoral systems for thirty-six national legislative elections. Such manipulations of the basic procedures of democracy do little to build citizen confidence.

As in Britain and other western democracies, voters appear more willing to shift their voting preferences from one election to the next. In 1981, the Left won the parliamentary election with 55 percent of the vote but by 1986 it lost with only 45 percent. By the 1988 presidential election, the leftwing candidate took 54 percent of the vote in the run-off ballot. But a few weeks later, the Left took only 49 percent of the National Assembly election vote. These are dramatic shifts in voter loyalties over short periods of time that suggest considerable voter volatility. These shifts also reflect a growing willingness of the voters to sanction a government that fails to please. It is only in the last fifteen years that voters have come to see the left-wing parties as an acceptable and viable alternative government. Before that, the Right ruled almost unchallenged because of voters' fears of the Communists, and the Left's inability to maintain a stable coalition majority made it an unattractive option. The 1981 Socialist victory and continued decline of the Communists now give French voters clear and credible alternatives at the polls.

Voting in France appears to be more influenced by personality factors than is the case in Britain. Presidential elections are largely personal clashes between very prominent figures who often distance themselves from their parties during the campaign. Even in legislative elections, the personality of the president may have important effects. When Charles de Gaulle was president, most voters claimed to base their decision to vote in legislative elections on the candidate's support or opposition to de Gaulle. More recently, François Mitterrand's popularity spilled over to the Socialist party in general. A Socialist National Assembly majority was elected in 1981 and a large Socialist plurality in 1988 due to voters' desires to support Mitterrand.

WOMEN IN POLITICS

In France, traditional femininity, not feminism has been the rule.[11] There was no counterpart of the British suffragette struggle, and the right to vote was not granted to women until 1945. Even then, female suffrage came about not in response to demands by women but as one of the Liberation reforms promulgated by the Provisional Government of General de Gaulle. Similarly, equal rights for wives *vis-à-vis* their husbands were only achieved recently. Until 1965 women needed their husband's permission to apply for passports, to open bank accounts, or to conduct other financial affairs. In divorce cases, infidelity on the part of the wife was much more readily accepted as grounds for divorce than was identical behavior by the husband. These inequities have now disappeared from the legal codes but the behavioral and attitudinal patterns are slow in disappearing.

Since their enfranchisement, French women continue to play a much less important part in politics than do men. Women first held junior minister posts in the Popular Front government of 1936, before they even had the right to vote. However, the number of women in the government has never been large. There have been a total of only fourteen women who have held full cabinet-rank portfolios; thirteen of them have served since 1974. The National Assembly elected in 1981 included twenty-eight women (5.7 percent), the highest share of women deputies ever. The number of women deputies rose to thirty-three after the 1986 elections but the percentage remained the same (5.7 percent) since the size of the assembly had increased. There are 1,445 women mayors, but this is out of a total of over 36,000, or only 4.0 percent. The percentage of women municipal councilors is somewhat higher with 14.1 percent of the nearly half-million positions. (See Table 7.7.)

The scarcity of women in elected positions is due to the infrequency with which they are nominated to elected office by major parties. In 1978, women made up 15.9 percent of the candidates in the National Assembly elections, more than twice the proportion in any previous election. Many of these women candidates were presented by minor parties with no chance

TABLE 7.7 Women in Elected Positions in France, 1947–1985

Women as a percentage of elected officials:[a]

	1946	1956	1967	1978	1985
Deputies in National Assembly	5.4%	3.1%	2.2%	3.7%	5.7%
Senators	3.6	1.9	1.8[b]	1.4	2.8
Department General Councilors	n.a.[c]	0.8[d]	2.3	2.3	4.5
Mayors	0.7[e]	1.0[f]	1.8[g]	2.3	4.0
Municipal Councilors	3.1[e]	2.4[f]	4.4[g]	8.3	14.0
European Parliament[h]					21.0

Notes:
[a] In the mid-1980's, women made up approximately 52% of the electorate.
[b] 1962 figure.
[c] Not available.
[d] 1958 figure.
[e] 1947 figures.
[f] 1959 figures.
[g] 1971 figures.
[h] The first election for the European Parliament was in 1979.

of electing anyone. Only 6.8 percent of the major party candidates were women, and they often ran in districts where their party had no chance of winning. To encourage greater political opportunity for women, a 1979 law established a quota of at least 20 percent of women candidates for each party in municipal elections. The Constitutional Council ruled this illegal but most parties accepted the quota as a target for the 1983 municipal elections.

There are counterparts to the American women's liberation movement in France, but they have won neither the influence nor the following the American movement has received. Women's movements in France have encountered several difficulties. Organizing women for joint action has been hampered by the lack of a tradition of women's clubs or sororities, which provided American, and to a lesser extent, British women with a sense of solidarity. Those women's groups that have emerged in France have had limited appeal due to their association with particular political currents, usually on the far Left. In addition, traditional values of women's roles in the home and community are still well established, and change is resisted by the women themselves. Indeed, 85 percent of French women declare themselves to be completely against joining any feminist movement, a higher percentage than in any other European country in the ten-nation poll.[12]

There is little evidence to suggest that the small number of women in politics is due to systematic political discrimination. Opinion surveys suggest that French public acceptance of women in politics is among the highest in Europe.[13] Other polls indicate that voters are as willing to vote for a woman candidate as for a man. The nature of social organization, however, limits the role of women in society as a whole, not just politics. Political activity is a luxury requiring time commitments away from the home or job that many French women simply cannot afford. Women are rarely found in the liberal professions or leadership positions in business or industry that permit free time for politics. Instead, they are occupied with household activities, childbearing, or outside jobs that give little spare time for political activities.

Very recently, growing numbers of women have been rebelling against these traditional roles, insisting upon recognition of their rights to political and social involvement on an equal footing with men. There is still a tendency for men to express more interest in politics than do women but this gender gap is declining. Recent studies show that French women define their political opinions independently and do not conform to the usual stereotype of simply following the beliefs of their husbands or fathers.[14] They are seeing major increases in their involvement in elected and appointed public offices. The growing importance of women in politics is evidenced by the fact that even when the conservative parties held power, the government pushed through a liberalized abortion law despite the opposition of the Catholic hierarchy in a still heavily Catholic country.

PARTICIPATION AND STABILITY

Many anxious observers of Western democracy have fretted over too much citizen participation, especially the growing tendency of citizens to engage in street politics. The fears are dual. Excessive political action is seen as overwhelming democratic procedures and as provoking backlash limitations that might curtail essential freedoms. The French case suggests that high levels of participation are not necessarily destabilizing, nor is unconventional participation automatically unsettling to democratic stability. French politics have always been more tumultuous than elsewhere, and yet, the Fifth Republic stands as one of the strongest and most effective political systems in postwar Europe. There is still the latent danger of a revolt coming from an attractive and romantic tradition of periodic rebellion. But the system has learned to adjust to these strains without serious threats to stability or democratic practices.

NOTES

1. Alexis de Tocqueville, *The Old Regime and the French Revolution*, trans. Stuart Gilbert (Garden City, NJ: Doubleday, 1955), pp. 210–211.
2. *L'Economie*, 9 July 1979, p. 6.
3. Michel Crozier, *The Stalled Society*, trans. Rupert Swyer (New York: Viking, 1973), p. 67.
4. See for example, Theodore Zeldin, *France 1848–1945: Politics and Anger* (London: Oxford University Press, 1979).
5. For example, a 1984 poll found that only a third of respondents believed that the political discourse was up to date. SOFRES, *Opinion publique 1985* (Paris: Gallimard, 1985), p. 22.
6. SOFRES, *Opinion publique 1986* (Paris: Gallimard, 1986), p. 241.
7. *Eurobarometer*, 19 (June 1983): 47.
8. See Charles Tilly, *The Contentious French* (Cambridge, MA: Harvard University Press, 1986) and Jack Hayward, "Dissentient France: The Counter-Political Culture," *West European Politics* 1(October 1978): 53–67.
9. Maurice Druon, cited by Alain Peyrefitte, *The Trouble With France* (New York: Knopf, 1981), p. 248.
10. Suzanne Berger, *Peasants Against Politics* (Cambridge, MA: Harvard University Press, 1972), pp. 237–38.
11. See John Ardagh, *France in the 1980s* (Harmondsworth, England: Penguin, 1983), pp. 347–367.
12. Commission of the European Communities, *European Women and Men in 1983* (Brussels: European Commission, 1983), p. 47.
13. Ibid.
14. Monica Charlot, "Women in Politics in France," in Howard Penniman, ed., *The French National Assembly Elections of 1978* (Washington, DC: American Enterprise Institute, 1980). See also Janine Mossuz-Lavau and Mariette Sineau, *Enquete sur les femmes et la politique en France* (Paris: Presses Universitaires de France, 1983).

CHAPTER EIGHT
FRENCH POLITICAL PARTIES AND INTEREST GROUPS

Recently, two teams of archaeologists were conducting separate digs within a few yards of each other in front of the Louvre in Paris. One team was headed by a conservative archaeologist, the other by a socialist. Far from cooperating in their research, the two sides engaged in vituperative exchanges that reached not only the French national media but also the international press. Each team denied the legitimacy of the other's academic credentials. Each accused the other of improper research methods and of conducting their project in such a way as to ruin future research of a more reliable nature. They decried each other's research objectives as misguided and worthless, and claimed that the rival team distorted its findings in accord with its preconceptions. Laced through their exchanges and clearly underlying the rancor were their different political orientations.

This battle and other similar clashes are not isolated incidents but examples of an apparently polarized society. The inability of these scholars to collaborate even in the study of centuries-old archaeological relics suggests the intensity of continuing political divisions in France. There is little support from the general public for such quarrels. As noted in Chapter seven, there is a broad and growing consensus among the general population on once divisive social and political questions. But among the political elites, the old passions prevail and give a distinctive color to French party politics and interest group politics.

POLITICAL PARTIES

In contrast to the relatively simple, two-party system in Britain, France has always had many parties clamoring for public support. De Gaulle once explained this extreme pluralism was only normal and expected in a country that prides itself on over 200 varieties of cheese. Indeed, the strong individualism of the French makes it natural for there to be so many different parties.

While there are still many parties in French politics, the number of politically relevant parties has shrunk to only four or five. The popular election of the president and the increased power of that office has led the party system to focus on prominent presidential candidates. A party without a credible presidential candidate faces real difficulties to convince voters that it is a serious political option. The electoral system with its second ballot run-off rule has made it difficult for smaller parties to survive. It has also encouraged the development of two broad coalitions: one on the Left and the other on the Right. Table 8.1 lists the major parties and their electoral strength in recent elections.[1]

French parties have usually been more ideological than their counterparts in other European countries. Ideas and abstract ideologies have long preoccupied French politicians of all persuasions. The Socialists debate regularly on ideology and issue lengthy statements of party doctrine that

TABLE 8.1   Political Parties in France

Percentage of vote in National Assembly Elections

	1978	1981	1986	1988
The Left				
Communists (PCF)	20.6%	16.2%	9.7%	11.3%
Socialists (PS)	22.6	37.5	31.6	37.5
Left-wing Radicals (MRG)	3.3		0.3	
Various leftists	6.2	1.9	2.4	0.3
Total for Left:	52.7	55.6	44.0	49.1
The Center-Right				
Gaullists (RPR)	22.6%	20.8%	41.0	40.4
Union for French Democracy(UDF)	21.5	19.2		
Various rightists	2.4	2.8	3.8	0.6
Far Right				
National Front (FN)	nil	0.4	9.8	9.8
Total for Right:	46.5	43.2	54.6	50.8

go unread by all but the most devoted party militants. They continue to use the rhetoric of class conflict in their political appeals when Socialist parties in most other countries have changed to more contemporary themes. Conservatives are also concerned with ideology. The Rally for the Republic discusses at length the meaning of Gaullism and the UDF Valery Giscard d'Estaing took time out from his duties as president of the republic to write a book on neoliberalism.[2]

Most of the general public takes little notice of these ideologies. Public disinterest and even hostility to abstract party doctrine have led the parties to move toward more pragmatism in word as well as deed. By the end of the 1980s, all parties, save the Communists, have decreased their attention to doctrinal discussions in favor of more issue-related and concrete policy proposals.

At the beginning of the 1980s, the distance between the French parties appeared to be great. The Left offered an entirely different vision of how society should be organized and spoke of the need to overthrow monopoly capitalism and to establish a genuine socialist society. However, Socialist leaders learned the limits of change while in office between 1981 and 1986. The crusading neoconservativism of the Center-Right has also been tempered by its experience in office between 1986 and 1988. Now, the policy options between Left and Right no longer appear to be entirely different social orders but simple differences in emphasis and details.

Despite the decline in the ideological distance separating major parties, there remains significant polarization. While not as easily measured, French parties are polarized from each other by psychological distance in the form of intense rivalries that are not rooted in different ideologies or issue differences. In part, this polarization comes out of the institutional conflict of two powerful political blocs. It also reflects a style of political dialogue and conflict that is filled with intemperate language. A conservative politician warned President Mitterrand what would happen when his coalition won a majority in the National Assembly.

> To François Mitterrand we say ahead of time: we will cut off your telephone, water, gas, and electricity and we will govern immediately and without sharing power.[3]

In fact, the cohabitation of a socialist president and conservative parliament and government after 1986 was tense but it took place more smoothly than the quoted politician had hoped.

Such intense political expression is commonplace in French politics. As one observer noted, French politicians use a vocabulary "charged with verbal violence."

> Even when they are basically gentle, like Raspail, they employ words which have an odor of powder, they create disquiet and animosities, and despite themselves they prepare for the bloody shocks of counterrevolution.[4]

The consequence has been a

> national nightmare: the confrontation of two irreducible blocs of almost equal strength, each struggling to become monolithic. Two sectarian forces ostracizing each other: a domestic cold war.[5]

This polarized dualism has prevailed since the early 1960s with a dogmatic Left and a principled Center-Right confronting each other as enemies, not just political rivals, in elections, in parliament, and in local politics.

There are some signs that this polarization may be diminishing. The cooperation of a Socialist president and a Conservative prime minister and parliament between 1986 and 1988 proved that these polarized political forces can work together when constrained to do so. Then, after the 1988 elections, a new centrist political force emerged vowing to try to work with both ends of the political spectrum. The Union of the Center (UDC) attracted about forty deputies. The prospects of the new UDC are uncertain; previous centrist groups were unsuccessful at the polls and merged with the rightwing parties. Furthermore, the reduction in psychological polarization will require much time and perhaps a new generation of political leaders.

The Gaullists

The Rally for the Republic (RPR) is the current name for the political party organized in 1958 to assemble supporters for Charles de Gaulle and his newly created Fifth Republic.[6] The Gaullist legacy includes a loyalty to the institutions of the Fifth Republic, as established by de Gaulle; national independence in foreign, defense, and economic policies; a nationalist element expressed in resistance to any threats to French national sovereignty coming from the United States or efforts to further European unification; a commitment to maintain at least on a symbolic level France's pretense of being a world power; and "participation," a vague ideal of involving citizens in making the political, social, and economic decisions that affect their lives.

The Gaullist philosophy makes it difficult to place the party on a Left-Right political spectrum. On the one hand, the Gaullists support political options traditionally associated with the Right: anticommunism, strong executive power, independent military strength, and French nationalism. And they draw support from social groups usually aligned with the Right: the middle class, faithful Catholics, and voters in the west and east of France. On the other hand, the Gaullists are committed to a modernist philosophy of change and adaptation alien to the traditional Right. During the Fifth Republic, the Gaullists: completed decolonization; enacted major university, agricultural, and economic reforms; pushed economic modernization against the vested interests of small businesses; installed new mechanisms for government direction of the economy; and pressed for fundamental changes in the free enterprise system to provide for the "association" and "participation" of workers in the profits and decisions of industry.

In the last decade, the RPR has moved more to the right of traditional Gaullist positions. The party has picked up Thatcher and Reagan's neo-liberal call for less government economic meddling and for more free market direction to the economy. It has worked for privatizing the public enterprises that were nationalized, not only by the Socialists in 1981, but also those firms nationalized by de Gaulle in 1945. Faced with competition from a powerful extreme right party, the Gaullists have also become more strident on the issue of law and order. Interest in social and economic reform has declined as many RPR leaders fear the disruptive effects of such changes on the social fabric of a country as unpredictable as France. The areas of greatest continuity with Gaullist traditions are in loyalty to the Fifth Republic political institutions and in foreign and defense policies. But these areas are now of general consensus that even leftwing parties accept. There have been subtle changes in foreign and defense viewpoints, notably a warmer attitude toward the United States and toward European unification.

The Gaullist movement is remarkably cohesive and well disciplined compared to other conservative political movements, past or present, in France. But within the party there are important differences over tone and some policies. The main difference is how to position the RPR in order to counter the electoral threat of the far-Right National Front. Some want the RPR to take a harder line on immigration and law and order so to win back the voters attracted by the National Front's exploitation of these issues. Others steadfastly insist on a more tolerant stand and oppose any alignment of the RPR with the National Front in local or regional politics.

The RPR is led by Jacques Chirac. Chirac has served as prime minister from 1974 to 1976 and again from 1986 to 1988. He is also mayor of Paris. He ran for the presidency unsuccessfully in 1981 and 1988. An ambitious and pragmatic politician, Chirac had demonstrated willingness to exert important government control over the economy but now espouses a staunch free market philosophy. His skills in party organization were demonstrated by his rebuilding the RPR after the party lost the presidency in 1974 and going into opposition when the Socialists won a National Assembly majority in 1981. Under his direction, the party took advantage of its period in opposition between 1981 and 1986 to largely renew its leadership ranks. These new leaders are loyal to Chirac and they also give the party a fresher and more youthful look than the other rightwing parties.

The Gaullist RPR claims over eight hundred thousand members. It stands in sharp contrast to the traditional conservative parties of France in the strength of its organization and the loyalty of its members. It can and has mobilized hundreds of thousands of party faithful to conduct elections and to take to the streets for political demonstrations. While it has seen the emergence of rival conservative parties on its flanks, the RPR remains the largest conservative party in the National Assembly and the dominant force on the Right.

The Union for French Democracy

The Gaullist movement's success in the first fifteen years of the Fifth Republic pushed other conservative and centrist parties to the political sidelines. In the developing rivalry between Gaullists and the Left, these small centrist and conservative parties tried unsuccessfully to be opposed to both. The one exception was the Independent Republican party formed by Valéry Giscard D'Estaing in the mid-1960s. This party, now known as the Republican party (PR), was founded by traditional conservatives who had rallied to de Gaulle but who had refused to affiliate with the Gaullist party. Giscard, de Gaulle's young finance minister, soon dominated the Republican party and it became a vehicle for his political ambitions. In return for their loyalty to de Gaulle, the Republicans were rewarded with important ministries in every government formed during the de Gaulle and Pompidou presidencies (1959 to 1974).

They nevertheless sought to define a separate identity from the Gaullists with the slogan *oui, mais*—"yes, but." Yes, they supported de Gaulle, but they had reservations about certain aspects of his policy agenda. The "buts" included: a stronger attachment to European unification and less hostility toward the United States and the Atlantic Alliance in foreign policy; more commitment to traditional conservative economic viewpoints than the Gaullist zeal for economic modernization; and uneasiness about de Gaulle's aloof and autocratic political style.

In 1974, Giscard defeated a Gaullist rival on the first ballot of the presidential election and went on to win the presidency. His victory was aided by the support of the smaller centrist and conservative parties who had previously avoided supporting the government out of distaste for the Gaullist political style. These parties were little more than the orphaned leaders of parties that had been important under the Fourth Republic but had not been able to survive under the Fifth Republic: the Christian democratic parties, the Radical party, and the sundry conservative personalities.

The Republican party tried to profit from Giscard's election by expanding its membership and by strengthening its party organization. These efforts produced some gains but failed in their ultimate objectives. The Republican party was unable to attract many members and its organization remained essentially the personal followings of local political notables. Giscard tried to enhance his party's reformist image by supporting several social adjustments, notably liberalization of abortion, the 18-year old vote, and some gestures toward consumer and environmental issues.[7] But the party's economic doctrine and basic orientation remained conservative.

The Giscardians also launched a vigorous campaign to become the largest party in the majority coalition by outvoting the Gaullists in the next legislative elections. To this end, the Republican party joined in 1978 with the smaller centrist and conservative parties in the Union for French

Democracy (UDF).[8] The Giscardian movement succeeded in nearly equalling the RPR vote in the 1978 elections but still fell short of matching the Gaullist parliamentary group in the National Assembly.[9] In addition, the frontal attack on the RPR soured relations between the two allied movements and ultimately contributed to Giscard's defeat when he ran for reelection in 1981.

The UDF remained a fragile coalition of weak parties. None of the parties in the UDF had a significant party organization; all were centered on a few key personalities. The various parties were concerned with maintaining their separate identities and accorded few real powers to the UDF central organization. After the 1981 defeat, internal disunion increased. Giscard still harbored hopes of another try at winning the presidency but other UDF leaders were interested in distancing the movement from its defeated leader. Raymond Barre, Giscard's prime minister from 1976 to 1981, was interested in building his own political base in the UDF and the Republican party for a run at the presidency. And a third presidential hopeful, François Léotard, tried to build support within the Republican party and the UDF.

It was once correct to talk of the UDF as the "Giscardian" movement because of its support for Giscard d'Estaing. But now the UDF is divided among older "Giscardians," ambitious "Barrists," and a growing number of "Léotardians." Since 1986, Léotard has become the leading figure in the Republican party. His support for the Gaullist prime minister Jacques Chirac won him a prominent ministry and other ministries for his PR and UDF supporters. But Barre was the more popular potential presidential candidate in preelection polls and developed a body of supporters within the UDF. Giscard's influence is on the wane but he still retains influence in the UDF as do several other older leaders. Policy differences among these leaders are small or nonexistent, but their ambition for high office pits them against each other. As these multiple leaders have jockeyed for position and appealed for support, they have divided and weakened the UDF and the Republican party.

The Right-Center Coalition

The Gaullists and their allies have dominated French politics since 1958 with the brief exception of the Socialist governments from 1981 to 1986 and since 1988. So enduring has been their control, that even after the 1981 Socialist victory, the press still wrote of the Gaullists and Giscardians as the "ex-majority." Within this coalition, the Gaullists have continued to be the "majority of the majority" despite the efforts of their allies to combine against them. Beyond the broader electoral support for the Gaullists, the RPR has the additional advantage of a strong party organization and mass membership.

While there are some slight nuances in policy positions between Gaullists and their partners, the electoral bases are the same. The same voters will support a Gaullist, a Giscardian, or another majority candidate depending upon which one happens to be running in their district. When there are two rightwing candidates on the first ballot, voters appear to make their choice on the basis of personality and style rather than substantive issue differences.

Despite regular internal clashes and personal rivalries, the Gaullist-Giscardian coalition has remained remarkably cohesive. It has permitted the same parties to dominate politics for twenty-five years despite occasional tensions. Relations between the two groups were at their worst in the late 1970s as a result of the Giscardian effort to challenge Gaullist hegemony. The Gaullists quite naturally reacted and clashed publicly with their ally in parliament and in election campaigns. The bitterness from this conflict contributed to Giscard's defeat in the 1981 presidential elections. The long campaign featured sharp competition for the first ballot contest between several candidates from the Gaullist-Giscardian coalition, and a Communist and a Socialist seeking the vote of the Left. The resulting contests on both the Left and the Right resembled a tennis doubles match in which the players seemed more interested in hitting their partners with the ball—or even with their racquets—rather than scoring points against the opposing side. In any case, when Giscard won the right to represent the coalition on the second ballot, many Gaullists calculated that they would do better with a Socialist president than risk another seven years of Giscard using the presidency to undermine their party. It was the abstention of such Gaullists on their second ballot vote that made the Socialist victory possible in 1981.

Once in opposition, the Gaullists and their allies quickly reforged their unity. It was easier to cooperate in opposing an increasingly unpopular government than to stay unified while fighting each other for ascendancy in the coalition. When these parties returned to government after the 1986 National Assembly elections, their very narrow majority meant that they could not afford internal feuds without the risk of losing power and giving the Socialist president an opportunity to reassert his. Thus, relations between the parties during the period 1986 to 1988 were tense but correct even as competition among three or four aspiring presidential candidates within their ranks began to intensify in preparation for the 1988 presidential election. In the event, the two Right-Center presidential candidates, Jacques Chirac and Raymond Barre, avoided a divisive battle on the first ballot. The parties were able to rally their votes for the second ballot and to unify their campaign for the National Assembly elections that came a month later. After defeats in the presidential election, the UDF and RPR entered a new period of opposition to a Socialist government with few problems to divide them.

The Union of the Center

However, a new political force emerged after the 1988 elections when several UDF politicians formed the Union of the Center (UDC). The UDC was a response to a new political situation created by the 1988 elections that had left no party or coalition with a majority in the National Assembly. Under the leadership of Pierre Mehaignerie, some of the centrists, Radicals, and Barrists from the UDF formed this new parliamentary group in the hope that they might play a key role in providing the needed votes for a parliamentary majority. They hoped to be a force for moderation; they also hoped that their centrist stance would make them likely candidates for ministerial positions in a new center-left government. They saw their new political group as a key pivot party at the center, like the German Free Democratic party, that could ally with either the Left or the Right as political circumstances dictated.

The UDC announced that it would be in opposition to the new Socialist minority government. However, it indicated that its deputies would examine individual bills presented by the government and vote on them according to their assessment of the merits of the legislation rather than on a predetermined partisan basis. When Mitterrand formed a new government under the Socialist Prime Minister Michel Rocard, he included several political leaders close to the UDC. The UDC remained formally in the opposition but it was ready to support the minority government when it felt the government's purposes matched the UDC's goals.

Prior to 1958, centrist forces controlled French politics because of the proliferation of small parties. Under the Fifth Republic, however, there has usually been a clear majority coalition in the National Assembly. The future of the UDC is unclear. First there is a problem establishing an electorate. Voters have been unwilling to support centrist parties in the past. The deputies who joined the UDC were elected on the RPR-UDF label in 1988; it is doubtful that many of them can be re-elected without the support of this coalition. Second, the current importance of the UDC comes from the absence of a majority in the National Assembly. This is the first time since 1962 that this has happened. If the Right-Center or the Left regains a majority in the future, the UDC will likely dissolve as its members return to the Right-Center alliance.

The Socialist Party

The Socialist party (PS) was first founded in 1905, but in many ways, the current party is the creation of François Mitterrand. After years of decline, the Socialist party was revived and redirected after 1972 under his leadership.[10] With new leaders and ideas, he turned the party into a powerful and effective political machine and nearly tripled its electoral strength over the next decade. In 1981, Mitterrand won the presidency and his party won 37.5 percent of the vote and an outright majority in the National Assembly. This was only the second time in five French Republics that a single party had a parliamentary majority of its own. Even after its loss of power in 1986, the PS remained the single party with the largest vote and parliamentary delegation.

Despite these achievements, the PS has been unable to overcome several problems. The party is ridden with factions, each of which has its own leaders, newsletters, and national network of followers.[11] Rivalries among these factions enliven the party but often lead to open divisions at the local and department levels. Its relatively open proceedings expose these divisions to the public more than do perhaps equally serious divisions in the internally less democratic parties of the Right. Its organization lacks the strength and funding of the Gaullist movement. Its rank-and-file members have failed to live up to the standards of militant activism expected by the party.

Until the mid-1980s, the PS stood apart from other European socialist parties because of its attachment to fundamental socialism and to the overthrow of what it saw as an oppressive capitalist society.[12] It continued to use the classic Marxist terminology of class warfare while even the radical elements of other European leftwing parties, such as the leftwing of the British Labour party, shunned that rhetoric as outdated. As recently as 1980, the PS produced a doctrinal statement that was aptly described as "a museum piece, a Marxist delirium in which most of the world's woes were blamed on imperialist exploitation, multinational enterprises, and capitalist contradictions."[13]

Despite its radical stance on social and economic issues, the PS has avoided the pacifist neutralism of the British Labour party and more recently of leftwing elements of the German Social Democrats. French Socialists remain firmly committed to the western alliance; they supported the deployment of new NATO nuclear armaments in the 1980s; they fully back the independent French nuclear weapons and the delivery systems. They support efforts to further unify the European Community. Even while the Socialist government included Communist ministers, it took a more forthright and critical stance on East/West issues than had the preceding conservative government. Indeed, the Socialist years 1981 to 1986 marked the best cooperation between the United States and France since World War II.

The explanation for the French Socialists' lack of support for neutralism is complex. In part, the French Socialists have always taken a strong pro-Western stance in order to differentiate themselves from a powerful Communist rival on their left. In Britain and Germany, the Labour and Social Democrats did not have that need since they faced no serious leftwing party. Paradoxically, support for the French nuclear force has also been a way of asserting independence from the United States which receives backing from all points on the political spectrum. Another aspect is that the doctrinal orthodoxy of the French Socialists made it unnecessary to prove their leftism by adopting a neutralist foreign and defense policy. In Britain and Germany, the leftwing parties embraced neutralism as a way of showing their leftist colors. These parties had conceded the inapplicability of traditional socialist socioeconomic reforms, but they needed a way to differentiate themselves from the center and right; neutralist postures were a way of showing a difference and of demonstrating loyalty to traditional socialist values.

Now, the PS is reevaluating its commitment to socioeconomic changes. When the PS came to power in 1981, it launched an energetic program of socioeconomic reform. The Socialist government nationalized all privately owned French banks and eleven major industrial groups. Social-welfare benefits and minimum wage requirements were immediately increased. Ambitious plans for increasing involvement of workers in plant decision-making were discussed and a modest effort toward this goal was launched in reforms of labor/management relations.[14]

The scope and speed of these changes demonstrated the sincerity of Socialist desires for changing society. But the results were less than expected. By 1983, the Socialist government had begun to slow its changes and back away from some of its earlier practices. At the end of its term in 1986, the economic and social policies of the Socialist government differed little in practice from that of earlier conservative governments. The experience in government appeared to have imbued the Socialist party leaders with a healthy dose of pragmatism and a sense of the real limits of social change in an unsupporting domestic and international setting. Thus, when the Socialists returned to power in 1988, they promised few of the structural reforms they had undertaken in 1981. Instead, the government of Michel Rocard pledged more continuity in the policies of the previous conservative government than change or ideologically driven reform.

The retreat from the party's socialist doctrine has disillusioned many PS activists. Ideological concerns have always been more important among the rank-and-file. As the leaders have become more pragmatic and less concerned with socialist dogma, these party members have fretted quietly. The inclusion of several centrists in the Rocard government in 1988 added to their uneasiness. There is a gap growing between Socialist party leaders, who have become moderate and pragmatic in response to the pressures of a moderate public and the experience of governing, and party activists still committed to a doctrinaire socialism.

Despite this gap, the PS remains strong in potential electoral strength. Its experience has proved to voters that a leftwing government is possible and that it will not result in catastrophe. However, it is a disparate party of many factions held together by the political skill and appeal of Mitterrand. The PS faces important difficulties in the immediate future. The first is the need to develop new leadership. Mitterrand's long dominance of the party and his late decision on entering the 1988 presidential contest made it difficult for other leaders to emerge. Already in his seventies, Mitterrand will soon leave the political scene. His absence will open a struggle among contending Socialist factions for control of the party. The most likely candidate to succeed is Prime Minister Michel Rocard. But while Rocard is popular with the general public, he is suspect in the eyes of many PS activists and the party hierarchy. Whether he can continue Mitterrand's magic in uniting a diverse party is still uncertain. In addition, the need to modify doctrine so it reflects the pragmatic direction of the PS's government practice, will likely cause a difficult period of adjustment. However, the party's growing electoral base and the collapse of its Communist rival on the Left will mean that the PS will remain a major and often attractive alternative to the conservative coalition.

The Communist Party

The French Communist party (PCF) once had the largest membership and tightest organization of any party in France. From 1946 to 1956, the PCF had the support of one out of every four French voters, polling more votes than any other single party. In 1958 under the new Fifth Republic, the PCF vote total fell but then stabilized at 20 to 22 percent of the vote through the 1970s. But in the 1981 election, the party's share of the vote fell to 16.2 percent and plummeted in 1986 to only 9.7 percent of the vote. On the first ballot of the 1988 presidential election, the Communist candidate polled only 6.8 percent. The PCF went up to 11.1 percent in the 1988 National Assembly elections, but this recovery was in no way a reversal of the party's declining electoral base.

One of the principal reasons for this rapid decline has been the PCF's failure to adopt a consistent policy. After 1958, the PCF began a twenty year effort to improve its public image and to build a coalition with other leftist parties, principally with the PS. It moderated its Marxist-Leninist doctrine by abandoning references to violent revolution and renouncing the key Communist notion of a dictatorship of the proletariat.[15] It committed itself to a distinctively French path to a communist society that would be compatible with French traditions of parliamentary democracy. The PCF also loosened its ties with the Soviet Union. While it remained loyal to the Soviet Union's foreign policy, the PCF regularly criticized Soviet violations of human rights. Perhaps most importantly, it committed itself to a political strategy based on winning office through free elections in a coalition with the Socialist party.

In moderating its stance, the PCF followed other Western communist parties in developing a European brand of communism dubbed "Euro-communism." But the French party lagged behind in moderating its doctrine and democratizing its practices. Many observers questioned the sincerity of the PCF's new commitment to democratic values.[16] These doubts were confirmed by the party's erratic behavior after 1977. The PCF ended its alliance with the Socialists and launched bitter attacks on Mitterrand and his party over the next four years. In addition, the PCF retreated from its moderate stance to champion revolution and radical change. The PCF mended its fences with the Soviet Union. It applauded the Soviet invasion of Afghanistan and the Soviet pressure on Poland in crushing the independent Polish labor movement Solidarity.

Then after the Socialist victories in 1981, the PCF reversed its position again. It renewed its alliance with the PS and entered the government for the first time since 1946 with three ministerial portfolios in the government of Prime Minister Pierre Mauroy. As the government's popularity declined, the PCF sought to put some distance between it and the government and finally left in 1984. Since that time, the PCF has resumed its hardline posture with sharp attacks on the Socialists, friendly words for the Soviet Union, and gradual retreat from the moderate policy positions it had adopted in the 1970s. When the Socialists lacked the seats for a majority after 1988, the PCF expressed no interest in a new alliance of the Left.

It voted with the Socialists in electing the leadership of the National Assembly in return for some leadership appointments. But the Communists indicated that they would support the minority Socialist government only when its policies coincided with those of the Communist party.

These sharp reversals in party strategy and especially the off and on affair with the Socialists led to the disaffection of many PCF activists, especially those from intellectual circles.[17] The party was riven with unparalleled internal conflict that demoralized even those members who were not alienated by the sudden shifts in political posture. The PCF leadership under Georges Marchais seemed out of touch with political reality and even the concerns of the party rank-and-file. But Marchais and his associates had firm hold on their positions and they steadfastly resisted demands from within the party for reform and moderation. The party elite's control of the PCF structure made it possible to ignore the clamor for change. But the party suffered the consequences. Party membership declined and the remaining members were less willing to devote themselves to defending the latest party line. The voters began to defect to other parties and the electoral defeats had further consequences on the PCF. Heavy losses in local elections eliminated the PCF's once large pool of professional activists since the patronage once available in local government was sharply reduced.

There are many reasons for the sudden decline of the French Communist party. There has been a general decline in communism's appeal throughout the world due to greater public awareness of the Soviet Union's economic problems and human rights' abuses. The PCF's leadership has been inept in responding to the problems. The leaders seem unable to identify the causes of the party's decline and to find a solution. The PCF also has suffered because workers who are basically content with the economic status quo have little interest in a revolutionary party. There have been changes in society that have cut into the PCF's usual voters as these social categories—notably workers in heavy industry—have diminished.

Perhaps the most important reason for the PCF's decline is the competition from a vigorous Socialist party. The Communists did well in the first thirty years after World War II because their party came to be identified as *the* party of the Left. The small and disorganized Socialist party of that period presented little competition to the PCF for the leftwing voters. But in the 1970s that changed with the revitalization of the Socialist party under François Mitterrand. As the Socialist party grew in strength, it came to be viewed as *the* party of the Left and increasingly cut into Communist strongholds. The critical point came at the end of the 1970s, when the PS, for the first time since the war, won the support of more voters than did the Communists. (See Figure 8.1.) It is the Socialist party that now stands for the Left in France.

The Communist party's recent electoral decline may be permanent. Elsewhere in Western Europe, as in West Germany, when the Communist party has faced competition from a dynamic left-of-center party, it has lost most of its political significance. There are some indications that this process is now well advanced in France with former Communist voters switching

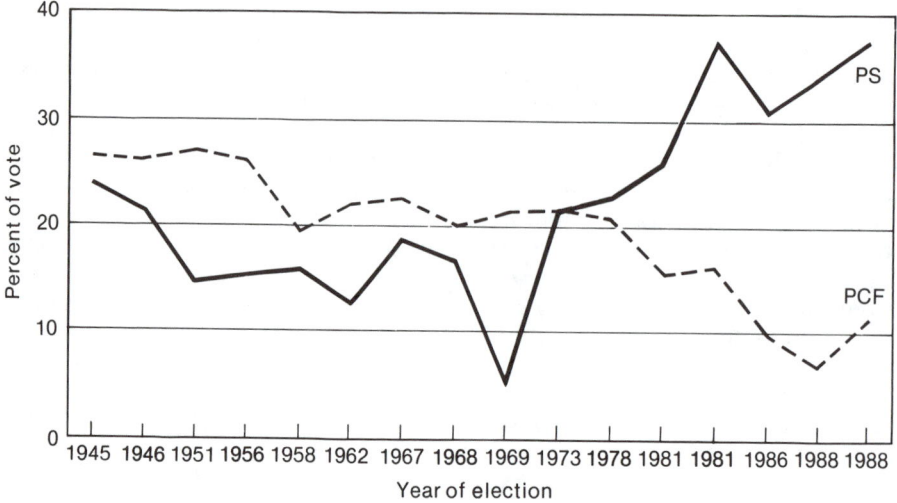

FIGURE 8.1   Percentage of Votes in National Elections for the French Communist and Socialist Parties.

to the Socialists. The return to a two-ballot electoral system (described in Chapter Seven) will further the decline of the PCF. Unwilling to form alliances with the PS, it will not be able to draw on Socialist voters for the run-off contests as it did between 1962 and 1981. Without that assistance, the PCF can expect to be virtually eliminated from the National Assembly even if its voting level does not drop any more.

While the PCF is unlikely to disappear completely, it is likely to become little more than an interesting relic from the past. It may occasionally make some noise on the margins of French politics, but its once great electoral and organizational power are no more. Barring some unforseen developments that would enable it to overcome its present crisis, the PCF will no longer have much impact on French politics.

The National Front

On the other political extreme, the National Front has emerged as an important political force. During the first twenty-five years of the Fifth Republic, political movements from the far Right had little consequence. Indeed, it was believed that one of the major accomplishments of the Gaullist era was the incorporation of the often antidemocratic French extreme Right into moderate and democratic parties. This achievement is cast into doubt by the stunning rise of the far rightist National Front (FN) of Jean-Marie Le Pen.[18]

Le Pen is an open admirer of the Vichy collaborator leader Marshal Pétain. His party advocates a slightly diluted dose of right-wing extremist themes intertwined with the populist rhetoric of the 1980s. It criticizes the press and electronic news media, the erosion of traditional virtues, the decline of public order and the rise in violent crimes, the aloof bureaucracy, big government, and the plight of the common citizen facing a distant, unresponsive state. Most importantly, the National Front skillfully exploits popular resentment against the large number of immigrant workers. They are held responsible for high unemployment, the rising crime rate, the drug problems, crowded public housing, overburdened social services, and the general decline in the quality of life in the cities where they congregate. In its strongly law-and-order and antiforeigner rhetoric, the National Front makes little attempt to disguise its appeal to the racist sentiments of many French citizens against the primarily North African and Middle Eastern immigrants.

Unfortunately, these racist attitudes do exist among the French people and appear to be becoming more powerful and widespread. The mainline parties, with only a few temporary lapses, have refused to exploit these sentiments. That has left the field open to the National Front. In the 1986 elections, the FN outpolled the PCF with nearly 10 percent of the vote. Those most likely to vote for FN candidates are the past supporters of far Right parties and those living in areas most heavily populated by the immigrants: Paris, Lyon-Grenoble, Marseille, Nice, and Toulon.

Like the Communist party, the National Front is largely isolated on the political extreme. The main conservative parties have refused to have any dealings with the FN at the national level despite their narrow parliamentary majority. There have been some coalitions between the FN and Gaullists or Giscardians at the local and regional levels. And there are some natural affinities. One of the reasons for the FN's good showing in the 1986 election was the presence among their candidates of prominent politicians who once were elected under Gaullist and Giscardian labels. In several cases, these were more senior candidates who were passed over by the main conservative parties in efforts to rejuvenate their ranks.

While racial tensions from the growing numbers of immigrants have mounted in many European countries, only in France have they been translated into a political movement. A National Front in Britain organized a few marches but could not translate that into electoral support; neofascist groups in Germany have been able to expand their minuscule support by appealing to the numerous Germans unsettled by the large number of guest workers in only a couple of state-level elections. The French success can be explained in two ways. First, the FN emerged at a time when there was growing and often passionate resentment to the then Socialist government. Voting for the FN—at the opposite end of the political spectrum—was a way to show how strongly voters opposed the incumbent government. Second, Le Pen has proved to be an attractive leader despite his extremism. He has been skilled in the use of the media that he condemns. Thus, the greatest voting success for the FN was Le Pen's 14.4 percent of the first ballot in the 1988 presidential election.

It is still too early to assess the full impact of the FN on the French party system. French politics has often witnessed the rise of "flash" parties which make spectacular entries onto the political scene only to disappear by the next election. The return to a two-ballot majority system is a serious disadvantage for a party like the National Front. With no allies, it can hope to win an absolute majority in only a very few districts. The voters know that and are reluctant to support these fringe parties. For example, only a few weeks after Le Pen had taken over 14 percent of the 1988 presidential vote, the FN candidates received only 9.8 percent of the National Assembly vote and elected only a single deputy. Without the ability to win seats in the National Assembly, the National Front will lose credibility and join other minor parties on the outskirts of Fifth Republic politics.

Political Parties and Political Stability

The French party system contributes friction and instability to the overall political scene. Some attribute this instability to the large number of parties, arguing that multiparty systems are inherently unstable and that two-party systems are always stable. However, the number of parties alone is not the crucial factor. Other democratic systems—the Netherlands, Sweden, Canada, and others—have stable party systems despite the presence of more than two parties. Where parties are polarized, whatever their number, the system is likely to be unstable. The degree of polarization between parties is much greater in France than in Britain or Germany and maybe even than in Italy. The Conservatives claim that the Socialists want to bring totalitarian collectivism to France; the Left denounces rule by the Right as authoritarian and fascist. The intensity of partisan feelings makes interparty cooperation and friendship difficult.

So far, the spread of more pragmatic values in the Socialist party has not affected this polarization. Differences on issues may be reduced but the psychological and emotional distances separating the parties and their activists remain great. Unlike in the United States where friendships cross the aisles in Congress, it is unusual for French politicians to develop close personal ties with those from opposing parties.

The problems of party polarization become more acute when the control of government shifts hands. When the Socialists took over in 1981, they immediately enacted major social and economic changes. They used their power to seek revenge in policy and personnel matters. The change, in 1986, back to a conservative government brought additional disruption. Much of the legislation passed by the Socialists was undone or ignored by the new government. Polarization also affects the operation of government when the president is from one camp and the parliamentary majority from another. There is not that easy cooperation found when an American president is from one party and Congress is controlled by the other. In France, such a situation raises the specter of a constitutional crisis. Despite problems, the system has survived the cohabitation era. This success will provide a precedent that should remove some of the uncertainty from future periods of cohabitation. In addition, the growing pragmatism and spreading sociopolitical consensus may also reduce polarization over the long term.

One of the important developments in the last decade has been the emergence of a viable leftwing alternative government. In spite of France's reputation as a haven for political radicalism, the Left has rarely governed. Between 1789 and 1981, the Left had held power alone for less than a half dozen years. The recent successes of the Socialist government demonstrated that the Left can govern and do so without danger to the overall political and social system.

This stability is important in developing the Left as a credible alternative government. For much of the Fifth Republic, despite dissatisfaction with the conservative government, voters often felt compelled to vote for the majority parties. They feared the radicalism of the Communists or the risk of destabilizing conflict between a governing Socialist party and its Communist ally. Now the Socialist party stands as a clear and attractive alternative to the conservatives.

In the section on Britain, concerns were noted about the apparent decay of the traditional British parties, the seeming public disinterest in them, and their organizational weaknesses in the 1980s. In France the parties experienced a period of public disapproval and disinterest in the early 1960s. By the 1970s, the French parties were revitalized and enjoyed greater public support than at any time since World War II. Party membership was up, party activities were well supported, and voter turnout was at an all-time high.[19] French parties resisted challenges from nationalist and environmental parties while in Britain and West Germany, similar parties disrupted the established systems.[20] The revitalization of the French parties suggests that any decline in Western democratic parties is not the inevitable product of modern society nor is it irreversible. Where party decline has occurred, it may more readily be explained in terms of a country's specific problems and the failure of its party leaders to respond effectively to them, not in terms of a general trend in Western democracy.

INTEREST GROUP POLITICS IN FRANCE

As in Britain and other Western democracies, interest groups play an active part in French politics.[21] Organized groups, such as labor unions, employers' associations, and farmers are involved in influencing policy making and implementation at all levels of government. From neighborhood protection associations and parent-teacher organizations to veterans' groups, environmentalists, and labor unions, groups seek to pressure government in order to shape policy to meet the needs of their members.

Among the most important of these interest groups are the major occupation-based associations listed in Table 8.2. As in Britain, these groups are peak associations, linking at the national level many regional and industry-based unions or associations. Smaller groups with narrow interest to defend are often very influential in the shaping of policies that affect them. As a case in point, the General Confederation of Beetgrowers representing approximately 150,000 beet producers, exercised inordinate political muscle for many years prior to the establishment of the Fifth

Republic. Sugar beets were used to make alcohol. The beet growers even succeeded for awhile in forcing the addition of alcohol to automobile gasoline, thus raising the cost and reducing the performance of the fuel. The political power of this small group stemmed from its financial resources, alliance with other powerful groups in the "alcohol lobby"— vintners, bar owners, and *bouilleurs de cru* (owners of fruit trees entitled to distill alcohol supposedly only for their own use)—and from its influence over many deputies from rural constituencies.

TABLE 8.2 Major Occupational Interest Groups in France

Labor Unions

Confédération Générale du Travail (CGT)
  Linked to Communist party
  1,500,000 members
Confédération Française Démocratique du Travail (CFDT)
  Leftist orientation
  740,000 members
Force Ouvrière (FO)
  Moderate leftist orientation
  900,000 members
Fédération d'Education Nationale (FEN)
  Leftist orientation
  550,000 members

Employers Associations

Conseil National du Patronat Français (CNPF)
  800,000 firms
Confédération Générale des Petites et Moyennes
  Entreprises (PME)
Centre des Jeunes Dirigeants d'Entreprise

Farmers Associations

Fédération Nationale des Syndicats d'Exploitation
  Agricole (FNSEA)
  Favorable to the Gaullist-Giscardian majority
  600,000 members
Centre National des Jeunes Agriculteurs (CNJA)
  Linked to FNSEA
  60,000 members
Mouvement de Défense de l'Exploitation Familiale
  (MODEF)
  Linked to Communist party
  200,000 members

Source: Rolf H. W. Theen and Frank L. Wilson, *Comparative Politics: An Introduction to Six Countries* (Englewood Cliffs, NJ: Prentice Hall, 1986), p. 164. Reprinted with permission.

Legislative lobbying, important during the Fourth Republic when parliament had considerable power and independence, is less important now because of the greater political power of the executive. As a result, French interest groups now direct their main efforts toward building contacts with ministers and senior civil servants in those departments concerned with issues affecting their members. This pressure is deflected in two ways.[22] First, government officials, and especially civil servants, feel that they represent the general will of the whole people while the groups push the views of only narrow, self-serving sections of the society. Second, much more so than in most other democratic nations, the government draws a distinction between "good" interest groups which represent important viewpoints in a reasonable way and "outside" groups which are seen as excessively preoccupied with their own privileges and with resisting needed social evolution. It is the first set that is most likely to receive a serious hearing by public officials while the outside groups are excluded or accorded only perfunctory opportunities to express their viewpoints.

While the executive is aloof and powerful, both political leaders and senior civil servants seek the opinions of affected interest groups even if they do not always follow their advice. Most interest groups, both those favorable to and those opposed to the governing parties, seem to feel that they are able to influence policy decisions to some degree.

The trend toward neocorporatist forms of interest group politics, groups that are involved directly in making and implementing policy decisions, is not as relevant in France as it has been in West Germany or even in Britain. There is an Economic and Social Council, which includes representatives from principal interest groups, and it must give parliament advisory opinions on all legislation dealing with economic or social issues. Parliament, however, frequently ignores the opinions of the Council, so its overall policy impact is very limited. Other quasi-corporatist bodies bringing together government officials and group representatives are usually consultative, at best, with no power over the decision process. Only in agriculture does there appear to be important formal ties involving the farmers' groups in making and administering public policy.[23] The social consensus and group unity necessary for this kind of institutionalized cooperation between groups and government are simply not present in France.

Occupational Groups

The polarized nature of French political elites results in the fragmentation of interest groups. Even where ideological differences are not great, personal rivalries produce multiple groups to speak for the same interests. Unlike the case in Britain and Germany where a single national body serves as a peak association for major occupational sectors, in France there are several bodies speaking for the workers, the employers, the doctors, and so on. The multiplicity of groups reduces their political influence. They spend much of their resources fighting each other. And the government can increase its control over policy by playing one group against its rival.

The labor movement is the best example of this fragmentation. There are three major national confederations: one close to the Communist party—the CGT; and two with moderate, leftist, political, orientations—the CFDT and the FO. In addition, there are many other smaller unions operating at the national, local, or industry levels. Their rivalries are intense. In the early 1980s, negotiations to end a serious automobile strike were delayed because representatives from different unions refused to sit with each other at the same bargaining table. The difficulty was resolved by negotiating via close circuit television with the bargaining teams from each union in separate rooms. This is an extreme example of the divisions among trade unions. But the intense competition that goes on among ideologically distinct unions at all levels, from the shop floor to national politics, weakens the cause of the working class.

As is the case of other industrial countries, the labor unions have experienced difficult times in the last decade.[24] The economic difficulties of the 1970s and 1980s with the decline of heavy industries, where union membership and militancy has always been strongest, have hurt the French unions. In addition, the involvement of the CGT and CFDT in leftwing politics has resulted in a loss of membership either due to disenchantment with the political positions or due to a preference for more job-related union efforts. Thus, membership declines have been particularly important in the Communist linked CGT and Socialist inclined CFDT. The more independent FO and job-related union has gained membership. In recent years, all unions have placed more stress on the bread-and-butter economic concerns of their members rather than longer-range political objectives. This more attuned stress has stopped the slump of the CFDT, but the CGT appears to be suffering the same plight as its Communist political party ally, the PCF.

They have proved able to present a common front on most political issues despite many potential sources of division among different kinds of employers. There are important differences between small and large enterprises as reflected in the presence of the separate organization to speak for small business, the PME. There are also divisions between employers who cling to the traditional paternalist employee-employer relation of the French *patronat* and those seeking good relations with employees and their unions. Within the CNPF, the major employers' organization, tensions between different sized enterprises or between rival industrial or commercial sectors often surface. Occasionally, disagreements over the strategy that the CNPF should take toward government results in an inability to take positions on controversial issues. As a result, the most influential representatives are often those from the industry-specific organizations who are able to concentrate their efforts on public officials who deal with the narrow legislation which affects their interests. For example, representatives from the insurance association have an important say in revisions of statutes governing their industry.

Agriculture is the exception to the fragmented pattern of interests. A single organization, the FNSEA, represents nearly all farmers. There are smaller leftwing and rightwing farm groups, but they have been unsuccessful in building much support even when given formal encouragement by sympathetic governments. The FNSEA has been highly successful in building close ties with the government. But it does not restrict its activities to formal consultation with the ministry of agriculture. It has the most extensive legislative lobby. When they fail to get their wishes from negotiations with the executive or from parliamentary lobbying, the farm groups are prepared to take to the streets in protest actions to press for their causes. A notable example of this multifaceted political action came when the FNSEA president had an interview with President Mitterrand to express farmers' concerns. Meanwhile in the provinces, on the same day, an angry group of farmers were demonstrating those concerns more dramatically by chasing the minister of agriculture through a field forcing a helicopter rescue of the mud-splattered minister.

New Social Movements

There has been a definite increase in group activities in France. Once the French were reputed to be hostile to joining groups, but in the last twenty years, there have been sharp increases in the number of associations and in the number of people participating in these group activities. In several European countries, similar increases have meant difficult times. They took the form of loosely organized movements pressing aggressively for government attention to issues such as women's rights, environmental protection, or nuclear disarmament. They challenged the established democratic politics by drawing members and voters from the political parties, by their uncompromising stands on single issues, by their willingness to resort to street politics, and by their impatience with, or their outright rejection of, normal democratic processes.

In France, the impact has been much less important. There are several reasons for this. First, the long tradition of protest politics denied these new movements of the shock effect they had in countries such as Britain or Germany which had experienced little protest prior to the rise of these new movements. Second, the rivalry in France between the sharply differentiated Left and Right reached its peak in the very years that these new movements were emerging in the 1970s. French citizens could not afford to affiliate with the new movements because the stakes in the party contests required that they devote their attention to the traditional parties. Finally, the Left had not yet governed in France; thus the new movements, such as ecologists, feminists, peace supporters, and consumer advocates, could hope that the Left would reflect their concerns once in office. Elsewhere, as in Britain and Germany, the Left had been in power during the 1970s and had proved that it would do little to meet the demands of these movements.

CONCLUSIONS

The French experience demonstrated that several of the supposedly inevitable problems of western democracies were not universal and thus were probably not unavoidable crises. There was no decline of parties in France; in fact, the parties were demonstrating surprising vitality. Despite their polarization, they brought greater political stability than France had experienced under four prior republics. Neocorporatism did not develop in France though there was much in France's historical background to suggest that it was a fertile field for corporatist politics. Even in agriculture, where this form of institutional interest group/government interaction was most developed, it did not compromise the autonomy of either the government or the group. The new social movements that caused concern in other countries found the political terrain in France much tougher to enter and to endure.

The French exceptions suggest that democracies have many resources to respond to new the challenges. Any crisis in democracy is not a crisis of democracy in general but a separate crisis coming from the vulnerability of a certain country.

NOTES

1. On French parties, see Frank L. Wilson, *French Political Parties Under the Fifth Republic* (New York: Praeger, 1982).
2. Valéry Giscard d'Estaing, *French Democracy* (Garden City, NJ: Doubleday, 1977).
3. *Le Monde*, 16 May 1985.
4. Val Lorwin, *The French Labor Movement* (Cambridge, MA: Harvard University Press, 1954), p. 33.
5. Alain Peyrefitte, *The Trouble With France* (New York: Alfred A. Knopf, 1981), pp. 218–219.
6. See William R. Schonfeld, "The RPR: From Rassemblement to Gaullist Movement," in William G. Andrews and Stanley Hoffmann, eds., *The Fifth Republic at Twenty* (Albany, NY: State University of New York Press, 1981).
7. J. R. Frears, *France in the Giscard Presidency* (London: George Allen & Unwin, 1981).
8. Jean Charlot, "The Majority," in Howard R. Pennimann, ed., *The French National Elections of 1978* (Washington, DC: American Enterprise Institute, 1980).
9. Ella Searls, "The Giscardians—the Republican Party," in *Continuity and Change in France*, ed. by Vincent Wright (London: George Allen & Unwin, 1984).
10. D. S. Bell and Byron Criddle, *The French Socialist Party*, 2nd ed., (London: Oxford University Press, 1988).
11. David Hanley, *Keeping Left: CERES and the French Socialist Party: A Contribution to the Study of Fractionalism in Political Parties* (Manchester, England: Manchester University Press, 1986).
12. See Bernard E. Brown, *Socialism of a Different Kind: Reshaping the Left in France* (Westport, CT: Greenwood Press, 1982).
13. Stanley Hoffmann, "French Politics: June-November 1979," *The Tocqueville Review* 2 (Winter 1980): 150.

14. For an assessment of the results of the labor reform legislation, see W. Rand Smith, "Towards Autogestion in Socialist France? The Impact of Industrial Relations Return," *West European Politics* 10 (January 1987): 46–62.

15. See George Ross, *Workers and Communists in France: From Popular Front to Eurocommunism* (Berkeley, CA: University of California Press, 1982).

16. Annie Kriegel, *Eurocommunism: A New Kind of Communism* (Stanford, CA: Hoover Institution Press, 1980).

17. For a fascinating account of the personal struggles of party members during these difficult times, see Jane Jensen and George Ross, *The View From Inside: A French Communist Cell in Crisis* (Berkeley, CA: University of California Press, 1985).

18. Martin Schain, "The National Front in France and the Construction of Political Legitimacy," *West European Politics* 10 (April 1987): 229–252.

19. Frank L. Wilson, "The Revitalization of French Parties," *Comparative Political Studies* 12 (April 1979): 82–103.

20. Frank L. Wilson, "When Parties Refuse to Fail: The Case of France," in Kay Lawson and Peter H. Merkl, eds., *When Parties Fail: Emerging Alternative Organizations* (Princeton, NJ: Princeton University Press, 1987).

21. See Frank L. Wilson, *Interest Group Politics in France* (Cambridge, England: Cambridge University Press, 1987).

22. Ezra N. Suleiman, *Politics, Power, and Bureaucracy in France: The Administrative Elite* (Princeton, NJ: Princeton University Press, 1974), pp. 316–351.

23. John T. S. Keeler, *The Politics of Neocorporatism in France: Farmers, the State, and Agricultural Policy-Making in the Fifth Republic* (London: Oxford University Press, 1987).

24. Frank L. Wilson, "Trade Unions and Economic Policy," in Howard Machin and Vincent Wright, eds., *Economic Policy and Policy-Making Under the Mitterrand Presidency 1981–1984* (London: Frances Pinter, 1985) and Mark Kesselman, ed., *The French Workers' Movement: Economic Crisis and Political Change* (London: George Allen & Unwin, 1984).

CHAPTER NINE
FRENCH POLICY MAKING

> The French lack, apparently, the gift of governability. . . . They love the notion of creating a state on the best rational principles, but they are temperamentally incapable of allowing it to work. The state is an intellectual glory, but is also the enemy.[1]

The French are reputed to view their country from two viewpoints. On the one hand, they see the *pays réel*—the real country—in a very positive way as the essence of France, worthy of respect and sacrifice on the part of its citizens. On the other hand, they view the *pays légal*—the legal country in the sense of its formal governmental institutions and leaders—with cynicism and contempt; citizens are justified in sabotaging or evading its acts since it discredits the *pays réel*. With such a dichotomy between the French people's attitude toward the country's abstract nature and its concrete reality, even the best drafted constitutions in France face skepticism and opposition.

The public's ambivalent attitude toward the state makes it difficult to find an appropriate political framework that can long endure. As we have seen, France has had a long series of different political frameworks in the past two centuries. Unlike the United States, where the Constitution enacted 200 years ago is revered, or in Britain where an unwritten Constitution produced by ages of practice and tradition is equally strong, the French have had difficulty in reaching a consensus on the basic political framework. Over 130 years ago, the transitory nature of French political frameworks was already the object of a popular joke: A Parisian bookseller explains to a potential customer that he cannot sell him a copy of the French constitution because he does not deal in periodical literature.

Despite the frequent change in regime, two basic patterns have prevailed and succeeded each other. The democratic pattern featured a powerful elected parliament dominating politics and a correspondingly weak executive. This pattern was found in the Third and Fourth Republics and earlier democratic regimes. The authoritarian pattern, found in the monarchies, the empires, and the Vichy era, emphasized the power of the executive. The legislature, when it still existed, was left with little or no power to check the executive actions.

The current regime, the Fifth Republic, established in 1958, attempts to blend these two patterns by increasing executive power but retaining the democratic controls of an independent legislature and free elections. After thirty years, the 1958 constitution enjoys broader support than have most earlier constitutions. It has worked well in both crisis and normal times. Its institutions have worked to correct some of the political problems of previous French democratic regimes. Indeed, there is now a broad popular consensus in support of the institutions established by this document that is shared by the political elite. Only the fringe parties on either extreme question its value and then only by suggesting slight amendments rather than wholesale constitutional revision.

For political scientists, one of the interesting aspects of recent constitutional developments in France is the use of constitutional reform to alter long-standing political features and practices. In Britain, the process was the opposite: Evolving political practices reshaped and redefined traditional political institutions. In contrast, the drafters of the French constitution hoped to change certain patterns of behavior and practices thought to be undesirable. The apparent success of some of this "constitutional engineering" illustrates that the relationship between political institutions and political attitudes and social settings is complex. If it is true that sometimes well-ingrained political attitudes and social structures determine the nature and operation of political institutions (as is the case to a great degree in Britain), it is also true that political institutions can shape and even radically transform political attitudes and behavior.

THE FRENCH CONSTITUTION
OF THE FIFTH REPUBLIC (1958)

When the Fourth Republic ground to a halt, Charles de Gaulle agreed to come back to power on condition that he be authorized to change the constitution. The drafters of the new constitution wanted to remedy what they thought were the shortcomings of earlier French democracies.[2] To correct for the past weakness of the executive, the constitution granted extensive independent power to the government (prime minister and council of ministers). To respond to the past problem of a seemingly overpowerful parliament, the 1958 constitution reduced the legislature's areas of competence and limited its power to oust the government through censure and votes of nonconfidence. In response to the chronic and excessive pluralism of the party system, the constitution included an electoral system that encouraged party coalitions and later added a system for presidential elections that forced parties to combine in order to elect a president.

In general, these efforts at "constitutional engineering" have succeeded in eliminating the problems they were designed to treat. The establishment of a powerful presidency has eliminated governmental instability; the electoral devices have contributed to the simplification of the party system. Not all efforts at constitutional engineering succeeded. The evolutions of the institutions in practice has produced some unforseen results, notably the great increases in presidential powers. But on balance, the institutions of the Fifth Republic do seem to have achieved the drafters' objectives of finding a more effective framework for democratic government.

A MIXED PRESIDENTIAL-PARLIAMENTARY STRUCTURE OF GOVERNMENT

To correct the governmental instability of past French democracies, the drafters of the Fifth Republic's constitution sought to mix the parliamentary and presidential political frameworks. The result is a unique hybrid with elements of both these basic governmental patterns. (See Figure 9.1.) The parliamentary elements include the presence of a prime minister and cabinet of ministers who are accountable to parliament and who can be ousted by a vote of censure in the National Assembly. The presidential elements include a popularly elected president who appoints the prime minister and has a variety of other constitutional prerogatives and powers. The mixed system results in a dual executive—a president and a prime minister—sharing responsibility in the direction of the government.

The system has worked well in remedying the problem of governmental instability that plagued the Third and Fourth Republics. For example, there were twenty-four prime ministers in the twelve years of the Fourth Republic; during the first thirty years of the Fifth Republic, there have been only eleven prime ministers. In addition, the presence of a powerful president gives added stability and continuity of government. As indicated in Table 9.1, the continuity of the French executive compares favorably with other Western democracies.

One of the principal and unusual features of this mixed system is the dual executive. In Germany, Italy, and most other democracies, the presidency is an honorific position with little real power. French presidents are very powerful but must share this power with their prime ministers. Normally, the president is the dominant figure in this dual executive, but

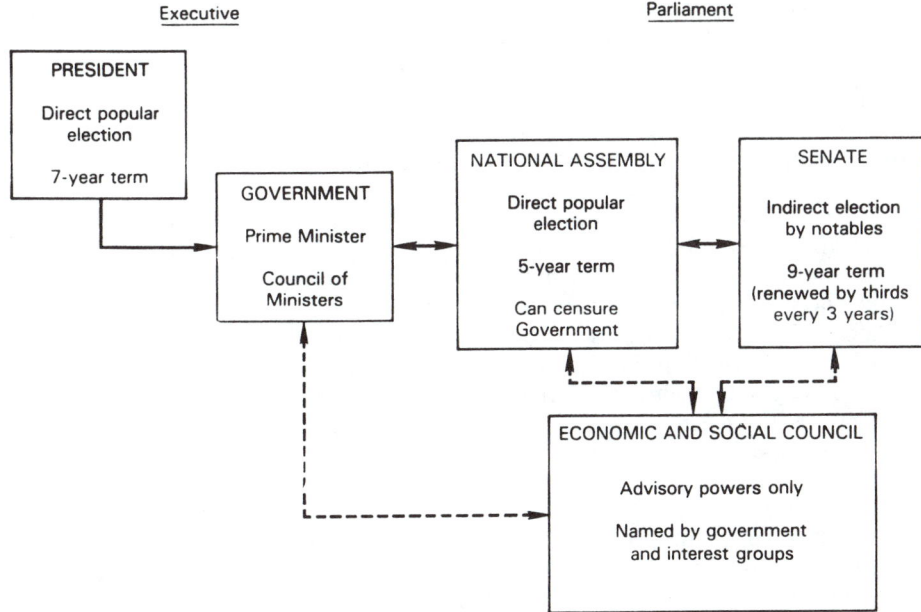

Executive   Parliament

FIGURE 9.1   **French Political Institutions.** *Source:* Rolf H. W. Theen and Frank L. Wilson, *Comparative Politics: An Introduction to Six Countries* (Englewood Cliffs, NJ: Prentice Hall, 1986), p. 139. Reprinted with permission.

TABLE 9.1   **Number of Chief Executives 1959–1988**

Britain	7 Prime Ministers
France	4 Presidents 12 Prime Ministers
West Germany	7 Chancellors
Italy	32 Prime Ministers
United States	7 Presidents

there are still problems of coordination and competing ambitions that mar the relationship between the president and the prime minister.

The President

The constitution provided for a presidency tailored to the political style and philosophy of its first occupant, Charles de Gaulle. As a war hero, de Gaulle envisioned himself as a man above the melee of daily politics. He believed, and many French did, that he was aloof from the normal partisan political passions that sometimes immobilized the French state. The constitution therefore called for the president to be an arbiter whose primary charge was to ensure "by his arbitration, the regular functioning of the governmental authorities, as well as the continuity of the state" (Article 5). The president should intervene when narrow and self-interested groups threaten to divert government from the general interest or paralyze its action.

In practice, the president's role has been much more than that of an aloof and neutral arbiter. Furthermore, presidential power has grown under each of the presidents.[3] With the growth of these powers has come the expansion in size and importance of the president's staff in the Elysée Palace.[4] By the 1980s, the supposedly mixed French system was clearly much more presidential than it was parliamentary.[5]

There are several explanations for the growth of presidential power in France. First, the constitution grants substantial power to the president. He is elected for a seven-year term with the possibility of reelection. The president has the power to appoint the prime minister. He presides over the meetings of the Council of Ministers. He can require parliament to reconsider legislation that it has passed and he can refer laws to the Constitutional Council for decisions on their constitutionality. He can dissolve the National Assembly and call new elections at his discretion. He may propose a referendum on any question. He has the right to declare a state of national emergency and to rule by decree "when the institutions of the Republic are threatened in a grave and immediate manner and when the regular functioning of the institutional public authority is interrupted" (Article 16).

Second, the popular election of the president accords additional political weight to the office. Originally, the president was elected by an electoral college of local and national officials. In 1962 a successful referendum replaced this indirect election with the direct election of the president by universal suffrage. Popular elections permit presidents to assert that they represent the nation as a whole. As one president put it: "I have legitimacy from the free election." All other elected officials come out of relatively small electoral districts; the president alone can claim a national constituency. In addition, the dynamics of a national election force him to be a powerful *political* leader and not just an impartial arbiter. The need to develop a national electoral majority forces the president to build a broad-based political party or coalition. Once elected, the president must continue to exert leadership over his political supporters both to achieve his policy goals and to prepare for reelection. To maintain the appearance of president aloofness, he generally controls his party through intermediaries. But this partisan leadership position makes it unlikely that the president can fulfill the arbiter role stipulated by the constitution. He is indeed the principal political leader and, as such, is very clearly a partisan leader rather than a neutral referee.

The election process contributes to the growing political role of the president in another way. To get elected, the president has to make a number of campaign pledges on what he will do once in office. After election, the president's sense of obligation to fulfill his campaign promises leads him to take an active and directing role in politics. French voters regard the presidential election as the most important electoral contest, the one that determines the political future of the country. The president is therefore impelled to lead the policy-making process.

A third factor in the growth of presidential power in France has been the presence of a sympathetic majority in the National Assembly through most of the Fifth Republic. In addition, the presidential majority has generally been cohesive and disciplined in parliamentary voting. Unlike the situation in the United States Congress, where presidents cannot rely automatically on support from legislators of their own party, French presidents can count on their supporters to give them a majority on virtually all of their major proposals. With the exception of 1986 to 1988, the majority in parliament is not only from the same political tendency as the president, it interprets one of its responsibilities as following the leadership of the president.

Because of the majority's loyalty, the president is able to control membership in the government. Presidents are able to go beyond the constitutional right of naming a prime minister to the virtual dictation of the composition of the whole council of ministers. It assures the president of the extraconstitutional power to dismiss prime ministers and ministers who are no longer satisfactory. Indeed, by the mid-1980s, it had become routine to clear all important appointments with the Elysée even when the powers of appointments were formally those of the prime minister or council of ministers. Because the majority looked to the Elysée for direction, the president set the agenda for meetings of the Council of Ministers and published the official minutes of those meetings.

All of these powers are contingent upon the presence of a sympathetic majority in the National Assembly. But the election sequence makes it likely that there will be times when the president does not have that parliamentary majority. Then the president faces a hostile majority and must assume a more modest role based more on the constitutional model of an arbiter rather than on the activist role that has evolved in practice. In the United States, a president can get along with an opposition controlling Congress because first, political differences between the Democratic and Republican parties are not that great. Second, the parties rarely vote along party lines in Congress; the president can build bipartisan support for his proposals since Republicans and Democrats cross party lines in congressional voting. Republican presidents are able to get their proposals through Congresses with Democratic majorities. In France, these two conditions are not present. Political parties are polarized, with party cohesion in parliamentary voting very tight. The opposition parties vote systematically against the government.

For many years, the issue of how to resolve a situation when the president did not have a supporting majority in the National Assembly was hypothetical. The only times that presidents lacked this majority (in 1962 when de Gaulle's initial coalition crumbled and in 1981 when a Socialist president was elected and the National Assembly conservative majority still had two more years in its term) were resolved when each president exercised his right to dissolve the National Assembly and the subsequent elections gave comfortable majorities to the president. Then, in 1986, voters elected a new conservative majority to the National Assembly when the Socialist François Mitterrand had two more years in the Elysée. This introduced a difficult era of "cohabitation" with the Socialist president contending with the conservative majority bent on undoing what he had accomplished during the first five years of his presidency.

Under cohabitation, Mitterrand found it impossible to exercise most of the informal and even some of the formal prerogatives of the presidency. Immediately after the election, he named a conservative prime minister because to do otherwise would have precipitated an unwanted constitutional crisis. The prime minister worked out the composition of the government with his political allies allowing Mitterrand only the right of veto over a couple of sensitive ministries. Mitterrand still presided over meetings of the Council of Ministers. But the real decisions were made in informal meetings of the government without Mitterrand present. The agenda was drawn up by the prime minister who also issued the public summary of the Council of Ministers' decisions. Mitterrand asserted that he had special powers in the fields of foreign and defense policies but he lacked the wherewithal to conduct independent policies even on these important issues. He did chastise or warn the government about its course of action and occasionally blocked the appointment of a particularly unwanted nominee sent up by the government. Mitterrand slowed some legislation by refusing to sign executive decrees but he lacked the power to veto legislation passed by parliament. Consequently Mitterrand was obliged to sign into law measures that undid many of the reforms his government had enacted earlier in the 1980s.

The reduction in presidential powers under cohabitation was only temporary. The same dynamics that produced the powerful presidency in earlier years brought a resumption of presidential primacy once there was harmony between the president and the National Assembly majority: the dynamics of a popular election, the cohesion and discipline of the parties, and the ambitions of the individuals who become president. The presidency attracts the top politicians. Once they are in that office, even those who in the past advocated reduced presidential powers—as Mitterrand had done—have acted to extend their powers and prerogatives. As long as the president is popularly elected and is seen as the pinnacle of politics, and as long as the most ambitious politicians seek that post, the presidency will be the seat of major policy decisions. There are likely to be future eras of cohabitation, but they will be the exception and short lived rather than a new direction in the evolution of the institutions of the Fifth Republic.

The Prime Minister
and Council of Ministers

Under normal circumstances, the president selects a prime minister and the Council of Ministers, collectively known as the government. The ministers head government departments such as Economy, Defense, Education, and Industry, with the prime minister serving as coordinator and director under the leadership of the president. The government directs the state administrative structures and handles the daily conduct of government affairs.

During earlier democratic eras in France, the government was often unable to perform effectively because of lack of support in parliament and its own precarious internal balance. To correct for these problems, the Constitution of the Fifth Republic provided the Council of Ministers with important new powers. The government can handle many manners through decrees issued on its own authority or on the basis of broad grants of decree powers given to it by specific acts of parliament. It can control the parliamentary agenda and give priority to questions it deems important. It can insist that parliament vote on government proposals without making any amendments. It is protected from parliamentary sanctions by a difficult censure procedure: The motion of censure must be signed by a tenth of the members of the National Assembly (who lose the right to sign another censure motion for the duration of that session). Voting is personal with no proxy votes accepted on censure motions and an absolute majority of the total membership is required for adoption of censure.

The development of cohesive majority coalitions has buttressed the position of the government. On nearly all issues, the government can count on the loyal support of a majority in parliament even when the margin is a narrow one. The Chirac government enacted major and controversial reforms in 1986 to 1987 with a majority of only two deputies. But the conservative coalition's discipline held firm on key votes. On censure motions, party unity in support of the government is near perfect: Since 1962 members of the government majority have voted for censure on only three occasions and in these cases the defectors were very few and had no effect on the outcome. The only time the National Assembly ousted a government under the Fifth Republic was in 1962 before the consolidation of the present party coalitions.

These constitutional and political developments have made governments more effective and more durable. Under the Fourth Republic the average government lasted for only a few months; since 1959, prime ministers have served an average of three years. In addition, presidential leadership added still more continuity to governments. Despite the fact that the prime minister acts often as the agent of the president rather than on his own initiative, the position is still much more powerful than that of the premier in the Fourth Republic, who faced continual threats to the very existence of his government.

The relationship between the government and the president is complex due to its mixed presidential-parliamentary nature. The Constitution assigns the government the responsibility of determining and conducting the nation's policies. In practice, save during the exceptional period of recent cohabitation, the president and his staff determine the major programs that are proposed by the government. The extent to which the presidential staff intervenes directly in a specific policy decision varies with the minister concerned and the importance of the issue at hand. Presidents can count on their governments to reflect accurately their own priorities and preferences in the conduct of state affairs.

In most parliamentary democracies, such as Britain or West Germany, the governments are accountable only to their parliaments which select them and can oust them through censure. In France, under the mixed presidential-parliamentary system, the government has dual responsibilities. On the one hand, the government is accountable to the president who normally appoints and dismisses the prime minister and other ministers. On the other hand, the government is also accountable to the National Assembly which can oust the government through a vote of censure. The National Assembly can also make life difficult for the government by slowing or obstructing the executive's proposals. In practice, except for the cohabitation era, the government's main accountability has been to the president. The president's secure majority in the National Assembly has given him the ability to select and remove governments without much concern for parliamentary reaction.

Even with the president selecting the prime minister, there has occasionally been major friction between the two executives. Popular and independently minded prime ministers can threaten presidential primacy. President de Gaulle, who benefited from enormous popular support, felt compelled to replace ambitious prime ministers with lesser-known figures. The problem is that the dual nature of the French executive, with a powerful president and a highly visible prime minister, leads to conflict between these two leaders even if they share the same political philosophy and partisan ties. The problem is much more acute during eras of cohabitation when they come from different political parties.

Parliament

The French parliament has two chambers. The *National Assembly* is the more powerful body, with its membership elected directly by the people for five-year terms.[6] Members of the *Senate* are elected indirectly by an electoral college made up of local elected public officials; senators serve nine-year terms. The government is accountable only to the popularly elected National Assembly; the Senate cannot censure the government. Both chambers act on all legislation. When there are differences between the texts adopted by the two houses or when one chamber adopts and the other rejects them, the prime minister may convene a joint committee to find a compromise settlement. If this move fails, the government can ask the National Assembly to decide the issue alone. This procedure permits the supremacy of the popularly elected National Assembly, but the important discretionary power of the government cannot be overlooked. When the government finds it is in its interests, it can let the Senate block a piece of legislation by not convening a joint committee; when it wants the proposal passed, it can ask the National Assembly to override the Senate's action. During the Socialist era, the government often faced opposition from the conservative-dominated Senate but was able to get all of its program implemented through the National Assembly, thus making the legislation a law without Senate approval.

As in Britain, where there is criticism of the aristocratic House of Lords, there are periodic attacks on the French Senate. The electoral college that elects the senators overrepresents rural and small-town interests; more than one half of the members of the electoral college come from towns and villages with less than fifteen hundred inhabitants, and where less than a third of the French population lives. The Senate often has an entirely different political composition than the popularly elected

TABLE 9.2 The Stages of a Bill in the French Parliament

National Assembly

1. Deposition of a bill
   Projets de loi (Introduced by the government)
   Propositions de loi (Introduced by member of parliament)
2. Consideration by the Economic and Social Council of all legislation dealing with social or economic issues
3. Action by parliamentary committee
   Consideration of amendments and alternative texts
   Preparation of a report on the legislation and amendments
4. Floor debate
   General discussion
   Discussion of each article
   Final vote on the whole text
5. Second consideration of all or part of the bill upon the request of the government or a member of parliament

Senate

Steps 1–5 Repeated

Final Stages

1. When the National Assembly and Senate versions are the same:
   a. Constitutionality verified by the Constitutional Council
   b. Promulgation of the law by the President of the Republic
   c. Publication of the law

2. When the National Assembly and Senate versions differ:
   a. Consideration of changes made in the second chamber by the first chamber to adopt the bill. If approved, bill goes through final stages described above.
   b. When differences remain, a joint committee *(navette)* is appointed to work out differences. The revised legislation must then be approved by both houses before going through the final stages.
   c. If agreement cannot be reached, the government may ask the National Assembly to decide the fate of the bill or it may simply let the bill die.

Source: David F. Roth and Frank L. Wilson, *The Comparative Study of Politics*, 2nd ed. (Englewood Cliffs, NJ: Prentice Hall, 1980), p. 359.

National Assembly, and it results in conflicts between the two chambers. An attempt to reduce the Senate's powers failed in a 1969 referendum and there has been little interest since in reforming or eliminating the Senate. The Socialists were often upset by the delays and obstruction their reforms encountered in the Senate. In case of clashes between the Senate and the National Assembly, the constitution allows the executive and the National Assembly to prevail over the upper chamber. That limited power of the Senate reduces the desire to abolish or further weaken that chamber even if it sometimes stands in opposition to the presidents and their National Assembly majorities.

Prior to 1959, the Palais Bourbon (where the French National Assembly meets) was the very heart of French politics. There laws were written and governments were made and unmade. Parliamentary debate was passionate, even tumultuous, with the fate of the nation in the hands of its deputies. The galleries were filled with lobbyists, who sometimes brazenly used hand signals to direct friendly deputies on how to vote, and with journalists and foreign diplomats interested to see whether the government would survive another day of parliamentary action. Nowadays, parliamentary debate is usually lower keyed and attracts much less interest. The seat of political power is now located in the Elysée presidential palace and the prime minister's residence at Matignon. Even the questioning of ministers (interpellation), a lively part of the British House of Commons' agenda, lacks excitement in France. The questions are routine, and ministers take pride in avoiding response to the embarrassing ones.

This shift of power from the legislature to the executive is by no means unique to France. It can be observed in Britain, West Germany, the United States, and other western democracies. The increased need for technical expertise in many policy areas has shifted lawmaking initiative to the executive. The development of disciplined parties has also reduced the legislature's ability to control the executive as long as it maintains the support of a majority.

These trends were accentuated in France by the deliberate effort of the constitutional drafters to reduce the powers of parliament. These restrictions included parliament's lawmaking powers. The Constitution specifies parliament's area of competence, with all issues not specifically assigned to parliament to be considered as regulatory matters that the government can handle by decree. In certain important legislative fields, the government can request authorization from parliament to legislate by decree, with only the broad outlines being specified by parliament. Even parliament's traditional control of the purse strings is limited by a constitutional provision barring it from increasing expenditures or decreasing revenues without the consent of the government.[7]

In addition to restricting the scope of lawmaking competence, the Constitution also changed procedures that have weakened parliament. Instead of meeting year-round as in the past and as in other European countries, the French parliament is limited to two three-month sessions each year. Parliamentary committees are fewer in number, larger in size, and much less powerful than in the past. The government controls the agenda and can insist on priority treatment for its proposals. It can avoid votes on amendments it opposes by forcing parliament to vote on its text without any parliamentary amendments (known as the "package vote"). When the government feels that one of its bills may face opposition in parliament, it can then declare that measure to be a matter of "confidence"—or an issue that the government believes is so essential that it cannot continue without its adoption. In such cases the legislation is considered as adopted even though no vote is taken. The only way to block such legislation is to introduce and adopt a motion of censure to oust the government. As noted earlier, the censure process is a difficult one and the difficulties are reinforced by feelings among deputies that ousting a government from your own party is political suicide for the individual and often the party.

Changes in the party system have also worked to reduce parliamentary influence. Parties are more disciplined in the sense that their members feel an obligation to vote together on most issues.[8] This discipline means that they follow their leaders in supporting or opposing the government not so much on the merits of the particular piece of legislation as out of duty to support or oppose the government across the board.

While these party/government links operate in such a way as to reduce parliamentary power, in the last analysis, the reduced role of parliament is due to self-denial rather than the actual loss of power. When the deputies from the majority choose to, they can force their government to modify or abandon projects that are given top priority. In fact, parliament still retains the ability to make life difficult and even impossible for any government. For most of the Fifth Republic it has chosen not to do so because of agreement between the majority in parliament and the government. Thus, a major part of the decline of parliament is the result of parliament's unwillingness to use the powers that it still has. Parliament can force the government to consider its amendments by voting down government-imposed package votes; it can block measures being forced through without a vote under the confidence procedures by voting to censure the government. It can exercise these controls but chooses not to because the majority accepts, albeit sometimes grudgingly, the dominance of the executive.

Despite the curtailment of its power, parliament still retains influence over policy. It has the ability to bring issues and ideas to the forefront of political debate.[9] Deputies often play important roles behind the scenes in shaping legislative proposals before they come to the floor of parliament. In the last decade, governments of all political stripes have become more solicitous of contributions from their supporters in parliament. Committees have modest staffs and are more effective in shaping legislation. On the floor of parliament, many bills are extensively modified; one recent budget was passed only after the National Assembly added 560 amendments.

Parliament's loss of power is relative. It is less powerful than the Third and Fourth Republic parliaments in the sense that it cannot topple governments as those unmanageable legislatures did with regularity. But legislature-dominated governments have not been good governments.[10]

Today's French parliament has the opportunity to debate major and controversial issues that in earlier republics were depoliticized by shifting them to the bureaucracy or handled by decree to avoid splitting shaky government coalitions. It has more influence over executive decrees than before.[11] Its public image has certainly improved from the low esteem prior to the 1960s with citizens now supportive of increasing the role of parliament. The French parliament may be less powerful than the unruly Italian parliament or the well-organized and professional German Bundestag, but it is probably no less powerful than the British Parliament and those of most other European democracies.

The Constitutional Council

In the last decade, the Constitutional Council has gained new prominence in French politics. The Council is composed of nine justices serving nine-year terms: three each appointed by the president of the republic, and the presiding officers of the Senate and the National Assembly. In addition, all former presidents have the right to sit on this body but no one has so far exercised that right. When created in 1958, the Council had a relatively modest role of assuring the regularity of elections and the constitutionality of major legislation.

Expansion of the role of the Council began in the early 1980s when it emerged as the most potent source of opposition to the Socialist reforms.[12] Socialist control of the presidency and National Assembly assured them of the ability to force through whatever legislation they wanted, but the Constitutional Council remained dominated by jurors named by earlier conservative presidents and parliamentary leaders. Opposition deputies and the conservative president of the Senate referred controversial reforms to the Council to delay or block them. The Council's workload increased dramatically.[13] The Council proved more willing to void legislation than in the past. It ruled that nearly half of the measures brought to it were at least partially unconstitutional. Beyond the actual voiding of legislation, the presence of the Council and its activism had deterrent effects on the legislative process. With the passage of time, the Socialists used their appointment powers to name their friends to the Council. By 1986, the Council had a majority favorable to the Socialists. Thus, when the Conservatives returned to power that year, they found the Council an obstacle to their efforts at undoing earlier Socialist reforms. Anticipated reaction of the Council has become a prominent concern as governments consider legislation.

The notion of judicial review is well established in the United States but it lacks depth in Europe. Here the tradition has been the supremacy of the popularly elected parliament as the manifestation of popular sovereignty. In the last decade, there has been a growing tendency for European courts to review the constitutionality of their government's actions and their parliament's laws. This is especially true in countries that introduced constitutional courts after World War II such as Germany, Italy, and, after 1958, France. But it has also happened in Britain where normal courts have begun to assert the supremacy of a constitutional law especially in the area of human rights.

The French experience with judicial review differs from the others in several ways. First, access is limited with the French Constitutional Council only handling questions referred to it by the President, the presiding officers of parliament, or by the joint appeal of sixty deputies or senators. Second, the Council can only deal with laws before promulgation; it cannot reverse laws already in force as can the courts of other countries. Third, the courts in other countries have emerged as potent defenders of individual civil liberties; the French Council has not dealt with human rights issues except in a most indirect manner. Fourth, the French Council has become a highly partisan body with controversy swirling around its actions while the other constitutional bodies have developed reputations for independence and impartiality.

Public reaction in France to the Constitutional Council's new assertiveness was initially favorable. Citizens saw the Council as a more neutral body guaranteeing continuity and constitutional regularity in times of rapid political change. But the increasingly apparent partisan nature of the Council has begun to erode its public support. The growing political controversies surrounding the Council and its decisions make it difficult to predict whether its new activism will remain a permanent feature of French politics or simply will provoke formal limits on its activities.

THE FRENCH CIVIL SERVICE

The French civil service has been both a source of strength and of political obstruction. Its centralization and hierarchy have helped assure the dominance of the national polity over local governments and narrow interests. It has also provided continuity in times of weak or divided government. On the negative side, its strength has permitted bureaucrats to ignore the directions of political leaders, especially during the earlier democratic republics when executive leadership was weak. Even now, with firm and durable executives, the bureaucracy can delay and sometimes block reforms proposed by the elected government but deemed inappropriate by bureaucrats.

The French civil service adheres much less strongly than its British counterpart to the norm of political nonpartisanship. To correct for this bias the French have a more extensive layer of politically appointed leaders. Each minister selects a *cabinet* of personal advisers, varying in size from ten (supposedly the limit) to as many as eighty people. The members of the cabinets, civil servants borrowed from other ministries, and younger politicians favored by the minister, form a body of advisers that compensates for the lack of innovation that is endemic of bureaucracies. They also help ministers master and control the bureaucrats who serve under them. In addition, the office of the president has a large staff of senior civil servants and political protegés. Both presidents and ministers use their cabinets to bypass the bureaucracies so firmly entrenched in the ministries, to avoid bureaucratic sabotage, and to develop innovative ideas.

Among the most important elements in seeking government control over the bureaucracy has been the presence, during much of the Fifth Republic, of a dominant party and a solid majority coalition.[14] With the presidency and parliament in the hands of a cohesive and durable majority, the government can in fact govern. There is still the possibility of bureaucratic obstruction due to the usual resistance of bureaucrats to change and to the presence of individual sympathizers of opposition parties at lower levels of the civil service. The government is usually able to overcome such resistance when it is determined to do so. For example, it forced through unwilling bureaucracies important reforms affecting education, agriculture, foreign affairs, and local administration. The government was able to prevail over bureaucratic obstruction because of strong executive leadership and because the political leaders could count on support from strong political parties to back their reforms in and out of parliament.

One of the most critical tests of bureaucracy obedience came with the Socialist victory in 1981. The Socialist government made changes in some senior civil service positions, notably department directors, university rectors, and prefects.[15] But the changes were modest and mostly brought in fresh faces rather than overtly Socialist partisans.[16] The bureaucracy respected these minor shifts, and posed no obstacle to the sweeping social and economic changes introduced by the Socialists between 1981 and 1986.[17] When power moved back to the hands of the conservatives in 1986, there were very few personnel changes in the ranks of the civil service. The new government found the bureaucrats ready to implement their new policies even though some of them were diametrically opposite to those adopted by the Socialists. The norm of bureaucratic loyalty to whatever government is in power appears well developed in contemporary France.

Open bureaucratic resistance to political leadership is now rare in France. There is still the danger that the range of policy options open to ministers can be restricted by unimaginative thinking, lack of rigorous and open-minded analysis of alternatives, and unsympathetic treatment from permanent officials in their ministries. Of course, an alert and dynamic minister can demand—and probably elicit—better treatment from bureaucrats. All too often, however, ministers are preoccupied with other concerns or simply lacking in the intellectual and technical abilities necessary to tell whether their officials are performing as they desire. In France the pool of potential ministers is somewhat larger than it is in Britain, Germany, or Italy because ministers can be selected from outside parliament. But the pressure to balance factions and parties, reward the faithful, and pay political debts limits the choice of the best ministers. Thus, by ministerial default, policy-making powers often slip from the hands of the politically accountable leaders into those of the bureaucrats.

The French bureaucracy is highly centralized but also compartmentalized. The various strata and divisions are insulated from each other, and the whole administrative system is prone to stalemate because of its lack of communication.[18] This danger is countered by informal links that tie together much of the political and administrative leaderships. Old boy networks made up of the alumni of the elite *grandes écoles* facilitate communication between bureaucrats, politicians, and business people.[19] In effect, the French bureaucratic system produces a high degree of interdependency between civil servants and politicians at all levels of government. Although this interdependency assures political leaders important roles in the administration of laws, the highly personalized nature of the politicians' involvement does not make for good democratic control.

THE ONE AND INDIVISIBLE REPUBLIC

To preserve national unity in the face of cultural and political diversity, both authoritarian and democratic regimes have sought to impose rigid centralized rule in France. All major political decisions still emanate from Paris. Local governments serve more to implement the decisions made by the central government than to solve local problems through their own initiative. The high degree of centralization in France is only slightly exaggerated by an anecdote about a Third Republic minister of education: Supposedly this official delighted in pulling out his pocket watch and telling visitors that at that moment every eight-year old in France was studying page so-and-so of a specific textbook.

Centralization not only promotes national unity in a diverse society, it also assures equality. Government policies and services are presumably uniform throughout the country. Citizens in one part of the country are treated in the same way and provided the same services by the government as in another part. The urge for equality is powerful in France and reinforces the centralization even at the cost of stifling local initiative and innovation. Recently, the minister of education terminated an innovative experiment in a Paris suburban public school involving special techniques and equipment with the explanation that "it is difficult to accept that teaching in one school should be very different from that in other schools."

The various layers of French government are illustrated in Table 9.3. They are not structured hierarchically in the sense that each level has control over the next lower level of government. Regional governments have no control over the department policies; the department general councils do not direct the municipal governments. Instead, each of these layers of government interacts directly with the central government in Paris. The specific competencies and responsibilities of the regional, departmental, and local governments are defined by the national government.

The Socialist government adopted a major reform in 1981 to decentralize French government.[20] The principal feature of the reform was the reduction in the formal power of the centrally appointed prefects. Prior to the reform, the prefects had vast powers.[21] They controlled the police, supervised the administration of national policies, and exercised control or "tutelage" over locally elected officials. After the decentralization reforms, the prefects were stripped of most of these powers. Currently, the

TABLE 9.3 Subnational Governments in France

Regions (22)

Executive	*President of the Regional Assembly* (elected by the Regional Assembly)
Legislative	*Regional Assembly* (direct popular election)

Departments (96)

Executive	*President of the General Council* (elected by the general council)
Legislative	*General Council* (direct popular election)

Local Governments or Communes (36,000)

Executive	*Mayor* (elected by the municipal council)
Legislative	*Municipal Council* (direct popular election)

president of the popularly elected general council, *conseil général,* exercises most executive powers in the department. The prefects, now retitled commissioners, serve as liaisons between the local government units and the national government.

There are some reasons for hesitancy in hailing these reforms as major transformations of French politics. To a large extent, they simply formalized changes already under way for at least ten years.[22] In practice, the prefects though powerful, worked cooperatively with local governments and only very rarely used the coercive powers at their disposal. And the commissioners are still very influential as links between central and local governments. Old practices are difficult to change. The new commissioners still wear the prefect's uniform and most are still addressed by the prestigious title of *Monsieur le préfet.* Besides the commissioners' strategic intermediary position, their contacts with the central bureaucracy and their skills in negotiating and bargaining continue to make them key political actors.[23]

Each department has a popularly elected general council which has powers to legislate on certain limited issues such as roads, public housing, and some welfare services.[24] The council elects a president from its members. The president serves as the chief executive of that department, setting the agenda, preparing the budget, and representing the department in negotiations with the central government. A general council votes on its departmental budget. The commissioners no longer have the prefects' power to propose the budget, but they do exercise audit control over expenditures and thus deter, as the prefects did, improper departmental expenditures. The ability of the general councils to control their budgets is also reduced by limited taxation powers and the absence of increased national funds.

At the local level, there are more than thirty-six thousand communes or municipal governments in France. This number is exceptionally large for the size of the country. France has more communes than are found in Belgium, the Netherlands, Italy, Luxembourg, and West Germany combined, even though these countries have a total population two and a half times larger. Each French commune elects a municipal council for a six-year term; the council in turn elects a mayor for the duration of its mandate. Once elected, the mayor dominates local government, with municipal councilors relegated to secondary roles of greater or lesser importance according to the mayor's desires.

Although the responsibilities of local government are circumscribed by central controls and the lack of independent finances, the mayors are powerful political figures. They serve as brokers mediating between individuals at the local level and the central government.[25] They compete with each other for resources offered by the central government and seek to adapt centrally decided policies to local situations. They work primarily through the prefectural and administrative channels to implement government projects and seek support for local projects. They also use their political contacts with parliamentarians to gain assistance for their communities. These contacts are facilitated by the possibility of holding concurrent elected positions. Thus, many members of parliament also serve simultaneously as mayors and/or members of a general council.[26] In contrast to the limited influence of British mayors, French mayors are important figures with more influence than might be expected in a state as centralized as France.

The regions were created in 1958. Originally designed to help in economic planning and regional development, they have only slowly accumulated other responsibilities. Both local and central authorities have resisted shifting any of their authority to the new regional bodies. Each region has an assembly elected directly by the people. There is also a regional economic and social council whose members are designated by labor unions, business groups, farmers' associations, and family and cultural associations. The executive officer of the region is the president of the regional assembly. The scope of activities for these regions is narrow, the most important act being the approval of the region's budget. But the funds available for regional governments are small.

Nearly everyone in France complains about excessive centralization and about its supposed social and political consequences. But there is usually stiff opposition to concrete proposals for decentralization. National politicians wish to preserve their control, and local politicians prefer the familiar pattern to experimentation. One observer notes accurately:

> Centralization survives because the notables who apply it know how to maneuvre their way around it; since they derive importance from the skill, they have little wish to overthrow it.[27]

There is, thus, a strong coalition of local and national politicians, reinforced by the powerful centralized state bureaucracy, that opposes decentralization as a threat to its established privileges and practices. Few political leaders dare to confront this coalition, and fewer succeed in even temporarily overcoming it.

Public interest in decentralization is somewhat ambivalent. Opinion surveys show overwhelming support when phrased in general terms, but reactions to specific proposals are much less positive. When public interest in decentralization was at a peak a few years ago, a poll showed that most French citizens were opposed to decentralizing control of public schools if it meant some variation in teaching content and methods. Important reservations surface, in the public as well as within the political elite, whenever it appears that decentralization may foster different qualities or levels of government services. Such efforts, which might facilitate greater responsiveness to local needs, would infringe upon the principle of equality that the French insist upon so strongly.[28]

THE PUBLIC AND THE POLICY-MAKING PROCESS

Many years ago, V.O. Key developed the notion of "opinion dikes" to explain the impact of public opinion on American policy making. Public opinion defines the general rules of the game and sets boundaries on the range of options available to the policy makers. Leaders can try to extend or move these limits by influencing public opinion. But these dikes of public opinion define the appropriate range of public action. They limit the discretion of government leaders in the selection of public policies to those policies that fit within the dikes.[29]

However, sensibility to these opinion dikes varies with the nature of the political institutions. France is correctly regarded as a strong state which is less responsive to public pressure than is a weaker state, such as the United States. Political leaders in France are less vulnerable because of the strength of its political institutions, the aloofness and dominant position of the executive, its disciplined parties and majority coalitions, the highly centralized state, and its integrated and hierarchical bureaucracy. Overuse of protest in the past reduces the shock effect and therefore its power. The result is that the government unhindered, can in fact govern.

This strength of the state does not mean that the opinion dikes are not in place. They are there and limit government action as the Socialists learned in 1984. They had to abandon their effort to force through a controversial and unpopular reduction in state funding for private church-run schools. But the dikes are wider than in other democracies and the government appears less sensitive in the short run to public opinion. This distance from popular demands gives the French state greater flexibility in responding to new situations. France has fewer signs of governmental overload and governmental incapacity to meet rising expectations of citizens than have other western democracies. Noncompliance with government policy decisions is occasionally a problem in France but not with the dramatic consequences that it had in the British coal miners' strike of 1973 to 1974, or in the blockage of key policies by vested interests in the United States and elsewhere.

The closed nature of French government appears to have aided in avoiding the expected ailments of modern democracies. It is often able to hold interest groups demanding attention to narrow concerns at a distance in making difficult but important policy decisions. This gives a continuity and consistency that is often lacking in other democratic countries. These other countries must be more responsive to shifting public interest and pressure groups and that often leads to policy by fits and starts and muddled policy compromises in these other countries. The French government can take action even if it sometimes makes mistakes or neglects certain interests. The insulation of the government from public demands makes it difficult for alternative groups—such as feminists, environmentalists, peace movements, and tax revolts which have disrupted normal politics in other industrial democracies—to establish themselves. The government can ignore them or grant concessions that appease the general public but for which these groups cannot take any credit.

The focus here is not to praise the limited role for public opinion in France, but to explain how such a faulted system of representation may have helped this country avoid the problems of decay that hit other democracies during the 1970s and 1980s. The French state is a limited, not a closed system; it remains democratic with officials competitively selected in free elections. Between elections, the government is much freer than most to function without paying heed to shifting public opinion or to clamoring interest groups. Some distance is probably desirable, especially in times when a government may need to take actions that are unpopular in the short run, but that are essential for the long-run health of the society. The situation in France, however, seems to offer too limited opportunities for interim representation between elections. This encourages unresponsiveness on the part of government. Executive dominance by an aloof president, a prime minister who is remarkably well insulated from parliamentary pressure, and a strong elitist bureaucracy leave few openings for the expression of public concerns.

NOTES

1. Anthony Burgess, "Le Mal Français: Is There a Reason for Being Cartesian?" *New York Times Magazine*, 29 May 1977, p. 52.
2. Michel Debré, "The Constitution of 1958: Its Raison d'Etre and How it Evolved," in *France at Twenty*, ed. William G. Andrews and Stanley Hoffmann (Albany, NY: State University of New York Press, 1981).
3. Ezra N. Suleiman, "Presidential Government in France," in *Presidents and Prime Ministers*, ed. Richard Rose and Ezra N. Suleiman (Washington, DC: American Enterprise Institute, 1981).
4. H. Machin, "The President's Men: Advisers and Assistants at the Elysée Palace," in Vincent Wright, ed., *Continuity and Change in France* (London: George Allen & Unwin, 1964).
5. On the growth of presidential power, see Vincent Wright, *The Government and Politics of France*, 2nd ed. (New York: Holmes & Meier, 1983), pp. 20–96 and François Goguel, "The Evolution of the Institution of the French Presidency,

1959–1981," in Fred Eidlin, ed. *Constitutional Democracy: Essays in Comparative Politics. A Festschrift in Honor of Henry W. Ehrmann* (Boulder, CO: Westview, 1983, pp. 49–61.

6. The actual term of office may be shorter since presidents can dissolve the National Assembly at their discretion.

7. A good summary of the evolution of executive-legislative relations in the formative years of the Fifth Republic is found in William G. Andrews, *Presidential Government in Gaullist France: A Study of Executive-Legislative Relations* (Albany, NY: State University of New York Press, 1982).

8. Frank L. Wilson and Richard Wiste, "Party Cohesion in the French National Assembly, 1958–1973," *Legislative Studies Quarterly* 1 (November 1976): 467–490.

9. See Frank R. Baumgartner, "Parliament's Capacity to Expand Political Controversy in France," *Legislative Studies Quarterly* 12 (February 1987): 33–54.

10. Anthony King, "How to Strengthen Legislatures—Assuming That We Want To," in *The Role of the Legislature in Western Democracies*, ed. Norman J. Ornstein (Washington, DC: American Enterprise Institute, 1981), p. 89.

11. Andrews, *Presidential Government in Gaullist France*.

12. John T. S. Keeler, "Toward a Government of Judges? The Constitutional Council as an Obstacle to Reform in Mitterrand's France," *French Politics and Society*, 11 (September 1985): 12–24. See also, Jack Hayward, "Separate and Rule—The Emerging Judicial Power in France," *Government and Opposition* 20 (Winter 1985): 104–11.

13. From 1959 to 1974, the Council handled an average of less than 1 case per year; from 1974 to 1981, the average rose to nearly 7 cases per year; between 1981 and 1984, the Council adjudicated nearly 14 cases per year. Keeler, "Toward a Government of Judges?" p. 16.

14. Ezra N. Suleiman, *Politics, Power, and Bureaucracy in France: The Administrative Elite* (Princeton, NJ: Princeton University Press, 1974), pp. 285–315.

15. See Anne Stevens, " '*L'Alternance*' and the Higher Civil Service," in Philip G. Cerny and Martin A. Schain, eds., *Socialism, the State and Public Policy in France* (New York: Meuthen, 1985), pp. 143–165.

16. Pierre Birnbaum, ed., *Les Elites socialistes au pouvoir, 1981–1985* (Paris: Presses Universitaires de France, 1986).

17. Socialist liberalization of law enforcement provoked some opposition from the police. But this declined after a 1983 clash that brought the forced retirement of the Paris police chief and the firing of the director-general of the national police.

18. Michel Crozier, *The Stalled Society* (New York: Viking, 1974).

19. Ezra N. Suleiman, *Elites in French Society: The Politics of Survival* (Princeton, NJ: Princeton University Press, 1978).

20. J. R. Frears, "The Decentralization Reforms in France," *Parliamentary Affairs* 36 (Winter 1983): 56–66.

21. Howard Machin, *The Prefect in French Public Administration* (New York: St. Martin's, 1977).

22. Yves Mény, "Decentralization in Socialist France: The Politics of Pragmatism," *West European Politics* 7 (January 1984): 65–79.

23. D. E. Ashford, "Reconstructing the French 'Etat': Progress of the *loi Defferre*," *West European Politics* 6 (July 1983): 263–270.

24. François Dupuy, "The Politico-Administrative System of the *Département* in France," in Yves Mény and Vincent Wright, eds., *Centre-Periphery Relations in Western Europe* (London: George Allen & Unwin, 1985), pp. 79–103.

25. Sidney Tarrow, *Between Center and Periphery: Grassroots Politicians in Italy and France* (New Haven, CT: Yale University Press, 1977).
26. Usually 75% or more of the members of parliament also serve in local governments.
27. Theodore Zeldin, *The French* (New York: Vintage, 1983), p. 173
28. For a presentation of important reservations about decentralization, see Wright, *The Government and Politics of France*, pp. 212–225.
29. V.O. Key, *Public Opinion and American Democracy* (New York: Alfred A. Knopf, 1964), pp. 552–553.

CHAPTER TEN
DEMOCRACY
IN FRANCE

The French are at once the most brilliant and the most dangerous of all European nations, and the best qualified to become, in the eyes of other peoples, an object of admiration, of hatred, of compassion, or alarm—never indifference.[1]

The Events of May 1968 shook French society and nearly toppled its regime. Student demonstrators and blue-collar strikers were joined by suit-clad business people, middle-level managers, sports heros, and entertainment stars in challenging the very essence of modern democracy and Western civilization. It was a revolt against the large and centralized society in which individuals seemed to be losing control over the things that affected their lives. While the revolt eventually collapsed, it was seen as a prototype of the kind of crisis of democracy and Western civilization that would not only recur in France but would likely hit other European democracies as well. It was thought that even if an actual revolt was avoided, the ideas and values of the sixty-eighters would inevitably change modern societies. The curious blending of libertarian, Marxist, and anarchist thoughts was to bring a drastic alteration if not the repudiation of liberal democracy.

Two decades later, such changes seem unlikely in France. The Events of May generation has now moved into influential positions and behave much like their predecessors. France has changed but not in the ways expected by the critics or Cassandras of democracy. Marxism, long regarded as essential for an individual in France to establish a reputation as an intellectual, is no longer fashionable among influential intellectual circles. The United States, which symbolized all that was bad about Western civilization to the sixty-eighters, is now seen as the most desirable model for development. The eagerly sought siting of a European Disneyland in France by both Socialist and conservative governments illustrates this point. Once suspicious of banks and contemptuous of profit, the French now flock to their stock market to speculate. There is a new realism and a pragmatism that has replaced traditional French rationalism and utopianism. Old battles over the very nature of the political regime have ended with a broader consensus supporting the current institutions than had ever been the case in the past.

The French are still wont to criticize their society for its propensity to stalemate or stall when faced with the need to adapt to a changing world. In fact, there is important evidence that indicates remarkable changes in France over the past thirty years that suggest greater dynamism than most French and foreign observers credit France with having.

A RETREAT FROM THE PLANNED ECONOMY

From the prerevolutionary times of Colbert to the Mitterrand years, the French state played an important part in developing and directing the economy. The state generously subsidized mining, banks, railroads, and heavy industry. Later, important parts of the economy were brought under direct ownership by the state: part of the automobile industry, all public utilities, much of the defense industry, tobacco, telecommunications, and over half of the banks and insurance firms. In addition, the government influenced the private sector through investment policies, subsidies, and economic planning.[2]

Economic performance over the last thirty years has been very positive. From the mid-1950s through the end of the 1970s, France's rate of economic growth was the highest in Western Europe, exceeding even the oft praised German economic record. During this period, the economy was transformed from one based largely on agriculture and small industry into a modern industrial state renowned for its achievements in such sophisticated fields as nuclear energy, automotive engineering, aircraft and missiles, and telecommunications.

A Socialist Alternative to Thatcherism

After resisting the oil crises of the early 1970s better than most European countries, the French economy began to falter at the end of that decade: Despite heavy subsidies, the steel industry was unprofitable; The once strong automotive industry slowed down; Other major industries began to show signs of overemployment. After first trying to encourage these large firms to avoid mass layoffs, the government eventually decided that international competition necessitated reducing the labor force and redirecting the economy toward more profitable enterprises. By 1980, unemployment was beginning to rise to postwar highs and the French economy slumped along with those of other industrial countries.[3]

When the Socialist party won power in mid-1981, its government adopted a sharply different strategy toward the economic crisis than that of Thatcher, Reagan, and indeed most other industrial leaders.[4] Instead of reducing government economic intervention, the French Socialists increased it. They expanded the public sector by nationalizing nearly all privately owned banks and eleven major industrial groups. With these new publicly owned firms, the government then controlled about 30 percent of the nation's industry. Beyond nationalizations, the Socialists took an active role in the rest of the economy by directing investment, controlling prices and wages, and regulating employment reductions in the public and private sectors.

While other countries were cutting public expenditures and reducing public employment, the Socialists in France substantially increased social-welfare benefits—especially for the neediest. New programs were created and old programs were administered with greater generosity. The Socialist government created thousands of new posts in public employment and increased the minimum wage level. It imposed a new, wealth tax and reduced taxes for lower income families in contrast to the British and American efforts to decrease taxes especially for the middle and upper income categories.

The results were initially positive—unemployment dipped slightly and the economy grew more rapidly than before and more rapidly than did the economies of many of France's neighbors. Disposable income grew, spurring consumer spending. But inflation also increased at a time when other countries rates were decreasing. Government indebtedness expanded, although it remained at a comparatively low level. Most importantly, the attempt to prod the French economy seemed to benefit trade competitors more than it helped the domestic economy. The increased consumer spending was for imported goods, such as Japanese videocassette recorders, rather than for domestic goods. The expected stimulus of domestic production did not occur. It also caused deterioration in France's trade balance and the weakening of the franc.

In effect, France suffered from following an isolated economic policy that was not in harmony with its trading partners.[5] The French government inflated its economy in anticipation of a worldwide economic recovery that did not take place. The difficulties of Mitterrand's economic policies did not necessarily prove the failure of a socialist alternative so much as they demonstrated the problems of following independent economic programs in an increasingly interdependent international economy. In addition, the French Socialists lacked the cooperation of their own business community. Business interests were alarmed by the Socialist nationalizations and anticapitalist rhetoric. The lack of confidence in the government, its economic policies, and the country's economic prospects discouraged new investment and risk-taking. Socialists felt businesses were making a deliberate attempt to sabotage their leftwing government. But a more accurate assessment of the decline in private investment would acknowledge the business community's anxieties about the economy rather than blame political motives. It was not so much a shortcoming of the economic policies as it was a political failure of the Socialists in selling their policies to those whose cooperation was essential to the programs' success.[6]

After less than two years, the Socialist government began to retreat from its initial economic strategy. A new policy of "rigor" stressed reduction in inflation, decreased public deficits, and defense of the franc. The Socialist policy of economic rigor closely resembled the austerity policies followed before 1981 by the conservative government and found in Thatcher's supply-side economics.

One lesson learned during this period was that the change of ownership from private hands into public hands did not have the dramatic effects on the overall economy hoped for by Socialists. The Socialist government soon found that the newly nationalized industries had to operate much the same as they did when they were privately owned: They had to be concerned with profitability; managers had to be able to make their decisions free from political considerations; public firms had to be able to reduce employment; they had to be as firm with unions as were competing private firms. Most importantly, the Socialists found that nationalizations did not mark a rupture with capitalism. Indeed, during their years in government, the Socialists seemed to rediscover the virtues of free enterprise. During the rest of the Socialist era, from 1983 to 1986, the Socialists tried to mend their relations with the business community. They gradually eased many of the economic controls they had earlier championed. During this later phase, Socialist policies were like those of conservative and centrist governments elsewhere.

Privatization and the Renaissance of the Market Economy

When the conservatives returned to power, they aggressively attacked longstanding mechanisms of state economic control. They eliminated most currency controls on the franc. They dropped government controls on laying off excess workers. They lifted price and wage controls and reduced controls on investment. Most importantly, they introduced a sweeping program to sell off most of the publicly owned industries. This meant denationalizing not only the firms the Socialists had nationalized in 1981, but also firms brought under public ownership by de Gaulle in 1945, and some enterprises, such as television networks, that had always been state-owned. To avoid depressing the prices for these nationalized corporations, the privatization sales were spread over several years. The initial sales were huge successes. When the first state-owned bank was put on sale, 3.8 million people wanted to buy 590 million shares—forty times the number offered to the public. The stock market thrived with an estimated 2 million new French investors coming into the market in 1986 alone.

Beyond public interest in the stock market, some observers have noted a new respect for entrepreneurship and even for profit that has often been absent in France. In the past, the best and the brightest tried to build their careers in the bureaucracy; while wealth was eagerly accumulated, profit-making was disdained. While success was desired, the appearance of success was shunned to the point that some wealthy French changed the emblems on their cars to make them look like less expensive models. Now, there is more interest in business as a respectable and prestigious career. There is a resurgence of popularity for free enterprise. It is still too early to determine if this is a passing fad or if it reflects changes in the traditional attitudes. But free enterprise notions are more popular now in France than they have been in the past forty years.

Similarly, it is not clear yet whether the current trend toward decreasing government's role in the economy is a temporary deviation or a real break with the past. It may simply represent an exaggerated reaction against the perceived excessive state-economic control under the Socialists that will wane when a traditional interventionist state rises again. The centuries' old tradition of state-economic intervention may yet reassert itself. There are forces within the government administrative ranks and within even conservative parties strongly attached to such an activist economic role for the state. While capitalism has gained new acceptance, public attitudes remain generally favorable to government economic intervention.

Privatization is clearly a success; the public has supported denationalization in principle and in fact by buying shares. For these reasons, the return of a Socialist government in 1988 did not bring concerns about a new wave of nationalizations. While Mitterrand and Rocard promised not to denationalize any other state-owned enterprises, they have tolerated the sale of minority shares in public firms to private investors. The Socialists have learned that state ownership is not necessary for state control, and the conservatives have long accepted the regulation of privately owned firms. At the end of the 1980s, such government economic control has not been fashionable. But the tradition of a state-directed economy has been a long one in France and is likely to continue.

THE SOCIAL-WELFARE STATE

Since the end of the Second World War, France has acquired an extensive system of social benefits, largely through the efforts of conservative and centrist governments. The government programs include unemployment and disability insurance, retirement benefits, health and hospitalization insurance, subsidized housing, subsidized public transportation, and direct family payments based on the number of children irrespective of income. These social-welfare benefits have received broad political support with conservative governments playing a major role in their creation and expansion.[7]

The programs are costly, amounting to nearly one fourth of the gross national product. Despite the extent and costliness of the benefits, there has been little discussion of a welfare state mentality in France like that which has preoccupied the British. In part, this is because the French economy has performed well and there has been no need to look for domestic causes of economic lethargy. It is also due to the format of French welfare programs. Unlike in Britain, where medicine was "nationalized" by creating a National Health Service, in France doctors and many hospitals remain private operations with the government paying for services through an insurance program rather than providing the services directly. The same is true in housing. In Britain, government-owned council housing makes up nearly a third of all dwellings. In France, government-owned housing accounted for less than one percent of total dwellings but the government provides households with generous subsidies for housing provided by nonprofit associations (HLMs—moderate price housing associations sponsored by the government) and private landlords.

The method of financing French programs is different from Britain. Nearly all of the British welfare programs are funded directly out of general state revenues; they are paid for with receipts from income, inheritance, and national sales taxes. In France, most of the programs are funded through employment taxes as a sort of insurance program. Both employers and employees pay a hefty percentage of the salary to social security funds. These funds are then used for retirement and disability benefits, for medical and dental care reimbursements. They also fund some educational and medical research and construction programs. One advantage of these taxes is that they tend to be less visible than income taxes. Workers are aware that part of their pay is deducted for the social security program, but few recognize that when the employers' share is added in the total cost, employment taxes amount to about a third of their income.

It should be stressed that these social-welfare programs are not poverty programs. They provide services and benefits for all, usually without any test of the individual's own means to afford them. The benefits tend to be more important to people of modest means in that the value of social benefits amounts to a much greater percentage of their total income. But the goal of these programs is not redistribution of wealth from the rich to the poor. For example, the generous system of family payments based on the number of children provide increasingly large payments as the number of children goes up without regard to family income. It is not so much a policy to provide assistance to needy people as it is one to encourage families to have more children in order to correct a too low birth rate.

Some of the programs are controversial. For example, government housing met an acute need in the 1970s by subsidizing construction of huge apartment tower complexes. However, these housing developments contributed to overcrowded neighborhoods with rising delinquency and crime. They also failed to meet the growing public desire for ownership of single family units. Social-welfare programs are also costly. As in other countries, these costs have grown rapidly with the prospect of paying for them out of employment taxes, as the population ages, posing a real challenge. The programs often involve complex and poorly coordinated administrative systems to implement them. But if a risk of government overload is created, it is well worth the problem. Most of the programs are very much appreciated by the public. Neither conservatives nor Socialists talk much of reducing benefits, of imposing user fees, or of eliminating programs. The social benefits are too popular for politicians to risk attacking them. In addition, political leaders remember that chief among the substantive complaints that fueled the tumultuous Events of May 1968 was a government imposed reduction in social security benefits announced nine months before the revolt.

The social-welfare state has helped to integrate less advantaged people into the capitalist system. Trade unions have pushed for these benefits and have been drawn into the system to promote them and administer them. The social-welfare programs reduce some of the uncertainties of a free enterprise system by providing for medical emergencies, income protection in cases of disability, and retirement benefits. Coupled with government programs to mandate a thirty-nine hour work week and five weeks of annual paid vacation for all workers, the social-welfare state promotes domestic tranquility by giving all a clear stake in the existing socioeconomic system.

There will continue to be changes in the social-welfare state. In recent years, both conservative and Socialist governments have worked to shift the pattern of benefits to favor the least advantaged portions of the population in the cause of national "solidarity." Such an orientation may be expected to continue in the future as a way of controlling rising costs. But there will be no broad retreat from the popular and stabilizing welfare state.

HUMAN RIGHTS

Among democratic peoples who value the notion of freedom, there are differences in emphasis and priorities. A recent international poll, for example, found that Americans tend to place greatest emphasis on freedom of religion while the French, along with most other Europeans, place greater importance on freedom of expression. These differences are reflected in societies. American towns are filled with churches of every denomination, and it is hard to find anything but the Catholic church in French towns. An American would have a hard time finding a journal on the local newsstand with anything other than ideas of the political mainstream, while a French citizen finds a full range of political magazines from Trotskyites to neo-fascists among the sports and gossip magazines in virtually every newsdealer's kiosk.

Americans regard it as inappropriate and illegal for the police to stop and question someone without having a reasonable suspicion that the individual has committed some crime. But the French accept as normal and desirable that their police have the right to stop people with no other motive than to check their identities. Criminal proceedings in France involve less protection for the rights of the accused than is the case in the United States. But trials are usually speedier in France. It has been said that if the accused is guilty, it would be best for them to be in the United States, where delays and technicalities may permit the guilty to escape; but if innocent, the accused would find the taint and suspicion of the accusation lifted more rapidly in France by pretrial judicial investigations that clear them without a trial.

Domestic and international human rights groups have little criticism of France's record in civil liberties. Until the early 1980s, the main shortcoming in the eyes of human rights activists was capital punishment—with executions still carried out by the guillotine. Capital punishment was rarely used (only five times between 1972 and 1982) and legally abolished in 1982. Another problem area has been the harsh treatment for conscientious objectors to France's obligatory national military service. While the draft applies to all young men, it affects most severely members of pacifist religious groups, such as Jehovah's Witnesses, who often find themselves imprisoned for refusing national service. One of the most important problems in human rights is discrimination against non-European foreign immigrants. While the government is genuinely attached to nondiscrimination and racial harmony, the anti-immigrant feelings of much of the population are reflected in intolerance and mistrust of the immigrants. As in Britain and West Germany, the laws bar such discrimination and the government promotes racial understanding. But such government efforts have little effect when faced with an intolerant public.

France has accepted the European Covenant of Human Rights, although, unlike most other adherents to this covenant, France does not permit individual citizens to take complaints to the European body when they feel that domestic channels are inadequate. Claims against France can only be taken to the European Commission or Court of Human Rights by other governments. Also, unlike other countries where constitutional courts have emerged as advocates of human rights, the French Constitutional Council has not moved into this area of law. But domestic legal recourses for those feeling their civil rights have been abused are adequate. Another check on possible civil rights abuse is a vigilant and independent press. In several recent cases, it has intervened on behalf of individuals and groups that have faced government abuse of their rights and succeeded in bringing relief through focusing public attention on the government's excesses.

State Controls and the Press

One area of concern has been the independence and impartiality of the written and electronic news. While it is true that a wide range of views appear in print, there are some problems for fringe political groups to get their views to the public.

For the written press, the problems have been financial. Increased costs and shifting public interests have affected the politically committed press. Nearly all newspapers now depend heavily on government subsidies for their income. There are worries that this financial assistance carries strings that prevent truly independent analysis.[8] The newspapers that prosper are those with minimal attention to political news. The mass circulation newspapers purport to be nonpartisan but, in fact, they reflect only the mainstream of public opinion. They give minimal coverage, if any at all, to advocates of more extreme political views or to those supporting policies or views outside the consensus.

In addition, Robert Hersant, a controversial conservative politician, has created a large press syndicate by purchasing many of the most successful Paris and provincial newspapers. His influence on editorial and news content has produced concern among leftwing politicians and even among centrist and conservative politicians. There are still important newspapers who support socialist viewpoints. While this helps to balance news coverage, there is a need for a genuinely independent source of political news. Newspapers hostile to the conservatives display that hostility in their news columns but fail to discuss the warts of their political friends; newspapers aligned with the conservatives are eager to show the faults of the Left but neglect the problems of their conservative allies. The result is that the informed public tends to expect and to ignore the criticism from committed newspapers. There are a few weekly magazines noted for their sharp criticism of governments of all political stripes and for their investigative reporting. But the committed nature of the press in general leads to public discounting of its political reporting.

The problem has even been more acute in broadcast news. Until the 1980s, radio and television were government monopolies. Unlike the renowned independence of the British Broadcasting Corporation, the French state-owned radio and television system acquired a reputation for clear bias toward their political masters. In the 1940s and 1950s, the bias operated against antisystem parties of the Left and Right: the Communists and Fourth Republic Gaullists. Once the Gaullists came to power under the Fifth Republic, they learned to use this power over broadcast news to their advantage. Their political rivals had difficulty in gaining access to television and when they did, it was their quarrels and divisions that caught the attention of television newscasters. It was common for the only televised pictures of Gaullist opponents to be taken from the rear showing them in rather uncomplimentary stances such as from the back as they walked up stairs or as they stooped to pick something up.

Over the past fifteen years, there have been a number of efforts to assure greater independence for television and radio news.[9] In practice though, these reforms have simply been a means of changing the political control of the media from one political camp to the other when political leadership has shifted. For example, after his election as president, Valéry Giscard d'Estaing undertook a substantial reform of the television system. The result was not greater independence but rather a new political bias favorable to Giscard and his associates. His foes, both in the opposition and within the ranks of his own majority, found it difficult to gain coverage on television news. Furthermore, the electronic media largely ignored stories and scandals that embarrassed Giscard and his government. François Mitterrand carried out an even more extensive reform of radio and television after 1981.[10] Again, the consequence was much more a shift in political bias rather than the creation of independent television and radio news.

There is now, however, hope that overt government intervention in television and radio will decline. Under Mitterrand, the government's monopoly over radio was abandoned. Numerous private stations have now emerged and their impact on the radio market has grown. While most have limited budgets and very small news staffs, if any at all, these private stations offer the potential, and in some cases the reality, of broadcasting independent, and even critical voices over the airwaves. Mitterrand also permitted the creation of two private television stations but they did not develop news coverage at first. Under the Chirac government, privatization extended also to television. The conservative government sold the largest state-owned channel to private investors.

The impact of privatization in both radio and television is uncertain. It is likely to mark a major step in decreasing overt government manipulation of the news. But the government's presence will still be felt through its supervision of these private stations. In addition, the shift to private hands may reduce government control, but it may increase the influence of economic and social forces. Stations may find it difficult to find sponsors for documentaries or controversial programs. They may be pressured to eliminate "bad" news or to support the status quo by the powerful private interests that now own them or pay for the advertising.

The assurance of broad access to a wide range of political views and to independent news coverage is a problem in all democracies. It has been a particularly thorny one in France. The shift of some radio and television to public hands will not eliminate the danger of news control, but it will shift that control out of the hands of government officials. The biases of the future will be less due to government news management than to the built-in economic and social biases of a consensual, free enterprise structure.

FRENCH RESPONSES
TO THE CHALLENGES OF THE 1980s

France is not one of the troubled democracies. Its performance compared to its earlier eras of political history and compared to contemporary neighboring democracies has been laudable in most regards. During the many years when French democracy was regarded as troubled, its weaknesses were often ascribed to exceptional circumstances peculiar to France. Now, that it is a more successful democracy to which more troubled democracies may look for lessons on resolving their problems, it may be that this same exceptionalism will limit the utility of the French experience.

Perhaps the most notable accomplishment has been the emergence of a consensus around the political institutions. After centuries of debate over the proper framework for government, there is now a broad consensus favorable to the institutions of the Fifth Republic. This broadness is surprising since that political framework was tailor-made for Charles de

Gaulle. Yet the constitution of the Fifth Republic has survived each of the crises that observers had predicted would end it: de Gaulle's departure from politics, a shift of political power out of the hands of the Gaullists, a shift of political power to the Socialists, and the challenge of the cohabitation of a president from one political camp and a parliamentary majority and government from its ardent opponents. At each of these bench marks, the institutions proved adaptable, flexible, and, most importantly, still desirable to both the political elite and to the general public.

The strength of these institutions and their ability to resist responding to whimsical changes in public opinion has enabled France to avoid the flux, the uncertainty, and the appearance of being overwhelmed by social change that have seemed to undermine support for democracy elsewhere. While Britain, Germany, and Italy have been troubled by systems that seemed to inhibit the emergence of strong executive leaders, the French system has provided a string of powerful and effective presidents and prime ministers. But the French hybrid presidential/parliamentary system is unlikely to be attractive to other countries. The French accept the aloof and sometimes authoritarian style of governing because of their coupling this acceptance with the tacit understanding that they have the right, even the duty, to resist the imposition of this authority that they grant to their leaders.

The long French tradition of popular contention[11] helped insulate France from the shock of the new and unconventional forms of political participation that had become standard in all democratic countries in the 1970s and 1980s. In France, these tactics were not unusual and the government was used to handling such disruptive forms of involvement. But these other countries have acquired their own experience with protest politics thus improving their abilities to control them and reducing their shock value.

The strength of the party system and its greater public acceptance add stability and flexibility to contemporary French democracy. The French party system was reviving while other countries were troubled by apparent party decline. The "older" party systems in Britain, Germany, and Italy were experiencing problems with their age and earlier successes to the point that many viewed them as in decline. While such worries about party decay now appear to be exaggerated, they nevertheless raised concerns about the viability of democracy in western democratic countries. Once again, the French experience in reviving the party system has only limited value for other democracies. The party revival was due to a serious but earlier decline of French parties. France did not avoid party decline; it simply occurred earlier. In developing a more disciplined, better organized, and less splintered party system in the 1970s, the French were simply catching up with much of the rest of Europe. The only lesson seems to be the likelihood that democratic competition will bring new parties when the old parties falter.

Terrorism in France

France has not escaped the plague of terrorism that has challenged other democracies.[12] Two categories of home-grown terrorist activities have occurred. The first, and most widespread, is terrorism from ethnic minorities in the cause of greater autonomy for their regions: Bretons, Corsicans, and Basques. The ethnic-based terrorists have usually targeted property rather than persons in their attacks, blowing up government offices, television towers, and other symbols of the central state. The second type is from extremist groups, nearly always on the far left of the political spectrum. These groups, such as Direct Action have been more willing, in recent years, to risk injury to persons with bombings of high speed trains and subway stations, attacks on military installations, and assassinations such as the 1986 killing of the head of Renault.

But added together, the ethnic and extreme left terrorists have not been as disruptive to the French political scene as have been IRA terrorists in Britain or political extremists in Germany or Italy. France has not had to resort to the extraordinary laws and judicial procedures that have been used in these other countries. The special terrorist laws, preventive detention, special terrorist courts, and other exceptional procedures that have been used elsewhere have no parallels in France. Indeed, the state security court, established in the early 1960s to try army mutineers who opposed Algerian independence and which later was used in a few terrorist cases, was disbanded in 1981.

As for international terrorism, the French have had a unique approach that has not been very appealing to other countries.[13] France has a large population of foreign exiles who have sought asylum in France. These former political leaders are often targets of attacks by agents from the new governments in their homelands, and these attacks take place on French territory; the political exiles are also often supporters of attacks on their homeland's embassies or other installations in France. While the French government tries to provide protection to these political refugees, it does not energetically pursue the terrorists as long as they do not harm French people or property. France also tried to reduce international terrorism through informal understandings with Arab terrorist organizations—the major source of international terrorism. The French succeeded in maintaining friendly ties with hard-line Arab states, such as Syria and Iraq, when tensions in the Middle East nearly ruptured these states' ties with other western countries. This "friendly nation" status helped to discourage Arab allies from promoting extensive terrorist activity within French boundaries. In return for this restraint, the French generally avoided extraditing suspected terrorists to other European countries. When they caught wanted terrorists, they got them out of the country rather than extradite them.

Eventually, this informal understanding broke down. By 1986 France was no longer immune from international terrorism. A rise in terrorism, both the domestic and the international types, alienated public opinion, and demands for stern antiterrorist action grew. As a consequence, France increased its cooperation with other countries and began to extradite accused terrorists. It imposed a requirement that all foreign visitors have visas in an attempt to regulate more closely the entry of potentially undesirable aliens. Police investigations and infiltrations of terrorist groups were increased. The new measures were successful. After a spurt of terrorist activity in the last half of 1986, terrorism abated. Police made a series of arrests of members of Direct Action, crippling that leftist group. But the terrorists' advantage and motivation is that even a few individuals can still wreak havoc with a few well-placed bombs.

Terrorism is not as great a problem in France as in other countries, but it is not absent. There will always be the possibility, even the probability, of a dramatic, headline-making terrorist episode to trouble the political scene and frighten the public.

Continuing Problems
of French Democracy

Perhaps the greatest risk, to the current and rather successful system, is the long tradition of revolt in France. There is a ritual of protest with the tactics, sites, and anthems of revolt well established by repeated use through the generations. These past revolts have a certain glamor and romance. Periodically, and often unpredictably, the French take it into their minds to rebel against the powers-that-be. Attracted by the desire to relive a glamorous past, they recreate earlier revolts and in doing so threaten the very existence of the current regime. The Events of May 1968 were such a "pyschodrama" with the participants more or less consciously acting out historical revolts.[14] It is likely that at some time in the future, the French will try to recreate the Events of May, the Liberation, the Paris Commune, and other revolutionary moments. Such a likelihood means that there will always be an unpredictable element in even the most stable of French regimes.

A second problem is the persistence of political polarization. Even as consensus has grown at the level of the general public, and even as party positions on specific issues have converged, the political elite has remained sharply polarized. Polarization poses two dangers: First, there is the risk of public alienation with a political elite that persists in fighting amongst each other in highly symbolic ways of little interest to a public more concerned with pragmatism and compromise; second, the intensity of the rhetoric is often taken seriously by the elite. Much of the problems that the Socialists faced from business circles was due to their revolutionary vocabulary and dogmatic posturing rather than to concrete policies that damaged the interests of private enterprise. Regarding your opponents as class enemies rather than simple rivals heightens tensions and discourages compromise.

The final problem is the remoteness of the regime from the people. While this distance has permitted decisive government action in France on issues, where divided public opinion has delayed decisions in other countries, it often appears that the French government is too well insulated from public opinion. The perception of an aloof and unresponsive government encourages protest and in extreme cases revolt. This problem is complicated by the extent of polarization among politicians. Not only do they not listen to each other, they do not listen to citizens with different viewpoints. Leaders talk of dialogue and consultation but prefer to proceed with their own projects. Then there is the public's disposition to resist involvement in order to guard one's right to oppose. One business leader expressed well the consequent problem in an interview with this writer:

> France is a country that is too rigid. . . . We tend to take for granted the anticipated reaction of others without trying to understand their reaction or their ideas. . . . The real problem is to try to truly establish dialogue. Will these contacts between groups and [citizens] lead government to take a different position than it would have and will my reaction be a bit different? These are the key questions.

NOTES

1. Alexis de Tocqueville, *The Old Regime and the French Revolution*, trans. Stuart Gilbert (Garden City, NY: Doubleday Anchor, 1955), p. 211.
2. Peter A. Hall, *Governing the Economy: Politics of State Intervention in Britain and France* (London: Oxford University Press, 1986) and Jack Hayward, *The State and the Market Economy: Industrial Patriotism and Economic Intervention in France* (Brighton, England: Wheatsheaf Books, 1985).
3. Volkmar Lauber, *The Political Economy of France: From Pompidou to Mitterrand* (New York: Praeger, 1983).
4. Howard Machin and Vincent Wright, eds., *Economic Policy and Policy-Making Under the Mitterrand Presidency, 1981–1984* (London: Frances Pinter, 1985).
5. John S. Ambler, "Is the French Left Doomed to Fail?" in John S. Ambler, ed., *The French Socialist Experiment* (Philadelphia: Institute for the Study of Human Issues, 1985).
6. Frank L. Wilson, "Socialism in France: A Failure of Politics Not a Failure of Policy," *Parliamentary Affairs* 38 (Spring 1985): 163–179.
7. X. Gardette, "The Social Policies of Giscard d'Estaing," in Vincent Wright, ed., *Continuity and Change in France* (London: George Allen & Unwin, 1984), pp. 129–138 and Gary Freeman, "Socialism and Social Security," in John Ambler, ed., *The French Socialist Experiment* (Philadelphia: Institute for the Study of Human Issues, 1985), pp. 92–115.
8. C. R. Eisendrath, "Press Freedom in France: Private Ownership and State Controls," in Jane Leftwich Curry and Joan R. Dassin, eds., *Press Control Around the World* (New York: Praeger, 1982), pp. 62–81.
9. Raymond Kuhn, "The Presidency and the Media, 1974–1982," in Vincent Wright, ed., *Continuity and Change in France* (London: George Allen & Unwin, 1984), pp. 178–201.
10. Raymond Kuhn, "France and the News Media," *West European Politics* 8 (April 1985): 50–66.
11. Charles Tilly, *The Contentious French* (Cambridge, MA: Harvard University Press, 1986).

12. Edward Moxon-Browne, "Terrorism in France," *Conflict Studies* No. 144 (1983).
13. Philip G. Cerny, "France: Non-Terrorism and the Politics of Repressive Tolerance," in Philip G. Cerny, ed., *Social Movements and Protest in France* (New York: St. Martin's, 1982), pp. 94–125.
14. Raymond Aron, *Anatomy of a Student Revolt* (New York: Praeger, 1969).

PART FOUR
FEDERAL REPUBLIC OF GERMANY

The Federal Republic of Germany, more commonly known as West Germany, lacks the historical roots that prepared the way for democracy in Britain and France. Democracy was imposed on the vanquished Germans after the Second World War by the conquering allies, hardly an auspicious beginning for a new democracy.

The challenges to maintain a stable democracy that countries experienced in the 1970s and 1980s prompted greater concern about the West German democracy than about the others. Would the threat of domestic terrorism, the end of the postwar economic boom, the rise of a new antiparliamentary party, and disruptive political patterns by a variety of new social movements undermine what many regarded as a still fragile system? West Germany's success in dealing with these and other challenges demonstrated the great strength of its political order and offered examples to other democracies on how to successfully meet the challenges of a changing society.

CHAPTER ELEVEN
DEMOCRACY IN A HOSTILE SETTING? GERMAN HISTORY AND SOCIETY

You hope in vain, Germans, to make yourselves a nation.
Train yourself, rather—you can do it—to be freer human beings.

Johan Goethe and
Frederich Schiller[1]

The British zeal in perpetuating the past has provided continuity and a sense of stability to their political system. The French, divided as they have been by their history, nonetheless celebrate it. The Germans, however, find their history a subject of great debate and even embarrassment. Certainly, they take pride in the cultural contributions of Beethoven, Dürer, Goethe, Kant, Luther, Schiller, and many others. But they struggle to understand how such a rich cultural heritage had failed to be accompanied by democratic political expression. Above all they are tormented by the need to explain how their parents and grandparents had permitted the horrors of the Nazi era. This anguish over their past makes history highly controversial. Whereas other peoples can celebrate the past, Germans worry if the exploration of the past, and especially the recent past, will lead to rationalizations of Hitler's atrocities.[2] Thus, recent proposals by the German government to establish historical museums in Bonn and West Berlin were met with strong opposition and renewed agonizing over how to treat modern and contemporary German history.

The German people are among the oldest peoples in Europe. But unlike other European nations that acquired their own unified states centuries ago, the Germans remained a people divided among many separate countries. Consequently, German unification was a goal that inspired poets and statesmen throughout the centuries. Other values such as social change, individual freedom, or representative democracy were ignored or delayed while the goal of national unity was sought. The results were slow in coming and then only short-lived: German unity was not achieved until 1870 and collapsed after 1945 in the enforced division of Germany into two separate and hostile countries.

In the western section of Germany, a democratic regime was established, the Federal Republic of Germany. Many observers, inside and outside of Germany, had worried about whether this democracy could establish roots in a setting where historical traditions and social structures seemed inhospitable. The only prior democratic experience in Germany had been the ill-fated Weimar regime that lasted only fourteen years. German history and society have been probed thoroughly for sources of threats or supports for their new democratic system. After forty years, the democratic government in West Germany seems to have found sufficient support in recent history and society to become enrooted. Questions still remain, however, on whether these roots have grown deep enough or spread wide enough to permit the democratic system to meet the challenges of the last decade of the twentieth century.

THE EMERGENCE OF MODERN GERMANY

After the division of Charlemagne's empire in A.D. 843, the western portion soon acquired a centralized and unified government that evolved into modern France. The eastern portions, however, received a lofty title, the Holy Roman Empire, but failed to develop a strong central government. Instead, the German-speaking peoples of central Europe soon divided into numerous sovereign states and free cities linked together only loosely in the Empire. By the thirteenth century, there were literally hundreds of separate German states. Their divisions and political underdevelopment made Germany the battlefield and wartime pawns for other European countries. For example, the Thirty Years War ravaged the German states between 1618 and 1648: One German region, the Palatinate, lost four fifths of its population; In Bohemia, 30,000 of its 35,000 villages ceased to exist during this total war; Other German states suffered similar devastation. There were other consequences because of this lack of unity. Without a strong central government, Germany lagged behind other European countries in establishing a distinctive identity, in creating a government bureaucracy and legal system, and in modernizing its economy and society.

The Quest for German Unity

It is not surprising that Germans yearned for a unity that would offer protection against external foes and direction in modernizing within. The eighteenth-century Enlightenment brought to much of Europe a concern for democratic values and the primacy of reason that inspired French revolutionaries and British reformers. But in a fragmented Germany, still recovering from the trauma of the Thirty Years War, the Enlightenment's main legacy was the fanning of nationalist aspirations and the beginning of the search for a strong state capable of imposing unity. These themes were then popularized by the much stronger German Romantic movement of the nineteenth century which exalted the notion of *Volk* or "the German people" to mystical levels.

The Napoleonic wars of the early nineteenth century also played an important part in the eventual unification of Germany. Napoleon's initial victories brought the formal end of the largely imaginary Holy Roman Empire and resulted in consolidating the three hundred or so German states into thirty-eight. Later, the role of Prussia and Austria in defeating Napoleon enhanced the potential for one of these powerful German states to serve as a focal point for unifying the rest. For the next sixty years, Prussia and Austria strove for ascendancy over the loose confederation of the German states. Because of its preoccupation with its own multinational empire, Austria showed less interest in the project of German unity. Prussia, on the other hand, with a well-disciplined standing army, prepared to bring unity through conquest if necessary.

French revolutionary ideals that were spread by Napoleon's armies and through intellectual circles found supporters in Germany as well as in other parts of Europe. A wave of liberal revolutions that swept across Europe in 1848 affected German states too. Many of the German liberals gathered in Frankfurt to establish a parliament. Faced with the twin needs of national unification and democratization, the liberals sought, but found little support in the population for their reform ideas. They also hesitated to carry through on their own revolutionary aspirations. When Prussia's Frederick William IV rejected their offer to support him in uniting Germany under a constitutional monarchy, the parliament dispersed. Elsewhere, Frederick William's troops suppressed liberal or popular uprisings and claimed to have saved Germany from chaos. Thus, Germany's earliest experiment with democracy was short-lived with even liberal reformers more concerned with national unification than with democracy or social change. The emperor tolerated the existence of a parliament with the trappings but not the reality of a democracy. Real political power was concentrated in the hands of the monarch and his political advisors.

In 1862, the Prussian King William I selected Otto von Bismarck as his chancellor. Unsupportive of liberal ideas, Bismarck countered an effort by the weak Prussian parliament to limit the military budget by simply dissolving that legislative body. Bismarck was a masterful diplomat but he showed no reluctance in seeking his ends through "blood and iron" when unable to achieve them through diplomacy. He often fomented war with neighboring countries on rather thin pretexts: against Denmark in 1864; against Austria in 1866; and against France in 1870. He enticed other German states to unite around Prussia in the face of threats, caused by the wars, from external enemies. Where that failed, he annexed them by force. The rapid and stunning victories of the Prussian armies in these wars further encouraged other German states to accord greater preeminence to the Prussians. At the end of the Franco-Prussian War, Bismarck was able to tell William I that the other German states wanted him to be emperor of the Second Reich.

German unity was accomplished after nearly a millenium of division. However, its achievement was accompanied by the consolidation of an archconservative and authoritarian rule at a time when most other European countries were making the transition to democratic forms of government. The new Germany began an energetic effort to modernize its economy, but there were few attempts to modernize its society or politics. Inordinate political and social power remained unchallenged in the hands of the Prussian aristocrats, the Prussian bureaucracy, the Prussian military, and large landowners. There was a parliament elected by universal manhood suffrage but its powers were strictly limited. At most, it offered a thin facade of democratic window dressing to an otherwise autocratic regime. Bismarck accommodated demands for social change by introducing social-welfare programs that were relatively advanced for their times. They were designed, however, to placate potential dissenters without engaging in fundamental social reforms. The result was a seriously "faulted nation" with new and old elements of the economy and society coexisting uneasily. Such intermingling of the old and new, common to every country, but in Germany, was so great as to be volcanic. There was hardly a single phenomenon that did not "display the faultings of old and new, of social traditions and economic requirements, of centralism and regionalism, of nationalism and rationalism.[3]

The Weimar Republic (1919 to 1933)

The imperial regime failed to endure the First World War. As the war developed into a costly stalemate, power shifted from the emperor and his chancellor into the hands of the military leaders. By 1916, effective political power was held by Field Marshal Paul von Hindenburg and General Erich Ludendorff. As they realized the inevitability of defeat, they returned power to the imperial chancellor, Prince Max von Baden, who, urged on by Hindenburg and Ludendorff, negotiated the armistice that ended the war. As the imperial regime toppled, power passed, by default, to a small band of liberal politicians who nearly by accident proclaimed a new republic. It was these aspiring democratic politicians who were left with the unpopular task of negotiating a final treaty with the victorious Allies.

By relinquishing power early, the military avoided responsibility for the defeat that they had earned both on the battlefield and in political power. In the mind of the public, the military still was associated with the earlier victories; the democratic politicians were associated with the defeat and humiliating terms of the Versailles Treaty. Within a few years, nationalists and the military spread the myth of a stab in the back to an otherwise powerful and undefeated military by conspiring democratic politicians. Despite the fact that there was no truth in this myth and that the Army High Command had urged an end of the war in 1918, the stab in the back thesis undermined the already shaky legitimacy of Germany's first democratic regime.

The new democratic system was known as the Weimar Republic, named after the small town where its constitution was drafted. The constitution was regarded as state of the art. It provided a democratic government through a parliamentary and federal system. Both the president and the parliamentary body, the Reichstag, were elected by universal suffrage. It provided guarantees of extensive political liberties. In retrospect though, it is easy to see the problems of this constitution: the broad emergency powers of the president, the ease of toppling the government, and a proportional representation system that encouraged the proliferation of small parties. But Weimar's problems were much deeper than simply defects in its written constitution.

First, the faulted nation that had developed under the empire was not united. The political changes were not accompanied by the sweeping social and economic changes that were needed to provide a supportive environment for democracy: The military and imperial bureaucracy remained untouched; The power of the old Prussian aristocracy was not affected; The economic structures retained the nationalist rather than capitalist character they had acquired under the empire; Above all, values remained more traditional, even feudal, instead of modern and democratic. Within weeks of the establishment of their new republic, democratic leaders were forced to forswear making urgently needed socioeconomic changes in order to win the support of key sections of society. The economic and political collapse that accompanied military defeat created a highly volatile social climate in which the fear of revolution or civil war flourished. The success of the Bolshevik Revolution in Russia encouraged discontented elements to attempt their own revolutions in various parts of Germany. On the far Right disgruntled nationalists organized counter-revolts or putsches of their own to protest the embarrassment of defeat. These were not abstract fears but founded on Germany's terrible turmoil: There were abortive Communist coups in 1919, 1921, and 1923, failed rightwing coups in 1920 and 1923, and a political climate punctuated by violence and assassinations.

In this highly explosive situation, democratic leaders were forced to agree to abstain from fundamentally reforming the economy and from reorganizing the military in exchange for support from the business community and from the military hierarchy. Both were suspicious if not openly hostile to the new democratic regime. The new political leaders needed the continuity and day-to-day services of the civil servants but they obtained them only at the cost of abstaining from reforming the old imperial bureaucracy. While these accords may have been essential for the immediate survival of the regime, they compromised the long-term prospects of democracy by preventing the social and economic changes that were needed to unite the faulted nation the democratic leaders had inherited from the empire. The emperor was gone but the democratic regime had to live with an imperial economy and society.

Second, the new democratic regime lacked public support from the beginning. Democracy was not achieved as a result of a popular uprising or even of broad public demands for political change. It came, almost by default, to fill a vacuum created by the fall of the imperial regime as the emperor fled from Germany, and to meet the demands of Allies that a democratic government be installed to negotiate a final treaty. The mass of the population felt no victory and showed little interest in the achievement of a pluralistic democracy.

The new government's ability to build legitimacy in the future was almost immediately undercut by the terms of the treaty ending the First World War. The democratic leaders, who had opposed the imperial regime's prewar policies, were forced to sign a treaty in which they accepted, on behalf of Germany, full responsibility for the war. Few historians now accept such a simplified account of the origins of World War I; a climate making war nearly inevitable had developed from the deeds and beliefs of leaders of most European countries. Whatever the objective facts, the Germans of the 1920s rejected this guilt and felt betrayed by their government's weakness in formally accepting such responsibility.

The Versailles Treaty imposed staggering war reparation costs on Germany. Since Germany was alone responsible, it must pay for every house, factory, or cow destroyed during the course of the war. The reparation payments would have been impossible even for a strong economy; for the struggling German economy after 1920, they spelled disaster. Eventually, the Weimar government simply printed money to meet its external and internal obligations with disastrous economic consequences. Inflation reached incredible rates: A magazine that cost 200 marks in April 1923 sold for 2000 marks in July, 150,000 marks in September, and 4,000,000 marks in October. When a new currency was introduced to end the spiraling inflation, 1 trillion old marks were exchanged for each new mark. This catastrophic inflation wiped out the savings of the middle class thus disaffecting the most likely source of popular backing for the new democratic regime. Only a few years after finally surmounting this economic disaster, the German economy was hit by the effects of the worldwide depression of the 1930s. In the minds of many Germans, democracy became linked with economic incompetence.

The third handicap to the Weimar democracy was the absence of a supportive political elite. Many of those who took part in politics had no commitment to democracy. Important political groupings on the Right—fascists, nationalists, and Nazis—and on the Left—communists—condemned democracy as fraudulent. But they fully used democratic freedoms of assembly and speech to attempt to destroy democracy. Beyond the normal electoral politics, they raised political militias to disrupt the meetings of their political rivals. Even those committed to democracy appeared unprepared to play constructive parts in the government. Divided into many small parties—for example, forty-one parties contested the 1928 election—they were unable to form stable government coalitions. Democratic forces fought with each other, less concerned with the looming danger of antidemocratic parties on the Right and the danger of Bolshevik style communism than with their own rivalries. In addition, the civil service, judiciary, military, and private businesses were filled with individuals with little sympathy for democracy and sometimes overtly opposed to it. In a very real sense, Weimar failed because it was a democracy without sufficient democrats in either the general public or the elite.

The Nazi Era (1933 to 1945)

Hitler came to power legally in 1933 under the provisions of the Weimar constitution. After a succession of short-lived governments, he was made chancellor by President Hindenburg. His party had become the largest party in the country but it was still far from having majority support. Once installed as chancellor, Hitler moved quickly and consolidated his power. Very soon he had effectively supplanted the discredited Weimar Republic with a Third Reich founded on unquestioning obedience to the Führer's will.[4] Terror and violence were used to isolate and eliminate Hitler's real and imagined rivals, first in Germany and then in other countries conquered by the German army. The Nazi regime's unspeakable brutality in dealing with the Jews left 6 million Jews dead by the end of the Second World War. And there were other victims: political rivals in Germany, resistance fighters in occupied countries, other supposedly inferior peoples such as the Slavs, gypsies, and the mentally ill.

In assessing the Nazi era, attention has rightly been directed first at the suffering the regime caused for all Europe. But it is also important to look at the consequences for the Germans themselves. In effect, Nazi rule and the Second World War carried out the social and economic revolution that previously had been escaped.[5] Partially, this was an intended change directed by Hitler to modernize the economy and to consolidate his political hold over all society. Also, it was the unintended consequences of total defeat. Together, Hitler and wartime destruction radically changed German society: The old Prussian aristocracy was virtually eliminated and its land lost to Poland and the Soviet Union; The imperial military elite had been replaced by a new Nazi military command which in turn was either killed off in the war or thoroughly discredited by its political ties; Old economic empires were broken down by Hitler's economic plans, the wartime destruction, or by postwar efforts to purge Nazi-tainted industrialists from resuming economic prominence; The bureaucracy and the judiciary were purged, first by Hitler and then by postwar occupation governments, of politically unacceptable elements; The devastation of the war and the flight of millions of German refugees from the East brought an important leveling of economic differences. The overall effect was revolutionary socioeconomic change. Unwittingly, Hitler produced a new Germany, one in many ways more suited for democracy than the Germany the Weimar regime faced after 1918.

The Birth of the Federal
Republic of Germany (1945 to 1949)

After the defeat of Nazi Germany, the country was redefined by the victors. Large parts of eastern Germany were given to the Soviet Union or Poland (to compensate the Poles for territory they were forced to concede to the Russians). Millions of Germans inhabiting these areas were forced to flee westward. What was left of Germany was divided into four occupation zones among the principal victors: Britain, France, the Soviet Union, and the United States. The old capital city, Berlin, was also divided into four occupation sectors. The task of the occupiers was to purge Germany of Nazis and reeducate the Germans in preparation for a return to self-government.[6] When it became apparent that the developing Cold War would make it impossible to write a treaty or settle on ultimate fate, the three western powers, Britain, France, and the United States, combined their three zones into one in 1948 and began moving toward German self-government in the western zones.[7]

Under the tutelage of the western occupying powers, the West Germans drew up a constitution. The occupying forces influenced the shape of the document both indirectly, through setting broad democratic parameters that the German constitution writers knew had to be observed, and directly, through interventions to add or eliminate clauses to the Germans' drafts. The end product was entitled the Basic Law, suggesting that it was a preliminary document to be used in the west only until a constitution could be drafted for all of Germany. Forty years later, this Basic Law remains the constitutional basis for the Federal Republic of Germany.

Meanwhile, in the eastern zone, the Russians guided their part of Germany toward a quite different and separate socioeconomic and political order.[8] The result has been the creation of two Germanies: the Federal Republic in the west and the German Democratic Republic in the east. Once again, Germany is divided.

LEGACIES OF THE PAST

The Nazi era and wartime defeat are huge dramatic episodes in German history. As a consequence, it is harder to find elements of continuity with the past in contemporary German politics than it is in Britain or France. This does not mean that historical forces are less important in Germany, but simply that the bench mark is 1945 instead of 1215 in Britain or 1789 in France. Indeed, the very effort to escape the past, as Germans sometimes appear to try to do, in itself has important political effects.

A New Division of Germany

The division of Germany imposed by the postwar settlement constitutes one of the key historical legacies for contemporary German politicians. The age-old quest for unity once again looms as a possible goal. The hope for ultimate reunification is clearly present and cultivated by West German politicians. Symbolic of this quest is the Basic Law which is still regarded as an interim document awaiting reunification and not the final constitution.

FIGURE 11.1 Map of Germany.

How to deal with the "other Germany"—not by the foreign ministry, incidentally, but by a special ministry of German affairs—remains an important challenge for West German politicians. Increasingly, German foreign policy has focused on ways to ease East-West tensions to keep open even a slight hope of reunification. As august a body as the Federal Constitutional Court has ruled that the government can do nothing that would hamper the prospects or diminish the demand for reunification.[9] And the federal government, concerned about young people growing up without an understanding of what Germany included, urged the return to using maps showing Germany's 1937 borders in school textbooks.

Lest there be concern that these aspirations might unleash yet another resurgence of German nationalism, it should be stressed that the goal of reunification is mainly a symbolic one, not one that seems likely to fuel passions for new conquest. Only a small portion of the population believes that reunification will ever be achieved (13 percent). Despite this realistic viewpoint, three out of four Germans want to retain the passages in the Basic Law expressing the goal of "unity and freedom of Germany."[10] Until the 1970s, there was real concern among observers about the ability of the West German polity to acquire acceptance in the minds and hearts of its people. Some feared that Germans were identifying themselves with an abstract and nonexistent German nation encompassing both West and East Germanies that they hoped might one day be realized in fact.[11] However, by the mid-1970s, evidence from opinion polls and other sources suggested that the German Federal Republic had developed its own loyal following among its people. Increasingly, West Germans were identifying with that regime and approving its social, economic, and political accomplishments. In a like manner, East Germans were becoming more and more different from their western relations and growing in their sense of identification with their regime.[12] It is no longer a problem of one German nation divided between two political units; now there are two Germanies and two increasingly different German peoples.

An Escape from History?

The Germans have consciously sought to escape their history in recent decades. So strong is the embarrassment about Germany's crimes during the Hitler era that for many Germans, only history beginning in 1945 can be tolerated. Public opinion polls indicate that three fourths of Germans unconditionally repudiate the Hitler era. Most of the rest, condemn his treatment of the Jews or his conduct of the war while seeing some positive features in his rule.[13] Now, nearly all Germans acknowledge the failure of the pre-1945 past and the need for new patterns. The legacy of Nazism is "a huge historical mortgage to burden the conscience of future generations."[14]

While the past is not denied, it is often ignored by a public unable to accept the collective guilt and shame for the Nazi era. The pride of West Germans in the cultural attainments of past Germans is reduced by their concern with "the German question": How did a nation that produced Beethoven, Dürer, Goethe, Kant, and Luther let itself engage in such barbarism as occurred under Hitler? While the public often dodges this question, it has been the object of intense examination by German intellectuals with sharp differences over the degree to which Hitler represented a tragic deviation from the development of German culture or its logical outcome.[15] The problem of coming to grips with the past brings tension and conflict to contemporary politics. Some young Germans in the late 1960s and early 1970s were so disgruntled by the attempts of intellectuals to explain the past and of the general public to escape thinking about it that they turned to terrorism. Such escapism and intellectualism, they believed, could only be rectified by overthrowing a democratic and capitalist system unable to properly atone for the social evils of the past.

Another dimension to the German attempt to escape from history has been more positive. The failures of the Weimar Republic and the excesses of the Nazi era have made contemporary Germans very sensitive to potential dangers to democracy. The determination never to let democracy fail again has led both citizens and politicians to be wary of developments that might endanger the regime. In a way, it has made Germans more vigilant about their democracy than other Europeans. Questionable political actions by government or citizens that in other countries would cause no concern become objects of careful examination in Germany as to whether or not they portend an erosion of democratic attachments.

In this way, the negative memories of the past have placed real constraints on contemporary politics. Hence, Germany has avoided the centralizing trends present in other countries because of fears about the danger of concentrating power in a few hands. Politicians who engage in demagoguery or appear too autocratic in style are shunned. For example, the Christian Democratic chancellor candidate in the 1980 elections—Franz-Joseph Strauss—was a man easily caricatured as too nationalistic and too authoritarian. The voting support for his parties dropped to their lowest level since 1949 largely because of voter rejection of his image of a too powerful leader. German voters have also rejected extremist parties of the Left and Right that evoke the memories of political extremism under Weimar and tragic consequences for Germany when extremists held power between 1933 and 1945. This kind of escaping from the past involves a repudiation of the political traits of the past and a determination to prevent them from recurring.

In many ways, the strength of the repudiation of the past has worked to legitimize a constitutional order that otherwise might have been regarded as foreign imposed and alien. The Basic Law, implemented under the guidance of the occupation officials, might well have been regarded as illegitimate in contrast to the Weimar constitution, which, despite its failings, was drawn up without foreign oversight. But the completeness of the defeat in 1945, the shame of the Nazi-era brutalities, and the recognition by most Germans of the need for a clean break with the past created an atmosphere in which the foreign-imposed Basic Law could be realized. Indeed, West Germany has proved much more receptive of foreign cultural, political, and economic models than other countries. Furthermore, the Basic Law has worked well in practice. It has provided public order and political stability within a democratic framework. Equally importantly, its early years were characterized by an economic prosperity diametrically opposite to the Weimar's disastrous economic conditions. As a result, the Federal Republic celebrated its fortieth anniversary with a broad public support that compensated for its foreign origins and the public's notable lack of enthusiasm at its inception.

GERMANY IN THE 1980s

Out of the rubble of wartime destruction, the Germans rapidly rebuilt their cities and villages. Where possible, they tried to preserve or recreate the charm of medieval architecture and decor with the result that Germany remains a popular tourist destination today. But the relations among the people that inhabit these cities and villages have changed radically and irreversibly. German society and economy have left the prewar mixture of almost feudal social stratification, traditional agriculture, and modern industry among the ignored and unwanted relics of the Nazi reign and war.

Social Class and Politics in the German Federal Republic

The social class structure in West Germany has changed from the prewar situation. The wartime destruction, the widespread poverty of the immediate postwar years, and the social dislocation produced by the movement of millions of refugees into West Germany all had important effects on patterns of social stratification. They brought major changes into a class system that earlier had been characterized by authoritarianism, rigidity, and immobility. Class mobility has increased opening up greater opportunities for individuals born into modest situations to improve their socioeconomic standing. But chances for improvement for those of the lower levels are still slim.[16]

One important change was the virtual disappearance of the prewar aristocracy of Prussian Junkers. Their wealth was based on large farms in eastern Prussia that are now part of Poland or the Soviet Union. The Junkers filled senior military officer ranks and many of these officers did not survive the war. The survivors lost their lands; those who are now in the Federal Republic arrived as refugees with little more than the clothes on their back. A new privileged class of industrialists and entrepreneurs has emerged, including some who were able to protect personal fortunes or enterprises from the prewar era. But the new privileged class lacks the exclusive social and political prestige that the Junkers once exercised. Instead, several sets of leaders share the political and social scene. Some leaders come from the economic sphere; others come from entertainment circles; politics provides yet another set of elite figures, and still others come from churches, associations, and clubs. These various elites are separate rather than overlapping. They compete with each other for prominence in the public eye and in influencing the shape of society.[17]

The farm population in Germany has changed in a way similar to France. The farm population constituted 28 percent of the German work force in 1950; by 1982, farmers made up only 5.5 percent of the work force. The consolidation of farms and the growth of agribusiness has reduced the number of farmers while better paying jobs lured others from the farms to the cities. Once a stronghold of conservative and nationalist values, the farm population has dwindled in size and political strength.

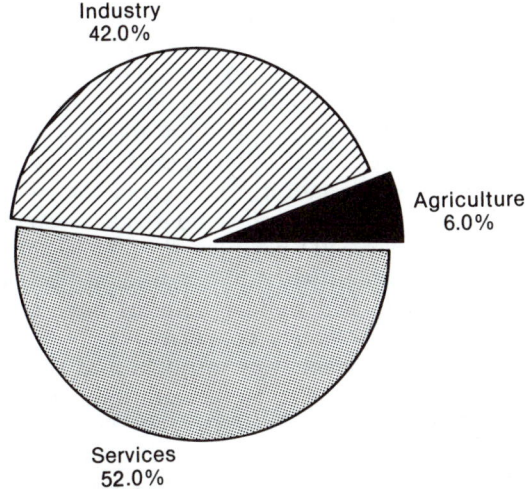

Industry
42.0%

Agriculture
6.0%

Services
52.0%

FIGURE 11.2   Employment by Economic Sector in West Germany. *Source: The World Almanac and Book of Facts* (New York: World Almanac, 1988).

As is true in Britain and France, the German middle class has evolved in the postwar period. Once made up of individuals who were self-employed business or professional people, often the proprietors of small family businesses, it is now a very heterogeneous class. The middle class now includes people from diverse occupations, from the private and public sectors, and with varying incomes. It is not surprising that its votes are widely dispersed among the major parties. By and large, the middle class is now mainly white-collar employees earning salaries: clerks, middle rank managers, engineers, and technicians. Their work conditions and income are usually better than those of factory workers but as employees, often working for large, impersonal firms or bureaucracies, they share some of the problems and frustrations of the blue-collar working class.[18] The younger, better educated members of this broadened middle class have been among the most dedicated advocates of social reform in recent years. More so than in Britain or Italy, where middle-class voters still remain loyal to center-right parties, important portions of the German middle class, especially those employed in the public sector, have aligned themselves with the left of center, Social Democratic party (SPD)[19] and more recently with the Greens. The reasons for the German exception are not clear but it may be due in part to the greater attention given by the majority of Germans to new issues such as environmental protection, citizen participation, and egalitarianism. These issues have been championed by the Greens and to a lesser degree by the SPD.

The industrial working class remains a larger proportion of the working population than in most other Western European democracies. Despite the absence of formal ties between the trade union movement and the SPD, German workers vote more heavily for this party than British workers vote for the trade union dominated Labour party. From a peak support of 70 percent of the workers in the 1972 elections, the SPD fell to only 59 percent of workers in 1983.[20] This decline of voting because of class influence corresponds to a general decline in the salience of social class such as noted in the discussion of Britain and France. It also seems in the case of Germany to reflect the emergence of new political issues such as the environment, participation, and relaxation of world tensions that have preempted the political agenda and weakened traditional class-based partisan loyalties. As the SPD has picked up these new issues, some workers who are still preoccupied with the traditional "bread and butter" concerns of economic security and welfare benefits have felt less at home with the Social Democrats' new policy concerns.

The weakness of working-class consciousness and the division of the middle class, between those attached to more traditional economic concerns who vote for the Christian Democrats (CDU/CSU) and those interested in the new issues of participation, ecology, and egalitarianism who are attracted to the SPD or the Greens, make the electorates of the major parties rather diverse. As Table 11.1 indicates, neither the SPD nor the CDU/CSU can rely alone on their natural classes for electoral support. Voting for the much smaller Free Democratic (FDP) and Green parties is also only loosely connected with social class. Workers make up 37 percent of the Christian Democratic electorate; middle-class voters account for over half of the Social Democratic electorate. The parties are catchall in the sense that they must appeal across class lines to voters from a broad range of socioeconomic backgrounds. German party leaders are not inclined to appeal to class themes in mobilizing their voters as happens in the British Labour party and the French Communist party.

As in other European countries, the postwar prosperity has reduced social-class tensions. The working class has shared fully in this prosperity. Consumer goods, once restricted to the privileged, are now broadly shared by Germans from all levels of the social hierarchy (See Table 11.2). In many ways, the German working-class movement is the best organized of the countries included in this text. Union membership is higher both in absolute numbers of members and in terms of membership as a percentage

TABLE 11.1 Social Class Composition of German Party Electorates

	CDU/CSU	SPD	FDP	Greens
Percentage of the parties' vote in 1983 drawn from				
Old middle class of self-employed	14%	5%	22%	4%
New middle class of employees	49	48	50	53
Workers	37	47	28	43

Source: Adapted from Russell J. Dalton and Kendall L. Baker, "The Contours of West German Opinion," in H. G. Peter Wallach and George K. Romoser, eds., *West German Politics in the Mid-Eighties: Crisis and Continuity* (New York: Praeger, 1985), p. 44.

of potential members. Unlike unions in Britain, France, or Italy, German union leaders have systematically avoided class-warfare rhetoric or themes in mobilizing their workers' workplace and political actions.

In part, this avoidance of evoking social-class conflict is due to the leaders' feelings that such rhetoric inflamed political tensions in the 1920s and early 1930s, and, thus, contributed to Hitler's rise. They have also found that prosperous German workers are not motivated by appeals to traditional class-warfare notions of working-class solidarity or fighting capitalism. In addition, German employers have avoided the rancorous conflicts that have poisoned labor/management relations in France and on occasion in Britain. German unions have been granted equal representation with shareholder representatives on the boards of directors for large enterprises. This system of codetermination has led workers and their representatives to believe that they have a real say in controlling their workplaces.[21] Taken together, the resulting moderation from the restraint of the union leaders and employers has virtually eliminated class conflict from the social and political agendas in Germany.

Religion and Politics

In prewar Germany, religion was often an important and divisive political issue. The majority of the population was Protestant, and Protestant dominance of politics often led to neglect or abuse of Catholic interests. In postwar West Germany, the population is almost equally divided since the Protestant strongholds are now in East Germany. Catholics make up about 41 percent of the total West German population; Protestants (predominantly Lutherans in the Evangelical Church of Germany) account for 52 percent; the rest either belong to other religions or are without a religion. There is no formal link between the church and the state in Germany like the ties between the Church of England and the British monarch. Nevertheless, the religion of the babies' parents is marked on their official birth certificates. Unless they later take legal steps to break their ties with that religion, they will pay a tax, collected by the government, to their church for the rest of their lives. In practice, few make the formal break with religion; 95 percent of the public pays the church tax, a

TABLE 11.2 Acess to Consumer Goods in West Germany

Percentage of households having

	1953	1979
Refrigerators	9%	98%
Automobiles	8	71
Televisions	32	94
Washing machines	34	83
Deep freezers	3	65

Source: Data from Lewis J. Edinger, *West German Politics* (New York: Columbia University Press, 1986), pp. 41–42.

surcharge amounting to about 10 percent of their income tax. This remains true despite a decline in religious practice: only 31 percent of Catholics and 8 percent of Protestants attend their churches regularly.[22]

Despite the secular trends in German society, religious leaders continue to play prominent roles in politics. They sit, by statutory right, on the boards that supervise radio and television broadcasting. They are members of government committees dealing with cultural and family affairs. They are frequently consulted by government policy makers on moral and family issues. The Christian Democratic parties, by their titles, are confessional parties and they seek the advice of clerics from both Catholic and Protestant churches. The Catholic church fought against abortion liberalization and through the CDU/CSU obtained a ruling by the Constitutional Court that overturned a 1974 federal law legalizing abortion. But Catholic groups have not been as successful at the state level where liberalization of abortion has often occurred.

Both Protestant and Catholic clergies feel guilt for the failure of their churches to oppose Nazism. There is a greater willingness on the part of German clerics to speak out on political and moral issues. Some religious leaders aligned themselves with student radicals during the late 1960s. Church leaders have spoken out on behalf of the rights of foreign workers and have worked to break down racial intolerance toward these immigrants. Others have championed greater support from Germany for better economic treatment of Third World peoples and even direct support for their revolutionary struggles. More recently, church leaders have taken prominent roles in the peace movement.[23] This new political activism, especially by Protestant clergy, has drawn criticism in many circles and reopened public discussion of the separation of church and state.

Despite this outspokeness, the influence of religion on voting behavior is less than it is in France or Italy. On occasion, German clerics have made appeals to their followers to vote for certain parties. As recently as the 1980 election, the Catholic hierarchy issued a pastoral letter making clear its feeling that good Catholics should oppose the SPD government of the day. But these electoral directions seem to have very little effect. Unlike Christian Democratic parties elsewhere in the world which have strong Roman Catholic links, the CDU/CSU deems itself an ecumenical Christian party with links to both Catholic and Protestant churches. Its electorate is almost evenly divided between Catholics and Protestants; in 1983 50 percent of CDU/CSU voters were Catholics and 46 percent were Protestants. The SPD, which inherited a Protestant and antireligious legacy from its pre-Nazi predecessor, has also had an extended appeal to Catholics; in 1983 36 percent of its voters were Catholics, 56 percent were Protestants.

Religious influence in politics declines as the number of faithful church members dwindles. But the institutional presence of the major churches and their willingness to speak out on controversial issues make it likely that they will continue to be prominent on the German political scene. And this moral leadership may not be entirely undesirable as the political agenda will contain difficult questions such as what constitutes life and death, the ethics of nuclear deterrence, the value of the human physical environment, and the role of the state in defending accepted moral stand-ards—issues which theologians are likely to be as able or better able to judge than politicians.

A New Racial Pluralism

Unlike Britain and France, Germany has had few problems since 1949 in maintaining internal unity. The population was and is ethnically ho-mogeneous without the kinds of divisions that caused tensions in parts of Britain and France. Despite their traditions of autonomy, the post-1949 German states have shown little interest in returning to the divisions of the past. The only partial exception is Bavaria, where early in the postwar era some politicians envisioned an independent Bavarian country. The adequacy of state controls over crucial cultural and educational policies under the Basic Law's federal framework and the need to maintain unity in the west to punctuate the "unnatural" separation of Communist-ruled East Germany from a united Germany have kept separatist feelings at a minimum throughout the Federal Republic.

One striking development in postwar Germany, as in France and Britain, has been the growth of a large immigrant population. The rapidly expanding economy of the 1960s soon exhausted local manpower sources and resulted in opening the frontiers to large numbers of immigrant "guest workers." From less than 400,000 immigrant workers in 1961, the guest worker population grew to over 2.5 million at its peak in 1973. Efforts to reduce the flow of immigrants, after the economy slowed down in the 1970s, proved unsuccessful. While new work permits were sharply reduced, guest workers already in the country remained and brought in family members. Government programs offering cash bonuses to guest workers who went home were largely spurned. In addition, refugees from Eastern Europe and Asia were admitted. By 1986, the foreign population residing in West Germany had risen to nearly 4.5 million or about 7 percent of the population.

There is little prospect that this foreign population will decrease. A 1986 poll of foreign residents found that less than one in six planned to return home.[24] Even if no new immigrants are admitted, the size of the non-German population is expected to grow dramatically. The birthrate of native Germans is the lowest of any people in Europe, and is well below the level needed to maintain the population at its current size. But the birthrate of foreigners living in Germany is high. Demographers expect that these trends will mean that the year 2000 at least 12 percent of the total population will be non-German.

Germany has thus far been spared the political consequences of the immigrant population that have occurred in Britain and France. There has been no German parallel to the French antiforeign National Front party. Some far right parties have attempted to exploit the immigration issue in state elections but their political impact has been minimal. Nor have the major German parties divided over the immigration issue the way the British Conservatives were divided in the 1970s. It appears to be an issue that transcends party alignments.[25] But the need to deal with the growing foreign population is fraught with important political issues. There have been incidents of violence directed at foreigners and even assassinations by small rightwing extremist groups. There is growing intolerance by Germans toward the foreign population and especially toward the large number of Turkish immigrants. The racial distinctiveness and Turkish unwillingness to integrate into German society have made them objects of fear and resentment for native Germans. As in other European countries, the increased foreign population is linked in many people's minds to the deterioration of the cleanliness and safety of urban centers.

The numbers of foreigners who have become German citizens are still very limited so the electoral impact of this new non-German population has yet to be felt. By the mid-1980s, only three out of one hundred non-German immigrants had been naturalized even though over half of the immigrant worker population had been in Germany for more than ten years.[26] Naturalization laws are currently the subject of debate. Some, notably the Greens party and some elements in the SPD, are calling for immigrant workers to have the right to vote in local elections even if they are not citizens. As elsewhere in Europe, the key problem remains guiding a population, which has never before had to deal with living alongside racially different peoples, toward tolerance and racial equality.

ECONOMICS AND POLITICS: GOOD ECONOMICS ARE GOOD POLITICS

Nowhere else in Europe has the health of the economy become more closely associated with the stability of democracy than it has in West Germany. The economic disasters that undermined the Weimar experiment had left deep-seated doubts in the minds of many Germans about the ability of a democracy to manage the economy. These doubts have died but only slowly with the economic successes of the Federal Republic of Germany.

Military defeat in 1945 had produced economic collapse and left much of the country in ruins; many of the factories not destroyed in the war were dismantled and shipped to the Soviet Union as war reparations. The economic infrastructure needed for economic recovery—highways and bridges, canals, ports, warehouses, railroads, communications networks—had been a primary military target and had been mostly destroyed. The disruption of farming and shipping of farm goods left much of the population near starvation by the end of the war. Added to this misery were the problems of feeding, housing, and finding jobs for the more than 12 million refugees from the east who arrived in West Germany between 1945 and 1950. The prevailing image of today's prosperous Germany leads us to forget that in the winter of 1946–47, Germans were close to starving with a caloric intake of 600 to 700 calories (compared to the 2400 calories required for a working adult); in the British zone 250,000 cases of tuberculosis were discovered and 90 percent of the children suffered from rickets. The task of cleaning up the wartime destruction itself was overwhelming. For instance, Kassel, a city with 181,000 inhabitants, was in shambles; it was estimated that it would take twenty-two years simply to clear up the 9 million cubic meters of rubble.

The rapid recovery of the German economy, rising within a decade during the 1950s like a phoenix from the rubble of the wartime destruction to become an international economic power, has rightly been called an economic miracle.[27] Recovery began in 1948 with an Allied imposed currency reform that prevented the kind of runaway inflation that had discredited Weimar. That same year marked the beginning of substantial American economic assistance through the Marshall Plan. Instead of the reparations bill handed Weimar, the new Federal Republic of Germany received financial aid to rebuild its economy. In the second half of 1948, German industrial production increased by 50 percent with an additional 25 percent increase the next year. Throughout the 1950s, the economy grew on average nearly 8 percent a year; in the 1960s, the growth was still an average of 5 percent a year. By 1953, the living standard had recovered its prewar level. By the 1960s, the German economy was the strongest in Europe with a healthy growth rate, full employment, virtually no inflation, and one of the strongest currencies in the world.

The miracle was made possible by the voluntary sacrifices of the German workers who deferred their demands for higher wages and better access to consumer goods while the economy was rebuilt. In contrast to the turbulent labor/management relations that plagued France in the 1940s and 1950s, there were very few strikes or other labor actions in West Germany. Instead, German workers were disciplined, orderly, and, most important, highly productive. As a result, Germans were able to reinvest 20 to 24 percent of the national gross product each year between 1949 and 1954. The large refugee population kept labor costs low and provided a reservoir of workers willing to move to the parts of Germany with job opportunities. Eventually, the workers began to share in the benefits of recovery. Real wages rose two and a half times between 1950 and 1973 giving German industrial workers the highest earnings in Western Europe throughout the 1960s.

This economic miracle has occurred within the framework of a capitalist system. While there is an important public sector in Germany, it is smaller than that in Britain or France. Nearly all industrial firms are privately owned. But the government plays a large role in directing economic recovery and in managing the economy, thus continuing a tradition of government guidance within a free enterprise system which dates back to the nineteenth century. The government has intervened freely and frequently to direct economic growth, to achieve certain social goals such as the protection of workers or refugees, and to respond to the needs of private entrepreneurs. The relationship between the government and the private sector is intimate and frequent. Government subsidies support new investments and prop up faltering industries; government policies encourage exports and industrial mergers. Private industry is highly centralized through large firms and closely organized associations of employers and industries.

The trade union movement is similarly centralized and well structured. Employers and union representatives have joined government officials in a broad range of parapublic bodies to coordinate and direct the economy. The result is a strong governmental presence even though the economy remains in private hands.

The German government has worked with labor and employer representatives to establish plans for economic expansion or adjustments. The federal government has invested its own funds and coordinated the investments of local and state governments as well as of private sources to promote industrial development and more recently industrial modernization or reconversion. Through partnership with labor and management successive German governments have attempted to administer wage and price controls to limit inflation.

CONCLUSION

One of the paradoxes of the postwar economic miracle was that the very success and rapidity of it left some Germans with a guilty conscience. Here again the heavy legacy of the Hitler era on the spirits of contemporary Germans is revealed. Parallel with this guilt about the short economic punishment for the sins of the Third Reich is the feeling that the speedy recovery prevented examining the possibility of deeper and more far-reaching changes in German society.

> With economic recovery came a sense of guilt, a feeling shared by many sensitive people . . . that it had all been too easy and too quick, that it had shut off the debate on options too soon, that it had foreclosed opportunities for fruitful innovation, and that it had brought not a brave new world but a Restoration, in which all the wrong things had been restored—a restored world of money and materialism and militarism . . . which would end the way all the other old worlds had ended.[28]

Such pessimism reflects uneasiness with the new consumerism and materialism that seem dominant in West Germany today. Germans worry that the old stereotype of heel-clicking, obedient Germans is being replaced with a new stereotype of complacent, self-satisfied, and prosperous Germans without a vision loftier than their own enrichment.

Along with such introspection though, it appears that the Germans have overcome their historical liabilities and indeed have learned to be free and democratic. They have not escaped their past; guilt provokes introspection and concern with their image. Above all, it leaves the legacy of a Germany once more divided. While West Germans have come to accept this division as an unchangeable fact of life, they have not entirely abandoned the centuries old hope of German unity.

NOTES

1. Translation in Gordon A. Craig, *The Germans* (New York: G.P. Putnam's Sons, 1982), p. 289.
2. For an examination of this debate, see Charles S. Maier, *The Unmasterable Past: History, Holocaust, and the German National Identity* (Cambridge, MA: Harvard University Press, 1988).
3. Ralf Dahrendorf, *Society and Democracy in Germany* (Garden City, NY: Doubleday Anchor, 1969), p. 52.
4. One of the best treatments of Hitler's rule is one of the oldest: Franz Neumann, *Behemoth: The Structure and Practice of National Socialism* (Oxford: Camden and Neworth, 1942). See also, Karl Dietrich Bracher, *The German Dictatorship: The Origins, Structures, and Effects of National Socialism* (New York: Praeger, 1970).
5. See David Schoenbaum, *Hitler's Social Revolution* (Garden City, NY: Doubleday Anchor, 1967).
6. See James E. Tent, *Mission on the Rhine: Reeducation and Denazification in American-Occupied Germany* (Princeton, NJ: Princeton University Press, 1983).
7. Peter H. Merkl, *The Origins of the West German Republic* (New York: Oxford University Press, 1965).
8. Gregory W. Sandford, *From Hitler to Ulbricht: The Communist Reconstruction of East Germany, 1945–46* (Princeton, NJ: Princeton University Press, 1983).
9. Jochen A. Frowein, "Legal Problems of the German Ostpolitik," *International and Comparative Law Quarterly* 23 (January 1974): 105–126.
10. Elisabeth Noelle-Neumann, ed., *The Germans: Public Opinion Polls, 1967–1980* (Westport, CT: Greenwood Press, 1981), p. 119.
11. See Dahrendorf, *Society and Democracy in Germany*.
12. Gerhard Ludwig Schweigler, *National Consciousness in Divided Germany* (Beverly Hills, CA: Sage, 1975).
13. Lewis Edinger, *West German Politics* (New York: Columbia University Press, 1986), p. 87.
14. Hans-Adolf Jacobsen, "The Third Reich, 1933–1945: A Sketch," in Charles Burdick, Hans Adolf Jacobsen, and Winfried Kudszus, eds., *Contemporary Germany: Politics and Culture* (Boulder, CO: Westview, 1984), p. 59.
15. For a recent summary of this debate, see Richard J. Evans, "Rethinking the German Past," in William E. Paterson and Gordon Smith, eds., *The West German Model: Perspectives on a Stable State* (London: Frank Cass, 1981). See also David Calleo, *The German Problem Reconsidered: German and the World Order, 1879 to the Present* (Cambridge, England: Cambridge University Press, 1978).
16. Edinger, *West German Politics*, pp. 44–45.
17. David Childs and Jeffrey Johnson, *West Germany: Politics and Society* (New York: St. Martin's, 1981), pp. 90–92.
18. Despite some similar concerns, one sociological study emphasizes the importance of the differences between white- and blue-collar workers. Christel Lane, "White Collar Workers in the Labour Process: The Case of the Federal Republic of Germany," *The Sociological Review* 33 (May 1985): 298–326.
19. Russell J. Dalton, "The West German Party System between Two Ages," in Russell J. Dalton, et al., eds., *Electoral Change in Advanced Industrial Democracies: Realignment or Dealignment?* (Princeton, NJ: Princeton University Press, 1984), pp. 120–122.

20. Ibid., p. 127.
21. Jutta A. Helm, "Codetermination in West Germany: What Difference Has It Made?" *West European Politics*, 9 (January 1986): 32–53.
22. Noelle-Neumann, *The Germans*, p. 235. The Protestant figure is down in 1980 from 15 percent in 1963; the Catholic percentage dropped from 55 percent in 1963.
23. Jürgen Moltmann, "Religion and State in Germany: West and East," *Annals*, No. 483 (January 1986): 110–117.
24. *Der Tagesspiegel* (Berlin), 8 August 1986.
25. Marilyn Hoskin, "Public Opinion and the Foreign Worker: Traditional and Nontraditional Bases in West Germany," *Comparative Politics* 17 (January 1985): 193–210.
26. Edinger, *West German Politics*, p. 56.
27. See Edwin Hartrich, *The Fourth and Richest Reich* (New York: Macmillan, 1980).
28. Craig, *The Germans*, p. 124.

CHAPTER TWELVE
CITIZENS AND POLITICS
IN WEST GERMANY

Every nation has its principal motive. In Germany, it is obedience; in England, freedom; in Holland, trade; in France, the honor of the king.
Karl Friedrich Moser, 1758

For centuries, the German people were known for their political passivity and their acquiescence to authoritarian regimes. This pattern of political obedience persisted well into the twentieth century. It is often cited as a principal explanation for Hitler's rise to power and for the people's acquiescence in the atrocities of his rule. The stereotype of the heel-clicking, dutiful German is, of course, an unfair and incomplete characterization of a whole nation but it does reflect a widespread German attitude about how citizens should respond to authority that is ill-suited for modern representative democracy.

Concerns about the Germans' political attitudes and values led Western occupation forces after the Second World War to take remedial measures.[1] In addition to purging Nazi elements throughout society, Western occupying forces also sought to teach Germans democratic values. This effort included not only supervision of the curriculum for the young, but also modest efforts to reeducate adults in democratic principles through the mass media and public forums. Prospective political leaders were screened by the occupiers, and those with apparently sincere democratic attachments were then groomed for leadership positions. The goal was to reshape German political culture and behavior to create a more supportive environment for democracy.

A NEW GERMAN POLITICAL CULTURE?

Political culture refers to the patterns of values, orientations, and feelings that people have about politics. Many political scientists feel that the prevailing political culture is an important factor in the success or failure of democracy. The success of British democracy, for example, is often traced to the underlying political values and orientations of the British people; France's more turbulent democracy is traced to French attitudes toward authority. Once established, political orientations are difficult to change. They develop typically during an individual's youth, changing somewhat through experience during one's lifetime but retaining most of the values acquired early in life. Earlier efforts in deliberately reshaping political culture, such as Stalin's effort to create a "new Soviet man," were often accompanied by violence or terror and still met with only limited success. Of course, a democratic political culture could not be created through coercion but only through persuasion. Many were pessimistic about the prospects for doing so in postwar Germany, especially since the rising generation had been so deliberately schooled in the antidemocratic values of Nazism.

By the end of the 1950s, a decade after the establishment of the Federal Republic of Germany, the outlook was still gloomy. A careful study of political culture in five nations revealed that Germany lagged behind in developing those civic values deemed important for Western democracy.[2] Germans remained more like subjects of the political system than active participants in its democratic processes. They were fearful of the consequences of political conflict, even those levels of conflict needed to sustain democratic competition. Criticism of public officials was frowned upon. Germans accepted the new political order but there was little sign of enthusiasm for it or democracy. While the political systems of the past were buried in the ashes of wartime defeat, the old values and orientations seemed to endure and to compromise the success of the new democracy.

However, by the beginning of the 1980s, the situation had changed dramatically. In thirty years of democratic government, West Germany had experienced a massive transformation of political and social norms and values, thus:

> . . . from a country plagued by severe conflicts and cleavages to a highly stable, integrated society in which the democratic political system constructed after World War II seems to enjoy substantial legitimacy.[3]

Democracy is now viewed positively and the regime itself has won near universal acceptance. Of equal importance, Germans have acquired orientations needed to support democratic government: an acceptance of the inevitability and even desirability of political conflict, a willingness to subject those in power to critical scrutiny, a tolerance of those who express political dissent, and a recognition of the essential nature of political competition.[4]

Several factors are accountable for this rapid revolution in political culture. First, total defeat in 1945 served to discredit previous political values. There were few defenders of the past political orientations, and those few were silenced by the postwar penitence for the excesses of the Hitler era. The self-examination brought on by the German question involved a public evaluation of old values and traditions. Second, the new political order earned public approval by its economic success. The economic miracle disproved the Germans' belief that democracy meant disorder and economic chaos, and it fostered a new faith in the ability of democracy to promote economic growth and prosperity. Third, the contrast with the communist regime in the German Democratic Republic promoted democratic attitudes in the west. The East Germans' absence of freedom and lower living standards further discredited the political values of obedience, discipline, and duty to the state in the eyes of West Germans. Fourth, the political leaders have been committed democrats who have played the game of politics according to the rules of a moderate democracy. They have spurned the violent rhetoric and tactics that often characterized Weimar politics. They have avoided demagoguery and exploiting divisions in their choice of campaign issues. Their moderate and responsible conduct promoted such values and behavior in the general public. Finally, a new generation of citizens has emerged since the 1950s, a generation of young people who have never experienced anything other than the successful democracy of the postwar era. The affluence and political stability of this period have helped develop social values more conducive to democracy than those of the previous generations. By the early 1980s, those who grew up under these more propitious conditions constituted a clear majority of the adult population.[5]

With the rise of this new generation comes new sets of political values that are different from the values of earlier generations. Growing up in times of political stability, economic plenty, and international peace, younger Germans seem less preoccupied with the materialist concerns such as their country's economic growth, political order, and defense matters than do older Germans. They are more interested in pursuing post-materialist values such as self-expression and participation, equality, and the quality of life. This appears to be an international trend, a "silent revolution" affecting most advanced industrial democracies.[6] Table 12.1 shows an estimate of the percentage of those with post-materialist values in relationship to the total population based on responses to polls on issue priorities. While Germany still has a large part of the population attached to traditional materialist values, the political impact of post-materialist attitudes has been greater here than in Britain, France, or Italy. An important section of the younger middle class of white-collar employees and civil servants has embraced these values. A variety of social movements have arisen to promote these causes. A new ecological party, the Greens, champions such values, and it made an entrance into the German parliament in 1983. The older parties find portions of their electorate attracted to political issues linked with these new values and are struggling to adjust their programs without alienating the old supporters still attached to materialist goals. There is some evidence to indicate that established voting coalitions already are weakening under the impact of these new issues.[7] As the proportion of the population born since the war continues to grow, the political effects of post-materialistic values are likely to increase.

Another important aspect of German political culture is the people's ambiguous attitude toward their country. The shame of the past still shows in the continued reluctance of Germans to profess pride in their country. With only 59 percent claiming to be very or quite proud of their country, Germany ranks lowest among West European countries. (See Table 1.1 in Chapter One.) In contrast, Germans now express broad satisfaction with the way democracy works in their country. In 1985, 69 percent declared they were very or quite happy with the way democracy works in Germany.[8] Only the Luxembourgers and Danes expressed greater satisfaction than did Germans on their country's political performance. Thus, despite the legacy of the past, contemporary Germans have developed a new political culture supportive of democracy. In a remarkable reversal in political values, Germans now express more confidence and trust in democracy than do the British or the French.

THE GERMANS IN POLITICS

In the first decade after the war, few Germans showed interest in taking part in the politics of their new democracy. Such reticence is understandable. The paramount need of the time was economic recovery; politics was a secondary concern at best. In addition, in the 1950s many Germans knew first hand of the sanctions hitting those who had engaged in politics in the past. Those who participated actively in the Weimar regime often found themselves in Hitler's jails; those who became politically involved under Hitler were punished after the defeat. Many Germans feared that

TABLE 12.1   Percentage of Population Holding Materialist and Post-Materialist Values, 1984

	Materialist	Post-Materialist	Mixed
Britain	24%	17%	59%
West Germany	22	20	58
France	36	13	51
Italy	44	9	47
Belgium	37	9	54
Netherlands	22	21	57

Source: Jacques-Rene Rabier, Helene Riffault, Ronald Inglehart, *Eurobarometer 21: Political Cleavages in the European Community, April 1984* (Ann Arbor, MI: Inter-University Consortium for Political and Social Research, 1984), p. 191.

yet another political change might bring penalties for those who joined in the politics of the Federal Republic.

This reluctance to participate in politics waned in the 1960s. Now, Germans are among the most politically interested people with over half the population claiming to be very or somewhat interested in politics. (See Table 2.1). A cross-national survey of five democracies found that by the end of the 1970s Germany was second only to the United States in the extent of individual political involvement.[9] Germans are also well informed on political matters. More Germans than any other European people claim to follow political developments in the newspapers on a daily basis (61 percent) or several times a week (18 percent).[10] There had been some ebbing of political involvement in national politics at the end of the 1980s. The turnout rate for the 1987 elections (83.4 percent) was at its lowest point since 1953. But the decline in national political involvement contrasted with continued and even growing interest in local political involvement. High political mobilization at the local level is indicated by the fact that in the mid-1980s, there were more Germans involved in local political action groups than in the established political parties.

The range of political activities is broad, with voting the most common act. Other political activities attract fewer people but nevertheless involve substantial portions of the German public. (See Table 12.2.) As in other democratic countries, the repertoire of political actions has expanded since the 1970s. In addition to the conventional methods of political activity— working to influence policy through the electoral process or by contacting elected officials, Germans have increasingly approved of unconventional, direct means of political action—demonstrations, sit-ins in public buildings, boycotts, and other forms of direct action.

Actual recourse to such extraordinary political actions is still unusual but the high rates of approval suggest that they may well become more common in the future. (See Table 12.3.) The extent of the use of these

TABLE 12.2 Political Actions of Germans, 1978

Nature of activity	Percent involved
Regularly votes in national and local elections	73%
Keeps informed on politics	46
Defends issues the individual believes in	40
Often discusses politics with others	39
Informs self in detail on certain political issues	31
Supports specific candidate or party in elections	18
Attends political lectures or discussions sometimes	9
Involved in political party, club, or association	7
Contacts representatives or public officials when concerned with specific goal	5
Participates on occasion in protests or supports protest group	3

Source: Adapted from Elisabeth Noelle-Neumann, ed., *The Germans: Public Opinion Polls, 1967–1980* (Westport, CT: Greenwood, 1981), pp. 40–42.

unconventional means of participation appears lower in Germany than in other European democracies. A 1984 poll found that the number of Germans reporting they had participated in a protest demonstration in the previous five years (11.9 percent) was lower than in any of the other ten countries covered, with the exception of Britain (9.6 percent).[11]

When some Germans began using these tactics in the late 1960s, they provoked consternation among their countrymen: Could their democracy tolerate these disruptive and often disorderly, new forms of political action? The dismay came not only from those with traditional values that were opposed to conflictual politics, but also from those who accepted conflict as natural in democracy. They feared that direct political confrontation might discredit the still fragile democratic order in Germany. By the 1980s, however, German citizens and political leaders had come to accept such direct political action as normal. Both the government security forces and the protesters had learned the ways to control demonstrations and protests to keep them within tolerable limits. German politics are livelier and more expressive than they were in the 1950s and early 1960s but no less stable.

There has been a disconcerting element, though, in German street politics. In recent years, a number of demonstrations that started out peacefully deteriorated into violent confrontations between demonstrators and security forces. In these cases, a small hard core of protestors have deliberately sought to use violence. Known as "Chaotics," these small groups of masked demonstrators have thrown paving stones, have shot off fireworks, and have even tossed Molotov cocktails. In one 1987 demonstration, which started as a peaceful environmental protest against the expansion of the Frankfort airport, two police officers were killed and others wounded when extremist elements used firearms. This violent turn to protest politics has prompted calls for new restrictions on demonstrations, and especially laws that would bar marchers wearing masks.

The overwhelming majority of Germans reject extremist politics not only in their selection of tactics but also in their objectives. In contemplating political change, very few Germans, less than most other Europeans, ad-

TABLE 12.3 German Acceptance of Unconventional Political Action

Type of Activity	Percent approving	Percent who have used tactic	Percent who would use
Lawful demonstrations	62%	9%	33%
Boycotts	36	4	24
Rent strikes	13	1	8
Blocking traffic	12	1	6
Unofficial strikes	9	0	4
Painting slogans on buildings	7	1	4
Occupying buildings	6	0	4
Personal violence	3	0	1
Damaging property	1	0	1

Source: Adapted from Samuel H. Barnes, Max Kaase, et al., *Political Action: Mass Political Action in Five Western Democracies* (Beverly Hills, CA and London: Sage, 1979), pp. 545, 549.

vocate revolutionary change; more Germans than any other people prefer maintaining the status quo. (See Table 12.4.) Most Germans can situate themselves on the usual Left/Right spectrum. The resulting profile of German political opinion indicates a clustering of most Germans slightly to the right of the political center. (See Figure 12.1.) The moderate character of the German citizen has been conveyed into the politics of the Bonn republic. In contrast to the tumultuous and often violent politics of the Weimar era, the Federal Republic has fostered participation without excess. Because of this basically moderate orientation, neither the extent of participation nor the extended repertoire of political actions has endangered German democracy.

Germans at the Polls

With voter turnout in excess of 90 percent for most national elections and only slightly lower rates in state elections, the Germans have among the highest levels of electoral participation. The act of voting is far more than simply the act of a dutiful people; over three quarters of the Germans

TABLE 12.4 Attitudes on Social Change

	Britain	France	Germany	Italy
Insist on change through revolutionary action	5%	6%	3%	7%
Call for changing society through gradual reform	65	68	51	71
Urge defending society as it is against subversive forces	22	24	36	19

Source: Eurobarometer, No. 24 (December 1985):39.

FIGURE 12.1 Self-Placement by West Germans on a Left/Right Political Spectrum.

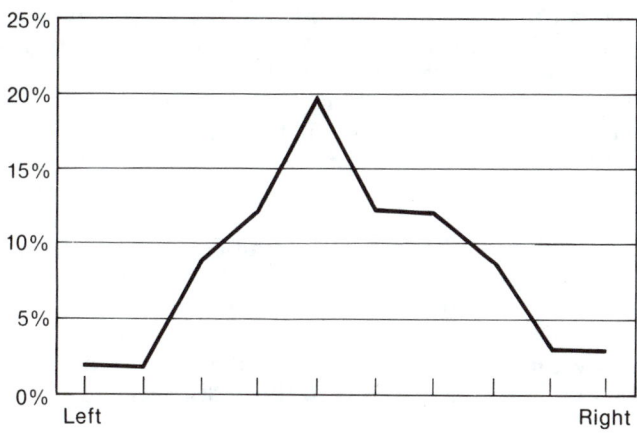

indicate that they vote as a means of showing preference for a particular party or candidate.[12]

The system used to organize national elections is relatively complicated.[13] At the polls, the voter has two choices to make: first, to vote for a representative for the district from among several candidates; second, to vote for one of the party lists of candidates to determine the parties' strength in the Bundestag. The first vote is for half the seats in the Bundestag (248 seats) which are decided in simple majority contests among candidates running in 248 equal-sized districts. In these contests, voters select among individuals to elect a district representative. Whichever candidate receives the most votes is elected whether or not the candidate had an absolute majority of votes cast.

The overall party balance in the chamber is determined, however, by the results of a second vote cast for lists of candidates from the separate parties. It is a system of proportional representation (PR) to assure a faithful reflection of the public's political views in the legislative body: a party receiving 45 percent of the vote wins approximately 45 percent of the seats; a party with 15 percent of the vote takes 15 percent of the seats; and so on. On the basis of this second vote, the number of seats each party is entitled to is calculated. Then the number of individual seats won by that party is deducted from that figure and the remainder of the earned seats are filled from candidates presented on the party lists. In this way, minor parties without a chance of winning a whole district are able to win parliamentary representation.[14] Table 12.5 illustrates the process with the results of a recent election. The column entitled "seats earned under PR" is equal to the percentage of votes won on the second vote. Since no party met that quota strictly from district victories, candidates placed by the parties on their lists were elected to bring party delegations up to the target.[15] The result is a very close alignment of party strength in accordance with the voters' preferences as indicated by comparing the size of delegation as a percentage of the total Bundestag membership in the final column with the percentage of votes on the second ballot in column three.

The advantage of proportional representation is that it assures an accurate reflection of the public's political preferences. In contrast to the distortions that have developed in Britain overrepresenting the major parties and seriously underrepresenting third parties, the German system has brought equitable representation of all of its political forces strong enough to garner at least 5 percent of the vote.

The chief problem with proportional representation is that it is sometimes seen as promoting minor parties and causing fragmentation of the party system. Many attribute the divided party system and consequent government instability of the Weimar Republic to the electoral system of proportional representation used at the time. The troublesome party system in contemporary Italy is often blamed on the proportional representation used there. The current German system discourages minor parties and party schisms by the requirement that a party receive at least 5 percent of the vote or win individual contests in three districts before being eligible

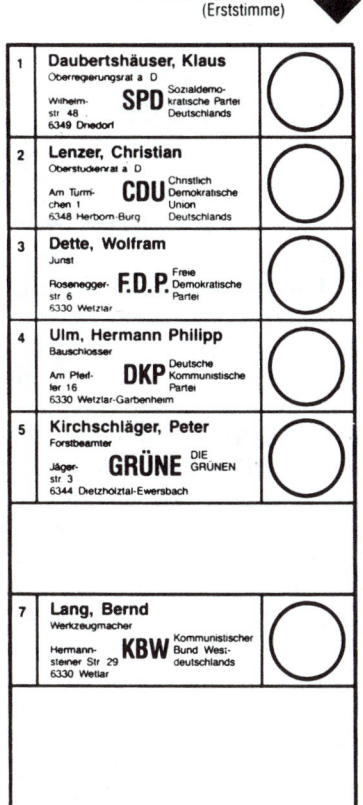

Stimmzettel
für die Wahl zum Deutschen Bunderstag im Wahlkreis 130 Lahn-Dill
am 5. October 1980

Sie haben 2 Stimmen

hier 1 Stimme
für die Wahl
eines Wahlkreisabgeordneten
(Erststimme)

hier 1 Stimme
für die Wahl
einer Landesliste (Partei)
(Zweitstimme)

#	Erststimme		#	Zweitstimme
1	**Daubertshäuser, Klaus** — Oberregierungsrat a D — Wilhelm-str 48, 6349 Dnedorf — **SPD** Sozialdemokratische Partei Deutschlands	○	1	○ **SPD** Sozialdemokratische Partei Deutschlands — Leber, Maithöfer, Jahn Frau Dr. Timm, Zander
2	**Lenzer, Christian** — Oberstudienrat a D — Am Turmchen 1, 6348 Herborn-Burg — **CDU** Christlich Demokratische Union Deutschlands	○	2	○ **CDU** Christlich Demokratische Union Deutschlands — Dr. Dregger, Zink, Dr. Schwarz Schilling, Frau Geier, Haase
3	**Dette, Wolfram** — Jurist — Rosenegger-str 6, 6330 Wetzlar — **F.D.P.** Freie Demokratische Partei	○	3	○ **F.D.P.** Freie Demokratische Partei — Mischick, von Schoeler, Hoffie, Wurbs, Dr. Prinz zu Sima-Hohensolms-Lich
4	**Ulm, Hermann Philipp** — Bauschlosser — Am Pfeiler 16, 6330 Wetzlar-Garbenheim — **DKP** Deutsche Kommunistische Partei	○	4	○ **DKP** Deutsche Kommunistische Partei — Mayer, Knopf, Frau Dr. Weber, Funk, Fray Schuster
5	**Kirchschläger, Peter** — Forstbeamter — Jäger-str 3, 6344 Dietzhölztal-Ewersbach — **GRÜNE** DIE GRÜNEN	○	5	○ **GRÜNE** DIE GRÜNEN — Frau Ibbeken, Hecker, Horacek, Kerschgens, Kuhnert
			6	○ **EAP** Europäische Arbeiterpartei — Frau Liebig, Haßmann, Stalleicher, Frau Kastner, Stalla
7	**Lang, Bernd** — Werkzeugmacher — Hermann-steiner Str 29, 6330 Wetlar — **KBW** Kommunistischer Bund Westdeutschlands	○	7	○ **KBW** Kommunistischer Bund Westdeutschland — Schmierer, Frau Nönich, Frau Eckardt, Dresler, Lang
			8	○ **NPD** Nationaldemokratische Partei Deutschlands — Phillipp, Brandt, Stürtz, Lauck, Bauer
			9	○ **V** VOLKSFRONT — Götz, Taufertshöfer, König, Riebe, Frau Weißert

FIGURE 12.2   German Ballot for Bunderstag Elections. The left side of the ballot offers the choice of individual candidates to represent the legislative district. The right side of the ballot offers party lists of candidates to be selected at the Land level in proportion to the votes received by each party. *Source:* Adapted from Rolf H. W. Theen and Frank L. Wilson, *Comparative Politics: An Introduction to Six Countries* (Englewood Cliffs, NJ: Prentice Hall, 1986), p. 270. Reprinted with permission.

TABLE 12.5   Distribution of Bundestag Seats in the 1987 Election

Party	First vote	Second vote	Seats earned under PR from second vote	Seats won on first vote	Number of seats taken from 2nd vote	Size of final delegation	Share of total Bundestag
CDU/CSU	47.7%	44.3%	222	169	54	223	44.9%
SPD	39.2	37.0	186	79	107	186	37.4
FDP	4.7	9.1	46	0	46	46	9.3
Greens	7.0	8.3	42	0	42	42	8.5
Others	1.4	1.3	0	0	0	0	0

to take part in the proportional division. This threshold prevented any minor party from entering the Bundestag from 1956 to 1983 when the Greens just barely exceeded that quota.

The German system has also avoided another complaint about proportional representation. Some contend that the use of lists of candidates in large districts tends to reduce the linkage between the elected representative and the voters. The German system provides for the election of half of the deputies in single member districts. This helps establish a feeling among voters that they have a representative to speak for them in Bonn.

The system does not, however, escape a third problem of proportional representation: The fact that the system is usually so complicated that voters do not understand what is happening and do not know how those elected actually win. In most countries using PR, this confusion is restricted to the technical formulas used to assure proportionality by allocating left over votes from one district to another. In Germany, the confusion is more critical. As should be apparent by this point, the most important part of the ballot is the vote for the party list, the second vote. The total of the second vote is used to determine the overall party balance. But most Germans do not understand this after forty years of using the system. Opinion polls show that they believe that the first vote is the most important. They then "lend" their second vote to an allied party or minor party to reinforce or restrain their preferred party, unaware that in doing so they weaken the final strength of their favorite party in the Bundestag.

Despite widespread confusion on the electoral system, there is evidence to suggest that German voters are becoming more rational in making their electoral choices. Many voters are still guided by loyalties derived from their social class, religion, or association memberships. But more voters are now shifting party loyalties from one election to the next apparently as they see differing parties responding better to the issues they view as important.[16] So far, economic performance has not seemed to have as important an effect on changing votes as elsewhere.[17] German voters blame external forces—the oil crisis, international trade situations, or recessions in other countries—rather than the incumbent party for economic problems. Instead, the emergence of new post-material issues—such as nuclear energy, ecology, participatory democracy, and disarmament—are the causes evoking issue voting among the better-educated, younger sections of the new middle class.

WOMEN AND POLITICS IN GERMANY

In most Western democracies, there have long been different patterns of political participation between men and women. In general, women have been less interested in politics, less involved, and more conservative in their partisan orientations. However, in the last fifteen years, these gender differences in political behavior have tended to diminish.[18] Germany has conformed to this general pattern with the very sharp differences in political conduct of men and women in the immediate postwar period waning by the 1970s. By the 1980s, the turnout rate for women voters has been approximately the same as for men in Germany. Once the level of religious commitment is accounted for, German women are as likely to vote for parties of the Left as are men.[19]

In comparison with other democracies, more German women serve in the national legislature. (See Table 12.6.) Many of the women deputies are from the small Green party which has made a special effort to represent women's issues. The number of women is likely to grow even more rapidly in the next decade. In 1988, the SPD party congress adopted a policy calling for women to fill at least 40 percent of all its party offices by 1994 and at least 40 percent of SPD seats in the Bundestag by 1998. These are ambitious goals accepted unanimously; whether they will be met by the target dates is still uncertain. In any case, the new SPD policy and the Greens' success in bringing women into the Bundestag make it likely that the number of women deputies will continue to grow rapidly in Germany. But few women have held major national government positions. Usually, German governments have had a single woman minister, often heading a stereotypical "women's" ministry such as education, health, or family. The Kohl government formed after the 1987 election had two women ministers, but neither headed key ministries. The only woman appointed to a major position, minister of economic cooperation, was forced to resign by hostile media reaction to the presence of a woman in such an office in the mid-1970s.[20]

Women make up over half the electorate (54 percent) but they still have not moved into political prominence. There are few formal restrictions on women in politics but attitudinal barriers among both men and women remain particularly strong in Germany.[21] A 1983 poll asking about attitudes toward women in politics showed that Germany ranked at the bottom in the development of egalitarian ideas on the political role of women. (See Table 12.7.) This poll indicated there has been progress compared to similar polls taken in the mid-1970s, but Germans seem more reticent about accepting women as equal participants in politics than do citizens in other Western European countries. Nevertheless, more than one out of four candidates for the 1987 Bundestag election were women.

TABLE 12.6   Women as National Legislators

Women as percent of total membership

COUNTRY	YEAR	UPPER HOUSE	LOWER HOUSE
Britain	1987	7%	6%
France	1988	3*	7
West Germany	1987	5*	16
Italy	1983	4	8
USA	1984	2	5

* 1983 figure.

Source: Adapted from Pippa Norris, "Women's Legislative Participation in Western Europe," *West European Politics* 8 (October 1985): 92.

TABLE 12.7   Attitudes on Women in Politics

COUNTRY	Percent rejecting idea that politics is more a man's business		Percent having at least equal confidence in a woman as a member of parliament	
	MEN	WOMEN	MEN	WOMEN
Britain	79%	81%	72%	70%
France	78	75	70	72
Germany	55	59	54	67
Italy	75	75	59	64

Source: Commission of the European Communities, *European Women and Men in 1983* (Brussels, 1984), p. 124.

In one rather unfortunate area, German women have taken the lead as political actors. Women played prominent roles in the domestic terrorist activities of the 1970s with Ulrike Meinhoff gaining international notoriety as the leader of a most prominent terrorist group. In a more positive way, women have been prominent in the Green party. Indeed, the record high number of women in the 1987 Bundestag was due largely to the fact that nearly half of the Green deputies were women.

The women's movement has languished in Germany.[22] It emerged in the late 1960s as a branch of the student movement, and shared the students' radical viewpoints which isolated the feminist cause from more moderately inclined women. It never moved beyond this base to attract broad and diverse support among women. The women's movement also suffered from one of the problems of radical causes: extreme fragmentation as the various ideological nuances went separate ways and challenged each other on doctrinal objectives and/or tactical choices. By the beginning of the 1980s, there were, in this small movement, over 140 different women's groups in Germany. There were important gains in moving toward sexual equality during the 1970s: liberalization of abortion and the attainment of financial and social equality before the law. But the fragmented and extremist women's movement can claim little credit for these achievements.

PEOPLE AND POLITICS IN WEST GERMANY

Germany's first experience with democracy during the Weimar era was faulted by attitudes and values in the political culture that were incompatible with democracy and by patterns of individual political activity that undermined democracy. The political culture and nature of political involvement is now much more supportive of representative democracy. In many ways, the German example suggests that the successes of the Bonn republic have developed a political culture and types of political action that sustain democracy. It appears that Germany has reversed the usual causal relationship given to explain stable democracy: Democratic values and behavior make effective and orderly democracy possible. The experience in postwar Germany suggests that a successful democracy may well create a positive political culture and foster constructive forms of political involvement. If a democracy can operate smoothly for a couple of decades, as Germany's did in the 1950s and 1960s, it may well be able to overcome the handicaps of unsympathetic political attitudes and lack of experience in appropriate forms of political action for individual citizens.

The higher levels of participation and the more turbulent, new, forms of political action have not unsettled the Bonn regime. Even the terrorist problems of the 1970s were handled with relative ease as will be demonstrated in Chapter Five. Germany now appears to have acquired desirable attitudinal and involvement patterns that will make survival of its democracy more likely in future troubled times.

NOTES

1. Walter Stahl, ed., *Education for Democracy in West Germany* (New York: Praeger, 1961).
2. Gabriel A. Almond and Sidney Verba, *The Civic Culture: Political Attitudes and Democracy in Five Nations* (Boston: Little, Brown, 1965). See also Sidney Verba, "Germany: The Remaking of Political Culture," in Lucien W. Pye and Sidney Verba, eds., *Political Culture and Political Development* (Princeton, NJ: Princeton University Press, 1965).
3. Kendall L. Baker, Russell J. Dalton, Kai Hildebrandt, *Germany Transformed: Political Culture and the New Politics* (Cambridge, MA: Harvard University Press, 1981), p. 9. See also David P. Conradt, "Changing German Political Culture," in Gabriel A. Almond and Sidney Verba, eds., *The Civic Culture Revisited* (Boston: Little, Brown, 1980).
4. See especially, Conradt, "Changing German Political Culture" and David P. Conradt, *The German Polity*, 3rd ed. (New York: Longman, 1986), pp. 49–58.
5. Baker et al., *Germany Transformed*, p. 13. In 1976, 52.1 percent of the adult population had grown up since the war.

6. See Ronald Inglehart, *The Silent Revolution: Changing Values and Political Styles Among Western Publics* (Princeton, NJ: Princeton University Press, 1977).
7. Russell J. Dalton, "The West German Party System Between Two Ages," in Russell J. Dalton, Scott C. Flanagan, and Paul Allen Beck, eds., *Electoral Change in Advanced Industrial Democracies: Alignment or Dealignment?* (Princeton, NJ: Princeton University Press, 1984). Others contend that traditional voting patterns remain intact. See Hans-Dieter Klingemann, "West Germany," in Ivor Crewe and David Denver, eds., *Electoral Change in Western Democracies: Patterns and Sources of Electoral Volatility* (New York: St. Martin's, 1985).
8. *Eurobarometer*, No. 24 (December 1985): 31.
9. Samuel H. Barnes, Max Kaase, et al., *Political Action: Mass Participation in Five Western Democracies* (Beverly Hills, CA and London: Sage, 1979), p. 84.
10. *Eurobarometer*, No. 19 (June 1983): 47.
11. Jacques-René Rabier, Helene Riffault, Ronald Inglehart, *Eurobarometer 21: Political Cleavages in the European Community, April 1984* (Ann Arbor, MI: Inter-University Consortium for Political and Social Research, 1985), pp. 116–117.
12. Elisabeth Noelle-Neumann, ed., *The Germans: Public Opinion Polls, 1967–1980* (Westport, CT: Greenwood Press, 1981), p. 210.
13. See Geoffrey K. Roberts, "The Federal Republic of Germany," in S.E. Finer, ed., *Adversary Politics and Electoral Reform* (London: Anthony Wigram, 1975).
14. Since 1957, the only parties winning at the district level have been the CDU/CSU and the SPD.
15. In this election, the SPD was awarded two extra seats because in two states, the number of seats earned in district contests exceeded the number of seats it was supposed to receive by the proportional allocation. In such cases, the size of the Bundestag is temporarily expanded beyond the usual 496 members.
16. Dalton, "The West German Party System Between Two Ages" and Klingemann, "West Germany."
17. Klaus von Beyme, *The Political System of the Federal Republic of Germany* (New York: St. Martin's, 1983), pp. 40–42.
18. See Margaret L. Inglehart, "Political Interest in West European Women: An Historical and Empirical Comparative Analysis," *Comparative Political Studies* 14 (October 1981): 299–326.
19. Lawrence Mayer and Roland E. Smith, "Feminism and Religiosity: Female Electoral Behaviour in Western Europe," *West European Politics* 8 (October 1985): 38–49.
20. Jane Hall, "West Germany," in Joni Lovenduski and Jill Hills, eds., *The Politics of the Second Electorate: Women and Public Participation* (London: Routledge & Kegan Paul, 1981).
21. Inglehart, "Political Interest in West European Women," and Donna S. Sanzone, "Women in Politics: A Study of Political Leadership in the United Kingdom, France, and the Federal Republic of Germany," in Cynthia Fuchs Epstein and Rose Laub Coser, eds., *Access to Power: Cross-National Studies of Women and Elites* (London: George Allen & Unwin, 1981).
22. Joni Lovenduski, *Women and European Politics: Contemporary Feminism and Public Policy* (Amherst, MA: University of Massachusetts Press, 1986), pp. 100–103.

CHAPTER THIRTEEN
GERMAN POLITICAL PARTIES AND INTEREST GROUPS

The actions of individual citizens cannot be ignored in democratic societies. But the political scene is nearly always dominated by the established political parties and the national interest groups. In Germany, the political party system enables individual citizens to participate by offering them options at election time and through opportunities for continuing participation in the parties' activities between elections. Because of the success of the CDU/CSU, SPD, and FDP in dominating the political scene, participation in their political activities is the most frequent and most effective form of political involvement. They have developed into strong links between the public and the political process.

In a like manner, strong interest groups have emerged. Those grouped together on the basis of their members' occupations have become important means of linking individuals into the processes that influence economic decisions such as wages and prices. The interest groups are important vehicles of political participation. Some have ties with a party sharing similar views and they try to influence its policy positions from within. All groups seek to exert influence on the government whatever their political complexion is. Together with the parties, they constitute the primary political actors in German politics.

THE GERMAN PARTY SYSTEM

The party system of the postwar German democracy is another area of sharp contrasts with the earlier experience under Weimar. Many analysts have traced several of Weimar's political problems to its party system: There were too many parties; Many of them were poorly organized and undisciplined; They were polarized from each other to the point that they often engaged in violence against their rivals. Far from supporting democracy, they are seen as largely responsible for its destruction.

The situation under the Bonn republic is entirely different. The party system has been simplified: Instead of the forty-one parties that competed in the 1928 elections, modern Germany has only three or four significant parties appealing to the voters. The two major parties, the Christian Democrats and the Social Democrats, control over eighty percent of the votes. The ideological politics of yore have largely been supplanted by the pragmatism of contemporary parties. Extremist parties have disappeared with the fascist parties outlawed and the Communist party destroyed by the unpopularity of the East German regime. Weimar's polarization of parties contrasts with the moderate interparty rivalries that are based more on policy nuances than on alternative views of society. This moderation prevails even though competition between the SPD and CDU/CSU is often intense with only a few percentage points separating them. There is a broad enough political consensus that, at one point or another during the last twenty-five years, each of the three major parties has joined with each of the other parties in government coalitions.

The Christian Democratic Parties

The Christian Democratic parties were new after the war.[1] They are in fact two separate parties, the Christian Social Union (CSU), which operates only in Bavaria, and the Christian Democratic Union (CDU), which operates in the rest of West Germany. They share a common heritage in the Catholic Center party from the Weimar era, a moderate party drawing approximately 11 to 13 percent of the vote between 1920 and 1933. But the postwar CDU/CSU is really a new political force that has avoided the denominational link with the Catholic Church and attracted a much broader spectrum of voters. The CDU/CSU grew rapidly in the early years of the Bonn republic. It benefitted from the sympathy of American occupation governors who liked the Christian Democratic mod-

TABLE 13.1   Party Strength in Recent Bundestag Elections

	1972	1976	1980	1983	1987
CDU/CSU	44.8%	48.6%	44.5%	48.6%	44.3%
SPD	45.2	42.6	42.9	38.2	37.0
FDP	8.4	7.9	10.6	6.9	9.1
Greens	–0–	–0–	1.5	5.6	8.3
Others	1.0	0.9	0.5	0.5	1.3

eration and who opposed extremist and regional parties. The CDU/CSU also drew strength from the popularity of its leader, Konrad Adenauer, who served as chancellor (or prime minister) from 1949 to 1963. It was successful in absorbing many of the smaller parties of the Center-Right that contested the first postwar elections. The CDU/CSU parties earned public support by the economic miracle that they led.

The CDU/CSU has won more votes than any other party in every election since 1949 with the sole exception of the 1972 election. Unwilling to rely on support from only Catholics as Christian Democratic parties in other countries did, the German Christian Democrats sought to be a "people's party" attractive to all Germans. The CDU/CSU carefully balanced leadership positions to assure equitable representation of Catholics and Protestants. Its appeal went beyond the traditional support of Center-Right parties to attract working-class voters. Its ability to attract diverse support from both Catholics and Protestants and from all social classes made it a "catch-all" party.[2]

The relationship between the two Christian Democratic parties has not always been easy. Since the CSU limits its activities to Bavaria and the CDU stays out of that state, there is none of the direct competition that produces the tension between the Gaullists and the Giscardians in France. But the two parties are separate and represent slightly different concerns. The CSU is more conservative, more Catholic, and more nationalistic than is the CDU. The CSU has taken stronger positions on law and order issues and has demanded greater controls over the immigration and naturalization of non-Germans. More importantly, personal rivalries between leaders in the two parties have produced tensions. The CSU was led for more than thirty years by Franz-Josef Strauss until his death in 1988. Strauss was a controversial and ambitious political leader. His authoritarian political style was an important handicap for him and, outside of his home state of Bavaria, for the CDU. When the CDU reluctantly put Strauss at the head of the CDU/CSU slate in 1980, the CDU/CSU vote dropped to its lowest point since 1949. But his strength at home—Bavaria is the most solidly Christian Democratic bastion and accounts for more than a fourth of overall Christian Democratic electoral strength—made him a powerful figure in the CDU/CSU. The accommodation of Strauss and his CSU friends through policy concessions and key ministerial appointments was always a difficult task for the CDU. However, the elected deputies from the two parties form a single group in parliament and vote together with near perfect unity.[3]

Tensions between the two parties rose in the late 1980s. After the 1987 election and subsequent state elections showed some electoral decline, Strauss challenged the moderate line adopted by CDU Chancellor and party leader, Helmut Kohl. In order to regain lost votes, Kohl argued that the party should target Center-Left voters who might be disaffected to the SPD. Strauss argued that the Christian Democrats would be better advised to adopt a more nationalistic and law-and-order position to attract right-wing voters unhappy with the CDU/CSU's moderation. Behind the tactical and ideological disputes laid an important personal rivalry between the two leaders. Strauss wanted to reassert his claim of greater influence in the coalition's government and over its general political strategy. While such intracoalition strife gained much press coverage, it had always been a part of the coalition's relationship without ever risking its end. The coalition had kept both parties in government for most of the 1980s. The union of the CDU and CSU was well described by Strauss as a strategy of "marching separately but striking together." Strauss's death in 1988 reduced coalition tensions as the new CSU leaders took a less abrasive stance in intracoalition relations and devoted more time to securing their own control of the CSU.

The CDU/CSU spurns doctrinal debates and prefers dealing pragmatically with specific issues rather than with ideologies. In its early years, the party attempted a compromise between an economic system based on free enterprise and concerns for social responsibility. It sought "capitalism with a conscience." The monumental task of rebuilding the economy after the war required Christian Democratic government officials to take leading roles in planning and directing the economic recovery. Like British Conservatives and French Gaullists (but unlike American conservatives), the CDU/CSU accepted an active role for the government in managing the economy while not altering its market and free enterprise orientations. It provided guidance and sometimes government funds to stimulate investment and industrial development. These practices continued long after the recovery from the war, becoming accepted CDU/CSU economic principles. In addition, the CDU/CSU sought to win broad acceptance for this economic order by reducing some of the uncertainties and tensions felt by the less advantaged. To this end, the CDU/CSU enacted a wide range of social insurance and welfare benefits giving Germany the most far-reaching and expensive social security system in the western world. It also welcomed the emergence of a powerful trade union movement and enacted labor legislation that helped provide trade union rights and employee job security.

In recent years, the CDU/CSU has followed other western conservative parties in de-emphasizing the government's role in the economy. It has worked toward selling some of Germany's few publicly owned enterprises to private buyers. The government's budget deficit has been less in Germany than elsewhere so the CDU/CSU has been less interested in pressing for cuts in government programs. Indeed, the party supported increased government appropriations for education, family benefits, and pension reform in the 1987 election campaign. The party has thus avoided the economic and social extremism of Thatcher, Reagan, or Chirac.

Christian Democrats have advocated close alignment of Germany with the United States in international politics. They have supported the controversial installation of new American medium-range missiles in Germany. They have also been among the most dedicated supporters of economic and political unification through the European Community or Common Market. But they have not excluded relations with Eastern Europe. The beginning of Germany's effort to regularize relations with the Soviet Union and other Eastern European countries (the Ostpolitik) came during the government of CDU Chancellor Kurt Kiesinger. More recently at the end of the 1980s, CDU officials have promoted further ties with the east, and especially with the German Democratic Republic. While loyal to the United States on foreign policy matters, they have quietly pressured American administrations to negotiate disarmament agreements with the Soviet Union.

During its first two decades, the organization and policies of the CDU were dominated by Chancellor Adenauer to the point that it was almost his personal party. So great was his control that Adenauer would not permit the emergence of a new leader to replace him when he retired in 1963. The search for new leadership and the adjustment to opposition after the Adenauer era was difficult. The next decade was a time of uncertainty and weakness as the CDU went through five party leaders and lost control of the government for the first time in the history of the Federal Republic.

Helmut Kohl became party leader in 1972. Despite his lack of personal public appeal, he slowly rebuilt the party. By the beginning of the 1980s, the CDU had more than doubled its membership since 1970. Its youth organization, "Young Union," increased its membership by two and a half times, attracting nonparty members as well as CDU members. New leaders emerged from this youth group and state level CDU governments. Thus, when the CDU regained the chancellorship in 1982, it was well situated to provide political backing for its government. In the 1983 elections, Chancellor Kohl led the CDU/CSU to its best showing at the polls since 1957 taking 48.8 percent of the votes. However, Kohl did not develop broad public appeal and his government was plagued with economic and political problems. The CDU/CSU vote fell in the 1987 elections to 44.3 percent of the vote—enough to hold on to control of the government (with the FDP) but it was its lowest percentage since 1949. Later that year, scandals involving CDU state governments further weakened the CDU's public standing. In many ways its political strength at the end of the 1980s came not so much from its own success and popular appeal as from the even greater problems of its main rival, the Social Democratic party.

The Social Democratic Party

The German Social Democratic party (SPD) dates back to the imperial era. Throughout its early history, the SPD struggled to reconcile its Marxist notions of revolution with its growing commitment to parliamentary democracy.[4] More often than not, the result was revolutionary rhetoric and reformist practice. After an initial return to Marxism in the first years after World War II, the SPD definitively abandoned the notion of a workers' party engaged in class conflict and instead, tried to create a broad people's party of the Center-Left. In 1959, the SPD met in a conference at Bad Godesberg and adopted a new party program which broke entirely with Marxist ideological principles and symbols. Urged on by Herbert Wehner and by Willy Brandt, the popular mayor of West Berlin, the SPD accepted the existing socioeconomic system and pledged to work within it to improve it, not replace it. Abandoned as well were such powerful socialist symbols as the red flag, the singing of *The International*, and class warfare vocabulary.

The SPD's moderation of its program and style paralleled a similar development at the same time in the British Labour party. The moderation was possible because, unlike socialists in France who faced competition from a strong Communist party, the SPD lacked any major rival on its Left to attract more radical elements disaffected by their party's new pragmatism. The SPD moved toward the political center confident that these leftists would still find the SPD more attractive than any other party. This permitted the SPD to broaden its political base beyond the traditional working-class support. In a final step to win public acceptance, the SPD agreed to join the CDU/CSU in a "grand coalition" government from 1966 to 1969 which demonstrated the ability and responsibility of SPD leadership in government position.

The SPD's moderate stance was successful: In every election from 1957 to 1972, the Social Democrats increased their voting support. They won over many middle-class voters, especially those employed in the civil service. By the 1970s, the SPD had become a catch-all party with a diverse electoral base. The party's share of the electorate had increased by nearly 20 percentage points from its standing in the early 1950s. In 1969, the Social Democrats led a coalition with the Free Democratic party to a parliamentary majority that governed the country for the next thirteen years.

In government, the SPD's economic programs varied little from those of the CDU/CSU: maintenance of competitiveness in international markets, a stable currency, and economic growth through the market economy. More attention was given to social reforms: liberalization of abortion, women's economic equality, worker representation in the factory and in the decision-making in the workplace (co-determination), and restructuring higher education. A major area of accomplishment was in foreign affairs where the SPD governments completed the process of reestablishing normal diplomatic relations with the communist countries of Eastern Europe. The Ostpolitik was started under a CDU-led government but it was fulfilled by Brandt's SPD in the early 1970s. The resulting detente in tensions between Germany and its neighbors helped to reduce German fears of becoming the battleground of a new war.

The moderate stance of the SPD bothered some of its left-wing activists, especially those inspired by the radical student movements of the late 1960s. By the late 1970s, this uneasiness within the party spread more broadly. After a decade in government, some felt that too few reforms were accomplished. Willy Brandt retired as chancellor in 1974 in a scandal precipitated by the discovery that his personal secretary was an East German spy. He was succeeded as chancellor by the less colorful and even more pragmatic Helmut Schmidt. The party's youth movement underwent a severe crisis in the early 1970s with many of its members lured away to radical movements on the political fringes. Other young radicals were brought into the party bureaucracy where they helped tilt the party toward more leftist positions.

There were growing tensions in many SPD local and state parties between the leftists and the supporters of Helmut Schmidt. These were exacerbated by the division of power in the SPD between the party leader, often a powerful figure, and the party's chancellor (when in power) or chancellor-designate (in opposition). After Willy Brandt stepped down as chancellor, he stayed on as party chairman. Soon tensions grew between him and Schmidt as Brandt followed the leftward swing of the grass-root elements of the party. At one point, Brandt was quoted as saying: "It isn't true that I don't get along with Helmut Schmidt. The fact is that I get along with him splendidly—as long as we don't talk politics."[5] The disagreements among these leaders spread through the party. The factional strife cost the party many members and contributed to the party's losses in local, state, and national elections.[6]

In the 1980s, the party struggled to redefine its goals. After the fall of the Schmidt government, the SPD designated, first Hans-Jochen Vogel, and then Johannes Rau as its chancellor candidates. The party moved slightly toward the left but with an emphasis on post-material issues rather than on radical economic changes. Broad public contentment with the economy and popular concern about fiscal responsibility limited the SPD's ability to call for changes in the basic economic structure. Instead, the party attempted to acquire a new leftist allure by picking up on public concerns about nuclear issues. The SPD pledged to press for negotiations for the withdrawal of American and Soviet nuclear weapons from East and West Germany. It called for the closing down of all nuclear energy plants in the country within ten years. More traditional party interests were represented in the call for the creation of new jobs to relieve high unemployment.

By the middle of the 1980s, the SPD faced a series of challenges.[7] First, the party's organization was stodgy and aging. After more than a decade in government, the SPD was tied to leaders who no longer had much appeal. Within the party, serious leadership rivalries produced tension. Struggles between party chairman Willy Brandt and Chancellor Schmidt, and later with chancellor-candidate Johannes Rau, produced uncertainty on doctrine and demoralized party activists. Brandt's retirement in 1987 brought some relief but did not heal the past divisions created by his rivalry with other party leaders. He was replaced by the more moderate Hans-Jochen Vogel. But the left-wing cause found a new champion in Oskar Lafontaine, premier of the Saarland and an aspirant for the party's leadership. The centralized power within the SPD kept the struggles for leadership more restrained than was the case in Britain.[8] But the rivalries tarnished the party's reputation with its rank-and-file members and voters.

Unlike the CDU/CSU's membership growth during the 1970s, SPD membership remained stagnant. Indeed, the party suffered some defections from its ranks. Its youth organization, the Young Socialists, had not recovered from the crisis of the early 1970s when many of its members had opted for more radical politics. Within the party, leadership positions shifted from the blue-collar workers from the trade union, movement to teachers and civil servants. This shift produced concern, among labor leaders, that the SPD might lose touch with its traditional core of trade union support.

Second, the SPD was the primary victim of the rise of the Greens. In 1987, the SPD vote fell to only 37.0 percent, its lowest level since 1961. Young, educated people from the new middle class with commitments to social change who might have been expected to vote SPD were, instead, attracted by the Greens. Attempts to regain this part of the electorate and to retain the loyalty of people still in the SPD by championing some of the post material causes, confused other elements of the party's electorate. Factory workers, for example, had little interest in environmental protection schemes that endangered their jobs. Reconciling the concerns of these two portions of the SPD electorate had been a major challenge through the 1980s.

Third, the SPD lost its coalition partner when the Free Democratic party (FDP) pulled out of Schmidt's government in 1982. The immediate result was the fall of the SPD-led government. The longer lasting problem was that the SPD was left without a strategy for returning to power. The party had never attained a majority on its own, and the challenge from the Greens has made the reaching of that goal virtually impossible in the foreseeable future. The SPD's prospects for finding a new coalition partner that offers hope of a parliamentary majority are slim. The FDP has aligned itself with the CDU and has shown no interest in returning to a coalition with the SPD in the near future. The prospect of an alliance with the Greens is remote and would bring problems of its own. The Greens are seriously divided over such a coalition at the national level. Should one be negotiated, a likely schism between pragmatic and radical Green activists would reduce the electoral effects. The SPD in turn has explicitly rejected such a coalition both to discourage wavering leftist voters from shifting to the Greens and to avoid association with the anti-establishment and often radical stances of the Greens.

The problems of the SPD are faced by several other European left-of-center parties. With the decreasing size of these parties' traditional electoral bases in the blue-collar working class, they must appeal to new groups of voters, especially among the better educated technicians and managers. Yet the political goals of these parties' traditional core supporters are often different from those of the new target groups. While the same problem faces the French Socialists and the British Labour party, the German SPD finds its predicament particularly difficult. It operates with an electoral system that permits parties winning as little as five percent of the vote to win seats in parliament. With a youthful and new image, the Greens thereby are a major rival to the SPD in its search for the crucial votes needed to regain power.

Without a strategy for returning to power, with sharp differences over priority issues and positions separating key parts of the party's leadership and electorate, and with continuing problems of internal party organization, the SPD did not profit from the problems and decline of the CDU/CSU in the late 1980s. Despite the continuing weakness of its main opponent, the SPD faces a trying period in the next decade. The federal structures in Germany will permit the party time to resolve these problems. Even though excluded from power at the national level, the SPD can win and has won control of state and local governments. At these lower levels, the party can groom new leaders, sort out its internal divisions, and experiment with different coalition possibilities.

The Free Democratic Party

The Free Democratic party (FDP) embodies the European liberal tradition. FDP liberalism, unlike American liberalism, is located at the political center. The party champions free-enterprise economic policies but is open to moderate social reforms and concerned about defense of civil liberties. Consequently, the FDP is a pivot party in that it can coalesce with the SPD on its left or the CDU/CSU on its right. Its strategic location and the inability of any party (except the CDU/CSU in 1957) to win a parliamentary majority on its own, enables the FDP to play a disproportionately important role in postwar German politics. With a vote that has varied between just over 5 percent to nearly 13 percent, the FDP has been part of every postwar government except for the Grand Coalition (1966 to 1969). It has traded its essential parliamentary votes for key political positions such as president, vice chancellor, foreign minister, interior minister, and economics minister. Thus, with less than 8 percent of the seats in the 1983 Bundestag, the FDP held 18 percent of the ministerial portfolios.

The problem with such a pivot position is that the party has difficulty in defining its own distinctive image. Voting for the FDP is less a support for its policies than it is a means of restraining its coalition partner. When the FDP is tied to the CDU/CSU, voters who may vote CDU or CSU for their first choice, cast their second vote for the FDP as a means of encouraging moderate reforms under an otherwise conservative government; they see the FDP as checking the right wing excesses of Strauss's CSU.[9] When the FDP was allied with the SPD, it was viewed as a check on the SPD's radical wing and as a voice of economic reason and moderation. And it is not only the voters who attribute this balancing role to the FDP; moderate party leaders from both major parties cite the FDP to refuse demands from radical elements within their own party.

Another problem stemming from the party's pivot position is that its voters' loyalty is tested when it shifts coalition partners as the FDP did in 1969 to ally with the SPD and then in 1982 to ally with the CDU/CSU. For two examples, its youth organization, the Young Democrats, opted for independence from the FDP when the party shifted to the Right in 1982, and a handful of its Bundestag deputies resigned from the party. Then, the party experienced a serious crisis in 1983 to 1984 with intense factional in-fighting and battles in the party's executive. Eventually, a new party leader was chosen, Martin Bangemann, minister of economics in the Kohl government.

The FDP is essentially a middle class party with its core support among white-collar workers, civil servants, and liberal professionals. FDP voters are predominantly, well educated, better off, Protestants.[10] The party organization is weak even when allowances are made for its small membership. It is very much the tool of a handful of its senior officials.

The major challenge for the FDP is to keep its vote above the 5 percent threshold required for sitting in parliament. Its electoral support is often unreliable and volatile. On occasion, notably in 1969, it came perilously close to falling below that barrier and losing its place in the Bundestag. Its survival depends largely on its ability to revive at the state level to develop the leadership and ideas needed for success in national politics.[11] Bangemann made some headway in reviving his party's fortune, and the party increased its share of the vote in the 1987 Bundestag elections to 9.1 percent. But many observers wonder if there is room for two minor parties and suggest that the rise of the Greens may spell the end of the FDP.

The Greens

The Greens are a political party that emerged out the environmental, feminist, peace, and antinuclear energy movements of the 1970s.[12] This new party brought together a varied mix of traditional conservationists, modern ecologists, and advocates of a wide range of radical left-wing and counterculture causes. It contains as a result, an often difficult mix of people ranging from conservatives to Marxists. The Greens reject the usual Left or Right political labels and claim to represent entirely new political and social interests. Their slogan is "We are not Right or Left; we are ahead!"

The Green party has developed a broad political platform that goes well beyond a narrow conception of environmental protection. The party prefers economic development to slow down so that humans might find ways to live in greater harmony with nature. The Green party believes that slower economic development would help in combatting environmental pollution and in overcoming the impersonal human environment in large industrial settings. It advocates decentralized, political, decision making that would shift the control of those decisions affecting people's lives to local community-based polities. The Greens are strongly opposed to both nuclear energy and nuclear weapons. In pursuit of a nuclear-free Germany, they would end West Germany's ties with NATO in preference for a neutral Germany. They are staunch advocates of civil liberties championing the feminist cause and more controversial causes such as gay rights, squatters' rights (rights for people occupying abandoned buildings), suffrage for immigrant workers, and political rights for accused terrorists.

The Greens draw most of their support from younger, university-educated, middle-class, Germans. Approximately 42 percent of 18 to 20 year old voters identified with the Greens in the early 1980s.[13] Beyond this core of young supporters, the Green party also succeeds in attracting votes from broader social categories in communities facing ecological challenges. Residents of areas adjacent to new nuclear energy plants, nuclear treatment plants, airport runways, or new highways often vote for the Greens. This support has important consequences in local and state elections. How durable this electorate will be is still uncertain. Many of those who vote Green out of opposition to specific, public-work projects seem to return to their normal partisan preferences once the issue loses its saliency. It is not certain whether young voters attracted by the Greens will remain loyal as they mature.

The party's loose structure may inhibit efforts to consolidate its support over the long run. The Greens deny that they are a party, claiming instead to be a voluntaristic social movement. Party membership is low with many Greens preferring to keep formal affiliation restricted to the truly devoted. The Greens espouse a strong anti-organizational, radical, egalitarian philosophy based on fears of oligarchic control if their organization acquires structure or permanent leadership. They blame the moderation of other once radical parties, such as the socialists or even the communists, on the emergence of entrenched party elites who acquire a stake in the status quo. The Greens want to prevent such a development in their own movement by keeping its organization to a minimum and in strengthening direct democracy within the party.

The Greens insist on rotation of leaders to prevent an elite from developing within their ranks. This does not always go over well with the leaders who are to be rotated out of position. For example, the Green deputies elected in 1983 were to step down two years later and let others on the list take their positions. Several refused to do so. The arrangements were changed for the 1987 elections allowing those elected to serve out full terms but barring reelection of incumbents. Some Greens—notably Petra Kelly, one of the party's most prominent personalities and one of those who had refused to step down midterm—ran again successfully. Nevertheless, the policy works well enough to hinder its ability to develop experienced and expert leaders.

Without experienced leaders and with a membership of populists more interested in self-expression than self-discipline, meetings of the Greens are often chaotic. Only those members actually present at a meeting or conference can vote. Since attendance varies from one time or location to another, there may be sharp changes in party policy from one meeting to the next depending on who actually shows up. To maintain a commitment to direct political action, it is standard practice for meetings to include a demonstration. The conference participants board buses and travel, often long distances, to demonstrate at the site of a controversial project. A 1985 meeting, for example, was interrupted by a 500 mile round trip to demonstrate against a nuclear recycling plant in Bavaria.

While the party is in the Bundestag, it does not yet accept parliamentary politics. Green deputies continue their direct political action. They spurn the decorum (and elitism) of other deputies by holding their party caucuses on the lawns of the parliament building rather than behind closed doors. The presence of Green deputies in parliament gives the movement visibility and legitimacy but not much impact on policy. The Greens place priority on direct action in demonstrations, sit-ins, or street politics rather than on affecting public policy through the legislative process. They eschew the accommodations on which parliamentary democracy is based. Like radical socialists of the late nineteenth century, they prefer loyalty to their principles rather than compromise. Their commitment to a radical participatory democracy may represent a real challenge to German democracy should their electoral strength increase.

A central concern is what will happen if the Greens win enough seats to prevent the formation of a parliamentary majority by either the CDU or the SPD. This situation has already occurred several times at the state and local levels with the Greens either tacitly supporting a minority SPD government or, more rarely, holding government offices themselves. (The first Green to serve as a minister in a state government took his oath of office in December 1985 attired in jeans and Nike sport shoes.)[14] The Greens are highly divided on what they should do when faced with the prospects of joining a government coalition. Some fundamentalists, known as "fundis", notably Thomas Ebermann, reject any coalition as inevitably involving compromise and betrayal of the movement's principles. More pragmatic Greens, "realos", such as Otto Schilly and Joschka Fischer, see the possibility of reforming and improving the system by working within it. The fundis control the party organization, such as it is, but the realos have strength in the party's Bundestag delegation. The contention between the two wings of the movement is bitter. Petra Kelly, described her party's division as "a kind of holy war, with mullahs of both camps throwing incredible personal slander."[15] With growing unhappiness of Green voters with this squabbling and schism a real prospect, the Greens' political impact may well have passed its peak.

A Party System in Crisis?

For three decades, the German party system seemed to be a principal source of strength for the new postwar democracy. In recent years, new questions on the health of the party system developed. One came from the sudden entry of the Greens onto the political stage and their effects on party politics. It appeared that the anti-establishment and unpredictable Greens might replace the FDP as the important third party of German politics. Unlike the FDP, which was committed to the existing democratic system and able to work with both major parties, the Greens lack the commitment to the system and reject coalition with either the CDU/CSU or the SPD. The near certain parliamentary majorities of the past were endangered by the possibility that the antisystem Greens might hold the balance of power after an election. The second question was about the health of the SPD itself. After a decade of power, the SPD was surprisingly weak and divided. Most of the voters attracted by the Greens were lured away from the SPD, and the party's prospects of winning back these voters were not bright.[16] There were also uncertainties about whether the SPD could reconcile the still materialist interests of its traditional working-class voters with the post-materialist concerns of the rest of its electorate. Finally, public confidence in the major parties—the CDU/CSU, SPD, and FDP—was shaken by a series of campaign contribution and financial scandals implicating leading personalities from all three.

Despite these challenges, the major parties show considerable resilience. The FDP adapted remarkably well to its shift in coalition partners; the CDU/CSU membership and electorate remain reasonably loyal despite the scandals and leadership rivalries. Even the SPD, perhaps the most seriously wounded of the three major parties, can expect to regain much of its strength as the Greens experience division and internal disarray. But the ebbing of the Greens should not lead one to neglect the very real political problems that led to their earlier successes. There can be little question about the anxieties of young voters who turned to the Greens. They were frustrated with the traditional parties' failure to deal with issues such as the destruction of Germany's beloved forests by acid rain, the danger of nuclear accidents like Chernobyl in a country with as many nuclear power plants as Germany has, and Germany's frontline position in the cold war. These are tremendous problems that the major parties will need to face more effectively if they are to avoid another challenge from a new party.

INTEREST GROUP POLITICS IN WEST GERMANY

Germans are as willing as British and French citizens to join groups to press for their political interests. Indeed, the relative autonomy of German local and state governments provides even greater incentives for such organizations. At the national level, more than eight hundred groups seek to influence national policy.[17] In comparison with British and French groups, German interest groups tend to be better organized with larger and more professional staffs. Under Weimar, ideologically grounded divisions separated German interest groups much as they still do in France or Italy; but under Bonn, the German interest groups have developed into some of the most unified in Europe, with strong "peak associations" in each major interest sector. German groups are more successful than their British or French counterparts in mobilizing potential members in most sectors.

German interest groups also appear better connected to the national policy process. The development of neocorporatist decision making, where groups join government officials in directly shaping public policy, has proceeded further in Germany than the other countries considered in this text.[18] There are extensive networks of consultative bodies drawing interest groups into collaboration with government officials at all levels of government. For example, the state level boards controlling radio and television broadcasting include trade union and business representatives along with political party leaders and government officials. In many federal ministries, the staffs are obliged by statute to consult with affected interests as draft legislation or regulations are prepared.

The peak of this neocorporatist group/government interaction was achieved in the Concerted Action conferences that were held through most of the 1970s. For a decade, they brought together government officials, trade unionists, and business representatives to discuss government economic policies. The participants agreed upon guidelines for price and wage increases and for the desired rate of government social expenditures and economic incentives to assure the desired level of economic growth. Many observers feel that the Concerted Action conferences explained the German success in minimizing the inflation and recession during the oil crises of the 1970s. Others, however, criticized the process as a means of preventing workers from achieving just wage increases. Indeed, the Concerted Action conferences ended in the late 1970s when the labor unions withdrew while criticizing the one-sided sacrifices being imposed on workers.

Despite the fact that such neocorporatist arrangements tend to bypass parliament and to shift policy making to inter-elite bargaining behind closed doors, they remain popular in Germany. There is a strong feeling there, and in other countries as well, that groups, whose interests are most directly affected by government policy, ought to be consulted and usually heeded when making public policy. But these institutionalized group/government contacts are not now, or likely to become, the most common or even successful forms of group pressure on government. In fact, with the exception of a few areas where small but powerful groups have a hold over narrow interests related to their members (notably, agriculture, German refugees from the east, and medicine), the predominant forms of group pressures are more traditional activities.[19]

German groups engage in a wide range of activities to bring their interests to the fore. They seek election of favorable candidates by endorsing sympathetic candidates. But they do not engage in the kind of financial backing of candidates as do interest groups in the United States or, to a lesser degree, in Britain. In Germany, campaign expenses for all parties are subsidized by the government. Interest groups nevertheless develop strong links with elected officials. Many members of the Bundestag are current members and past leaders of interest groups. Indeed, employment by interest groups is second only to the civil service in listings of the deputies' occupations.[20] The primary targets of group action, however, are the ministries. There, interest groups cultivate ties with both civil servants and politicians to press their ideas and concerns. Ministers are eager for affected groups to accept the policies they develop. Such acceptance heightens the legitimacy of the policy and improves the chances that those affected will cooperate in making it work. To get this support, ministers and their aides solicit and, sometimes, incorporate the ideas of concerned groups. In some cases, ministries become advocates of their clienteles with, for an example, the ministry of agriculture championing the cause of German farmers within the government.

There are concerns about the government's independence from such key groups. But civil servants and ministers have their own interests as well. They are usually able to transform the group's interests, as they incorporate them into their policies, in ways that bring them into line with the government's perspective. The strength of major economic and occupational groups gives the government latitude as it tries to strike a balance between the interests of labor and business or between agriculture and industry. Germany contrasts with France and Italy where the weaknesses of the trade union movements have left the governments more beholden to business interests. And, German groups that feel abused by the process are able to withdraw and press for their interests in other forums as the trade unions did when they withdrew from the Concerted Action conferences.

Occupational Interest Groups

Among the hundreds of German interest groups, the ones with the most importance are those based on occupations. These groups have broad interests covering economic, social, and even cultural concerns. Narrower advocacy groups, such as the Forest Owners' Association or the League of War Victims, have much more restricted and particularistic interests to defend. Combined, these occupational groups speak out on macroeconomic policies, social policies, and a variety of other public issues. They have strong organizations and highly professional staffs to conduct relations with the government. They are well situated to influence government policy making. Interest group politics in Bonn are more reminiscent of Washington lobbying than interest group politics in London, Paris, or Rome. The German versions are more subtle but no less effective than the highly visible actions of American lobbyists.

The labor unions are represented by a peak association, the German Federation of Labor (DGB). In contrast to the weakness of the British Trade Union Congress or the divisions of the French labor movement, the DGB remains a powerful voice for labor in German politics. With a membership of nearly 8 million, it has over nine thousand, full-time, officials. Nearly 40 percent of eligible German workers are members of a trade union, a figure much higher than in most other European countries despite Germany's lack of union shops. The DGB represents 85 percent of the unionized workers.

The DGB has close links with the SPD but not the integral ones that tie the British TUC to the Labour party. The German federation has attempted to keep good relations with the CDU/CSU even though most of its leaders prefer dealing with the SPD. The absence of dogmatic critiques of the existing social order—such as those that have often isolated French unions from conservative governments—make such relations easier and more common in Germany. After its return to power, the CDU/CSU made a conscious effort to build a new partnership with the DGB.[21] Both sides recognize that the vitality of the German economy depends upon maintenance of its competitive standing with respect to other industrial exporters. This realization plus the unions' avoidance of dogmatic critiques help pave the way for smooth relations and continued union influence under conservative governments.

During the past three decades, the DGB acquired a strong reputation in Germany and abroad for its moderation. Union leaders won agreement from their workers to forgo strikes and keep wage increases to a minimum while the economy recovered from the war. By the end of the 1960s, wages began to rise and working-class access to the benefits of the strong economy improved. Unlike the French and British unions which still retain the class warfare vocabulary and mentality, the DGB definitively abandoned Marxist class conflict in 1963. While the DGB was uninterested in radical economic changes, it pressed for worker participation in management decision making. The unions won limited co-determination in the 1970s and continue to seek a greater voice for labor in workplace councils. Co-determination mandates the involvement of trade union representatives on an equal footing with shareholder representatives on the boards of directors of large firms. Questions exist about whether co-determination brings greater worker participation in policy decisions or whether the trade union delegates are simply co-opted, giving the guise of participation without any real power over key issues such as employment and wages.[22]

Trade union militancy did increase at the end of the 1970s.[23] There were a series of often lengthy strikes over wages and job retention in the early 1980s. Such strikes would not be unusual in France or Britain but they marked a major departure from normalcy for Germany. Growing unemployment and declining heavy industry made job security a major concern for the German workers. Recently, the DGB has made the reduction of the work week to 35 hours without pay cuts a key demand in political and strike actions. This demand is not only so the workers profit from greater leisure time, but also that the lower maximum work week will create jobs for the unemployed. With the exception of a few factories, little headway has been made in winning the 35 hour week. But the continued commitment to this goal makes more lengthy strikes a likelihood in coming years.

The trade union crisis that has hit other European countries had much less impact on the German labor movement. As elsewhere, the decline of heavy industries reduced DGB membership. Between 1982 and 1987, overall DGB membership fell two hundred thousand, and the rate of unionization dropped from 35 to 32.3 percent of all workers.[24] The drop in Germany was much less than in Britain or France due, in part, to the better resistance of German industry and, in part, to the traditional strength of the DGB. A more serious threat to the health of the trade union movement came from the failure of a union-owned housing firm. The firm, *Neue Heimat,* was the largest, single-home construction company in the country. Its failure combined with the malfeasance and corruption of several of its directors discredited the trade union's claim to be able to manage business as effectively as a private owner. The scandal dragged over several years, embarrassing the union and its SPD friends. Nevertheless, the trade union movement remains a powerful political voice heeded by governments of all political stripes.

In a comparative sense, German business appears better organized and more unified than in other democratic systems.[25] The business community is represented by three peak associations: the Federation of German Industry (BDI) speaking for the interests of industry; the German Industrial and Trade Conference (DIHT) protecting the interests of small businesses and craftsmen; and the Federation of German Employers' Associations (BDA). The interests of these three are usually, but not always, complementary. The BDI has been the most important of the three in recent years because of its broad ranging economic and social interests. It claims the membership of 98 percent of all industry. The DIHT advocates the special needs and concerns of the small and medium-sized enterprises. The BDA focuses more on wage policies and labor relations. Many enterprises have membership in more than one association that links them with two or more of these peak organizations. Leaders of one organization are often leaders in another as well. Informal gatherings in business clubs or discussion groups extend opportunities for coordination of their political action. In most instances, the BDI, BDA, and DIHT collaborate closely on major policy decisions.

As might be expected, there is a natural affinity between the business community and the CDU/CSU. But the business groups also maintain cordial ties with the SPD, especially during those years when the SPD governed. A financial scandal in the early 1980s, the Flick affair, revealed extensive illegal business financing for all parties, including the SPD. The years when the SPD was in power were good years for the BDI and other business groups. Business leaders felt then a greater need to strengthen their organization than when friendlier politicians held power.[26]

The influence of business interests in politics is evident. It was not able to prevent the implementation of codetermination but it did limit its impact. Business pressure led to modification of the antimonopoly legislation left over from the occupation era. Informal pressure from business leaders appeared to have contributed to the FDP's 1982 decision to shift coalition partners from the SPD to the CDU/CSU. This influence does not mean that business dominates politics. In many cases, the surface unity of the business community is maintained only by taking no position, or by taking ambiguous stands on controversial public policies which divide different business interests. The government is also skilled in using other interests to counterbalance business interests and to defend its own viewpoints. But business is well situated to present its positions in a persuasive manner.

German businesses and trade unions do not exhaust the occupational groups. Farmers are well organized and their influence permits the 750 thousand full-time farmers to have an extraordinary influence on the entire country's agricultture and food policies.[27] Professionals such as doctors, pharmacists, lawyers, and others are well organized and highly influential on public issues touching their activities. But labor unions and business groups hold the public's and the government's attention because of the breadth and diversity of their interests, because of the strength of their membership numbers, and their control over the economy.

Citizen Initiative Groups

The 1970s produced the rise of large numbers of new, locally based, citizen initiative groups advocating a broad variety of specific causes. By the early 1980s, there were approximately fifty thousand such citizen lobbies with an estimated total membership of 1.5 million.[28] Many were focused on environmental issues; others addressed social and cultural issues ranging from tenants' rights to day care centers.[29] They usually had little formal structure and small memberships. The life of the typical citizen lobby was a short one; few lasted more than a couple of years.[30] Only a few made the transition from a local protest to a broad-based social movement.

Supporters of the citizen lobbies and new social movements often resorted to unconventional means of political action: protest marches, boycotts, sit-ins, and demonstrations. In their early years, the unexpected militancy and surprising new political tactics won them victories. Particularly important was the success of the German antinuclear movement in halting, at least temporarily, the construction of new nuclear energy plants. French antinuclear protests failed to slow development of nuclear power in their country.[31]

The citizen lobbies and new social movements attract more attention in Germany than elsewhere. The success of the Greens—the electoral manifestation of many of these counterculture movements—brings more attention to the German social movements than is the case in Britain, France, or Italy. But some evidence suggests that they are no more prominent in Germany than in other countries. (See Table 13.2). The greater impact of these groups in Germany seems to be due to their unexpected appearance, the ability of the Greens to mobilize their various strands of support behind their political party, and their early success in swaying government policy. With few developments in the party system during the 1970s, these new groups had attracted media attention. Larger citizen groups in other countries where party change was underway created less of a political sensation in the media and did not seem to have the same success.

In recent years, the Greens have claimed to represent these citizen initiative groups in the Bundestag. Not all of these citizen lobbies welcome

TABLE 13.2 Membership in Citizen Lobbies, 1984

Percentage of respondents claiming membership in

	Britain	France	Germany	Italy
Environmental group	0.3%	0.3%	0.5%	0.9%
Antinuclear energy group	0.3	0.3	0.5	0.9
Antiwar group	2.0	0.3	1.6	1.2

Source: Jacques-Rene Rabier, Hélène Riffault, Ronald Inglehart, *Eurobarometer 21: Political Cleavages in the European Community, April 1984* (Ann Arbor, MI: Inter-University Consortium for Political and Social Research, 1985), pp. 106–108.

the Greens' self-proclaimed representation. They see, and correctly so in many cases, that alignment with a partisan movement, especially one as controversial and marginal as the Greens, limits their appeal and their prospects for winning concessions from local, state, and federal governments that are still dominated by parties who see the Greens as dangerous rivals. Many citizen initiative groups also feel that the Greens do little to defend their interests in parliament and are too preoccupied with their own internal divisions to represent others.

In the past decade, the most visible of the citizen lobbies was the peace movement. Based on German uneasiness with American security policies during the Reagan era, the peace movement attracted followers from a broad range of political beliefs. The German peace movement lacked the political sponsorship that the Labour party gave the British movement. The peace demonstrators included many religious leaders, traditional pacifists, and a variety of socialists. The movement reached a peak in the early 1980s when the United States and European countries were debating the deployment of new nuclear weapons in Europe. The issue was particularly crucial in Germany because its citizens are located on the "front line" of the cold war and, thus, were particularly affected by increased East-West tensions. In addition, the bulk of the new weapons were to be stationed on German territory.

Hundreds of thousands participated in mass demonstrations to protest the deployment of the new missiles between 1981 and 1984. By the mid-1980s, the issue had become moot: The missiles were deployed despite the public outcry. With the issue no longer a pressing one and economic pressures redirecting attention to employment concerns, the peace movement lost much of its momentum. At the end of the 1980s, the Soviet-American agreement on the elimination of all intermediate range missiles in Europe put an end to what was left of the peace movement. It left behind a legacy of a new hesitancy about Germany's role as the launching pad for the conventional, as well as nuclear, defense of the West.

CONCLUSION

The image of the quiescent German of yore who placidly obeyed the powers that be is a thing of the past. Contemporary German politics are characterized by levels of citizen involvement that match or exceed those of other democracies. Numerous citizens have demonstrated their willingness to challenge established norms of political behavior even at the risk of unsettling the social and economic climate. After some initial problems in accommodating these new participants and their often, unconventional methods of political action, the regime now seems capable of managing the greater participation without disrupting overall political stability and public order.

There has been little evidence of a crisis in the party system. Public acceptance of the parties has remained strong and patterns of partisan loyalty have only slightly changed. The successful rotation of parties in and out of power at the national and state levels has created a healthy pattern for democracy. The SPD has had some difficulties in the last decade but not fateful or on the order of those that afflicted the British Labour party. The Greens have represented a challenge both in the electoral threat that they pose for the SPD and FDP and in their anti-establishment attitudes that seem to preclude their involvement in government coalitions. But parties can become stronger from such challenges, and there has been no reason to believe that the major German parties will be unable to prevail over the long run.

As stressed in this chapter, the numbers of people involved in political movements with anti-establishment goals and disruptive tactics remain quite small. What is troubling is

> the fanatic intensity of feeling animating the crowds. . . . The rage possessing them showed clearly that theirs was not a rational movement and that the slogans on their banners were mostly unconscious pretexts for something deeper. What they wanted was some vociferous expression for deep pent-up emotions, for their collective malaise, for their unhappiness.[32]

This malaise stems from the gap between utopian ideals and the reality of the world in which people live. It comes from concerns about Germany's future: its continued division, its exposed position on the cold war, the deterioration of the environment, misgivings about the extent of American influence in Germany, and the absence of inner satisfaction from the material advantages provided by economic prosperity. The malaise is particularly important among young, well-educated Germans—those groups which will provide tomorrow's leaders. If these sources of discontent are not addressed by the political parties and leaders of today, they may well pose more important political problems in the future.

NOTES

1. Geoffrey Pridham, *Christian Democracy in Western Germany* (New York: St. Martin's, 1977).
2. See Gordon Smith, "The German *Volkspartei* and the Career of the Catch-All Concept," in Herbert Doring and Gordon Smith, eds., *Party Government and Political Culture in Western Germany* (New York: St. Martin's, 1982).
3. See R.E.M. Irving, *The Christian Democratic Parties of Western Europe* (London: George Allen & Unwin, 1979), pp. 149–161.
4. See W.L. Guttsman, *The German Social Democratic Party, 1875–1933: From Ghetto to Government* (Winchester, MA: George Allen & Unwin, 1981) and Richard Breitman, *German Socialism and Weimar Democracy* (Boulder, CO: Westview Press, 1983).
5. *Hamburger Abendblatt*, 31 December 1981.
6. Gerard Braunthal, "The West German Social Democrats: Factionalism at the Local Level," *West European Politics* 7 (January 1984): 47–64.
7. William E. Paterson, "The German Social Democratic Party," in William E. Paterson and Alastair H. Thomas, eds., *The Future of Social Democracy: Problems and Prospects of Social Democratic Parties in Western Europe* (Oxford: Oxford

University Press, 1986); See also Gerard Braunthal, "The Social Democratic Party," in H. G. Peter Wallach and George K. Romoser, eds., *West German Politics in the Mid-Eighties* (New York: Praeger, 1985).

8. Thomas A. Koelbe, "Trade Unionists, Party Activists, and Politicians: The Struggle for Power over Party Rules in the British Labour Party and the West German Social Democratic Party," *Comparative Politics* 19 (April 1987): 253–266.

9. The FDP's second ballot vote is usually much greater than its first ballot results. In 1983, only 2.8 percent voted FDP for a constituency representative but 7 percent voted for FDP party lists.

10. Eva Kolinsky, *Parties, Opposition, and Society in West Germany* (London: Croom Helm, 1984), pp. 59–60, 106–113.

11. Christian Søe, "The Free Democratic Party," in Wallach and Romoser, eds. *West German Politics in the Mid-Eighties*, pp. 161–171.

12. Elin Papdakis, *The Green Movement in West Germany* (London: Croom Helm, 1984).

13. Kolinsky, *Parties, Opposition, and Society in West Germany*, pp. 312–319. See also Wilhlem P. Burklin, "The Split Between the Established and the Non-established Left in Germany," *European Journal of Political Research* 13 (September 1985): 283–293.

14. There was a touch of capitalist commercialism in Fischer's act: He wore Nike shoes because Adidas refused to give him a free pair of their jogging shoes for the occasion.

15. *New York Times,* 11 October, 1987, p. 8.

16. Ferdinand Muller-Rommel, "Social Movements and the Greens: New Internal Politics in Germany," *European Journal of Political Behavior* 13 (March 1985): 53–67.

17. Lewis J. Edinger, *West German Politics* (New York: Columbia University Press, 1986), p. 185.

18. See Gerhard Lehmbruch, "Introduction: Neo-Corporatism in Comparative Perspective," in Gerhard Lehmbruch and Philippe C. Schmitter, eds., *Patterns of Corporatist Policy-Making* (Beverly Hills, CA and London: Sage, 1982); See also Claus Offe, "The Attribution of Public Status to Interest Groups: Observations on the West German Case," in Suzanne Berger, ed., *Organizing Interests in Western Europe: Pluralism, Corporatism, and the Transformation of Politics* (Cambridge, England: Cambridge University Press, 1981).

19. Klaus von Beyme, *The Political System of the Federal Republic of Germany* (New York: St. Martin's, 1983), pp, 90–92.

20. Ibid., p. 85.

21. Josef Essen, "State, Business and Trade Unions in West Germany after the 'Political Wende'," *West European Politics* 9 (April 1986): 198–214.

22. Jutta A. Helm, "Codetermination in West Germany: What Difference Has It Made?" *West European Politics* 9 (January 1986): 32–53.

23. *Nürnberger Nachrichten,* 1 May, 1987.

24. See Andrei S. Markovits and Christopher S. Allen, "Power and Dissent: The Trade Unions in the Federal Republic of Germany Re-Examined," *West European Politics* 3 (January 1980): 68–86.

25. Graham K. Wilson, *Business and Politics: A Comparative Introduction* (Chatham, NJ: Chatham House, 1986).

26. Ibid., p. 54.

27. Erich Andrlik, "The Farmer and the State: Agricultural Interests in West German Politics," *West European Politics* 4 (January 1981): 104–119.

28. Von Beyme, *The Political System of the Federal Republic of Germany,* pp. 75–76.
29. Jutta Helm, "Citizen Lobbies in West Germany," in Peter H. Merkl, ed., *Western European Party Systems* (New York: Free Press, 1980), pp. 578–579.
30. Herbert Doring, "A Crisis of the Party System? An Assessment," in Doring and Smith, eds., *Party Government and Political Culture in Western Germany,* pp. 212–214.
31. Dorothy Nelkin and Michael Pollak, *The Atom Besieged: Extraparliamentary Dissent in France and Germany* (Cambridge, MA: The MIT Press, 1981).
32. Luigi Barzini, *The Europeans* (Harmondsworth, England: Penguin Books, 1983), p. 111.

CHAPTER FOURTEEN
GERMAN POLICY MAKING

West Germany, like France, has gone through four political regimes during the twentieth century: the imperial monarchy, the Weimar democracy, Hitler's dictatorship, and the postwar democratic regime, known formally as the Federal Republic of Germany. The current regime is the product of deliberate postwar constitutional engineering. The Germans involved in preparing the 1949 constitution and their occupation-force advisors made conscious efforts to rectify the institutional features of the past that seemed responsible for the failure of the Weimar democracy. From this perspective, the Basic Law is a "backward looking document conditioned, above all, by the determination to avoid the errors of the Weimar Republic's constitution."[1]

Many observers were skeptical of the chances of the new regime. The lack of public enthusiasm for the democratic order in 1949, the near total absence of citizen participation in preparing the constitution, and the important role played by foreign occupiers in drafting the constitution led many to scoff at the chances for its success. Those drafting the constitution did not feel that it should be a permanent document, but, rather, a provisional statute until reunification made possible the preparation of a constitution for all of Germany. Hence, the document was called the Basic Law, rather than a constitution, to reflect its temporary nature. Bonn, a small university city on the Rhine, was selected as the capital, presumably only until the government could return to its normal quarters in Berlin.

Despite these disadvantages, the Basic Law has proved durable and successful. In the forty years since its adoption, the Basic Law has assumed full constitutional status in all but a strictly formal sense. More importantly, it has acquired legitimacy in the eyes of the political elite and the general public. The institutions established by the Basic Law have provided exceptional governmental stability within a democratic context.

THE BONN REPUBLIC

The Federal Republic is a parliamentary and federal system. Figure 14.1 illustrates the basic institutional relationships. Political power is vested in a popularly elected legislative body—the Bundestag. A second chamber, the Bundesrat, has some legislative powers but is more important as an agency for maintaining the balance between the federal government and the state governments. As is typical of parliamentary systems, executive powers are divded between a head of state—the president and the government—the chancellor and the cabinet of ministers.

The President

The President of the Federal Republic lacks the political power of the French president and instead, exercises limited powers comparable to those of the British monarch. Because of the Weimar experience with a powerful, popularly elected president who challenged both the government and parliament, postwar constitutional framers were wary of giving too much responsibility or the endorsement of direct election to the head of state. Unlike the popularly elected French president and different too from the hereditary British monarchy, the German president is now elected by

FIGURE 14.1 Political institutions of the Federal Republic.

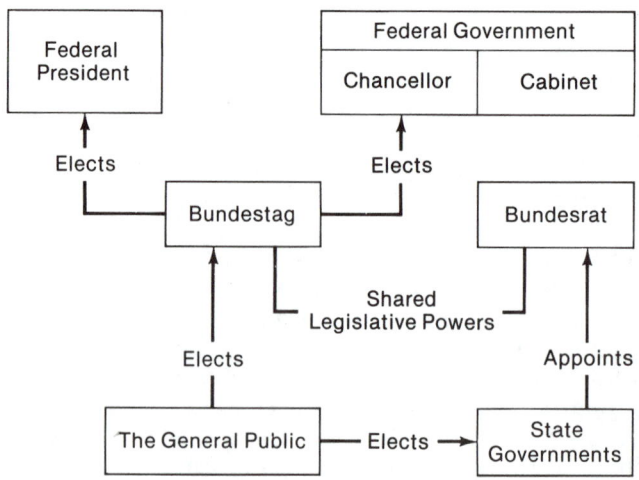

a federal convention made up of all the members of the Bundestag and an equal number of delegates named by the ten state legislatures. The term of office is five years with the possibility of reelection one time for an additional term. Unlike the divisive elections that frequently disrupt Italian politics, the elections for the German president proceed smoothly. Those nominated for the position are usually senior, respected politicians near the end of their careers. Usually only two candidates (in the 1984 election, there was a single candidate presented for the office) are presented with the outcome apparent beforehand to all because of the coalition alignments and agreements.

These elections are fitting for an office with little more than ceremonial powers. The president symbolizes the state but is not a powerful, independent actor. While their signatures are necessary for the promulgation of all legislation, decrees, and most major appointments, presidents must act on the direction of the government: They do not have the power to veto or even delay legislation. A few presidents attempted to expand their powers by delaying signature or raising public reservations. Such tentative efforts at increasing presidential powers were steadfastly and successfully resisted by the government and parliament.[2] Presidents are able to use their public prominence and their right to be consulted by the government to raise issues, express concerns, or warn the public of dangers. But such intervention must be circumspect or there is conflict with the government that usually results in embarrassment for the president.

The Chancellor

The most important responsibility of the president is the formal nomination to the Bundestag of a candidate for chancellor. There is usually little choice since the major parties announce their candidates before the election. After the election, the president takes note of the results and submits the name of the leader of the winning coalition for the Bundestag's endorsement. If no party or coalition has a majority, the president's discretionary powers may increase. But the Bundestag can always reject the presidential nominee and then proceed to elect its own preferred chancellor. The chancellor needs only a simple plurality (more votes than any other candidate but not necessarily an absolute majority), of votes in the Bundestag for election. However, if the chancellor fails to muster an absolute majority, the president then has the option of appointing that person or dissolving the Bundestag for new elections. These details may seem complicated but they are largely hypothetical. So far, presidents have had no opportunity to exercise these options. They have always had to name the already known candidate of the victorious coalition.

Once named, the chancellor is the chief functioning executive officer in Germany. The chancellor names the other members of the cabinet and can create or abolish federal ministerial departments. The chancellor can also remove cabinet ministers. In practice, these decisions are limited by the need to satisfy coalition partners, party factions, regional and religious balances, and a variety of other political concerns. Nevertheless, chancellors can exercise important control over government policy through the power of appointing and dismissing fellow ministers. The Basic Law gives legitimacy to the leadership of the chancellor: He is charged with defining general policy guidelines. His ability to carry out this task is facilitated by a large staff of his own. The office of the chancellor includes nearly five hundred employees of whom over a hundred are senior, policy-level civil servants.[3] In addition, the chancellor has the political support of a disciplined party that has a near majority in the Bundestag and is a strong organization throughout the country.

In practice, the exercise of power has varied according to the political style of the individual holding the office of chancellor. The first chancellor of the postwar era, Konrad Adenauer, exercised his powers to their fullest extent, largely dominating the policy-making process during the thirteen years he served. He was a determined man with a mission and a vision of a new Germany to fulfill. Fears that Adenauer's style might revive the traditional German pattern of strong executive leadership were largely laid to rest by the performance of the chancellors who succeeded Adenauer. His successors have been powerful leaders but their styles have emphasized greater collaboration with their fellow ministers and their colleagues in parliament and the party. They have been coordinators and mediators of interministerial or intracoalition relations rather than forceful leaders controlling large areas of policy making.

Chancellors exercise leadership through arbitration and occasional vetoes of their ministers' proposals.[4] The negotiating role often overrides the leadership role. One chancellor was mockingly labelled "a strolling mediation committee" by one of his own ministers. Much of the chancellors' efforts are directed toward building a consensus within the government majority and toward persuading the public to also support that consensus.[5] Their party base of support is not unconditional; they must constantly cultivate their own party and that of their coalition partner.[6] When they try to leave a personal imprint on policy, they usually concentrate on one or two issues rather than exerting broad policy direction. For example, Helmut Kohl, chancellor from 1982 to the present, has no policy master plan that he is pursuing. He is a pragmatist more adept at coordination than command. He works through his ministers and stresses frequent consultations with party and parliamentary leaders. Indeed, he has been criticized for the absence of central control when it appeared that the parties in the coalition separately determined the policies for the ministries. Some claimed the FDP set general policy guidelines in foreign, economic, and legal affairs, the CSU shaped interior and farm policies, and the CDU covered the rest. Those concerned with such dispersion of executive power felt that Kohl had failed to exercise the chancellor's prerogatives to oversee all policy and to coordinate all government action.

The German chancellorship is a powerful political institution. But its actual influence has varied with the personalities and political styles of the individuals who have held that office. While the executive has the powers needed to govern effectively, the chancellors have found important and inescapable democratic constraints on their exercise of those powers.

The Cabinet

The typical German government includes the chancellor and fifteen to sixteen ministers. It is therefore considerably smaller than the British or French governments. The cabinet meets weekly under the presidency of the chancellor. Cabinet politics in Germany are more like American or French cabinet meetings than the collegial, decision-making process of the British cabinet. They are more for coordination than for collective decision making. In fact, few votes are ever taken in cabinet meetings. Junior ministers often attend cabinet meetings for their minister. There are not numerous cabinet committees like in Britain and France. Instead, most government policies are hammered out in bilateral negotiations between the appropriate minister and the chancellor. The meetings of the cabinet are more often occasions where the results of these bilateral discussions are announced than opportunities for all ministers to participate in the decision.

The notion of collective responsibility is not as well developed in Germany as it is in Britain. In a formal sense, the chancellor, alone, is accountable to the Bundestag as he is the only member of the cabinet elected by that body; other members are accountable through him as his appointees. But decisions made by individual ministers do not compel others to resign if they disagree. Despite the potential for conflict in such a loose system of government coordination, there have been few breaches of cabinet solidarity. German cabinet ministers tend to hold the same portfolios for long periods of time, much longer than British or French ministers. Their longer tenure permits them to develop substantial technical expertise. The result is that the Federal Government resembles more a "board of technical directors rather than a collective political leadership."[7]

The minister and his senior advisors in the ministry shape policy within their sphere of responsibility. This policy-making often involves obligatory consultations with concerned interest groups. It always means extensive deliberation with the chancellor's office and other ministries, especially the finance ministry. These other bodies limit the extent to which an individual minister can personally influence public policy.

In addition to their policy-making roles, ministers are also charged with directing the administration of their departments. Managing a large and organizationally complex bureaucracy is a formidable task. Ministers must devote much of their time to handling personnel duties and coordinating the actions of the various divisions under their supervision. Indeed, they are more preoccupied with these responsibilities than with integrating separate department policies into a coherent, overall government program.[8] They are assisted by parliamentary secretaries (junior ministers) selected from the ranks of the government's Bundestag deputies and state secretaries (senior civil servants). All these are political appointments that end with the tenure of the minister. It is not uncommon for the state secretaries to continue on under the new minister, even when the party in control changes. Unlike French ministers who are often selected from outside parliament, German cabinet ministers are nearly always members of the

Bundestag. They rise through the ranks after serving apprenticeships in parliament, local or state governments, party, or interest groups close to the party in power.

All cabinets formed since 1949 have been based on coalitions of two or more parties. There have been three patterns: the Christian-Liberal alliance of the CDU/CSU and the FDP that governed from 1949 to 1966, and from 1982 to the present; the Social-Liberal alliance of the SPD and the FDP that governed from 1969 to 1982; and the Grand Coalition of the CDU/CSU and the SPD that governed from 1966 to 1969. Unlike the fleeting government coalitions in Italy, the German coalitions have been durable. On only two occasions have coalition changes brought the premature end of a government. In 1966, the FDP pulled out of the coalition with the CDU/CSU. The CDU/CSU was forced to turn to the SPD to form a grand coalition government. Then in 1982, the FDP switched its coalition with the SPD to the CDU/CSU and helped elect Helmut Kohl as the new chancellor. Coalition pressures are always important influences on the selection of ministers and the broad contours of policy.

The Bundestag

The principal legislative chamber is the Bundestag. Its 496 popularly elected deputies serve four-year terms.[9] They are vested with chief legislative powers and with the tasks of representing the public in the political process and controlling the executive. All legislation must go through the Bundestag. It elects the chancellor and can replace the government by electing a new chancellor. It shares the task of electing the president with representatives from state legislatures.

As the near-exclusive source of ministers and ultimately chancellors, the Bundestag deputies compose the top level of the German political elite. They come from a broad range of backgrounds, but the most frequent occupations among the deputies are civil servants, educators, and interest group administrators. Together, these three occupations accounted for over 60 percent of the deputies elected in 1983.[10] The Bundestag has not succeeded in attracting policy experts or even well-versed citizens into its ranks. Instead, deputies are more often party professionals employed as civil servants or as representatives for the major interest groups.

As in Britain and France, it is unusual for legislation to originate in the Bundestag. Nearly all the legislation that is finally enacted is drafted by the ministries and proposed by the government. Party discipline among deputies is very strong assuring the government of a loyal majority to support its proposals. The government wins Bundestag approval for about 80 percent of its proposals. Unlike the practice in most legislatures, individual German deputies are not entitled to introduce legislative proposals; a minimum of twenty-six deputies must sponsor a nongovernment bill. Such private bills are fewer than government bills. They receive less deliberation, and only about 12 percent of the bills introduced by deputies are enacted.[11]

The Bundestag has been described as a working legislature rather than a debating legislature. Debate on the floor of the Bundestag is usually low-keyed and lackluster (in contrast to the often lively exchanges in the British House of Commons or the French National Assembly). Even on issues of vital national importance, the discussion is uninformed and unimpassioned. Parliamentary debates are, thus, of limited value in educating the public on the issues and the parties' different approaches to them even though the debates are televised. The arrival of the Greens in parliament enliven things a bit. The anti-establishment Greens show up for parliamentary sessions attired in blue jeans and open-neck shirts. They occasionally disrupt Bundestag deliberations by spontaneous demonstrations on the floor of the chamber. But such activities do not bring greater public esteem to the Bundestag nor do they improve the quality of debate.

The more important work of the Bundestag is done in its committees.[12] The Bundestag committees are much more powerful than their counterparts in Britain or France. They hold public hearings on pending legislation. They suggest amendments or refinements to the government, many of which are incorporated into the final versions of the laws. They also hold private sessions where deputies can work out differences in secret. These powerful committees are also key points for interest group influence. Several of the key ministries are "colonized" by deputies who are members or sympathizers of affected groups. The Federation of German Industry is well represented on the Economic Committee; the German Farmers Union controls the Agriculture Committee; the Home Affairs Committee is dominated by deputies close to the German Federation of Officials.[13] These Bundestag committees have specialized staffs to assist them in evaluating policy proposals. These committee staffs are not as large or as professional as those in the United States Congress but they are much more developed than elsewhere in Europe.

Another important point of deliberation happens in the party groups. Each party has a parliamentary group or causus that meets regularly. The groups have their own leaders and specialized subcommittees of concerned deputies to develop party positions on key issues. More so than in Britain or France, the meetings of the parliamentary party groups deal with substantive policy issues. The caucuses of the majority parties can be quite assertive in pressing their colleagues, in ministerial positions, to change proposed government bills in response to the concerns of the deputies.[14] This influence is exerted both while the legislation is being formulated in the ministries and after it is introduced on the floor of the Bundestag.

Parliamentary power over legislation may be limited by party discipline in Germany. But members of parliament have developed means of influencing the government's policy proposals. The situation may be that they react more to the government's initiatives rather than propose their own laws, but deputies from the majority in the Bundestag do have the ability to shape the bills both before and after they are introduced into parliament.

Government-Parliament Relations

The German government lacks many of the powers that permit the British and French governments to control the agendas of their parliaments. The extraordinary powers that the French government has to bypass amendments and to force through measures without votes by the motion of confidence procedures are absent. So too is a government's ability to set the order of debate and to limit its length. It is, not the German government but, a committee of Bundestag leaders that sets the timetable and the limits on debate. As a result of the power of the Bundestag and the party committees, the German government must accord a much larger partnership role to the Bundestag than other European governments do to their parliaments.

At times though, the German Bundestag appears more restricted in its ability to exercise control over the executive. Interpellation—the questioning of ministers on the floor of parliament about their conduct in office—has only recently developed as an important means of checking government power, and it still lacks the impact that it has in Britain. While there are large numbers of parliamentary questions, most are written questions that attract little interest, and the oral questions usually lack drama. Rather than the lively exchanges that they occasion in the British House of Commons, in the Bundestag they involve two statements: one by the questioner followed by a second statement by the minister. They do little to aid the Bundestag in maintaining the accountability of the government.

The Bundestag has limited powers over the making and unmaking of governments. It does have an important role in selecting the chancellor in that it must vote to accept the new head of government. It does not vote on the chancellor's selection of cabinet ministers. Once a government is in place, the Bundestag lacks the power to oust it through a censure motion as can happen in both France and Britain. The difficulty of organizing governments under Weimar led the framers of the Basic Law to restrict the censure powers of the Bundestag to a "positive vote of censure." The Bundestag can only oust the incumbent government by electing a new chancellor. When that occurs, the old chancellor and his ministers must step down. This positive vote was designed to limit the toppling of governments by diverse opponents by forcing them to agree first on a replacement. The constructive vote of censure has been tried only twice since the inception of the Federal Republic: unsuccessfully in 1972, and successfully in 1982.

The chancellor's power to dissolve the Bundestag is also limited. Unlike his counterparts in Britain and France who can dissolve the parliament at their discretion, the German chancellor can ask the president to dissolve the Bundestag only after the government introduces a motion of confidence, and that confidence is rejected by a majority of the deputies. Even then, the chancellor's right of dissolution can be checked if the Bundestag elects a new chancellor.

These unusual limits on the normal censure and dissolution powers of parliamentary systems have proved unnecessary and cumbersome. The discipline and simplicity of the German party system have made these restraints unneeded; there have been very few occasions when the government's existence was endangered. The restraints have made it difficult to adjust the executive according to the political balance within the parliament. Flexibility is needed to keep executive-legislative harmony, which is one of the chief virtues of a parliamentary system. For example, in 1972, defections from the FDP left the SPD-FDP coalition government of Willy Brandt with a deadlocked Bundestag. An attempt to elect a new chancellor failed with a tie vote. But the Brandt government was unable to get Bundestag approval for its budget. After several months of deadlock, the government had to engineer a failed vote of confidence in order to dissolve the stalemated Bundestag. Brandt introduced a motion of confidence and then assured its failure by ordering the government ministers not to vote for it. The failure of the confidence motion gave Brandt the right to dissolve the Bundestag and call new elections to determine the majority. (The SPD-FDP coalition in fact won a comfortable majority in the ensuing election.)

There were similar problems in 1982. The shift of the FDP from a coalition with the SPD to an alliance with the CDU/CSU brought about the first successful use of the positive vote of confidence. A new chancellor was elected, Helmut Kohl, and the old chancellor and his ministers had to resign. But the new CDU/CSU-FDP coalition government felt that it was important for it to win public endorsement of this change in government as soon as possible through parliamentary elections. However, the limits on dissolution made this difficult. In Britain or France, the executive has only to announce the dissolution of the chamber; but in Germany, the chancellor has to arrange to lose a motion of confidence and then ask the president to dissolve the Bundestag.[15]

The Bundestag's ability to control the executive seems limited in comparison to those of other parliaments. Debates on the floor of the chamber rarely excite public interest or inform the public of key issues even though sessions are televised. But the Bundestag has developed extensive influence in the legislative process. More so than in Britain or France, the deputies have earned a partnership with the executive in shaping legislation. Their performance has won public approval and support for parliament.

The Bundesrat

The Bundesrat, or Federal Council, represents state interests at the federal level of politics. In many regards, the Bundesrat resembles the old United States Senate when Senators were chosen by the state legislatures rather than by popular election. The forty-five members of the Bundesrat are named by the state governments with each state having between three to five members according to population size. They are all from the majority coalition that is in the state legislature at the time. They are often serving as members of the state government too. They vote as state blocs according to the wishes of their state governments; all representatives from a state thus must vote together. Conceived as a place for the defense of state interests, the Bundesrat has become a much more powerful and partisan body than anticipated by the constitutional founders. All legislation that affects the states must go through the Bundesrat. Since the state bureaucracies implement federal policies, most legislation falls into this category. The Bundesrat has an absolute or suspensory veto over the legislation affecting the states.

All legislation must be submitted first to the Bundesrat for its preliminary opinion. This initial reaction gives added impact to the Bundesrat's role in the legislative process. In the Bundestag, the deputies and government are likely to reshape the bill to avoid clashes with the Bundesrat. Once passed by the Bundestag, the bill goes back to the Bundesrat for the formal decision. If the Bundesrat wants changes in the bill, a conciliation committee made up of equal numbers from each chamber tries to work out an agreement. For laws that have direct impact on the states, approval from the Bundesrat is mandatory. For other laws, a negative vote in the Bundesrat can be overridden by a positive vote of the same proportion in the Bundestag. For example, if the Bundesrat rejects a bill by a 55 percent margin, it takes a 55 percent positive vote in the Bundestag to adopt the legislation. In practice, the Bundesrat veto is still the exception being exercised on only about 10 percent of the bills.[16] On the one hand, the threats of delays and a possible veto often force the government to make concessions to its opponents in the Bundesrat that it otherwise would not have to grant. On the other hand, the Bundesrat is also restrained in using its veto powers, recognizing that a veto not only stops the undesirable clauses but kills the entire legislative package that states may need or want.[17]

The drafters of the Basic Law had anticipated that the Bundesrat would have veto powers on just about 10 percent of all legislation; the Bundesrat has acquired veto power on over 60 percent of the laws coming out of the Bundestag.[18] Of course, it does not actually veto all of that legislation, but its broadened scope of jurisdiction makes it a potent force in the legislative process. Its powers expanded notably during the 1970s when the CDU/CSU majority in the Bundesrat sought to temper or thwart the reforms enacted by the SPD-dominated Bundestag. In the two year period, 1972 to 1974, there were more clashes between the Bundesrat and the Bundestag than the total for the previous twenty-five years. Out of these conflicts came a 1974 ruling by the Constitutional Court that the Bundesrat was "not a second chamber" on an equal footing with the Bundestag. Nevertheless, the Bundesrat was able to continue to delay enactments of SPD proposals and to force the government to dilute its legislation in anticipation of problems from the Bundesrat.

The partisan dimension of the Bundesrat should not be overstressed. While party politics are present, there are also divisions within the party alignments based on different state interests. For example, the heavily industrial states often share concerns regardless of which party controls their state governments; poor states have an interest in cooperating with one another other in spite of partisan differences in order to get more aid diverted toward them from the richer states. In addition, the small states are highly dependent on the federal government and are therefore reluctant to oppose it cavalierly in an openly partisan manner.

The Bundesrat has less impact now that the Christian Democrats are back in power in the Bundestag, and the majorities of the two are the same. The allocation of seats favors smaller states and results in a CDU/CSU majority most of the time. Despite its power, more than half of the Germans do not know what the Bundesrat does or have even heard of it.[19] Intended as a means of protecting state prerogatives, it has become instead a potent tool of "party federalism."[20]

The Federal Constitutional Court

The Basic Law established a constitutional court to serve as a court of last resort in the defense of civil liberties and to maintain the balance of power between the states and the federal government. The Federal Constitutional Court is composed of sixteen members. Half are appointed by the Bundesrat and half by the Bundestag to 12 year terms. The court is divided into two senates or chambers, one which deals with civil liberties and the other with federal/state relations and judicial review or questions of the constitutionality of government actions and laws. Politics intrude into the operation of the court especially through the selection process with some judges having had political careers before being named to the court. In general, the quality of appointees is high and they act independently and in a nonpartisan manner after they take office. But the success of the court is tied to the broad consensus politics that the major parties have established in postwar Germany.[21] The court usually avoids dissenting opinions by seeking an agreement that balances conflicting interests and basically reflects the national political consensus.

The German Federal Constitutional Court is a much more powerful body than the French Constitutional Council. The German court has jurisdiction over claims of abuse of human rights, an area of judicial action left to ordinary courts in France. Its powers of judicial review are broader. Unlike the French court which must intercede before promulgation of a law, the German Constitutional Court can determine the constitutionality of laws already in force. The right of appeal to the French court is limited to the president, prime minister, and groups of deputies or senators. In Germany, individuals, both local and state governments, and even political parties as well as members of parliament can bring cases to the Constitutional Court. It is not an appeals court but lower courts can and do refer cases to the Constitutional Court.

The court has proved to be an influential force in postwar German politics.[22] It has not hesitated to overrule the actions of the government or to overturn the laws adopted by parliament. It has emerged as a forceful defender of civil liberties and a protector of the division of responsibilities between the federal and state governments. The bulk of its work has been in these areas, especially the protection of human rights. Its effects have been felt not only directly in the cases that it has adjudicated but indirectly as a deterrent against abuse of the constitution by its presence in the policy-making process.[23] It has ruled on such contentious issues as abortion (which it initially struck down on the basis of a "right to life" clause inserted in the Basic Law to hinder future Hitler-like atrocities) and German reunification; it has angered both advocates of state rights and the federal government. Nevertheless, the German Constitutional Court has earned broad public acceptance as a valued protector of the constitution and civil liberties.

THE CIVIL SERVICE

The Prussian bureaucracy was noted for its discipline, organization, efficiency, and effectiveness. But its hostility to the Weimar democracy and its connivance with Hitler during the Nazi era destroyed its reputation. In the postwar era, the first task was to eliminate the thousands of senior civil servants who had joined the Nazi party. While the purge was never complete and its results were partially negated by the desire for a rapid return to normalcy, it did open up opportunities at the top for a new generation of civil servants.

Unlike the situation in Britain and France where senior civil servants come from a few very elite schools, the German senior administrators come from many universities across the country. In addition to those who have come up through the ranks of the civil service, there are also growing numbers of "outsiders" coming into the senior civil service from backgrounds different from those of the usual recruits.[24] The civil servants tend to provide viewpoints and skills that complement rather than challenge those of the elected public officials.[25] They have more regular contacts with deputies and other politicians than do bureaucrats elsewhere in Western democracies.[26] The federal bureaucracy is relatively small since the German administrative system is based on the principle of state bureaucracies implementing both federal and state policies. But the combined number of all levels of civil servants is in excess of 4 million and accounts for nearly 15 percent of employed adults. The reliance on separate state bureaucracies has not prevented the development of a unified and uniform administration of federal policies.[27]

The postwar bureaucracy has not regained its prestige and that may be an advantage since the social standing of bureaucrats contributed to their highhanded treatment of citizens and their disposition to ignore less prestigious politicians during the Weimar regime. But the bureaucracy has once again earned plaudits for its efficiency. Most important, it has demonstrated a commitment to democratic principles and to the existing regime.

There is no spoils system as in the United States but approximately two hundred division heads at the federal level are political appointees subject to change as the chancellor or the ministers change.[28] Those who fill these positions are senior civil servants who serve under both parties but whose specific responsibilities change with new political leaders. The changes are usually minimal: only sixty of these division heads were replaced when power shifted to the SPD for the first time in 1969 and about forty were transferred after the 1982 return of the CDU/CSU. While civil servants with partisan ties to one of the major parties have found few impediments to their careers even when the opposing party is in power, those from fringe parties risk the loss of their jobs. A controversial decree adopted in the early 1970s bars the entry into the civil service of radicals who reject the usual democratic norms.

In the British and French sections, the issue of maintaining political controls over the bureaucracy was discussed. In Germany, the concern is different. The Nazi experience when civil servants followed the political leadership in executing atrocities has made observers more concerned with blind obedience to inappropriate directions than with bureaucratic loyalty. Studies of postwar German bureaucrats suggest that the lesson has been learned: Blind obedience is no longer seen as a virtue. Civil servants today seem to accept the obligation of loyalty to the political leaders but within the context of an overriding duty to the democratic order and human rights.

In practice, there are few instances that test the willingness of civil servants to resist improper directives from their political leaders. Nor is the new willingness of civil servants to examine their directions before obeying them leading to resistance to the government's appropriate decisions. The civil service is responsive to the political leadership offered by the governments of both major parties. Both political parties recruit members and leaders from the ranks of the civil service. Unlike the formal restrictions on political activities by civil servants that exist in Britain and the United States, there are generous leave provisions in Germany that facilitate political involvement for their bureaucrats.[29] Consequently, civil servants make up a large proportion of the deputies in the Bundestag, state assemblies, and other elected offices. The strength of the party system within the civil service and outside as a check on the civil servants' loyalty help make the German administration highly responsive to political directions.

GERMAN FEDERALISM

Unlike the centralized systems in Britain, France, and Italy, the Basic Law established a federal system in West Germany and guaranteed extensive powers and prerogatives to the state governments. The Federal Republic of Germany is composed of ten states plus West Berlin which has a particular status that will be discussed. The federalism of the Bonn Republic builds on federalist traditions of past regimes. However, the current states differ from earlier German states. Only Bavaria started out with borders resembling those of a historical German state. The inhabitants of the other states lacked a sense of identification with these political units. Over the years, these state loyalties have begun to develop.

The federal structure is reinforced by the geographical dispersion of political and economic centers. Unlike the political, economic, and cultural dominance of Paris and London, Germany has no real central city. Bonn is the present but "provisional" capital. But many key political departments are not even located there: the Constitutional Court is in Karlsruhe; the Federal Bank in Frankfurt; the Federal Labor Office in Nuremberg; the Statistical Office in Wiesbaden; and the Federal Environmental Office in West Berlin. The traditional capital, Berlin, is cut off from the rest of the country and formally is still not a part of the Federal Republic. Even before the war, Berlin faced competition from a half dozen other cities. The cultural, political, and economic dispersion is even greater now and assists in maintaining an effective decentralization of power in the Federal Republic.

The states vary much in size and population, ranging from tiny Bremen to large North Rhine-Westphalia which has over a quarter of the nation's population. This range poses problems since policies adopted by the large states, and especially by North Rhine-Westphalia, tend to set precedents that smaller states resent but cannot resist. The states vary also in economic strength. For example, the per capita income in Hamburg is nearly twice that of Saarland. Because of these financial inequities, the Constitutional Court ruled in 1986 that the tax system had to be revised by 1988 to assure a more equitable distribution between rich and poor states.

State Politics

Each state has its own elected legislative body. That assembly selects a minister-president (or a mayor in the city-states). The minister-president selects a number of ministers to complete the state government. The state governments are accountable to the current majority in the state assemblies as is the national parliamentary pattern. State government has become a training ground for national politics with many leaders from state politics moving up to national political leadership. Three of the six postwar chancellors—Kiesinger, Brandt, and Kohl—had served previously as heads of their state governments.

TABLE 14.1   German States

Name	Population (in Millions)	Party in Control (January 1988)	Seats in the Bundesrat
Baden-Württemberg	9.2	CDU	5
Bavaria	11.0	CSU	5
Bremen	0.7	SPD	3
Hamburg	1.6	SPD	3
Hesse	5.5	CDU-FDP	4
Lower Saxony	7.2	CDU-FDP	5
North Rhine-Westphalia	16.7	SPD	5
Rhineland-Palatinate	3.6	CDU-FDP	4
Saarland	1.1	SPD	3
Schleswig-Holstein	2.6	CDU	4
Berlin (West)	1.9	CDU	4

Elections for the state legislatures occur at different times rather than all at once as in local elections in Britain and France. These state legislative elections are highly competitive with party control shifting often in most of the states. Voters take them seriously and turn out to vote at nearly the same high level as for the Bundestag elections. While the elections are usually contested on local issues, they are seen as indicators of the public mood for national politics as well. For example, the CDU/CSU victories in Bavaria and Hamburg in late 1986 were interpreted as a good sign for these parties in the national elections that were held a few months later. The usual pattern—as in by-elections in Britain and off-year elections in the United States—is for the party controlling the national government to lose in state elections.

State elections also have impact on national politics through the Bundesrat. Christian Democratic victories in state elections in the late 1970s brought nearly a two-thirds CDU/CSU majority in the Bundesrat that negatively influenced the SPD policy agenda. Finally, coalition patterns at the local level may portend shifts in the national coalitions that provide a government majority. In the late 1970s, the return of CDU-FDP coalitions in a couple of state governments foreshadowed the 1982 return of the Christian Democrat-Liberal coalition at the national level. Social Democrat experiments with alliances with the Greens in the state of Hesse may prepare the formation of a similar national alliance sometime in the future.

Federal-State Relations

German federalism is described as "functional federalism" in that the governmental responsibilities are divided between the federal and state levels: The federal government is primarily responsible for setting policy; The state governments are charged with implementing and administering policy. In practice, this division of duties is often only partly respected. Notably, as was pointed out earlier in this chapter, the states exercise important influence over the legislative process through the Bundesrat. But federalism assures policy uniformity across the country while allowing states to alter it to fit local needs and circumstances.

The division of policy competency in the Basic Law assigns the bulk of policy sectors to the federal government. State governments reserve power over education, law enforcement, cultural matters including radio and television, environmental protection, local governments in their jurisdiction, and the civil service. In addition, states may enact policies in any other issue area where the federal government has not acted. Where states share responsibilities with the federal government, the federal policies prevail.

In practice, the federal government's arena has steadily expanded over the years leaving the states fewer areas for independent action. In part, the expansion of the centralized government has resulted from efforts to solve problems like terrorism, pollution, and economic modernization that cannot be handled by individual states. Centralization has also come from the states voluntarily passing up to the federal government decisions that are unpopular or difficult. For example, states have often deferred to the central government the final decision on whether to construct a nuclear energy facility rather than make the politically difficult decision themselves.

The states have jealously guarded other assigned areas of responsibility with the support of the Constitutional Court. Education has been an especially sensitive area since different religious backgrounds of the various states have resulted in quite different educational structures even though standards and curricula have been coordinated by a committee of state ministers of education. States have successfully resisted various government and private efforts to unify the television and radio system. In police matters, the states have protected their prerogatives in law enforcement but they have approved federal efforts to unify antiterrorist action.

The federal government's control over most policy areas is furthered by the fact that the states do not have independent sources of revenue. All taxes are raised by the federal government and then disbursed to the states, often with many strings attached. There are also provisions for horizontal transfers from wealthy states to poorer ones to reduce economic inequalities. The results are often complicated and there are intense disagreements between the states and the federal government and among the states themselves over the formula for dividing revenues.[30]

Federalism as a Path to Decentralization

In both Britain and France, there have been efforts to decentralize the highly centralized governments. These reforms have been hampered by the absence of a meaningful intermediate layer of government between the central government and local governments. The German federal system provides that needed layer: The state governments provide additional opportunities for citizen participation; they facilitate the adjustment of centrally legislated policies to local needs; they help to reduce the gap between citizens and government by at least bringing geographic proximity to policy administration.

There are disadvantages that result from this federal arrangement. One such problem was evident in the attempts to counter the terrorist threat in the 1970s. The campaign was severely handicapped by the absence of a federal police force and inadequate means of coordinating the separate state police forces.[31] It was only after new means of coordination and the establishment of two federal level law enforcement agencies that the battle against terrorism began to succeed. Environmental protection is another issue where the federal government finds itself restricted in its ability to respond to the acid rain that is threatening Germany's forests or the pollution of the Rhine that troubles not only the Germans but the other riparian countries as well. The federal government lacks competence to take action in the states where the polluters are seen as essential to economic health.

Another problem with federalism is that it is less efficient than centralized government. Even in Germany's functional federalism, there is duplication of services. The federal processes slow policy making. Conflicts between and within levels of government are inevitable. Innovation and reform are more difficult to enact. Despite these disadvantages, the federal structure is still strongly supported by the German people. A 1980 poll found only 9 percent favoring a shift from federalism to a centralized form of government.[32] It appears that many Germans have linked federalism with successful democracy and see it as useful in preventing an autocratic government. For others, the federal structure offers a framework for a possible reunification of Germany at some point in the future.

The Special Status of Berlin

The Basic Law lists Berlin as one of the states in the Federal Republic. But the Western Allies blocked the inclusion of West Berlin in the new German state. Because of its exposed position as a exclave surrounded by the German Democratic Republic and vulnerable to economic and military pressure from the East, the Western allies preferred that Berlin retain its formal status as an occupied territory under the jurisdiction of the Four Powers—Britain, France, the United States, and the USSR. This is seen as the best way of protecting Berlin from blockades, pressures, and even invasion. Indeed, the overlapping jurisdictions of occupation bodies, the governments of the Federal Republic and the German Democratic Republic, the governments of East and West Berlin, and the boroughs create an incredibly complicated political pattern.[33]

As a result, West Berlin is not formally part of the Federal Republic. But the practical ties make it so in all but a strictly legal sense. West Berlin sends twenty-two delegates to the Bundestag. They are not publicly elected but named by their parties. Like the four representatives to the Bundesrat, they are appointed by the Berlin government. The Berlin deputies do not have the right to vote but they may participate in floor debates and serve on committees. Occasionally, meetings of parliamentary committees are held in West Berlin but full sessions of the Bundestag, Bundesrat, or federal cabinet can not be held there. West Berliners carry passports from the Federal Republic and can use its consular services throughout the world. Laws passed in the Federal Republic are automatically enacted in West Berlin by the covering law procedure. The covering law procedure is the way in which laws adopted by the West German Bundestag are extended to the formally independent western parts of Berlin. Since West Berlin is technically out of the country, the West Berlin legislature automatically passes a two to three line statement that the law adopted in the Federal Republic shall apply to West Berlin as well. With very rare exception, these laws are passed in a pro forma manner without debate. This covering law procedure is mandatory for all laws designated by the Federal government that are applicable to Berlin. Occasionally, the Allied Powers, still the formal sovereign body, reject specific items of legislation provoking declarations of outrage from West Berliners.

The government of West Berlin is similar to that of other West German states. Politics are linked with the parties and issues of the rest of Germany. Berlin politicians often go on to distinguished public service in the Federal Republic. The most notable example was Willy Brandt who used his position as mayor of Berlin to build a national political career that took him to the chancellorship. Over the last decade, Berlin has been the location for many citizen protests, notably over the issue of low-cost housing. The Greens have profited from this political activism winning over 11 percent of the 1985 West Berlin elections—their highest score anywhere in Germany.

Local Government in Germany

There is a strong heritage of local self-government in Germany. Organization patterns for local government vary in different states in accordance with often centuries-old traditions. In general, local politics attempt to be nonpartisan with greater emphasis on the personality of the mayor or council members than on party affiliations. However, party considerations, especially in the large cities, are often important.

The jurisdiction and power of local governments vary from state to state.[34] Generally, they have responsibility for maintenance of schools, roads, sanitation, and some aspects of public safety. They administer social and economic policies set by the federal and state governments. In addition, local governments have the authority to enact legislation covering local matters. The range of these local activities varies according to local traditions and the party in control. Local government undertakings often include activities that are most unusual by American standards: city-owned markets, cemeteries, orchestras, banks, and even breweries. As is the case in Britain and France, many of the small towns and villages of Germany are declining due to social changes.[35] As in Britain, the Germans carried out a sweeping reform of local government consolidating the 24,000 local governments that existed at the end of the 1960s into 8,500 by the mid-1980s.[36] The new units are more efficient but they lost some of the homogeneity and proximity to the citizens that were the strong points of traditional local government. The reforms strengthened the role of civil servants and diminished the influence of local elected officials. The consolidation appears to have encouraged the formation of citizen initiative groups to protest decisions that people no longer feel able to influence through local governments.

THE PUBLIC AND POLICY MAKING

Despite its legacy of authoritarian political systems and aloof bureaucracies, contemporary Germany has opened up the political process to allow much broader public involvement than it had in its own past and than what is found in many other Western democracies. The strong party system assures stable majorities in the Bundestag and clear lines of accountability for government action and inaction. In the shaping of policy, the extensive interaction between coalition parties and deputies from the majority party makes the German political system more open and accessible than other European democracies. The federal structure affords many opportunities for citizens to attempt to wield influence over policies that concern them.

In contrast to the strong state encountered in France and to a lesser extent in Britain, the German state is more responsive to public pressure. The orientation of both civil servants and politicians in Germany is more favorable to seeking consensus, unlike in France where confrontation and aloofness are more frequently viewed as normal. In seeking this consensus, German policy makers are willing to engage in genuine dialogue with concerned citizens and groups.[37] This communication means greater influence for organized interest groups and less organized citizen initiative groups. The decentralized administrative structure offers more points of access for citizens. The court system is relatively open, and its judges are willing to challenge the executive. The courts thus provide another avenue of appeal for those unable to find satisfaction through the normal political channels.

The evidence of this greater responsiveness can be seen in the German reaction to public protests against nuclear energy. Despite the initial commitment of both politicians and technical experts in the bureaucracy to a vast system of nuclear generators, the German government was forced to impose a moratorium on construction of new nuclear facilities because of public outcry. The antinuclear demonstrations precipitated lengthy debates in the Bundestag and in the major political parties. Comparative studies suggest that the German system is among the most open and responsive to public pressure on the issue of nuclear energy.[38] Highly visible successes of the citizen groups in shaping public policy, such as this victory in nuclear energy, encourage citizens to undertake other efforts to influence government.[39]

Government responsiveness to citizen views is a virtue of a democracy. But excessive vulnerability to public pressures may leave a government the captive of some small, unrepresentative minorities. Too much concern for consensus or a government's unwillingness to risk public outcry may deprive it of policy initiative and leadership. When governments are too open, they may be unable to defend the broader public interests against the noisy demands of small, unrepresentative, but dedicated minorities. For instance, a group of forty property owners were able to block the construction of a highway bypass designed to reduce congestion and divert traffic out of the medieval streets of a small Bavarian town.

The degree of openness in government can be the outcome of leaders' policy styles or the consequence of institutional arrangements. In Britain, government responsiveness changed sharply from the open, consensus style of the former Prime Minister Callaghan to the more assertive and aloof style of Margaret Thatcher when she gained power. In Germany, whatever the individual political style of the chancellor, the institutional framework—with its more powerful parliament, federalism, and decentralized administration—nurtures a more open policy-making style.

CONCLUSIONS

The record of the postwar political institutions in bringing a stable democracy to a nation without any democratic heritage is a major triumph for West Germany. It is easy to overemphasize the importance of institutional arrangements in making democracy work well, more important though are the attitudes of the public and the leaders. But the success of the postwar German regime in overcoming Weimar's institutional weaknesses suggests that constitutional engineering can be useful in strengthening democracy. Just as the Constitution of the French Fifth Republic remedied some of the problems of previous democratic regimes, the Basic Law remedied the faults of Weimar's regime. The experience of these two countries suggests that, under some circumstances, constitutional provisions can have important effects on the success or failure of democracy.

NOTES

1. David P. Conradt, *The German Polity*, 3rd. ed., (New York: Longman, 1986), p. 236.
2. After the first president delayed signing a treaty ratification while he awaited a ruling from the courts on its constitutionality, an amendment to the Basic Law was enacted forbidding the president from delaying signature of laws or treaties, even to consult the courts.
3. Renate Mayntz, "Executive Leadership in Germany: Dispersion of Power or *Kanzlerdemokratie?*" in Richard Rose and Ezra N. Suleiman, eds., *Presidents and Prime Ministers* (Washington, DC: American Enterprise Institute, 1981), p. 142.
4. Nevil Johnson, *State and Government in the Federal Republic of Germany: The Executive at Work*, 2nd ed., (Oxford, England: Pergammon Press, 1982), pp. 58–63.
5. Mayntz, "Executive Leadership in Germany," p. 147.
6. William E. Paterson, "The Chancellor and His Party: Political Leadership in the Federal Republic," in William E. Paterson and Gordon Smith, eds., *The West German Model: Perspectives on a Stable State* (London: Frank Cass, 1981), pp. 3–18.
7. Johnson, *State and Government in the Federal Republic*, p. 71.
8. David Southern, "Germany," in F.F. Ridley, ed., *Government and Administration in Western Europe* (London: Martin Robertson, 1979), p. 129.
9. The number of deputies can go up by two or three in order to meet the requirements of proportional representation. See pp. 00.
10. Conradt, *The German Polity*, p. 147.
11. Klaus Von Beyme, "Policy-making in the Federal Republic of Germany: A Systematic Introduction," in Klaus von Beyme and Manfred Schmidt, eds., *Policy and Politics in the Federal Republic of Germany* (New York: St. Martin's, 1985), p. 4.
12. Nevil Johnson, "Committees in the West German Bundestag," in John D. Lees and Malcolm Shaw, eds., *Committees in Legislatures: A Comparative Analysis* (Durham, NC: Duke University Press, 1979.)
13. Southern, "Germany," p. 148.

14. Gerhard Loewenberg and Samuel C. Patterson, *Comparing Legislatures* (Boston: Little, Brown, 1979), pp. 257–258.
15. An uncooperative president may first try to appoint a new chancellor and if he is ratified by the Bundestag the dissolution cannot take place. Party discipline and tacit understandings between the president and the chancellor eliminated that risk in both 1972 and 1983.
16. Klaus von Beyme, *The Political System of the Federal Republic* (New York: St. Martin's, 1983) p. 164.
17. Jörn Alwes, "Participation of the Laender in Decision Making at the Federal Level with Special Reference to the Bundesrat," in R. L. Matthews, ed., *Federalism in Australia and the Federal Republic of Germany: A Comparative Study* (Canberra, Australia: Australian National University Press, 1980), pp. 37–38.
18. Conradt, *The German Polity*, p. 155.
19. Elisabeth Nöelle-Neumann, ed., *The Germans: Public Opinion Polls, 1967–1980* (Westport, CT: Greenwood Press, 1981), p. 175.
20. Gordon Smith, *Democracy in Western Germany: Party and Politics in the Federal Republic* (New York: Holmes & Meier, 1979), p. 54.
21. Nevil Johnson, "The Interdependence of Law and Politics: Judges and the Constitution in West Germany," *West European Politics* 5 (July 1982): 236–252.
22. Donald P. Kommers, *Judicial Politics in West Germany: A Study of the Federal Constitutional Court* (Beverly Hills, CA and London: Sage, 1976).
23. Hans N. Weiler, "Equal Protection, Legitimacy and the Legalization of Education: The Role of the Federal Constitutional Court in West Germany," *Review of Politics* 47(January 1985): 113–166.
24. Renate Mayntz, "German Federal Bureaucrats: A Functional Elite Between Politics and Administration," in Ezra N. Suleiman, ed., *Bureaucrats and Policy Making: A Comparative Overview* (New York: Holmes & Meier, 1984), p. 187.
25. Joel D. Aberbach, Robert D. Putnam, Bert A. Rockman, *Bureaucrats and Politicians in Western Democracies* (Cambridge, MA: Harvard University Press, 1981).
26. Ibid., p. 230.
27. Southern, "Germany," p. 136.
28. Von Beyme, *The Political System of the Federal Republic*, p. 190.
29. Civil servants may take a temporary retirement to engage in political activity. While in politics, the former civil servants receive 60 percent of their salary (in addition to any payment they may receive for service in elected office) and regular promotions. Their original jobs are then available when they leave politics. See Renate Mayntz, "The Political Role of the Higher Civil Service in the German Federal Government," in Bruce L. R. Smith, ed., *The Higher Civil Service in Europe: Lessons for the United States* (Washington, DC: The Brookings Institution, 1984).
30. See Bernd Reissert and Gunther A. Schaefer, "Centre-Periphery Relations in the Federal Republic of Germany," in Yves Mény and Vincent Wright, eds., *Centre-Periphery Relations in Western Europe* (London: George Allen & Unwin, 1985.)
31. The absence of a central police force and national emergency procedures was due to sensitivities about the potential for abuse of the state's coercive powers. The legacy of the Hitler era made many Germans uneasy about the creation of a new national police force.
32. Nöelle-Neumann, ed., *The Germans*, p. 175.
33. The complex legal and diplomatic status of Berlin is covered well by Martin J. Hillenbrand, ed., *The Future of Berlin* (Montclair, NJ: Alanheld, Osmun,

1980) and Richard L. Merritt and Anna J. Merritt, eds., *Living With the Wall: West Berlin, 1961–1985* (Durham, NC: Duke University Press, 1985).

34. Arthur B. Gunlicks, *Local Government in the German Federal System* (Durham, NC: Duke University Press, 1986).

35. See the account of declining Bavarian cities in Peter H. Merkl, "How Communities Decline," in Peter H. Merkl, ed., *New Local Centers in Centralized States* (Lanham, MD: University Press of America, 1985).

36. For an evaluation of this reform, see Patricia Gibson, "Local Territorial Reform in Bavaria," and Peter H. Merkl, "Territorial Reform and Bavarian Local Politics: Patterns of Resistance," in Merkl, ed., *New Local Centers in Centralized States.*

37. Peter J. Katzenstein, *Policy and Politics in West Germany: The Growth of a Semisovereign State* (Philadelphia, PA: Temple University Press, 1987).

38. Herbert P. Kitschelt, "Political Opportunity Structures and Political Protest: Anti-Nuclear Movements in Four Democracies," *British Journal of Political Science* 16 (January 1986); Dorothy Nelkin and Michael Pollak, *The Atom Besieged: Extraparliamentary Dissent in France and Germany* (Cambridge, MA: The MIT Press, 1981).

39. Gadi Wolsfeld, "Political Action Repertoires: The Role of Efficacy," *Comparative Political Quarterly* 19 (April 1986): 104–129.

CHAPTER FIFTEEN
FROM
"THE GERMAN PROBLEM"
TO
"MODEL GERMANY?"

During the first two decades after the Second World War, scholars in and out of Germany sought the social and historical origins of the "German problem" and fretted about the durability of the new democratic regime. Over the past decade, they have probed "model Germany," as an example of stable democracy, social cohesion, and economic prosperity. The successes of the Federal Republic, while other democracies have undergone crises, have led some to see Germany as no longer a problem but rather an example for other European democracies. Judgments on the performance of the Federal Republic are by no means unanimously positive. Some see implicit weaknesses and dangers in both the economic and political features that make model Germany undesirable for other countries and even dangerous for Germany's democratic future. Most, however, see Germany now as a strong democracy with the ability to offer other countries examples in coping with the crises of the modern era.

THE GERMAN ECONOMY AND POLITICS

As already noted, one of the great miracles of the postwar era was the rapid recovery of the German economy. From the rubble of 1945 emerged the world's third strongest economy. Its success helped overcome the association between economic chaos and democracy left from the Weimar era. It built broad-based support for the democratic regime and for the parties that had promoted it. Even as economic problems developed, the earlier successes helped maintain public confidence in the political leadership and the political and economic system.

One of the strengths of German democracy has been the broad social consensus on economic questions. The economy is a market economy based on private ownership and free enterprise. But there is also widespread acceptance of a prominent role for the government in directing and promoting that economy. German trade unions have avoided the adversarial, anticapitalist stances of their counterparts in France and Britain. Even as economic problems have forced difficult decisions that have closed down entire industries in the interest of economic modernization, the German unions have preferred working with the employers and the government in adjusting to the new economic situation. For their part, German employers and government officials have been more interested in working with the unions to ease these economic adjustments. In contrast to the public debates in Britain and France over the basic nature of the economic system with the Left and Right proposing sharply different economic orders, discussion in Germany on economic matters has usually been restricted to differences in ways of managing the existing economic order.

Neither Thatcherism nor Socialism

The German economy was affected by the worldwide recession of the 1970s and 1980s. The Germans were relatively successful in restraining the inflationary trends that weakened the British and French economies but were unable to escape the unemployment problems of the 1980s. Compared to other European democracies, Germany's unemployment figures were still low: 9 percent in 1986 compared to 11 percent in France; 12 percent in Britain; and 13 percent in Italy. But in comparison to earlier performance the numbers were alarmingly high. German heavy industry proved more competitive than other European countries, and job losses in the industrial sector were lower than elsewhere. But the loss in industrial employment was still nearly 20 percent.[1] The general recession of the mid-1970s virtually ended economic expansion in West Germany.

In Britain, with the economic problems came a sharp move to the right and the experiment in Thatcherism; in France, there was a sharp move to the left and Mitterrand's short-lived experiment of a more state-centered, socialist economic policy. In Germany, the political balance shifted bringing the CDU/CSU back to power but policy changes were much less pronounced than in either France or Britain. In the face of the economic slowdown, both Social Democratic and Christian Democratic governments tried using tax incentives to promote investment, government funds for retraining those who lost jobs through economic modernization, and slight cuts in federal spending on social benefits.

This stability is explained by the unwillingness of any of the major parties or of the trade unions to advocate wholesale change in the existing economic system. The economic problems have not been serious enough to undermine confidence in the system that brought the economic miracle of the 1950s. Of equal importance is the consensus-based system of policy making for economics. Even though formal institutions of cooperation, such as the Concerted Action of the 1960s and early 1970s, have disappeared, economic policy is the product of broad consultation among employers, financial circles, trade unions, and government officials. Powerful semipublic bodies that bring together government officials with the representatives from trade unions and employers have important places in Germany's economic life. They include the Federal Reserve (which controls banking and fiscal policies), the Labor Office (which regulates labor/management relations), and the Social-Welfare Fund boards which administer social benefits. Compromise and accommodation are common and part of the normal process for setting economic policy.

These consensual policy-making procedures assure continuity in the nation's economic policies but there are costs as well. First, the emphasis on accommodation among affected groups and the government usually means incremental changes that simply adjust the system to deal with the immediate effects of the problems rather than the sweeping alterations needed to remedy the causes. The involvement of unions, employers, financial circles, and the government leads to policy changes that will hurt no one when appropriate corrective measures might well require sacrifices from one of them. Finally, the setting of national economic policies through consensus usually involves secret negotiations among the elites. When that occurs, it shifts public policy-making from visible and accountable elected officials to hidden and unrepresentative power brokers.

While these problems ought not to be ignored, they need to be placed in the context of the still impressive economic achievements of the Federal Republic. Despite the economic problems of the 1970s and 1980s, Germany still has one of the strongest economies and currencies in the industrial world. The incremental changes and compromises seem to be sufficient thus far in maintaining the country's economic position.

International Economic Restraints

German economic power is often resented by its neighbors and trading partners. In its nastiest forms, this animosity recalls wartime memories by seeing Germany's exercise of its economic power in the same aggressive way that it once used its military strength. In milder forms, the resentment focuses on Germany's large trade surplus and on claims that the mark is undervalued. Much of this criticism is exaggerated. It is true that the German government has often been reluctant to revalue the mark or to stimulate its economy in order to increase imports. But it has cooperated with several countries, including Britain, France, Italy, and the United States, by defending their currencies when they were under pressure. Germany has been a consistent advocate of free trade, with fewer informal and formal trade barriers than most other major industrial countries.

West Germany is a founding member of the European Economic Community, the European Common Market. It has been among the most enthusiastic and loyal supporters of the European Community's efforts to promote free trade and economic integration. It has not had the economic problems that have, from time to time, reduced the willingness of Britain, France, and Italy to promote free trade. Germany's economic strength (Germany has 30 percent of the gross product of the Community which is made up of twelve countries) has been used with restraint in Community affairs. But its role in promoting economic stability beyond its borders has brought it new responsibilities which it has exercised with restraint:

> West Germany will not play the role of the strong locomotive pulling others out of their economic troubles; more likely it will attempt to become the engine switching trains in the yard and heading them in the direction of stability.[2]

Its willingness to support on occasions a troubled neighboring economy stems less from altruism than from the recognition that Germany has profited from the trade opportunities of the Common Market.

Germany has not experienced the kinds of direct economic pressure from international or foreign financial circles that have affected British and Italian economic and social policies. But the indirect effects have been important. Germany's economy depends heavily on foreign exports; 25 percent of all industrial production is linked with exports. Governments of all political parties have felt constrained by the need to maintain a competitive position in international markets. They have curtailed domestic social policies and economic priorities to protect this export advantage. They have won concessions from both employers and trade unions to pursue this end.

Economic Performance and Political Stability

The economic reverses of the 1970s and 1980s caused Germany its own special concerns. The memory of economic mismanagement during the Weimar era still was present in people's minds, and many feared that renewed doubts about the ability of the democratic system to provide economic security would undermine popular support for the regime. Some insisted that the public support for the Federal Republic was based less on genuine commitment to its democratic principles and more on its economic success. If that success should end, they felt that the legitimacy of the whole system would be weakened. They believed prolonged economic problems might very well destroy this second experiment with democracy in Germany.

There are three reasons why such arguments are inaccurate. First, while the German economy has had its problems, it has done relatively well compared to the performance of its neighbors. This fact is known and regarded by the public as a credit to their leaders in difficult economic times. In addition, the economic slump and unemployment have not produced the kind of misery that destroyed Weimar's support. In today's

Germany, there is unemployment insurance, retraining programs for those laid off because of industrial modernization, and a full range of social-welfare benefits that alleviate the suffering of those experiencing economic hardships.

Second, studies of public attitudes toward democracy in Germany show a steady growth of democratic orientation since the 1950s. Even when the economy has faltered and even when the public is dissatisfied with government's economic policies, the trend toward greater attachment to democratic attitudes has continued.[3] Third, the success of the Federal Republic in leading the economic miracle during postwar recovery and in providing orderly government has created a "reserve of goodwill." This four-decades-old reservoir of public satisfaction appears likely to sustain public approbation of the regime even as it encounters economic hard times.

SOCIAL POLICIES IN WEST GERMANY

As in Britain and France, West Germany has vast social-welfare programs that account for more than 53 percent of all government expenditures. Despite its conservative and even reactionary past, Germany has often led the way in developing social-welfare policies. Indeed, the beginnings of the modern welfare state are conventionally identified with Bismarck's introduction of compulsory health insurance in 1883.[4] Over the next century and under diverse political regimes, a wide range of social programs have been added and benefits expanded. Once obtained, these social benefits have continued even though the regime that introduced them has fallen and is otherwise disgraced. The range of programs is wide including direct payments based on the number of children, paid maternity leaves, unemployment benefits, job retraining, retirement benefits, and full medical care. The specific benefits are also impressive. For example, the medical program covers lengthy stays for "cures" in popular health spas that are as much social and recreational centers as they are genuine medical treatment centers. While enjoying the benefits of the spa at the expense of the state medical program, the "patient" continues to draw full salary from the employer's sick pay program.

Most German social benefits are entitlement programs based on insurance principles where individuals and their employers pay into funds used to pay for the benefits. This system is similar to the French program but contrasts with the British social service that is funded mainly from the government's general tax revenues. There are relatively few direct benefits intended for the truly poverty stricken in Germany. In part, this is because there are few very poor people and those that are impoverished are often foreign immigrants whose plight has not attracted much government or popular sympathy. For the genuinely impoverished—such as the physically handicapped, single women with children, or the chronically ill—there are direct payments for food, housing, clothing, and other necessities. But these welfare programs account for no more than 4 percent of the total social budget.[5] The relatively small needs and costs mean that welfare has not become the controversial issue that it has been in American politics over the last decade.

Social insurance programs have been popular means of bidding for electoral support. Even conservative parties have found it good for election politics to promise and later deliver new programs or higher benefits. Competitive outbidding, with each party matching or exceeding the social promises of its rivals, has meant the steady expansion of these programs over the years. Often the more conservative parties have been the initiating forces in setting up new programs in order to undercut the appeal of the more progressive parties. For example, the CDU Chancellor Adenauer introduced the indexing of pensions to wage levels in the 1950s despite the opposition of business and financial interests because he felt he could then outbid the SPD and prolong the CDU political dominance. Adenauer also saw the pension programs as showpieces of a humane capitalism to East Germany.[6] In addition, both CDU- and SPD-led governments traded social programs in exchange for wage restraint from union workers during postwar reconstruction and in the mid-1970s recession. The retention of artifically low wages kept German manufactured goods very competitive on international markets while the new or higher social benefits compensated workers for their wage restraint. Thus, the modern social-welfare state is not the product of the socialist parties but rather of all the parties.[7]

The Crisis of the Welfare State

Expansion of the welfare state posed few problems while the economy was vigorous but with economic problems of the 1970s, more critical assessments were made of the social-welfare state that had been created. Unlike in Britain, where critics blamed much of that country's economic and social problems on the welfare state, the reexamination in Germany focused mainly on the costs of the programs.

The cost issue grew in importance because unemployment and economic slowdown reduced payments into the social insurance funds and increased payments for unemployment and retraining programs. In addition, rapid inflation in the cost of the welfare programs, especially the expensive health programs, escalated the crisis. A deficit in the government's own budget, not as large as those of Italy and some other European countries, was worrisome for Germany. The country's preoccupation with a stable currency, made a bailout from tax funds unacceptable. Demographic trends caused additional concern: The very low birthrate and increasing longevity meant that in the near future, fewer employed people would be paying benefits for people who would be retiring earlier and living longer.

The result has been efforts by both the SPD and the CDU governments to reevaluate and to consider retreating somewhat from the extensive social programs. Any retreat has proved a difficult task. The public strongly supports the existing programs and is unwilling to see any of the major programs eliminated. Powerful vested interests oppose major cutbacks.

Doctors, for example, resist reductions in their often generous fees; spa owners block the elimination of medical payments for cures despite the paucity of scientific evidence to support the curative effects of their waters or mud. Employer and employee contributions to the social insurance programs cannot be increased since they are already very high and amount to about 20 percent of an individual's pay.

Consequently, the thrust of the German effort to deal with the crisis in the welfare state has been to attempt modest cost cutting. Some programs, such as medical prescriptions, now impose small user fees. Other benefits have been reduced (pensions no longer rise automatically at the same rate as wage increases of the employed) or are determined by financial need. But the wholesale attack on the welfare state that Thatcher launched in Britain has not occurred in Germany.

The Limits of Equality

The destruction of World War II had an important leveling effect on German society and on the pattern of income distribution. While the previous privileged social groups did regain their positions by the end of the 1960s, the poorer sections of the population still controlled more of the nation's income than was the case in most other European democracies. By the mid-1970s, a comparative study indicated that Germany was among the most equal democratic countries in terms of the pattern of income distribution.[8] However, the economic equality found during the early postwar era had changed by the 1970s. There were signs of growing economic differences in Germany.

There have been few efforts to undertake a redistribution of income in Germany. The tax system includes a modest progressive income tax but much of the government's income is derived from direct value added taxes on sales. Thus, the tax system has only limited redistributive effects. As noted above, the social programs are nearly entirely funded by employer and employee insurance payments rather than by the government's general funds. There has been public support for heavier taxes for the wealthy but no government has been willing or able to tackle the issue. Pressure for more income redistribution has been minimal since the expanding economy has meant better living standards for all without redistribution. The economic slowdowns of the 1970s and 1980s led some observers to believe that public pressure for redistribution would grow as the economic pie stopped growing. But this has not happened so far. Germans from all socioeconomic strata correctly perceive themselves to be well off compared to other Europeans. The relative and absolute strength of the German economy has continued to meet most demands for improved living standards.

In the past, the educational system tended to perpetuate economic and class differences. By the age of ten years, the child was tested. On the basis of these test results and other factors such as parents' preferences, the child was then placed in one of three educational tracks: a general school which led to an end to formal education by the age of fifteen or sixteen and then vocational training; a middle school with options for either academic preparation or vocational training; or the gymnasium for university preparatory academic education. Transfers between educational tracks were possible but rare.[9]

There has been some improvement in what was once a very rigid educational structure. The percentage of students receiving only a basic education in the general schools dropped from 72 to 47 percent from 1955 to 1981.[10] As in Britain, Germany has also experimented with comprehensive education, with all groups of children attending the same school. But these comprehensive schools have remained experimental in all but a few states that have been controlled by SPD governments. Only 4 percent of children were attending such schools by the early 1980s.[11]

There has been a vast expansion in higher education in the postwar era. Between 1960 and 1974, the number of students in higher education increased threefold. By the mid-1980s, one out of every five young people was attending higher education, the largest proportion in Europe. With higher education fully paid for by the government and with more accessible university preparatory programs, opportunities for children from working-class backgrounds to attend university have increased. About 16 percent of all university students come from the working class, another relatively high figure compared to other European countries but much below the comparable figure for the United States.

The universities were not able to keep up with the rapid growth in numbers of students during the 1960s and 1970s. Overcrowded facilities and rigid academic regulations contributed to a student revolt that disrupted the universities' operations for nearly a decade. The student movement radicalized many students. In actions reminiscent of Nazi students in the 1930s, the radical leftist students

> prowled through the departments, breaking up lectures, restructuring seminars and colloquia that had no relevance to the realities of the world as they saw it, changing rules for examinations, and homogenizing all subjects into one endless disquisition on *'faschismus theorie.'*[12]

A small but visible portion of this radical student Left turned to terrorism. It was not until the end of the 1970s that reforms in university governance and a decline in student activism permitted university life to return to normal.

As the number of university graduates has increased, the value of the university degree has decreased. In addition, German universities graduate too many humanity majors for whom it is very difficult to find jobs. As in France, the dilution of the value of the degree has meant a return to other criteria such as social backgrounds or family and school networks in competing for the best jobs.

CIVIL LIBERTIES
IN THE FEDERAL REPUBLIC

The horrendous abuses of human rights during the Nazi era have made observers particularly vigilant of respect for civil liberties under the Bonn republic. The legacy of the past led to an emphasis on clearly stating these rights and on assuring ample opportunities to defend them. The Basic Law begins with a long list of political and economic rights that are guaranteed for all citizens. It is as clear and as extensive a list of rights as to be found in any country's constitution. In addition, West Germany subscribes to the United Nations Declaration of Human Rights and to the European Convention of Human Rights.

The test of a country's commitment to human rights involves more than checking on the rights government is supposed to be observed. It must also include an evaluation of the means for defending these rights when citizens feel that they have been abused. Germany has developed several effective channels for those claiming abuse of their rights. The Federal Constitutional Court has emerged as a strong advocate of human rights. Access to the court is available to individuals with human rights cases. In practice, the court has proved sympathetic to those citizens claiming government violation of their rights. It tends to interpret these civil liberties broadly. The Constitutional Court has not hesitated to decide against all levels of government in protecting these rights. Individuals who feel that they have not received adequate help from German courts have the right to take their case to the European Commission of Human Rights and ultimately to the European Court of Human Rights. The legal remedies in Germany have been adequate so that only a very few German cases have reached the European Court.

In addition to the legal protection, civil liberties have received broad public support. There have been several controversial issues about human rights in the last decade involving both legislative proposals and actual incidents of alleged violations. These issues have fully been aired in the press and in parliament. The tenor of the discussions have indicated a watchful public concerned with defending its rights even against abstract future threats. Political leaders from all parties have shown similar wariness of any erosion of basic rights. Their criticism of even the minor abuses that have taken place indicate the broad acceptance by the political elite of the need to operate within the limits of broadly defined civil liberties. An example of surveillance of even potential human rights dangers came in the early 1980s when civil libertarians raised the alarm about questions on the proposed census that might give law enforcement and government officials information about individuals. The ensuing public debate delayed the census and eventually, with backing from the Constitutional Court, eliminated the offensive questions.

A Delicate Trade-Off: Internal Security and Civil Liberties

One of the principal causes for concern about German respect for civil liberties was the battle against terrorism. The serious terrorist threat of the 1970s brought new legislation that contained provisions that if broadly applied would have been a potential threat to civil liberties. No democracy has an easy time in controlling terrorism while restricting its actions to remain within the limits of civil rights. Terrorists often use those democratic rights to attack democracy. A good case in point was the abuse of the lawyer/client privileges by members of the Baader-Meinhof group in the 1970s. Once the police had jailed several leaders of this terrorist band, the leaders continued to direct their group's activities by choosing attorneys sympathetic to their cause. These attorneys served as couriers between the imprisoned leaders and their comrades still at large. This communication was possible because of the constitutional right of the accused to counsel of their choice. Eventually legislation was passed depriving accused terrorists of this right under certain circumstances. If broadly used, that law might well deny other citizens accused of civil crimes from adequate legal assistance. In practice, the "incommunicado" law has been used narrowly in only those cases where accused terrorists were likely to abuse the right. Its provisions were relaxed in 1983 when the worst of the terrorist threat was over.

The most controversial issue was the adoption of a policy in the 1970s that excluded radicals from civil service positions. West Germany's geographic location on the frontier with eastern bloc countries contributed to a siege climate. There was a fear of the "enemy at the gate." In addition, East Germany has succeeded in placing many agents in sensitive positions in West Germany's civil service. In the 1970s, there was evidence to suggest that East Germany was preparing a new generation of such agents through its influence in the radical student movement. To hinder this, the federal and state governments agreed to block the recruitment of radicals into the civil service.[13]

Political screening for loyalty to the Federal Republic was required of all civil service job applicants. With literally hundreds of thousands applying over a decade, the potential for abuse was great. Definitions of key terms such as "radical" or "loyalty" were not clear nor consistently applied in all states. In practice, the loyalty test was used with restraint with most of the cases involving purportedly radical teachers in elementary and secondary schools.[14] The Constitutional Court has sustained the loyalty test but the SPD government that originated it tried to abolish it. The law to repeal the loyalty test passed in the Bundestag, but it was vetoed by the CDU-dominated Bundesrat.

Shortly after its return to power, the CDU/CSU government pushed through parliament another controversial law. The law has made individuals participating in demonstrations criminally liable if they refuse to obey a police order to disband because of violence. Individual states have also added their own antidemonstration laws. Several states have passed legislation allowing the government to recover the costs of any special deployments to assure the peace from organizers of demonstrations. The inhibiting effect of such provisions may well represent an abridgement in the right of assembly. But the Federal Constitutional Court affirmed in 1985 the right of citizens to demonstrate peacefully and restricted the police's power to ban demonstrations that it feared may provoke violence. And state courts have overturned some of the "demonstration fee" laws.

In part, these laws are a reaction to unusually violent actions on the part of political dissidents. Over the past decade, a small but determined handful of radicals has seemed bent on the violent expression of their political views. They have engaged in actions to provoke physical repression from police forces. Faced with such an extraordinary challenge, the government has responded with new limitations on political demonstrations, not with the intent of suppressing freedom of political expression but with the intent of controlling political violence. In the 1920s and early 1930s, the inability of the democratic government to control similar political violence led many to support antidemocratic groups promising to restore order while at the same time actively participating in the disorder. The Bonn government has sought to prevent such a collapse of public order without using repressive means that would be incompatible with democracy.

Some observers see in these antidemonstration measures a reflection of German intolerance for political dissent. The range of acceptable political beliefs and political action appears narrower in Germany than in other Western European countries. On rare occasions, this intolerance has produced official responses reminiscent in style but not in severity of Germany's past. For example, in 1985, the Bavarian state government was angered by the participation of many Austrians in demonstrations against a nuclear reprocessing center in Bavaria. In a fit of pique, the Bavarian government intruded on federal prerogatives by ordering the closure of the frontier. When this was reversed, the Bavarian minister-president tried to pressure the federal government into revoking the permission granted many years earlier for Austrian military aircraft to fly over Germany in the approach to the Salzburg airfield.[15] This "Alpine War" was ended by the federal government's refusal to support the Bavarian government. But the clash revealed the persistence of political intolerance in certain influential political circles. As one German commentator noted:

> We have not yet developed that measure of calm composure in the face of extreme political opinions that is characteristic of older mature democracies, in spite of their often incomparably more difficult social problems.[16]

These laws reflect the clash between the new radical groups who are dissatisfied with the system and ready to use disruptive tactics and traditionalists who are hostile to political dissidence and are concerned about disrupting the system whose stability provides prosperity and security. If the official response of governments has sometimes been excessive or illiberal, the courts and public opinion have emerged as powerful advocates of civil liberties. With few exceptions, the political leaders have shown strong attachment to generous definitions of human rights even if at times they have erred in seeking ways to handle the disruptive new forms of political action.

The greatest threat to civil rights does not come from the government but rather from the general public. As was noted in Chapter One of this section, Germans have displayed intolerance toward foreign guest workers and refugee racial minorities who have settled in Germany. Both SPD- and CDU-led governments have promoted racial understanding. The parties have avoided exploiting the issue but, as in Britain and France, there is no doubting the presence of a large number of Germans who have exhibited intolerance and prejudice in their attitudes toward these nonwhite alien residents.

Government and the Media

Germany has a vigorous and independent press. The mass circulation newspapers are largely apolitical with a focus on sensational crimes, sports, and human interest stories rather than political news and analysis. Radical critics allege that the newspapers thus serve to depoliticize the public and to lull citizens into complacent acceptance of the existing regime. Most other observers contend that the newspapers are simply following the public's tastes.

The largest newspaper chain, with its papers read by 60 percent of the public, was controlled by Axel Springer until his death a few years ago. Springer's conservative and nationalist political philosophy was featured in his newspapers. His bitter criticism of the student movement of the late 1960s made his newspapers the targets of some of the most violent student demonstrations in those years. The impact of his views seems to have been limited; there was little sympathy for his extreme opposition to improved relations with eastern bloc countries or with his strident anti-SPD rhetoric. People seemed to buy his papers more for their sensational news than for his political views.

While investigative reporting has not reached the important scale of that in the United States, it has been more common in Germany than in most other European countries. Newspapers and magazines have played important parts in discovering and probing several recent political scandals such as the Flick affair, which involved illegal political contributions by industrialists and the financial problems of the trade unions' housing construction firm, *Neue Heimat.*

The electronic media are still largely in the hands of the government. Private broadcasting did not begin until 1981.[17] Unlike the situation in Britain and France, radio and television is highly decentralized with control vested in the states rather than the central government. Each state has a broadcasting board made up of representatives from all the parties and from key social groups such as trade unions, business, and churches. These boards supervise the radio and television stations and assure political neutrality.

The record has been remarkably good. Germany has avoided the ongoing controversies over political control of the television news that have been constant in France and occasional in Britain. The decentralization of control has meant that abuse of its monopoly to control the news is limited at least, to the state governments and not uniform throughout the country. Federal and state courts have been vigilant in acting quickly to counter even the slightest hints of political interference in the electronic media. As private commercial stations have begun to appear and as new technologies such as cable and satellite television have emerged, the courts have ruled frequently in defense of pluralism and neutrality within the context of the state rights to control the media.

GERMAN RESPONSES
TO THE CHALLENGES OF GOVERNANCE

West German democracy has faced its share of the challenges to democratic stability that have troubled all democracies. It has proved flexible and durable despite the misgivings of many about the grafting of democracy onto Germany's troubled history.

Political Stability
in Troubled Times

Germans have been more sensitive to the dangers of the disruption that occasionally accompanies political action by new social movements than have been the citizens of other European democracies. The ghosts of the Weimar era contributed in part to this greater sensitivity. The Weimar regime was destroyed by excessive politicization and political violence. It was not only the disruption itself that weakened the regime but also its inability to control violence that destroyed the public confidence in its ability to govern. Those memories have haunted the present regime as it has had to cope with the aggressive actions of new social movements. In addition, West Germany's position on the front line of a, never too cool, cold war makes its leaders particularly mindful of the dangers of political extremes. East German espionage and sabotage are well-documented realities; eastern bloc funding of radical leftist groups in the Federal Republic is also a fact.

The greater awareness of the risks posed by the new politics has contributed to efforts to impose legal restraints on political demonstrations as was just pointed out. But there have been other more positive consequences of recent political activism. Important issues that otherwise might have been ignored have been brought into the political scene. Groups that might have been neglected—such as women, students, and advocates for the rights of guest workers—have been able to present their demands. In several instances, the German government has been more responsive to these new demands than have been the more aloof French government and the more hard line British government.

It sometimes appears that Germany has more problems than they do with new social movements and their unconventional forms of political action. Comparative statistics presented in Chapter Twelve suggest that the numbers of Germans involved in political action in both conventional and unconventional forms are no higher and often lower than those in other European countries. A variety of factors have made the new social movements appear more important than they are. Critics' uncertainty about the durability of German democracy attracted unmerited attention to groups and activities because they seemed to endanger democratic stability. The turmoil of the 1970s contrasted sharply with the tranquil nature of the first twenty years of the Bonn republic and invited apocalyptic interpretations of political trends in Germany. The electoral system's five percent threshold was high enough to stimulate lengthy discussions in the media about the inability of fringe groups to enter parliament. But it was low enough for the Greens to reach it and appear victorious. All of these factors have contributed to a disproportionate focus on new politics, crises, and destabilizing trends in West Germany. In fact, the system seems to have adjusted rather well to the new levels and forms of political participation.

Terrorism

The rise of terrorism in Germany was unsettling because it was a domestic terrorism aimed at the overthrow of the Federal Republic. Much of the terrorism elsewhere in Europe was the work of international terrorists concerned with causes far from the locale of their violent acts. In Britain and France, the principal domestic forms of terrorism came from separatist groups seeking to break off a part of these countries but not attacking the political systems as such. Germany too had its share of international terrorism but, as in Italy, its domestic terrorists directly attacked the whole system. The Baader-Meinhof terrorist band and other similar groups repudiated the German's way of life. Their philosophy was well captured in their global condemnation of the main parties. "There is only one difference between the Social Democratic party of Germany and the Christian Democratic Union, and that is the difference between plague and cholera."[18] For these extremists, the death of "bourgeois democracy" was a necessary first step to the creation of a "genuinely just and democratic" order.

The rise of terrorism in the 1970s caught the regime off guard and ill prepared. There were no federal police so the means of coordinating actions and information of the separate state police forces were poorly developed. With a series of daring and spectacular attacks—including bank robberies, bombings, kidnappings, and assassinations—the terrorists seized the headlines and spread uncertainty among political leaders and the public in general. The federal and state governments fought back with the creation of antiterrorist squads and a new federal police force (the Office for the Protection of the Constitution). It still took several years for the government to regain control and confidence. But by the end of the decade, most of the first generation of terrorists were either dead or imprisoned.

The terrorist threat is still present. A new generation of terrorists has emerged. Normally acting under the title of Red Army Faction, these terrorists carried out over two hundred attacks during 1985. They form a tight circle of individuals who have known each other for years from school, neighborhoods, and political protests. The network has proved more difficult for the police to infiltrate and destroy. The number of actual terrorists is very small, twenty to twenty-five, according to police estimates. They are supported by another two hundred or so who aid them in their activities by providing safe houses, cars, and other direct assistance. An outer circle of two thousand to three thousand sympathize with the terrorist cause, attending rallies, putting up posters, scribbling political grafitti on walls, and generally providing moral support.

As tragic as are the consequences of these terrorist acts for the individuals directly affected, terrorism no longer is as regime-threatening as it appeared a decade ago. Terrorists are not seen as vanguards of a mass movement that could overthrow democracy. They are now recognized for what they are: a small band of fanatics with very limited public support but with the ability to inflict isolated violence on selected targets.

In a way, the stability of the Federal Republic of Germany is today stronger than it was before it faced the challenges of political protest and terrorism of the last two decades. Before, the stability had a sort of fairyland unreality and complacency that led people to wonder if the regime could really stand up to a serious challenge. It has now faced several serious challenges and still retains its essential stability and order. The regime has acquired the character of being able to control threats to its order and to tolerate the periodic probes of antisystem extremists.

Strength of the Institutions

The institutions of the Federal Republic have worked well. Along with the strong party system that has emerged, these institutions have permitted governments to respond to both normal and crisis situations. There have been few signs of problems with governance or overload in the Federal Republic. Of equal importance has been the success of the institutions and the parties in establishing responsible government. Periodic elections have permitted citizens to express approval or disapproval of the government's stewardship in office. They have offered voters choices between real policy alternatives. The voters have exercised these rights bringing changes in government at both the national and state levels.

Additional support for the system is found in the very rapid development of democratic attitudes and values. In a remarkably short time, West German political culture changed from attitudes supportive of authoritarianism to values and attitudes conducive to democratic stability.[19] At first, the rapidity of the transformation raised questions about the permanence of the new democratic values. The challenge to these values from radical groups seemed to give credence to the skepticism. But the very acts, that at first impression seem to be signs of an uncertain democratic commitment, are in fact evidence of a repudiation of traditional political values thought to be inimical to democracy. Political protest, citizen initiative groups, and public prominence of dissident political views betoken the decline of antidemocratic values which stressed stability, obedience, and intolerance of political deviations and which were long seen as part of the German character. Germans seem to have learned that too much as well as too little stability may endanger democracy and peace.[20] Above all, Germany offers proof that "democratic stability does not necessarily require the centuries-long evolution characteristic of the 'classical' democracies of Great Britain and the United States."[21]

Public opinion polls indicate that the antidemocratic fringe is a very small one. Germans demonstrate vigilance over potential human rights abuses or misuse of political power. Comparative opinion studies indicate that Germans hold democratic attitudes as strongly or more strongly than do the peoples of other European countries. With the exception of small dissident minorities, Germans strongly back the democratic system and are content with the political regime that has emerged since the war.

PROBLEM AREAS IN GERMAN POLITICS

As well as the West German system has operated over the past decades, there remain important challenges to be faced. These challenges can be seen in the economic, political, and international areas.

Economic Problems

It is paradoxical to discuss economic problems in Germany given its outstanding economic record. But in the late 1980s, one of the most important challenges facing West Germany was that of unemployment. At the end of 1988, unemployment stood near 9 percent. This figure was low in comparison to other major European countries, but high for Germany. As elsewhere in Europe, the unemployed included many who had been without work for long periods as a result of economic changes that had rendered their jobs redundant. The problem appears likely to remain. More so than in other European countries, German employment depends upon the traditional heavy industries that have declined and that are likely to shed even more workers. The service sector has not expanded to absorb more of the population. Unemployment does not seem likely to become a regime-threatening problem, but it will pose continuing needs to adapt both economic policies and political practices.

The trade union movement has long been a source of stability and strength for German democracy. The DGB has provided discipline and productivity in the work force that have contributed to the country's economic strength. It has earned worker confidence by its ability to win social benefits from the government and good wages with good working conditions from employers through tough negotiations but with few strikes or work interruptions. Now, there is a risk that the trade unions may become a victim of the economic crisis. They have lost membership in the last decade. Their ability to maintain the economic standing of their members has been threatened, and they have been unable to assure job security. The confidence of union members has been further shaken by corruption and mismanagement in DGB-owned housing concerns. Should the DGB fail to recover from these crises, German democracy will lose one of its strongest assets in a powerful and constructive trade union movement that has done much to keep the working class well off and content with democracy. Without a strong DGB, the maintenance of the political and social consensus that has been the foundation of the current regime's success may be endangered.

Over the long run, the unemployment problem could well solve itself. Current unemployment is swollen by the large postwar baby boom. But the birthrate fell by the 1960s and that means that the working population will shrink over the next couple of decades. The demographics indicate that another labor shortage could appear by the end of the century. In the meantime, politicians, trade unionists, and employers will struggle to readjust German industry to provide jobs for the unemployed.

The Challenge of New Politics

The new politics of increased and unconventional participation have been discussed at several points in this section on Germany. It is not a problem that is unique to Germany; indeed, the levels of activity and attitudes associated with new politics appear lower in Germany than elsewhere. But the new politics have had more important consequences in Germany than in other countries.

The Greens pose the most immediate probable trial coming from the rise of new politics. Their political strength makes it possible that they will one day hold the balance of political power at the national level. The danger of the Greens is not that they are antidemocratic, although they have occasionally drawn into their ranks the voters and leaders of antidemocratic elements.[22] What makes their holding the political balance risky is the fact that the Greens do not see themselves as a party like the others; while not antidemocratic, they are antisystem. They prefer an oppositional stance to constructive participation in governing the nation. They recognize correctly that governing would involve compromise and accommodation that might betray their principles. Neither the Christian Democrats nor the Social Democrats are interested in allying with such a party.

Thus, if the Greens were to hold the balance needed for a majority after a Bundestag election, the result might be either a minority government headed by the SPD or CDU or a grand coalition of the SPD and CDU. Neither option would be as stable or as desirable as the traditional alliances of one of these parties with the small but amenable FDP. It is possible that the Greens will evolve under the pressure of such a situation into an acceptable alliance partner. Such an alliance has happened at the state level on one occasion with mixed results. There is a "realist" minority in the Green party favorable to such an evolution and it may yet prevail.

As noted earlier, the popularity of the ideals of new politics has posed a direct challenge to the SPD. This party has felt the loss of part of its electorate to the Greens. Younger citizens who might otherwise have been expected to support the Social Democrats have been drawn to the Greens. The SPD has been limited in its ability to adjust its agenda and program to win back these voters by the continued interest of its traditional, working-class, electorate in bread and butter issues. Those voters who are tempted to support the Greens give priority to environmental protection over economic growth, while the blue-collar SPD voters believe strongly in the need to expand the economy in order to combat unemployment.

More fundamentally, the German parties must respond to some of the popular issues that have been captured by the Greens if they hope to limit the Greens' political influence. The issue of environmental protection is important and cannot be ignored. Germans are rightfully proud of the beauty of their country. They are troubled by the pollution of their rivers and by the death of their beloved forests due to acid rain and automobile exhaust. These are not easy problems to address, not the least because they involve international cooperation as well as the cooperation of private and public bodies in Germany.

The International Challenge

The division of Germany into two separate countries is not a pressing political concern for the German Federal Republic. After nearly forty-five years of separate existence for the two German states, it is no longer correct to view the situation as an artificial division of a single people. A reunification of Germany would no doubt involve as much chaos as its separation did in 1945 to 1949. While West German politicians sometimes invoke the symbol of a united Germany, there is a pragmatic acceptance of the post-1945 division and boundaries as permanent for the foreseeable future.

More so than any other country, Germany is the front line of the cold war. East-West hostilities or rapprochement do not seem to have a direct effect on German domestic stability. But they do contribute to a climate of security or crisis among German people. Germany's geographic situation makes issues of armament and disarmament in Europe very important in domestic politics. For much of the postwar period, defense and foreign policies have been defused as partisan issues by a bipartisan consensus based on loyalty to the United States in defense and foreign policy positions coupled with efforts to ease tensions with the eastern bloc through diplomacy and trade.

That consensus has weakened in the 1980s due to the SPD's new interest in disarmament and to uncertainties shared by both parties about the reliability and stability of American policies. It has no longer been clear that the economic and political interests of the United States are identical to those of the Federal Republic. In addition, the rapprochement with Eastern Europe has reached its limits. The trade expansion into Eastern markets has ended as East European countries have experienced their own economic crises and as the Soviet Union tightened its grip on some of them. Despite these new concerns, the popular consensus on loyalty to the West while promoting detente with the East remains. If this bipartisan agreement on foreign policy should succumb to the changing international situation, foreign policy may become a volatile and even polarizing issue for German domestic politics.

Another international concern is Germany's place in world economics. Germany's economy is dominant in that domestic economic and fiscal policies have important consequences among its neighbors and trading partners. Its very success has engendered envious resentment among those countries that have not fared as well. There is sometimes the feeling that German prosperity has been purchased at the cost of others. Such attitudes reinforce, still present, animosities from the past. The government's ability to conduct its own domestic economic policies is sometimes constrained by its desire to avoid the appearance of an economic bully to neighboring countries. The dilemma is that domestic political groups see the government as caving in to these international forces too often while foreigners feel it does so too rarely.

CONCLUSIONS

For over one hundred years, German advocates of democracy turned to Britain for a model of successful democratic society and politics. By the end of the twentieth century, however, the roles have been reversed. At the height of the economic and political travails of the 1970s, the British government sent Royal Commissions to the Federal Republic of Germany to study its solutions to combining economic growth and democratic stability.[23] The success of the institutions of the Bonn Republic in gaining public confidence and in handling both ordinary and crisis situations has helped to compensate for the lack of a democratic tradition in the past. With nearly forty years of successful operation, the regime has built up a reservoir of good will and experience that should aid it in weathering future crises. This outstanding achievement gives confidence to both the leaders and the public in general. Crises will come and go but uncertainties about the viability of German democracy should be set aside. Its record portends not disaster but an ability to adapt and respond to challenges. As former Chancellor Helmut Schmidt indicated a decade ago, West Germany "now has a history of its own. It is the best and most dignified part of German history."[24]

NOTES

1. The losses in industrial employment were 26 percent in Britain and 21 percent in France between 1973 and 1985. *The Economist* (London), 8 February, 1986, p. 99.
2. Peter J. Katzenstein, "Germany as Number Two: Reflections on the West German Model," in Andrei S. Markovits, ed., *The Political Economy of West Germany: Modell Deutschland* (New York: Praeger, 1982), p. 208.
3. David P. Conradt, "Changing German Political Culture," in Gabriel A. Almond and Sidney Verba, eds., *The Civic Culture Revisited* (Boston: Little, Brown, 1980), pp. 262–263.
4. Arnold J. Heidenheimer, Hugh Heclo, Carolyn Teich Adams, *Comparative Public Policy: The Politics of Social Choice in Europe and America* 2nd ed. (New York: St. Martin's Press, 1983), p. 311.
5. Lewis J. Edinger, *West German Politics* (New York: Columbia University Press, 1986), pp. 299–300.
6. Gosta Esping-Andersen and Walter Korpi, "Social Policy as Class Politics in Post-War Capitalism: Scandinavia, Austria, and Germany," in John H. Goldthorpe, ed., *Order and Conflict in Contemporary Capitalism* (Oxford: Clarendon Press, 1984), p. 197.

7. Helga Michalsky, "The Politics of Social Policy," in Klaus Von Beyme and Manfred G. Schmidt, eds., *Policy and Politics in the Federal Republic of Germany* (New York: St. Martin's, 1985).

8. Malcolm Sawyer, "Income Distribution in OECD Countries," *OECD Economic Outlook: Occasional Studies,* July 1976.

9. David P. Conradt, *The German Polity,* 3rd ed. (New York and London: Longman, 1986), pp. 37–39.

10. Edinger, *West German Politics,* p. 50.

11. Ibid.

12. Gordon A. Craig, *The Germans* (New York: Putnam's, 1982), p. 187.

13. See Roger Tilford, "The State, University Reform, and the 'Berufsverbot,' " in William E. Paterson and Gordon Smith, eds., *The West German Model: Perspectives on a Stable State* (London: Frank Cass, 1981) and Kenneth Dyson, "Anti-Communism in the Federal Republic of Germany: The Case of the 'Berufsverbot,' " *Parliamentary Affairs* 28 (Winter 1975): 51–67.

14. Conradt, *The German Polity,* pp. 65–67.

15. The minister-president was Franz-Joseph Strauss who had been involved, in the 1950s, in an even more serious abuse of civil liberties. While defense minister in the federal government, he was irritated by a series of critical articles in the popular news magazine *Der Spiegel.* He concocted charges that the magazine had leaked national security secrets and ordered the predawn arrest of the editors and the seizure of the magazine's files. The charges were soon dropped and Strauss was forced to resign.

16. Wolfgang J. Mommsen, cited in Craig, *The Germans,* p. 297.

17. See Arthur Williams, "West Germany: The Search for the Way Forward," in Raymond Kuhn, *The Politics of Broadcasting* (New York: St. Martin's, 1985).

18. Gunther Wegelhner, *Motivation for Political Terror in Germany* (Westport, CT: Greenwood, 1978), p. 200.

19. Kendall L. Baker, Russell J. Dalton, Kai Hildebrandt, *Germany Transformed: Political Culture and the New Politics* (Cambridge, MA: Harvard University Press, 1981).

20. Katzenstein, "West Germany as Number Two," p. 211.

21. Conradt, *The German Polity,* p. 245.

22. See Perry Anderson and others, *Rudolf Bahro: From Red to Green* (London: Thetford Press, 1984).

23. Klaus Von Beyme, *The Political System of the Federal Republic of Germany* (New York: St. Martin's, 1983), pp. 195–196.

24. *The Washington Post,* 22 May 1979.

PART FIVE
ITALY

Like West Germany, Italy is a relatively new democracy, created on the ruins of a fascist regime. In contrast to the stability of the postwar German state, Italy continues to be plagued by considerable instability. Whether or not an Italian democracy will survive has been a pressing question since the birth of the Italian Republic.

Two problems have been especially difficult for Italy: governmental instability which has brought a succession of short-lived governments, and the challenge of controlling a serious threat from domestic terrorists. In the process of responding to these challenges, Italian democracy has proved much more resilient and robust than many had expected.

CHAPTER SIXTEEN
THE BACKGROUND
TO ITALIAN POLITICS

The French want to preserve. The Germans want to become. The Italians want to recreate.

Paul Valéry

On the surface, there are a number of similarities in the Italian and German paths to democracy. Both countries underwent unsuccessful democratic revolutions in 1848. Italy and Germany attained national unity at the same time in 1870, centuries later than the rest of Western Europe. This delay led reformers in both countries to stress nationalism rather than democratization during much of the nineteenth century. When democracy came, it was the result of revolts at the elite level and was not accompanied by the economic and social changes needed to provide support for the political changes. These democracies gave way in both countries to fascism and totalitarian dictatorships. Only after the Second World War did Italy and West Germany acquire reasonably stable democratic polities. Beneath these similarities, however, there are important differences.

In contrast to Germany, Italy looks back on a glorious past. Living amid the stone ruins of Imperial Rome, Italians remember the power of ancient Rome. Contemporary religious ceremonies remind them of the political and spiritual leadership of the papal Rome during Medieval times. The city states of Genoa and Venice give a legacy of commercial and political dominance from the fourteenth and fifteenth centuries. And all

Italians take pride in the artistic achievements of the Italian-born renaissance even though the political systems sponsoring the arts were decadent and are an embarrassment. Such a proud history might have served to stimulate the nationalist sentiments which can produce imperialism and aggression. But such lapses are rare in modern Italy. Mussolini tried to exploit the hope for a new Roman empire with his tragicomic efforts at military colonization but met with only modest success with his countrymen. Instead, this legacy builds pride in Italy and hope for future greatness even when their current political system is a cause for embarrassment and frustration.

THE EMERGENCE OF MODERN ITALY

As recently as 1860, the Italian peninsula was a patchwork of small, autonomous, and quarrelsome states with few relationships with each other. The Italian states were tied to different European countries through a variety of alliances. They often became the pawns and the battle sites of confrontations between the major European powers. Prince von Metternich, the famous nineteenth-century Austrian statesman, contemptuously dismissed Italy as a geographic expression, not a real nation.

The Risorgimento

The Napoleonic invasions at the end of the eighteenth century ignited Italian nationalism. Italians were stung by the occupation of Italy, by first the French and then after postwar settlements by other countries. They were humiliated by the post-Napoleon settlements that determined the fate of Italy based on the power calculations of the European powers rather than on Italian needs or desires. These early nationalists made up of intellectuals and people from the liberal professions formed secret societies such as Guiseppe Mazzini's Young Italy and began to search for ways to renew Italy and to rebuild its integrity. Eventually their discussions moved to action in conspiracies and plots to force change. Swept along by the continentally wide revolutionary spirit of 1848, the nationalists succeeded in temporarily ousting the Austrians from Milan and in establishing short-lived republics in Rome and Venice. Just as the 1848 revolts failed in Frankfurt and Paris, they quickly faltered in Italy as well. But the national resurgence, or *Risorgimento,* was under way and difficult to resist. The nationalists were a mixed lot of romantic revolutionaries such as Guiseppe Garibaldi, republican political theorists such as Guiseppe Mazzini, and moderate power brokers such as Camillo Bensa di Cavour. They agreed on the goal of a united Italy but differed on its ultimate form and on the methods to achieve it.[1]

Unification came by conquest as the Kingdom of Sardinia, which despite its formal name was centered in the northwest state of Piedmont, took the lead in pressing for a united Italy. Under Piedmont's King Victor Emmanuel II and his prime minister, Cavour, Piedmontese troops first defeated Austria to win Lombardy and then extended control over much of central Italy.[2] In the south, another nationalist, Garibaldi, led a thousand men in battle to seize Sicily and then Naples. Seeing a chance for further expansion, Piedmont sent troops south, uniting the papal states to their cause on their way. Despite his republican predilections, Garibaldi agreed to the incorporation of his conquests in the south with the new Italian nation-state, dominated by the Kingdom of Sardinia (Piedmont). Piedmont allied with Prussia in its 1866 war against Austria and, as a reward, was able to incorporate the northeastern provinces around Venice. The final step in Italy's unification was the incorporation of Rome and its surrounding province when the French were forced to end their protection of the pope during the Franco-Prussian War of 1870.

The *Risorgimento* was the product of a narrow, educated, and relatively affluent, middle-class, elite. It never acquired a mass following, nor did it try to. There was no popular uprising as in revolutionary France; the battle for Italian unity was fought by professional troops with the aid of foreign powers. As each area was incorporated into Italy through conquest, its residents were invited to legitimize the incorporation by rigged referendums. It was a revolution from above with the limited goal of political change without social or economic revolution. Its leaders were moderate liberals who avoided referring to their success as a "revolution" but insisted on the use of the term "rebirth" to stress the continuity and not a break with the past.[3] With unification achieved, the new Italian state firmly squelched any popular uprisings which tried to extend the rebirth to the social or economic domains. In response to the *Brigandage,* a peasant uprising in the south that tried to achieve land reform and social revolution, the new state acted ruthlessly to suppress it in a campaign that took more lives than did all the wars of the unification process.[4]

Constitutional Monarchy: The Liberal Era (1870 to 1922)

The dominant role played by Piedmont in the unification process made it the master of the new Italian state. Italy thus inherited the Piedmontese Constitution of a limited monarchy. There was an elected parliament and a government headed by the prime minister, but the monarch retained important powers. The state was highly centralized with few concessions to the political and cultural peculiarities of the once individual states.

The new kingdom of Italy faced the formidable opposition of the Catholic Church. In 1864, Pope Pius IX had identified democracy as one of the world's worst evils. His hostility increased as the unification process had stripped the Pope of the last shreds of his secular power, leaving him only the few acres of Vatican City as his temporal power base. In response, he ordered loyal Catholics to abstain from voting or otherwise taking part in the new state. This doctrine of *non expedit* lasted formally until 1929 although some relaxation took place after 1904. But in the first forty years of Italian democracy, the Church withheld its support and urged its followers to do the same. Such ecclesiastical hostility to democracy was a serious impediment to its success in a country as religious and as Catholic as Italy.

The democratic content of the parliamentary government was limited. Only a small elite had made the revolution, and only a small portion of the population was allowed to participate in the new state. While parliament was elected, those allowed to vote made up only a small proportion of the adult population. Property, educational, and other restrictions limited the electorate in 1861 to only 2 percent of the population; in 1882, the eligible

FIGURE 16.1   Map of Italy.

electorate had expanded to 7 percent of the population; and as late as 1913, only 25 percent could vote.

It was only after the First World War that universal manhood suffrage was attained. At the same time, the Church began to relax its strictures against its members taking part in Italian politics. Citizen involvement in public affairs expanded so rapidly in the first two decades of the twentieth century that the political system was not prepared for the strain of this vast increase in participation. The established political parties were elitist clubs incapable of attracting the new voters. The mass-based Socialist party was eager to appeal to these new voters but its radical, revolutionary stance meant that Socialist voters were aligned against the system instead of being brought into constructive participatory roles. A new Catholic-oriented party, the Popular party, emerged and attracted a mass following. In the 1919 elections, the new system of proportional representation awarded these two parties more than half the seats in the Chamber of Deputies. The older political groupings, really loose gatherings of political notables without doctrine or organization, lost their dominant role and were pushed to the political sidelines by the new mass parties. The political cleavages between these parties and the personal rivalries among their contending leaders led to governmental instability and incompetence. The last moderate premier before Mussolini was a political nonentity chosen because other politicians were too jealous of each other's power to cooperate in an effective antifascist front. Thus, the democratic government remained paralyzed as the social and political climate became more tumultuous.

The Fascist State (1922 to 1943)

This participation explosion after World War I produced chaos. The Socialist party eschewed participation in any government while awaiting the inevitable workers' revolution. The Popular party lacked experienced politicians in parliament. Furthermore, its Catholic orientation prevented it from forging durable alliances with the staunchly anticlerical, traditional, politicians. Political turmoil and threatened Bolshevik coups in Italy, and elsewhere in Europe, added to a climate of uncertainty. In this setting of growing domestic and international crisis, Benito Mussolini's bombastic pledges to restore order and prevent revolution seemed appealing to many.[5] His fascist party rapidly mobilized tens of thousands of followers who were willing to engage in violence to disrupt the meetings of political rivals or to intimidate those who spoke out against him. The fascists thus contributed significantly to the collapse of public order and to the climate of revolutionary fear that they blamed on democracy.

The end of the Italian democracy came without a struggle. In October 1922, fascist squads began an insurrection. King Victor Emmanuel II spurned his government's decision to declare a state of emergency and use the army to quell the fascist revolt. Instead, he appointed Mussolini prime minister. The new leader, accompanied by his blackshirt-shirted party thugs, entered Rome in triumph. Mussolini then moved quickly to consolidate power. A fraudulent and violence-filled election delivered 65 percent of the vote to the fascists in 1924. Not content with this overwhelming majority, Mussolini's thugs brutally murdered the outspoken leader of the Socialist party. When Mussolini suspended meetings of the parliament, Socialist and Popular opposition deputies withdrew from the Chamber of Deputies, an act known as the Aventine secession, leaving Mussolini facing only a handful of submissive moderate opponents as he consolidated his authoritarian rule.

Mussolini coined the term totalitarian to describe his rule. But his ineptness, the inefficiency of his followers, and the continued resistance from autonomous parts of society prevented the achievement of the total social, economic, and political control suggested by the label. In comparison to the totalitarian dictatorships of Stalin and Hitler, the Italian fascist dictatorship was moderate if only out of ineptness. Mussolini's pompous behavior, his strutting posture, and his bungling should not result in underestimating his brutality.[6] He ruled openly admiring violence and willing to engage in atrocities against his own people and those of the countries he tried to incorporate into his new empire.

The Italian Republic
(1946 to the present)

Shortly after the Allied invasion of Italy in 1943, a palace coup led by King Victor Emmanuel II replaced Mussolini with Marshal Badoglio. The new government quickly arranged an armistice and joined the Allied powers in the war against Hitler. Germany reacted by occupying most of Italy and installing a puppet regime headed by Mussolini. There was an active resistance movement made up of Communists, Christian Democrats, and others that challenged first, domestic fascism and then, the Germans. It was these resistance forces, including the Communists, who joined in the provisional government that governed Italy at the end of World War II.[7]

King Victor Emmanuel's actions spared Italy the disgrace of a postwar occupation such as those installed in Germany, Austria, and Japan. But they did not save the monarchy. Once the war was over, a referendum was held on whether to maintain the monarchy or establish a republic. The monarch's role in bringing Mussolini to power and in his complicity through twenty years of fascist rule left a bad memory that was not dispelled by the old king's later effort in 1943 or even his abdication in favor of his son. Italians voted by a narrow majority to replace the constitutional monarchy with a new republican form of government. In 1947, a Constituent Assembly drafted the new Constitution and it took effect in January 1948. The Constitution provided new democratic controls that had been absent in the earlier constitution. But it failed to resolve the key problems that had discredited democracy in the early 1920s: the fractious disputes of the parties and their inability to join in durable coalitions to support effective executives. The resulting disorderly democracy has led many to wonder about its ability to survive. But forty years later, it appears that

Italian democracy has achieved a certain degree of stability and durability in spite of its inherent destabilizing elements.

LEGACIES OF THE PAST

One of the important features of modern Italy has been the absorption of successive generations of outsiders and subversives into a moderate political entity with the sole exception of the fascists.[8] The four political patterns experienced by Italy over the past 125 years have been the patchwork of small client states before unification, a constitutional monarchy, a fascist dictatorship, and finally, a sometimes troubled parliamentary republic. Despite the often dramatic differences between these regimes, there are certain continuities that provide an important historical legacy to contemporary Italian politicians as they seek to respond to today's challenges.

Centralization

As unification was achieved in the 1860s, the masters of the new Italian state imposed a highly centralized political framework. Instead of the federalism adopted by those who united Germany, the Italian leaders opted for the Bonapartist pattern of centralized rule. For centuries, the people of Italy lived along side each other and called themselves Italians but they "were almost as different as inhabitants of foreign countries."[9] The process of integrating these people into a single nation, something accomplished elsewhere in Europe centuries earlier, required a strong, hierarchical state. The leaders feared a possible revival of the petty disputes and provincial loyalties of the old separate Italian states if there was not a firm, central control.

To prevent any return to the fragmented pattern of the past, one of the first steps was to divide Italy up into new political units. Just as revolutionary France had done in the 1790s, the Italian government ignored the traditional boundaries and created new and often arbitrary provinces that bore little relationship to the preexisting autonomous principalities and states. Each of the ninety-odd provinces was dominated by a powerful prefect whose loyalty was to the central government.

Besides the fear of the disintegration of the newly unified Italy, there were other reasons for the extreme centralization. The avowed opposition of the Catholic Church posed a major threat to the new regime that could only be confronted by a unified and coherent response. In the South, centralization was needed to counter the influence of traditional forces which remained skeptical of the union. Finally, the political changes had encouraged those advocating social revolution and the *Risorgimento* leaders wanted none of that. The centralized state was a weapon to assure that revolutionary movements were squelched throughout the land.

The fascist regime made no effort to break down the centralized state it inherited. Indeed, the extreme centralization was well suited to

Mussolini's plans to build a totalitarian state. Only after the Second World War, with the new republican Constitution, was there a commitment to decentralize the state. This commitment went unfulfilled for nearly thirty years before the promised regions were created. Still, many of the key elements of a centralized state remained. Thus, in contrast to the decentralization of police powers and education in West Germany, the Italian Republic retained control over the police and public schools at the center.

Oligarchic Rule

In Italy there has been continuity in the limited role accorded to the general citizens under both democratic and authoritarian regimes. Both ventures in democratic government resulted from "revolts from the top" rather than from genuine popular mass movements. The *Risorgimento* was a movement of the educated middle class with little mass following among the peasants or working class. Once in power, the heirs of the *Risorgimento* regarded the common classes as dangerous and as unworthy to participate in democratic politics. They were seen as easily manipulated by traditional forces hostile to the new regime, notably the Church. Or, the new rulers of Italy feared that the commoners would be attracted to the revolutionary movements, that also endangered the regime. Thus, the right to vote was highly restricted until after the First World War.

The end of fascism came by royal decree rather than by a mass uprising. The resistance movement was successful in attracting a fair percentage of workers to its ranks, but it remained a middle-class and intellectual movement. The conspiratorial nature of the resistance movement was elitist and secretive by necessity. While the social base of the resistance movement was broader than earlier Italian political elites in that many resistance workers were drawn from the working class as well as the usual middle class, its small size and clandestine nature made it elitist.

With this persistent tendency to restrict political control to a narrow elite, Italian democracy was characterized by its elitist nature and by the modest role allowed the average citizen. With such an orientation, it is not surprising that so many of the critics of democratic oligarchy and elitism are Italians: Roberto Michels, Viltredo Pareto, and Gaetano Mosca, all of whom criticized how easily narrow elites dominated democracies. The distance of the people from the democratic political system produced a setting of "unrelieved political alienation and of social isolation and distrust" among Italians in the late 1950s.[10] Despite such oligarchical tendencies, Italians are very much involved in politics, although in forms not common in other European democracies.

Absence of Social Revolution

The *Risorgimento* leaders sought political change by unifying Italy but, with few exceptions, they were dedicated to avoiding revolution in a broader sense. They believed such sweeping changes might disrupt the existing social and economic structures which were generally accepted by the liberal reformers of the nineteenth century. The few revolutionary leaders of this era were soon won over to a more conservative stance or shunted off to the sidelines. When the prospects of social revolution became threatening again after World War I, fascism won supporters as staunch enemies of revolution. The fascist era was a counterrevolution against a revolution that had never taken place. In the postwar era, the promises of far-reaching social reform of the resistance movement were soon forgotten in the struggle to reestablish Italian unity and integrity after the fascist debacle. The monarchy was eliminated but other traditional social and economic forms went unchallenged.

Without dramatic social change, Italian democracy was forced to operate with an antiquated system of land tenure in much of Italy that produced discontent in the large peasant population. Feudal structures had given way to a rural, bourgeois, propertied, elite of absentee landowners. The peasants had no land or very small plots of their own and suffered under inequitable sharecrop arrangements with the wealthy. Industrial workers felt oppressed by their employers and were tempted to turn to unions and parties that advocated entirely different economic structures. The nation's wealth was distributed inequitably with a small elite enjoying great wealth while the mass of the population experienced poverty. The Church retained a powerful and conservative political and social influence barring the creation of a modern secular society. In the forty years of republican government, some of these problems have been addressed in a gradual and piecemeal manner. But the absence of a reformed society and economy continues to pose challenges for the political system.

Uneven Development: The Problem of the South

The unification of Italy forced northerners for the first time to come to grips with the poverty of the South or the Mezzogiorno, essentially all of Italy south of Rome. Northerners seemed genuinely surprised at the extent of suffering in the South and compared it to the conditions of the African territories that were about to be carved up into colonies by Italy's neighbors. A special fund for the development of the South was soon established. But its success was hindered by political control of the funds. Politicians used the money more to assure their political futures by rewarding their supporters than to resolve any problems. In addition, heavy taxes were imposed on all Italy but their overall effect was to draw funds out of the South to support industrialization in the North.

The gap between the industrialized, relatively affluent North and the rural, poverty-stricken South has actually grown as the South has modernized but has not developed.[11] Ambitious plans for the industrialization of the South did bring some new factories but not economic development. Isolated from major markets and labor sources, the new plants became "cathedrals in the desert" and often eventually failed. One celebrated failure was the decade long effort to build a steel plant in Calabria during the 1970s, a time when Italian steel plants were already operating at only

65% capacity because of low demand. The new plant cost tens of millions of dollars and destroyed the relatively prosperous farms on its site. By 1979, the plant was closed never having reached its potential production and never having turned a profit.

The disparity between the North and the South remains striking. For example, in 1975 the average income per inhabitant in the South was only 56 percent of the national average for Italy as a whole.[12] In the mid-1980s, the per capita gross domestic product in the South was 7.4 million lira compared to 12.6 million lira in the more prosperous North and Center; unemployment in the South was twice the national figure. By every measure of the standard of living—energy use, number of cars, television sets, level of education, infant mortality—the South remains sharply worse off than the rest of the nation.

Economic and social structures in the South fostered the development of particularly strong patron-client relationships. The limited size of the electorate and the absence of clearly differentiated political parties between the time of unification and the First World War produced clientelistic politics. Politicians exchanged political favors in the forms of government jobs, contracts, subsidies, and even pensions for political support. They built extensive followings (or clienteles) through such distribution of state funds. While widespread in all parts of Italy, clientelism was especially strong in the South and it has remained so. As the electorate expanded and mass-based political parties grew in the South, especially the Christian Democratic party, local notables became key agents who gathered votes for their deputies. In return, the deputies were accorded state benefits to distribute to those who had helped gather the votes. Clientelism remains a key political feature of the South. Out of these powerful political machines have emerged politicians who have gone on to important national positions. Indeed, while northerners generally predominate in business, southerners make up a disproportionate share of government officials.

ITALY IN THE 1980s

As significant as these legacies are, Italy has experienced important social and economic changes in the last two decades. Without the brutal break with the past that revolutions often necessitate, a series of changes are occurring that may reshape the legacy that today's Italy passes on to the future. Clearly, the social and economic setting, both the elements of continuity and the elements of change, have important political consequences.

Cultural Homogeneity

Despite its lack of a centrally unified existence in the past, Italy is a remarkably homogeneous country. While there are some regional dialects and cultural differences, there are very few indications of separate ethnic identities. Thus, Italy has been spared the revival of ethnic awareness that occurred in France and Britain among even well-integrated groups. There is a small German-speaking Tyrolese population in Alto Adige (along the Austrian border). There has been some violence between South Tyroleans and Italians but the ethnic conflict is far less by comparison than the problems encountered by the British and the French. On the island of Sardinia, a party advocating greater autonomy took 14 percent of the vote in the 1984 regional elections. But the reasons seem to be more related to Sardinia's economic problems than to important separatist sentiments. There is no other national identity to challenge the dominant identification as Italian. From the religious perspective, Italians are solidly Roman Catholic with only 50,000 Protestants and even fewer Jews in a population of 60 million. Thus, Italy is "one of the most homogeneous countries of Europe."[13]

From the end of the war until the end of the 1970s, Italy was a major "exporter" of workers with many Italians finding employment in France, Germany, and elsewhere in Western Europe. Indeed, emigration has been a traditional Italian response to poverty. Between 1861 and 1975, approximately 29 million people emigrated with nearly 20 million later returning to Italy for a net loss of 9 million permanent emigrants.[14] In recent years, Italy has begun to receive a number of foreign immigrants, although nowhere near as important a flow as elsewhere in Western Europe. In 1986, there were an estimated 1 million foreigners living in Italy, which included some 4 hundred thousand with work permits and at least an additional 2 hundred thousand illegal immigrant workers.

Many of these illegal aliens are Arabs and their presence provokes fear stemming from the growing incidence of international terror in Italy by Middle Easterners. Anti-Arab graffiti have started to appear along with acts of intolerance and a few violent attacks on Arabs. But the problems in Italy are not as severe compared to the racial tensions that have come to plague Britain, France, and West Germany in the last decade.

Church and State in Politics

The absence of different religions in Italy has not eliminated religious conflict as an important source of political cleavage. From the Renaissance on, and especially after the French Revolution, Italy has faced a conflict between pious Catholics and nonpracticing Catholics over the influence of the church in secular and political matters. Anticlericals played the major roles in the *Risorgimento,* and the battle to unify Italy meant a direct and sometimes military confrontation with papal forces. The Church reacted with opposition to the new Italian state that was not formally lifted until Pope Pius XI negotiated the Lateran Treaty and the Concordat with Mussolini in 1929. The treaty gave the pope secular control of Vatican City, and the pope in exchange renounced his old claims to a much broader territorial sovereignty. The Concordat resolved a series of social issues of interest to the Catholic hierarchy: Church preeminence in marriage law (with papal annulments the only way to dissolve a marriage bond), recognition of Church property, legalization of religious associations, and an important role for the Church in education. it also provided for state subsidization of the maintenance of Church buildings and state salaries for the clergy.

After the Second World War, the new Constitution declared Roman Catholicism to be the only official religion. The Concordat, negotiated by Mussolini, remained the basis for relations between the Italian Republic and the Church for forty years. The Church gained additional political power through the influence that it had in the Christian Democratic party (DC). It encouraged loyal Catholics to support the DC, openly in early years, more subtly in recent years. It intervened frequently in DC party matters to influence policy positions and the selection of leaders. It also spoke out directly in attempting to influence legislative programs that overlapped with its social interests in: education, divorce law, birth control laws, and abortion. With nearly half the Italian population still regularly practicing their Catholic religion (only one fourth of French Catholics still practice their religion regularly), the Church was able to play an important role in postwar Italian politics.

This role has declined over the past fifteen years. The Church's influence is waning as the number of Italians who are faithful Catholics is dropping. Even among those who continue to practice regularly, there is a growing disposition to make political choices independent of the Church's directions. This independence was shown in two recent referendums involving issues on which the Church had intervened. In 1974, only 40 percent of Italians voted to repeal a divorce law the way the Vatican urged; in 1981, the Church found only 30 percent willing to join it in trying to overturn a liberalized abortion law. These campaigns by the Church also damaged its influence in the DC. Many DC deputies in parliament had joined in voting for the 1970 divorce law only to be forced by Vatican pressure into opposing it in the 1974 referendum. The defeat left the DC in an awkward position and built resentment within the party toward Church influence. The 1981 defeat on abortion was even more damaging and reinforced the position of those within the party who favored greater distance from the Church. The selection of a non-Italian as pope for the first time in modern history was another element diminishing the political role of the Church.

The growing secular trend was confirmed by a rewriting of the Concordat. The delicate negotiations between the Vatican and the Italian government took about nineteen years before its enactment in 1985. Under the new Concordat, Catholicism ceased to be the official state religion. Catholic religious instruction is no longer mandatory in public schools, but it is still the only religion enjoying the right to teach its precepts to public education pupils on a released time basis during the school day. Church annulments of marriages must now have state approval to be valid divorces. The system of state subsidies for the salaries of the clergy (amounting to $183 million in 1983) will be gradually suppressed, but the state will continue to provide tax funds to maintain churches open to the general public and citizens will be able to direct a portion of their income tax to the Church. Simultaneously with these political agreements, two major financial scandals involving Vatican City banks that were closely linked with the Church brought a concession from the Vatican to place these banks under the financial and legal surveillance of the government of Italy.[15]

Taken together, the provisions of the revised Concordat and the assertion of state control over Vatican banks, represent major victories for the further secularization of the Italian state. The implementation of change can produce tensions such as those that almost toppled the coalition government of Giovanni Goria in October 1987. When the Goria government proposed scheduling religious classes at the beginning or the end of the school day, the Vatican objected. Church leaders realized that most children would skip the optional religious classes if the choice was to go home or to attend the religious class. They forced the Goria government to revise the legislation requiring students who chose not to participate in religious classes to attend some other alternative course. Some government coalition supporters in parliament, angered by the Church's intervention and by Goria's acquiescence, threatened at first to vote against the measure which endangered the government's survival. Eventually, the fall of the government was avoided when these deputies instead simply abstained.

The legal change in the status of the Church will have long-term effects but has not eliminated its political significance. In France, the formal separation of church and state was consummated in 1905 but religion still remains a significant political variable. As in France, there is a strong link between religious commitment and voting behavior. The stronger the individual's attachment to the Church, the more likely he or she will vote for the DC (See Table 16.1). Indeed, the Church has renewed its efforts in recent elections to make certain that its political and even partisan preferences are known by its loyal adherents.

Religious loyalty is of prime importance in understanding political divisions in contemporary Italy.[16] Such partisan associations are durable and unlikely to change soon. The Church shapes the attitudes and behavior

TABLE 16.1 Religious Commitment and Voting Behavior, 1985

Party preference according to religious practice

	Attend Mass Regularly	Never go to Mass
Far Left (PDUP)	0.4%	1.6%
Radical party	0.8	2.7
Communist party (PCI)	5.6	32.0
Socialist party (PSI)	13.9	13.3
Social Democratic party (PSDI)	0.4	1.0
Republican party (PRI)	5.0	5.1
Christian Democrats (DC)	36.8	13.6
Liberal party (PLI)	2.2	1.3
Neo-Fascists (MSI)	1.8	3.9

Source: Adapted from Frederic Spotts and Theodor Wieser, *Italy: A Difficult Democracy* (Cambridge, England: Cambridge University Press, 1986), p. 302.

of its large and loyal membership in Italy and thus, has a continuing indirect influence over politics. For example, the slowness of implementing the abortion reform has been due to the Vatican's barring faithful doctors and nurses from participating in abortions. While the Church's political influence will continue to decline, its remaining strength and its traditional presence will preserve its power in Italian politics for decades to come.

Social Class

As in other European countries, the postwar era in Italy has been a time of important shifts in social structures. Perhaps the most important change in Italian society was the dramatic reduction in the size of the farm population. In 1951, approximately 42 percent of the employed population was engaged in agriculture; thirty-five years later, only 10 percent were farmers. This striking change produced enormous dislocations as former peasants left the countryside and moved to industrial centers in search of jobs in industry and commerce. Much of this internal migration involved the movement of southern peasants to the industrial centers of the northwest.

The dislocations of this migration were eased by several factors. Economic growth and industrialization provided jobs in other economic sectors for the millions of Italians who left their farms. The European Community's farm programs assured the remaining farmers an adequate and growing income. Social security benefits and retirement programs were extended to cover independent farmers and agricultural workers.

Despite the dramatic population shift away from the farms, the nature of farm land tenure has changed remarkably little.[17] In northern Italy, there are large, mechanized farms and agribusinesses. In the South, farming is dominated by small landholders and sharecroppers working the fields for absentee landowners. Well over half the farms are smaller than 5 hectares (12 acres), but all these small farms together constitute only 16.5 percent of the cultivated land. This disparity reflects the continuation of old preunification patterns of agriculture and the absence of significant land reform. The European Community provided large amounts of aid for restructuring Italian agriculture but they were underutilized because of administrative inefficiency in Italy.[18]

Postwar economic development has changed Italy from a basically agricultural state into an industrial and service oriented society. One study, for example, suggested that the industrial working class expanded from 23 percent of the total labor force in 1951 to 33 percent in 1971.[19] Then in the 1970s and 1980s, the service occupations grew rapidly as traditional blue-collar employment declined. These changes in class structure and size have political consequences. They explain in part the gradual decline in electoral support for the Christian Democratic party which has had an important electoral base in the rural areas since the early 1950s. They help to account for the rise in electoral strength of the Communist party, which is particularly effective in urban industrial settings, through the end of the 1970s.

More important than the electoral shifts has been the social and political unrest associated with the dramatic socioeconomic transformations. The tensions reached a peak in the series of events called the Hot Autumn of 1969 that triggered student and industrial conflict that continued through the next decade. Italy's Hot Autumn paralleled the Events of May 1968 in France. Student activism spilled over into broad challenges, by larger groups of the population, to the social and economic status quo.[20] The Hot Autumn lacked the drama and concentrated effect of the Events of May. But it did bring a sense of prolonged social crisis and fostered the terrorism that pervaded Italy during the 1970s.

Student discontent with the universities and the American war in Vietnam spilled over into a much more sweeping indictment of postwar Italian society. Higher education had become available to a broad new section of the population, but university students found its facilities inadequate for their growing numbers. They found job opportunities for graduates limited. Student radicals tried, with greater success than in France, to link up their grievances with those of the working class. The student uprising and the example of French workers provoked greater worker discontent. Young workers in factories, urged on by the radical students, became more assertive. They ignored traditional trade union channels to press demands for wage and other benefits, and protested in spontaneous and difficult to control strikes. They claimed a greater share of Italy's postwar prosperity should go to the workers who made that economic growth possible. The absence of social and economic reforms created a climate of growing social agitation. The spurts and sputters of the Italian economy during the 1970s added a sense of economic uncertainty to the unrest. The unions lost control of the situation as wildcat strikes and work stoppages led by student-worker committees disrupted industry.

Eventually, the unions responded by accepting the new demands and leading their own strike movements. The new militant stand gained the trade union movement many new members. The percentage of the eligible work force belonging to unions rose from 33.5 percent in 1968 to 50.7 percent in 1979.[21] Italian workers had long financed the country's rapid economic growth by working for substantially lower wages than their counterparts elsewhere in Europe. Lower wages had permitted Italian manufactured goods to capture large markets in Europe but at the expense of the underpaid workers. The consequences of worker dissatisfaction and the Hot Autumn were a series of militant strikes during much of the 1970s. Throughout the decade, Italy led the nine European Community countries in terms of days lost through work stoppages. Italy alone accounted for over 54 percent of all the days lost in strikes in 1973 and 45 percent in 1974.[22] The labor situation was the worst that Italy had experienced since 1920. There were more strike incidents, longer strikes, and more diffuse and radical demands than at any time since the end of the Second World War.

Given these tensions, what was surprising was that the crisis was not more extensive than it was. In fact, social class tensions gradually relaxed by the end of the 1970s. Order was slowly restored as employers made major wage concessions. The labor scene returned to peace; indeed, the early 1980s marked a period of exceptional calm in worker/management relations with fewer strikes and fewer days lost due to labor unrest. There were five reasons for this. First, the working class decreased in size as more people found jobs in the service sector, which usually afforded them more prestige if not always higher salaries. Second, the economy entered a new era of growth in the 1980s. Overall, postwar economic prosperity has brought benefits to all social categories. Italians from all classes have a better standard of living at the end of the 1980s than any of their parents would have dared to dream of thirty years ago. Nearly all Italians now have access to goods that once were restricted to the elite. For example, there is a private automobile for every three Italians and a vast system of superhighways second only to Germany's, a television set for every four people, and a telephone for every two and one half people. With the availability and affordability of such consumer goods, the sense of deprivation among lower classes has diminished. Third, the poorest Italians tend to be the small farmers and farm workers in the South. They are strongly attached to traditional values and are not readily mobilized despite their deprived status. Fourth, broad public repugnance at the terrorist excesses of those advocating radical social change have led to more moderate attitudes and greater self-discipline. Finally, the political elites avoid fomenting class conflict. The moderation of the Italian Communist party (PCI) is particularly striking in this regard. In contrast to the French Communists' continued efforts to stir up class awareness through the use of class-conflict rhetoric, the Italian Communists have moderated their stance and have generally avoided using traditional class conflict-themes.

The turbulence of 1969 to 1978 has had a lasting impact on Italian politics. In the 1970s, the spirit of the Hot Autumn prodded politicians into making a number of long delayed, progressive reforms in labor relations laws, in wage indexation linked with inflation, and in social matters such as divorce and women's rights. A more sinister consequence of the Hot Autumn was the emergence of leftwing terrorists. Some of the student and young worker radicals rejected the reformist aftermath of the Hot Autumn and turned to violence to bring the revolution that they felt was essential to real change.

While class tensions did stir unrest, class lines are not reflected in the party system. The relatively low salience of class in partisan matters is shown by the social class background of party supporters (see Table 16.2). Instead of serving as voices for a particular social class, each of the major parties draws its support from a broad range of social classes. The alignment between classes and parties is not a direct one. Table 16.3 shows how each class divides its vote among several parties. Both the Christian Democratic party and the Communist party have been successful in attracting voters from a wide range of socioeconomic backgrounds. Their broad support coming from many sections of Italian life makes them "catchall parties."

The working class divides its vote among several parties with religious commitment and membership in a leftist union the variables that determine

TABLE 16.2 Social Class of Party Supporters

	PCI	PSI	PSDI	PRI	DC	PLI	MSI
Big business	1%	1%	1%	9%	1%	8%	3%
Farmers	10	8	7	5	13	3	8
Shopkeepers & craftsmen	8	10	19	16	7	17	17
White collar workers	11	14	–0–	23	9	17	17
Workers	35	26	15	7	10	5	14
Housewives	23	22	34	21	35	29	18
Retired	15	18	17	13	23	19	18
Students	4	2	5	6	2	2	5

Source: Adapted from Paolo Farneti, *The Italian Party System (1945–1980).* (New York: St. Martin's Press, 1985), pp. 92–93.

TABLE 16.3 Voting Preference of Italians by Socioeconomic Background

Percent of industrial workers' vote

	Far Left	PCI	PSI	PSDI	PRI	DC	PLI	MSI
Farm workers	5%	21%	21%		1%	48%	3%	1%
Farmers	8	19	15		—	54	3	1
Employers and small business	2	19	17	4	7	44	3	4
White collar workers	9	22	22	5	7	30	3	2
Industrial workers	5	45	19	2	3	25	—	1
Housewives	1	24	5	14	2	49	2	3

Source: Adapted from Paolo Farneti, *The Italian Party System (1945–1980),* (New York: St. Martin's Press, 1985), p. 98. (All figures are for 1978 except for 1968 figures for farmers and farm workers. In 1968, the PSI and PSDI were combined in a single party.

specific party choices (See Table 16.3).[23] Workers who are loyal Catholics tend to vote for the DC or other moderate parties. Nonreligious workers who have joined the communist-influenced General Confederation of Italian Labor (CGIL) vote for the PCI and those with few Church ties and who have avoided the CGIL vote for the PSI or PSDI. Similar divisions exist in each sociooccupational category with the two major parties, the DC and the PCI drawing broad-based support across class lines.

ECONOMICS AND POLITICS

During the first three decades after World War II, Italy experienced very rapid economic change. The predominantly agricultural economy was transformed into a modern economy with large industrial and service sectors. The Italian rate of economic growth as measured by gross national product was among the highest in Western Europe through the 1970s. This rapid growth was somewhat offset by the difficulty in controlling inflation. And while Italy's rate of growth was often substantially higher than its major European economic partners, its starting point was so much lower than most other European countries that it still lagged considerably behind all these other countries.

Italy was one of the founding members of the European Economic Community. The European Common Market provided important benefits for Italy, especially during its early years. Italy's lower labor costs gave it a trade advantage on many industrial goods once tariffs were eliminated. Thus, its exports more than doubled between 1963 and 1969. But Italy was a net importer of food products, and the EEC Common Agricultural Policy brought higher prices for food products purchased from France, Germany, and the Netherlands as the Community's farm programs took effect at the end of the 1960s. Higher food prices fueled Italian inflation. Then the industrial edge enjoyed by Italy began to slip due to improved industrial wages and the declining markets for the consumer goods of medium-level technology, where Italy excelled, and the growing market for high-technology goods, where Italy was weak.

Such trends began to affect the Italian economy in the 1970s. The effects of the first oil crisis were also damaging as shown by Italy's negative GNP growth rate in 1975. It was the first decline since the postwar economic recovery had begun. The 1970s continued as a time of economic difficulty with very high inflation, serious unemployment, growing government deficits, a weak lire, and trade imbalances. These problems followed Italy into the 1980s.

Among the problems was a lag in industrial growth. The Italian economy did well in absorbing the millions of rural migrants who left the countryside to seek jobs in the urban industrial centers. But many of these workers found jobs in the less productive service sector rather than in industry where more economic expansion might be expected from the increased employment (See Figure 16.2). Instead, the results were the growth of a large, inefficient bureaucracy and overemployment in commercial and distributive firms leading to higher consumer prices.

The state has played a major economic role in postwar Italy. Much of its role has been enacted through the Institute for Industrial Reconstruction (IRI). Originally founded by Mussolini in 1933 as a structure to assist Italian banks recovering from the Great Depression, the IRI has become a giant conglomerate linking about a thousand publicly owned enterprises and over half a million employees together.[24] It controls banks, airlines, communications firms, steel manufacturers, engineering firms, food processors, highway builders and the vast network of toll roads, shipping, and ship builders. Unlike the recent moves to sell off public enterprises in Britain and France, the popularity and success of the IRI has limited Italian interest in privatization. There are three other large state-owned holding companies of which the most important is ENI, the National Corporation for Hydrocarbons. ENI controls the state petroleum company, much of the country's chemical industries, and nuclear energy industries.[25] Together, the four state conglomerates account for a third of all sales and one half of all investment.[26] Through their large involvement they offer

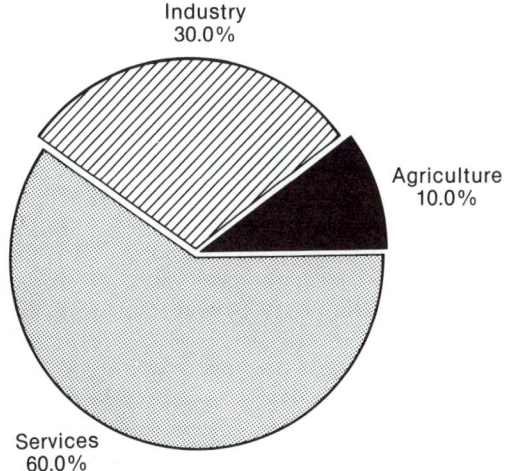

FIGURE 16.2 Employment by Economic Sector in Italy. *Source: The World Almanac and Book of Facts* (New York: World Almanac, 1988).

the state a means of exerting guidance over the entire economy. Top executives in these giant firms usually have close ties with the Christian Democratic party. However, the independence of both the IRI and the ENI in making economic decisions has meant that government and parliament have not always been able to exercise these economic tools in the way politicians have wanted to.

The reconstruction and modernization of the Italian economy was not accompanied by changes in political patterns. The strong clientelistic relationship that remains between politicians and their supporters is much more typical of a less-developed economy. The exchange of government contracts, subsidies, and other benefits for political support continues to characterize Italian politics and economics. It leads to inefficient use of public resources. Often ambitious and creative plans for economic growth are thwarted as politicians distribute the needed funds according to political considerations (coming from traditional clientelistic obligations) rather than to calculations of which firms or regions would be most able to profit from the government's assistance. Given the persistence of such practices, the economic successes of the postwar era are a tribute to the hard-working nature of the Italian people.

It is necessary, once again, to bring up the inequities in the pattern of economic development. This uneven development has produced a dualism with several dimensions.[27] First, there is the regional dualism between the industrial-developed North and the underdeveloped South. Second, there is the dualism between the part of the economy based on modern, advanced, and productive industry and the part of the economy still rooted in traditional and inefficient activities. Third, there is a dualism in the labor market between those in secure and well-paid jobs and those finding work in marginal and poorly paid jobs. Such dualism can be found in other countries, notably there is a similar pattern in Britain. But in Italy the pattern of uneven development is more pronounced and long-lasting than in any other European country.

It is more than uneven development that besets modern Italy. Italy is facing the same modern challenges as are other Western European countries: the restructuring and modernization of aging heavy industries, promotion of new high-technology industries, financing the costs of popular but expensive social-welfare programs, inflation, and protection of the value of their currencies. The special challenge in Italy is it has to face these problems in a more volatile political setting than is found elsewhere. Extreme fragmentation of the party system, shifting coalitions, and transitory governments all contribute to a less than predictable political framework for meeting new social and economic challenges. Given this uncertain political, economic, and social heritage and the fragility of the Italian state, the endurance of its political unit is surprising. How it survives despite these handicaps will be useful in understanding the underlying strength of contemporary European democracy.

NOTES

1. Clara M. Lovett, *The Democratic Movement in Italy 1830–1876* (Cambridge, MA: Harvard University Press, 1982).
2. Denis Mack Smith, *Cavour* (New York: Knopf, 1985).
3. Lovett, *The Democratic Movement in Italy*, p. 1.
4. Denis Mack Smith, *Italy: A Modern History* (Ann Arbor, MI: University of Michigan Press, 1969), pp. 40–42, 69–75.
5. Christopher Seton-Watson, *Italy From Liberalism to Fascism* (London: Meuthen, 1967) and Adrian Lyttleton, *The Seizure of Power: Fascism in Italy 1918–1929* (London: Weidenfeld and Nicolson, 1973).
6. On Mussolini's life and rule, see Denis Mack Smith, *Mussolini* (New York: Vintage, 1983).
7. On the founding of the postwar regime, see Norman Kogan, *Italy and the Allies* (Westport, CT: Greenwood Press, 1982).
8. Martin Clark, *Modern Italy: 1871–1982* (New York and London: Longman, 1984).
9. Luigi Barzini, *The Europeans* (Harmondsworth, England: Penguin, 1984), p. 181.
10. Gabriel A. Almond and Sidney Verba, *The Civic Culture: Political Attitudes and Democracy in Five Nations* (Princeton, NJ: Princeton University Press, 1963), p. 402.
11. Judith Chubb, *Patronage, Power, and Poverty in Southern Italy* (Cambridge, England: Cambridge University Press, 1982), pp. 28–33.
12. Jacques Bethemont and Jean Pelletier, *Italy: A Geographical Introduction* (London: Longman, 1983), p. 105.
13. H. Stuart Hughes, *The United States and Italy*, 3rd ed., (Cambridge, MA: Harvard University Press, 1979), p. 28.
14. Bethemont and Pelletier, *Italy: A Geographical Introduction*, p. 41.
15. Frederic Spotts and Theodore Wieser, *Italy: A Difficult Democracy* (Cambridge, England: Cambridge University Press, 1986), pp. 251–252.

16. See Samuel H. Barnes, "Italy: Religion and Class in Electoral Behavior," in Richard Rose, ed., *Electoral Behavior: A Comparative Handbook* (New York: The Free Press, 1974), pp. 208–210.
17. Bethemont and Pelletier, *Italy: A Geographical Introduction*, pp. 68–71.
18. Norman Kogan, *A Political History of Postwar Italy: From the Old to the New Center-Left* (New York: Praeger, 1981), p. 23.
19. Paolo Sylos Labini, *Saggio sulle classi sociali* (Rome: Laterza, 1974). For an English summary of the controversy about these statistics, see Donald Sassoon, *Contemporary Italy: Politics, Economy and Society since 1945* (New York and London: Longman, 1986), pp. 90–94.
20. See Michele Salavati, "May 1968 and the Hot Autumn of 1969: The Responses of Two Ruling Classes," in Suzanne Berger, ed., *Organizing Interests in Western Europe: Pluralism, Corporatism, and the Transformation of Politics* (Cambridge, England: Cambridge University Press, 1981).
21. Jean-Pierre Dumont, "Les Syndicats: une crise de croissance," in Le Monde, *Economie italienne sans miracle* (Paris: Economica, 1980), p. 172.
22. Guiseppe di Palma, *Surviving Without Governing: The Italian Parties in Parliament* (Berkeley, CA: University of California Press, 1977), p. xi.
23. Barnes, "Religion and Class in Electoral Behavior," pp. 210–218.
24. Stuart Holland, ed., *The State as Entrepreneur: New Dimension for Public Enterprise, The IRI State Shareholding Formula* (London: Weidenfeld and Nicolson, 1972).
25. Charles R. Dechert, *Ente Nazionale Idrocarburi: Profile of a State Corporation* (Leiden, the Netherlands: E.J. Brill, 1963) and Dow Votaw, *The Six-Legged Dog: Mattei and ENI* (Berkeley, CA: University of California Press, 1964).
26. Spotts and Weiser, *Italy: A Difficult Democracy*, p. 130.
27. Vittorio Valli, *L'Economia e la politica economica italiana (1945–1979)* (Milan, Italy: Etas Libri, 1979).

CHAPTER SEVENTEEN
CITIZENS
AND POLITICS
IN ITALY

> Is there any other country in Europe where the character of the people seems to have been so little changed by political and technological change?
> W. H. Auden

The contemporary poet, W. H. Auden, penned these words in an introduction to a new edition of Goethe's *Italian Journey*. He notes the striking continuity between attitudes of mid–twentieth-century Italians and those of early nineteenth-century Italians. Despite the impact of the *Risorgimento*, the rise and fall of a would-be totalitarian dictator, and the establishment of the postwar republic, the people have remained little changed. This continuity in Italian political culture—attitudes, values, and orientations about politics—poses a problem for democracy. Over twenty-five years ago, an important study of democratic political cultures concluded that the Italian political culture was "one of unrelieved political alienation and of social isolation and distrust."[1] So troubling were the Italian attitudes that observers maintained grave doubts about the ability of democracy to long survive in such an inhospitable political culture.

The passing years do not seem to have brought any dramatic changes in the civic attitudes of Italians.[2] The Italians have generally been negative in their evaluations of the state of democracy in their country. The dissatisfaction has remained a constant over the last dozen years despite the rise and fall of terrorism and the changing of governments. In this high level of dissatisfaction with democracy, Italians are strikingly different from other Europeans (See Table 17.1). Whereas the overwhelming majority of Italians have consistently declared themselves to be dissatisfied with their democracy, in every other Western European country the percentage satisfied with democracy has exceeded that of those dissatisfied with only rare and temporary exceptions.

The stability of this public disapproval through both bad and good times suggests that there may be other causes for the Italians' negative assessment of their government than governmental performance. Perhaps part of the explanation of the poor comparison of Italian views of democracy to that of other Europeans is due to a tendency to report negative evaluations of life in general. In fact, Italy also ranks lowest among Europeans with regard to their reported evaluations of satisfaction with life in general. The Italians' long experience with bad government that stretches back many centuries is also likely part of the explanation for their disapproval of the current government. It has left "a century-old ineradicable suspicion and mistrust of all governments, laws, regulations, and official authorities."[3] In addition, Italians demonstrate a basic mistrust of other people, whether in government or not. An often-used Italian proverb runs: *Fidarsi è bene, non fidarsi è meglio,* (To trust is good; not to trust is better). This general mistrust of each other spills over into their evaluation of those who run the government and of the institutions themselves. In the last analysis, though, much of the blame for the low level of support for Italian democracy is found in its real failings.

> In brief, the citizenry is not paranoic or unduly pessimistic. The political discourse *is* byzantine and almost incomprehensible to the uninitiated; the burden of taxation *is* poorly distributed; the bureaucracy *is* inefficient; the squandering of public monies *has* occurred, and so on.[4]

Political actions often reflect these skeptical and hostile attitudes towards politics and politicians. A long history of living under the yoke of foreign control has left a legacy of silent resistance to public officials.

TABLE 17.1 Satisfaction with Democracy in Italy

	Very Satisfied	Satisfied	Dissatisfied	Very Dissatisfied	Don't Know
1973					
Italy	2%	25%	42%	30%	1%
European Community	5	36	37	18	4
1985					
Italy	2	23	45	27	3
European Community	8	42	31	14	5

Source: Eurobarometer, No. 23 (June 1985): 6. The question was: "On the whole, are you very satisfied, satisfied, dissatisfied, or very dissatisfied with the way democracy works in your country?" European Community figure is a weighted average for the 10–11 member countries, including Italy.

As in France, a strong sense of individualism sometimes leads to undiscipline and disregard for the rights of others. Italian drivers, for example, are reputed for their often reckless failure to observe traffic regulations. While Britons and Germans line up in an orderly fashion when waiting their turns, Italians mill around and maneuver to edge ahead of others.

The growing expectations people place on government have increased causes for this silent resistance and discontent in Italy. Many of the government activities that are regarded by Italians as most important are those that they also believe that the government handles poorly. For examples: A poll in the mid-1970s found that 78 percent felt the government had a great responsibility in assuring jobs for all but only 18 percent thought the government was doing an adequate job; eighty-three percent identified crime prevention as another area of major government responsibility with only 13 percent evaluating the government's actual performance as positive; And 81 percent thought the government had a major responsibility in controlling inflation but only 7 percent thought it did that job well.[5] It appears that the changing society is bringing new expectations that the government is unable to meet.

There is reason to believe that the publicly expressed hostility to the political scene reflects a self-critical attitude characteristic of the Italian political culture. There is a general tendency on the part of Italians to be hypercritical in analyses of their country and its political system. They tend to be "less idealistic and more cynical than the citizens of other democracies, even the French."[6] Above all, they tend to be overly suspicious of their public institutions and their performance. For example, the poll cited above on government performance in various issue areas showed strong negative evaluations by Italians; most outside observers, however, would be much more generous in evaluating the performance of the Italian economy and law enforcement.

While the Italians have little pride in their political institutions, they are nonetheless proud of their country. With one poll showing 80 percent of the public proud of Italy, they exceed many countries whose people give a much more positive evaluation of their government (See Table 1.1, p. 25). This pride comes from their past history, their artistic contributions, and the physical beauty of their country rather than any great esteem for their political system. This national pride does counteract, in part, some of the dissatisfaction with the political world. But there is a danger in this gap between national pride and respect for the political system. In other countries, the gap has led citizens to draw a distinction between the virtuous "real" country and the corrupt existing state. Then there is the danger that citizens will withdraw support from the state which has betrayed the potential of the real country and turn to some alternative system that promises to achieve that potential.

Italians may draw this distinction but they have yet to indicate any propensity to turn to alternative political orders. Those favoring a radical break with the status quo are only marginally more numerous than in other countries (See Table 17.2). There are antisystem parties on both the far left and far right which promise alternative political systems but they have found little support in Italy. So strong has the current system become entrenched that even the Communist party has accepted the existing democratic system rather than insisting on its replacement by a new order. Thus, there is a paradox of a people who tell their pollsters they dislike the political system and then continue to vote for parties dedicated to it rather than for the antisystem parties.

The general lack of trust toward other people contrasts with the marked loyalty within the family. The Italian family remains strong despite the effects of important social changes which have elsewhere weakened the family. Thirty years ago, a sociologist described the ethics of a small southern Italian village as "amoral familism": a strong loyalty to family coupled with an absence of moral strictures on behavior in the community.[7] There is no reason to believe that amoral familism was typical of all Italian villages and certainly not all Italians. The importance of loyalty to family has been more important in Italy than elsewhere. But the Italian extended family, as family in most modern societies, is affected by the trend toward secular values.

The negative attitudes expressed by Italians toward the political system spill over to hostility toward politicians. Seventy-five percent of Italians believe that the parties are interested only in getting votes from the people, that "politicians are not very interested in what the average person thinks," and that over 85 percent agree that the people elected to parliament very quickly lose contact with the electors.[8]

The verbal dissatisfaction with the regime and its politicians are used by Italians to justify their manipulation of the system. Their strong individualism leads them to seek exceptions and loopholes in regulations. They make the system work through "quite creative accommodations."[9] In the process, they find themselves committed to the system that they verbally berate. Their professed disillusionment does not lead them to take the kinds of political action that would lead to a change in the regime. Even the vast majority of the discontented neither support antiregime parties

TABLE 17.2 Attitudes toward Changing Society

Country	Favor Radical Change	Favor Reform	Favor Defense of Status Quo	Don't Know
Britain	4%	66%	23%	7%
France	6	63	28	3
West Germany	3	52	37	8
Italy	8	62	25	5

The text of the question for this item reads:
On this card there are three basic kinds of attitudes vis-a-vis the society we live in. Please choose the one which best describes your own opinion:
1. The entire way our society is organized must be radically changed by revolutionary action. [Labelled here as advocates of radical change]
2. Our society must be gradually improved by reforms. [Advocates of gradual reform]
3. Our present society must be valiantly defended against all subversive forces. [Advocates of defending the status quo]
Source: Eurobarometer, No. 25 (June 1986): 17.

nor join revolutionary movements. Their deep-seated cynicism seems to incline them to accept the present political system with its evident faults rather than to support an alternative whose vices are unknown and might even be worse than the existing ones.

THE ITALIANS IN POLITICS

Improved education and urbanization since World War II have helped produce a more politically alert Italian citizenry. But there still remains an important part of the public with little or no political interest and knowledge. One scholar estimates that approximately a third of the adult population is unaware of any political information.[10] This uninformed section of the population is likely to shrink in coming years as improved education continues to bring greater political awareness.

The Italians that are politically aware are often pictured, and correctly so, as intensely partisan in their behavior. The number of Italian citizens having partisan loyalties, even among the young, is significantly greater than in other democratic countries: 72 percent (67 percent of those are under twenty-five years of age) identify with a particular party.[11] Partisan ties have deep supporting roots in the individual's peer group, family, and group associations. Even presumably nonpolitical groups have partisan ties with the major parties. Notably the Communists, Socialists, and Catholic-Christian Democrats sponsor their own women's associations, student groups, trade unions, sports clubs, and other mass organizations. At the local level, partisan considerations are often important in finding a public job, winning a government contract or subsidy, or even receiving social-welfare benefits.[12]

In effect, there is an elaborate set of distinctive political subcultures in Italy.[13] The three principal subcultures are the Catholic, the secular (now principally Socialist), and the Communist cultures. Each is rooted in a long history dating back to the early years of the Italian state with its battle between it and the church. Each subculture has extensive social, cultural, and political organizations that reach into all aspects of the individual's life. The auxiliary groups convey the party ideology into the other social organizations. Patronage and well-developed party machines bring material advantages to the faithful supporters of the party controlling politics at the local, regional, or national levels. The strength and influence of the various mass organizations linked with the subcultures vary. For example, the once powerful Catholic Action has been eclipsed by a newer organization, Communion and Liberation, in the Catholic subculture; the once powerful Communist youth movement has dwindled to a mere skeleton organization. What is significant is the persistence of such partisan bodies in Italy, while in other countries there is a trend away from party-linked mass organizations. These cultural roots tend to reinforce and perpetuate partisan loyalties. The strength of the Catholic, secular, and Communist subcultures insulate Italian parties from the electoral volatility of voters shifting their loyalties that has plagued and weakened parties in other countries.

Despite the depth and persistence of these different political subcultures, they are not reflected in the Left/Right distribution of Italians. As Figure 17.1 indicates, most Italians place themselves at or near the center of the political spectrum. The percentage of Italians placing themselves at the left end of the spectrum is slightly higher than in the other three countries that have been examined. What is surprising is that in a country where nearly one out of three voters support the Communist party, there is not a greater number of people who identify with the Far Left. The general pattern of Left/Right placement is quite similar to what we saw in Britain, France, and Germany.

The Citizen at the Polls

With such strong partisan ties, it is not surprising that Italy has one of the highest turn-out rates for national elections. The participation level is close to 90 percent for national elections (See Table 17.3). It is nearly as high in other elections, for example, the turnout for the 1985 regional and local elections was 88.9 percent. This unusually high rate of electoral participation leads some to speculate that Italians must believe that voting is required by law. But such legal incentives are not necessary for the high voting turnout. There has been some decline in turnout in the last few national elections. Rather than an indication of growing political alienation, most see less worrisome causes behind the slightly higher levels of those not voting. Part of the explanation is that the increased mobility leaves many newly moved or travelling citizens ineligible to vote since there is

FIGURE 17.1   The Self-Placement of Italian Voters on a Left/Right Spectrum. *Source: Jacques-René Rabier, Hélène Riffault, Ronald Inglehart, Eurobarometer 23: The European Currency Unit and Working Conditions, April 1985* (Ann Arbor, MI: Inter-University Consortium for Political and Social Research) 1986, pp. 81–82.

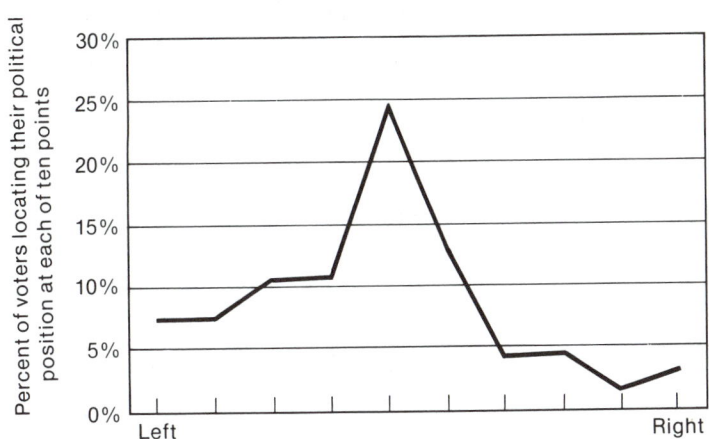

no absentee or no mail ballot. In addition, the larger number of new voters due to the enfranchisement of 18-year-olds in the mid-1970s has also reduced turn-out percentage numbers since these young citizens are the ones least likely to vote.

The electoral system used in Italy is the d'Hondt highest average version of proportional representation.[14] Since the districts are very large, electing as many as fifty deputies, the Italian system accurately reflects the political spectrum of the population: A party with 25 percent of the vote ends up with close to 25 percent of the parliamentary seats. There is no minimum threshold such as the 5 percent requirement in Germany. Even parties obtaining as few as 1 or 2 percent of the total vote still win representation in the Chamber of Deputies. Such a system encourages party fragmentation since a dissident party leader with even minimal support can threaten to form a new party and still hope to win reelection. Since proportional representation minimizes the impact of the slight variations in political support that are usually the case in Italy (and elsewhere), the electoral system complicates the process of bringing political change: It is always the same parties, each of which have gained or lost a handful of seats, which must form the government. Instead of deciding political issues, elections simply hand the issues back to the same politicians who try again to resolve them.

The electoral rules also specify that voters can express preference for specific candidates on the list they vote for in Chamber of Deputies elections. This permits voters to reorder the list of candidates established by the parties and to select individual candidates who were not highly ranked by the party. Everywhere, these preference votes are a means of factional infighting within the parties. In the South, preference voting is widespread as it is a part of the strong clientele relationships. One study suggests that preference voting may be a sign of the continued importance of personalism as a means of simplifying voting choices among relatively uninformed voters.[15] The large number of voters making candidate preferences is also due to factionalism in the DC as various factions draw upon their supporters and clients to enhance their candidate's chance of being elected. Approximately 30 percent of all Italian voters express a preference

TABLE 17.3 Voter Turnout in National Elections

Italy		Britain		France		Germany		United States	
1953	93.8%	1966	75.8%	1967	80.9%	1965	86.7%	1965	62.1%
1963	92.9	1970	71.5	1968	80.0	1969	86.7	1968	61.0
1972	93.2	1974	78.7	1973	80.9	1972	91.2	1972	54.5
1976	93.4	1974	72.8	1978	82.8	1976	91.0	1976	53.3
1979	90.6	1979	76.0	1981	70.4	1980	88.7	1980	52.6
1983	89.0	1983	72.6	1986	79.5	1983	89.1	1984	53.0
1987	88.8	1987	76.0	1988	65.8	1987	84.3	1988	50.0

Figures are for turnout in parliamentary elections, except for the United States where the figure is for presidential elections.

but it is especially important among DC voters, where 40 percent indicate a preferred candidate.[16]

The strength of party loyalties has meant fairly stable patterns of political power for the major parties over the years. However, there is some evidence of greater volatility among voters in recent elections with more Italians willing to shift their party loyalty from one election to the next. This fluidity appeared greatest in the 1970s and contributed to the growing strength of the Left.[17] Other studies suggest a growing readiness of Italian voters to reflect issue positions in their voting decisions.[18] But the general economic conditions that have come to play important roles in American, British, French, and German elections seem to have only a limited impact on Italian voters.[19] Overall, in comparison with other European countries, the Italian electorate seems much more stable due in large part to the strength of the subcultures underlying the party system.[20]

Direct Participation

The Hot Autumn of 1969 marked the beginning of new political activism for many Italians. No longer content to work through the established parties or their associated women's, student, or labor organizations, a small section of society begin to press for government attention through new forms of participation. There is growing acceptance of the right to join in a peaceful demonstration (75 percent approve of that) and a significant portion of the public claim to have taken part in at least one such protest (17 percent).[21] But most other unconventional forms of participation still have only marginal acceptance.

The visible nature of such political acts makes them seem more common than they in fact are. Less than half the population approve of even the modest act of signing a petition, with 10 percent claiming to have signed one. A third approve of building sit-ins, with 4 percent claiming to have participated in one. Blocking traffic is accepted by 14 percent, with 2 percent saying they had done so; and painting graffiti is approved by 6 percent and has been done by 2 percent. More extreme forms involving property damage and violence are overwhelmingly rejected by Italians as appropriate forms of political action.[22]

One new form of political action has played an important part in recent politics. The Constitution authorizes the holding of a national referendum whenever 500,000 citizens sign a petition calling for the repeal of a specific law passed by the Parliament. This contrasts with the French referendum procedure and the British advisory referendums since the Italian referendum procedure is invoked by the population. Also, it is used to abrogate existing legislation rather than to adopt a new law. The procedure went unused for nearly thirty years before the laws were implemented, in 1974, to make the use of the referendum possible. Since then, there have been five referendums, including three that have had multiple issues. In the first four tries, none succeeded. But in November 1987, the voters passed, by large majorities, referendums that voided five laws.

TABLE 17.4 List of Italian Referendums

Date	Issue	Sponsoring Party	Vote for Repeal	Turn-out
1974	To repeal law permitting divorce	DC	41%	91%
1978	To repeal antiterrorist law	Radicals	22	82
	To revoke law giving public financing to political parties	Radicals	44	82
1981	To repeal liberalized abortion law	DC	32	82
	To repeal restrictions on abortion	Radicals	12	82
	To repeal antiterrorist laws	Radicals	15	82
	To restrict power of prefects	Radicals	14	82
	To abolish life prison sentences	Radicals	23	82
1985	To repeal government decree reducing wage escalator provisions	PCI	46	78
1987	To deny legal immunity to judges	Radicals	80	65
	To end trials by parliamentary commissions of ministers and exministers	Radicals	85	65
	To end subsidies to local governments building nuclear power plants	Radicals	80	65
	To deny government the ability to override local opposition to building nuclear power plants	Radicals	81	65
	To bar the energy board from signing international agreements	Radicals	72	65

At first, Italian citizens seemed to approve of this form of participation with turnout around 80 percent for each of the first four referendums. But with the five referendums in 1987, turnout dropped sharply to sixty-five percent of the eligible voters. This drop exceeded the constitutionally mandated 50 percent turnout so the referendum was valid, but it also showed waning interest in this approach to direct democracy. The 1987 referendum included three provisions limiting the development of nuclear energy in Italy (never a major issue in a country with great potential for hydroelectric energy), a fourth would permit citizens to file civil suits against magistrates they feel are guilty of misconduct, and a fifth measure abolished a special parliamentary committee that investigated political corruption and turned that task over to the parliament itself.

None of these issues had the same emotional or political intensity of previous referendums. Two of the earlier referendums that focused on religious issues were pressed on the DC by the Church and had damaging political consequences since they demonstrated the slipping social and political power of the Church. The 1985 referendum sponsored by the PCI was an attempt to overturn the government's restrictions on the *scala mobile,* a wage indexation that linked increases with inflation. Most economists contended that the *scala mobile* had an important part in Italy's rampant inflation. But the PCI insisted on its need as a protection for the worker against declining purchasing power. The defeat on such a popular issue was an important blow to the PCI.

The Radical party, a small, new Left, party with very limited electoral appeal, has used the referendum process to attract attention and to try to demonstrate a political influence beyond the handful of voters who support its legislative lists. The party is a very small one that is excluded from a meaningful role in parliament. As a result, it has sponsored popular referendum measures for which it can claim credit when they are approved by the public. The four Radical proposals in 1981 were only half the propositions that the party had tried to put on the ballot. The Constitutional Court rejected four others including a Radical proposal to abolish hunting and to legalize soft drugs. When the Radical party introduced the five measures voted on in 1987, the five main parties first fought the referendums in the Constitutional Court. When they lost there, the major parties rallied to support the repeal of the laws they had earlier supported in parliament. Thus, the success in these referendums was claimed by all parties.

The use of the referendum is always subject to criticism in parliamentary democracies because the voters' recourse to direct democracy challenges the principle of parliamentary supremacy, a basic precept of democratic government. Many Italians also feel that there has been an abuse of the referendum process, notably by the Radical party. But for small parties, the referendum offers a way of capturing public attention by picking up on popular issues to prevail over the much larger parties. The 1987 referendums, even though they were the first to be approved by the voters, were disappointing. Some explanations of the voter apathy found in these referendums, centered on sentiments that these were complicated issues that parliament ought to have resolved. With all parties claiming a share of the victory and with voter participation at its lowest level in postwar Italy, the referendums were limited successes at best.

Terror as a Form of Political Action

Besides the general expansion in political action and awareness that came out the troubled era of the Hot Autumn, a more sinister product was the emergence of a small handful of radicals who turned to terrorism when the rest of the society began to return to normalcy in the early 1970s. The most important of several terrorist groups were the Red Brigades. They were domestic terrorists with domestic political objectives behind their acts. While the Red Brigades were the most notorious of Italian terrorists, other smaller leftwing groups also engaged in terrorism such as the Armed Proletarian Nuclei and the Front Line. There was also an important number of rightwing or neo-fascist terrorists whose organizations and goals were much less well defined. Rightist terrorists were less discriminating in their targets, often exploding bombs in public places. International terrorists also carried out attacks in Italy with the 1985 shooting at the Rome airport by Middle Eastern terrorists as one of the most serious such incidents.

Terrorism in Italy differed from the terrorist violence in Britain and France. In these two countries, much of the domestic terrorism was linked with ethnic causes—the Irish, Bretons, and Corsicans—who used violence to draw attention to their demands for autonomy. The Italian problem was more like that of Germany in that the goal of both right and left terrorism was to topple the existing regime. The apparent fragility of the Italian state and the seeming low levels of popular support made this a much more realistic objective than in Germany. There, terrorists had to envisage several stages before the regime might collapse in revolutionary violence. In Italy, such a revolution, whether conceived of as a mass uprising or as an elitist or military coup, seemed much closer to realization.

The number of actual terrorists combined from all the causes was never very large. Their toll in human lives though was important: Between 1968 and 1983, two hundred ninety-six civilians, ninety-two policemen, and forty-two terrorists died in terrorist incidents. As tragic as such losses were, the numbers were not great for a fifteen year period in a country of 57 million people. The toll was much smaller, for example, than British victims of terrorism. The fifteen year total of terrorist fatalities in Italy was far fewer than what die in automobile accidents on Italian roads in two or three months. Yet the domestic and political nature of Italian terrorism, coupled with that country's seemingly weak democratic process, made terrorism appear to be a real threat to the existence of the regime.

After 1978, the government began to have success in its counter-terrorist campaign. (This discussion will be in Chapter Twenty.) But domestic and international terrorism remain a problem for Italy despite the near eradication of the Red Brigades and other terrorist organizations. Unfortunately, as few as one or two devoted activists can perpetrate a terrorist act that will bring more attention to their cause than would the most persuasive arguments of a skilled orator. Because of this attention, terrorism will remain a form of political participation for a small handful of extremists even if it no longer poses the danger of destroying the regime.

Italian Women in Politics

Italian men have traditionally manifested the *machismo* of most Mediterranean people and have relegated women to a clearly second-class social status. A Sicilian proverb captures this attitude, *La donna non è gente* (The woman is not a person). Changes in this social status for women have come only recently and slowly. Italian women, as in France, did not receive the right to vote until after the Second World War.

The real changes in moving toward the equal legal status of women did not begin until the 1970s. The first step was the legalization of divorce in 1970. The Church and other traditional forces challenged this law in a referendum, but the failure of the referendum confirmed the readiness of Italians for a change in women's rights. A series of laws in 1975 gave women social and economic equality, and brought Italy into line with the most socially advanced European states on the legal matters of women's rights. In 1978, abortion was legalized and this law too survived the challenge of a Church-backed referendum with opponents of abortion only able to muster less than a third of the votes.

Changes in behavior by both women and men have not kept up with the legal advances. Traditional values in the home and society still restrict women's opportunities. In politics, the two major parties have tried since 1945 to attract women voters by organizing their own women's movements: The Christian Democrats sponsor the Center of Italian Women (CIF) and the Communist party has the Union of Italian Women (UDI). The CIF stresses assisting women in their traditional roles as wives and mothers while the UDI presses for change in women's social role.[23]

The percentage of women serving in the Italian parliament (8 percent of the Chamber of Deputies elected in 1983) is among the highest in Western Europe but still far from an equitable share. The PCI party accounts for most of the women in parliament, but the DC is clearly committed to presenting women candidates for election although often in positions on the ballot where election is unlikely. This does not seem to have affected the loyalty of the DC women voters. With women making up about 51 percent of the population, they account for 60.5 percent of DC voters despite that party's lack of interest in the popular social changes benefiting women.

Differences in voting behavior between men and women have declined in other countries but still remain important in Italy (See Table 17.5.). This contrast is due largely to the continued influence of religiosity on Italian voting patterns, that is, the greater loyalty of women than men to the Church.[24] Women still provide a disproportionate share of the vote for the Christian Democrats. Leftwing parties that support feminist issues receive little electoral reward from women voters. Despite its championing of women's issues and presenting a large number of women candidates, the PCI is unable to attract more women voters because of the Church's great influence. But women voters did desert the Church on the Church-backed referendums to prevent the legalization of divorce and abortion. It was women voters, by their numbers, who assured the rejection of these referendums.

While not as popular or as successful as the American feminist movements, there has been an important Italian women's movement in recent years. The movement has helped to bring feminist issues and perspectives to the forefront of Italian politics.[25] The women's movement reached its peak of influence between 1975 and 1981 in the battle to legalize abortion. The women's movement, however, soon undermined its success by radical feminist and leftist positions that were out of touch with the vast majority of Italian women. Italian women have shied away from the extreme demands of the feminists and the leftwing political predilections of their movements in a "pervasive spirit of diffidence."[26] Even the PCI has ex-

TABLE 17.5 Gender and Voting Preferences, 1978

VOTING PREFERENCES OF	MEN	WOMEN
Far Left (DP)	6%	3%
PCI	29	26
PSI	19	14
PSDI	3	4
PRI	5	2
DC	32	47
PLI	2	2
MSI	3	2

Source: Data from Paolo Farneti, *The Italian Party System (1945–1960).* (New York: St. Martin's Press, 1985), p. 100.

perienced tense relations with its women's movement, the UDI, because of its radical feminism.[27] Most of all, the strength of traditional values have placed limits on the real accomplishments of the women's movement. For example, the new legal status of women has not changed their situation in most of their marriages. Legalizing divorce was not followed by a flood of divorces. While the laws have changed, traditional values ingrained in the minds of both women and men in this society have persisted, and have thus limited the political and social role of women nearly as effectively as the old laws did.

People and Politics in Italy

Italians express much cynicism about their politicians and their political system. But some observers of Italian politics see this hostility toward the political world as less serious than it first appears. The frequent verbal expressions of antipathy to the democratic order and its leadership are not accompanied by any action that translates this fashionable grumbling about the political world into a real attack on the political status quo. In some ways, this antagonism toward politics may well be a healthy sign of potential resistance to abuse of power or authoritarianism. Above all, one has to look at the rhetoric in its cultural setting. As Joseph LaPalombara has observed

> A taciturn Dane who quietly expresses negative feelings about the polity may be prepared to overthrow it. A wildly gesticulating Italian who shouts obscenities about politics may actually like the polity very much, particularly if he can attack it openly with impunity.[28]

Life in Italy is highly political; it is a society "saturated by politics."[29] Even such seemingly nonpolitical parts of life such as the arts are, in fact, politicized. Decisions, on which opera or theatrical companies will appear in a city, depend on those companies' political connections. The pervasiveness of politics in daily life means that Italians experience partisan politics more directly than do citizens in the United States and most of the other democracies that have been studied in this textbook. This exposure makes Italians more critical of politics, but it also means that they sense that things are not as bad as they appear.[30]

NOTES

1. Gabriel A. Almond and Sidney Verba, *The Civic Culture: Political Attitudes and Democracy in Five Nations* (Princeton, NJ: Princeton University Press, 1963), p. 402.
2. Giacomo Sani, "The Political Culture of Italy: Continuity and Change," in Gabriel A. Almond and Sidney Verba, eds., *The Civic Culture Revisited* (Boston: Little, Brown & Co., 1980).
3. Luigi Barzini, *The Europeans* (Harmondsworth, England: Penguin Books, 1983), p. 178.
4. Sani, "The Political Culture of Italy," p. 309.
5. Ibid., p. 310.
6. Joseph LaPalombara, *Democracy Italian Style* (New Haven, CT: Yale University Press, 1987), p. 27.
7. Edward C. Banfield, *The Moral Basis of a Backward Society* (Glencoe, IL: The Free Press, 1958).
8. Leondardo Morlino, "The Changing Relationship Between Parties and Society in Italy," *West European Politics* 7 (October 1984), 58.
9. LaPalombara, *Democracy Italian Style*, p. 29.
10. Sani, "The Italian Political Culture," p. 307.
11. Samuel H. Barnes, "Secular Trends and Partisan Realignment in Italy," in Russell J. Dalton, et al., *Electoral Change in Advanced Industrial Democracies Realignment or Dealignment* (Princeton, NJ: Princeton University Press, 1984), pp. 214–216.
12. Sidney Tarrow, *Between Center and Periphery: Grassroots Politicians in Italy and France* (New Haven, CT: Yale University Press, 1977).
13. These subcultures were first described in Joseph LaPalombara, "Italy: Fragmentation, Isolation, and Alienation," in Lucien W. Pye and Sidney Verba, eds., *Political Culture and Political Development* (Princeton, NJ: Princeton University Press, 1965). For his recent evaluation of the persistence of these subcultures, see LaPalombara, *Democracy Italian Style*, pp. 35–43.
14. The system is slightly different in the Senate where individual candidates are presented (instead of party lists). A candidate must win 65% of the vote to be elected as an individual. Such occurrences are rare, with, usually, only a couple each election. Where no candidate receives 65%, the d'Hondt system is used with the individual candidates placed in rank list order according to their own vote totals. For a description of the Italian system, see Douglas Wertman, "The Italian Electoral Process: The Elections of 1976," in Howard R. Penniman, ed., *Italy at the Polls: The Parliamentary Elections of 1976* (Washington, DC: American Enterprise Institute, 1977), pp. 44–51, 74–79.
15. Richard S. Katz, "Preference Voting in Italy: Votes of Opinion, Belonging, or Exchange," *Comparative Political Studies* 18 (July 1985): 229–249.
16. Wertman, "The Italian Electoral Process," p. 75.
17. Giacomo Sani, "The Electorate: An Ambiguous Verdict," in Howard Penniman, ed., *Italy at the Polls, 1983: A Study of the National Elections* (Durham, NC: Duke University Press, 1987); and Barnes, "Secular Trends and Partisan Realignment in Italy," pp. 217–222; and Percy Allum and Renato Man-

heimer, "Italy," in Ivor Crewe and David Denver, eds., *Electoral Change in Western Democracies: Patterns and Sources of Electoral Volatility* (New York: St. Martin's, 1985).

18. Morlino, "The Changing Relationships Between Parties and Society in Italy," pp. 48–51; and Katz, "Preference Voting in Italy."

19. Walter Santagata, "The Demand Side of Politico-Economic Models and Politicians' Beliefs: The Italian Case," *European Journal of Political Research* 13 (June 1985): 121–134.

20. Guido Martinotti, "Electoral Trends in Italy: The Cycle 1970–85," *West European Politics* 9 (April 1986): 253–281.

21. Sani, "The Political Culture of Italy," pp. 310–313.

22. Ibid.

23. Karen Beckwith, "Women and Parliamentary Politics in Italy, 1946–1979," in Howard R. Penniman, ed., *Italy at the Polls, 1979* (Washington, DC: American Enterprise Institute, 1981), pp. 230–241.

24. Lawrence Mayer and Roland E. Smith, "Feminism and Religiosity: Female Electoral Behaviour in Western Europe," *West European Politics* 8 (October 1985): 38–49.

25. See Lucia Birnbaum, *Liberzione della Donna: Feminism in Italy* (Middletown, CT: Wesleyan Press, 1986) and Judith Adler Hellman, *Journeys Among Women: Feminism in Five Italian Cities* (London: Oxford University Press, 1987).

26. Annarita Buttafuoco, "Italy: The Feminist Challenge," in Carl Boggs and David Plotke, eds., *The Politics of Eurocommunism: Socialism in Transition* (Boston: South End Press, 1980), p. 216.

27. Karen Beckwith, "Feminism and Leftist Politics in Italy: The Case of UDI-PCI Relations," *West European Politics* 8 (October 1985): 19–37.

28. LaPalombara, *Democracy Italian Style*, p. 89.

29. Ibid., p. 83.

30. Ibid., p. 57.

CHAPTER EIGHTEEN
ITALIAN
POLITICAL PARTIES
AND INTEREST GROUPS

In all of the countries that have been examined so far, political parties are the central actors in the political scene. This is the case in Italy too, but only more so. The strong partisan subcultures (Catholic or Christian Democrat; secular or Socialist; and Left or Communist) have waned in other countries but pervade all aspects of life in Italy. The parties' influence is extended by their auxiliary organizations for workers, students, farmers, women, and others. The weakness of the ~~executive~~ executive branch of government enhances the roles of the parties—both large and small—in determining state policy and the success and fall of the government. Party-based political patronage extends partisan influence into the economy to a much greater extent than elsewhere in Europe. Parties colonize the bureaucracy and the public sector of the economy, and also they intrude into the private sector. Americans would find party control of the television networks unacceptable, but Italians find it natural that the three publicly owned television channels are divided informally among the major three parties: Channel One to the Christian Democrats, Channel Two to the Socialists, and Channel Three to the Communists. Thus, Italian parties have remained much more important than the electoral machines and parliamentary clubs that have evolved in the other European countries.

The centrality of political parties is a fact, but not one that is accepted by all Italians. Many grumble about "partyocracy" and the political and economic ills that it presumably creates. New groups claiming freedom or aloofness from the traditional parties have emerged: ecology groups, women's movements, local action groups, and the like. But they have not won extensive public support. Perhaps, as is suggested in this chapter, the oft-criticized Italian parties serve well the interests of their citizens even if they do not win their love or admiration.

THE POLITICAL PARTY SYSTEM

The Italian political party system is above all characterized by the large number of parties playing important political roles. As Table 18.1 shows, even very small parties are able to win legislative seats under Italy's system of proportional representation with the resulting presence in the Chamber of eleven parties. Despite this fragmentation, two parties clearly are dominant: the Christian Democrats (DC) and the Communists (PCI). These two parties alone account for nearly two thirds of the vote and of the deputies. None of the other parties comes close to these figures. Only the Socialist party (PSI) gains as much as 10 percent of the vote. Thus, despite its pluralism, there is an element of dualism in Italian politics with the chief political dialogue taking place between the DC and the PCI.

The political spectrum runs the full length from Marxist revolutionaries on the far Left who despise the Communist party's moderation to dedicated neo-fascists on the far Right. There is no doubt that ideology is important to most of the Italian parties. Nevertheless, there is much less polarization among political elites than is found in the French political elite.[1] Interaction among party leaders is fairly common with only a few radical parties excluded, notably the neo-fascist MSI and, more recently, the Radical party. Much of the low level of partisan hostility is due to the moderation of the Communist party over the last two decades. This major

TABLE 18.1   Party Strength in Recent Chamber of Deputies Elections

	1987		1983		1979		1976	
	Percentage of vote	Number of seats	Percentage of vote	Number of seats	Percentage of vote	Number of seats	Percentage of vote	Number of seats
Far Left (DP)	1.7%	8	1.5%	7	2.2	6	1.5	6
Communists (PCI)	26.6	177	29.9	198	30.4	201	34.4	228
Radicals (PR)	2.6	13	2.2	11	3.4	13	1.1	4
Socialists (PSI)	14.3	94	11.4	73	9.8	62	9.7	57
Social Democrats (PSDI)	3.0	17	4.1	23	3.8	20	3.4	15
Republicans (PRI)	3.7	21	5.1	29	3.0	16	3.1	14
Christian Democrats (DC)	34.3	234	32.9	225	38.3	262	38.8	262
Liberals (PLI)	2.1	11	2.9	16	2.2	9	1.3	5
Neo-fascists (MSI)	5.9	35	6.8	42	5.9	30	6.1	35
Greens	2.5	13	–0–		–0–		–0–	
Others	3.3	7	2.8	6	1.3	6	0.6	3

political actor no longer opposes the regime nor does it seek revolutionary change. Unlike the ideological appeals of the French Communist party which in turn preserves the French Socialists' ideological attachments, the PCI avoids ideological arguments or slogans. Thus, it contributes to a low level of political polarization both within the elite and within the general public.

There are other reasons for the lack of partisan hostility. Over the last twenty years, every party, except the pariahs on the far Right and Left, have taken part in government with each other or, in the case of the PCI, at least supported such a government through its votes in parliament. The spread of the Italian political spectrum is illustrated by Figure 18.1. The five parties in the brackets are the ones available for participation in a government. The two parties on the ideological flanks—the PCI on the Left and the PLI on the Right—have come and gone depending on whether the coalition is centrist or center-left. But the other four have been part of most governments formed since 1947. They must overlook their ideological differences if Italy is to be governed since a parliamentary majority is not possible without all of them working together. Stronger than differences among them is their resistance to including any party from either the Left or Right extreme. Since the early 1970s, the PCI has nearly been included in this circle of principal political actors. Although still not trusted with ministerial portfolios, it has supported governments on several occasions and stands ready to participate again under the right circumstances.

Internal party factionalism is another source of moderation in the Italian party system. The major parties are all riven by well-developed factions. This factionalism reduces control from the party headquarters. Instead of the disciplined and hierarchical parties unified in pursuit of certain objectives that prevail in other European countries, the Italian parties are delicate coalitions of diverse factions which guard their autonomy as much as possible. Often the distance between factions within a party are as great or greater than the distance between parties. For example, left-wing Christian Democrats share many values and objectives with elements of the Socialist party and even some with the Communists. These affinities often result in cooperation to pass or oppose legislation and to form coalitions that support local or national governments.

Another source for the relaxed partisan tensions is a system of government at the national and local levels that has always stressed mutual back scratching. Dating back to pre-fascist Italy is the tradition of *trasfor-*

FIGURE 18.1 **Italian Political Parties on a Left/Right Spectrum. Parties in brackets are those parties that take part in government coalitions.**

Parties in brackets are those parties that take part in government coalitions.

Proletarian Democracy	Radicals	Communists		Socialists	Social Democrats	Republicans	Christian Democrats	Liberals		Monarchists
Left										Right

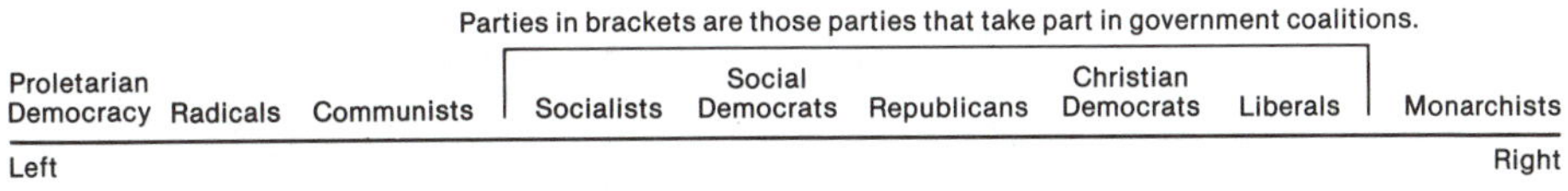

mismo that built legislative and government coalitions on deals with each of the various parties gaining something. In its modern variant, even the Communists are co-opted in legislative deals that provide them, as well as the other parties, with symbolic and material advantages to distribute to their supporters.[2] Such practices exist also at the local level. They build bridges across the party lines.[3]

The collaboration at the elite level is reciprocated by the often instrumental nature of partisanship at the grassroots level. Many voters choose their party loyalty more out of the practical necessity of getting along with the local dominant political force than out of firm ideological commitments. There remains, however, important popular uneasiness about a national-level grand coalition that links the Communists to the government.[4] However, the old ideological wars are largely passed. Among political elites, there is now more competition than antagonism.[5]

The Christian Democrats

The Christian Democratic party has been the dominant party in Italian politics since the end of the Second World War. It has taken part in every government formed since then and one of its leaders has headed all but two of the forty-three postwar governments. It was not until 1981 that a politician from some other party had the opportunity to be premier. As was the case with the Gaullist-Giscardian twenty-three years of hegemony in France, the even longer dominance of the Italian DC produced complacency, leadership stagnation, and vulnerability to corruption.

The DC is a Catholic party. It is a moderate right-of-center party comparable in doctrine to the German Christian Democrats or the pre-Thatcher British Conservatives. In contrast to the loose ties between the German CDU and the Church, the Italian DC has had and continues to have close ties with the Vatican hierarchy. A DC meeting often begins with the singing of a hymn in praise of the Virgin Mary, *Salve Regina,* before the party faithful turn to political rhetoric. Of course, the overwhelming dominance of Catholicism in this country makes this religious character an advantage rather than a disadvantage for the Italian Christian Democrats. The Church tie has provided the party with a secure electorate among practicing Catholics. It is strongest in the devout Catholic areas of northeastern Italy and the South. But the party has a broad-base of support cutting across class and regional lines. It draws at least 20 percent of the vote in every region in the country.

Beyond its religious support, the DC has built an impressive political machine around the country that permits it to mobilize large numbers of supporters for electoral and other political duties. Its political strength throughout the country has permitted it to develop an extensive system of rewards for its followers. The DC has built a powerful organization based on political clientelism similar, in some respects, to the American urban political machines of the past. Profiting from their ties with the national government that provides access to state resources and from their control of local governments, local and national DC notables exchange political favors in the form of jobs, government contracts, subsidies, welfare assistance, and so on for political support.[6] The DC clientelism is not restricted to the South; it is a common feature of DC politics throughout the country.[7]

This clientelism is unusual in Europe although it is widely found in developing countries. Its importance in Italy has derived in part, from the *trasformismo* patterns inherited from the constitutional monarchy and from traditional practices in the south of Italy that have affected all of Italy. It has been facilitated by the absence of a strong, civil service, tradition such as that West Germany inherited from the Prussians and the French from Napoleon's reforms. Finally, the long political dominance of the DC has meant that the same party has had control of many state resources and therefore, has been able to distribute them as its factions pleased without effective challenge.

This clientelist network is reinforced by a well-developed system of auxiliary groups that reach out to all social sectors. Thus, the DC is linked with a Catholic trade union, a teachers' association, a women's movement, youth organizations, the lay Catholic Action, a business and employers' group, an association of Catholic lawyers, and so on. The party has used these auxiliaries to develop a broad-based, catchall, party that has appealed successfully to voters across social-class lines.

The DC is riven with factions.[8] Organized by support of a particular ideological viewpoint, of a certain coalition strategy, or frequently simply of a particular leader, each faction has its own headquarters, newsletter, and internal organization. Party congresses are times for assessing the changing strength of these factions, for determining which faction or combination of factions has sufficient strength to control the national party organization, and for rallying as many factions as possible behind some sort of synthesis of the different views. The balancing of factions when forming the party executive and distributing ministries in the government is a delicate but crucial task. It is not unusual for factional disputes within the DC to lead to the fall of a government or to delay the formation of a new government coalition. As one observer notes, "every Christian Democratic faction constitutes a margin of insecurity for the DC, at least to the extent that each one is capable of threatening the life of a DC-led government."[9]

There are some positive aspects to the factional struggles. These rivalries encourage party activity as each faction seeks to recruit members to strengthen it *vis-à-vis* other factions. Their constant jockeying for position heightens interest in party activities for DC members. In addition, the debate over issues and alternative leaders brings elements of democratic discussion and control into the party. The openness of the party debate and the unseemly squabbling among factions does not appear to affect the party's public image the way similar struggles in the British Labour party damaged it. Perhaps it is because the many DC factions make it impossible for any one faction, let alone an extreme one, to dominate the party as the left wing did in the British Labour party. Another explanation may be that the prevailing low esteem in which politicians are held in Italy cannot be worsened by factional disputes.

The factional diversity of the Christian Democrats makes it difficult to summarize their party's political positions. It is a centrist party with ties to traditional conservative forces, notably the Church, but with a record of supporting major socioeconomic reforms. Christian Democrat-led governments have directed the overhauling of the country's agricultural structures, the development of an extensive system of social-welfare benefits, an expansion of the public economic sector and the role of the state in economic management, regional decentralization, expansion of the rights of women, and educational reforms. The Italian DC has not had a close association with big business interests like that of German Social Democrats or British Conservatives. Only in the last five years or so has the business community warmed to the DC as the party has advocated more economic "rigor" such as slowing inflation and cutting government social expenditures. But the DC has not joined other European conservative parties in pressing for privatization of Italy's large public sector. In foreign policy, the party has stressed loyalty to the Atlantic Alliance and support for the development of European economic unity and cooperation. In recent years, the DC has tried to renew its religious links by focussing on such themes as the family and traditional morality. One critic has referred to this as the "revirginization" of the Christian Democrats.

After thirty-five years of political dominance, the DC faced severe challenges in the 1980s. Part of its problem came from the decline of the "Communist menace." Many Italians voted for the DC as the major obstacle to Communist ascendancy in Italy. But by the end of the 1970s, the Italian Communists no longer appeared as dangerous, and other parties emerged as alternative checks on the Communist party for those who were still concerned about that danger.

But the major source of the Christian Democratic decline came simply from the fact that it had been in power too long. Too close of attachment to the reins of power for too many years had made the party sloppy and left its officials tainted by widespread political corruption. A series of spectacular scandals tarred the reputations of the party's leading figures and undermined public confidence in the DC's ability to continue to provide reasonably honest government. Its leadership was aging and new leaders were unable to emerge from the factional politics dominated by old party barons who constituted "a gerontocracy without successors."[10] The Italian Christian Democratic party had not had the benefit of a time in opposition to review its doctrine and renew its leadership in the way that the French conservatives profited from the five-year Socialist ascendancy after twenty-three years of Gaullist and Giscardian preeminence. Parties usually change their approach and their leaders when they lose elections; the DC's long years of success had left it with tired doctrines and familiar but aging and not always popular leaders.

Public discontent with the DC had begun in the 1970s but really became evident in the 1980s. The major shock was at the polls. The DC's political base in local politics was shaken by losses in the 1975 local and regional elections when every city in the north and center with a population over two hundred thousand elected leftist local governments. The party's support in national elections had held steady at 38 to 39 percent through the 1960s and the 1970s and then plummeted to only 33 percent. Meanwhile, its chief rival, the PCI, had increased its position from 25 percent in the 1950s and 1960s to 30 to 32 percent in the 1970s. In the 1984 European parliament election, the PCI actually outpolled the DC, the first time that had happened in the history of the party. There were also indications that the party's organization was weakening. The party claimed a membership of 1.3 million in 1983, down from 1.9 million a decade earlier. That is a loss of a third of its members.

In response to its growing problems, the DC party leader, Ciriaco de Mita, undertook a major battle to reform the party.[11] He selected factional disputes and inept local and regional party leaders as his first targets. The struggle was a difficult one with factions still vital and interested in preserving their prerogatives and their loyalties to the tried and sure leaders, even if they had passed their prime. Another important obstacle to DC recovery was the loss of the premiership. There was no DC leader to rival the Socialist Premier Bettino Craxi's popularity. At the local level, the loss of control in municipal and regional governments had cost the party the political base it needed to pay off its supporters in the traditional manner. Finally, the general secularization of Italian society was undermining the DC's most loyal electorate, the faithful, church-attending Catholic.

De Mita's efforts began to bring results by the end of the 1980s. The party regained most of its municipal and regional strongholds and with them, control over their patronage positions. It won new support from conservative business circles that, in the past, had been suspicious of the DC's vague commitment to social change. At the national level, a Christian Democrat, Giovanni Goria replaced Craxi as the youngest premier in postwar Italy. Most importantly, the party reversed the declining electoral strength in the 1987 elections when the DC increased its share of the vote for the first time in two decades. The DC still faced major challenges but it was clear that it was back in a position to continue its domination of Italian politics.

The Communist Party

Since 1947, the PCI has been the largest Communist party operating in a democratic setting, both in terms of members and voting support. With a membership in 1983 of 1.6 million and the backing of 30 percent of the voters, the Italian Communist party clearly is a major political power. The party's base of support is broad. It is not simply a beneficiary of negative or protest voting. Its strongest bases of support are in the industrial cities in the North and in the "red belt" across the center of Italy. In the North, the party's support comes from the large population of industrial workers. In the red belt of Tuscany, Emilia-Romagna, and Umbria, the Communist party benefits from a historical tradition of leftwing voting and draws a broader cross section of voters from all social backgrounds.

The PCI also draws some voters from most of the social classes in all regions.

The PCI has had the advantage of having its own ideologists—Antonio Gramsci and Palmiro Togliatti—whose humanism took the rough edges off of the Marxist-Leninist doctrine. The PCI soon accepted a gradualist or reformist path to social change in Italy. Under the guidance of party leader Enrico Berlinguer (1972 to 1984), the PCI pioneered in the development of Eurocommunism in the 1970s.

The Italian brand of Eurocommunism had three features that distinguished it from earlier European Communist strategies. One was the rejection of the Soviet model. In a way, the Eurocommunist movement which Italy led represented a second major schism in the International Communist Movement, which was as nearly as significant as the split between the Chinese and the Soviet Communist parties. Italian Communists rejected the validity of the Soviet model in their country and implicitly in other Western European democracies. Furthermore, the PCI moved beyond that rejection to publicly criticize the Soviet Communist party for serious shortcomings in the USSR. It began with attacks on Soviet infringements on the civil rights of its people, and moved on to criticize Soviet foreign policy. Thus, the PCI came to accept the European Common Market, which was denounced by the Soviet Union as a club of monopolists. It also supported the Western defense alliance, with party leader Berlinguer insisting that NATO was Eurocommunism's shield. Finally, and most significantly, the PCI denounced the Soviet Union's economic and social policies which it charged had betrayed the hope of the workers. The PCI thus, asserted its total independence from the Soviet Union in shaping its foreign and domestic policy orientations.

The Italian Communists also moved to accept the democratic process that it had earlier decried as a false bourgeois democracy. The Leninist notion of a dictatorship of the proletariat was abandoned as the party accepted the parliamentary democracy that had developed in postwar Italy. When Italy faced threats from terrorism and even economic failure, the PCI participated in a responsible way trying to work out the problems through the usual parliamentary channels. Fears that a Communist victory might lead to a single party system were allayed as the party insisted that it endorsed political pluralism and that it accepted the notion of a rotation of parties in and out of power.

The PCI repudiated the notion of political change coming through a violent revolution. Instead, it sought to develop a strategy for coming to power through democratic procedures. Party theorists reckoned that major social reform in a country where conservative forces were as deeply ingrained as they were in Italy can only be achieved without violence if they were supported by a very broad coalition. (The violent end of Allende's Socialist-Communist government in Chile in 1973 confirmed this belief.) So the Italian Communists called for a "historic compromise" linking the DC and the PCI in a governing coalition.

Another reason for the PCI's choice of a conservative ally in its search for power was the weakness of the more likely allies on the Left. Unlike the French Communists who could hope to win a majority within a coalition with the French Socialists, the Italian Socialist party was too small to provide that hope to the PCI. Thus, the Christian Democrats were the most desirable ally, both from the standpoint of overcoming public fears of the Communist party and from the practical standpoint of finding a partner capable of providing the coalition with an electoral majority. DC hesitancy prevented the formal achievement of a coalition but the PCI openly supported several DC governments in the late 1970s and played a role of constructive opposition in several others.[12] While not formally in the government coalition, the PCI has voted with several governments on some issues and avoided all-out or systematic opposition to the government.

The result of the PCI's evolution was that it offered a distinctively Italian form of communism that was different from that of the Soviet Union or other Communist countries. It succeeded in persuading many voters of the sincerity of this commitment to an Italian model. One Communist mayor captured the party's approach well:

> The Italian Communist party is unlike any other Communist party, anywhere. When we think of socialism, we don't think of the Soviet Union, China, of Yugoslavia, of Cuba, or of any other orthodoxy. We think of Italy.[13]

In the early 1980s, the party's commitment to the historic compromise wavered as it considered other options.[14] Its gains during the 1970s led some of its leaders to hope that the PCI alone could muster a parliamentary majority. Others hoped for a leftwing alliance, like the one that brought the Left to power in France. Other leaders were concerned when the party experienced some losses in voting strength. They attributed these setbacks to the disillusionment of the party's traditional electorate in seeing the PCI support the conservative DC. Besides, it was increasingly clear that the prospects of the DC accepting the "historic compromise" were remote.

In 1984, the party's popular leader and principal architect of Euro-communism, Enrico Berlinguer, died. Under a new party leader, Alessandro Natta, the PCI hesitated briefly, but then resumed its moderate and independent course. The PCI's strategy was clouded since the historic compromise seemed distant and an alliance of the Left seemed unlikely.[15] Italian Communists showed little sympathy for the government led by the Socialist Bettino Craxi with whom Berlinguer had a long-standing personal rivalry.

The PCI is more open in its internal politics. There are several well-developed factions in the party representing different political strategies and policy approaches. The more open style means that factional disputes are more intense and more public than in other communist parties: Some advocate a more revolutionary stance; others would like greater loyalty to the Soviet Union; others advocate the Eurocommunist strategy; and still others would like to see even more moderation of the party's position. At the end of the 1980s, the party was still struggling to find the best strategy. In 1988, Natta resigned as PCI leader because of ill health. He was replaced by a young party leader, Achille Occeheto, who was not associated with any of the main factions. The party is still loyal though, to its moderate course.

The PCI's loyalty to Eurocommunism is in striking contrast to the French Communists' retreat from their moderate Eurocommunist stance after 1977. Most observers regard the Italian party's changes as real and irreversible. There are several reasons for the different courses followed by these two Communist parties.[16] The French party lacked the independent thinkers that have enriched the Italian Communist party throughout its history. French Communists have instead been suspicious of intellectuals in their ranks. The Italian party was forced underground early in its existence by the triumph of fascism, while the French Communists underwent the purges and struggles in the 1920s and early 1930s that made their party Moscow's most loyal Western European party. More recently, the PCI became Italy's second largest party, and in the trying period of the 1970s it found that it controlled the fate of the republic. The PCI was forced to decide whether to prop the presiding regime up and seek to achieve its ends in the democratic procedures or to risk a change in the regime. The PCI chose to work within the existing system. The French party never had to openly make that choice. It opposed de Gaulle's establishment of the Fifth Republic and continued as an advocate of a regime change. Perhaps most importantly, the Italian Communists saw their efforts at moderation rewarded by a growing electorate while the French PCF found that its moderation brought no new voters but instead bolstered the electoral chances of the rival Socialist party.

The PCI suffered serious setbacks in the late 1980s: first in losses in the regional elections; then in the defeat of its referendum measure to repeal the government's limit on the wage escalator clause; and lastly, in the sharp electoral decline in the 1987 national elections. The party's electoral reverses came from a number of developments. First, the PCI lost its appeal as the "party with clean hands." In earlier decades, the exclusion of the PCI from the patronage games protected it from corruption and scandal. But broader sharing of patronage and the local election victories of the 1970s exposed the party to the same perils of political corruption that the DC had long confronted. Several major scandals in Communist-run communities left the PCI unable to tout its ability to fight political corruption. Second, the PCI no longer seemed to have the appeal to young voters and workers that it once had. The decline of the heavy industries once the stronghold of unions and the PCI hurt its electoral base. Third, the Socialist party, for the first time since the Second World War, now appeared as an attractive alternative to many left-wing voters who otherwise might have voted Communist. Finally, with the demise of the "historic compromise" and the inability of the Communist leaders to find a new coalition strategy, the party lacked a credible program for coming to power and governing. Despite these problems, there is little chance that the PCI will experience the decline that has befallen the French party. The PCI has made its adjustment to democracy and to the new social setting of the 1980s, while the French party has not. It will remain a powerful influence in Italian politics and may recover political strength should the Socialists and Christian Democrats falter again.

The Socialist Party

Among the chief beneficiaries of the Communist losses is the small Socialist party, the PSI. For the first two decades of the Republic, the PSI stumbled trying to maintain its own identity and unity. Torn by disputes between factions advocating different policies and political strategies, the party seemed to have little future. For the first fifteen years or so after the Second World War, the Socialists allied themselves, not without dissension and misgiving, with the Communist party. The result of this alliance was the decline of the Socialists and the success of the Communists in becoming the party representing the left-wing subculture in Italian politics. It was only in the 1960s, that a severely weakened PSI sought an independent role. But the major issue in national politics for the next decade was the cooperation between the DC and the PCI in the historic compromise, an issue that left the PSI on the sidelines. It was a small party without a strategy for coming to power.

In 1976, the Socialist party selected Bettino Craxi as its new leader. He soon consolidated his position as the dominant figure in a previously divided party but still faced some resistance from local Socialist notables that were more tied to old political patterns than the new approaches favored by Craxi. Nevertheless, under his guidance, the party modernized its doctrine by eliminating most of the class warfare rhetoric and by focusing on concrete issues rather than dogma. The party organization was renewed and centralized.[17] Until then, the PSI, despite its small size and electorate, was divided by numerous factions. Craxi succeeded in overcoming many of the factional divisions and in giving the party greater unity than at any time since the war. By 1983, his party began to reap the electoral benefits, rising from 9.2 percent in 1972 to 11.4 percent in 1983, or almost a 25 percent increase in its share of the vote.[18] Craxi's popularity increased during the period of his long and successful government. His party registered important gains in the 1985 regional elections. Then, in 1987, after nearly four years of a Craxi-led national government, the PSI increased its strength to 14.3 percent of the total vote, another 25 percent increase.

The result was an Italian Socialist party that was more like the German Social Democrats than the French Socialists. The difference between the changes in the PSI and those in the French party illustrate the impact of different personalities in key leadership positions. Mitterrand sought to win votes from the French Communists. Craxi seemingly targeted Center-Left voters dissatisfied with the DC as well as wooing former Communist voters willing to shift their support to a party with government ties. Mitterrand changed the French party by first radicalizing it and then, by allying it with a basically unreformed Communist party; Craxi chose to move in a more moderate direction, reducing ideological commitments and rejecting an alliance with the Italian Communists. Beyond the personalities of leaders, another factor in the more moderate course of the

Italian Socialists may have been the PSI's ties with the PCI from 1945 through the early 1960s. In seeking to give the PSI a new image from its past collaboration with the Communists, Craxi had to break clearly with its earlier practices.

The Socialist vote was still small but the 1983 gains coupled with the DC's political problems permitted Craxi to form a government after the 1983 election. He succeeded in becoming postwar Italy's first Socialist prime minister, although he headed a government still preponderantly Christian Democratic. But he was able to give his government a distinctive Socialist image through his reforms and his skills in managing the coalition. He proved to be a dynamic and resourceful leader as evidenced by the life of his government. It set the record as the longest-lived government since 1946. Craxi pushed through parliament a series of important reforms: the new concordat with the Church; a reduction in the *scala mobile*—the automatic salary and pension increases tied to rises in the cost of living; a new antiterrorist law; approval of deployment of new American missiles; and a economic austerity policy. Avoiding the new issues—such as ecology, peace and nuclear disarmament, and feminist causes—that have caused divisions in the German Social Democratic and the British Labour parties, the PSI emerged as a powerful and attractive moderate voice of the Center-Left.

With its new program and moderate image, the PSI has started to develop a more secure niche in Italian politics. Excluded by the PCI from its traditional place as the political voice for the left-wing or Marxist subculture, the PSI has begun to emerge now as the dominant party in the lay or secular subculture. It has eclipsed the traditional parties of this ideological family: the Republicans, Social Democrats, and Liberals.

The Socialists are far from challenging the two major parties, but they now constitute an important political force. Craxi's own popularity is high and will likely be enhanced by contrast with his less durable and resourceful successors in the premiership. The ability of the PSI to expand its electoral strength even further depends upon Craxi's ability to counter the cultural and organizational holds that the DC and PCI have over much of the population.[19] A beginning was made with the Socialist victories in the local and regional elections of the mid-1980s. These wins greatly increased the PSI access to the prestige and patronage of local government. The party has also succeeded in developing a strong base of support among younger voters. In 1987, the PSI outpolled every party, except the DC, with voters under 25-years-old: the PSI took 23 percent of the younger voters compared to 17 percent of the once youthful PCI.[20] The Socialists also cut into the PCI working-class support. While much of the recent PSI success has come at the expense of the PCI, the Italian Socialists still have a long way to go to match the French Socialists' success in shunting the Communists to the political side lines.

The Other Parties

Flanking the DC are three "lay" or anticlerical parties: the Social Democrats (PSDI) and the Republicans (PRI) slightly to the Left of the DC, and the Liberals (PLI) slightly to its Right. While these parties have only modest electoral support, their position on the political spectrum makes them key players in building parliamentary majorities. While these parties are close ideologically, there are important personality, historical, and issue differences that keep them apart. These three parties have traditionally served as the political voice of the lay subculture. However, in recent years, they have faced competition for this role from the revived and newly moderate Socialist party.

The Social Democratic party is the product of a schism in the early postwar years when the right wing of the Socialist party broke off in opposition to the PSI's coalition with the Communists. The party was left a legacy of strident anti-Communism and resentment toward the PSI. By now, however, it is difficult to distinguish significant differences between the PSDI positions and those of the PSI. But personality clashes and traditions keep it a separate party. The PSDI has its strongest support among independent small shop owners, craft people, lower-level civil servants, and pensioners. Its preoccupation with defending its distinctiveness and the undisciplined behavior of its parliamentary deputies and senators often make this small party a difficult but needed partner in government coalitions. In 1987, the PSDI appeared to lose support to the PSI as that party profited from Craxi's popularity and political skill.

The Republican party dates back to the 1890s with a similar legacy to that of other European liberal parties such as the German FDP and the British Liberal party. The PRI is committed to the secular state, democratic and parliamentary values, and modest social reforms.[21] Its position at the political center assures it a place in nearly all government coalitions. The Republican party leader, Giovanni Spadolini, became the first non-DC prime minister in 1981, followed by PSI's Craxi in 1983. He owed this position to internal divisions in the DC and the feeling that he was an innocuous leader who would not offend anyone, a characterization that also fits his party's image. The party draws support from middle-class professionals, technocrats, and business people. The Republicans gained slightly in 1983, reaching its postwar peak in electoral support with 5.1 percent of the vote. This gain was due to dissatisfaction with the larger parties and to the personal attraction of Spadolini after his term as premier.[22] In the 1987 elections, the Republican support slipped back to 3.7 percent of the vote.

The more conservative PLI's presence in government is felt when the DC shifts to the Center-Right. It also draws on the liberal heritage but with a greater emphasis on laissez-faire economic values than on social and democratic reforms. It defends the interests of big business and wealthy property holders. With only 2.1 percent of the vote in 1987, it is the smallest of the governing parties. As small as it is, the PLI has four factions that contend with each other as much as with their rival parties.[23]

There are also several small parties whose extreme views leave them on the margins of Italian politics. On the far Left is the Proletarian Democracy. This small party (1.7 percent of the 1987 vote) has attracted a variety of leftists—Trotskyites, anarchists, Maoists,—that are dissatisfied with the moderation of both the PCI and the PSI. It has very limited electoral appeal and no significant role in the Chamber.

On the far Right is the neo-fascist Italian Social Movement (MSI). It is the largest of the small parties polling 6 to 7 percent of the vote. Once it was possible to discount the neo-fascist vote as simply reflecting nostalgia for Mussolini's more assertive Italy. Now few voters can remember that era firsthand. The MSI's continued electoral appeal comes from its staunch opposition to the regime, one of the few such parties now that the PCI has joined the ranks of the constitutional parties. It also wins votes, like the French National Front does, from a law-and-order backlash against the presumed decadence of modern life and against deteriorating public order. The situation is paradoxical since neo-fascists are linked with an important share of terrorism. But the links between these rightist terrorists and the MSI are distant. Despite its important bloc of seats in parliament, the extreme positions of the MSI makes it an unacceptable participant in parliamentary coalitions. But in recent years, some parties, including the PSI and DC, have made tentative gestures toward the MSI. With the passage of time, the MSI may yet emerge from its political ghetto.

The Radicals are so eccentric that they are difficult to place on the political spectrum. The Radical party emerged in the mid-1970s as a vehicle for the political actions of the new Left, the heirs of the Hot Autumn. With some loose resemblance to the German Greens, the Italian Radical party advocates environmental issues, disarmament and withdrawal from NATO, feminist causes, and the rights of such outsiders as homosexuals, conscientious objectors, and accused terrorists. It has championed the use of referendums to promote participatory democracy. As a result the party has brought a number of controversial issues to a vote. While these measures have usually been defeated, they have always attracted far more support than the 2 percent the Radical party musters in legislative elections. It draws its greatest support from young intellectuals and far Left outsiders.

The Radical party has won public attention, if not always approbation, by nominating unusual candidates. In 1983, it listed the reputed leader of the terrorist Red Brigade, Toni Negri, for that year's parliamentary election. Since the candidate was at the top of the list, he was elected and freed from prison. When his parliamentary immunity was lifted to permit his trial on terrorist charges, he fled the country.[24] In 1985, the Radicals elected a newly convicted drug peddler as party president. In 1987, the party put a star of pornographic films at the top of its list. She won wide press coverage for baring her body in addition to her political program at election rallies.

Such eccentricities keep the party in the press but have done little to win it either votes or a meaningful role in building a parliamentary coalition. In parliament, it has engaged in obstruction rather than constructive debate. To delay unwanted legislation, the Radicals will organize an Italian variant of the filibuster by introducing thousands of amendments to pending bills. For all the problems that they have caused, the Radicals have played important roles in defending divorce and abortion reforms and in their unrelenting criticism of political corruption.

Italian Parties
and Political Instability

Among the most widespread beliefs among students of political science has been the notion that too many parties leads to difficulties in forming durable government coalitions. Italy is almost always an example of the perils of multiparty systems. Recent research has shown that there are many multiparty systems that are successful in supporting stable governments.[25] Italy, no doubt, faces extra challenges because of the large number of parties in parliament and because of the fact that it needs at least four or five of them to build a parliamentary majority. Italian governments are difficult to form and fragile once they are in existence.

But the causes of governmental instability are deeper than the number of parties: the weaknesses and internal divisions of the parties, the intensity of personal rivalries, ideological differences, and most important of all, the fear and hostility that keep the PCI, with its nearly one third of the deputies, from being accepted as a potential participant in a government. The consequence of these reasons combined is that elections change little in Italy. It is always the DC that forms the core of the government and is usually the party of the prime minister. The same small parties must also join the DC in order to have a majority. The absence of rotation in power creates an environment in which corruption flourishes and which prevents those parties in government from renewing their leadership and their ideas. Voters have difficulty in sanctioning a government that displeases them because there is no alternative to replace the existing coalition.

Perhaps the most important change in Italian party politics has been the moderation of the Communist party. As it has become a respected and responsible participant in the political process, it has contributed to a relaxation of the once highly polarized party system.[26] The full potential of this change has yet to be reached since the PCI has not yet been accepted as a full participant in a government coalition. It has tacitly and even publicly supported specific governments in the past. It seems likely they will offer this support again or even play a more important role as a full partner with ministerial portfolios for its leaders in some future government. When this rise happens, it will not only further the trend toward moderate party politics but also give Italians the choice between alternative parties or coalitions that their party system has thus far failed to provide.

INTEREST GROUPS
AND ITALIAN POLITICS

Until recently, Italian interest groups have reflected the divisions within the party system. The divisions are particularly marked in the labor movement with separate and competing unions based on the three political subcultures: the General Confederation of Italian Labor (CGIL) with ties to the Communist party; the Social Confederation of Italian Labor (CISL) linked to the DC; and the Union of Italian Labor (UIL) aligned principally with the Republican and Social-Democratic parties. Similar party-associated groups seek to represent farmers, women, students, veterans, and so on. These political links are useful in gaining access to party officials with control over government resources at both the national and local levels.[27] Business interests were the one major set that seemed to avoid partisan alignment. The principal group, Confindustria, established good contacts with appropriate government ministries and agencies but avoided partisan entanglement, notably with the DC.

During the 1970s, party linkages in many of these groups weakened.[28] As a result, greater cooperation among previously divided groups representing similar issues became possible, as was the case of the labor movement. In some instances nonpartisan groups emerged to replace or absorb the old party-based groups. The 1970s marked an era of unprecedented labor unity as the three major unions put aside their differences in pursuit of specific workplace-related demands.[29] This unity was accompanied by greater consultation with the government on major economic policies but with only limited additional weight for the views of the trade unions.[30] Unity broke down in the 1980s over the issue of defending the *scala mobile.* When the Craxi government issued a decree limiting such increases to a maximum of 10 percent, the CGIL mobilized its supporters against the new policy while the other unions backed the government with greater or lesser enthusiasm. The PCI and CGIL pressed the issue in a referendum to repeal the decree, but the referendum was rejected by the voters. In the aftermath of this defeat, all unions suffered a loss of influence and the Confindustria exploited their weaknesses to press for further concessions.

As elsewhere in Europe, the trade unions were also facing losses in membership from the protracted economic crisis and unemployment. Italian unions had never had extensive political influence but they had grown in strength, at least temporarily, during the 1970s.[31] This power ended during the 1980s when the Craxi's Socialist-led government imposed austerity on the unions and returned to the more familiar pattern of excluding the trade unions from the political decision-making process.[32] Their diminished power, in the late 1980s undermined their ability to integrate potentially disaffected workers into the existing political and social system.

As in all western democracies, there are numerous other interest groups active in Italian politics using a variety of methods in attempting to influence policy. Italian interest groups are active both in parliament and in government offices. To some extent, party ties shield elected officials and bureaucrats from opposing partisan-linked interest groups. But most agencies and departments have an established set of client groups with which they must regularly work with in the implementation of government policy. They have developed symbiotic relationships of mutual support and understanding so that the interest groups provide political support for the government agency and the bureaucrats work to accommodate the demands of these clients. These ties between government departments and the groups affected by their policies even include amicable relations with groups aligned with the opposition parties and that may oppose the overall policy or orientation of the government in power. They nevertheless can reach agreement on issues of mutual concern. Thus, Communist trade unions will provide political support to the Ministry of Labor or other departments in order to promote the interests of their workers. This clientelism goes beyond the ties between notables and individual citizens to bind governments and parties with control over public policy on the one hand to large groups on the other.[33]

The number of associations in Italy is large and activity is generally high. But, with the exception of the emergence of neighborhood associations, there has not been a rise of new, alternative groups to challenge either the major interests or the political parties. The feminist movement has little mass following and has avoided overt political challenges to the existing parties. The ecologists have only limited support. They contested national elections for the first time in 1987 and took 2.5 percent of the vote. They appear unlikely to grow to become the political force that the German Greens have become. The Italian peace movement has limited appeal and did little to oppose the government's decision in the early 1980s to permit the installation of new NATO missiles in Italy. The political scene is still dominated by the traditional parties and groups.

This lack of change or growth is surprising since the electoral system facilitates entry of new parties. There is no convincing explanation for the absence of a real electoral challenge by parties reflecting contemporary social movements such as the German Greens or the Scottish or Welsh nationalist parties. But one possible explanation is that the terrorist threat preempted the political agenda. Public attention was focused on this challenge to the regime and on the major parties' efforts to counter it. Voters may have been too anxious about terrorism to support the efforts or direct votes to new parties or social movements.

STABLE PATTERNS OF POLITICAL PARTICIPATION AND INSTABILITY

One of the striking features of Italian politics is the stability of its patterns of political participation. Apart from the social explosion of the Hot Autumn in 1969, Italians engage in politics just as they have since the war. The surge in terrorism, especially its domestic form, disturbed politics, but it was not novel if one remembers the turmoil and terrorism of Italy in the early 1920s or the continuous violence of organized crime in southern Italy. The new social movements that have appeared elsewhere in Europe have failed to penetrate Italian politics. Citizens are strongly negative in their evaluations of the political system but they continue to vote heavily for the parties that have produced that system.

This chapter has noted certain traces of dynamism in the party system and even in citizen actions. But the prevailing pattern of politics dominated by the two main party rivals—the DC and PCI—with a coterie of smaller parties remains unchanged. With the parties firmly anchored in durable political subcultures, this party system exhibits considerable stability in a country reputed for its instability as voter loyalties to their parties and subcultures remain comparatively firm. Over the last forty years, the average shift in vote support for a party between successive elections is a remarkably low 1.6 percent.[34] It is this lack of change in patterns of political participation that brings continuity and order to a political system that on the surface looks turbulent and unstable.

NOTES

1. See Robert Putnam, *The Beliefs of Politicians: Ideology, Conflict, and Democracy in Britain and Italy* (New Haven, CT: Yale University Press, 1973).
2. See Guiseppe di Palma, *Surviving Without Governing: Italian Parties in Parliament* (Berkeley, CA: University of California Press, 1977).
3. Sidney Tarrow, *Between Center and Periphery: Grassroots Politicians in Italy and France* (New Haven, CT: Yale University Press, 1977).
4. Paolo Farneti, *The Italian Party System (1945–1980)* (New York: St. Martin's, 1985), pp. 101–113.
5. Geoffrey Pridham, *The Nature of the Italian Party System: A Regional Case Study* (London: Croom Helm, 1981), pp. 184–248.
6. See Judith Chubb, *Patronage, Power, and Poverty in Southern Italy: A Tale of Two Cities* (Cambridge, England: Cambridge University Press, 1982).
7. For an example of a study of the DC in Tuscany, see Pridham, *The Nature of the Italian Party System*, pp. 120–144.
8. Alan S. Zuckerman, *The Politics of Faction: Christian Democratic Rule in Italy* (New Haven, CT: Yale University Press, 1979).
9. Frank P. Belloni, "Factionalism, the Party System, and Italian Politics," in Frank P. Belloni and Dennis C. Beller, eds., *Faction Politics: Political Parties and Factionalism in Comparative Perspective* (Santa Barbara, CA: ABC-Clio, 1978), p. 103.
10. Frederic Spotts and Theodor Wieser, *Italy: A Difficult Democracy* (Cambridge, England: Cambridge University Press, 1986).
11. Douglas A. Wertman, "The Christian Democrats: The Big Losers," in Howard Penniman, ed., *Italy at the Polls, 1983: A Study of the National Elections* (Durham, NC: Duke University Press, 1987).
12. See Gianfranco Pasquino, "From Togliatti to the *Compresso Storico*: A Party with a Governmental Vocation," in Simon Serfaty and Lawrence Gray, eds., *The Italian Communist Party: Yesterday, Today, and Tomorrow* (Westport, CT: Greenwood Press, 1980).
13. *The Christian Science Monitor*, 17 April 1987.
14. James Ruscoe, *The Italian Communist Party, 1976–81: On the Threshold of Government* (London: Macmillan, 1982).
15. Steven Hellman, "The Italian Communist Party Between Berlinguer and the Seventeenth Congress," in Sidney Tarrow, ed., *Italian Politics: A Review* (New York: St. Martin's, 1986).
16. For an earlier contrast of these parties, see Thomas H. Greene, "The Communist Parties of Italy and France: A Study of Comparative Communism," *World Politics* 21 (October 1968): 1–38.
17. Joseph LaPalombara, "Socialist Alternatives: The Italian Variant," *Foreign Affairs* 60 (Spring 1984): 924–942.

18. K. Robert Nilsson, "The Italian Socialist Party: An Indispensable Hostage," in Penniman, *Italy at the Polls, 1983.*
19. Gianfranco Pasquino, "Modernity and Reforms: The PSI Between Political Entrepreneur and Gambler," *West European Politics* 9 (January 1986): 120–141.
20. Robert H. Evans, "The Italian Election of June 1987," *Italian Journal* (September 1987): 9–27.
21. Norman Kogan, "The Italian Republican Party," *Conference Group on Italian Politics & Society Newsletter,* 23 (February 1988): pp. 1–4.
22. Robert Leonardi, "The Changing Balance: The Rise of the Small Parties in the 1983 Elections," in Penniman, *Italy at the Polls, 1983.*
23. Joseph LaPalombara, *Democracy Italian Style* (New Haven, CT: Yale University Press, 1987), p. 23.
24. Ibid., p. 20. A few years later and still in exile to avoid prosecution, Negri complained that the Italian government was only sending him half of his parliamentary salary because of nonattendance in the Chamber of Deputies!
25. Gregory M. Luebbert, "Coalition Theory and Government Formation in Multiparty Democracies," *Comparative Politics* 15 (January 1983): 235–249; and G. Bingham Powell, Jr., *Contemporary Democracies: Participation, Stability, and Violence* (Cambridge, MA: Harvard University Press, 1982).
26. Geoffrey Pridham, "Opposition in Italy: From Polarized Pluralism to Centripetal Pluralism," in Eva Kolinsky, ed., *Opposition in Western Europe* (London: Croom Helm, 1987).
27. Joseph LaPalombara, *Interest Groups in Italian Politics* (Princeton, NJ: Princeton University Press, 1964).
28. Belloni, "Factionalism, the Party System, and Italian Politics," pp. 80–81.
29. Peter Lange, et al., *Unions, Change and Crisis: French and Italian Union Strategy and the Political Economy, 1945–1980* (London: George Allen & Unwin, 1982).
30. Marino Regini, "Changing Relations Between Labour and the State in Italy: Towards a Neo-Corporatist System?" in Gerhard Lehmbruch and Philippe C. Schmitter, eds., *Patterns of Corporatist Policy-Making* (Beverly Hills, CA and London: Sage, 1982).
31. Ibid.
32. Miriam A. Golden, "Interest Representation, Party Style, and the State: Italy in Comparative Perspective," *Comparative Politics* 18 (April 1986): 279–301.
33. Mario Caciagli and Frank P. Belloni, "The 'New' Clientelism in Southern Italy: The Christian Democratic Party in Catania," in S. N. Eisenstadt and René Lemarchand, eds., *Political Clientelism, Patronage and Development* (Beverly Hills, CA and London: Sage, 1981), pp. 36–42.
34. LaPalombara, *Democracy Italian Style,* p. 140.

CHAPTER NINETEEN
ITALIAN
POLICY MAKING

For decades, Italy has been used as a stereotype of the dangers of governmental instability and chaos in a multiparty state. The instability has been so great that observers have described Italy as a "republic without government", or its parties as "surviving without governing."[1] And yet, despite these problems, the regime somehow has muddled through hard times and avoided the ultimate, regime threatening, crisis to persist for over four decades.

ITALIAN REPUBLICAN GOVERNMENT

After the Second World War, Italian voters were asked in a referendum to decide on whether to retain the monarchy or to switch to a republican form of government. By a narrow margin, voters disgusted with the monarchy's collaboration with fascism until 1943 opted for a republic. As a result, sovereignty was transferred to the parliament in a system that resembles in many ways the British and West German political frameworks. Political power is divided among the parliament, the president of the republic, and the government composed of the council of ministers and its president, the prime minister. (See Figure 19.1)

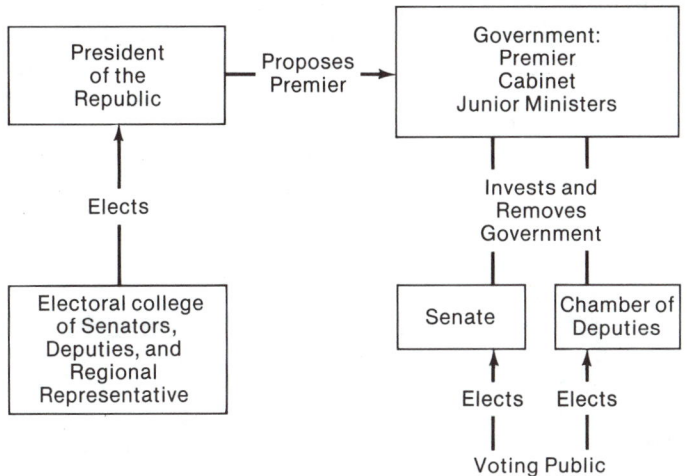

FIGURE 19.1   Basic Political Institutions in Italy.

Parliament

In the other countries that have been examined, the power of the executive has come to prevail over the legislature under normal circumstances: in Britain, people talk of prime ministerial government; in France, the powers of the president and prime minister give one or the other control over policy; in Germany, "chancellor democracy" prevails. In Italy, however, the traditional parliamentary preeminence continues. There is not a single party having a majority in parliament and parliamentary coalitions are fragile and transient. Still the parliament has succeeded in retaining control over policy and the executive.

The Italian parliament is composed of two houses: the Chamber of Deputies and the Senate. Deputies and senators are elected at the same time for five year terms although their tenure in office may be cut short by dissolutions as has been the case in each of the last five elections. The electorates for the two houses are slightly different since voters must be at least 25-years-old to vote for the Senate while 18-year-olds may vote for the Chamber of Deputies. But this age difference has little effect on the composition of the two bodies. The party strength in the two houses is virtually identical. There are 630 members of the Chamber of Deputies. In the Senate, there are 315 directly elected members plus the presidentially appointed senators-for-life. Each president is entitled to name five such senators; in 1985 there were eight appointed senators serving in the Senate. The two houses have similar powers. Both the Senate and the Chamber are required to pass a law for its adoption and both are able to oust the government through a vote of censure.

The similar nature of the powers and electorate of the Senate and Chamber has raised questions about the need for two houses. It is bicameralism without reason. Bicameralism in each of the other three countries that have been examined is based on a difference in power and a political base for the second chamber: in Britain, a weak House of Lords is based on an hereditary aristocracy; in France, an indirectly elected Senate is unable to block National Assembly laws; and in West Germany, a Bundesrat is designated by state governments to defend state interests. Without a different selection basis, the Italian Senate simply replicates the Chamber and has little to offer in the way of a unique contribution to the legislative process.

Informally, the Chamber has greater influence. While there is no constitutional stipulation establishing the priority of the Chamber, by tradition, the prime minister and most ministers come from its membership. Governments tend to pay more attention to legislative defeats and votes of nonconfidence in the Chamber than they do to those in the Senate. Sometimes they await the outcome of the Chamber after a defeat in the Senate before stepping down. When there are disagreements between the two houses on the wording or provisions of legislation, there is no constitutional procedure to resolve these differences, such as the conference committees or shuttle processes that are found in Britain, France, and West Germany. Instead, in Italy legislation disputed between the Senate and Chamber simply is sent back and forth from one house to the other in the hope that eventually the differences will disappear. If they do not, the bill dies only when a new election brings a new parliament.

In constitutional theory, the Italian parliament is all powerful. On the surface, it appears very active and powerful, enacting many more laws than legislative bodies in other European countries, taking greater initiative in legislation and adopting more amendments, and causing the fall of governments on regular occasions. But in fact, the parliament is ineffective as a decision maker.[2] Its ineffectiveness derives from disagreements among deputies and senators on policy content, and also from their inability to agree upon procedures for making the decisions. The volume of legislation that is produced represents incomplete legislative packages and marginal laws that are designed more to serve the political interests of incongruous assemblies of deputies from many parties than to provide the nation with coherent policies. Despite parliament's great powers, its proceedings are usually uninspired, even boring because government and party spokespersons deliberately avoid blunt exchanges. It is clear that while parliament is the locus of power, decisions on how and when to use that power are notably made elsewhere, such as in the caucuses and headquarters of the political parties.

Party loyalty in parliament is high with deputies and senators from the same party nearly always voting as a bloc. No single party has a majority, however, nor are there stable majority coalitions. Consequently, majorities for each major and minor pieces of legislation must be constructed through the Italian variation on logrolling, *trasformismo*. Italian parliament members draw on nearly one hundred years of experience in putting together unlikely coalitions drawn from sharply opposed parties who, nevertheless, find some redeeming value in a part of the legislative package. Consequently, a surprisingly large share of the legislation is passed with strong majorities, that often include the support of extremist parties. For example, the PCI voted for 71 percent of the laws passed by parliament between 1948 and 1968.[3] And most of this period was before the PCI's moderation. Today, it is rare for a major piece of legislation to go forward without the concurrence of the Communists even though they are part of the formal opposition.[4]

Since the parties vote as a bloc, the party group leaders in parliament are key figures with important power over the legislative decisions. These officials also control the legislative agenda.[5] This power in Britain, France, and Germany has been acquired by the government and is used there to assure preferential treatment of government proposals. Such attention to the government's priorities is not assured in Italy, and if it does happen it is because of the wills of these party leaders rather than because of the government's own decision. Another source of power is the committee structure. The standing committees have been delegated the right to pass legislation on behalf of the whole house. A surprisingly large percentage of the legislative output, about three out of four bills, is passed in this manner. Such measures are usually not major or controversial bills but they do reflect the pervasive importance of acceptance by Italian parliamentarians of negotiated, compromised, logrolling legislation. In addition, the committees often completely rewrite the government's proposals. The government has none of the powers that prevents the rewriting of its proposals as is the case in Britain and France. It is in the secrecy of the committees that the intricate balances among competing interests, parties, and party factions are struck to serve the interest of the parties' clients.

There is one peculiar feature of Italian parliamentary procedure that makes governments highly vulnerable: The final vote on all legislation that goes to the floor of parliament is a secret ballot. Designed to allow individual members to vote according to their consciences rather than the party line, the secret ballot has in fact become the means for members of a party to weaken or overthrow a government headed by one of their own leaders because of factional disputes or personal rivalries. Thus, legislation may go through initial votes with little problem only to be voted down by such "snipers" on the final secret ballot. Occasionally such votes bring the fall of a government. For example, in June 1986, such a legislative defeat at the hands of unidentifiable snipers provoked a two-week crisis that nearly toppled the Craxi government.

The frequent fall of Italian governments suggests that the parliament makes ample use of its ability to oversee the executive. But in fact, direct parliamentary action is not the principal cause of the governments' resignations. Of the more than forty governments that have fallen, only a handful have been toppled by votes of censure. Most governments have resigned because of internal disunity or their calculations that they have lost majority parliamentary support without actually awaiting verification by parliamentary action. The Craxi government finally fell in March 1987 as a result of a dispute among the coalition parties rather than a direct vote in parliament. Interpellation, the powerful check on the British prime minister through regular question times, is scarcely developed in Italy with most questions being posed in writing and all answered in writing rather than before a full house of skeptical political rivals.

Debate is lively but it is faulted. It is either highly ideological in content—and therefore not likely to do more than confirm the prejudices of the believers—or it is directed at minutiae—of interest to those who might benefit materially from the law's provisions but too narrow to raise the crucial political and economic issues at stake. Without discussion of concrete but broad political principles, parliamentary debate neither educates the public nor provides for informed discussion on the issues among policy makers. In fact, despite its constitutional standing as the paramount political institution, what goes on in the Italian parliament is not nearly as important as the interaction among parties, citizens, special interest groups, and the bureaucracy outside of parliament in the important coalition and clientelistic politics.[6] The tradition of clientelism, reinforced by the preference voting possible under Italy's electoral system, does encourage deputies to maintain close links with their constituents.[7]

The President

As is true of other parliamentary systems, such as Britain and West Germany, the powers of the executive are divided between the head of the government (the prime minister or chancellor) and the head of state. The Italian head of state is the president. Italian presidents lack the power that French presidents have accumulated in their mixed parliamentary-presidential system. But they exercise more power than German presidents or British monarchs because of the greater fluidity of party coalitions and majorities in Italy.

Presidential elections are often prolonged and tortuous affairs. The president is elected by an electoral college composed of the 630 deputies, 323 senators, and 58 representatives from the regions. For the first three ballots, a two-thirds majority is required to be elected; on successive ballots an absolute majority suffices. That majority can be difficult to muster. In the 1978 presidential election, it took sixteen ballots to elect Sando Pertini president, and that was not a record; it took twenty-three ballots to find a president in 1972.

The 1985 presidential election set a record in the other direction. The Christian Democrat Francisco Cossiga was elected on the first ballot with the support of a broad five-party majority plus the Communists. And at fifty-six years of age, Cossiga was also the youngest of the eight preceding presidents. In previous elections, older senior politicians were honored by the presidency almost as a retirement benefit. As a result of the difficult process of finding a majority to elect the president, the electors typically gave preference to old, less controversial, even marginal political leaders who might have emerged in later ballots as compromise candidates. This selection process was also reinforced by the desire of deputies and senators to avoid voting for too ambitious or powerful presidential candidates. The propensity to turn to noncontroversial leaders for the presidency also explains why the Christian Democrats have not dominated the presidency as they have the rest of the government. Non-Christian Democrats have held the presidency for twenty-one of the last forty years.

Beyond the ceremonial powers exercised by all heads of state, the Italian president also plays an important part in the selection of a new prime minister. In Britain and Germany, the role of the head of state in selecting the prime minister or chancellor is very restricted since elections nearly always produce solid parliamentary majorities with party leaders designated beforehand in that role should their parties win the majority. In Italy no single party or preelection coalition has won a majority since the early 1950s. Nor has the DC, the largest single party, yet contested in an election with a single leader known publicly ahead of time as the prime minister designate. Consequently, after an election or after the fall of a government between elections, the president has considerable leeway in deciding which of several DC leaders to ask to form a government. And in the last decade, with the DC no longer enjoying the dominant position it once had, the president's options have extended to other parties as well.

It is clear that the president's political and personal preferences influence the selection of prime minister candidates. For example, Socialist President Sando Pertini named fellow Socialist Bettino Craxi in 1983 instead of several other possible candidates. Other presidents have scorned powerful leaders whom they have personally disliked or whose political inclinations they have opposed. Some presidents have gone beyond simply asking an individual to try to form a government by dictating the general political tendency of the new government. For example, a president may direct the prime minister designate to build a Center-Left or Center-Right government. The president's powers in shaping the government, both in nominating the prime minister and in suggesting its composition, are limited by the willingness of the leaders, parties, their factions, and eventually parliament to accept his choices. And, as shall be seen, such acceptance is often difficult to obtain with the president forced to nominate several prime ministers before finding one capable of forming a government. Nevertheless, the Italian president has greater influence over the choice of the head of government than does either the German president or the British monarch. But French presidents, at least when they are supported by a favorable majority in the National Assembly, have even wider options in selecting their prime ministers. The president's role in selecting the new prime minister is thus a key power with important consequences on Italian politics.

Other powers of the president include a suspensive veto which temporarily delays promulgation of a law while parliament reconsiders the legislation. Presidents have used this power sparingly and usually in a noncontroversial manner such as to call attention to badly drafted laws. The president also has some important appointive powers including the naming of five senators for life to the Senate and five members to the Supreme Court. An important presidential power that has emerged only in the past fifteen years is the president's power to dissolve parliament and call for new elections. A presumed popular antipathy to premature elections dissuaded presidents from using the power until 1972. But since that year, presidents have dissolved every parliament before the full term of five years has elapsed. The purpose of such a dissolution is to get a fresh reading of the voters' feelings when stalemate and governmental crisis seem to have exhausted the possible government coalitions. While presidents have made use of this power regularly, the utility of dissolution in resolving political stalemate is limited by the tendency for the new parliament to resemble the old one both in faces and in the relative strength of the parties. For example, after the 1979 dissolution, the parliamentary elections did little to resolve the *imbroglio,* and it took three months to form a government. The problem has been that parties rarely lose or gain more than a handful of seats in an election so the stalemate is simply perpetuated from one parliament to the next. As was noted in Chapter Eighteen, there is some change in this stalemate with greater swings among parties in recent elections. If this trend toward greater voter volatility continues, the president's power of dissolution may become a more useful device in coping with the chronic government instability.

Italian presidents do not have the arbiter powers accorded to the French president to deal with government crisis. They, nevertheless, have important influence on politics through their role in forming new governments and their power to dissolve parliament. In both these areas, presidential influence is likely to increase due to the waning of the once predominant position of the DC, the broadening spectrum of possible government parties, and the growing volatility of voters who now do seem more willing to shift party loyalties between elections. The president may well emerge as a more powerful stabilizing force in the coming years.

The Government

The government is composed of about one hundred political leaders: a prime minister, a cabinet of approximately twenty ministers, and a large number of junior ministers. They assume collective responsibility for the main executive functions: conducting foreign relations, proposing legislation, appointing key public officials, executing laws, and directing and the bureaucracy.

Perhaps the greatest weakness of Italian political institutions has been chronic governmental instability. Government instability means that the prime minister and cabinet are toppled regularly by internal divisions or by the loss of their parliamentary majority. Italy has, by far, the worst record in this regard of any Western European government. Between 1946 and 1988, the Italian republic went through forty-eight premiers and governments. The average life of a government is 10.6 months with some lasting less than two weeks and the longest-lived government, that of Bettino Craxi, enduring nearly four years.

Beneath this pattern of constant change in prime ministers and governments is some continuity. The personnel of governments are much more stable since it is the same group of party leaders who have to form every government. Sometimes they remain in the same posts, other times they remain in the government but with new duties. Often the same individuals have served as heads of several different governments: Four men have, between them, presided over one-third of the forty-eight postwar governments (De Gasperi—eight times premier, and Moro, Rumor, and Andreoti—five times each). Many of the most important ministerial posts are not changed even as prime ministers come and go. Thus, the average tenure for key ministers in Italy is twenty months which compares favorably with the usually stable Britain's twenty-six months.[8] Some leaders have had remarkably long tenures in the same ministry; some ministries have remained under the control of the same party for many of the forty-five years since the creation of the republic.[9] Thus, despite the coming and going of governments, there is much more continuity and stability than often believed to be the case.

Unlike in the other three countries that have been looked at where collegial decision making takes place in weekly meetings of the cabinet, in Italy the cabinet does not meet regularly for a collective discussion of major policy decisions. Coordination can occur through informal and bilateral contacts between ministers or their representatives. Other devices for coordination are the interministerial committees, but these committees lack the political influence necessary to assure that decisions reached in their meetings are, in fact, implemented by the affected ministers once they get back to their own ministries. In recent years, cabinet meetings occur more regularly but without any increase in collective decision making. Instead, all ministers have important controls over their respective departments both in terms of administrative matters and in terms of the nature of policy.

Consequently, the Italian prime minister does not have the control over policy like that of the British prime minister or German chancellor. The prime minister's control is limited, not only by the delegation of decision making to the various ministers, but also by the nature of the people who compose the government. Unlike in Britain, Germany, and even France where the personalities are selected by the prime minister and are therefore beholden to the leader, in Italy the prime minister is more constrained in the selection of ministers by the difficult process of forming a majority coalition. Often powerful party or faction leaders with little or no sympathy for the prime minister must be included in order to win the needed support of a party or a DC faction. The result is a government cabinet made up of "a chorus of prima donnas."[10] In many cases, the prime minister is not even a prominent figure but a compromise leader selected to avoid more powerful but controversial leaders. Such weak prime ministers obviously have little success in imposing their will on their colleagues. The more successful prime ministers, such as Aldo Moro and Alcide de Gasperi, have not been commanders but mediators capable of holding together otherwise incompatible political elements.[11]

But there are some indications of growing prime ministerial influence. For one thing, the size of the prime minister's office has grown substantially: from about three hundred in 1963 to about eight hundred at the beginning of the 1980s[12] and even larger under Craxi. One observer notes accurately that the prime minister's power has grown not because of constitutional provisions but because of the prime minister's emerging role as coordinator of the disparate government elements. It is the prime minister who gives central direction and coherence to government.[13] Under Bettino Craxi, the head of the longest-lived Italian government, the prime minister's power grew substantially. Unlike other governments which have sometimes avoided action to perpetuate their longevity, Craxi was an activist prime minister pushing ahead even with very controversial issues (such as the reduction in the wage escalator clause).[14] He had a program in mind which, although not always fully shared by his government colleagues, nevertheless formed the agenda for their collective efforts. He was clearly an activist prime minister such as Italy has rarely experienced: shaping a response to the economic recession; concluding the new concordat with the Church; conducting an ambitious and sometimes controversial foreign policy. He pressed forward even when faced with internal opposition and won greater public esteem in doing so. With regard to detractors inside his government, Craxi self-confidently proclaimed

> The ship is on the right course. I remain at my post holding high the flag. If the other officers do not wish to follow orders . . . they can be let off at the first port.[15]

His immediate successors were unable to carry on this activist style. Four governments came and went in the next year. But Craxi's leadership offers a precedent for a possibly stronger leadership role for future prime ministers.

The drama of the overthrow of Italian governments leads observers to focus on the weakness of the executive in Italy. And in comparison with the executives in Britain, France, and Germany, the Italian premier and government are less powerful. However, divisions within parliament leave more latitude to the Italian executive than is usually enjoyed by American presidents. The Italian government has broad decree powers that recent cabinets have used with greater frequency. Deadlock in parliament provides the necessity and the justification for such executive action. While the Italian executive may often be crippled by partyocracy, the Craxi government proved that it is capable of a long and powerful policy-making term when in the hands of a capable leader.

Making and Breaking Governments in Italy

The Italian Constitution offers the government less protection from votes of censure than is the case in either the German Federal Republic or France. In Germany, the Bundestag cannot oust a government without electing first a new chancellor; in France, votes of censure require an absolute majority of the total membership in the National Assembly. In Italy, a simple majority of those present and voting in either the Senate or the Chamber of Deputies on a vote of nonconfidence or a vote of censure brings the fall of the government. Despite the relative ease of this procedure, it is not the explanation of the frequent falling of Italian governments.

Far more often, the government simply resigns because it becomes aware that it has lost its majority in parliament. A party participating in the coalition may indicate that it intends to leave the government; a DC faction may announce that it is dissatisfied with the conduct of the existing government; or an important piece of government legislation may be deadlocked or defeated outright in parliament. Such crises may evolve out of genuine disagreement over policies and the conduct of the government, or they may simply come from the exhaustion of the original agreement that brought the various elements together in the first place. The government's fall may also be the product of personal rivalries or result from hopes for improved representation in a new government on the part of individuals, factions, or parties.

When a government falls, the president calls upon a party figure of his choice to try to form a government. Unlike the formation of governments in France, the president plays little part in the selecting of the other ministers. While the French have tried to minimize the role of parties in the formation of governments, the Italian government formation process centers upon negotiation with the parties in what some call a partyocracy. The prime minister designate consults with leaders from other parties regarded as "permissible partners" by his or her party to explore the conditions of their participation in a new government coalition.[16] In nearly all cases, this means consultation with most parties except the PCI and neo-fascist MSI. A DC prime minister designate must also negotiate with the various factions inside the Christian Democratic party. Issues that are involved include the policies that the government will seek to implement and the distribution of ministerial posts and other key appointive offices (such as parliamentary committee leadership and administrative posts in government and in public corporations). Each party or faction wants to assure maximum appointments for its leaders both in numbers and in terms of the importance of a ministry or other appointment. Thus, the prime minister designate must try to balance different parties, factions within parties, powerful personalities, and considerations of regional balance in forming the coalition. With so many political factors at stake, it is not surprising that ministerial competency—the ability of an individual political leader to administer a department in an effective manner—is often slighted in the process of selecting ministers. In many cases, the individuals named to head important government departments lack any administrative experience.[17]

If the prime minister designate fails to find the needed majority, the president acts again by either asking the leader to try again or, more frequently, selecting another leader to try to put together a government coalition. The achievement of this coalition is often a prolonged and difficult process leaving the country with caretaker governments for long periods of time. Such interim governments—sometimes headed by the defeated premier, other times by temporary premiers—handle routine matters and enact needed policies but they are unable to deal with the more controversial issues. In the first twenty-five years of the Italian Republic, there were 680 days of "governmental crisis" between the formation of governments. That is almost two years without a formally installed government. In recent years, there have been some exceptionally long governmental crises. For example, for much of 1979 there was only an interim caretaker government while a series of leaders sought to form a durable coalition. Even an election did not resolve the situation: After the parliamentary elections in June 1979, a new government was not formed for more than three months. The crisis, before and after the elections left Italy without a formally invested government for seven months.

Once a prime minister believes that he or she has achieved a workable coalition, the president proceeds to swear in the new government. The new government then tests its majority by proposing votes of confidence in both houses of parliament. Failure to win a majority of those voting in either chamber results in the fall of the government with the whole process starting over. Even after the successful formation of the coalition, negotiations among party leaders in the government continue at frequent intervals to resolve tensions, adjust policy stands, and renew understandings on the important matter of distributing patronage appointments.

There are six typical structures of Italian governments:

1. Single party (or monocolor) minority coalitions
2. Center-Left coalitions
3. Centrist coalitions
4. Center-Right coalitions
5. The "five party coalition"
6. Grand coalitions

When the parties are unable to reach an agreement on a new government, the DC has on occasion ruled alone in a minority government made up of its supporters. Such governments are able to win passage of the confidence motion due to the voluntary abstention or even positive votes from parties who are formally not part of the government but who acquiesce, at least temporarily, to its existence. Such silent partners are often rewarded with nonministerial appointments and the government's acceptance of their policy constraints. More typically, one finds the kind of multi-party coalitions indicated in types two through five. A Center-Left government generally includes the DC, PSI, PSDI, and PRI. A Centrist government is made up of the DC, PSDI, PRI, and possibly the PLI. A Center-Right coalition includes the DC, PRI, and PLI. In the 1980s, the predominant coalition pattern—the one used in every permanent government between 1980 and 1988—was the five party coalition based on the Christian Democrats and the Socialists with support from the Social Democrats, Liberals, and Republicans.

At the end of the 1970s, a new option was added: that of the grand coalition of the DC and the PCI in the historic compromise advocated by the Communists.[18] There has not yet been such a government formed with direct PCI participation in holding ministerial portfolios. But the PCI has supported DC governments on several occasions through its votes in parliament. In return, it has been rewarded with parliamentary leadership positions and appointments of its supporters to administrative and public corporation positions. The emergence of the Communist party opens new opportunities for coalition formation that have, thus far, not been explored in practice. But the continued hostility to such an option by the DC and the PCI's recent decline, make it unlikely that this option of the grand coalition will develop further. Instead, there is now often discussion of a coalition of the Left with the reinvigorated Socialist party of Bettino Craxi playing the leading role.

THE CONSTITUTIONAL COURT

The ease with which Mussolini distorted the democratic constitution to permit authoritarian rule and the serious abuse of human rights led those who drafted the postwar Constitution to create a judicial body responsible for overseeing the compatibility of government laws and actions with the Constitution. Because of the absence of a tradition of judicial review in Italy and the resistance of both legislators and judges to competition from a Constitutional Court, it took nearly a decade to pass the legislation needed to bring the Court into actual existence. Once in existence, its prerogatives were initially restricted by the reluctance typical of all parliamentary regimes to see the legislature's supremacy as the elected representatives of the sovereign people challenged by any body, juridical or otherwise.

The Constitutional Court is composed of fifteen judges. The president names five judges; five are elected by a joint session of parliament with a three-fifth's vote required; the remaining five are named by the jurists in the higher civil and administrative courts. They serve nine-year terms and are not eligible for immediate reselection. The Constitutional Court is responsible for assuring the constitutionality of legislation, the respect for human rights, and the resolution of jurisdictional disputes between branches and layers of the government. Access to this court is much more open than is access to parallel bodies in either France or West Germany since cases may be appealed by individuals, groups, or regional governments by simply raising a constitutional issue. In its first decade, lower level appelate courts, especially the Court of Cassation which viewed the Council as a potential rival to its authority, resisted the referral of these cases by regularly disallowing such constitutional appeals. But in the last two decades, this obstacle has diminished as a new and more sympathetic attitude toward the Constitutional Court has developed among Italian jurists. Consequently, the case load of the Court has increased sharply since the early 1970s.

Parallel with its larger workload has been the growth in political influence of the Court. After an initial period of hesitancy, the Italian Constitutional Court has become one of Europe's most active and politically involved high court. In the 1970s, it led in the effort to secularize Italian society in a series of decisions that reduced Church influence: overturning adultery laws on grounds that they discriminated against women; ruling that divorce reform did not require a constitutional amendment; voiding fascist era laws which barred the publication of information on contraception and sale of contraceptives; overturning fascist era antiabortion laws. In 1974, the Court ruled that the government's monopoly of radio and television violated the freedom of press and of speech, touching off a genuine revolution in Italian radio and television as literally thousands of new stations were opened by private firms, local governments, and political groupings. The Court has also played an important role in supervising referendums, invalidating, for example, half of the referendum proposals that the erratic Radical party tried to get on the ballot.

In these and other major decisions, the Italian Constitutional Court has emerged as a powerful body fully able to use its powers of judicial review to protect civil liberties and to assure the constitutionality of laws. It is now much more powerful than either the French or German Constitutional Courts. The Italian Court's prestige and activism seem likely to assure it an important role in the coming decade.

THE BUREAUCRACY

The Italian state in its various forms—ministries and agencies, local governments, the military, schools, and publicly-owned corporations—employs over 4 million people out of a total active population of 19 million.[19] In theory, these posts are filled through competitive examinations on nonpartisan grounds. In practice, due to the use of temporary staffs and the neglect of competitive examination procedures, many of these positions are filled through patronage. Thus, nearly a third of those presumed to be career civil servants have avoided the formal competition when entering public service.[20] Perhaps because of this political tainting, Italian civil servants lack the social prestige of their counterparts in Britain, France, and Germany. This lower prestige does not reduce, however, the civil service's tendency to assume a condescending attitude toward the public with evidence that the structure and organization of the civil service takes precedence over service to the public.[21]

Whatever their origins, the civil servants become part of the vast political, party-interest, group-bureaucracy, networks or the *parentella* and *clientella* relationships.[22] Political parties—especially the DC but others too—develop broad coalitions (or *parentella* relationships) with interest groups as a base for political operations. The parties—again, especially the DC but others too in recent years including even the PCI at local levels—colonize various government agencies or offices with officials who align themselves with the party or who owe their jobs to it. These party activists working for the government or public firms are expected "to serve as a conduit for party policies and preferences in the administrative apparatus of the state."[23] The parties and their bureaucratic friends also build close relationships with groups representing the interests of those whom the agency serves. Such *clientella* ties serve the interests of parties, bureaucracies, and the affected interest groups. This partisan influence is virtually nonexistent in the British or German bureaucracies but it can be seen in the French bureaucracy. The party influence in the civil service is far greater in Italy than in all other European democracies.

The parties' penetration of the bureaucracy provides only an indirect means of political control by the government. The permanence of the present party balance and the growing tendency to divide patronage up among the various government parties means that there are few changes in the partisan personnel after elections such as the vast shifts that take place in Washington after an American presidential election. In seeking to exercise control over the bureaucracy, the Italian government must therefore often work through party channels. The government's ability to monitor the bureaucracy it supposedly heads is further reduced by the transient nature of governments and ministers. Control and coordination is also hampered by the high degree of compartmentalization with various agencies and departments hesitant or unable to communicate with each other. Even the potential for control through the budget is restricted by the ability of individual parts of the bureaucracy to use their political ties to bypass the Treasury or the government by direct action in parliament. Indeed, the centralized budget control was a relatively recent development as there was no unified budget until the mid-1960s. Before that, numerous separate budgets were passed by parliament for each part of government.

While the issue of political control is of central theoretic importance for democracy, the average Italian citizen is more upset by the inefficiency, the red tape and the delays of the civil service. The Italian bureaucracy is notoriously slow in its operation. For example, claims for damage suffered in the great 1906 earthquake were still being processed in the mid-1970s.[24] Its compartmentalization and extreme centralization are inefficient. It is plagued also by a reputation for corruption. Formal rules seem to take precedence over citizen needs. Thus, a mayor's request for emergency relief in the aftermath of recent earthquakes in Sicily was returned because the application was not bound with an official ribbon using the colors of the nation's flag.[25] The arrogances and delays that citizens face in daily encounters with bureaucrats in the post office and other government bureaus contribute significantly to the Italians' disregard for their political system and its representatives.

Despite its problems, the Italian bureaucracy has proved able to resist the few and relatively feeble efforts by postwar governments to reform it. A comprehensive analysis of the weaknesses of the administration along with a proposal for reforms was prepared in 1979 by the Minister of Public Administration, Massimo Severo Giannini. But Giannini later explained the lack of action on his proposals, "There is no political will to solve the problems."[26] No government is seriously interested in changing a system that provides the patronage needed to reward party loyalists. No Italian government has the strength or durability to impose structural reforms on the large and well-entrenched bureaucracy.

DECENTRALIZATION

One of the legacies of the *Risorgimento* was the highly centralized state. Because of the ease with which Mussolini used this centralization to consolidate his authoritarian rule, the postwar Constitution called for the decentralization of power to twenty regions. However, there was a long lag in bringing the regions into being. Five "special" regions were created promptly to provide measures of decentralized rule to areas with ethnic or regional needs: Val d'Aosta, Trenton-Alto Adige, Friuli-Venezia Giulia, Sicily, and Sardinia. But it was not until the 1970s that the fifteen ordinary regions actually came into existence as operative political entities.[27] In part, the delay was due to fear that the Communists might win control of some regional governments, which in fact happened although without the predicted dire consequences. In the meantime, the national government continued its highly centralized practices. The centrally appointed prefect held power to overrule or actually oust mayors or local councils if they violated their constitutional powers. As in France, important political restraints limited the use of these powers.[28] In addition, the Italian prefects lacked the coordinating powers of French prefects since the separate ministries in Italy operated their own local offices and enjoyed autonomy from the prefects.

The regional governments are composed of a regional Council elected by the public using a system of proportional representation. The Council then selects an executive committee or regional Junta and a regional president from among its membership. These regional governments are relatively young entities beginning to function at the end of the 1970s. The definition of their powers and the development of their relationships with each other and with other layers of government are evolving slowly through trial and error. Some critics have already labelled the regional experiment as a failure due to the central government's refusal to grant real powers to the regional units and the regions' hesitancy to assert those powers they have received.[29]

The central government therefore still has important powers throughout the country and retains the key power of control over law enforcement at all levels. The regional governments have a limited economic base; the financial resources of all regional and local governments combined amounts to slightly more than one third of the budget of the national government. The relationships between the central government and the regional governments, between the central government and the 95 provincial and 8000 local governments, and between the regional governments and provincial and local governments are still evolving. Early indications suggest some differences from the evolving pattern in France. In France, the regional bodies have yet to challenge the power of the central departments. In Italy the provinces, which are comparable to the French departments but which have never had their political importance, have posed no threat to the regional governments. Whereas in France the regional governments seem to be eclipsed by the preexisting departmental and local governments, in Italy it appears that the regional governments are beginning to exercise the same centralized control over provincial and local governments that Rome used to maintain over local authorities.[30] Regional bodies now have the surveillance control over local authorities that the prefect used to exercise. Such a trend raises doubts about the ability of regional decentralization to in fact increase local autonomy and greater citizen control.

These doubts are strengthened by an examination of the early trends in the evolution of expenditures by the various levels of government. A surprising development was the growth of the central government's share of public expenditures. Table 19.1 shows these trends in the early years of decentralization. Despite the creation of this new layer of government, the central government's power continues to grow with the regional governments in effect assuming functions and control once exercised by local or provincial governments. In addition, the funds for all levels of government are raised by the central government alone (See Table 19.2) and then doled out by it to the regional and lower level units. In distributing these funds, the central government often attaches conditions or stipulates programs or standards that must be followed as the money is used.

One advantage of decentralization is that it has offered additional opportunities for experimentation in political cooperation. For example, the grand coalition of the PCI and DC that has remained a hypothetical possibility on the national level has been implemented at the regional level. In other regions, left-wing alliances of Communists and Socialists, which

TABLE 19.1   Public Expenditures by Level of Government

Percentage of total public expenditures

	1974	1977	1980
Central government	67.1%	69.8%	77.5%
Regional governments	6.6	11.3	10.6
Provincial governments	4.1	3.0	1.6
Local governments	22.2	15.9	10.3

Source: Adapted from: Bruno Dente, "Centre-Local Relations in Italy: The Impact of the Legal and Political Structures," in Yves Meny and Vincent Wright, eds., *Centre-Periphery Relations in Western Europe* (London: George Allen & Unwin, 1985), p. 130.

TABLE 19.2   Source of Government Revenues in Selected Countries, 1981

Country	% raised by central government	% raised by regional and local governments
Italy	99%	1%
France	93	7
Britain	90	10
USA	70	30
West Germany	68	32

Source: Adapted from Richard Rose, "From Government at the Centre to Nationwide Government," in Yves Meny and Vincent Wright, *Centre-Periphery Relations in Western Europe* (London: George Allen & Unwin, 1985), p. 27.

have not been possible on the national level since the early 1960s, have been tried. But the strongly centralized and disciplined parties remain instruments for imposing central control over the new regions, bringing if not a state centralism then party centralism.[31]

CITIZEN CONTROL
IN ITALIAN POLITICS

In Britain and West Germany, citizen control over government is assured by the presence of disciplined parties which form cohesive governments that are generally able to continue in office throughout the life of the legislature. The individual who will head the government from each of the major competing parties is known ahead of time so that voters know the choices of not only the policy differences but also the likely prime minister or chancellor and can express their feelings at the polls. The situation is similar in France for presidential elections: The electoral choices are real as the parties can and have rotated in and out of power. Voters are given the opportunity to exert control by approving or sanctioning parties and leaders they like or dislike through their votes. Such features facilitate government responsibility to the electorate.

In Italy, the situation is quite different. Because the choice of a prime minister is the result of intricate negotiations and secret bargains after and between elections, voters rarely have any idea who will be the next prime minister when they go to the polls. Policies and priorities are also established after the elections through this same secret negotiating process over which voters have little or no control. The voters know that the same parties that were in government before the elections will be in government afterwards. The voters' ability to sanction a government they feel has betrayed their hopes is eliminated. The prime minister and government are likely to change four or more times between elections, and again the voters' impact on such changes is nil.

During these various negotiations over government composition, policies, and patronage, the parties and their internal factions are the central actors. One study of Italian legislators found that they tended to equate voters with their party membership and organization.

> As the party takes the center stage, the term *electorate* loses its undifferentiated features, and becomes progressively identified . . . with the base, the rank and file, the organized and active membership of each party. In the extreme, the term is a synonym for the party organization and apparatus.[32]

Of course, such images of the electorate are distorted since the parties are representative neither of the general public nor even of the voters for a particular party. The point is that when party elites struggle with each other behind closed doors to form governments and establish policy priorities after the election instead of before it, the public loses its means to control government through electoral checks. At best, the public determines through elections who will play the postelection game of creating and destroying a government and establishing policy. But the public has little impact on the crucial issue of who will win that game.[33]

While the public is excluded from much of the game of determining national politics, clientelist politics does bring the presence of government into the lives of many Italians. The parties are well organized with extensive networks that affect the lives of many citizens in the sense of bartering government services and benefits for political support. Clientelism, or the subtle exchanges between powerful political brokers and their supporters, continues to be an important part of Italian politics. Because the local party officials have an immediate and tangible effect, many citizens give preference to these local party notables or faction leaders over elected deputies. Thus, clientelism provides an alternative means of linking the mass with the elite policy makers through local party officials. Unlike the linkage through elections of deputies or senators which should influence the actors in democratic policy making, this clientelistic link is one oriented toward government output or the implementation of policy as they affect individuals.[34]

It is easy to be critical of the Italian system of clientelistic politics. It is demeaning to the individuals involved who are forced to "pay" with their political support for government services and benefits that ought to be provided to all. It leads to inefficient distribution and allocation of government resources. It is prone to outright corruption. But clientelism *does* provide real benefits to many people, benefits that can perceptibly be seen to affect their lives. Such benefits are more popular than the less tangible benefits of ideological satisfaction with the orientation of a government in distant Rome. It helps citizens to escape the delays and rigidities of the bureaucracy. One study explored the efforts of a PCI local government in Naples to escape the clientelistic pattern of politics that had prevailed before the Communist party came to power. After five years of a PCI government that avoided clientelism, observers noted a nostalgia for the old pattern of politics, "Better a clientelistic system than no system at all."[35] In a political system where national politics are often stalemated by fragmented and polarized parties, an alternative system of particularistic relations linking people with government, even in an imperfect manner, has some distinct advantages.

NOTES

1. P. A. Allum, *Italy—Republic Without Government* (New York: Norton, 1973) and Giuseppe di Palma, *Surviving Without Governing: The Italian Parties in Parliament* (Berkeley, CA: University of California Press, 1977).
2. Di Palma, *Surviving Without Governing.*
3. Ibid., pp. 48–57.
4. Joseph LaPalombara, *Democracy Italian Style* (New Haven, CT: Yale University Press, 1987), pp. 213–224.

5. Robert Leonardi, et al., "Institutionalization of Parliament and Parliamentarization of Parties in Italy," *Legislative Studies Quarterly* 3 (February 1978):163–169.
6. Samuel H. Barnes, *Representation in Italy: Institutionalized Tradition and Electoral Choice* (Chicago: University of Chicago Press, 1977), p. 14.
7. Geoffrey Pridham, "Parliamentarians and their Constituents in Italy's Party Democracy," in Vernon Bogdonar, ed., *Representatives of the People? Parliamentarians and Constituents in Western Democracies* (London: Gower, 1985).
8. Statistic is based on 1955–1970. Allum, *Italy—Republic Without Government*, p. 120.
9. Sabino Cassese, "Is There a Government in Italy? Politics and Administration at the Top," in Richard Rose and Ezra N. Suleiman, eds., *Presidents and Prime Ministers* (Washington, DC: American Enterprise Institute, 1980), pp. 172–173.
10. Carlo Donolo, "Social Change and Transformation of the State in Italy," in Richard Scase, ed., *The State in Western Europe* (New York: St. Martin's, 1980), p. 166.
11. Frederic Spotts and Theodor Wieser, *Italy: A Difficult Democracy* (Cambridge, England: Cambridge University Press, 1986), p. 117.
12. Donolo, "Social Change and Transformation of the State in Italy," p. 176.
13. Cassese, "Is There a Government in Italy?" pp. 180–181.
14. Vincenzo Guizzi, "Craxi's Italy," *Government and Opposition* 20 (Spring 1985): 166–177.
15. *Christian Science Monitor,* 4 March 1985.
16. Alberto Marradi, "Italy: From 'Centrism' to Crisis of the Center-Left Coalitions," in Eric C. Browne and John Dreijmanis, eds., *Government Coalitions in Western Democracies* (London: Longman, 1982), p. 57.
17. Cassese, "Is There a Government in Italy?" p. 176.
18. Sidney Tarrow, "Transforming Enemies into Allies: Nonruling Communist Parties in Multiparty Coalitions," *Journal of Politics* 44 (1982): 924–954.
19. David Hine, "Italy," in F.F. Ridley, ed., *Government and Administration in Western Europe* (London: Martin Robertson, 1979), pp. 178–179.
20. Ibid., p. 183.
21. Frank Tripi, "Client Power and Italian Bureaucracy: Time Delays and Its Costs to Clients," *Social Science Journal* 22 (April 1985): 95–104.
22. Joseph LaPalombara, *Interest Groups in Italian Politics* (Princeton, NJ: Princeton University Press, 1964).
23. Robert Leonardi, "Political Power Linkages in Italy: The Nature of the Christian Democratic Party Organization," in Kay Lawson, ed., *Political Parties and Linkage: A Comparative Perspective* (New Haven, CT: Yale University Press, 1980), p. 264.
24. Raphael Zariski, *Italy: The Politics of Uneven Development* (Hinsdale, IL: Dryden Press, 1972), p. 285.
25. Spotts and Wieser, *Italy: A Difficult Democracy,* pp. 127–128.
26. Ibid., pp. 135–136.
27. See Robert Leonardi, et al., "Devolution as a Political Process: The Case of Italy," *Publius* 11 (Winter 1981): 95–117.
28. See Robert C. Fried, *The Italian Prefects: A Study in Administrative Power* (New Haven, CT: Yale University Press, 1963).
29. Donald Sassoon, *Contemporary Italy: Politics, Economy, and Society Since 1945* (New York and London: Longman, 1986), pp. 211–213.
30. Raphael Zariski, "Approaches to the Problem of Local Autonomy: The Lessons of Italian Regional Devolution," *West European Politics* 8 (July 1985), 64–81,

and Raphael Zariski, "The Impact of Regional Devolution on Local Autonomy: A New Chapter in Italian Center-Periphery Relations," in Peter H. Merkl, ed., *New Local Centers in Centralized States* (Lanham, MD: University Press of America, 1985).

31. Bruno Dente, "Centre-Periphery Relations in Italy: The Impact of the Legal and Political Structures," in Yves Mény and Vincent Wright, eds., *Centre-Periphery Relations in Western Europe* (London: George Allen & Unwin, 1985), pp. 146–147.

32. Di Palma, *Surviving Without Governing*, p. 163.

33. Samuel H. Barnes, *Representation in Italy: Institutionalized Tradition and Electoral Choice* (Chicago: University of Chicago Press, 1977), p. 159.

34. See Leonardi, "Political Power Linkages in Italy."

35. Cited by Judith Chubb, "Naples Under the Left: The Limits of Local Change," in S. N. Eisenstadt and René Lemarchand, eds., *Political Clientelism, Patronage, and Development* (Beverly Hills, CA: Sage, 1981), p. 119.

CHAPTER TWENTY
THE PERFORMANCE
OF THE "UNSTABLE"
ITALIAN REPUBLIC

A country that seems to lean into the void but never really falls into it may actually be firmly anchored there, like the Tower of Pisa.[1]

Italy suffers in comparison with the company that it keeps. As a founding member of the European Community, observers are prone to evaluate Italy's democracy and its socioeconomic accomplishments by reference to neighboring European industrial democracies. The comparisons are not always favorable: Italy has more governmental instability, party fragmentation and factionalism, greater inefficiency and political corruption, a weaker economy, and a currency with far too many digits. A more just analysis of Italian political performance would make previous Italian experience the point of reference. In comparison with the performance of prior Italian regimes—Mussolini's fascism, the liberal monarchy, and the fragmented preunification Italian states—the current democratic regime looks very good from virtually every point of evaluation. There is more public order, unprecedented economic growth and prosperity, greater citizen control of politics, and a strong respect for civil liberties. This point should be kept in mind as this chapter proceeds because the analysis that follows will often make reference to Italy's record in comparison with its more prosperous neighbors.

POLITICS AND THE ECONOMY

Italy has moved from relative economic backwardness to a modern economy "at a faster speed than any other country in western Europe."[2] Italy's rapid economic growth in the 1950s and 1960s is the second "economic miracle" of the postwar era, even if much less frequently acknowledged than the more widely praised German economic recovery.[3] Indeed, given the weaker initial economic base and Italy's lack of key natural resources, Italian economic modernization may be even more miraculous than that in Germany. Italy has also developed a modern set of social-welfare benefits to protect its citizens against the vagaries of modern capitalism.

A Troubled Economy

The Italian state has played an important part in this socioeconomic transformation. It has fostered private enterprise and, in addition, it has promoted economic growth through its own activities in the large public sector of the economy. In the 1950s and 1960s, large public holding companies—notably the ENI, a petrochemical combination, and the IRI, which controls over 150 firms ranging from steel production to public utilities and from banks to automobile manufacturers—promoted economic modernization and development through public and private investment. The public sector has remained a leading element in the Italian economy accounting for 25 percent of the gross domestic product. Government employees make up 15.6 percent of the workforce. The impact of the public sector is enhanced by the fact that the key large industries are state owned. Their decisions have broad impact on the privately owned firms.

The economic impact of government and politics is not only felt at the level of macroeconomic policies and state-owned enterprises. At every level of Italian politics, public officials and party dignitaries mete out public funds, contracts and other favors in exchange for political support. This clientelistic politics is inefficient and contributes to corruption, but it also promotes strong parties and permits the remedying of some of the economic and political blockages that otherwise might slow the economy.

Given the important role of the state in the economy, many have concerns about the impact of Italy's frequent political instability on the functioning of the economy. During the period of rapid growth in the 1950s and 1960s, there was little evidence of economic repercussions from Italy's chronic governmental instability. Despite the coming and going of prime ministers and the sometimes lengthy intervals of caretaker government, the economy was largely unaffected. There were two reasons for this stability. First, there was a general agreement on the broad outlines of economic policy during this era. The comparatively "easy" economic decisions needed were usually not politically divisive. Second, the public sector was insulated from the political leadership and continued its policies while governments were organized and toppled. Energetic and autonomous leaders, notably ENI's Enrico Mattei, pushed ahead with their plans for economic development even when the government lacked its own vision or when the government itself was absent.

It was much more difficult to insulate the economy from the uncertainties of governmental politicking during the economic crises of the 1970s. The multifaceted challenges of simultaneous inflation and economic recession, the shortage of natural resources, the skyrocketing costs of petroleum and other key resources, growing public deficits, and eventually high unemployment left governments everywhere struggling to find solutions. Without new growth, economic decisions became harder as they involved taking increasingly scarce funds or resources from one group or economic activity to give to another.

In Italy, the regular change of prime ministers only complicated the search of new policies. Successive governments would try stimulating and then cooling the economy. Difficult decisions were not made at all because the governments were too fragile to make them or because they preferred to defer such decisions to their successors. All of the governments during this era in Italy capitulated to the temptation to finance inherited deficits and their own overspending by simply printing more money. The dramatic reversals in credit, investment, and monetary policies sent mixed and conflicting signals to private investors and foreign economic partners. As each new government tried to find its own solution during its few months in office, it was impossible for any consistent approach to the deepening crisis to develop. The simultaneous weakening of public order from the growing terrorist problem reduced public confidence and further worsened the economic milieu. So great was the confusion, that one observer noted that "it is not clear in what sense we can talk of the [Italian] state responding even in a superficially coherent short-term manner to successive crises."[4]

Italy's membership in the European Community also placed limits on its ability to respond to its economic problems. In the past, Italian governments responded by competing with its neighbors by autarchic or self-sufficiency policies. Such protectionist solutions used by Italy in the past (and still used by some countries) such as the imposition of tariffs, import quotas, or agricultural subsidies, are barred by Community rules. The use of other solutions, such as the manipulation of the currency, were restricted. Additional international economic forces impinged on Italian sovereignty. For example, the International Monetary Fund imposed stringent restrictions on government social-welfare programs in 1975 as a condition for loans needed to support the lira during a period of extraordinary inflation. This incident was the primary cause of the fall of the government of the time.

But the benefits that come from both the European Common Market and from full participation in the International Economic Community compensate for the occasional infringements on Italian sovereignty. Indeed, Italy has benefitted more from the European Community than any other of its original members: European Community funds have helped support economic development in the South; Neighboring countries have accepted millions of Italians as workers; Italian exporters profited from low salaries in the 1960s to develop large new markets throughout the Community for their manufactured goods. Italian statesmen have recognized these advantages and the long-run potential for even greater opportunities. Italy has thus been one of the most ardent and constant supporters of European economic unification.

In fact, despite Italy's political problems, the economy has survived its difficulties of the 1970s and has performed rather well. One commentator states that the economy shows "persistent vigor and dynamism even under the most difficult circumstances."[5] Italy stood up well to the economic and political shocks of the 1970s.[6] Between 1978 and 1982, Italy's economic productivity grew by 4.4 percent, a higher rate than in any other industrial democracy including even Japan. In 1979 to 1980, Italy led the European Community in the rate of economic growth. But serious problems remained, especially inflation, rapidly growing public deficits, and unemployment. By the mid-1980s, inflation dropped to a single digit figure for the first time in a decade and the halving of the *scala mobile* promised to assist in keeping inflation under control. But Italy's inflation rate was still substantially higher than that of most of its trading partners. The government budget deficit continued to grow reaching 10 percent of gross domestic product by the early 1980s, higher than any other industrial nation (See Table 20.1). In 1987, the accumulated public debt had reached 97 percent of that year's estimated gross domestic product. Unemployment also rose to over 12 percent, which was less than in Britain or the Netherlands but higher than many other European countries. The restructuring or modernization of basic industries proceeded very slowly as the IRI, the government holding company, bought up failing industries and propped them up with funds from the public coffers.

There is another important aspect of the Italian economy that has both positive and negative consequences. It is the flourishing "black economy" of illegal or unreported economic activity. In every country, there are moonlighters, part-time workers, and others who avoid social security, income taxes, and labor union dues by failing to report their activities and income. But in Italy, the black economy represents a major portion of the nation's economic efforts. One recent estimate placed the unrecorded economic activity in Italy as somewhere between 25 to 35 percent of the official figures on domestic output.[7] The black economy includes manufacturing as well as services. The extent of unreported economic activity

TABLE 20.1   Government Debt in 1987. Annual Budget Deficit as percentage of Gross Domestic Product

Country	Percent
Britain	2.4%
France	2.8
West Germany	1.7
Italy	10.4
United States	2.7

Source: OECD figures.

means that Italy's unemployment is not as bad as the official statistics suggest and that its economic output is considerably larger than shown in the records.

Italy's postwar economic performance is impressive when compared to its prewar performance and when the limits of its resource base are considered. What is surprising is that its economic record in many dimensions looks good statistically even in comparison with the stronger economies of Germany and France and with the once much stronger British economy.

An Advanced but Costly Welfare State

The most important concern about the Italian economy, the continuing growth of public indebtedness, is directly linked with one of the most popular achievements of the postwar era, the provision of a broad range of social-welfare programs. Italians are now provided with government-sponsored pensions, health insurance, housing, unemployment and disability insurance, and direct cash payments to families with minor children according to the number of children. These programs amount to a sizable drain on the government's expenditures and consume an important portion of the gross domestic product—nearly 30 percent in 1981. As Table 20.2 indicates, Italy's expenditures for social-welfare programs are comparable to those of its neighbors but significantly higher than in the United States. The benefits are very popular with voters who have come to view them as rights. Reductions in these programs would be politically difficult for any government to handle. They are easy to adopt but then neither the users nor the government are eager to pay for them.

One of the more recent social-welfare programs was the introduction in 1978 of a new health insurance system. Adopted at a time of economic austerity, the new health service was a reward to workers for their wage restraints and to the PSI and PCI for their support of the government's economic policy. It was patterned after the British National Health Service

TABLE 20.2 Welfare Expenditures as Percentage of Gross Domestic Product, 1981

	Britain	France	Germany	Italy	USA
Education	5.1%	5.9%	5.2%	6.1%	5.7
Health	4.4	6.4	6.8	6.0	3.7
Community and social services	0.6	0.9	0.9	0.4	0.4
Pensions	6.5	11.9	12.6	13.1	6.7
Sickness benefits	0.4	1.2	0.6	0.8	0.1
Family allowances	1.4	1.9	1.4	1.2	0.4
Unemployment compensation	0.7	1.9	1.4	0.6	0.4
Other	0.0	0.0	0.9	0.0	0.0
TOTAL	22.7	33.2	31.0	29.8	18.0

Source: OECD figures. British data are for 1979; U.S. data are for 1978.

with the goal of providing a uniform level of medical care throughout the country at no cost to the individual patient. But it came into existence simultaneously with a steep rise in medical costs. In addition, the complicated system of regional based "mutuals" that was to administer the new health system proved to be far more expensive, more vulnerable to political manipulation, and more inefficient than anticipated.[8] Despite the need for economies, the Italian government, like other Western European governments, found it difficult to cut back on popular social benefits. The Craxi government talked about ways to reduce the siphoning of public funds into the health system, but it moved much more slowly to actually cut the services or impose user fees for this new but popular program.

Many other aspects of the social-welfare system reflect these same problems of the costly programs, inefficient administration, political influence from clientelist networks, and often deteriorating public services. Once a program is installed, however, it acquires a constituency and a momentum that keep it going despite its problems. Also the weak governments resist broad reforms.

Education is another area that reveals the problems of policy stagnation at a time of expanding public service. The education system has grown to accommodate a large number of new students. For example, the university system had 750,000 students in 1978 compared to one-third that number fifteen years earlier. There have been some changes in the education system to align it with modern social and economic realities. But much of the system remains unreformed. Thus, "the primary school curriculum was last changed in 1955 and dates predominantly from 1928, while the crucial upper-secondary curriculum, though the subject of many reform attempts, is substantially unaltered since 1923."[9] These cases of chronic problems which have not been confronted by Italian governments illustrate the problems of policy making where the prime minister shifts frequently. Governments in Italy are too weak to face divisive issues. Where there is no consensus on both the need for change and the direction of such change, there is likely to be immobilism, or the absence of government action.

Despite these continuing problems, Italy has succeeded in establishing comprehensive programs for the protection of the public welfare. Even in comparison to its wealthier neighbors, these programs are impressive in their coverage and benefits. The efficiency of these programs may compare unfavorably with other countries, but this comparison reflects the grafting of these programs onto traditional party and political practices. The presence of the public welfare's pledges of security and protection builds support for the regime. Few Italians, no matter where they are on the social hierarchy, want to endanger their pensions or health programs or their children's educational opportunities by toppling the regime.

Toward a More Equitable Society

The uneven pattern of economic development has left important pockets of impoverished Italians. Most of the poverty is found in the South where the economy was originally and remains today the most underdeveloped. This pattern is reflected in the still stark differences between the conditions of the South compared to the North on a variety of social indicators: per capita income; unemployment; level of education; access to consumer goods such as automobiles, television sets, and telephones; hospital beds per inhabitant; infant mortality; and so on. The diminution of these differences has remained an objective of every Italian government but progress has been slow. The South accounts for about 40 percent of the land area and has approximately 35 percent of the population. But it provided only about 25 percent of the country's gross domestic output in 1984 despite decades of effort to improve the industrial base there. In the same year, the average per capita production of southerners was only 60 percent of the average production in the North.

The problems of poverty are not restricted to the South. Elsewhere in Italy, especially around urban industrial centers, there are large impoverished populations made up of southern emigrants who have come North in search of jobs and better opportunities. Through the 1960s, Italy's industrial expansion was facilitated by its unusually low wages for the workers. These low wages helped Italian manufactured goods find competitive new markets all over Europe as the European Community eliminated tariff barriers. Since the 1970s, there has been important progress toward improving the wage and work conditions for industrial workers but with some reduction in the competitiveness of Italian goods on the European market.

Some of the economic gap has been filled by social-welfare programs. Also trade unions grew in strength and militancy in the 1970s and won important wage increases. Indeed, there has been a surprisingly rapid narrowing of the gap between the wealthy and the poor in recent years, especially during the troubled decade of the 1970s. For example, in 1973, the average salary of a middle-class employee was 7.75 times that of the average farm worker's (who earn the lowest wages in Italy) earnings; by 1977, the difference had shrunk two full points so that the middle-class employee earned 5.45 times the income of the farm worker.[10] Another study showed that in 1967, the most privileged 20 percent of Italians controlled 46 percent of total income while the poorest 20 percent had only 5.2 percent of total income. That meant that the wealthiest controlled 9.6 times as much income. By 1972, the gap had been lowered to only 8.5 times more.[11]

Consumer goods are now widely available to people of all socioeconomic backgrounds. By the early 1980s, there were 346 passenger cars for every 1000 Italians, a higher figure than in Britain. Italians from all walks of life have access to automobiles and enjoy travelling their country's extensive and impressively engineered super highways. There are 234 television sets per 1000 people and 434 telephones for every 1000 Italians. These figures are only slightly under comparable statistics for Britain, France, and Germany. Despite its economic and political problems, Italy is a far more prosperous and a more equal society than it was twenty-five years ago.

STABILITY AND INSTABILITY
IN CONTEMPORARY ITALY

The importance of Italy's governmental instability has frequently been noted here. The fall of governments contributes to the public disdain for the political system, but there are surprisingly few other consequences. Underlying the shifting top of the political world is an administrative system that plods along and maintains the basic governmental services which more directly affect people's lives. The fall of a government, the prolonged ministerial crises with caretaker governments, premature dissolutions of parliament, and stalemates in the choice of a new president have virtually no consequences on the lives of the vast majority of Italians. While the press labels such events "crises," they affect only the political elite. Meanwhile, the civil service continues to operate, and the unofficial administrative processes of clientelistic exchanges function without missing a beat. It is at these two points that the citizen interacts with government. The continuation of their activities means that there is little popular perception of a crisis when a government topples.

Furthermore, the frequency of such governmental shifts in the past has eliminated much of the shock of seeing a government fall or waiting for weeks while a new coalition is patched together. The 1979 ouster of the British prime minister was alarming to some Britons because it had not happened for over a half-century. Governments fall so regularly in Italy that few pay much attention.

There is a serious problem underlying these governmental shifts that is not widely perceived. That is the absence of any substantial political change despite the rise and fall of new governments. Nearly all the parties clustered at or near the political center must participate in a coalition government in order to muster the requisite parliamentary majority. The DC must be part of that coalition. What is needed is an alternative coalition to which voters might turn to when disappointed with the present coalition. The moderation of the PCI theoretically makes a leftist alliance possible that might offer a genuine alternative. But so far, the other left-wing parties have shown very little interest in taking part in a coalition in which they would be dwarfed by the much larger Communist party. The historic compromise of a DC-PCI coalition would represent some change but it would not accomplish the expulsion of the Christian Democrats from government. Both the DC party and Italy would probably benefit from a period of time when the DC was out of power for what would be for the first time since 1945.

Another much more clearly perceived crisis among the public in general was created by the surge in political terrorism during the 1970s.[12] As was the case in West Germany, a portion of young Italians that mobilized during the student turmoil of the late 1960s turned to political violence when the radicalism of the Hot Autumn waned without producing the hoped for revolution. These youthful radicals were often from middle-class backgrounds, but they were sensitive to the plight of the underprivileged. They had witnessed the crowded tenements and slums in which the migrants from the South were often forced to live in as they came to the North for the benefits of an industrial society. They rejected the enormous gap between the few rich and the many poor that persisted even as Italy modernized. For these few, but dedicated radicals, the only hope was in a total rupture with the existing capitalist society through violent revolution.

The moderation of the PCI left such radicals in search of political vehicles to promote their revolution. They turned to terrorism to weaken the capitalist system and disrupt what they regarded as a phony bourgeois democracy. Eventually, many affiliated in a loose network of radical terrorists known as the Red Brigades. There were other terrorist groups at work as well over the next dozen turbulent years: the Armed Proletarian Nuclei, the Front Line, the Proletarian Fighting Squads, the Communist Liberation Army, the Workers' Autonomy Movement, and splinter groups with more colorful names such as the Savage Cats. In 1978, at the height of the terrorist threat there were an estimated 209 terrorist groups: 181 on the far Left, 28 on the far Right.[13] Right-wing terrorism also increased during this period, partly to counter leftist terror and partly to add to the climate of disorder in the hopes that it might bring a reaction against democracy by the military. But the leftist Red Brigades were most prominent and active in a series of terrorist attacks that marked "the professionalization of violent protest."[14] The actual number of terrorists was never high. A 1980 estimate suggested that there were approximately 1,000 leftist terrorists backed by about 10,000 actual supporters and perhaps 40,000 ideological sympathizers.[15]

The terrorists first targeted property as the objects of their attacks: the automobiles and homes of the wealthy, shops, and factories. Next the terrorists began to kidnap prominent industrialists, especially those whose firms had poor labor relations. Then the terrorists directed their attacks at journalists who were critical of them. At first, the victims were held for ransom but by 1974, the Red Brigades became more violent. They maimed their victims by shooting them in the knees or executed them. As the violence spread, some prominent Red Brigade leaders were arrested. In the hope of winning the release of their captured comrades through habeas corpus in the absence of prompt trials, the Red Brigades attacked the judges and lawyers involved in the court proceedings. Finally, the Red Brigades aimed their attacks at politicians.

The culmination of these attacks came in the kidnapping of Aldo Moro. Moro, who had been prime minister five times, was an attractive target because he was the principal DC architect of a coalition with the Communists. While not prime minister at the time, he was nonetheless the single most important political figure in Italy. To strike against him was to strike at the heart of the democratic system and indirectly at the Communist party, which the radicals believed had betrayed the revolution by allying with the Christian Democrats. Moro was held prisoner for nearly two months and subjected to a "proletarian trial" in which he was found guilty of being "the political godfather and most faithful executant of the directives issued by the imperialist centers of power."[16] He was finally executed and his body left in the trunk of a car symbolically parked halfway between the Rome party headquarters of the DC and of the PCI.

Right-wing terrorism was a much more shadowy subject. Terrorists from the far Right were much less willing to claim responsibility for their attacks, and they sought less publicity than the left-wing terrorists. But their attacks were often less discriminating in choice of targets. They often bombed public places causing indiscriminate deaths rather than selecting ideological enemies for attacks. Consequently, their attacks were among the most costly in terms of lost lives. For example, they bombed the Bologna railway station in 1980 which took eighty-four lives, and the neo-fascists carried out the 1984 bombing of the Rome-Milan train killing fifteen passengers. Their purpose was to demonstrate the impotence of the government in the hope of prodding the military into seizing power. In the 1960s, there was a military officer, General Giovanni de Lorenzo, who accumulated substantial power and appeared tempted to carry out such a coup d'état. But he had little support from his fellow officers and was eventually shunted aside. In the mid-1970s, the neo-fascists deliberately increased their own terrorism to add to that of the Left in a vain effort to provoke the military into intervening in the interest of public order.

Public confidence and, equally important, the confidence of political leaders in the democratic instituituions were shaken by these events. Indeed, the goal of terrorists on the Left and the Right was to discredit democracy in order to bring the fall of the regime and a new authoritarian system to power. The political malaise was furthered by the spreading political corruption, including one scandal that brought the resignation of President Giovanni Leone. The nation's economic problems, notably rapid inflation, further complicated the situation.

The Moro tragedy marked the peak of the terrorist threat and, indeed, helped bring about the defeat of terrorism. It brought the alliance of constitutional parties from the Communists on the Left to the Liberals on the Right into a common front against terrorism. They joined together to assure overwhelmingly the public endorsement of the antiterrorist Reale laws in the 1978 referendum: 78 percent voted to reject the Radical party's attempt to repeal these laws. The PCI had opposed the Reale laws when they were considered in parliament but, after the Moro incident, the PCI rallied to their support. The Reale laws gave the police extraordinary powers to deal with terrorism. It broadened their rights to arrest suspected terrorists, gave them greater freedom in conducting searches of premises linked with suspected terrorists, and extended the policeman's right to carry and use firearms. Another law, passed in 1977, lengthened the time that suspected terrorists could be held without trial when legal proceedings were disrupted by threats of violence. Such individuals could be held for as long as the sentence for the crime they were accused of committing or up to four years (lengthened in 1979 to ten years). New laws in 1978 and 1979 gave the police the right to tap telephones, to interrogate accused terrorists without the presence of their lawyers, and to hold suspected terrorists without formal charges for up to forty-eight hours.

Beyond the new legal tools, the police developed a strong, centralized antiterrorist unit thus, correcting the lack of coordination of the several police forces that had plagued earlier efforts to deal with terrorism. The police infiltrated the ranks of the terrorist units and used paid informants to obtain the location of the terrorist bases and the names of members. As the number of arrests mounted, the police encouraged imprisoned terrorists to name their associates with appeals to their consciences and with promises of reduced sentences. The ineptness of the terrorist groups also helped bring their demise. They were plagued by internal ideological divisions that encouraged informants to betray their rivals; they also stockpiled incriminating documents and future plans in unsafe locations.

By 1982, the terrorist threat was largely over. There continued to be isolated incidents of terrorist violence but the danger to the regime was no longer there. The success was so great that the head of the antiterrorist effort was given the more challenging task of combatting organized crime in southern Italy.[17] The total elimination of terrorism in open societies observing democratic procedures is probably impossible. But after 1980, terrorist incidents dropped sharply in Italy: from over 2500 in 1978, to 217 in 1983, 310 in 1984, and fewer than 100 in 1985, 1986, and 1987. There are still isolated incidents of domestic terrorism, such as the 1988 shooting of a prominent DC politician, but these tragic events no longer have the regime-threatening overtones that they did in the late 1970s.

With the decline of domestic terrorism, international terrorist incidents in Italy, such as the 1985 shootings at the Rome airport, stand out as the more serious problem. While such terrorist episodes have foreign objectives, usually linked with the Middle East, they can have important domestic political consequences. For example, disputes over the handling of the hijacking of the Italian liner, Achille Lauro, nearly toppled the Craxi government in October 1985. But the threat to the whole democratic regime is no longer present.

Italian democracy seemed particularly vulnerable to the terrorist danger. Its weak and unstable executive was prone to collapse and paralysis even under normal conditions. Public opinion polls suggested very low level of support for the regime and widespread disrespect for the officials that ran it. Thus, when Italy was struck by the heaviest outburst of terrorism anywhere in the western world, and when the terrorists had the explicit objective of overthrowing the political system, many feared for the future of Italian democracy. In the 1970s, it was easy to scoff at the foibles of the Italian police as they struggled vainly to stem the terrorist tide. But the picture was much different by the 1980s. Indeed, Italy offers an example to other Western democracies of how to conduct a successful antiterrorist campaign and to accomplish the objective of controlling terrorism without heavy-handed counter-violence and without compromising basic human rights. The successful handling of terrorism demonstrated that the Italian political system was much stronger than many had believed.

HUMAN RIGHTS

Italy has a very good record in observing basic human rights. The Constitution provides a full slate of civil liberties, and the government has, in fact, respected these rights. There is a Constitutional Court which has begun to play a more important role in defending individual rights. The strength of the tradition of parliamentary supremacy will probably place limits on the Constitutional Court's expanding role. It is also unlikely that this court will ever match the importance of the United States Supreme Court. But the Constitutional Court has emerged as a new advocate of human rights.

For those who feel their rights have been neglected by Italian national bodies, it is possible to appeal to an international body. Italy subscribes to the European Convention of Human Rights. Italian citizens have the right to appeal to the European Court of Human Rights when national remedies have been exhausted. The Italian government has agreed in advance to accept as binding all rulings by this court.

The Impact of a State Church

The presence of the Catholic Church and its continuing strength in politics and society has occasionally imposed limits on human rights. For example, until the new concordat of 1985, Rome had a "special" status as seat of the Church. The Church was used to justify laws on pornography and on other moral issues presumably incompatible with its presence. These restrictions occasionally involved infringements on the freedom of speech and the freedom of the press. As an illustration, in the mid-1960s, the papacy intervened and succeeded in persuading the civil authorities in Rome to ban performances of Rolf Hochuth's play, *The Deputy*, because of its criticism of the role of the pope during World War II.

The restraints on the Church have often come from the Constitutional Court. For example, one of the early landmark decisions of the Italian Constitutional Court involved a ruling in favor of religious liberty in a case involving persecution of Pentecostals. The Court has played a major role in furthering women's rights by invalidating laws reflecting the country's Catholic heritage: laws against adultery and laws barring the advertisement or distribution of contraceptives. The growing secularization of Italian politics and society should bring more parliamentary action to limit Church influence. Non-Catholics may continue to feel overwhelmed by the Church's influence, but its direct intervention in politics will no doubt continue to diminish with growing secularization and the spreading implementation of the new concordat.

Politics and the Media

Government control of the radio and television has in the past been a source of concern. In the 1970s, it was common for opposition parties to be denied coverage in the radio and television news. In the mid-1970s, the publicly owned television channels were brought under parliamentary control with the consequence that they were quickly colonized by the parties. An informal agreement between the Christian Democrats and the Socialists led to the division of the two channels, with each party gaining control of one national channel. Later, the Communist party gained influence over a third national channel.

However, the parties' ability to exploit this television control for political advantage was limited. In 1976, the Constitutional Court ruled that while the national electronic media could be monopolized by the state, there could be no monopoly at the local level. The door was opened for private interests and political groupings to start up their own locally based radio and television stations. Since that time, there has been a literal explosion of private television and radio stations. In 1983, there were approximately 350 to 400 private television stations with regular programs and an equal number with sporadic programming. In addition, there were some 6,000 to 8,000 private radio stations throughout Italy.[18] There is virtually no regulation of this vast new industry with the only enforced limit being that the private station's signal not interfere with those of the state-owned stations. As a result, even the state monopoly at the national level authorized by the Council has disappeared. In addition to the state-owned national television channels, there are now four national companies or networks linking 125 television channels across the country.

There is another important political consequence of this privatization of television and radio. In other European countries, political campaign advertisements on radio and television are either not allowed at all or severely restricted. But there is good election coverage in these countries through news reporting, candidate debates or forums, and free time to each party. In Italy, similar official coverage on the public channels is supplemented by coverage on private stations plus spot advertisements such as those familiar to observers of American elections. By the 1983 election, television and radio had become the principal media for campaign activities. The result is the escalation of campaign costs and the growing importance of telegenic politicians.[19]

In the last decade, the Italian written press has become less partisan and more responsible in its coverage of political developments.[20] As recently as the mid-1970s, Italian newspapers were highly partisan and passionate in their political reporting. Now, economic pressures have made papers more competitive and less inclined to restrict their potential market and advertising appeal to a single party. Newspaper staffs have acquired more influence over content and editorials and have often counterbalanced the partisan prejudices of the publisher. The continuing financial crisis of many newspapers, including some of the most prestigious, has left the newspaper industry in a state of uncertainty. But even if they recover financially, they have been eclipsed as political forces by the electronic media.

Civil Liberties
and the Control of Terrorism

One of the tests of a democracy is its ability to maintain public order and security without infringing upon the rights of its citizens to exercise their freedoms without state inhibition. The serious terrorist threat necessitated draconian laws to combat it. The details of these laws were previously stated. They provided antiterrorist police with important powers of arrest, preventive detention, search and seizure, detention without trial when judicial proceedings were disrupted, interference in client-attorney relations, and a variety of other powers. While the extraordinary danger may have justified them, all of these provisions held the danger of undermining civil liberties for ordinary citizens if they were abused by the law enforcement officers. Indeed, terrorists often hoped for such a severe police reaction in the belief that it would weaken civil liberties for all and build sympathy for the oppressed terrorists among the general public.

There is little evidence of abuse of these special powers by the Italian authorities. Most observers have praised the restraint that was used. There have been a couple of prominent terrorists whose trials were delayed an unusually lengthy time, but the circumstances were extenuating. One Red Brigade leader, Antonio Negri, accused in several crimes including the Moro murder, won release after he was elected to parliament on the list of the quirky little Radical party. The Radicals thought that he had been held too long without a trial and so put him on their list to be elected. After he was, the Radicals then voted, with other parties, to lift his parliamentary immunity so that he could be tried. Negri, meanwhile, had fled the country. The actual numbers held under provisions of the special antiterrorist laws were quite small. Democratic control over this preventive detention was maintained by the obligation of the minister of interior to read the list of those so detained to parliament every three months. Even in 1980, when the threat was still near its peak, the number of detainees was only sixteen.

The major criticism of these laws has not been about their abuse but their existence. Some critics have complained that there was no need for the special legislation and that it was designed more to appease the public by giving the appearance of action than to actually fight the terrorist menace. In retrospect, the crucial elements in the antiterrorist battle do not appear to have been these laws but, rather, better trained and organized police and the purchase of information through money or reduced sentences. But at the time these laws were adopted, the battle was still very uncertain. Even if the purpose were only to allay the fears of the public, such a motive was sufficient with the state literally trembling from the shocks of the Moro case and the seemingly uncontrollable terrorism.

Indeed, the most serious abuse of civil rights through the absence of a speedy trial may be occurring not in the case of terrorists but in the case of approximately twenty thousand ordinary prisoners who are in jail awaiting trials. They often spend months in prison waiting their day in court because of the severely overcrowded criminal dockets.

Another threat to civil liberties coming from the terrorist threat emerged in the mid-1980s. As noted above, the decline in domestic terrorism was followed by a rise in international terrorism. The result was a growing racial intolerance in a country whose people have long been regarded as free of racial prejudice. Many Italians seemed unable to draw the line between immigrants and terrorists, especially Arab immigrants.

The government pushed through parliament new laws to control immigration and to crack down on illegal immigrants. Racial intolerance in Italy is still far from the tensions that have troubled Britain, France, and Germany in recent years. But the likelihood of a continued increase in the number of immigrants, especially those coming from unstable regions of the world, may mean that Italy will face the same challenge of learning to accept different races and cultures in their society.

A PECULIAR STABILITY

Italy offers the paradox of a political system with ample problems that has nonetheless done an admirable job of overseeing important improvements in the lives of its people. The postwar era offers a remarkable record of accomplishment in economic, social, and human rights when compared to Mussolini's Italy. Even in comparison with its European partners, the Italian record is a strong one. That this record has been achieved by a political regime that is so widely maligned suggests that behind the turbulent surface of Italian politics there are some important strengths. That nearly all Italian citizens steadily vote for parties that back the current system despite the presence on the ballots of clear alternatives on the Left or Right indicates that behind the carping about their politicians is a solid support for the current regime.

There are a number of problems that plague Italian democracy: governmental instability, political corruption, absence of a rotation of parties in and out of power, economic weakness, and the North-South regional differences. For the most part, they are not the kinds of challenges predicted by the prophets of a decline of democracy nor are they the ones faced by other European countries in the 1970s and 1980s. Many of the crisis of democracy problems have not affected Italy. Despite their weaknesses, the Italian parties have not experienced any decline beyond the normal shifts in popular support; alternative social movements have neither challenged the existing parties nor posed difficulties for government. Some symptoms present in Italy of the crisis of democracy are not the novelties that they have been elsewhere in Europe. Governmental overload is not a new problem for Italy since its weak and fragile governments have had to muddle through difficult issues with partial or no policies since the end of the war. The crisis of public confidence that hit other democracies in the 1970s has been a constant feature of postwar Italy with deep roots in the political cynicism of its people. Finally, the major threat of terrorism has successfully been faced and overcome.

Some claim that Italian democracy still survives not because of its strengths but because it has yet to face a real challenge. When that crisis comes, as it surely must, these people argue, the citizens' poor attitudes toward their regime will assure its democracy's rapid failure. That possibility cannot be discounted entirely. But Italy has survived a series of challenges in the 1970s and 1980s which might well have become such a regime-ending crisis: the Hot Autumn of 1969, the assassination of Aldo Moro, or the very high unemployment of the 1980s. In fact, the regime showed previously unrecognized strength in facing these challenges. It has emerged from these crises with new self-confidence and new public esteem. Even if the public persists in expressing cynical views of their politicians and institutions, they seem to acknowledge grudgingly and silently the desirability of the current system.

Perhaps this acceptance is due to the absence of attractive alternatives. Authoritarian fascism still is tarnished by its failure in Mussolini's Italy; communism, as it has been practiced elsewhere in Europe, has very limited appeal even to Italy's Communists. Even if the democratic system is faulted, it looks better to most Italians than any of its alternatives.

NOTES

1. Joseph LaPalombara, *Democracy Italian Style* (New Haven, CT: Yale University Press, 1987), p. 1.
2. Geoffrey Parker, *The Countries of Community Europe: A Geographic Survey of Contemporary Issues* (London: Macmillan, 1979), p. 115.
3. On Italy's economy, see D. C. Tempelman, *The Italian Economy* (New York: Praeger, 1981).
4. Paul Furlong, "Political Underdevelopment and Economic Recession in Italy," in Andrew Cox, ed., *Politics, Policy and the European Recession* (London: Macmillan, 1982), p. 167.
5. Ibid., p. 190.
6. Guido Carli, "The Italian Crisis," in Ralf Dahrendorf, ed., *Europe's Economy in Crisis* (New York: Holmes & Meier, 1982).
7. "A Survey of the Italian Economy," *The Economist*, (London) 27 February 1988, p. 9.
8. See P. F. Furlong, "Italy," in F. F. Ridley, ed., *Policies and Politics in Western Europe: The Impact of the Recession* (London: Croom Helm, 1984), pp. 143–146.
9. Ibid. p. 149.
10. Gilbert Mathieu, "Une formidable réduction des inégalités de salaires," in Le Monde, *L'Economie italienne sans miracle* (Paris: Economica, 1980), p. 193.
11. Malcolm Sawyer, "Income Distribution in OECD Countries," *OECD Economic Outlook: Occasional Studies* (July 1976), pp. 3–36.
12. For a good survey of the development of the terrorist threat, see Dominick J. Coyle, *Minorities in Revolt: Political Violence in Ireland, Italy, and Cyprus* (Rutherford, NJ: Fairleigh Dickinson University Press, 1983), pp. 113–147.
13. Ibid., p. 146.
14. Sidney Tarrow, "Three Years of Italian Democracy," in Howard R. Penniman, ed., *Italy at the Polls, 1979: A Study of the Parliamentary Elections* (Washington, DC: American Enterprise Institute, 1981), pp. 16–17.
15. *The Economist*, 22 November 1980, p. 54.
16. Coyle, *Minorities in Revolt*, p. 138.
17. The Mafia, with the links between organized crime and politicians, posed a more important danger than terrorists. Indeed, even at the height of the terrorist threat, there were far more lives lost at the hands of Mafia hit men than in terrorist attacks. Shortly after his assignment to Sicily, General Dalla Chiesa and his wife were gunned down by the Mafia. The subsequent popular

and official reaction to these brutal murders led to the jailing of over a thousand Mafia in Italy and the United States.

18. Donald Sasson, "Politics and Market Forces in Italian Broadcasting," *West European Politics* 8 (April 1985): 67–83.

19. William E. Porter, "The Mass Media in Italian Elections," in Howard Penniman, ed., *Italy at the Polls, 1983* (Durham, NC: Duke University Press, 1987), pp. 155–161.

20. See William E. Porter, "The Mass Media in the Italian Elections of 1979," in Penniman, *Italy at the Polls, 1979.*

PART SIX
THE OTHER EUROPE

Charles de Gaulle used to dream of an association of all Europe "from the Atlantic to the Urals." The geographic definition of Europe does place its eastern frontier far to the east of the countries that have been the focus of this book's attention thus far. Historically and culturally, Eastern Germany, Russia, Poland, Czechoslovakia, Bulgaria, Romania, Hungary, Yugoslavia, and even Albania have been considered a part of Europe. But in 1917, the Bolshevik Revolution started Russia on a quite different course of political and economic development than that followed by the rest of Europe. Then, after World War II, Communist regimes in Eastern Europe gave these countries distinctive patterns from countries to their west. After forty-five years of separate development, Europe is very clearly divided not only by ideology but also now quite different cultural, economic, and social outlooks.

Despite the iron curtain that separates these two parts of Europe, many of the same trends that have caused political adjustments in the West are occurring also in the East. This section is not intended to be a comprehensive examination of politics in Eastern Europe but rather a brief summary of the ways in which these similar trends have affected politics in the East, and how the responses of these Communist regimes differ from the reactions in the democratic settings.

CHAPTER TWENTY-ONE
A DIFFERENT
POLITICAL SETTING

We all live under the same sky but we do not all see the same horizon.
Konrad Adenauer

In the spring of 1987, promoters scheduled a rock concert in Berlin just on the western side of the infamous Berlin wall. As in the United States, rock radio stations advertised the concert for days before. On the day of the event, crowds gathered for the outdoor concert—including several thousand East Berlin youth who had heard the radio advertisements and hoped to hear the concert from their side of the wall, only 100 meters from the stage. Unable to hear clearly and angered by police harassment, the East Berliners began to chant "down with the wall" and "we want freedom." Eventually, East Berlin police arrested fifty or so demonstrators and drove the rest away from the Wall—and the concert.

What was significant about this episode was not the size of the demonstration—West Berlin had been the site of far larger and more destructive street violence only a few days earlier. The event was important because it reminds the world how porous is the wall separating East and West Europe. Much as Eastern European leaders might like to cut their people off from the West, it is less and less possible to do so. Trends, fashions, and ideas circulate across the most highly defended frontiers. In a very real sense the old Europe, from the Atlantic to the Urals, is reemerging.

regime to include intense efforts to inculcate the correct values into the minds of adults as well. The party prepares and distributes an enormous volume of literature to explain its positions and to develop correct ideas. It exposes most citizens to regular sessions in political education. Formal and informal sanctions are applied to those who fail to incorporate socialist values into their personal behavior.

Such campaigns have brought some changes in political and social orientations. However, most observers stress the limited success of Communist regimes in breaking with past value structures. Attitudes and values that have developed over centuries have proved difficult to change despite conscious manipulation of the socialization process. Even the political leaders themselves have seemed unable to overcome traditional political viewpoints, attitudes, and styles after several decades of communist rule.[9]

Political attitudes, however, are by no means fixed; they do change, but often in ways unintended and undesired by the political elite. There is no evidence yet in Eastern Europe of the emergence of a kind of postmaterialist value system such as that affecting Western Europe. But the growing experience of East Europeans with their political systems has resulted in adaptations in their political orientations to cope with, not always to follow, the Communist party elite. Inured by lifetimes of party propaganda that has reduced ideology to slogans and platitudes, the people of Eastern Europe are now disinterested in Marxist-Leninist ideology. Public awareness of the standard of living outside their countries leads to growing public impatience with shortages and poor quality in consumer goods.

EASTERN EUROPE IN THE 1980s

Marxist theory always placed heavy stress on the interrelationship between economics and politics. The installation of Communist states in Russia and Eastern Europe brought revolutionary changes in these countries' economic and social structures. Ideology and aspirations for complete political mastery have led Communist leaders to seek to control of all of society by bringing various social groups under party control. Communist regimes are sometimes referred to as totalitarian because of this desire for complete subjugation of society to the party. It is part of the official ideology that there should be no group or organization, political or social, beyond the control of the Communist party. But absolute social control always remains a desire and not a reality. Soviet and East European societies are not monistic ones under the party's control. There remain important social, ethnic, and religious divisions which manifest themselves in ways that the party can neither predict nor prevent.

Social Class and Politics in Eastern Europe

Among the many social changes in Eastern Europe, one of the most important is the shift of people from rural locations and occupations to urban-industrial settings. Tables 21.1 and 21.2 show these dramatic shifts.

East European populations are still more agrarian than those in Western Europe, but the trend has been in the same direction and nearly as intense.

The structural changes in agriculture, notably the collectivization of farmland in the 1930s in the USSR and in the 1950s in Eastern Europe, has transformed the traditional peasant life in these countries. But it has not eliminated the peasants. Indeed, in several East European countries, there has been a retreat from the emphasis on collective farms by encouraging peasants to work on their private plots. These small plots accorded to collective and state farmers are far more productive than the large collective farms and often are the major source of garden vegetables and meat. With handsome profits available from their sales in the open market, farmers devote more time and care to their private plots than they do to their collective farm duties. The produce from these plots is sold by the farmers and provides important supplements to the farmers' earnings.

With Marxist-Leninist ideology stressing the need to represent the interests of the industrial working class, the farm population has often received short shrift in Communist states. The average income for peasants is considerably less than their counterparts in industry; in the USSR, peasants earn half the salary of industrial workers. Living standards in the countryside are sharply lower than those in the cities and industrial towns. Investment in agriculture has lagged so that the agrarian revolution that has occurred in the West has not happened in the East. For all these

TABLE 21.1 Agriculture as a Percent of National Income in Eastern Europe

	1960	1975
Bulgaria	32.2%	22.0%
Czechoslovakia	14.7	8.3
German Democratic Republic	16.4	10.0
Hungary	30.8	16.3
Poland	30.3	12.6
Romania	34.9	16.6

Source: Adapted from David Turnock, *Eastern Europe* (Boulder, CO: Westview Press, 1978), p. 112.

TABLE 21.2 Farmers as Percent of Total Workforce in Selected East European Countries

	1965	1975	1985
Bulgaria	45%	26%	23%
Czechoslovakia	20	14	17
Romania	57	37	29

Source: Robin Okey, *Eastern Europe 1740–1985: Feudalism to Communism*, 2nd ed., (Minneapolis, MN: University of Minnesota Press, 1986), p. 218; and *The 1987 Information Please Almanac* (Boston: Houghton Mifflin, 1987), pp. 156, 173, 241.

reasons, the peasant class is usually the least content section of Communist societies.

But the plight of the working class is often not much better.[10] The party claims that it represents the proletariat and that it has set up a "workers' state," but the reality is often far from that. The worker may be subject to constant pressure from management, the party, and even the trade union to maximize production. The choice of training, location, and job is often limited or preempted by the party and state. Industrialization in the USSR and postwar reconstruction in Eastern Europe was financed by long work hours, low pay, and strict labor discipline. Workers are now enjoying some of the benefits of these sacrifices. If workers in the Communist countries of Europe are less affluent than their counterparts in Western Europe, they are much better off than they or their parents were twenty years ago.

In the first decade or so after Communist regimes were established, there was much evidence of class mobility with individuals from very modest backgrounds assuming positions of prestige and responsibility in the new Communist states. Rapid industrialization and economic growth as well as the ouster of prior elites opened up many opportunities for the upward mobility of talented workers and peasants. However, the classless society was not ushered in as anticipated by Communist ideology. Instead, a new privileged class began to emerge made up of Communist party members, technocrats and administrators favored by the party, and their sons and daughters.[11] The typical worker remained underpaid and without much hope of improving his or her social standing or economic situation.[12] One estimate suggested that two fifths of the nonpeasant labor force earned less than the amount needed for subsistence.[13] Despite efforts to recruit workers and, failing this, to inflate the number of workers by loosely applying occupational descriptions to its members, workers and peasants still remain underrepresented in the party and especially in the leadership positions.

An intelligentsia of bureaucrats, engineers and technical experts, and intellectuals has emerged throughout Eastern Europe. Also included in this social stratum is the growing body of the *apparatchiki*, fulltime, paid, party workers. The most privileged part of this elite is "the new class"[14] of top party leaders and senior bureaucrats.

While the intelligentsia parallels to some extent the broadening middle class in Western societies, its privileges appear more important in contrast to the lack of opportunities and benefits of the workers and peasants. Salary differences between the intelligentsia and workers in Communist countries are usually far less significant than in the West; income equalization has in fact been a real accomplishment of Communist regimes. The significance of equitable income distribution, however, is sharply diminished by the highly developed system of nonsalary privileges accorded to the intelligentsia. These privileges include access to consumer goods in short supply or imported from the West, better housing, special vacation resorts, travel abroad, ability to get medical treatment by the best doctors when needed, private showings of Western movies, and a host of other privileges not available to the general public. Differential access to privileges is common in all types of societies. What distinguishes the Communist pattern from that in Western Europe is that money is the means of access in the West, while social status as defined by the party elite is the means of access in the East. An impoverished West German may use up all his savings to get the best pediatrician to treat his sick daughter, but an East German who had saved up his money could not have access to the finest medical care unless he is part of the privileged elite entitled to treatment at that clinic.

Open class conflict between these privileged strata and the workers and peasants is minimal. The party line stresses the unity of the party elite with the interests of the working class. Many workers may not share that assessment, but they have few opportunities to express their dissatisfaction in their controlled societies that lack independent trade unions or free presses. In most Communist regimes, special attention is devoted to controlling dissidents in the working class. Workers who attempt to organize protests are usually quickly arrested and receive harsher sentences than the more publicized cases of dissidence among intellectuals. Worker dissidence cannot be tolerated because it would cast doubt on the party's claim to its establishment of a workers' state. More important in understanding the lack of class tensions is the widespread satisfaction with the system as it is. While social inequalities and even inequities are acknowledged, the large majority of citizens in the Soviet Union and in most East European countries is content. Workers appreciate the "paternalistic state." In exchange for no more than the routine performance of their duties and political passivity, the Communist state provides them with job security, assured retirement, and a modest but improving standard of living.[15]

The most notable example of worker discontent was the Solidarity movement in Poland from 1980 to 1982. A variety of working class-grievances underlay the formation of this independent trade union in 1980, but the movement came into being to protest government plans to cut subsidies for meat and other foods. Within a few months, Solidarity attracted 10 million members, and became so powerful a force that the Communist party leadership was unable to stem its rise. The inability of the leadership to control Solidarity brought the fall of several premiers and eventually the selection of a Communist military leader, General Wojciech Jaruzelski, to run the country. Encouraged by the Soviet Union, Jaruzelski imposed martial law and ordered the dissolution of Solidarity.[16] Solidarity leaders were imprisoned and the independent trade union movement, leaderless and exhausted by eighteen months of struggle, collapsed. However, persistent economic distress in Poland led to a revival of Solidarity in 1988. Workers took up the Solidarity label as they struggled for higher wages and better access to consumer goods.

There have been other less spectacular instances of worker protest. They usually occur in Eastern Europe rather than in the USSR where worker protest is rare and isolated.[17] But these uprisings are exceptions to the general passivity of the workers in the Communist states. For most Soviet and East European workers, the Communist regimes have met their need for secure jobs, social guarantees, and domestic tranquillity. They may feel disadvantaged compared to others in their societies or to workers in the West, but they feel far better off than their parents and even than their own situation a decade or so ago.

Ethnic Minorities

More so than in the western portions of Europe, the East has long been characterized by ethnic conflicts in its states that include several nationalities. In the Soviet Union, where Russians account for less than 52 percent of the total population, the nationality issue of maintaining harmony and unity among the more than one hundred different ethnic groups within its borders is a major preoccupation. Some problems have notably been alleviated by the postwar expulsion of the Germans who had been an important minority in most East European countries for the past 200 years. The wartime exaltation of nationalism and ethnic conflict was followed by twenty years of relative ethnic tranquillity. But now there is a resurgence of ethnic nationalism among minorities in several East European countries.

The revival of ethnic nationalism has been particularly important in the Soviet Union. Ukrainians in the west, Lithuanians and Latvians in the Baltic area, and Zakakhs, Tartars, and other Muslims in central Asia have all been sources of concern about resurgent nationalism in the last decade. Gorbachev's *glasnost* era seems to have fanned these ethnic disputes. After decades of repression of most political dimensions of ethnicity, the opening of the Soviet system has brought more public expression of demands for greater autonomy for ethnic minorities. One of the most dramatic of these disputes was that in Armenia where the Armenian Socialist Republic tried to force a change in its boundaries to include a portion of the neighboring Azerbaijan Socialist Republic which has a large population of Armenians.

The federal structure is based on ethnic divisions and seems to accord considerable autonomy to the major ethnic groups. In fact, the centralized nature of the Communist party renders the federal structure null and void. Slavs, and especially Great Russians dominate the party: Since 1964 nearly all secretaries of the party's Central Committee have been Russians. Ethnic tensions in the Soviet Union may well become more difficult in the immediate future. The non-Russian population is growing much more rapidly than is the Russian and Slavic population. There is fear that the Moslem fundamentalist revival along Soviet borders may stimulate Moslem nationalism in the USSR. Finally, a resurgence of nationalism among Great Russians[18] may exacerbate relations between them and their many minorities.

Religion and Politics

The official atheism of Communist regimes fails to eliminate religion as a significant political factor. Early in their histories, European Communist regimes launched vigorous attacks on religion as a holdover from reactionary pasts. However, more recently, individual religious practice has been regarded as a matter of official indifference to the state as long as the religion has pledged full subservience to the Communist regime in secular matters. Occasionally, the Communist leadership will use the churches for their own political ends, as they did in the peace movements of the early 1980s.

The antireligious stance of the Communist party has often made religious practice a primary manifestation of political dissent. In Poland, for example, Catholic clergy have been prominent among those supporting the Solidarity labor movement. The fact that the pope is Polish has reinforced the Polish nationalist elements of Catholicism against the internationalist, pro-Soviet communism. Consequently, Catholicism has experienced a revival as many Poles have come to see attending mass as more than simply a sign of religious devotion. When the Solidarity trade union emerged as a challenge to the Communist regime, the Catholic Church viewed it as a useful ally in defending human rights in Poland. As tensions have risen, the Church has played the role of a mediator seeking to avoid conflict and repression. The Church's independence from the regime and its political influence have been heightened by this crucial political action.[19] The strength of Catholicism in Poland has made the Church a powerful political force that even an authoritarian Communist regime cannot ignore or subjugate.

In the USSR, the Russian Orthodox Church practices a centuries-old tradition of subservience to the political powers that be. Other religions sometimes pose political difficulties. The unrest of Central Asian ethnic groups is related to the revival of Islamic fundamentalism. As in Poland, Catholicism in Lithuania and among some Ukrainians is often an expression of the ethnic feelings of these minorities. It is also suspect in official circles because its ultimate loyalty is to Rome and not Moscow. Religious groups, notably Jews and Pentecostals, have protested official restrictions on their religious practice. Indeed, 300,000 Soviet Jews have left the USSR over the past fifteen years and an equal number have unsuccessfully applied to leave in search of religious freedom.

Perhaps because of such linkages between political dissidence and religion, the Soviet state is more aggressive than East European countries in attacking organized religion. Unregistered churches, those who have refused to accept state supervision, are subject to open persecution. Some patriotic zealots at the local level have fined believers for going to church. In some cases, religious practice is viewed as a sign of mental breakdown and is treated with confinement in mental hospitals. Religious instruction for children is prohibited. Less than one-hundred synagogues remain open to serve the nearly 2 million Jews still in the USSR. As recently as 1980, a university instructor had her degree revoked because she "believed in God" and announced this belief to her students.[20] In a more positive approach, the Soviet leaders have tried to develop secular rituals to wean people away from religious pageantry and rites.[21] To provide dignity and ritual to state weddings, for example, many Soviet couples now culminate their exchanging of marital vows with a visit to the local monument to the unknown soldier where they place a memorial wreath. Despite the negative sanctions for religious practices and the positive encouragement for atheism, many observers note a revival of religion in the Soviet Union, not only among the elderly but especially among the young.[22]

More so than other social groups, churches have a real potential for challenging the Communist monopoly over society. They offer their adherents a separate and competing loyalty. It is not surprising that Communist leaders feel the need to keep religions, and especially those which resist pledging subservience to the party, under close surveillance. So far, the Polish Catholic Church stands as the only truly independent social force in Eastern Europe. Its success will no doubt heighten antireligious sentiments among Communist leaders there and elsewhere in Eastern Europe.

CONCLUSIONS

Despite the attraction of a Europe from the Atlantic to the Urals, the eastern parts of this continent have always been sharply different from its western parts. Political, economic, and social patterns have differed throughout history with West European countries resembling each other much more closely than they have East European countries. Nevertheless, despite their distinctive socioeconomic features, many of the same social trends evident in West Europe since 1945 can also be seen in Eastern countries.

One observer contends that by the 1970s Eastern Europe had come to resemble Western Europe more closely than had been the case for centuries before.[23] It is true that political and economic trends affecting the West have influenced the East as well. But the effects are often sharply different in Eastern Europe. Exposure to modern education and industrial settings has altered traditional values and social-role definitions in the Soviet Union.[24] But new patterns of political behavior have not been brought, as in the West. Class structures are changing in both settings but with different consequences: In the West, social-class distinctions appear to have fewer consequences on political behavior; In the East, social-class distinctions may have more political consequences. Both areas have seen an expansion in the numbers and privileges of technical experts, engineers, and managers. But the East European intelligentsia is significantly different from the new middle-class in Western Europe. Ethnic nationalism has revived in both parts of Europe but the manifestations of this new nationalism is more open and dramatic in the West than in the East. New values, such as concern for environmental protection, are emerging everywhere. But in West Germany they lead to new ecological political forces, while in East Germany they encourage existing elites to calculate ecological costs when making policy decisions.

There are some observers who note growing signs of pluralism in Communist societies. But this pluralism is different in quantity and quality from the free formation and interaction of autonomous elements in Western societies. Old notions of monistic societies in Communist states are no doubt inaccurate, but the pluralism that is found in these countries is due to the party's inability to quash it rather than to the state's tolerance or fostering of such autonomous social forces.

NOTES

1. See Nathan Leites, *A Study of Bolshevism* (Glencoe, IL: Free Press, 1953), pp. 93–103.
2. Susan Jacoby, "Reforming Soviet Education," *Saturday Review/World,* 12 February 1973.
3. Richard Pipes, "The USSR or Russia? The Historical Perspective," in Uri Ra'anan and Charles M. Perry, eds., *The USSR Today and Tomorrow: Problems and Challenges* (Lexington, MA: Lexington Books, 1987), p. 27.
4. For a discussion of the effects of such experience on contemporary political attitudes, see Stephen White, *Political Culture and Soviet Politics* (New York: St. Martin's, 1979) pp. 22–63.
5. Henry Krisch, "Changing Political Culture and the Culture of the Apparatchiki," *Studies in Comparative Communism* 19 (Spring 1986): 25–39.
6. Martin McCauley, "Legitimation in the German Democratic Republic," in Paul G. Lewis, ed., *Eastern Europe: Political Crisis and Legitimation* (New York: St. Martin's, 1984), pp. 42–67.
7. Archie Brown and Jack Gray, eds., *Political Culture and Political Change in Communist States* (New York: Holmes & Meier, 1977).
8. White, *Political Culture and Soviet Politics,* pp. 64–83.
9. Stephen R. Burant, "The Influence of Russian Tradition on the Political Style of the Soviet Elite," *Political Science Quarterly* 102 (Summer 1987), 273–293.
10. For an East European dissident's views of the conditions of the working class, see Miklos Haraszti, *A Worker in a Worker's State* (Harmondsworth, England: Penguin, 1971).
11. François Fejto, *A History of the People's Democracies: Eastern Europe Since Stalin* (New York: Praeger, 1971), pp. 272–273.
12. A more favorable view of class mobility is offered in Jerry F. Hough and Merle Fainsod, *How the Soviet Union is Governed* (Cambridge, MA: Harvard University Press, 1979), pp. 561–563.
13. Mervyn Matthews, *Poverty in the Soviet Union: The Life-Styles of the Underprivileged in Recent Years* (Cambridge, England: Cambridge University Press, 1986), p. 176. This was the figure for small families; the incidence of poverty among larger families, peasants, and retired persons was even higher.
14. Milovan Djilas, *The New Class* (New York: Praeger, 1957).
15. White, *Political Culture and Soviet Politics,* pp. 104–106.
16. Jacques Rupnik, "The Military and 'Normalisation' in Poland," in Lewis, *Eastern Europe: Political Crisis and Legitimation.*
17. Betsey Gidwitz, "Worker Unrest in the Soviet Union," *Problems of Communism,* 31 (November-December 1982): 32–35.
18. John B. Dunlop, *The Faces of Contemporary Russian Nationalism* (Princeton, NJ: Princeton University Press, 1983).
19. J. Nowak, "The Church in Poland," *Problems of Communism,* January-February 1982.
20. Radio Liberty, *Current Abstracts and Annotations,* 1980, no. 6; p. 11.
21. See Christel Lane, *The Rites of Rulers: Ritual in Industrial Society—The Soviet Case* (Cambridge, England: Cambridge University Press, 1981).

22. Paul A. Lucey, "Religion," in James Cracraft, ed., *The Soviet Union Today* (Chicago: Bulletin of the Atomic Scientists, 1983), pp. 293–303.
23. Robin Okey, *Eastern Europe 1740–1980* (Minneapolis, MN: University of Minnesota Press, 1982) pp. 218–22.
24. Ellen Jones and Fred W. Grupp, "Modernization and Traditionality in a Multiethnic Society: The Soviet Case," *American Political Science Review,* 79 (June 1985): 474–490.

CHAPTER TWENTY-TWO
THE CITIZEN
AND POLITICS
IN COMMUNIST SYSTEMS

Some years ago, the Soviet leadership launched a major public debate over the need for a new constitution. For a couple of years, meetings were held all over the country to discuss the existing constitution and possible changes in it. Tens of millions of Soviet citizens took part in these meetings although there was little to suggest that their participation had any effect whatsoever on the new Constitution that was adopted in 1977 or that the resulting Constitution was any more accurate in describing the real pattern of power and policy making than was the old document. One of the central paradoxes of Communist politics is there is a very high rate of citizen involvement in political activities—probably higher than in most West European countries—but there is also much doubt about the efficacy of this participation in shaping policy or controlling the government.

The high level of citizen political involvement distinguishes Communist systems from traditional authoritarian regimes. Instead of stifling all citizen participation, the Communist party attempts to promote it and to channel it into forms and directions compatible with the party elite's agenda. The party seeks to mobilize the citizens so as to give legitimacy to its claim to rule in their behalf and to tap the human resources available through voluntary civic action. This participation is a different form than what is found in Western democracies, but nevertheless an important form of citizen political involvement.

THE INDIVIDUAL AND POLITICS

The nature of citizen involvement in the politics of Communist systems is the object of debate among Western scholars.[1] Some contend that the limits on citizen influence are such that one ought to talk of "mobilization" rather than "participation." Others have found a variety of ways in which citizens' independent and organized political actions influence the elite's political options and choices. Most observers agree, however, that the significance of participation in Communist states tends to be less than in Western democracies in terms of affecting the elite's actions and policies.

There are three categories of individual citizen political participation in East European Communist regimes. There are those forms of participation that are officially encouraged and directed by the Communist party: voting in elections, membership in mass organizations, volunteer civic activities, and participation in political education programs. There are also informal patterns of participation which, while not discouraged, are not the direct product of party citizen mobilization. Finally, there are the acts of political dissidence that are opposed by the political elite.

Party-Directed Political Participation

In Western democracies, the most common and, in some ways, the most important form of individual political participation is the act of voting. In Eastern Europe and the Soviet Union, elections are held at regular intervals. Although the outcome is never in doubt, these elections are taken seriously by the party leadership. The election campaign is well publicized and party members make special efforts to use the campaign to reiterate their list of accomplishments. On election day, citizens are strongly urged to vote; by early afternoon, party workers visit the homes of those who have not voted to see why and to encourage them to fulfill their duty as citizens. Those who are hospitalized or too ill to leave home are brought ballots and urns to vote from their bedsides. Consequently, turnout is always reported at a nearly perfect 99.9 percent in the elections in the Communist states. With an extensive system of mobilizing all voters, "it is virtually impossible to avoid voting."[2]

In form, these elections follow democratic procedures. But in reality they fall short of the requirements of free elections in three ways. First, there is no competition. The old Bolshevik leader, Georgi Molotov, is reported to have complained to a British politician, "The disadvantage of free elections is that you can never be sure who is going to win them."[3] In Communist states, the party does not run such a risk. The ballot contains the name of a single candidate. There is no provision for write-in candidates; voters vote against a candidate by marking his or her name out on the ballot.[4] One of the few attempts to open the electoral process in the Soviet Union was made in 1989 but it is not clear whether this will continue. With only one candidate, officials are elected by overwhelming margins of 99.5 percent or more of the voters. Not all candidates are Communist party members; in fact, in Eastern Europe, there are often candidates from other parties. But the presence of a candidate on the ballot, whether or not an actual Communist party member, indicates that the candidate has been approved by the Communist leadership. In recent years, there has been talk of permitting contested elections as part of Soviet Party Leader Mikhail Gorbachev's *glasnost* (the opening of the regime). It is doubtful that such a reform would bring much additional competition since all candidates would still need the approval of the Communist party. Already, in Poland and Hungary, party leaders have nominated more candidates than there have been seats contested. But these multiple candidacies did not increase competition since all candidates were party approved.[5]

Second, free elections involve the selection of the key policy-making personnel. Elections in Communist countries are for members of powerless parliaments; real political power is controlled by the party elite. While these party leaders may also be candidates in these elections, they derive their power not from the government office to which they are elected, but rather, from the unelected party positions they hold.

Third, these elections in Communist states are not free elections because the secrecy of the ballot is dubious. Voting booths are available but few voters use them. To do so is to invite speculation by neighbors and party election-monitors that those using the booth do so to conceal their voting against the party's candidate. Even with the decline of terror as a means of political control, few citizens are willing to publicly mark themselves as probable opponents of the regime. Most voters simply pick up their ballots and place them unmarked in the ballot boxes without using the booths.

Despite the predictability of the outcome, these Communist regime elections are important political events involving careful preparation by party workers. The goal of elections is much different than in the West where control over the government may change hands. In the East, elections are "tangible demonstrations of popular unity and support for the re-gimes."[6] Elections do nothing to change the composition of government or the balance of political power in the country. Instead, they have im-portant roles in the political education of the people. The party uses the campaign to explain its goals to the public and builds hope for an even more magnificent socialist future. Elections serve to enhance the legitimacy of the system. The overwhelming endorsement for the party's candidates in the election is used to publicly legitimize the regime to both internal and external audiences. Those discontent with the regime are demoralized by the overwhelming odds against them as they see 99.5 percent of their fellow citizens endorse the existing government. Elections bring a renewal of patriotism. Election day is a holiday with patriotic celebrations to build pride in the Communist country and party.

In recent years, there has been some evidence that voter turnout, especially in local elections, can give signs of public attitudes toward the regime. Thus, the 1984 local elections and the 1985 national elections in Poland were used to gauge the success of normalization campaigns after the turmoil of the first era of Solidarity-stirred unrest. In both elections, there was considerable abstention compared to results in previous years leading many to believe that the regime had not yet regained the confidence of the Polish people.

Another channel of approved political participation is through membership in mass organizations. On the surface, these organizations resemble some Western interest groups; they include youth groups, women's organizations, trade unions, collective farmers' associations, and other such groups. In practice, they are very different from their Western counterparts. They are designed to broaden the party's appeal and control beyond its formal membership to all parts of society. Sometimes the role of these mass organizations is compared to that of a transmission belt. The organization transmits to its mass membership the directions and priorities of the party elite and mobilizes its members to achieve the party's goals. Directed by party officials who are their leaders, these mass organizations assist the party in carrying its message to all citizens. Thus, trade unions are not the agents of citizen participation and representation that they are in Western Europe. Instead, "the primary task of the East European trade unions is to organize the labor force to increase production effort and fulfill various national goals."[7]

These transmission belts primarily convey directives from the party elite to the mass public. But they also serve as means for the party leadership to keep a finger on the pulse of the nation. Trade union leaders (who are also party leaders) bring to inner party circles impressions on the mood and needs of the workers; women's leaders (though rarely in top party circles) are able to communicate concerns of women to party leaders. The leaders have a representative task, but it is nearly always secondary to the primary task of social control that is expected of these bodies by the Communist elites. Above all, these organizations are to support the party's leadership.

> No organization in Eastern Europe is allowed to challenge the policies and decisions of the party. Furthermore, no organization is ever permitted to ask questions that can embarrass the authorities. After all, there can be no conflict of interests when the party of the working people is the ruling party.[8]

Citizens in Communist countries are well informed on political issues if informed is defined to mean knowledge of the party's position. It is difficult to get information beyond that dispensed by the party; it is even more difficult to avoid the party's version of current issues. Citizens are subjected to a constant barrage of political education emanating from the party: It is on the television and in the newspapers; It is pressed on them in the party propaganda centers present in virtually every work place; Clubs and community centers offer heavy doses of party indoctrination along with their social activities. For example, during a rest break in a factory, a party member will read an editorial from the party newspaper on the current party "line" to fellow workers "lest they idle away their time."[9] As a result, nearly all citizens attend political meetings or hear political presentations regularly.

The party encourages civic volunteer work. The volunteer activities range from self-administration committees to run apartments, advise schools, assist libraries, and so forth to citizen street cleaning and sanitation work, and to social-control activities such as volunteer police and citizen courts for minor offenders. The result is broad citizen involvement in the acts of government, especially local government.

Such volunteer activities permit the state to tap human resources at minimal costs and to give citizens a sense of civic involvement with a stake in the community. The best example is the Soviet practice of designating one Saturday each year, currently the Saturday nearest Lenin's birthday, as a day when citizens will voluntarily work without pay. In addition, citizens may be called upon to devote other Saturdays to *subbotnik* work, "volunteer" civic action. Such *subbotnik* work may mean involvement in some special civic project; but it often means simply working in their usual jobs for a day without pay. This volunteer civic work permits building patriotism and using patriotic impulses to extract practical services for the state.

One of the most common forms of citizen political expression is through letters to the editors of the newspapers. Such letters are encouraged by the regime. Party leaders urge citizens to report corrupt party officials or managers in this manner. These letters also give the party leadership a way of gauging public opinion: they aid in identifying policies that are unpopular or ineffective; they give citizens a way to vent their ire at inept or corrupt officials without threatening the regime; they provide the party with a way of identifying corrupt lower-level officials in order to remove them and thus avoid public disapproval.

The sheer volume of this form of political communication is overwhelming. In the USSR, the central radio and television offices receive over two million letters a year; *Pravda* receives well over 500,000 letters.[10] In addition to printing chosen letters, the press provides summaries of themes and concerns in their columns. They also pass on more extensive analyses of this mail to the party central committee. Since the beginning of *glasnost,* the number and critical level of these letters to the editor have increased as citizens have responded to Gorbachev's call to be more critical of official abuses of power.

In the absence of more extensive means of participation, media letters are important means of policy debate in Communist states, but they are imperfect means of citizen involvement. As in all societies, those who write letters to the editor are not representative of the range or incidence of opinions in society at large. In addition, there are certain issues and personalities that are not impeachable in a letter that will actually be published. A letter criticizing top party leaders, openly attacking major policy decisions already taken, or questioning the Communist system is very unlikely to be read in the press.

There are indications that the use of these formally approved methods of participation has increased in recent years.[11] This increase is not at all displeasing to the party in the age of *glasnost* and reform. Party leaders encourage letter writing, civic involvement at the local level, and volunteer service. Their efforts have been rewarded as growing number of citizens avail themselves of these limited channels of political action. In addition, as in the West, improved access to schooling means a better educated public, and with greater education comes a greater willingness to become politically involved.

Nonsanctioned Forms of Participation

Despite the growth in political participation, Communist systems have not experienced the crisis of participation that has been felt by Western democracies as people that had previously been politically uninvolved shift into political action. There has been increased evidence, however, that not all the new participation is contained in the party-approved channels. The most dramatic example of this form was the independent Solidarity trade union that flourished in Poland until suppressed by the military. Solidarity gathered broad support and manifested unhappiness with the regime in massive street demonstrations. Twice, this protest brought the resignation of the Communist premier.

To be sure, Solidarity was an exceptional case with few other protest movements having anywhere near this importance. But there have been other less spectacular signs of participation beyond the party's control. Indeed, spontaneous participation has increased in the last few years as citizens in the Soviet Union and other East European countries have tried to explore the limits of *glasnost* and the seemingly more tolerant attitude of leaders toward more spontaneous participation. There has been an increase in the number of demonstrations by political and ethnic dissidents. Perhaps of equal importance, these demonstrations have been reported in the official media. Such reporting may encourage further political demonstrations as a means of attracting public attention to problems that closed societies otherwise might ignore.

As in virtually all kinds of political systems, citizens in the Soviet Union and Eastern Europe have developed skills in finding how to work within the system to smooth out its abrasive aspects. One recent study suggests that Soviet citizens "go through the motions of participation" in the formal, party-sanctioned, channels, but "put far more serious effort into trying to influence the way decisions are implemented."[12] The resulting pattern involves extensive covert participation in which citizens use unapproved or blatantly illegal means to shape or escape the implementation of policies that affect them. This development is not surprising; without effective means of affecting policy making, citizens in Communist countries find it more practical to emphasize efforts that buffer themselves from the effects of unwanted policies or to extract individual benefits from the policies they cannot shape. Thus, personal ties are used to obtain favors; and bribery is "a common way of handling difficult situations."[13] Clientele relationships, like those in Italy, have developed that permit individuals to exchange favors.

There have been official attempts to curtail this form of participation. While the Western press has focused on the hopes of economic and political liberalization in the recent Gorbachev era of reform, one of the major thrusts affecting citizens in the Soviet Union and other Communist states has been a vigorous attack on such corrupt practices. It is paradoxical that in systems stressing the importance of collective values, the most meaningful form of citizen participation has been the individual's extra-legal or illegal efforts to secure his or her private welfare.

Citizen attempts to challenge the political system are much rarer. But small and sometimes noisy dissident movements exist in all Communist countries.[14] Political dissidence takes a number of forms: sincere Marxist-Leninists disillusioned by the reality of the Communist regimes; ethnic minorities concerned with greater autonomy and cultural preservation; religious dissidents seeking greater freedom to practice their beliefs; human rights advocates concerned with compelling the state to defend the liberties and rights specified in the existing Constitutions; and anti-Communists opposed to the entire Marxist-Leninist system.

The dissident causes that have mobilized the most people in the Soviet Union have tended to be those emanating from the discontent of national minorities. A recent example that was exceptional in its numbers and the general restraint of law enforcement bodies, was the series of Tatar demonstrations in Moscow and elsewhere in 1987. There were also a series of disturbances in 1987 and 1988 in Kazakstan reflecting the opposition of another Central Asian people to Soviet centralization. Other protest causes have attracted much less support despite often extensive coverage of the dissidence in the Western press.

The lack of popular interest in opposing Communist regimes is due in part to the difficulties of mobilizing opposition in states which do not have a free press. There are also heavy penalties in the form of harassment, loss of jobs or education opportunities, social exclusion, and even arrest that discourage citizens from expressing sympathy with dissident causes. In East European countries, a sense of helplessness stemming from Soviet suppression of dissident movements that were, at least initially tolerated by their own Communist parties, dissuades individuals from engaging in protest activities. The crushing of revolts in East Germany, Poland (on two occasions), Hungary, and Czechoslovakia by Soviet pressure or troops leads citizens of these countries to the belief that a change in their domestic politics is unlikely in the present system. Finally, and most importantly, dissident causes mobilize few followers because of the widespread feelings that the current regimes provide economic growth and security that had not been experienced under previous non-Communist governments. Citizens may not be satisfied with many of their government's oppressive policies, but they do not want to endanger the economic successes or give up the social-welfare benefits the Communist regimes provide by engaging in political disruption.

The Dilemmas of Participation
in Communist Regimes

Communist leaders currently face two dilemmas as patterns of citizen participation in their countries evolve. First, just as West European leaders have had to learn to cope with new and unconventional forms of participation, leaders in East Europe and the Soviet Union have had to adapt to higher levels of dissidence than they have faced in the past. Second, while eager to advance technologically, they have discovered that innovation requires more freedom to create and more interaction with the rest of the world than occurred in the past. Gorbachev's advocacy of *glasnost*, or opening up of the regime, is a recognition of the need for such liberalization in order to advance economically and technologically.

During the Stalinist era, indiscriminate terror was used as a means of paralyzing all political dissent. The terror included among its victims, not only those with suspect political backgrounds, but also random innocent victims. While the average citizen could understand the disappearance of political figures, the arrest of their nonpolitical neighbors for no apparent reason had a paralyzing effect. To avoid the same fate, the individuals would try to avoid even negative thoughts and would work harder at appearing to conform to the party's prescribed behavior in their public and private acts. Terror was an effective technique then for virtually eliminating opposition.

Now, the Soviet Union and all other Communist countries have repudiated the terrorist tactics of their pasts by forswearing the use of terror. In doing so, they have deprived themselves of the only way of totally eliminating dissent. They have gone further in proclaiming a more tolerant attitude toward some expression of diverse opinions within their countries. Yet they have not yet reached a point where they are ready to tolerate the dissent that they can no longer totally eliminate. The result is that most Communist states now vacillate between eras of relative tolerance of dissidence and eras of vigorous repression. In the Soviet Union, the repressive tactics of Brezhnev have been replaced by a more indulgent attitude toward dissidence under Gorbachev. This variable response to protest tempts dissidents to constantly check the current policy by pressing acceptable protest to its limit. The Communist leadership, often divided on the issue, gives off mixed and confusing signals on how it regards its internal opponents.

The second technological dilemma is equally difficult. As their economies and societies become more complex, Communist leaders are discovering the need for greater freedom of individual creativity in order to keep up with the technological change. Giving scientists, engineers, economists, and managers the leeway they need to keep up with changing technologies and complex societies means the social controls, that in the past limited individual political participation, must be relaxed. More highly educated populations are more interested in political questions than their less educated predecessors. Communist party leaders also accept the need to pay heed to the advice of technical experts in the increasingly complex social and economic policy making.[15]

In a very real sense, the populist revolt that brought greater political involvement and new forms of participation in the West has had its effect in the East as well. The extent and nature of this new populism is quite different in Communist countries. But the expansion of participation at the local level, the increased volume of political mail to newspapers and public officials, the growth of dissidence and even street politics, and the covert participation in altering policy as it affects the individual, all suggest important changes in the pattern of participation in Eastern Europe. Whether these changes will lead to greater participation or new attempts to limit it remains to be seen.

COMMUNIST PARTIES IN POWER

Unlike the multiple parties found in Western Europe, East European regimes are single-party systems dominated by the Communist parties. In several East European countries, non-Communist parties exist but their presence has no political significance. These purportedly autonomous parties are there because they serve to legitimize rule by the Communist party. Even if they always lose or if they have allied with the dominant party, their presence adds credibility to the claim that the regime is approved by the voters in a free choice. Their presence in no way challenges the political monopoly of the Communist party.[16]

Ruling Communist parties are entirely different entities than political parties in Western democracies, even if Communist. Their fundamental tasks are different. In the West, parties exist in a competitive environment where they must constantly prepare for the next election. Their primary task is to conduct and win these elections. To affect policy, to place their leaders in positions of official responsibility, Western parties must win elections. The electoral preoccupation is essential because the public and party leaders themselves evaluate the health of a party by how well it is doing at the polls. By contrast, in Eastern Europe, while the Communist parties do pay attention to the electoral process, their primary task is to exercise social control on behalf of the party elite. Thus, the duties of members of the Communist party of the Soviet Union include

> To put Party decisions firmly and steadfastly into effect. . . . To combat vigorously all manifestations of bourgeois ideology, remnants of a private-property psychology, religious prejudices, and other survivals of the past . . . to resist all actions injurious to the Party and the state, and to give information of them to Party bodies. . . .[17]

Party Organization and Discipline

Lenin's original concept of the party called for a small elite of professional revolutionaries to lead the proletariat to a revolution it could not achieve by itself. These few party members were to be highly disciplined, ideologically aware, and totally committed to bringing a socialist society into reality. The small size of the party is now largely a feature of the past as the task of seizing power was replaced by the task of governing. Ruling Communist parties have expanded their memberships in order to have the personnel needed for their social control duties. Party membership in Communist countries is thus higher than the combined membership of all parties in Western democracies. In the West, usually no more than 5 percent of the adults are formal members of various parties; Soviet party membership is about 10 percent of the adult population and East European Communist parties include 7 to 8 percent of the population.

In addition to their burgeoning general membership, ruling Communist parties have acquired very large bodies of full-time salaried party workers. Known in the Soviet Union as the *apparatchiki*, these professional party people make up a large and powerful bureaucracy that runs the party. This large army of party officials monitors the state bureaucracy, the military, the police, and other important forces. It assures compliance with the directions of the party elite by all parts of society. The exact size of these party apparatuses is not known but estimates for the Soviet Union run from 200,000 to 500,000 party employees.

Despite their parties' sizes, Communist party leaders still try to maintain very tight discipline and high levels of involvement. The key organizational principle in Communist parties is the Leninist notion of "democratic centralism." The "democratic" elements include the notion that party officials are elected by the membership directly below them and are expected to report regularly on their stewardships to those who elected them. The "centralizing" elements are strict party discipline, the subordination of the minority to the majority, and the obligatory acceptance of the decisions made by the higher party officials. There is to be free debate within the party prior to the making of a decision; once the decision is made all discussion ends and all levels of the party work together to carry out that decision. In practice, the centralizing elements are carefully preserved and the democratic elements frequently ignored. Party officials are formally elected. But since they face no open competition and are nominated at the higher levels, the process is more that of co-optation than election. Party officers do report on their activities to the bodies that elected them, but these reports are perfunctory and rarely debated or voted upon. In short, democratic centralism is a device to promote the centralism needed to monitor society effectively.

There are important material advantages and social prestige that come from Communist party membership. The leaders use these as incentives to keep party members loyal and active. Periodic purges of less active members are used to encourage the desired level of commitment and activity.[18] In these "gentle" purges, party membership cards are renewed, and less active members do not receive new cards thereby losing their party membership. Party discipline is furthered by the encouragement of criticism and self-criticism. Party members criticize their own shortcomings and the failings of other members. Criticism of the regime, top-level leaders, or policies is usually not tolerated. Relatively free criticism of middle- and lower-level party leaders serves to keep these officials efficient, increases their vulnerability to hierarchical control, and provides scapegoats for party failings.

Party Decline
in Communist Countries

The risk of party stagnation is greater in single-party states than it is in multiparty systems. In a democratic setting, elections alert parties to the need for reform and review of their doctrine and style. In single-party states, such warning signals are much more difficult to identify, but the need for them is probably greater. Long and secure tenure in public office breeds complacency and corruption; party membership becomes a means of social and economic advancement that has little relationship to the party's principles or in attuning the party to the needs of the general public. Party workers develop vested interests that creep into their public, policy decisions.

One sign of party stagnation is the near universal decline of ideological fervor of the ruling Communist parties. Ideological discourse continues, but even within the party discussions of doctrine and ideology are perfunctory and unenthusiastic. Enforced orthodoxy reduces the prospects for revitalizing old doctrine to meet the demands of changing societies. There are few party leaders left in Eastern Europe or the Soviet Union who are ideologists; most are pragmatists and technocrats. Pragmatism and technocracy suffice in ordinary times but they do not provide answers for times of change such as those presently facing Communist regimes. The dearth of new ideas and doctrinal development leave the party encumbered with a nineteenth-century ideology out of touch with the needs of society in the 1990s.

Even apart from the absence of ideological renewal, ruling Communist parties are not likely places for innovative individuals. Democratic centralism imposes a hierarchical control that discourages individual party members from trying to find creative ways to adjust the party or its policies to meet new social and political milieus. The best way to get ahead in the party is not to be innovative but to find a rising party leader and link oneself to him or her. Such recruitment patterns foster sycophancy, not creativity.

The size of the parties in most countries continues to grow, but this growth is in itself an impediment to party adaptation to new needs. The parties have acquired large and elaborate organizations which tend more to inertia than to reform. Add the vested interests of the party apparatus in the status quo and the party becomes an obstacle to, not a promoter of, social change. Thus, Soviet leader Mikhail Gorbachev has encountered powerful resistance within the party to the reforms he is trying to introduce.[19]

In most Communist parties, the membership is aging. In the Soviet party, for example, the percentage of members older than fifty grew from 22.9 percent in 1967 to 35.1 percent in 1981.[20] At the top level of leadership, many Communist parties resemble gerontocracies rather than vital revolutionary bands. Rejuvenation of top leadership ranks occurs when a new top leader emerges but rarely in the midst of the often long tenure of a party leader.

Finally, the parties often stagnate because of these long tenures. While the vicious struggle for power by Stalin is now discredited, no alternative mode for selecting the top leader has developed. The result is an extraordinary length of service for most Communist party leaders. Until 1987, only one East European Communist leader had voluntarily retired (East Germany's Walter Ulbricht); the rest either died in office or were pushed out by rivals within the party (See Table 22.1).

The unwillingness of senior party officials to risk political instability or uncontrolled struggle over power produces very cautious successions of leaderships. The most senior party leader or the least threatening one is granted the top position, rather than the most innovative or creative. The result is often near paralysis of policy under aging and unimaginative leaders. This stagnation was particularly evident in the Soviet Union during the first half of the 1980s. The last four years of Leonid Brezhnev's eighteen years of rule were characterized by policy stagnation and political uncertainty due to the leader's declining health and the inability to replace him. Brezhnev was succeeded by Yuri Andropov who fell ill a few months after becoming party leader and died after only fifteen months in office. He was succeeded by the even older Konstantin Chernenko who was ill throughout his thirteen month tenure. For much of this time, the Soviet Union lacked a leader who could respond to the international and domestic economic and political changes.

This discussion should not suggest that ruling Communist parties are crumbling. In fact, they have remarkable resilience and durability. But they do not have the verve and energy that they once might have had to bring change to their societies. Instead, they have become very conservative and stodgy bodies more concerned with protecting their privileged positions than with adjusting themselves or their countries to changing settings. This decline is a different kind than that menacing Western parties.

TABLE 22.1   The Years in Office of Communist Leaders in 1987

Country	Leader	Years in Office
Albania	Ramiz Alia	5[a]
Bulgaria	Todor Zhivkov	32
Czechoslovakia	Gustav Husak	18
German Democratic Republic	Erich Honecker	16
Hungary	Janos Kadar[b]	30
Poland	Wojciech Jaruzelski	6
Romania	Nicolae Ceausescu	21

[a] Alia's predecessor, Enver Hoxha, died in 1982 after ruling 37 years.
[b] Kadar retired voluntarily in 1988.

But it is perhaps more threatening since there are no rival parties to prod the ruling Communists into adaptation or to replace them if they fail.

NOTES

1. See D. Richard Little, "Mass Political Participation in the US and the USSR: A Conceptual Analysis," *Comparative Political Studies* 8 (1976).
2. Paul Hollander, "Soviet Elections: For What Purpose?" in Harry G. Shaffer, ed, *The Soviet System in Theory and Practice*, 2nd ed. (New York: Frederick Ungar, 1984), p. 287.
3. Cited in R. L. Leonard, *Elections in Britain* (New York: Van Nostrand, 1968), p. 1.
4. On rare occasions, candidates in local elections have failed to win their seat because more voters crossed out their names than voted for them. (In the 1980 Soviet local elections, 77 of the 2.3 million candidates were rejected by the voters.) But this rejection has never happened in a national election in the Soviet Union or in any of the East European countries. In the Soviet Union, there appears to be a trend toward a decline in the willingness of citizens to vote against candidates in the national elections. See John N. Hazard, "Soviet Elections: Controlled Mass Participation," in Shaffer, ed., *The Soviet System in Theory and Practice*, pp. 283–286.
5. In Poland, for example, 646 candidates ran for the 460 seats in the Polish parliament. But the results were predetermined since a list system was used and the party had set beforehand the order of the candidates on that list. See Baruch A. Hazan, *The East European Political System: Instruments of Power* (Boulder, CO: Westview Press, 1985), p. 14.
6. Joni Lovenduski and Jean Woodall, *Politics and Society in Eastern Europe* (Bloomington, IN: Indiana University Press, 1987), p. 288.
7. Baruch A. Hazan, *The East European Political System: Instruments of Power*, p. 317.
8. Ibid.
9. John A. Armstrong, *Ideology, Politics, and Government in the Soviet Union: An Introduction*, 4th ed. (New York: Praeger, 1978), p. 62–63.
10. Ellen Mickiewicz, "Political Communication and the Soviet Media System," in Joseph Nogee, ed., *Soviet Politics: Russia After Brezhnev* (New York: Praeger, 1985), p. 46.
11. Theodore H. Friedgut, *Political Participation in the USSR* (Princeton, NJ: Princeton University Press, 1979). See also Jerry F. Hough and Merle Fainsod, *How the Soviet Union is Governed* (Cambridge, MA: Harvard University Press, 1979), pp. 277–319.
12. Wayne DiFranceisco and Zvi Gitelman, "Soviet Political Culture and 'Covert Participation' in Policy Implementation," *American Political Science Review* 78 (September 1984): 605.
13. Ibid., p. 611. See also Konstantin M. Simis, *USSR: The Corrupt Society* (New York: Simon and Schuster, 1982).
14. Iain Elliot, "Dissent, Opposition and Instability," in Martin McCauley, ed., *The Soviet Union After Brezhnev* (New York: Holmes & Meier, 1983), pp. 40–61, and Olga A. Narkiewicz, *Eastern Europe 1968–1984* (Totawa, NJ: Barnes & Noble, 1986), pp. 84–114.
15. Erik P. Hoffmann and Robbin F. Laird, *Technocratic Socialism: The Soviet Union in the Advanced Industrial Era* (Durham, NC: Duke University Press, 1985).

16. Lovenduski and Woodall, *Politics and Society in Eastern Europe,* pp. 191–192.

17. "The Rules of the Communist Party of the Soviet Union," *Soviet Union,* March 1981, p. 8.

18. These are "gentle" purges which simply deprive insufficiently committed individuals of their party membership, not the Stalinist kind of purge that cost individuals their freedom or lives. See Hough and Fainsod, *How the Soviet Union is Governed,* pp. 323, 335–336.

19. Robert C. Tucker, "Gorbachev and the Fight for Soviet Reform," *World Policy Journal* (Spring 1987), pp. 179–206 and Timothy J. Colton, *The Dilemma of Reform in the Soviet Union,* rev. ed. (New York: Council on Foreign Relations, 1986).

20. John H. Miller, "The Communist Party: Trends and Problems," in Archie Brown and Michael Kaser, eds., *Soviet Policy for the 1980s* (Bloomington: Indiana University Press, 1982), p. 8.

CHAPTER TWENTY-THREE
POLICY MAKING
IN EASTERN EUROPE
AND THE SOVIET UNION

Unlike the situation in Western democracies where political parties do not make the policies, the Communist parties in Eastern Europe and the Soviet Union directly dominate the policy-making processes. Western democratic parties propose policies as part of their electoral platforms or programs. These proposals must then be translated into authoritative decisions by government bodies. Translation often leads to significant revisions from a party's actual proposal, even when that single party controls the parliament. In Communist countries the policy decisions are not made by government bodies but in party councils and then transmitted to the official government bodies for implementation.

The party's dominant position is no secret; it is confirmed by the constitutions of all Communist countries. Formal governmental institutions exist and have important tasks to perform, but real power is always held by the party elite. This priority of the party over constitutional institutions is indicated by the fact that it is often that body that requests or receives the resignation of key political leaders, ministers and even the premier, rather than the parliamentary body. All notions of divisions of power are inapplicable in Communist systems, whether it be the American separation of power among different branches of government or the less rigid division between parliament and government found in other democracies. In Communist systems all power is concentrated in the hands of senior party officials.

These party-dominated policy processes brought about enormous socioeconomic changes in the European Communist states permitting the modernization of the Soviet Union and the rapid recoveries in devastated Eastern Europe after the Second World War. But growing economic and social problems in the 1980s led to an ongoing search for new approaches and an era of reform.

PARTY POLICY-MAKING BODIES

The basic structure of Communist party organization is shown in Figure 23.1. While the figure describes the party organs in the USSR, nearly identical party bodies are found in all the East European states. In principle, control over these bodies resides in the large Party Congress that meets at four to five year intervals. In practice, the flow of control is from the top to the bottom. The Secretariat, especially the General Secretary, designates which individuals are to be elected to the Central Committee and then, which are to be elected by the Central Committee to the Politburo and the Secretariat. Meetings of the Party Congress are very important political events. The importance comes not in the charade of controlling or electing party officials but, rather, in the ceremony and the policy directions indicated by the leaders in their addresses to the Congress.

FIGURE 23.1 Organization of the Communist Party of the Soviet Union.

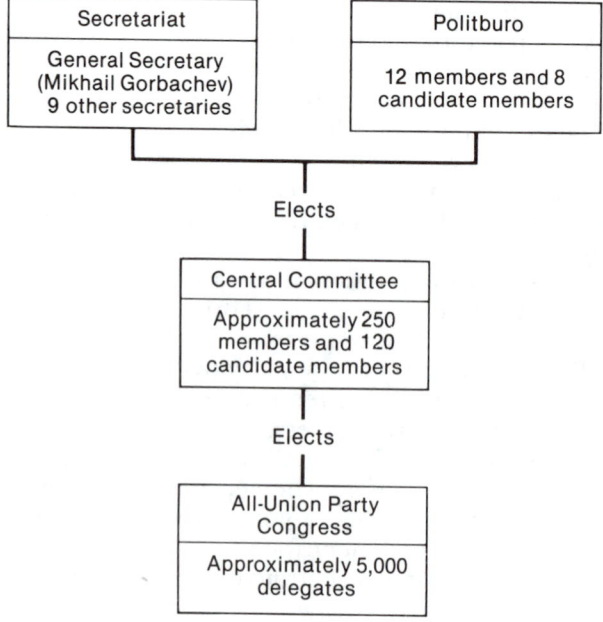

The Central Committee

The Central Committees are powerful political bodies in their own right. They usually have about five hundred full and candidate members that include all of the most powerful figures in the country. Because of its large size, the Central Committee meets in plenary sessions only two or three times a year. In the interim, an extensive system of specialized departments and subcommittees explore virtually every area of public policy and make recommendations for policy changes to the Politburo. Public debate by the Central Committee is usually limited with its plenary sessions being ceremonial rather than real decision-making sessions. However, behind the subcommittees' closed doors wide-ranging discussions with a full airing of diverse views is often the case.

Ordinarily, the Central Committee prepares, rather than makes, major policy and personnel decisions deferring key choices to the higher party body. On rare occasions, notably at times of leadership conflict, the Central Committee can play an important role. For example, during the Khrushchev era, the Central Committee was twice involved in major power struggles: the first to overrule an anti-Khrushchev majority in the Politburo in 1957; the second to confirm the Politburo's decision to oust Khrushchev in 1964. More recently, the Polish Central Committee was deeply involved in trying to resolve the Solidarity crisis. The Committee in 1980 dismissed the Polish premier and several Politburo members.

The Politburo and Secretariat

The Politburo and Secretariat are the key decision-making bodies. The exact division of responsibilities between these two bodies varies. The Politburo has the formal task of assuring the work of the Central Committee between its plenary sessions. In fact, it is usually the site of all major policy decisions.[1] The Secretariat manages the party apparatus, names key party and government personnel, and assures the execution of Politburo decisions. In a way, the division is not important because there is considerable overlap of people between these two supreme party organs. In 1989, for example, 21 party leaders filled the 30 positions in the Soviet Union's Politburo and Secretariat with several leaders sitting in both bodies. In addition, Secretariat members who are not formally on the Politburo nevertheless have the right to attend its meetings. Those members with the greatest influence are those who are members of both of these powerful party bodies and, particularly, the party leader, the General Secretary.

Politburo and Secretariat members are generally a heterogeneous group drawn from different clienteles of the party—its apparatus, the secret police, and the military—and from various regions of the country. Whether or not these individuals hold formal government positions, they are at the pinnacle of political power in their country. Politburo members are more likely to be recruited on the basis of their service in party bodies rather than in government ministries. Unlike Western politicians who come and go with the tide of electoral results, Communist political leaders who reach top positions usually stay there the rest of their political careers. Removal nearly always means a permanent end to the individual's political life.

Little is known about the operation of the Politburo and the Secretariat. Only recently have the presses been able to note even the fact that they are meeting. Most Politburos appear to meet regularly, usually once a week, with the sessions often lengthy. The party's General Secretary presides over the meetings of the Politburo. There is some evidence that the discussions in the Politburo and Secretariat are free and open with leaders working to achieve consensus among themselves on policy and personnel choices. A senior Soviet official told Western reporters how the Politburo works.

> At practically every session of the Politburo, nearly all members express their opinions. But there is virtually no disagreement in the Politburo. We never vote, because after we have all worked together to arrive at an opinion, there are no objectors left. And if there is still someone with his own opinion, we discuss it and work out some kind of convergence so that there will be unity.[2]

Despite such statements, consensus is often achieved only with great difficulty. Behind the consensus, there may be sharp disagreements on specific policies and strategies. A good illustration is the contention between Gorbachev and leaders such as Yegor Ligachev who opposed Gorbachev's reforms. These opponents may be forced to go along with a collegial decision on one issue but can and do fight again on the next issue. Yet, their position in the party may make it impossible for the party leader to expel them from these policy-making bodies. Gorbachev was apparently compelled by circumstances to allow his rival, Ligachev, to organize and chair the Secretariat while he chaired the Politburo. Everywhere in Eastern Europe and the Soviet Union, the presence of powerful party leaders on the Politburo and the Secretariat make them important policy-making bodies that do much more than rubber-stamp proposals from the party General Secretary.

General Secretary

The General Secretary is the head of the party and the most powerful political leader.[3] General secretaries no longer have the absolute dictatorial power that Stalin and his East European contemporaries had, but they are the most influential members of the small body of supreme party leaders. This fact is true whether or not they hold a key government position. For example, when Mikhail Gorbachev became General Secretary in 1985, he had not taken the position of President of the Presidium or of premier— the two key government posts according to the Soviet constitution. Some saw this lack as an indication that he had not yet fully consolidated his power since his predecessors—Brezhnev, Chernenko, and Andropov—all had held these posts. But his ability to control the political system was not significantly affected. Nor was Gorbachev's authority significantly altered when he did become President of the Presidium in 1988.

The General Secretary shares power with his associates in the Politburo and Secretariat. His influence is increased by the fact that over time he has been able to bring into these bodies individuals who are favorable to him and beholden to him for their appointments. Gorbachev moved quickly to consolidate his power by bringing an unusually large number of new members into the Central Committee. At the 1986 Party Congress, only 59 percent of the members of the preceding Central Committee, who were still alive, were reelected to the Central Committee.[4] Gorbachev was fortunate in that the top party bodies were filled with old men who had either died or retired shortly after his selection as the General Secretary. Within twenty-four months of his appointment, Gorbachev had named nine of the twelve members of the Secretariat and eleven of the nineteen members of the Politburo giving him a powerful base in these bodies.[5]

The influence of the General Secretary is enhanced by the diversity of the membership in the top leadership bodies. His leadership can change the balance among competing tendencies.[6] In addition, virtually every Communist leader has eventually permitted or insisted upon a cult of personality.[7] A cult of personality involves efforts to develop personal loyalties to a leader in the minds of general citizens and party workers: The leader's portrait is displayed everywhere; Laudatory biographies are prepared and given wide circulation; His writings become obligatory reading for all party members and upwardly mobile citizens; His public addresses and press releases dominate political news.

The influence of the party leader is likely to depend in part on his interest in change. Gorbachev has appeared to be unusually influential because of his reform agenda. He has not been interested simply in maintaining the course as Brezhnev did during much of his reign. As Gorbachev presses for change, he has had to try to assure a positive reaction throughout the party and state by making personnel changes.

Policy-Making Styles

Despite personality cults, Communist countries are usually not personal dictatorships but oligarchies that are made up of small numbers of party leaders. The General Secretary is the most powerful out of a group of powerful individuals. There are some exceptions in Eastern Europe. Nicolae Ceausescu has dominated Romania and has appeared tempted to create a personal dynasty with many top positions being held by his relatives. So many of his relatives have held public office that a joke has circulated that the only difference between the Austro-Hungarian royal Hohenzollern family and the Ceauscecus is that the old imperial Hohenzollern dynasty ruled Romania one after another while the Ceauscecus have ruled all together.[8] Walter Ulbricht's power in the German Democratic Republic was also near absolute. But these are exceptions to a more general pattern of party oligarchy rather than personal dictatorship.

Such shared power facilitates easy transfers when the General Secretary dies or steps down. The other party leaders quickly agree among themselves on a replacement from their ranks with seniority often among the most important criteria for selection.[9] The leader is gone but the party structure selects and legitimizes the successor. The common crises and instability of more traditional dictatorships that occur when the leader dies are thus avoided.

While the routine permits easy succession, it often leads to unimaginative decision making. Most decisions are the products not of a single person, but collective ones of the top elite. For example, during Brezhnev's reign, policy making followed "a style of rule which produced a lowest common denominator of agreement within the elite."[10] The emphasis is still often on elite consensus and the avoidance of elite division. More often than not, the consensus is reached by finding a common ground rather than the resolution of different opinions or factional conflicts. It sometimes appears that consensual decision making is stressed even at the cost of policy consistency and coherence.[11]

There is a lively debate among Western specialists on Communist politics as to the extent and significance of this collective decision making. Some see it as evidence of a much more open, even pluralist, society in which various interests acquire some autonomy and are able to press freely for their viewpoints in party decision-making circles.[12] Others insist that such a view overlooks the essential nature of the Communist system which is that society is dominated by the party and that no decision is taken against the will of the party.[13]

With few exceptions, however, the experts agree that whatever the influence of these contending interests, they differ dramatically in nature and in tactics from West European interest groups. The group actors in Communist politics are not structured associations of farmers, workers, or employers but formal and informal groups of individuals sharing common interests: party *apparatchiki,* secret police, the military, economic planners, plant managers, and government bureaucrats. They press for their needs through party channels, often relying on top officials drawn from their ranks to "represent" their interests in the Central Committee or Politburo. Less frequently, other groups become points of reference for policy makers who feel it wise to anticipate their reaction to policies: collective farmers, factory workers, teachers, and so forth. In some East European countries, notably Poland, the views of autonomous or semiautonomous churches must also be taken into account.

How effective these groups are in influencing policy decisions is controversial. The hierarchical and closed nature of the political elite certainly restricts such interests from the degree of influence that they can exercise in Western democracies. But even the authoritarian regimes of Eastern Europe and the Soviet Union are responsive to the demands of key sectors of their societies. There are some who argue that the resulting pattern of policy making in Communist parties is similar to the kind of neocorporatist policy making that has developed in some West European democracies. This corporatist pattern is characterized by intense interaction between powerful groups that have a vested interest and the government officials as policies are made and implemented. But most see the corporatist model as of limited value in understanding politics in Communist systems.[14] There are few examples of the formal institutions of corporatist collaboration with genuine policy-making power that are associated with that model. Instead, the interaction takes place in party councils. The state and the party have the strength to impose their will, and this power leaves the ultimate decisions in their hands.

In the final analysis, the influence of all such groups depends upon the willingness of the top party leaders to grant concessions to them. The elite is not compelled to do so and often refuses to even when the political costs are high. Stalinist dictatorial power is no longer the rule. This change does not mean a new participatory system but, rather, a new collegial dominance of politics by the small party elite.

FORMAL GOVERNMENT INSTITUTIONS

A reading of a constitution of any East European country or of that of the Soviet Union would reveal an elaborate parliamentary framework very much like those found in Western Europe. There is the usual arrangement of a popularly elected parliament which selects from among its members a premier and ministers. As in the West, these parliaments have the power to censure their governments—although no parliament has ever even held such a vote—and to vote on all legislation—although in practice the legislation is at best only ratified and is often not even brought before the parliament. Though these parliamentary institutions are, in fact, present, they are not the locus of political power; that power is monopolized by the party.

Parliaments in Communist Europe

While political power is concentrated in the hands of the political elite, the formal government institutions have political significance even if they do not make the key policy decisions. In part, they contribute to the legitimizing of these regimes. The parliamentary institutions provide a facade of democratic organization that masks the party's control.[15] The parliamentary bodies and the elections of these bodies help convey the impression of democracy to the citizens. They are used to sustain the legitimacy of these regimes to their own citizens and to the outside world in an era where parliamentary democracy is seen as desirable.

Instead of bodies for deliberating and debating public policy, the parliaments of Communist countries are assemblies of notable citizens. "Representatives" of diverse social classes and ethnic groups, athletes, and entertainment personalities are brought together more to show their support of the regime than to shape the regime's priorities. The presence of these outstanding individuals in parliament, many of whom are not Communist party members, is supposed to enhance the state's legitimacy. In addition, their election to parliament rewards them for the service they have provided to the country.

Parliamentary sessions occur two to four times a year and last only a few days each time. In such short periods, the parliaments have no time for serious consideration of public policy. Their debates are characterized by formal speeches by party leaders outlining their achievements. Beyond listening to such addresses, the members of Communist parliaments simply endorse by unanimous votes the acts of the party and government leadership.[16] There is some evidence that legislative committees and subcommittees are increasingly involved in overseeing implementation of policy in several Communist regimes, especially in Eastern Europe but also in the USSR.[17] In 1989, Gorbachev reformed the Supreme Soviet to give it greater political influence. It remains to be seen if this reform will last and if it actually increases Parliament's powers.

Premiers and the Council of Ministers

More important than the legitimizing functions of the formal political institutions are their roles in implementing and administering the party's decisions. The legislative body formalizes the selections for the premier and the Council of Ministers much like in Western parliamentary governments. Most Communist countries have very large Council of Ministers with highly specialized portfolios such as separate ministers for the automotive industry, general machine building, geology, and the gas industry along with the more traditional ministers of foreign affairs, defense, and finance. The State Councils or Councils of Ministers are in effect miniparliaments formally adopting state policies in place of the parliaments. When the parliaments do convene, they routinely ratify these policy decisions of the ministers.

The Council of Ministers is not a collective decision-making body like the cabinets in West European democracies. In Communist countries, the council meets infrequently in plenary sessions. The ministers take directives from the Politburo and appropriate Central Committee subcommittees and try to implement them. There are also smaller groups of key ministers who do meet regularly—such as the Presidium of the Council of Ministers in the USSR.

The Chairman, or premier, of the Council of Ministers is equivalent in rank to a Western premier or prime minister. The premier has important power due to his control of the vast state bureaucracy. Because of its key control over the state apparatus, the post is a potential source of rivalry to the party secretary. For this reason, the party leader often takes that position himself or fills it with a close ally. In the Soviet Union, Gorbachev named Nikolai Ryzhkov premier shortly after assuming control of the party. Ryzhkov is a full member of the Politburo but, more importantly, he is a strong backer of Gorbachev.

There are ministries that parallel those in West European countries: defense, interior, foreign affairs, communications and information, and so forth. But the total number is much greater and the areas of responsibility are more detailed. In effect, these ministries run the economy of the country. Thus, a typical Communist government includes ministries for the many sectors of the economy: mines, industrial construction, light industry, chemical industry, and electric power. The breadth of ministerial responsibilities is much greater than in a western democracy.

> [Ministries] set wages and prices, manage all financial institutions, run the factories and farms, and oversee the operation of all retail and wholesale stores, from the smallest general store to the largest supermarket.[18]

With the state in control of the economy, ministries must establish salaries and prices. They oversee the management of all factories, shops, and stores.

Heads of State

As in Western parliamentary systems, the Soviet and East European constitutions provide for a president who serves as the head of state. These executives are theoretically elected by the parliaments, but as with the other key officials they are actually selected by the party Secretariat with only formal election by the parliaments. The political significance of these officials varies from country to country and even within the same system. For example, Brezhnev held this position in the Soviet Union after 1977 and his immediate successors, Andropov and Chernenko, also took that office. Gorbachev initally turned the position over to the aging Andrei Gromyko as an honor to his long service to the country. However, in 1988 he assumed the post himself and pressed for changes to increase the powers of the head of state.

How powerful the president is, is not a function of the office itself but rather the person who fills the office. When the president is the top ranking party leader, then the office has added significance. But the office does not seem to add additional strength to the party leader. Gorbachev, for example, did not suffer politically from not taking the presidency as had his predecessors. Nor did his powers increase when he became President. All this is simply a restatement of the basic principle of politics in Communist states: The key to political power is not found in government position but in party rank. Whatever his formal state office, it is the party's General Secretary who is *the* leader.

The Means of Party Control Over the State

In each Communist country, the party devotes considerable effort to convincing the general public that it alone represents the will of the people. Nearly all their Constitutions declare the party's privileged position and a barrage of propaganda repeats that message incessantly. Loyalty to the party's policies is a basic principle that all employees of Communist states are expected to endorse, just as civil servants in Western Europe are expected to maintain political neutrality. The legitimacy of the regime varies from country to country.[19] But it is fair to say that throughout Eastern Europe and the Soviet Union a substantial majority of the general public and an even greater proportion of those in positions of influence in the state bureaucracy accept the party's claim to speak for the people. This acceptance provides the party leadership with an important advantage in trying to assert control over the state bureaucracy.

To maintain this initial edge of control over the bureaucracy the party has at its disposal several additional instruments.[20] Perhaps the most important is the power of controlling all key appointments. In the Soviet Union, for example, this power over appointments is known as the *nomenklatura* system.[21] Lists of key posts are compiled with specific units assigned to assure that the people serving in these posts are completely loyal to the party. The naming of people to fill virtually every position of even modest importance in Soviet society is thus subject to the direct or indirect control of the party.

A second related point is the surveillance of government personnel by the various party units. The party bureaucracy parallels the state bureaucracy and checks on the state officials' obedience to party directives. At the highest levels, the Central Committee oversees the actions of the national ministerial staffs. At the grass roots level, the party unit verifies the obedience of officials from government agencies and ministries as well as of plant managers, collective farm operators, trade union officials, and so on. Throughout society, promotions, dismissals, and transfers of state employees are subject to the recommendations of the surveilling party unit regarding the individual's compliance with the desires of the party leadership.

Thirdly, the party's influence in the bureaucracy is enhanced by the fact that so many of the key officials are themselves party members. As such, they are subject to party discipline and expected to not only obey the party leaders' directives but to assure that others do so too. At every level, there is considerable overlap of personnel in leadership positions in the state agencies and at the same level in the party organization.

Finally, the party encourages public surveillance of government officials. Individual citizens can and do report on ministry officials, managers, group leaders, and others who are believed to deviate from the party line. The press is full of letters denouncing public officials who have failed to live up to the spirit and the letter of party guidelines.

Despite these various controls, the massive size of the bureaucracies in Communist countries makes them difficult to be totally controlled. Indeed, the checks themselves engender efforts to escape party restraints. Party officials and bureaucrats find that they share common purposes: A plant or government office that is seen as performing well brings praise not only to the bureaucrat but to the party official overseeing it. The converse is also true: A poor performance diminishes the reputation of the manager responsible and the party person in charge. As a result, there are incentives for both sides to make the other one look good whatever the reality may be. Such mutual protection arrangements may frustrate party controls.

In addition, the cumbersome nature of the vast bureaucracy means that officials may be tempted to make it more responsive to an individual's needs by granting exceptions or special treatment. In the worst cases, this means extensive corruption as officials accept bribes. These exchanges of favors mean the evading of party control. Yet, such activity is needed to reduce individual hardship and to prevent bureaucratic rigidity. It makes the system tolerable and workable and therefore cannot be eliminated. Of course, such activities do mean breaches in party control over the implementation of its policies. In 1986, General Secretary Gorbachev issued a scathing attack on the Soviet planning agency, *Gosplan,* for its corruption and its deviation from party-dictated priorities. Despite severe penalties for corruption, the prospects for controlling this kind of bureaucratic activity are not good.

The extensive interweaving of the party and its monitors into the bureaucracies of Communist systems takes away some of the usual concern about the subservience of the civil servants to political guidance. In general, the party's presence and its control mechanisms assure that the bureaucracy will make loyal efforts to implement the leadership's preferences. However, as is the case in Western bureaucracies, the East European and Soviet civil servants are especially loathe to accept changes that threaten their prerogatives or disrupt their established patterns. It is not surprising, then, that a principal source of resistance to recent reforms in the Soviet Union and Eastern Europe comes from the bureaucrats who see the changes as endangering their privileged situation.

PARTIES WITH STATES OF THEIR OWN

In Western Europe, political parties sometimes hold the power and may even temporarily dominate the state. But the parties always remain distinct and separate entities from the state. They hold sway only for the time until another party replaces them. In Eastern Europe and the Soviet Union, the Communist parties have so dominated their states that the distinction between the state and the party loses significance. The parties are so pervasive that in a very real sense, they have become parties with states of their own. They are therefore very different from Western parties; they are preoccupied with assuring their permanent control over their states and societies.

The policy processes in both democratic Western Europe and Communist Eastern Europe are dominated by relatively small elites whose socioeconomic traits are much different from those of the general public. But the character of rule by these elites is sharply different. In the West, the competitive political situation in which politicians exist force them to be responsive to shifting public opinion; they rotate in and out of public office as they please or displease the majority of voters. In the Communist setting, however, the elite remains in power permanently. Changes generally come only when the top leader dies.

A noted scholar on Soviet politics caught the difference between the competitive elitism of the West and the closed elitism in the East in an analogy to a bus travelling through time.

> In a society in which the elite is relatively open to new entrants, elite status might be compared to a bus that travels through time: various passengers get on the bus at its stops, ride for differing lengths of time, and get out again. In a society in which the political elite is relatively closed, either because it is formed by traditional, ascriptive criteria or because it is made up of a power-monopolizing and self-selecting core, the membership of the elite is rather stable over time.[22]

This closed and unchanging nature of the political elite is, of course, a principal characteristic of Communist states. But it is a chief obstacle not only to building more responsiveness to citizen concerns but also to responding to pressures for change and reform.

NOTES

1. John Lowenhardt, *The Soviet Politburo* (New York: St. Martin's, 1982).
2. Lev Kaikov, third ranking member of the Politburo in an interview with *Newsweek*, 4 April 1988, p. 9.
3. Archie Brown, "The Power of the General Secretary of the CPSU," in T.H. Rigby, et al, eds., *Authority, Power and Policy in the USSR* (New York: St. Martin's, 1980).
4. Thomas Gustafson and Dawn Mann, "Gorbachev's First Year: Building Power and Authority," *Problems of Communism* 35 (May-June 1986). In contrast, at the preceding party congress in 1981, over 90 percent of the Central Committee members elected in 1976, who were still alive, were reelected. Robert H. Donaldson, "Political Leadership and Succession: The Passing of the Brezhnev Generation," in Joseph L. Nogee, ed., *Soviet Politics: Russia After Brezhnev* (New York: Praeger, 1985), p. 9.
5. Archie Brown, "Gorbachev and the Reform of the Soviet System," *Political Quarterly* 58 (April-June 1987): 139–151.
6. Ibid.
7. See, for example, George W. Breslauer, *Khrushchev and Brezhnev as Leaders: Building Authority in Soviet Politics* (London: George Allen & Unwin, 1982).
8. Baruch A. Hazan, *The East European Political System: Instruments of Power* (Boulder, CO: Westview Press, 1985), p. 224.
9. In Eastern Europe, the selection of the new General Secretary also involves the informal consent of the Soviet Union to the party's choice. Hazan, *The East European Political System*, pp. 212–213.
10. Brown, "Gorbachev and the Reform of the Soviet System," p. 141.
11. Roger A. Blough and Philip D. Stewart, "Political Obstacles to Reform and Innovation in Soviet Economic Policy: Brezhnev's Political Legacy," *Comparative Political Studies* 20 (April 1987): 83–84.
12. See Susan Gross Solomon, ed., *Pluralism in the Soviet Union* (London: Macmillan, 1983).

13. A. L. Unger, *The Totalitarian Party* (Cambridge, England: Cambridge University Press, 1974), pp. 62–63. See also W. E. Odom, "A Dissenting View on the Group Approach to Soviet Politics," *World Politics* 28 (July 1976): 542–567.
14. See Valerie Bunce, "The Political Economy of the Brezhnev Era: The Rise and Fall of Corporatism," *British Journal of Political Science* 13 (April 1983): 129–158.
15. On parliamentary bodies, see Daniel Nelson and Stephen White, eds., *Communist Legislatures in Comparative Perspective* (London: Macmillan, 1982).
16. Stephen White, "The USSR Supreme Soviet: A Developmental Perspective," in Daniel Nelson and Stephen White, eds., *Communist Legislatures in Comparative Perspective* (London: Macmillan, 1982).
17. Ibid.
18. Ivan Volgyes, *Politics in Eastern Europe* (Chicago, IL: Dorsey Press, 1986), p. 173.
19. Paul G. Lewis, ed., *Eastern Europe: Political Crisis and Legitimation* (New York: St. Martin's, 1984).
20. On party control of the bureaucracy, see Rolf H. W. Theen, "Party and Bureaucracy," in Erik P. Hoffmann and Robbin F. Laird, eds., *The Soviet Polity in the Modern Era* (Hawthorne, NY: Aldine, 1984), pp. 131–166.
21. See Bohdan Harasymiw, *Political Recruitment in the Soviet Union* (New York: St. Martin's, 1984).
22. Frederick C. Barghoorn and Thomas F. Remington, *Politics in the USSR*, 3rd ed. (Boston: Little, Brown, 1986), pp. 202–203.

CHAPTER TWENTY-FOUR
REFORM
IN
REVOLUTIONARY REGIMES

A prominent Czech dissident, Vaclav Havel, tells of a talented brewer he once worked for who wanted his brewery to produce the finest beer. The brewer was a skilled craftsman who took pride in his product; he worked hard, spending extra, unpaid hours improving his ability to perfect his ale. His zeal in his job and his evident talent were eventually seen as threats by his superiors who were managers, not brewers. They labeled him a "political saboteur" and had the brewer transferred to another job which required no skill to perform.[1] These kinds of situations, where political considerations can be used as excuses to defend bureaucratic mediocrity, plague the economies and societies of Eastern Europe and the Soviet Union.

The revolutionary visionaries who saw communism as a way to improve and modernize their countries' societies and economies have disappeared in the Soviet Union and, with only a few exceptions, have passed from the political scene in Eastern Europe as well. The political leaders have been replaced by party men (and very few women) who have lost that vision by their concern for maintaining their privileges and prestige. They are products of the party apparatus, well skilled in its internal politics and often effective managers, but so attached to the current political and economic arrangements that they abhor thoughts of change. They are honestly committed to Communist ideology but they are no longer inspired by it; they expound it endlessly but are not able to arouse public passions to enact the oft-repeated precepts.[2]

The result is a crisis of Communist Europe that coincides with and parallels the crisis of capitalist Europe. The Communist economies were stagnant, and those in Eastern Europe were plagued by heavy debts to Western banks. There were serious social problems including malaise among workers and serious problems of alcoholism. Political dissent appeared on the rise with workers in Poland, minorities in the Soviet Union, and intellectual dissidents everywhere expressing open dissatisfaction with the realities of the socialist state. Aged leaders in most of the European Communist countries seemed uninterested in, or threatened by, the kind of changes needed to overcome these problems.

The era of *glasnost* (openness) and *peristroika* (reform) opened hesitantly in the early 1980s. But it was only after Mikhail Gorbachev ascended to power in 1985 that these efforts to respond to the spreading crisis really flourished. He set a broad agenda for his changes.

> *Peristroika* means initiative and creative endeavor, improved order and discipline, more *glasnost*, criticism and self-criticism in all aspects of our society. The essence of *peristroika* lies in the fact that it unites socialism with democracy.[3]

Two problems quickly developed: First, could Gorbachev impose the changes on those who had benefited from the old system in the Soviet Union and on the Communist leaders in other countries whose careers had been built on the old system? Second, if the changes were brought about, would they be sufficient to correct the socioeconomic and political problems? It is too early to answer either of these questions. But it is possible to look at the achievements and problems of the Communist regimes in Eastern Europe and the Soviet Union noting the direction of the changes promised by Gorbachev.

THE SOCIALIST ECONOMY

The economy of Eastern Europe and the Soviet Union is characterized by the near absence of private entrepreneurship. All industry and nearly all agricultural operations are owned and operated by the state in conformity with the guidelines developed by the Communist party. There are a few exceptions to the state-dominated economies: small private plots tilled by collective farmers in their spare time; some farming operations in Eastern Europe;[4] and some individual craft people providing services or products on a local basis. The economies are centrally organized with planners dictating to each plant the item to be produced, its price, and its purchaser. This central planning requires a massive bureaucracy to make all the economic decisions that in Western economies are made by the interplay of supply and demand and other market forces. Such deliberate decisions obviously increase central control over the economy, but they also bring the risk of massive blockages if the decisions are poor, not carried out at all levels, or not made at all. Since the plans are very detailed, even a slight error—and such errors are inevitable—can mushroom into serious proportions as it moves from the central planner to the plant level. Moreover, suppliers deal with distant central planners rather than with those who actually use their product. There is often an irresistible temptation to follow to the letter the plan by producing the desired quantities without respecting its assumption of good quality.

In the 1940s and 1950s, the economies of Eastern Europe and the Soviet Union grew at record rates, far outstripping the United States and rivalling the "economic miracle" in West Germany. Central planning and state investment in heavy industry fostered the rapid economic growth of economies that had been ravaged by war or that had not been industrialized earlier. However, by the 1960s, economic growth had substantially slowed and by the 1970s, the Eastern economies began to import products and investment funds from the West. East European debt to the West grew from $10 billion in 1976, to $56 billion in 1980 and to $90 billion at the beginning of 1988.[5] Labor shortages and, especially, shortages of essential natural resources began to impinge on economic performance. Yet Communist notions of economic value (which define value essentially in terms of labor costs alone) did not encourage the best allocation of investment funds or natural resources. These shortages coincided with agricultural problems caused, in part, by poor management of collective farms and, in part, by a series of poor harvests in the Soviet Union and grain-producing areas of Eastern Europe.

The earlier preoccupation with the building of heavy industry had meant that citizens had to endure shortages of consumer goods that were readily available in the Western world. The patience of these citizens was tested when the growing economic problems forced the ending of subsidies on food. In Poland, the uprising that gave birth to the Solidarity movement was the result; elsewhere in Eastern Europe and even in the Soviet Union, leaders began to feel more urgency in responding to pressure for more readily available consumer goods and goods of better quality.

There is a sharp gap between the standard of living of East Europeans and that of West Europeans, which is seen by comparing per capita gross national product (See Table 24.1). But since East European currencies are not directly convertible with Western currencies, the comparisons do not accurately portray the extent of the differences. In terms of access to basic consumer goods, the differences are even more striking. Table 24.2 shows the gap more clearly by comparing the time that citizens must work to earn enough to purchase an actual commodity. With a very few exceptions, notably housing,[6] the costs of living, in terms of working time necessary to purchase key items, are much higher in the Soviet Union and other East European countries than in Western countries. In addition, whatever the cost, there are often serious shortages of basic items that result in lines for meat, or matches, shoes that often do not fit, and occasional recourses to rationing to allocate short supplies of necessities. Moreover, key consumer products that are taken for granted in the West are in very short supply in the East. For example, in the United States, there are 580 automobiles for every 1,000 inhabitants; in the USSR, there are only 48 cars per 1,000 people; there are 791 telephones for every 1,000 Americans but only 90 per 1,000 Soviets; and there are 794 television sets per 1,000 in the US but only 300 per 1,000 in the USSR.[7]

To a large extent, the lower living standards in Communist countries reflect deliberate decisions by policy makers to stress investment in heavy industry rather than to promote consumer goods. The ability of these leaders to continue such a priority appears to be diminishing as pressure for consumer goods rises among people. The Polish crisis in 1980 is the most dramatic of several episodes that show the growing public desire for more and better quality consumer goods. Of equal importance is a growing unwillingness on the part of the workers to give their best efforts when they know that however dedicated their work, the rewards in terms of improved access to consumer goods will be slight. A popular Russian joke captures the resulting spirit, "They pretend to pay us and we pretend to work."

The slowing of economic growth in Communist countries can be explained in several ways. Some of the economic problems can be traced to the basic nature of Communist economics.[8] Marxist economics attributes all value of a product or service to the labor cost. No value is placed on capital or natural resources. This system leads to inefficient use of scarce resources. Thus, energy poor Poland consumes three times as much energy to produce each $1000 in gross domestic power than does France.[9] Rational economic planning is hindered by the ideologically mandated neglect of the costs of capital and natural resources.

Also linked to basic Communist precepts is the insistence on central planning. In and of itself, this enormous planning process consumes the time of skilled economists. Its comprehensive nature brings inevitable delays and errors that multiply into economic nightmares. In addition, centralization reduces local initiative and innovation that are the source of much of the vitality of Western economies. Such centrally planned economies lack the ability to respond to changes in needs. For example, many of the current economic problems in the Soviet Union can be traced to decisions

TABLE 24.1 Comparison of Per Capita Income for Selected Countries

Country	Per capita income in 1986 U.S. dollars
Czechoslovakia	$ 5,914
German Democratic Republic	9,800
Hungary	7,200
Poland	6,190
Romania	5,200
USSR	6,763
Britain	7,640
France	10,400
German Federal Republic	10,672
Italy	7,151
USA	13,451

Source: The 1987 Information Please Almanac (Boston: Houghton Mifflin, 1986).

TABLE 24.2   Work Time Required to Purchase Selected Consumer Items in 1986
(Minutes of work unless otherwise noted)

Item	US	UK	France	FRG	USSR
Rye bread	18	14	34	19	11
Sirloin steak	83	123	109	93	195
Sugar	6	8	11	8	52
Milk	4	6	8	6	20
Grapefruit	6	7	7	13	112
Instant coffee	18	27	48	28	335
Vodka	78	78	97	61	569
Beer	13	21	15	9	14
Small car (months)	5	8	8	7	45
Bicycle (hours)	17	23	29	17	49
10 liters gasoline	17	64	66	47	167
T-shirt	28	56	55	70	184
Panty hose	16	14	17	16	279
Man's shoes (hours)	6	6	9	11	37
Man's suit (hours)	18	16	34	33	118
Refrigerator (hours)	44	30	30	31	102
Washing machine (hours)	46	52	61	49	177
Color TV (hours)	30	75	106	54	669
Month rent in subsidized apartment (hours)	55	26	15	24	11
Man's hair cut	62	61	92	75	34
Shampoo and set	62	61	91	135	167

Source: Keith Bush, "Retail Prices in Moscow and Four Western Cities in October 1986,"
Radio Liberty Research Bulletin, Supplement, January 21, 1987, pp. 23–30.

made in the 1970s to expand heavy industrial output in anticipation of continued need for large machinery and steel. However, by the early 1980s, existing industrial production was exceeding demands and shortages were becoming acute in consumer goods and services. But the planning mechanisms continued to include annual increments in the production of the very heavy industrial goods that were already in surplus.

In the rest of the world, economic growth has been stimulated by international transfers of technology. Firms from one country "import" their technology into other countries where they build plants or develop new markets. The closed nature of the Communist states and, above all, their hesitations when considering significant joint ventures with foreign firms has reduced their ability to share in these technology transfers. Several East European countries, notably Poland, did encourage foreign investment in their countries during the 1970s. But by the 1980s, when interest rates increased sharply, they had accumulated very large foreign debts that they had difficulty meeting. Another related problem is the fact that Soviet and East European currencies are set at arbitrary values and cannot freely be exchanged in world money markets. Thus, the interest and ability of foreigners to buy or sell to these countries are limited.

Finally, there is a growing problem of labor productivity coming from workers who are insufficiently motivated. With consumer goods in short supply and even staples difficult to obtain, worker morale and incentive is low. Worker morale has declined as inflation has hit many East European countries. The once remote fear of unemployment has again arisen among workers in the heavy industries of Poland, Czechoslovakia, and elsewhere.

The economic situation is bad as Gorbachev admitted bluntly in his critique of the Soviet economy. He was equally outspoken in his assessment of the economies of his East European allies: In 1987, he referred to their economies as "a garbage can."[10] The economic problems can be summarized succinctly.

> The Soviet economic problem lies essentially in producing, at excessive cost and waste, low-quality items that arrive too late at production points with the psychological effects of fostering a managerial style of fulfilling the plan mainly in formal terms and a workers' style of working slowly, intermittently, and carelessly.[11]

One of the main difficulties in addressing these impediments to renewed economic growth is that many of them are intimately linked with Communist doctrine.[12] The remedying of these problems depends upon repudiating, at least implicitly if not explicitly, many elements of Communist economic theory. There is also the simple hesitancy to tamper with economies as large and as complex as the Communist states have acquired. There is a "reluctance to undertake the awesome task of changing something big that is moving."[13] There is fear that any change may not work or may produce unexpected and unwanted economic and social consequences.

Consequently, those Communist countries which have experimented with economic reforms have cautiously done so and with only limited results. Perhaps the most important reforms were in Hungary during the 1970s when central economic controls were relaxed and some experiments with private enterprise in the service sector were undertaken.[14] Poland followed more timidly, but most of the Polish reforms were lost in the repression of Solidarity. In East Germany, an effort to avoid the cumbersome central planning, while still maintaining it, has led to the creation of large "cartels." Central planners delegate some of the specific planning to these cartels. Elsewhere, progress toward overcoming the basic economic dilemmas has been minimal.

The most promising opportunity for change has come with Gorbachev's championing of *peristroika* or reform in the Soviet Union. After a decade of minor tinkering with economic structures by his predecessors, Gorbachev has undertaken major economic reform. He has talked about loosening central controls, promoting local initiative, and developing more rational bases for making economic decisions. There are three phases to his reforms. The first phase, between 1985 and 1988, involved the tightening of worker discipline, campaigns against alcohol abuse, replacement of inept managers and bureaucrats, improved quality control, a modest expansion of opportunities for small private enterprises, and major investments in technology and modern equipment. The second phase began in 1988 to bring more independence to local plant managers. They acquired the authority to make their own investment and production decisions, including eventual control over setting their prices. It will take time for the party, civil servants, and plant managers to put the new system into full operation and then to learn how to make it function well. By 1991 the transition process is supposed to end with the achievement of a more modern, decentralized, and productive economy that can provide for accelerated economic growth.

The changes, if achieved, will bring some market mechanisms into play that encourage greater efficiency: prices that more accurately reflect real costs and demands; and encouragement of profits as an incentive to plant managers to increase production and to evaluate their effectiveness. The Soviet Union has also shown new interest in fostering joint economic ventures with private foreign firms. In 1987, the Soviet embassy in the United States went so far as to purchase a nine-page advertising supplement for the *Wall Street Journal* touting the advantages of investing in the USSR. The publication was often pilloried in the past by Soviet leaders as the voice of monopolist exploiters.

The actual implementation of these changes has been slow. In part, the slow pace of reform is possibly due to obstruction from conservative elements within the Soviet hierarchy. But it is also due to a recognition by Gorbachev and other advocates of reform that such changes must be deliberate and well conceived to avoid failure or unwanted consequences. Too rapid change might bring unemployment and other economic ills that would undermine support in the public and the bureaucracy for the reforms. Even if all the changes are carried through, the fundamental nature of the economy will not be changed. Despite the new openness to the use of market mechanisms, the Soviet economy will remain a centrally planned economy with ownership of nearly all means of production and property still in the hands of the state.

If reform succeeds in the USSR, there may also be new impetus for change in the East European countries. Their economies are plagued with similar problems. The leaders in many of these countries are old and not interested in undertaking major economic reforms at this point in their political careers. But they will face pressure to respond to their countries' economic problems and to follow the lead of the USSR in undertaking major reforms. In addition, these aged leaders are likely to be replaced in the next few years. New leaders in Eastern Europe might base their claim for position and legitimacy on their willingness to undertake the same economic liberalizations in their countries that Gorbachev has championed in the Soviet Union. Already, some leaders of East European countries have followed the Soviet lead in loosening central economic controls or have justified their prior reforms on the Soviet leader's new directions.

Radical critics of Western economies saw in the economic malaise of the 1970s and 1980s portents of the ultimate and inevitable collapse of capitalism. But the simultaneous economic stagnation and decline in Eastern Europe and the Soviet Union suggest that economic recessions are not restricted to capitalist nations. The sources and symptoms of the recessions in the East and West have been different. In Eastern Europe, the economies have suffered from overcentralization, inability to meet quality and quantity standards, and, in most countries, labor shortages while heavy industry continues to produce well. In Western Europe, the economies have been plagued by excess capacity, unemployment, and the need for modernization of inefficient heavy industry.

TOTAL WELFARE STATES

The Western view of emigrants from East European countries finding a world of freedom and plenty in the West is very much exaggerated. In fact, most recent Soviet and East European emigrants find life in the West to be unexpectedly hard. They find themselves in a highly competitive setting in which the most productive and efficient thrive and those less able or less dedicated often experience difficulties in keeping a job, finding adequate housing, or paying for expensive medical services. In their Communist homelands, they enjoyed a secure environment in which they were assured jobs, low-cost housing, free medical care, and a comfortable retirement whatever their skills or efficiency. They find much greater gaps between the living standards of the poor and the very wealthy than what they experienced in their East European homes.

Indeed, there appears to be great popular support for the socialist economic and social rights given priority in Eastern Europe and the Soviet Union: the right to a job, the right to needed medical care, the right to low-cost housing, the right to a comfortable retirement, and the freedom from fears of losing out in a competitive economic setting. The sense of security that comes from collective, as opposed to individual, undertakings is important to people which have long histories of economic and political troubles. Frequent press reports of unemployment and poverty in capitalist socieities remind East Europeans of the uncertainties of life in the West. There is in effect, an implicit social contract in Eastern Europe between workers who grant political compliance with the regime in exchange for economic security.[15]

The social benefits are extensive. There is no official unemployment in most European Communist states with the exception of some seasonable unemployment of farm workers. Housing is heavily subsidized and is now more available than a decade ago. Paid vacations are assured to all with the additional benefit of public access to subsidized vacation villages; not only are workers paid on vacations, but their costs are reduced because of state-provided vacation plans. Retirement benefits are modest, but women may retire at 55-years-old and men at 60-years-old in the Soviet Union and several other East European states.[16] Citizens enjoy free medical care

certain policy positions or to enhance the political careers of leaders preferred by the Soviet Union.

Indirect methods are also important. Over the past thirty years, the close interaction of Eastern Europe and the Soviet Union has developed a corps of leaders whose political careers have been built around links with the Soviet Union. Many young administrators or party officials serve "apprenticeships" in the Soviet Union.[19] They are accustomed to deferring to Soviet leadership on ideological matters and in decisions on economic and social policies. Their compliance with Soviet directions is spontaneous and voluntary.

Above all, the fragility of these countries' legitimacy leaves them dependent upon the Soviet Union. With the possible exception of Bulgaria, East Germany, and Romania, the existence of these Communist states is directly dependent upon their support from the Soviet Union. The leaders of Czechoslovakia, Hungary, and Poland know that their regimes would not long survive if for some reason the Soviet Union no longer felt it necessary to support their Communist governments. This dependence makes them beholden to their patrons in the Kremlin and thus, willing to follow their guidelines.

Control is also exercised through two formal organizations. The Warsaw Treaty Organization is a mutual defense arrangement similar in appearance, but not in reality, to the North Atlantic Treaty Organization, NATO. Through the Warsaw pact agreements, large number of Soviet troops are stationed in all East European countries save Romania and the super-loyal Bulgaria. Extensive joint military maneuvers thoroughly integrate East European armies into the Soviet defense plans. East European military leaders are trained in the Soviet Union. In the process they acquire a loyalty to the Soviet Union that sometimes seems to overpower their loyalties to their homelands.

There is also an East European parallel to the West European Common Market. Comecon or the Council for Mutual Economic Assistance, CEMA, was designed to promote trade and joint economic planning among East European states. It has achieved a significant economic interdependence that discourages any country's abandonment of the Eastern bloc. Comecon serves to encourage trade among the member countries and to discourage trade with Western countries. While Comecon has a role to play in integrating Eastern Europe with the Soviet Union, the arrangements are not always disadvantageous for the Soviet Union's smaller allies. Through Comecon agreements, Eastern Europe acquires low-cost natural resources, notably energy ones from the Soviet Union. This agreement remained even when the international oil crisis made the selling of that oil more profitable outside of Comecon. The smaller East European Communist states also have assured markets for the low-quality manufactured goods that they would have difficulty in selling in open world-markets.

The degree of economic coordination undertaken by Comecon is still minimal. Some states resist the economic directions decided by Comecon. For example, Romania refused Comecon's suggestion that it focus on oil production and agriculture; instead its leader, Ceausescu, pushed for a more broadly based industrialization in his country. Unlike the multinational integration of the Common Market in the West, Comecon relies more on bilateral agreements that deal with specific exchanges between its members. Comecon integration decreased during the 1970s as separate East European countries tried encouraging greater investment from the West in their economies. This move proved disappointing when East Europe accumulated large debts to Western banks and countries and failed to develop the expected markets for their goods in the West. The result was renewed interest in the 1980s in promoting greater economic cooperation through Comecon. However, genuine economic integration is still far off as Comecon persists in deferring to political, rather than economic, considerations.

POLITICAL STABILITY

There is little doubt that the Soviet Union and Eastern Europe had experienced at least as great an era of crisis at the end of the 1970s and into the early 1980s as many had thought had occurred in Western Europe. One did not have to listen to westerners whose anti-Communist sentiments may have colored their description of the regimes in crisis. The words of Gorbachev and other reform-minded leaders have clearly spelled out the extent of the crisis and the urgent need for fundamental political and socioeconomic change.

Economic stagnation and decline, aging and uninspired leaders who seem to have lost confidence in their own ideology's answers to social and economic problems, and growing public unrest have all suggested serious political problems that over the long run might erode the political stability that has largely prevailed in Eastern Europe since the Second World War. This stability, an unusual political feature for this part of the world, has been the product of the Communist party. The party's discipline, its organization, and its skills in mobilizing popular support have made these regimes secure. When disorder has threatened, the Soviet army has loomed as the ultimate guarantor of the stability of East Europe. With the Soviet Union still present in the shadows of nearly every East European regime, dissidents recognize their limits in pressing for change. Thus, forty years after their founding, the security of the East European Communist regimes still depends primarily upon the authority of the USSR.[20]

However, in the 1980s, that stability seemed to falter. Communist parties have emerged as the principal obstacles to the needed social and political reforms. The party apparatus has resisted needed adaptations that might compromise their existing privileged political and social roles. The centralization, discipline, and hierarchy of these party organizations served well in the initial postwar political and economic recovery. But these features now stand in the way of decentralization, individual initiatives, and innovation, all of which are needed to breathe life into both the economic and political institutions of Eastern Europe. Yet if change is to come to Eastern Europe or the Soviet Union, it must come through these very parties.

While they may have lost their vision and dynamism, they have not lost the monopoly of political power or their ability to dominate society. The real challenge for Gorbachev and reformers in other East European countries will not be to reform the economy or society but to reform the Stalinist parties that brought them to power.

NOTES

1. Jan Vladislav, ed., *Vaclav Havel: Or Living in Truth* (London: Faber & Faber 1987).
2. Alfred G. Meyer, "Assessing the Ideological Commitment of a Regime," in Joseph L. Nogee, ed., *Soviet Politics: Russia After Brezhnev* (New York: Praeger, 1985), pp. 107–121.
3. See Mikhail Gorbachev, *Peristroika and the New Thinking* (New York: Harper & Row, 1987).
4. Before recent reforms, only 3 percent of the farm land in the USSR was outside of the state and collective farm system. In Eastern Europe, about 15 percent remained in private hands, except in Poland and Yugoslavia where 85 percent of farm land was privately owned and operated. Sophia M. Miskieiwicz, "Social and Economic Rights in Eastern Europe," *Survey* 29 (August 1987): 75.
5. Robin Okey, *Eastern Europe: 1740–1985* (Minneapolis, MN: University of Minnesota Press, 1986), p. 234 and International Debt Problems, *Background Brief* (London: Foreign and Commonwealth Office, June 1988), p. 6.
6. Housing is often in short supply and requires long waits. For example, in Moscow, 20 percent of families are forced to share apartments with others, usually relatives.
7. *The Economist,* "Survey of the Soviet Economy," 9 April 1988, p. 4.
8. Marshall I. Goldman, *USSR in Crisis: The Failure of the Economic System* (New York: W. W. Norton, 1983).
9. Jan Winiecki, *Economic Prospects, East and West* (London: Centre for Research into Communist Economies, 1987).
10. *The New York Times,* 4 October, 1987.
11. Karl W. Ryavec, "Economic Reform: Prospects and Possibilities," in Nogee, *Soviet Politics,* p. 184.
12. Marshal I. Goldman, "The Burden of the Stalinist Model: The Case of Soviet Agriculture, Industry, and Consumer Goods," in Uri Ra'anan and Charles M. Perry, eds., *The USSR Today and Tomorrow: Problems and Challenges* (Lexington, MA: Lexington Books, 1987), pp. 63–75.
13. Karl W. Ryavec, "Economic Reform: Prospects and Possibilities," in Nogee, *Soviet Politics: Russia After Brezhnev* (New York: Praeger, 1985), pp. 203–204.
14. Bill Lomax, "Hungary—The Quest for Legitimacy," in Paul G. Lewis, ed., *Eastern Europe: Political Crisis and Legitimation* (New York: St. Martin's, 1984), pp. 84–101.
15. C. Gati and J. F. Triska, *Blue Collar Workers in Eastern Europe* (London: George Allen & Unwin, 1981).
16. The low pensions force many retirees to find part-time work to sustain themselves. See Mervyn Matthews, *Poverty in the Soviet Union: The Life-Styles of the Underprivileged in Recent Years* (Cambridge, England: Cambridge University Press, 1986).

17. Murray Feshbach, "Soviet Health Problems," in Erik P. Hoffmann, ed., *The Soviet Union in the 1980s,* Proceedings of the Academy of Political Science, v. 35, no. 3 (New York: Academy of Political Science, 1984), pp. 81–97.
18. Alastair McAuley, "Social Policy," in Archie Brown and Michael Kaser, eds., *Soviet Policy for the 1980s* (Bloomington, IN: Indiana University Press, 1982), pp. 146–169.
19. George Schopflin, "Soviet-East European Relations," in Martin McCauley, ed., *The Soviet Union After Brezhnev* (New York: Holmes & Meier, 1983), p. 124.
20. Robin Okey, *Eastern Europe 1740–1985: Feudalism to Communism,* 2nd ed. (Minneapolis, MN: University of Minnesota, 1986), p. 240.

PART SEVEN
CONCLUSION

Democracy is the worst form of government—except for all the others.

Winston S. Churchill

The fact that Communist regimes in Eastern Europe have as many and perhaps more serious problems than West European countries may be some consolation to advocates of democracy. But the problems of others do not dispell the West's need to confront the challenges that face its democratic governments. Many saw these governments as embattled and endangered during the period from 1968 to the early 1980s.

Perhaps the most important lesson to be drawn from this difficult era is that democracies are not as fragile as once believed. Despite the seeming decline in public confidence, the prolonged economic decline, the terrorist explosions, and the other problems faced by Western European democracies, not a single one has come close to failing. No West European country has experienced a shift from one to another political extreme, nor has one sacrificed civil liberties to counter threats to its existence. Indeed, the troublesome experiences of the last fifteen years may well have strengthened these democracies. They have faced new challenges. They have effectively responded to changing circumstances even if the adaptations have not always been graceful, speedy, or the result of deliberate action by government leaders; they have, nonetheless, met their challenges.

Regimes tend to grow in stability as they face and surmount crises. They develop flexibility when dealing with changing and demanding circumstances. Furthermore, they demonstrate to their citizens their ability to avoid or overcome chaos and disorder. Italian democracy has won support despite its shifting government coalitions because of its successful response to terrorism and its contributions to economic growth. The Bonn Basic Law has acquired greater reverence from its citizens as it has assured democratic procedures and liberties and while the people have shifted priorities in their political values. British democracy has muddled through economic decline and political stagnation to emerge with a new energetic leadership and fresh, if not always convincing, answers to social and economic challenges. In France, the Fifth Republic has witnessed the decline of political passions that divided the French for over two hundred years.

CHALLENGE AND RESPONSE: EUROPEAN DEMOCRACY AND THE CRISES OF THE 1970s TO THE 1980s

The strength of West European democracies at the end of the 1980s may lead to questions about how real was the purported crisis of the previous fifteen years. Indeed, there is some reason to believe that the crisis was exaggerated. The troubled years, from 1968 to the early 1980s, followed a period of exceptional serenity in Western Europe. The unparalleled economic prosperity and the exhaustion of old international divisions after two world wars produced political tranquility and stability. It was this unnaturally calm era that served as the point of comparison for the more troubled period that followed. Had the comparison been made with the politically turbulent 1920s and 1930s, European democracy would not have seemed as troubled in the 1970s and 1980s as it did when contrasted with the postwar serenity. What is not clear is whether the calm era is any more "typical" of good democratic government than the more turbulent eras.

Democracy is a form of government that is dependent on conflict. Citizens have to make real choices at election time. Even where a broad political consensus emerges, important differences remain over the definition of that consensus and the ways of implementing that consensus into concrete actions.[1] It is not surprising that such conflict becomes heated and volatile from time to time. A look back at the various elements of the crisis as depicted in the early 1970s can assess the reality of the challenges and Western Europe's responses to them.

Governmental Overload

Governments have retreated from some of the responsibilities that they had earlier been called upon to absorb. The best example is the widespread interest in selling state-owned enterprises to private buyers. In addition, nearly all governments have accepted the rhetoric of reducing state functions. But such trends have been misleading. Privatization has meant a change in ownership but usually not of the governments' abilities to control firms still deemed to be of public interest. Bureaucracies have remained large and unreformed. The talk of reducing the central state has been much greater than the actual eliminations of government activities. Public attitudes on such reductions have generally been unenthusiastic. Citizens in Western Europe seem to want some cutbacks as long as the reductions do not affect them personally. Above all, the public is hostile to any diminution in the costly and complicated social-welfare programs that had, a decade ago, fed fears of overload.

Part of the problem is that democratic politics encourage modest short-term changes rather than dramatic, but more long-term, corrections. This trait is best illustrated by the difficulty of managing the economy. Democratic governments face special problems when establishing coherent economic programs and sticking to them if they are adopted. Leaders face periodic challenges in the form of regular elections when they must justify their record before the voters. This timetable provides a powerful incentive for the incumbent government to seek short-term results to demonstrate their abilities at election time. The periodic electoral tests and the possibility that the election might bring a change in government control make it difficult for democratic governments to develop long-term economic policies that go beyond a single electoral cycle.

The problems persist, but the public perception of the crisis of government overload has markedly changed. No longer do political analysts wring their hands in despair over the governments' inability to meet the demands placed upon them. These perceptions have changed for two reasons. First, the sense of overload in the 1970s was due largely to the unprecedented economic conditions of simultaneous inflation and recession that governments of all political varieties seemed unable to handle. As the economic situation changed, public judgments on the incapacity of their governments eased. Later, citizens have seemed more tolerant of their governments' struggles in finding solutions to the problems of industrial reconversion and stiff economic competition from the newly industrialized states.

Second, democratic publics seem to have grown more understanding of the difficulties governments have in confronting hard social and economic issues. Instead of expecting miracle results from government programs or actions, they now are more tolerant of slow and uneven steps in dealing with social problems. Thus, incumbent governments are returned to office despite poor records of unemployment and slow economic growth. To some extent, there is a "retreat from the state" in the sense that citizens are less sanguine about their government's ability to solve their problems and more willing to look for nongovernmental avenues when confronting continuing difficulties.

The issue of overload has thus declined in importance, not because governments have increased their capacities or decreased their work, but rather, because the impression of crisis and paralysis has disappeared. Concern about too much government intrusion into the private lives of citizens remains, but the feeling is more that interference is something to guard against rather than something posing the imminent loss of individual freedom or privacy.

The Crisis of Public Confidence

Public opinion polls continue to show that confidence in government institutions and officials is lower, often much lower, than it was in the 1950s and early 1960s. The downward trend appears to have ended. Some countries have shown slight increases in expressions of confidence in the 1980s. More importantly, the decline did not have any of the adverse consequences in political behavior that was anticipated in the 1970s. Voters have not acted on their supposed mistrust by voting for extremist candidates or by not voting at all. The vote for radical parties has been modest and, in most countries, has declined; electoral turnout remains at approximately the same level in the 1980s that it did in the 1960s with only a couple of minor exceptions. In short, voters, in most countries, continue to vote back into office the same officials whom they claim not to trust when they talk to pollsters.

This discrepancy suggests that much of the decline in trust may be more fashionable cynicism than fundamental disaffection with the institutions or personnel of government. The poll results may also be due to heightened partisan feelings. When statistics on confidence in government are broken down by party, the most negative sentiments are expressed by people identifying with parties opposed to the government and shift as parties rotate in office. Thus, the responses, that the social scientists take to mean declining confidence in government, may mean little more than a partisan preference for the opposition.

Public skepticism about their rulers is not necessarily bad. As the ancient Greek orator Demosthenes said,

> There is one safeguard known generally to the wise, which is an advantage and security to all, but especially to democracies as against despots. What is it? Distrust.[2]

Such distrust is especially useful when it is not accompanied by a general rejection of the system, as appears to be the case in Western Europe. It promotes citizen vigilance and elite awareness of the costs of abusing their powers.

Decline of Representative Bodies

The evidence of party decline differs from country to country according to political tendency. The clearest evidence of decline is found in the left-wing parties and the trade unions associated with them. Communist parties in Italy and, especially, in France have suffered serious decline in electoral support and organizational strength. The decline of such anti-system parties may very well have positive effects for Western democracy. The more threatening problem has been the difficulty of the moderate, social-democratic parties, notably in West Germany and Britain, in adjusting to the divisions between the advocates of new values among the hard-won middle-class sections of their electorates and their working-class voters who are still attached to traditional bread-and-butter economic issues. To the extent that party decline has occurred, it is in these social-democratic parties struggling with this adjustment that the decline has taken place.

The situation of moderate and conservative parties has been quite positive. The British Conservative party, the Gaullist party, the Christian Democrats in Italy and the Federal Republic have all shown strength in reaching out to new voters, especially young voters. Their party organizations are, in most cases, now stronger than they were fifteen years ago, and their elected deputies still loyal in parliamentary voting. In fact, even weak and divided parties have proved remarkably resilient in the face of challenges from new parties. For example, the British Labour party has fended off the challenge from the Social-Democratic/Liberal Alliance. The challenger is now more divided and moribund than the old Labour party it tried to replace. The German Social Democratic party may yet prove as adaptable in responding to the threat of the Greens. Thus, twenty-five years after the time party decline was first proclaimed to be a serious threat to democracy, the same parties are found still dominating politics in all West European countries. The newcomers of the 1970s, whether ethnic parties, antitax movements, or ecologists, have been the ones that have disappeared or have been pressed to the margins rather than the mainline parties that dominated politics since the end of the Second World War.

Instead of the alarmist notion that this decline endangers democracy, it is possible to see the fall of some parties as a natural and even desirable part of free electoral competition. Those parties that fail to adjust to changing public moods ought to be replaced or sanctioned so that they make adjustments. Therefore, the threats of the 1970s have strengthened, rather than toppled, most of the main parties of West Europe.

The Participation Crisis

The increased levels of public political involvement combined with the tendency to use unconventional methods of political action have not had the anticipated effects. The expansion of participation to include groups from the political sidelines has not led to overburdened government officials. New institutions that foster dialogue between government and concerned citizens have developed, especially on the local level.

There was initially surprise and even panic on the part of the government officials who had to deal with unexpectedly large numbers of citizens taking to the streets to press for their causes. This early astonished paralysis in the face of street politics has now passed. Governments have learned how to control such participants to avoid unnecessary clashes or disorder. The passing of the crisis of participation involved more than governments simply devising better tactics to contain street politics and even terrorism. The frequency of demonstrations and the other forms of unconventional political action has eliminated the shock effect. The ability of groups to use such tactics to attract the public's attention has been reduced. A small demonstration in Hamburg in the 1960s brought nationwide press coverage; at the end of the 1980s, moderately large demonstrations fail to attract even the local press beyond the simple notation that another march of this or that group has occurred.

As these unconventional forms of political action become more common, governments and the public have tended to become inurred to them. Wide use, and sometimes, overuse have rendered such actions ineffective in prompting responses from governments. Whereas in the past, a single political demonstration in Britain would capture the public's attention and might provoke prompt government reaction, current demonstrations are not likely to bring a change in government policy. There is a risk in this indifference. While political protest was rare in the past, it was an option for severely dissatisfied groups to use after exhausting all other approaches. Governments would pay heed to such exhibitions of extreme political frustration. Now, with groups demonstrating about everything from an unsafe school crossing to nuclear arsenals, the alienated no longer have a unique and effective way of expressing their distress.

In any case, the West European democracies have demonstrated the ability to accommodate higher levels of participation and to sustain more political turbulence without the risk of political instability. After some initial anxiety and miscues, they have successfully adapted to the participation explosion with a mixture of openings for the voices of previously excluded social sectors, new forums for dialogue, and new skills in managing protest. Concerns that too much participation would overwhelm democracies, are not present today. The political systems in Western Europe have proved capable of dealing with both new participants and unconventional political action. Elitist notions that political stability is best served by a combination of political roles for the more knowledgeable minority and passive acceptance by the masses appear outmoded in the light of this successful accommodation of democracy to the new participation.

Institutional Sclerosis

The decay of political institutions that had been perceived to be occurring in the late 1960s and 1970s has been followed by a revival of the very institutions that had seemed to be in decline. Thus, after decades of ebbing power, parliaments have begun to reclaim some of the power they had earlier surrendered to political executives. Parliamentary committees have acquired new strength in Britain and West Germany; question time has become more vital in France and West Germany; better salaries, more spacious offices, and funds for secretaries and legislative aides have contributed to greater competence on the part of those elected to parliament. Parliaments now attract younger politicians interested in pursuing politics as a career rather than as an avocation. Their professional aspirations make them less content to continue the deference their predecessors had once granted party and government leaders.

Executives have also proved more effective than the often lackluster leaders of the 1970s. In Britain, Margaret Thatcher won public backing by appealing to the people's desire for strong and capable leadership. Her policies were not nearly as popular as her image of personal strength, independence, and determination. She is readily acknowledged by friends and foes as Britain's most forceful and successful prime minister since the Second World War. Even in Italy where governments change frequently, Bettino Craxi served thirty-two continuous months as premier between 1983 and 1987 easily setting the postwar record of government longevity. It was a time of such strong personal leadership that Craxi made a mark as the most effective premier since Alcide de Gasperi.

In Italy, West Germany, and France, constitutional courts that had remained moribund since their creation after World War II have begun to assume greater political importance. They have slowly but consistently pressed toward grafting the American notion of judicial review onto the European parliamentary tradition. They voided laws that were deemed to be incompatible with their constitutions. These courts have also emerged as new judicial defenders of human rights.

Similarly, governments have responded to public interest in decentralization. Regional governments, promised by the Italian Constitution in 1947 and by French reforms of the early 1960s, laid unimplemented for two to three decades. In these countries, these regional governments are now a reality even if their powers are still evolving. In Germany during the late 1970s, the Bundesrat extended the powers of the states beyond what was granted by the drafters of the Basic Law. In Britain, government's offers of devolution to the Scots, Welsh, and the people of Northern Ireland were turned down, but they represent a government more attuned to regional and ethnic interests than ever.

It may well be that the serenity of the 1950s and early 1960s brought a generation of political leaders fit to rule only under such unchallenging conditions. The more troubled times seem to have, at last, produced a set of more energetic and forceful leaders. With these new politicians found in parliament, courts, regional offices, and premierships, the talk of institutional sclerosis has declined.

Erosion of Civil Liberties

Fears about threats to personal freedom and privacy from the computer revolution, mounting government social regulation, and antiterror campaigns have also largely abated. For example, nearly every French household now has a minicomputer with videotext capability. There has been no sacrifice of privacy or any imposition of new government controls. Europeans enjoy full health protection provided by the state without losing the right to select doctors or hospitals for their medical care. The battle against terrorism sometimes brings legislation that lifts some civil liberties from accused terrorists. But there is little evidence to suggest that these powers are abused or applied in an inappropriate way to the general public. In all countries, courts have placed a new emphasis on the individual's rights as opposed to the government's in contrast to their traditional emphasis on the integrity and immunity of the state. In addition, external checks on civil liberty abuse are present both in the abstract fear of antagonizing international public opinion and in the more concrete form of the European Court of Human Rights.

Human rights advocates still can not relax their vigilance; there are always civil rights issues in each country. Perhaps the most important human rights problem (in all countries except Italy) is not a threat from government, but popular intolerance toward racially distinct, recent, immigrants. Indeed, public resistance to government programs to foster better race relations indicates how difficult it is for democratic governments to try to reshape their citizen's values and attitudes. Such a discovery is unfortunate in efforts to promote racial understanding, but it may reveal an important strength of democratic people in resisting potential government efforts to change the public's commitment to basic rights.

And the Next Crisis?

Lest this discussion seem unduly positive, it is important to note that some of the governmental adjustments have only been partial and others may well engender new problems in the future. There is not only the possibility but the virtual certainty that new dangers, not even thought of so far, will develop to challenge these democracies.

However, their successes in dealing with the troubled 1970s and 1980s will give West European democracies strength and tools to confront these new challenges. In addition, their past successes will provide them each with a measure of good will among their citizens that will allow them time to cope with any new menace. The fact that democracy has responded to past crises has led citizens to expect their governments to again succeed and to allow time to find the correct remedies for future problems.

DEMOCRACY WITHOUT A VISION

West European democracies survived the crisis years in part because of the adaptations noted above. But there is another important reason for their success in weathering those troubled times: the absence of an attractive alternative. The political extremisms of both the Right and the Left have little attraction. Fascism is still discredited for its atrocities and for its failure during World War II. Communism has lost its appeal. Soviet leaders themselves have revealed the excesses and ineptitude of their Communist predecessors. The economic, political, and social crisis that Communist regimes are currently experiencing has further dulled the once shiny hope of a workers' state. Democratic socialism has also failed to develop a successful example of its promised regime that would combine the freedom of Western capitalism with a socialist equality. Anarchism has little appeal in a day when people count heavily on their governments to alleviate the undesirable and unpredictable elements of their environment. The radical ecologists' vision of humans living in complete harmony with nature attracts only those with very secure backgrounds.

The vision of a united democratic Europe has dimmed as the enlargement of the Common Market has brought together increasingly diverse people. It was conceivable that a United States of Europe might have emerged among the six original members of the European Community; very few, however, harbor the illusion of a political unification of Britons and French, Spaniards and Portuguese, or Greeks with anyone and certainly never with the Turks who are now aspiring to join the Community too. European unity no longer impassions people with the hope of a single political entity; the Community is simply a means to expand markets and promote prosperity among traditional trading partners.

Democracy is valued not because it is viewed as an ideal form of government but because it meets the needs of people better than the less attractive alternatives. It is seen as providing orderly and competent government for Western societies. But the vision of democracy ushering in a better life for its peoples has perished and, with it, the enthusiasm and optimism that once characterized Western democracy. Thus, the hope that democracy would bring fair government to all people and provide the basis for lasting world peace has also vanished. Democracy is secure in Western Europe (and the United States) not because it offers the lofty vision of a better world, not because democracy makes better human beings, but because there is no better alternative.

The decline of hope for a political utopia is desirable in some ways. The waning of old ideologies has lowered political passion and promoted compromise and accommodation rather than extremism. Zealous pursuit of these ideological and political promised lands often brought intolerance of those seen as obstructing progress toward the millenial goal. Concentration on pragmatic solutions to the real problems of today instead of ignoring them to struggle for some distant panacea usually means more effective and responsive government.

But without a higher goal, citizens in Western democracies are free to pursue their own selfish interests regardless of the consequences on the less advantaged in their own societies or on the rest of the world. Many observers are concerned about the consequences of the death of the old visionary ideologies. The absence of a commitment to a vision of a better world leads citizens to concentrate on the here and now. Their activities center on personal gain rather than on community improvement. Stanley Hoffmann notes that if

> . . . the old ideologies are dead or dying, one is left immersed in a dreary present, a jungle of group conflicts with no standard for their solution. And the very intensity of the struggle for power and product, the very absence of any grand cause, the very myopia of each class, profession, and association concentrating on its claims makes it almost impossible for any vision of the future to emerge.[3]

Thus, the dilemma of democracy at the end of the century is not its survival but whether its survival will mean a better world. If democracy endures only to provide a convenient framework in which each individual or group seeks selfish goals, it will only face new dangers should the deprived revolt. If it does not provide a vision for improving the world, it will also fail to fulfill even the prosperous citizens by leaving them uninspired and unmotivated.

Can democratic leaders find goals to inspire commitment in their citizenries? Can they persuade them to sacrifice some immediate consumption to make a better future for themselves and for less advantaged peoples everywhere? These are difficult questions to answer as the "me generation" of Europe and North America comes to the age when they will take the leading positions in politics and society.

NOTES

1. Seymour Martin Lipset, *Consensus and Conflict: Essays in Political Sociology* (New Brunswick, NJ: Transaction Books, 1986).
2. Cited by Vivien Hart, *Distrust and Democracy: Political Distrust in Britain and America* (Cambridge, England: Cambridge University Press, 1978), p. xi.
3. Stanley Hoffmann, "Fragments Floating in the Here and Now," *Daedalus* (Winter 1979), p. 18.

INDEX

A

Accountability:
  Britain, 87–88
  France, 178, 188–189, 204–205
  Germany, 271, 285
  Italy, 361, 382–383
  U.S., 88
Acton, Lord, 88
Adenauer, Konrad, 247, 249, 294, 270, 404
Alain (Emile Chartier), 119
Algeria, 123–124
Alia, Ramiz, 428
Allende, Salvador, 354
Alliance Party (Britain), 53, 55ff, 59–61, 108
Andreoti, Giulio, 373
Andropov, Yuri, 428, 434, 439
Ashdown, Paddy, 61

Attlee, Clement, 57

B

Baden, Max von, 212
Badoglio, Marshal, 316
Bagehot, Walter, 23f, 69, 70, 253
Bangemann, Martin, 253
Barbie, Klaus, 116–117
Barre, Raymond, 153–155
Barzini, Luigi, 109
Basques, 129–130, 203
Beethoven, Ludwig von, 209, 218
Berlin, 216, 280, 283–284
Berlinguer, Enrico, 355
Bismark, Otto von, 211
Brandt, Willy, 249ff, 275, 280, 284

Brezhnev, Leonid, 424, 428, 434, 436, 439, 453
Britain:
  accountability, 87–88
  bureaucracy, 14, 81–83, 88, 278f
  civil liberties, 102–105, 110
  class, 26–28, 47, 124
  constitution, 69–71, 102, 107
  decentralization, 31, 47, 85–87, 94, 97
  economy, 36–38, 92–100, 307, 447–448
  education, 27–28, 102
  elections, 46–48, 53–54, 87
  ethnicity, 28–38, 47, 98, 107
  and European Economic, 37–38, 48, 98–100, 107
  government debt, 389
  history, 21–26
  immigration, 34–35, 104
  interest groups, 62–67
  legitimacy, 88, 136
  local government, 47, 84–87, 187
  map, 30
  media and politics, 47, 85, 103–104
  monarch, 22, 25, 36, 42, 70–72, 75
  national pride, 25
  and NATO, 66–67, 99–100
  neocorporatism, 63
  new social movements, 65–67, 167
  parliament, 70f, 75–81
  political culture, 22–25, 41–43, 88–89, 106–109, 135, 232, 334f
  political participation, 43–49, 66–67
  political parties, 52–62, 87–88, 107–108, 110
  post-materialism, 234
  prime minister, 71–75ff
  protest politics, 12, 45–46, 65–67
  public employment, 6
  public opinion, 74, 87
  Question Time, 78, 180
  racism, 34–35, 104
  referendum, 47, 87
  religion, 35–36, 56, 79f, 223
  social welfare programs, 93–98, 100–102, 390
  taxes, 6, 381
  television, 47, 104
  terrorism, 32–34, 46–47
  trade unions, 57f, 64–65, 95, 259–260, 290
  voter turnout, 338
  Whitehall, 81–83
  women in politics, 48–49, 242
"British disease," 93–97
Brittany, 129–130, 203
Bulgaria, 454
Bundesrat (Germany), 268, 275–277, 283
Bundestag (Germany), 182, 268–270, 272–277, 283

  elections, 238–240
  women in, 241–242
Bureaucracy:
  Britain, 14, 81–83, 88, 278f
  control of, 14–15
  France, 82f, 117, 165, 183–185, 278f
  Germany, 83, 212, 215, 271, 278–279
  Italy, 362–363, 378–379
  problems of, 7, 14–15
  size of, 7
  Soviet Union, 440
  U.S., 83

C

Callaghan, James, 285
Campaign for Nuclear Disarmament, 66–67
Cavour, Camillo Bensa di, 312ff
CDU/CSU (*see* Christian Democratic Party—Germany)
Ceausescu, Nicolae, 428, 435, 454
Chamber of Deputies (Italy), 338, 343, 367–370, 374–377
Charlemagne, 210
Chernenko, Konstantin, 428, 434, 439
Chirac, Jacques, 151, 153–155, 201, 248
Christian Democratic Party—CDU/CSU (Germany):
  and business, 261
  and the Church, 246
  doctrine and positions, 246–249, 294–295
  and the Greens, 305
  support, 222, 224, 245, 246–249
  and trade unions, 259
Christian Democratic Party—DC (Italy)
  and bureaucracy, 351–353, 378
  and Communist Party, 352, 354–355, 381–382, 393–395
  doctrine and policies, 351–352
  governing coalition, 375–376
  organization, 351–353, 375
  political control, 352–353, 370–371
  support, 323–324, 326–327, 336, 340, 343–344, 348–353, 362
Christian Social Union—CSU (Germany), 246–249 (*see also* Christian Democratic Party—CDU/CSU)
Churchill, Winston, 108, 460
Civil liberties, 15–16, 466
  Britain, 102–105, 110
  Czechoslovakia, 452
  France, 198–201
  Germany, 16, 277–278, 296–301
  Hungary, 452
  Italy, 397–400
  Poland, 452
  Soviet Union, 452

U.S., 198
Clientelism, 336, 347, 351
  Italy, 378–379, 383
  Soviet Union, 422–423
Codetermination, 223, 260
Cohabitation, 150, 176–178
Colbert, Jean-Baptiste, 193
Collective responsibility, 73–75, 271
Comecon, 454–455
Common Market (*see* European Economic Community)
Commonwealth, 72
Communist Party—PCF (France)
  alliance with Socialists, 158–160
  compared, 222
  doctrine, 149, 158–160
  and Fifth Republic, 124
  and Italian Communist Party, 355–356
  organization, 158–160
  support, 126, 128–129, 148, 158–160
  and unions, 165
Communist Party—PCI (Italy)
  and bureaucracy, 356–357, 378
  and Christian Democratic Party, 352, 354–355, 376–377, 381–382, 393–395
  doctrine, 353
  moderation, 326, 335, 354–356, 393–395, 401
  organization, 353–356
  and referendum, 340–341
  support, 323–324, 326–327, 336–337, 343–344, 348–349, 353–354, 362
Communist Party (Soviet Union)
  history, 425
  ideology, 427
  membership privileges, 410–411
  organization, 425–428, 432–437
  as policy maker, 432–437, 439–442
Concerted Action, 258–259
Concordat, 321f
Confederation of British Industry, 65
Conservative Party (Britain)
  and business, 65
  doctrine, 55–56, 92, 94–95, 101
  organization, 55–56
  support, 26–27, 42, 48, 53–54, 98
Constitutional court:
  France, 145, 174, 182–183, 277
  Germany, 217, 277–278, 280, 282, 297f
  Italy, 371, 377–378, 398
Corsica, 123, 129–130, 203
Cossiga, Francisco, 370
Craxi, Bettino, 353, 355, 357–359, 362
  fall of, 369
  as prime minister, 371, 372–374, 465
Crisis of democracy, 2–17, 92, 105–110
Cromwell, Oliver, 21
Czechoslovakia:

civil liberties, 452
economy, 449f
revolt, 423
and Soviet Union, 454

D

DC (*see* Christian Democratic Party, Italy)
Decentralization, 195–196, 465–466
  advantages, 282–283
  Britain, 31, 47, 85–87, 94, 97
  disadvantages, 86, 186, 188
  France, 129–130, 185–188, 195–196
  Germany, 279–285
  Italy, 317–318, 380–382
Deference, 23–24, 42, 135
De Gasperi, Alcide, 372, 465
De Gaulle, Charles:
  as president, 143, 173–175, 178, 404
  and Algeria, 123–124
  and Fifth Republic, 123–124, 171, 201–202
  doctrine, 121
  and Giscard, 152
  and May 1968, 120
  party of, 150
  provisional government, 195
  as reformer, 143
Delinquent community, 135–137
De Mita, Ciriaco, 353
Democracy:
  Conditions for, 2
  Crisis of, 2–17, 92, 105–110
  Defined, 2
Democratic centralism, 426–427
Denationalization, 201
  Britain, 36, 95–97
  France, 151, 201
  Italy, 328–329, 352
D'Estaing, Valery Giscard, 152–153, 161, 200
Devolution, 85–87
Dickens, Charles, 26
Direct Action, 203, 204
Disraeli, Benjamin, 108
Durer, Albrecht, 209, 218

E

Ebermann, Thomas, 256
Economic and Social Council (France), 165
Education:
  Britain, 127
  France, 127f, 185
Elections:
  Britain, 46–48, 53–54, 87
  France, 120, 131, 140–143, 174–175
  Germany, 235, 237–243, 281

Elections: *(cont.)*
  Italy, 337–341
  Poland, 419–420
  Soviet Union, 418–420
Electoral system:
  Britain, 46–47, 87
  France, 141–143, 148, 160ff
  Germany, 238–240, 301–302
  Italy, 338
"Embouregoisement," 26–28, 124–127
Ethnicity:
  Britain, 28–35, 38, 103, 105–107
  France, 129–131, 199, 203
  Germany, 225–226
  Italy, 320–321
  Soviet Union, 412–413, 423
Eurocommunism, 158, 354–356
European Commission on Human Rights, 102ff, 199, 297, 397, 466
European Economic Community, 467
  Britain, 37–38, 47, 98, 107
  and Communist Party (Italy), 354
  Germany, 291–292
  Italy, 328, 388–389
European Parliament, 100
Events of May 1968, 198, 325

F

FDP (*see* Free Democratic Party)
Federalism:
  Germany, 275–278, 279–285, 298–300
  U.S., 84
Fischer, Joshka, 256
Foot, Michael, 58
Ford, Gerald, 8
France:
  accountability, 178, 188–189, 204–205
  bureaucracy, 82f, 117, 165, 183–185, 278f
  civil liberties, 198–201
  class, 124–127
  cohabitation, 150, 176–178
  constitution, 170–173
  Constitutional Council, 145, 174, 182–183, 277
  Council of Ministers, 172–182
  decentralization, 129–130, 185–188, 195–196
  denationalization, 151, 201
  economy, 93–94, 96, 117, 131–133, 151, 193–196, 447–448
  education, 102, 127f, 185
  elections, 120, 131, 140–143, 174–175
  electoral system, 141–143, 148, 160ff
  ethnicity, 129–131, 199, 203
  government debt, 389
  history, 115–124
  ideology, 118–119, 125–129, 137, 147, 148ff, 192–193
  immigration, 129–131, 161, 199
  interest groups, 118–119, 163–168
  legitimacy, 124, 136
  local government, 85, 137, 185–188
  map, 122
  May 1968, 119–121, 139, 192
  media and politics, 137, 199–201
  national pride, 25
  nationalism, 121
  nationalization, 131–133, 194–195
  new social movements, 167–168, 189
  parliament, 79, 123, 141, 144–145, 172–182, 242, 273
  polarization, 147, 149–150, 162–163, 175–178, 204–205, 232, 334f
  political culture, 117, 119–120, 135–137, 170, 232, 334f
  political interest, 137–138
  political participation, 43, 137–146
  political parties, 118–119, 125–126, 137, 147–163, 175, 177, 202
  post-materialism, 234
  presidency, 172–176, 183, 268
  prime minister, 172–173
  protest politics, 115–116, 119–120, 138–140, 146, 167–168, 192, 202
  public employment, 6
  public opinion, 188–189
  racism, 129–131, 161, 199
  religion, 118, 127–128, 145, 150
  Senate, 173, 178–180
  social programs, 96, 196–198, 390
  student revolt of 1968, 119–121, 139, 192
  taxes, 6, 96, 136, 186, 381
  terrorism, 130, 203–204
  trade unions, 126, 136–137, 164–166, 260, 290
  voter turnout, 338
  voting, 140–143
  women in politics, 143–145, 167, 189, 242
Frederick the Great, 407
Frederick William IV, 211
Free Democratic Party—FDP (Germany), 155, 245, 253–254
  and Christian Democrats, 252–253, 261
  and Greens, 256, 305
  and Social Democrats, 252, 253, 261
  support, 222, 254
Fulton Committee, 83

G

Garibaldi, Guiseppe, 312ff
Gaullist Party—RPR (France)
  doctrine, 149, 150–151, 153–154, 198

and Giscardians, 152–155
and National Front, 161
organization, 151–152
and press, 200
support, 126, 128–129, 148, 150–152, 153–154
German Democratic Republic (*see* Germany (East))
German Federal Republic (*see* Germany (West))
Germany (East):
and West Germany, 216–217, 223, 233, 249, 298, 301, 306
and the Soviet Union, 454
economy, 409, 411, 446–449f
history, 216–217, 223, 407
leadership, 428, 435
policy making, 414, 435
political participation, 404, 407
political protest, 405, 414, 423
Germany (West):
accountability, 271, 285
bureaucracy, 83, 212, 215, 271, 278–279, 298
cabinet, 268, 270–272
chancellor, 268–272
civil liberties, 16, 277–278, 296–301
class, 220–223, 295–296
constitution, 213, 216, 218, 219, 267
Constitutional Court, 217, 277–278, 280, 282, 297f
economy, 93, 226–228, 289–293, 304–305, 306–307, 447–448
education, 102, 282, 295–296
elections, 235, 237–243, 281
electoral system, 238–240, 301–302
federalism, 275–278, 279–285, 298–300
government debt, 389
history, 209–220, 267, 307
immigration, 225–226, 299–301
interest groups, 257–263, 271f, 273, 291
legitimacy, 136, 232
local government, 85, 235, 280–285
map, 217
media, 235, 282, 300
national pride, 25
new social movements, 67, 262–263, 285, 301–303, 305–306
parliament, 79, 182, 268–270, 272–277, 283
political culture, 231–234, 303–304, 335
political participation, 43, 234–243, 263–264, 282
political parties, 221–225, 245–257, 294–295
political protest, 236–237, 301–303
post-materialism, 234
presidency, 172, 268–269f
protest, 236–237, 296, 298–299

public employment, 6
racism, 226
religion, 223–225, 246
reunification, 215–218
social programs, 96, 293–296, 390
taxes, 6, 96, 295, 381
television, 282, 300
terrorism, 46, 242, 282, 296–298, 302–303
trade unions, 222–223, 228, 252, 258–260, 290f, 304
voter turnout, 338
Weimar, 88, 210, 212–215, 219, 227, 257, 267, 274, 289ff
women in politics, 241–243, 254, 301
Giannini, Massimo Severo, 379
Giscardian Party (France), 148–149, 152–153
Goethe, Johan, 209, 218
Goldwater, Barry, 58
Gorbachev, Mikhail:
and dissidence, 424
as party leader, 419, 434–435
as president, 439
reforms, 423f, 441, 445, 449–450
resistance to, 427
Goria, Giovanni, 323, 353
Government:
growth of, 5–7
overload, 5–7, 100–102, 461–462
Gramsci, Antonio, 354
grandes ecoles, 127, 185
Greens Party (Germany)
compared, 305–306
doctrine, 254–255, 257
and Free Democrats, 256
mentioned, 16, 302
in parliament, 273
and Social Democrats, 252, 256
support, 221–222, 233–234, 254–256, 257
and women, 242, 254
Gromyko, Andrei, 439

H

Havel, Vaclav, 444
Heath, Edward, 42
Hersant, Robert, 200
Hindenburg, Paul von, 212
Hitler, Adolf, 3, 21, 88, 209, 215, 218, 223
Hoffmann, Stanley, 468
Honecker, Erich, 428
Hot Autumn, 325–326, 360, 363, 393, 400
House of Commons (Britain), 22, 70f, 75–81, 107, 242, 273f
House of Lords (Britain), 22, 70, 75f, 79–81, 107, 179, 242
Hoxha, Enver, 428
Human rights (*see* Civil liberties)

Hungary, 407, 419, 423, 449f, 452
Husak, Gustav

I

Immigration, 16
  Britain, 34–35, 104
  France, 129–131, 161, 199
  Germany, 225–226, 299–301
  Italy, 321, 399–400
Interest groups:
  Britain, 62–67
  France, 118–119, 163–168
  Germany, 257–263, 271f, 273, 291
  Italy, 361–363
  Soviet Union, 420, 436–437
  U.S., 62, 258
International Monetary Fund (IMF), 37, 93, 99, 388
Ireland, 31–34, 106
Italian Social Movement (MSI), 323, 327, 348–349, 360
Italy:
  accountability, 361, 382–383
  bureaucracy, 362–363, 378–379
  civil liberties, 397–400
  class, 319, 324–327
  clientelism, 378–379, 383
  constitution, 316, 366–367
  constitutional court, 371, 377–378, 398
  decentralization, 317–318, 380–382
  economy, 93, 96f, 327–330, 387–390
  education, 391
  elections, 337–341
  electoral system, 338
  ethnicity, 320–321
  and European Economic Community, 328, 388–389
  government debt, 389
  history, 311–320, 386
  immigration, 321, 399–400
  interest groups, 361–363
  legitimacy, 136
  local government, 85
  map, 314
  media and politics, 347, 397–398
  national pride, 25
  new social movements, 363
  Parliament, 79, 338, 367
  political culture, 332–336, 344–345
  political participation, 43, 336–345, 347–364
  political parties, 368–370, 374–376, 382–383, 393–396
  post-materialism, 234
  presidency, 172, 370–373
  prime minister, 372–377
  protest politics, 339
  public employment, 6
  referendum, 339–341, 378
  regionalism, 317–318, 319–320, 326, 329–330, 391–392, 400
  religion, 313–315, 317f, 321–324, 336, 340–341ff, 347, 351f
  social programs, 96, 390–392
  taxes, 6, 96, 381
  television, 347, 397–398
  terrorism, 46, 341–342, 363, 393–396, 397–400, 460
  trade unions, 325–327, 361–363
  voter turnout, 338
  women, 242, 342–344, 363, 377–378

J

Jaruzelski, Wojciech, 411, 428
Jenkins, Roy, 60
Judicial review, 182–183

K

Kadar, Janos, 428
Kant, Immanuel, 3, 209, 218
Kelly, Petra, 256
Kiesinger, Kurt, 249, 280
Kinnock, Neil, 58–59, 66, 76
Kohl, Helmut, 241, 247ff, 253, 270, 272, 275, 280

L

Labour Party (Britain):
  and trade unions, 57f, 259
  compared, 156, 222
  doctrine, 57–59, 66, 79, 86, 93, 99
  economic policies, 36
  history, 57
  organization, 57–59
  sources of support, 26–27, 48, 53–54, 58, 98
Lafontaine, Oskar, 251
LaPalombra, Joseph, 344
Lateran Treaty, 321ff
Le Pen, Jean-Marie, 160–162
Legitimacy, 108
  Britain, 88, 136
  crisis of, 7–9
  defined, 88
  France, 124, 136
  Germany, 136, 232
  Italy, 136
Leone, Giovanni, 395

Leotard, Francois, 153–155
Liberal Party (Britain), 55, 59–61, 86
Liberal Party—PLI (Italy), 323, 327, 348–350, 358–359, 376
Ligachev, Yegor, 434
Lincoln, Abraham, 2
local government:
  Britain, 47, 84–87, 187
  France, 85, 137, 185–189
  Germany, 85, 235, 280–285
  Italy, 85, 380–382
  Northern Ireland, 84, 86
Locke, John, 3
Lorenzo, Giovanni de, 395
Ludendorff, Erich von, 212
Luther, Martin, 209, 218, 407

M

Madison, James, 84
Magna Carta, 22
Marchais, Georges, 159
Marshall Plan, 227
Marx, Karl, 26
Mattei, Enrico, 387
Mauroy, Pierre, 158
Mazzini, Guiseppe, 312
McGovern, George, 58
Media, 8–9
  Britain, 47, 85, 103–104
  France, 137, 199–201
  Germany, 235, 282, 300
  Italy, 347, 397–398
  Soviet Union, 421, 423
Mehaignerie, Pierre, 154
Metternich, Clement Furst von, 312
Mezzogiorno, 319–320
Michels, Roberto, 318
"Militant Tendency," 57
Mill, John Stuart, 3
Mitterand, Francois:
  and Communist Party (France), 158–160
  opposition to, 149
  party leader, 155–158, 159
  popularity, 143
  as president, 167, 176, 193–196
  and press, 200–201
  and Rocard, 155
Molotov, Georgi, 418
Moro, Aldo, 372, 394–395, 400
Mosca, Gaetano, 318
Moser, Karl Friedrich, 231
Mussolini, Benito, 3, 312, 315–316, 318, 328

N

National Assembly (France), 79, 123, 141, 172–180, 273

women in, 144–145, 242
National Front (Britain), 35, 42
National Front (France), 35, 131, 225
  doctrine, 151, 160–161
  support, 148, 160–162
National Health Service (Britain), 62, 101
nationalization, 194–195
  France, 131–133, 156–157
NATO, 66–67, 99–100, 254
Natta, Alessandro, 355
Negri, Toni, 360
neocorporatism, 63, 165, 168, 257–259
new social movements:
  Britain, 65–67, 167
  France, 167–168, 189
  Germany, 167, 262–263, 285, 301–303, 305–306
  Italy, 363
noblesse oblige, 23, 42
nomenklatura system, 440
Northern Ireland, 25, 35–36
  conflict, 29, 31–34, 108
  constitutional reform, 47
  local government, 84, 86
  terrorism, 46, 103–106

O

Occheto, Achille, 356
Official Secrets Act of 1911, 103–104
Overload, 5–7, 100–102, 461–462
Owen, David, 60

P

Pareto, Viltredo, 318
Parliament:
  Britain, 20, 70f, 75–81, 107, 242, 273f
  decline of, 13–15
  France, 79, 123, 141, 144–145, 172–182, 242, 273
  Germany, 79, 182, 268–270, 272–277, 283
  Italy, 79, 182, 338, 366–367
  Soviet Union, 437–438
Party government, 87–88
PCF (*see* Communist Party—France)
PCI (*see* Communist Party—Italy)
"Peak associations," 257
Pertini, Sando, 371
Petain, Marshal, 160
Pius IX, 313
Pius XI, 321
PLI (*see* Liberal Party—Italy)
Poland:
  civil liberties, 452
  economy, 448–449f

Poland :*cont.*)
elections, 419–420
political participation, 419–420
religion, 413f
social class, 411
and Soviet Union, 454
trade unions, 411
Polarization, 162–163, 175, 204–205
Politburo (Soviet Union), 433–434
Political culture:
Britain, 22–25, 41–43, 88–89, 106–109, 135, 232, 334f
defined, 41
France, 117, 119–120, 135–137, 170, 232, 334f
Germany, 231–234, 303–304, 335
Italy, 332–336, 344–345
Soviet Union, 232, 407–408
Political interest, 43–44
Political participation:
Britain, 43–49, 66–67
expansion of, 464–465
France, 43, 137–146
Germany, 43, 234–243, 263–264, 282
Hungary, 419
Italy, 43, 336–345, 347–364
Poland, 419–420
Soviet Union, 418–425, 453
unconventional, 12–13, 464
Political parties:
and political stability, 162–163
Britain, 52–62, 87–88, 107–108, 110
decline of, 9–10, 61–62, 107, 110, 163, 202, 256–257, 263–264
East Germany, 405
expansion of, 10–13
France, 118–119, 123–124, 125–126, 137, 147–163, 175, 177, 202
Germany, 221–225, 245–257, 294–295
Italy, 368–370, 374–376, 382–383, 393–396
Soviet Union, 439–442
U.S., 53, 58, 88, 175
Political recruitment:
Britain, 48–49, 73, 85, 87, 108, 127, 278
France, 127, 144–145, 185, 278
Germany, 231–232, 241–243, 255, 258, 272, 278, 280
Soviet Union, 440
U.S., 278
Political trust, 7–9
Post-materialism, 41, 233–234
Powell, Enoch, 35
PRI (*see* Republican Party—Italy)
Proletarian Democracy (Italy), 323, 327, 348–349, 359–360
Proportional representation, 47, 141–142, 238, 240
Protest:
Britain, 12, 45–46, 65–67

France, 115–116, 119–120, 138–140, 146, 167–168, 192, 202
Germany, 236–237, 296, 298–299
Italy, 339
Poland, 422
Soviet Union, 422–424
PS (*see* Socialist Party—France)
PSDI (*see* Social Democratic Party—Italy)
PSI (*see* Socialist Party—Italy)
Public opinion:
Britain, 74, 87
France, 188–189

Q

Quangos, 63
Question Time:
Britain, 78, 180
France, 180
Germany, 274

R

Radical Party (Italy), 341, 344, 360
support, 323, 327, 348–349
and terrorism, 194, 395, 399
Reagan, Ronald, 5, 194, 248
Referendum:
Britain, 47, 87
France, 141
Italy, 339–341
Religion:
Britain, 35–36, 56, 79f, 223
France, 118, 127–129, 145, 150
Germany, 223–225, 246
Italy, 313–315, 317f, 321–324, 336, 340–341ff, 347, 351f
Poland, 413
Soviet Union, 412–414
Republican Party (France), 152–153
Republican Party—PRI (Italy), 323, 327, 348–350, 358–359, 376
Risorgimento, 312–313, 317f, 321
Rocard, Michel, 155, 157
Romania, 435, 449f, 454
RPR (*see* Gaullist Party—France)
Rumor, Mariano, 372
Ryzhkov, Nikolai, 438

S

Schiller, Frederich, 209
Schilly, Otto, 256
Schmidt, Helmut, 250–252, 307
Scotland, 28–33, 47, 84, 87, 107ff
SDP (*see* Social Democrats—Britain)

Secretariat (Soviet Union), 433–434
Senate:
  France, 173, 178–180
  Italy, 367–370, 374–377
Social class:
  Britain, 26–27, 47, 124
  embourgeoisement, 26–28, 124–127
  France, 124–127
  Germany, 220–223, 295–296
  Italy, 319, 324–327
  Poland, 411
  Soviet Union, 408–412
  U.S., 124
Social Democratic Party—SDP (Britain), 55ff,
  59–61
Social Democratic Party—SPD (Germany),
  156, 245
  and business, 261
  decline of, 264
  doctrine, 249–253, 294–295
  and Greens, 252, 256, 305
  support, 221–222, 224, 250–253
  and trade unions, 252, 259–260
  and women, 241
Social Democratic Party—PSDI (Italy), 323,
  327, 348–350, 358–359, 376
Socialist Party—PS (France)
  alliance with Communists, 158–160
  and bureaucracy, 184
  and Constitutional Council, 182
  doctrine, 94, 128, 131, 142–143, 149,
    156–157, 180, 194–195, 198
  factions, 155–156
  and Fifth Republic, 124
  organization, 155–158
  reforms, 184f
  support, 126, 128–129, 148, 155–158, 160
  and unions, 166
Socialist Party—PSI (Italy)
  and French Socialists, 357
  and government, 376–377
  organization, 357–358
  support, 323, 327, 336, 344, 357–358,
    348–349
Solidarity, 411, 413, 419, 449
Solzhenitsyn, Alexander, 4
Soviet Union:
  bureaucracy, 439–441
  civil liberties, 452
  class, 408–412
  clientelism, 422
  economy, 409, 445–451
  ethnicity, 412–413, 423
  history, 406–407
  interest groups, 420, 436–437
  parliament, 437–438
  and PCF, 158–159
  political culture, 232, 407–408
  political participation, 418–425, 453

  political parties, 439–442
  protest, 422–424
  religion, 412–414
  social program, 451–452
  trade unions, 420
Spadolini, Giovanni, 359
SPD (*see* Social Democratic Party—Germany)
Springer, Axel, 300
Stalin, Josef, 3, 406f
Steel, David, 60
Strauss, Franz-Josef, 247f
Sweden, 6, 28

T

Television, 8–9
  Britain, 47, 104
  Germany, 282, 300
  Italy, 347, 397–398
Terrorism, 12–13
  Britain, 32–34, 46–47
  and civil liberties, 103–106, 460
  France, 130, 203–204
  Germany, 49, 242, 282, 296–298, 302–303,
    326
  Italy, 46, 341–342, 363, 393–396, 397–400,
    460
  Northern Ireland, 103–106
Thatcher, Margaret:
  doctrine, 36, 54–56, 94–95, 97, 101
  and feminism, 49
  government action, 77
  leadership, 24, 108
  mentioned, 5, 42, 194f, 248
  and monarch, 72
  party leader, 54–56, 76
  as prime minister, 73–75, 78, 465
  and religion, 36
  style, 45, 285
Tocqueville, Alexis de, 109, 135
Togliatti, Palmiro, 354
Trade unions:
  Britain, 57f, 64–65, 95, 259–260, 290
  France, 126, 136–137, 164–166, 260, 290
  Germany, 222–223, 228, 252, 258–260,
    290f, 304
  Italy, 325–327, 361–363
  Poland, 411
  Soviet Union, 420
Trades Union Congress, 64–65
  and Labour Party (Britain), 57f, 64

U

Ulbricht, Walter, 429, 435
Union for French Democracy—UDF (France),
  152–155

Union of the Center, 150, 154–155
United States:
  accountability, 88
  bureaucracy, 83
  civil liberties, 198
  class, 124
  Congress, 77, 79, 175
  constitution 170
  democracy in, 2
  economy, 93f
  education, 102
  federalism, 84
  government debt, 289
  interest groups, 62, 258
  national pride, 25
  political parties, 53, 58, 88, 175
  presidency, 78, 175
  public employment, 6
  revolution, 115
  social programs, 390
  taxes, 6, 96
  voter turnout, 338
  women in politics, 242
USSR (*see* Soviet Union)

V

Valery, Paul, 311
Victor Emmanuel II, 312, 315, 316
Vogel, Hans-Jochen, 251

W

Wales, 28–33, 47, 84, 87, 107f
Wehner, Herbert, 249ff
Weimar, 88, 210, 212–215, 219, 227, 257, 267, 274, 289ff
Whitehall, 81–83
William, King I, 211
Women, 10
  Britain, 48–49, 242
  France, 143–145, 167, 189, 242
  Germany, 241–243, 254, 301
  Italy, 242, 342–344, 363, 377–378
  in national legislatures, 242
  Soviet Union, 420
U.S., 242
Wright, Peter, 103

Z

Zhivkov, Todor, 428